The Life of William Faulkner

The Life of
WILL
IAM

THE PAST IS NEVER DEAD, 1897–1934

FAUL
KNER

VOLUME 1

CARL ROLLYSON

UNIVERSITY OF VIRGINIA PRESS

Charlottesville & London

University of Virginia Press
© 2020 by Carl Rollyson
All rights reserved
Printed in the United States of America on acid-free paper

First published 2020

1 3 5 7 9 8 6 4 2

Library of Congress Cataloging-in-Publication Data
Names: Rollyson, Carl E. (Carl Edmund), author.
Title: The life of William Faulkner / Carl Rollyson.
Description: Charlottesville : University of Virginia Press, 2020. |
Includes bibliographical references and index. | Contents: Volume 1.
The past is never dead, 1897–1934.
Identifiers: LCCN 2019032254 (print) | LCCN 2019032255 (ebook) |
ISBN 9780813943824 (hardback ; volume 1) | ISBN 9780813943831 (epub ; volume 1)
Subjects: LCSH: Faulkner, William, 1897–1962. | Authors, American—20th
century—Biography. | Novelists, American—20th century—Biography.
Classification: LCC PS3511.A86 Z9619 2020 (print) | LCC PS3511.A86 (ebook) |
DDC 813/.52 [B]—dc23
LC record available at https://lccn.loc.gov/2019032254
LC ebook record available at https://lccn.loc.gov/2019032255

Cover art: Faulkner in 1931. (William Faulkner Related Material
from the Library of William Boozer, Albert and Shirley Small
Special Collections, University of Virginia Library)

I would have preferred nothing at all prior to the instant I began to write, as though Faulkner and Typewriter were concomitant, coadjutant and without past on the moment they first faced each other at the suitable (nameless) table.
                    —William Faulkner to Malcolm Cowley, February 18, 1946

Faulkner wrote as if there were no literature written in English before him, no century and more of convention and literary tradition established before he put pen to paper. He recreated fiction anew and set the novel free to better serve the twentieth century through a powerful, discordant, and irresistible torrent of language that crashed through time, space, and experience to tell the story of modern mankind in ways both tragic and comic. Faulkner would have written the way he did whether or not James Joyce, Virginia Woolf, Joseph Conrad, and the others had ever existed.
                    —M. Thomas Inge, *William Faulkner* (Overlook Illustrated Lives)

Contents

Gallery follows page 234.

Preface

Why read another biography of William Faulkner? New facts, new interpretations. I also wanted to write in the light and dark of previous narratives. His biographers remain silent on what they do not know and retreat to what "must have been." Long stretches of even the longest biographies have not told me what I want to know. What did it mean to Faulkner to expend so much energy not only on his fiction but on his screenplays? What did his wife, Estelle, think, and what was she doing at crucial periods when only her husband's testimony is available? What is a biographer to do with her erasure—sometimes self-inflicted?

As in a Faulkner novel, it is important to preserve the mysteries and not to pretend to know what is not or cannot be known, although, like his characters, I speculate, submitting questions that perhaps others will be able to answer or clarify. Identifying gaps in the evidence can reveal as much about Faulkner as what can be sourced. Minor figures abound because they reveal sides of the quotidian man ignored in previous biographies. I am that species of biographer who believes in presenting the whole man, not just those aspects of his life that pertain to the literary figure.

Although, like most biographers, I take a chronological approach, at times I backtrack, flash back, and flash forward because, as Faulkner said, all of time is inherent in every moment of time—the past, the present, and what is to come. To never deviate from chronology is to suppose life is a matter of just one damn thing after another. Even if that is so, books should not be so. Too many times stories are interrupted in a biography simply because of what happens next. Sometimes chronology has to be broken badly in order for the story to survive.

Like my predecessors, I owe an enormous debt to Joseph Blotner. Some paragraphs of this biography would need a note to Blotner for nearly every sentence, and that would be tedious and counterproductive. So I have not notated facts and details derived from Blotner's two-volume and one-volume biographies, but in many cases I have cited his papers, when I can access the raw data that he later transformed on the printed page. Blotner, for a whole range of reasons, chose not to use certain discoveries about Faulkner's life that become an important part of my narrative. As his daughter Jill said, he told "hundreds of little white lies" that "lovingly protected" the family.[1]

They needed protection, she made clear, from another biographer: Carvel Collins, whose immense collection at the University of Texas is a treasure of primary sources, including interviews with people who had passed away by the time Blotner began his work. Judging by the notes in previous biographies, I am the first biographer to look at every one of the 105 boxes in the Collins collection. His interviews often corroborate Blotner but also add a good deal of texture to this biography. Collins began in the late 1940s to collect everything. By the summer of 1967, he had made more than thirty visits to Oxford,[2] and he continued to work on his biography until his death in 1990, never even beginning to write a narrative, so far as I know, but interviewing Faulkner, his mother, his brother John, and many other family members and virtually anyone who could contribute the minute particulars that Boswell and Johnson extolled in their conception of biography. Collins spoke with anyone who had contact with his subject. He remained an independent, and that was held against him. "Neither Bill Faulkner nor his family ever authorized Prof. Collins to do a biography," Blotner explained to Morton Goldman, Faulkner's former agent. "As a matter of fact, Bill expressed to me in conversation his anger over what he considered Prof. Collins' intrusions into his private life."[3] Blotner routinely offered to remove material that offended his sources.

As for the other biographers, they all have their uses. Anyone wishing to understand Faulkner's southern background and family history had better read Joel Williamson. For acute psychological analysis, Fred Karl is the go-to biographer. Judith Sensibar restores Estelle Faulkner to an importance that other biographers have occluded. The reasons for her eclipse have their origins in Joseph Blotner's reluctance to press her on several important issues. "It is true that I felt the need for tact, not only because she had been a faithful friend, and I think, generally a good informant, but for Jill's sake too," Blotner wrote to fellow scholar Floyd Watkins. "In a way, for his [Faulkner's] sake—you can imagine my feelings of general ambivalence writing an intimate account of the life of my friend who in life had trusted me and whose trust I had tried to deserve."[4] No subsequent biographer had Blotner's access to Estelle, who died in 1972.

No one writes more incisively about Faulkner than Philip Weinstein. In smaller measure, I have profited from my reading of biographies by Judith Wittenberg, David Minter, Jay Parini, David Rampton, André Bleikasten, and Kirk Curnutt. I have also drawn on the short biographies of Faulkner by M. Thomas Inge, Carolyn Porter, and Robert W. Hamblin. Of necessity, what I write overlaps with previous books, but no one except a lazy reviewer could not see how my arrangement of events and discussion of Faulkner's work differs from previous narratives. To do complete justice to this biography, you would need to place it page by page against the others, and who has time for that?

In spite of all this previous biographical work, no biographer has integrated Faulkner's screenplays, fiction, and life into one narrative.[5] To do so has resulted in a biography much longer than I originally projected. In the last two decades Faulkner scholars have shown how Faulkner's work in Hollywood contributed to the creation of his novels, but only recently have they looked at his screenplays in their own right. As Ben Robbins notes: "Most studies of Faulkner and film do not immediately take into account the idea that a craft as plastic as Faulkner's could in fact be advanced through the exertion of new conventional conditions within Hollywood, overtly commercial or otherwise. . . . Faulkner both reshaped and was shaped by the alien territories of commercial film."[6] How the plasticity of all his work relates to the whole man has been one of my chief concerns. Certain screenplays like "The De Gaulle Story" and "Battle Cry" changed the nature of Faulkner's writing, as Robbins argues as well for *To Have and Have Not* and *Mildred Pierce:* "Though his screenplays may not be as formally ground-breaking as his prose, the presentation of new social realities within his work for film is in fact at times more progressive than equivalent presentations in his novels."[7]

All Faulkner biographers have to confront his drinking. Why did he do it? He advanced some answers, and friends, biographers, readers, and scholars have advanced others. I report on what they said and what Faulkner did, but I do not attempt to offer a diagnosis. I don't see how it could be done while he was alive or now that he is no longer with us. He seemed singularly uninterested in why he drank and showed scarcely any interest in stopping. In the end, I have to side with King Lear: "reason not the need."

I abjure one primary function of the literary critic. I refrain, in most cases, from dwelling on the flaws in Faulkner's work, except insofar as contemporary reviews rendered such judgments, thus providing a view of his evolving reputation. Faulkner biographers and critics have assessed his strengths and weaknesses, but my main concern is to understand how his work functions and to explain how his life and work can be coordinated in narrative terms. I don't believe, at this advanced stage in the work on William Faulkner's life and career, that readers need my opinion, except to state the obvious: I believe he is a great writer, and all of his work fascinates me and has done so for more than fifty years. Similarly, with the exception of *Absalom, Absalom!,* which seems caught up in the very process of revision, I have not tried to trace in detail Faulkner's process of composition, even though Michael Millgate and other scholars have shown how studying various drafts of his work enriches our understanding of his genius. To replicate their work, or even to add to it, would make this long biography even longer and truly test the patience of even the most dedicated Faulkner reader. Nevertheless, I have included crucial details about Faulkner's working methods and drafts, relying, in the main, on the Digital Yoknapatawpha site: http://faulkner.iath.virginia.edu/.

That Faulkner was a paradox, and one that should not be too easily explained, is the point of this biography. Or to put it another way: What you think you know about William Faulkner may be true, and everything you think you know about him has to change.

I began my work on Faulkner as an undergraduate, inspired by M. Thomas Inge at Michigan State University, and then continued on with Michael Mill- gate at the University of Toronto, producing a dissertation and my first book, *Uses of the Past in the Novels of William Faulkner.* The debt owed to these fine scholars is immeasurable. I owe many other debts to Faulkner critics, which I have acknowledged in my narrative and notes.

Right from the beginning, when I had only a book proposal and a sample chapter to show, I had the invaluable support of Linda Wagner-Martin, who wrote in support of my work and has been a continuing inspiration. In the summer of 2014, during a stay in Oxford, I had the pleasure of lunching with Jay Watson, the Howry Professor of Faulkner Studies at the University of Mississippi, who patiently listened to my plans for a new Faulkner biogra- phy and provided much-needed encouragement and the invitation to give a keynote talk at the summer 2015 Faulkner and Yoknapatawpha Conference. On that same trip, I met and interviewed Larry Wells, the husband of Dean Faulkner Wells, and a fount of information and contacts that I sorely needed. Larry generously put me in touch with William Lewis Jr., the current owner of Neilson's Department Store, where Faulkner was a customer. Mr. Lewis knew Faulkner and was most welcoming and informative during our inter- view. Just as important was Tommy Freeland, another Larry Wells contact and the son of Phil Stone's law partner. Mr. Freeland gave me a tour of the Stone law office and told me a good deal about his father's dealings with Wil- liam Faulkner. Through Larry I was also able to contact Sandra Baker Moore for her memories of the Faulkners and of what it was like for her to live next door to Rowan Oak in the 1940s, when her mother, Kate Baker, owned a dress shop in Oxford. I have been extremely fortunate to find those still living with memories of Faulkner, including Salley Knight, whose recollection of Faulkner in Virginia came to me via my contact with Scott Beauchamp.

Thanks to Jay Watson's invitation to Gloria Burgess, who spoke at the 2016 Faulkner and Yoknapatawpha Conference, I was able to interview her and continue a correspondence that has yielded a significant insight into Faulkner's efforts to help people of color.

Steve Railton, who has done so much to further Faulkner studies with Digital Yoknapatawpha, helped me out at a crucial moment when a website went down and has been a strong supporter of my biography. I relied on the estimable Molly Schwartzberg, Curator of the Albert and Shirley Small Special Collections at the University of Virginia, not only for much help with the vast Faulkner archive but also with connecting me to members of the university and Charlottesville community who had memories of William Faulkner. Ellie Sohm shared with me her University of Virginia undergraduate paper about Faulkner's relationship with his daughter Jill at a crucial time in the development of my biography. Sara Barnes was a wonderful tour guide and all-around facilitator during my visit to the university to deliver the first William and Rosemary MacIlwaine Lecture in American Literature. That lecture, I'm happy to say, prompted an email to Richard Garcia from Donald Nuechterlein about his experience with William Faulkner in Iceland that was forwarded to me. After my lecture, "Faulkner's Virginia Persona," I had the pleasure of speaking with George Thomas about those Faulkner days on the University of Virginia grounds. Others in the audience for my lecture came forward with their own William Faulkner stories. I am grateful to all of them.

Robert Hamblin, former Director of the Center for Faulkner Studies at Southeast Missouri State University, has been an invaluable source of information as he guided me through their indispensable Faulkner collection. Christopher Rieger, the current Director, has been equally helpful and generous. He made available to me a grant that allowed extended stays at the Center for Faulkner Studies so that I could complete my research in a timely fashion. On the premises, I had the excellent help of Roxanne Dunne, and of the indispensable Tyson Koenig, who sorted out many of the photographs reproduced in this biography.

Archivist Rick Watson, the son of eminent Faulkner scholar James G. Watson, helped me navigate my way through the Carvel Collins Papers at the Harry Ransom Humanities Research Center, University of Texas at Austin. Rick saved me a lot of time by expediting my access to the papers. I owe thanks as well to Ned Comstock at the Cinematic Arts Library, University of Southern California. I have known Ned since the mid-1980s, and he has remained an important source of archival material for many of my biographies. He has sent me copies of vital items that I did not know existed. Jenny Romero and the rest of the staff at the Academy of Motion Picture Arts and

Sciences have always proven a boon to my research, and that was true in this case as well, pointing me to a script not mentioned in previous accounts of Faulkner's career. Todd Goddard at Utah Valley University hosted my talk on "Faulkner as Screenwriter" and secured funding for a trip to Salt Lake City so that I could examine the Faulkner-authored scripts in the Howard Hawks Collection at Brigham Young University.

Similarly, through a generous invitation from Faulkner scholar Stephen Hahn at William Patterson University, I was able to examine the important work Donald Philip Duclos did on William C. Falkner, the old Colonel.

Jennifer Ford, Jessica Leming, and Lauren Rogers, in Special Collections at the University of Mississippi Library, facilitated my work in its Meta Carpenter Wilde Collection and other choice items such as Faulkner's hand-written script "Wooden Crosses," a first-draft screenplay that became *The Road to Glory*. And thanks to Gerald Walton for helping me out on my interest in the Ole Miss golf course that Faulkner played on. I'm grateful to William D. Griffith for a splendid tour of Rowan Oak and for answers to my questions.

Elizabeth Sudduth, Director of the Irvin Department of Rare Books and Special Collections, University of South Carolina Libraries, made my visit to consult the Frederick R. Karl Archive and Malcolm Argyle Franklin Collection efficient and profitable.

Matthew Turi, Manuscripts Research and Instruction Librarian, Research and Instructional Services Department, Louis Round Wilson Special Collections Library at the University of North Carolina, helped to facilitate my work in the Robert H. Moore Papers.

Meredith Mann in the Brooke Russell Astor Reading Room for Rare Books and Manuscripts at the New York Public Library helped me navigate through the Joel Sayre Papers, as did Mary Catherine Kinniburgh in the Berg Collection for various Faulkner items.

David Harper and Jessica Stock made my visit to the M. Thomas Inge Faulkner Collection at West Point a delight and an edification. I was able to follow Faulkner's walking route to his talk.

Penny White, reference librarian, and the Digital Production Group at the University of Virginia Library aided in acquiring the volume 1 cover image and several of the images in the galleries.

Edward Perry and Marcus Gray, two Faulkner scholars, have stuck with me over several years, making important suggestions about items essential to this biography. I thank Patrik Andersson for answering my query about the correspondence between Faulkner and Else Jonsson, and John Waters for answering my questions about Jean Stein.

Other Faulkner scholars, including Ted Atkinson, Sarah Gleeson-White, Arthur Kinney, Claude Pruitt, D. Matthew Ramsay, Timothy Ryan, Stefan Solomon, and Sally Wolff-King have responded to my queries and have contributed to the completion of my biography. I'm grateful to Jack Elliott for sending me an advance copy of his valuable work on Faulkner's last days, and for his last-minute corrections of material relating to Faulkner's ancestry and his early years. I should have consulted Jack sooner.

For sound advice about matters related to Faulkner and publishing, I'm grateful to Craig Gill, the Director of the University Press of Mississippi.

My fellow biographers Jonathan Alter, James Atlas, Kate Buford, Betty Caroli, Mary Dearborn, Gayle Feldman, Anne Heller, Justin Martin, Marion Meade, Sydney Stern, Will Swift, and Amanda Vail have given me much good advice, encouragement, and items to mull over for this biography.

Thank you, Barbara Barnett, for helping me with my rudimentary French and figuring out a Faulkner caption, and William Crawley for speaking with me about Faulkner's visit to Mary Washington University. And to Rosemary Clark, for untold great finds and research assistance, I am immeasurably indebted.

Several research award grants from Baruch College and the PSC-CUNY Research Fund made it possible to travel to archives and to conduct interviews for this book. Biography is an expensive endeavor, and without such help I don't see how I could have taken on so many research projects.

I'm very pleased that my shrewd agent, Colleen Mohyde, and my astute editor, Eric Brandt, combined to make this a better book. To Susan Murray, my magnificent copyeditor, and to the vigilant Morgan Myers, my heartfelt thanks for making this book, line by line, and chapter by chapter, better than I could make it myself. And it is gratifying to say here how much I valued the support of the late Mark Saunders, the former Director of the University of Virginia Press.

Lisa Paddock, my wife and a wonderful Faulkner scholar, patiently listened to my plans for the biography and made many excellent suggestions. I'm sure it was a trial, at times, to put up with my obsession, but she has borne it pretty well.

The Life of William Faulkner

1

Beginnings

1825–1910

THE BIG DOG

Because William Faulkner's characters are obsessed with the past, the same has been said of their author. Biographers dwell on his family history, especially the example of his great-grandfather, the old Colonel, William C. Falkner (1825–1889),[1] who embodied the "three major legends of the South: the Cavalier Legend, about family origins and personal style; the Plantation Legend, about 'the golden age' before the war; and the Redeemers Legend, about the glorious unseating of the carpetbaggers."[2] Biographers quote young Willie's public avowal that he wanted to be a writer like his great-granddaddy, and they have assiduously investigated the old Colonel's life, exhuming details that Faulkner may not have known or have cared to examine. When Donald Philip Duclos pressed Faulkner for details, the novelist suggested the scholar fill out the record with fiction, which is precisely what Faulkner had already done—as Duclos pointed out to him.[3]

The elements of Faulkner's southern heritage, and particularly his family history, do not come fully into play until his third novel, *Flags in the Dust,* published as *Sartoris,* a truncation that magnifies, sometimes simplifies, and debunks Falkner family lore. The old Colonel figure, John Sartoris, embodies the myth more than the man William C. Falkner. The man, more townsman than plantation owner, and certainly no cavalier with legions of slaves, was a lawyer and businessman who came out of the war with a fortune—how, no one knew, although he may have acquired his wealth as a blockade-runner after leaving the Confederate army in 1863. And what did

William C. Falkner have to do with Reconstruction? In *Flags in the Dust* and *The Unvanquished* John Sartoris shoots carpetbaggers attempting to win an election with black votes. Nothing like this episode occurred in William C. Falkner's life. William Faulkner carefully selected the fictional value in his great-grandfather's career and scorned the biographer's search for evidence. Here is what mattered, Faulkner told Robert Cantwell, who published a *Life* magazine profile in 1938: The old Colonel was "overbearing" and "had to be big dog. He built the railroad after the Civil War because he wanted to make a lot of money." This man was not fit for Faulkner's fiction. Money as such does not enter into John Sartoris's calculations. Faulkner's fiction never examines the man too carefully and favors deploying him through the veils of memory and nostalgia. The old Colonel, "a grasping, pushing stinker," resembled a robber baron, "exemplifying the social Darwinism of the late nineteenth century."[4]

Was Faulkner "haunted" by his great ancestor?[5] The legend suited him insofar as it was good material for a story. He told Cantwell about the Colonel's big marble statue in the Ripley cemetery, still there in the capital of the old Colonel's enterprises. Faulkner pictured his great ancestor riding through "that country like a living force. I like it better that way. I never read any history. I talked to people. If I got it straight it is because I didn't worry with other people's ideas about it." Absorbed in his own creation, he lost track of what was Falkner and what was Sartoris. He would have to go through the novel page by page and ask himself, "Did I hear this or did I imagine this?"[6] He used what played well on the page. Like Bayard Sartoris in *The Unvanquished,* who rejects and honors his father's legacy, William Faulkner repudiated but also revered his heritage.

The legend of the old Colonel and his exploits during the war were part of Uncle Ned Barnett's repertoire. Born in 1865 and raised to serve the old Colonel and the next generations of Falkners, Ned had an air of authority stemming from his propinquity to the past. Ned appears with his own name in *The Reivers,* the novel that brings Faulkner full circle back to family history. "He is a cantankerous old man," Faulkner told Cantwell, "who approves of nothing I do." When Faulkner introduced Cantwell to the reserved, almost formal Ned, the mention of the old Colonel's name seemed to "make Ned older." Asked to provide details about his master, Ned grew silent; the "recollections seemed troubling," Cantwell observed. Perhaps most telling is Cantwell's conclusion that "Colonel Falkner's life brooded almost oppressively over that cabin in the woods. . . . I sensed its reality, not so much to Faulkner as to the old man."

Like John Sartoris, the old Colonel had been shot down in the street, the murder victim not only of rivalry with a former business partner, Richard Thurmond, but also of Falkner's own unrelenting torment of his competitor. His great-grandson remembered how those on the Thurmond side would cross the street rather than acknowledge a Falkner.[7] It was precisely this kind of bad blood that Lincoln sought to allay in his postwar policy and that Faulkner assuaged in stories like "An Odor of Verbena," based upon the old Colonel's murder.

Faulkner imbibed much of his family history from his great-aunt, Alabama Falkner McLean, the old Colonel's last surviving child. Bama, as the family called her, was his favorite, to whom he felt he must account, and for whom he named his firstborn child. He enjoyed her "charming grand-duchess air" and her habit of making "penetrating stage asides." She intimidated her family, as one Falkner put it, but Bama was also a "stimulating person who read much, talked about what she read, and inspired you to do likewise."[8] She would later say that she could see the old Colonel's facial expressions in his great-grandson.[9]

Through his Aunt Bama, William Faulkner also accessed the playful side of the old Colonel, especially in evidence in *Rapid Ramblings in Europe*. In a dedication to baby Roy, his affectionate appellation for Bama, the "pet of the household," Falkner quotes from her unintentionally funny letter to him: "Mama and I are well; my big doll had its nose broken clear off. Hoping these few lines will find you enjoying the same blessing." The author then turns to us: "I don't think she meant to express a wish that the letter would find my nose broken, consequently I inscribe this work to her." This delightful, idiosyncratic book presents a boasting hero who also casts a skeptical eye on himself and even engages in buffoonery. In short, he is a comic figure whose commentary is not so different from his great-grandson's humorous exposures of vainglory and chicanery. The old Colonel was a trickster—never forget that when assessing William Faulkner's presentation of himself and his ancestry. In the old Colonel's famous novel *The White Rose of Memphis,* set aboard a steamboat, virtually every character masquerades as someone else, leading a double life, pretending to be royalty, cloaking in the costumery of a party baser motivations and commonness that have to be redeemed by the nobility of women fighting for their men.

Faulkner scoffed at his great-grandfather's famous melodramatic novel: "The men all brave and the women all pure."[10] But he also said the book was better than the general impression of it. The novel may have at least provided the great-grandson with an antidote to the acrimony that infested southern accounts of the war. For Colonel Falkner began his best-known work in a spirit of reconciliation:

> Let the past bury the past—let us cultivate a feeling of friendship between the North and South. Both parties committed errors—let both parties get back to the right track. Let us try to profit by our sad experience—let us teach forgiveness and patriotism, and look forward to the time when the cruel war shall be forgotten. We have a great and glorious nation, of which we are very proud, and we will make it greater by our love and support. It was a family quarrel, and the family has settled it, and woe be to the outsider who shall dare to interfere!

The Falkner desire to defend the South's case ended with the old Colonel, and William Faulkner's fiction reflects the same attitude, although the past could not be so easily buried as the old Colonel hoped.

If Colonel Falkner sought reconciliation in his prose, he perpetuated divisiveness in both his private and public life. He had been a slaveholder and most likely miscegenetic. In *The Siege of Monterey* (1851), before he had become reconciled to defeat, Falkner admonished the North: "Do you wish to rob us of our slaves? / If so, give us our bloody graves." Yet the old Colonel was not like those South Carolina fire-breathing rebels. He suggested the North might yet offer redress of grievances and that "secession is a serious undertaking, / It will set the whole globe to shaking."[11] More was at stake than economic losses resulting from the abolition of slavery. The peculiar institution represented a way of life that had evolved in a sort of morganatic way. William C. Falkner and Richard Thurmond may have shared a black mistress, and their possession of her may have contributed to the acrimony that ended in Falkner's death. He is reported to have said, while dying, "What did you do it for, Dick?"[12] The question signifies, perhaps, not merely Falkner's shock and baffling inability to understand how he had alienated friends, family, and foe alike,[13] but also a certain intimacy, a shared experience with Thurmond, that contributed to Falkner's plaintive last words, although the evidence for such an intimacy has been disputed by Jack Elliott, now writing a revisionist biography of the old Colonel.[14]

To explain why the old Colonel had to die as he did requires a narrative nearly as convoluted and fragmented as *Absalom, Absalom!* or *Go Down, Moses*. In fact, biography might contribute to understanding those historiographical novels by revealing that, like his characters, Faulkner could only know his family's past by intuiting and imagining it—just as the connection between Thomas Sutpen, slave owner, and his black son, Charles Bon, is established through deduction and insight. The story begins in 1859, when

Colonel Falkner settled a lawsuit in favor of his client Benjamin E. W. Harris and as a fee took possession of his client's slave, Emeline, and her three children.[15] Falkner acquired several slaves in the same manner. Among Emeline's progeny, it has always been told that Colonel Falkner fathered her fourth child, named Fannie Forrest Falkner, the first name perhaps the sobriquet of his sister Frances, and the middle name in honor of Nathan Bedford Forrest, that wily scourge of the invading Yankees who appears in his great-grandson's Civil War fiction.

Fannie's birth most likely occurred in 1863, in Pontotoc, Mississippi, thirty miles south of Ripley. Colonel Falkner had retired from his role as military man, aggrieved that he had not received the recognition and higher rank that his heroic efforts deserved. He was apparently estranged from his wife, Elizabeth Vance, who moved permanently to Memphis. In Pontotoc, he might have resorted to lucrative blockade-running that provided for his postwar investments. Colonel Falkner suffered from physical complaints that might have been bleeding ulcers. He may have found emotional support in Emeline, then twenty-seven or twenty-eight. The author of *The White Rose of Memphis* and other sentimental novels and poems, and known to indulge in emotional public reminiscences about his early life and struggles, created male characters who are simply at a loss without the women in their lives, women who express a purity and patience that their impulsive and imprudent male lovers can never match. Only women in *The White Rose of Memphis* have the stamina, tolerance, and conviction to prevail. For all their simplistic characterization, the female characters in Falkner's most famous novel are the avatars of women like Clytie and Judith in *Absalom, Absalom!*[16]

After Emeline's death in 1898, her Ripley cemetery tombstone identified her as Mrs. Emeline Falkner, and although no record of an actual marriage has been found, she has been memorialized as such by a family that has always believed, like the descendants of Sally Hemings, in both their black and white progenitors. Alfreda Hughes, Emeline's great-granddaughter, grew up in West Baltimore with the understanding that she shared the same great-grandfather with William Faulkner.[17] The black Falkners believe that only Fannie, among Emeline's children, was sent to college with Colonel Falkner's support. Deaths in the black community were not news, and yet the *Ripley Standard* reported: "'Aunt' Emeline Falkner, one of the good old ante-bellum colored women of Ripley, died Monday at the home of Sam Edgerton, her son-in-law." Calling Emeline "Aunt" was itself a tribute, since most black people were not addressed as Mr., Miss, or Mrs. and were acknowledged only by their first names or by nicknames, if not simply referred to as "boy" and "girl."[18] Williamson notes that Emeline is the "only Mrs. Falkner in the [Ripley] cemetery" where the old Colonel's "marble self rises above all."

After Colonel Falkner's death, a mulatto woman (Emeline?) was rumored to have visited Thurmond in jail before he made bail, though the historian Jack Elliott attributes the rumor to an effort to discredit Thurmond.[19] For a fact, both Emeline and her daughter Fannie worked as servants in Thurmond's house. These fraught connections between Thurmond and Falkner result in Williamson's suggestion that the "failure of the jury to convict Thurmond was not simply a matter of money spent overtly and covertly in his defense." To Jack Elliott, however, "too much has been made about possible irregularities in Thurmond's trial," and acquittal was "based upon convincing the jury that the defendant was in fear of his life."[20] The *Tupelo Journal* reported the "deadly feud" between the two men, and any gesture on Falkner's part that Thurmond might have considered threatening may have been enough to convince the jury that Thurmond acted in self-defense.

The Falkner family never spoke of black relatives or liaisons, so far as is known. Jim Crow laws enforced stricter racial segregation than in slavery. Reconstruction resulted in a riven family stripped of a bloodline. A certain history died with Colonel Falkner, and his great-grandson spent a lifetime trying in his fiction to recover a displaced past. In *The Unvanquished*, Colonel Sartoris is a relic of an old era, remote even from his own son. He rarely appears in a fatherly role but instead strides or gallops in as a figure of myth, just as the old Colonel was not much of an actual father to his own son, even if that son was called the "young Colonel." The vaunted past that was supposedly proximate to William Faulkner was, in certain vital respects, remote and, if not entirely forgotten, then at the very least occluded. No wonder Isaac McCaslin in *Go Down, Moses* is so stunned to touch the hand of a distant relative, a black woman, part of the Great Black Migration to the North, who has had an affair with his nephew Roth Edmonds. She has no place in his white family.

Faulkner had his suspicions. The old Colonel's fictional counterpart, John Sartoris, has a black daughter, Elnora, in the short story "There Was a Queen." And though she is not directly linked to John Sartoris, another black character named Elnora is an abiding presence in *Flags in the Dust*, which shows the indissoluble and yet camouflaged connection between black and white lives in the post–Civil War South. Elnora comments on the action, saying of old Bayard, "He's gittin' old." Her singing is a choral accompaniment to the Sartoris saga, with lyrics about sinners and preachers and women, foreshadowing the murder of old Simon, old Bayard's black retainer and a prominent member of his church, in a lovers' tryst. Elnora's voice "floated in meaningless minor suspense," which is perhaps not meaningless or minor but is rather the minority report on what is happening to the Sartorises. "All folks talkin' 'bout heaven ain't gwine dere," she sings in a "dying fall." While her brother Caspey tries to assert himself after his service in World War I, Elnora tries to protect him, assuring old Bayard that her brother will fall in line, even as old Bayard seems thwarted by Simon, his black shadow, who manipulates the banker into paying Simon's debts to his church. Faulkner understood how the lives of his family were, in part, the possession of those who served them. The novelist understood the "notion of a working space, within the constraining stereotype."[21] Or, as Faulkner said of Simon: his environment had taught him that "Negroes got along better if they act like black-faced comedians when white people were looking at them."[22]

The Falkners did not seem to agonize over the legacy of slavery, and that is, to some extent, remarkable. Faulkner's Mississippi contemporary Stark Young noted that "as a child I could only sense that my family was forever troubled in their minds about it; and I understood that people like us did not hate the Negroes." Neither did the Falkners, who nevertheless remained as implacable as the Youngs in opposing integration.[23]

Faulkner's treatment of race may have been influenced by what Bama told him about his great-grandfather's benefactions to Ripley's black citizens who paid him tribute. One of them, Gus Green, wrote to his sisters on December 16, 1948:

> I borrowed $50.00, a lot of money in those days from Col. W. C. Falkner . . . during my stay in college and would pay him back when I taught a country summer school. . . . I restate these few things so you may see I have many good things to recollect about my old home. The fact is *there* was no real hatred on the part of either race toward the other in those days. We neither learned to hate or to fear each other. And these attitudes have helped me to go through the world in a good way.

Bama made sure that Donald Philip Duclos, researching the life of the old Colonel, saw Green's letter, which attested to the "wonderful side of my father's character." She stressed his "consideration for the unfortunate."[24] She had grown up as her adoring father's favorite, "the Colonel's Baby," the servants said.[25] And Bama, speaking about her father to Duclos, became tearful as she described "what a wonderful man he was."[26] When he returned from Europe, she told Carvel Collins, "the whole town of Ripley would turn out as though he were a hero to be welcomed because he had been on a long trip and was such a prominent man."[27] Did his great-grandson, absorbing such stories, remember them when the town turned out to attend the world premiere of *Intruder in the Dust*?

One of Faulkner's earliest memories shows his profound sensitivity to place, to the shifts, disruptions, and displacements that disturb children, and that seemed always to dog him, no matter where he might land. In this case, he recalled a moment in the town where his great-grandfather had made his mark. On his first trip to Europe he wrote to his Aunt Bama that he would be "awful glad to see Vannye again," the daughter of Bama's elder sister, Willie Madora: "The last time I remember seeing her was when I was 3, I suppose. I had gone to spend the night with Aunt Willie (in Ripley) and I was suddenly taken with one of those spells of loneliness and nameless sorrow that children suffer, for what or because of what they do not know." At such moments, children may feel homeless, no matter how temporary the dislocation may be. Outside the proper sense of order the child has already established, the world turns to chaos, as it does for Benjy in *The Sound and the Fury* when Luster reverses the customary route around the courthouse square. "And Vannye and Natalie [Vannye's elder sister] brought me home, with a kerosene lamp," Faulkner continues, with an image—the kind of scene that often stimulated the writing of a new story or novel. "I remember how Vannye's hair looked in the light—like honey. Vannye was impersonal; quite aloof: she was holding the lamp. Natalie was quick and dark. She was touching me. She must have carried me."[28] The two maternal figures, light and dark, cold and warm, pre-figure Mrs. Compson and Dilsey, and are reminiscent of Faulkner's mother, Maud, and his Mammy Callie (Caroline Barr).

The detail that Faulkner puts into his letter confirms Aunt Bama's memory of him as a three-year-old with extraordinary powers of perception and understanding. She remembered his asking for a "blow-tow," and when the family could not understand what he was saying, he drew a picture of the object with "all the recognizable parts." He had been watching some workman use a blowtorch, and he wanted one for himself. This ability to observe and record is evident especially in his first published short stories, which are full of the kinds of details about machine parts in planes and boats that make his work seem especially authentic. This talent set him apart from other children. He was "always different" and "just smarter," his mother emphasized.[29]

So to begin with, he liked to draw. Across from him at a two-sided desk sat Myrtle Ramey, perhaps the first playmate to recognize he had a style different from everybody else's. He tossed bits of his poetry and drawings over to her, and she would send them back in approval. After he began to publish, he sent her copies, signing books before shipping them to Florida, where she had moved with her husband.[30]

One of his cartoons featured a werewolf-like Abraham Lincoln, at the mercy of Miss Ella Wright, history teacher, putting the president through her Demerit Mill, while at his knee a Union soldier advances on the much smaller Confederate defender. Another teacher, Annie Chandler, presented her pupil with a copy of Thomas Dixon's *The Clansman: An Historical Romance of the Ku Klux Klan*,[31] depicting the "great North, with its millions of sturdy people and their exhaustless resources," overwhelming the gallant if undersized South, just as the British had crushed the Highlanders at Culloden. The book may have had some initial appeal to the undersized Billy, a small child in a family of male six-footers, but Dixon focused on the defeated South and its painful rebirth.

Annie Chandler and women of her generation instated the restoration of the Confederacy in monuments erected in the South and North, appealing not merely to a romantic sense of the Lost Cause but to the sentiments of northerners who wanted reconciliation with a recalcitrant region that had to be reintegrated into the national economy and mythology. The well-funded Daughters of the Confederacy sponsored a network of Jefferson Davis highways in projects that localities, seeking financial support, could not resist, which is why even in California, Arizona, and Washington State roads named after the president of the Confederacy proliferated.[32]

Thomas Dixon, Woodrow Wilson's good friend, incensed at the negative portrayal of southerners and slave owners in *Uncle Tom's Cabin,* wanted to turn defeat into triumph as he announced his mission: "How the young South, led by the reincarnated souls of the Clansmen of Old Scotland, went forth under this cover and against overwhelming odds, daring exile, imprisonment, and a felon's death, and saved the life of a people, forms one of the most dramatic chapters in the history of the Aryan race." Faulkner grew up on this story but chose not to tell it in his fiction, knowing full well what his mammy, Callie Barr, had told him about her family's dread of the Ku Klux Klan—terrorists who rode at night, prompting black families to be home before dark and bar their windows and doors. She kept a knife at the ready, which in her fierce, commanding presence seemed more than just a relic of the evil past. Unlike the melodramatic Dixon or Margaret Mitchell, Faulkner presents a nuanced narrative of Reconstruction in *The Unvanquished* and in the "Compson Appendix," a mordant depiction of Old Scotland and its revival in the Old and the New South. The Scottish propensity for lost causes, culminating in the Highlanders' defeat at Culloden, is a defining historical moment that provides the backdrop not only for the Compson family's failures but also for exposing the bogus southern idea of postwar redemption. The southerners who regarded themselves as building a new civilization are viewed ironically in terms of the other displaced peoples, such as the Chickasaws. Faulkner understood that even as his ancestors established their towns and plantations, and the Chickasaws were pushed out and sent to reservations, the antebellum South was committing itself to defeat.

Underneath Billy's Lincoln cartoon is a caption: "Them's My Sentiments." Whose sentiments? The obvious answer is Miss Wright's, who seems triumphant in her takedown of the tyrant, the Lincoln depicted in the poetry of the Confederacy. Billy may well have shared his teacher's convictions, but it is striking how he is already making his own material out of history. Was he also making fun of school? He had begun well in the lower grades—so well that a teacher had accused his mother of doing his homework. But by his teens, bored with classes, he became a truant, preferring to read on his own. Was he already ridiculing the sentimental version of the war against northern aggression? The caption is redneck folksy, prefiguring, perhaps, a sensibility unbound by chauvinistic pedagogy, but also amused and aroused by the redneck simplification of history. Even if Billy had read no more than the first three chapters of *The Clansman,* he would have encountered a sympathetic portrait of Lincoln, who is depicted as having southern qualities, a nobility as seen through a southern woman's witness of his "goodness, tenderness, sorrow, canny shrewdness, and a strange lurking smile all haunting his mouth and eye." If Lincoln had lived, the novel argues, Reconstruction would have meant reconciliation with the South, not revenge upon it. This Lincoln, whose magnanimity is heralded in the screen and dramatic adaptations of *Birth of a Nation* (1915), presented in Oxford onstage and in a movie theater, has his counterpart in *The Unvanquished* when Bayard reports: "I heard Father say to Drusilla, 'We were promised Federal troops; Lincoln himself promised to send us troops. Then things will be all right.'" Lincoln's spirit of reconciliation is also evident when an unarmed Bayard Sartoris refuses to perpetuate his father's penchant for violence and faces his father's killer, who flees, putting an end to the blood feud that has divided the community. The white-sheeted knights of the South make only the briefest of appearances in *The Unvanquished* in Bayard's reference to Thomas Sutpen: "how when Father and the other men organised the night riders to keep the carpet baggers from organising the negroes into an insurrection, he refused to have anything to do with it."

Like Bayard and Ringo in *The Unvanquished,* Faulkner and a black childhood playmate joined in Civil War games based on what the old veterans had told them.[33] In his fiction, Faulkner never rationalized the evils of slavery, but he did depict certain slaves like Ringo who identified with their white families and regarded the Yankees as invaders, even as others, like Loosh, collaborated with the Union army and provided intelligence about the whereabouts of Confederate armies and treasure.

There are moments in Faulkner's fiction, as in *Intruder in the Dust,* when the Civil War and the imagination of that war coalesce, so that one is bound to believe in the all-encompassing grasp of the past:

> It's all *now* you see. Yesterday won't be over until tomorrow and tomorrow began ten thousand years ago. For every Southern boy fourteen years old, not once but whenever he wants it, there is the instant when it's still not yet two o'clock on that July afternoon in 1863, the brigades are in position behind the rail fence, the guns are laid and ready in the woods and the furled flags are already loosened to break out and Pickett himself with his long oiled ringlets and his hat in one hand probably and his sword in the other looking up the hill waiting for Longstreet to give the word and it's all in the balance, it hasn't happened yet, it hasn't even begun yet, it not only hasn't begun yet but there is still time for it not to begin against that position and those circumstances which made more men than Garnett and Kemper and Armistead and Wilcox look grave yet it's going to begin, we all know that, we have come too far with too much at stake and that moment doesn't need even a fourteen-year-old boy to think *This time. Maybe this time* with all this much to lose and all this much to gain: Pennsylvania, Maryland, the world, the golden dome of Washington itself to crown with desperate and unbelievable victory the desperate gamble, the cast made two years ago; or to anyone who ever sailed a skiff under a quilt sail, the moment in 1492 when somebody thought *This is it:* the absolute edge of no return, to turn back now and make home or sail irrevocably on and either find land or plunge over the world's roaring rim.

Faulkner describes an instant, a world-historical event, that is simultaneously all of time, but he is also evoking a sense of a pregnant moment that is a work of the imagination, when facts are transmuted into story, so that the past recurs as if it has yet to happen, and as if it is alterable. A contemporary reader might balk at the third sentence. Every southern boy? Black ones as well? In Faulkner's childhood experience, the answer is yes. Not only Callie, but others like Earl Wortham, an African American blacksmith,[34] shared stories of the war that would have encouraged Faulkner to think in terms of a common heritage. The "probably" in the passage from *Intruder in the Dust* is the imagination at work, supplying details that history does not divulge. The South's desperate gamble, Faulkner suggests, is that of every new beginning, the birth of a nation that D. W. Griffith elegizes in his film, not questioning the rightness of the cause so much as extolling an achievement on the brink of chaos.

In school, Billy read books about southern war heroes. The Stonewall Jackson biography praised the "blaze of his matchless military genius, the unchanging rectitude of his conduct, the stern will-power by which he conquered all difficulties, his firm belief in an overruling Providence, and his entire submission to the Divine Will." The Lee biographer treated him as a benevolent slave master: "When he came home from West Point, he found his mother's old coachman, Nat, very ill. He took him at once to the South and nursed him with great care. But the springtime saw the good old slave laid in the grave by the hand of his kind young master." William Falkner, so close to his own mother, read about Lee: "If he was a good boy, it was his mother who kept him so." A Faulkner classmate remembered these books and their teacher, "Miss Laura," who made the reading and lengthy discussion of these books "extra special": "She was a Confederate patriot of the first order! I leave you to imagine," she wrote to Carvel Collins, "the zeal and enthusiasm she exhibited in teaching about Lee and Jackson. All in the third grade must remember that book."[35]

Two Mothers

If Maud Falkner fostered the stoical silences of her son, who could read every day over her door a sign saying, "Don't Complain, Don't Explain," then Mammy Callie (Caroline Barr) did the reverse in story after story, regaling Billy and his brothers with tales about slavery and the war and olden times. To outsiders, she was circumspect. In the old slave quarters behind Faulkner's house, Robert Cantwell spoke with her: "She was a bright-eyed, small, high-voiced old lady, and I got an impression of her as shrewd and humorous, but we did not have much to say to each other."[36] This woman could stop most anyone in an Oxford street, of whatever race or class, and hold a conversation. Caroline Barr brought the past with her every day to work. "Matriarchal and imperial," she had "forgotten nothing."[37] Even in old age, she disallowed electricity and saw her way with kerosene lamps. She was opinionated and severe but also affectionate and hands-on.

Maud gave her son stories to read, and like Mammy Callie, Maud was her own woman. She shared with her mother, Lelia Butler, whom the Falkner boys called Damuddy, a visual and aesthetic sense expressed on canvas, doing a sensitive portrait of Mammy Callie that suggested Maud understood and appreciated the black woman who had done so much to bring up her boys.[38] These three women dominated Billy's earliest years, taking more of an interest in him than did the men in the family until he was old enough to hunt and talk and carouse with them. While Mammy Callie walked Billy through the woods, pointing out and naming flowers, Damuddy played in the backyard with her grandchildren, helping them build stockades, huts, stores, streets, and churches. She used whatever the boys found: grass, stones, pebbles, and broken glass. Like his grandmother, Billy was a hands-on builder and became the chief backyard architect.[39]

Damuddy's slow death, when Billy was nine, is powerfully evoked in *The Sound and the Fury* as the children try to comprehend what is happening to their grandmother, who can no longer sit in her chair, who eats in bed, as they hear their mother crying, and Jason cries because he cannot sleep with Damuddy. The children worry about what is going to happen to her body, and if the buzzards will undress her. Yet they expect her to get well and that they will have a picnic. Like Jason's crying, Quentin's and Benjy's grief is terrifying to them as they sense the disorder of Damuddy's departure. Caddy sits down in water that muddies her drawers, and Quentin says he will take his own life after he takes hers. These scenes suggest a trauma induced by an early sense of mortality and the destruction of the female triumvirate that had stabilized the Falkner home. Damuddy's death was a sickening experience. Sallie Murry, Faulkner's cousin, recalled that Damuddy suffered from "one of those female cancers with a horrible odor." The Falkner boys were sent to Sallie Murry's for a week after Damuddy died so that the house could be fumigated.[40]

Faulkner wrote more about Mammy Callie than he did about his own mother, although as a grown man in Oxford he visited Maud nearly every day. He thought of how these two women, weighing together less than two hundred pounds, had commanded his childhood in a house "roaring with five men," his father, three younger brothers, and himself. Caroline Barr and Maud Falkner fused present and past, as did Uncle Ned Barnett, wearing the old Colonel's clothing, including a "blue brass-buttoned frock coat and the plug hat in which he had been great-grandfather's and the grandfather's coachman." Ned had "two tremendous trunks" full of costumes for all occasions, showing Billy—who also liked to dress up and dress down—how to put on a performance. In style and manner, William Faulkner grew up in a theatrical household, which he made more theatrical in the telling of it.

To Faulkner, it would always seem that Callie and Ned had chosen to stay with the Falkners, as though an honor had been conferred on the family. Whatever Callie and Ned actually thought of their places, their presence undoubtedly reified a certain sentimental view of the Old South that Faulkner could never quite relinquish even as his writing revealed a past that gave the lie to much of the *Gone with the Wind* celebration of antebellum society.

Callie and Ned belonged to a hierarchical system built into slavery but that had evolved to a point where they had certain rights and privileges, if not the kind of freedom their white contemporaries enjoyed. When Faulkner later made his remarks on race, he could not entirely forsake a certain patronizing tone that derived from the enormous comfort he relished in the company of family retainers like Callie and Ned. He could not think of a home without them. And yet he certainly sensed that they had lives of their own and in many ways were in command of the Falkner household, shaping a code of behavior as much as they were responding to white hegemony, as can be seen in *Go Down, Moses* and *The Reivers*. Mammy Callie's stories about the terrifying night-riding Klan, even without overt criticism of the Jim Crow counter-reformation, provided a decidedly different version of history than what Billy heard in Oxford's courthouse and square.

The Code of the Gentleman

Perhaps one indirect result of slavery's legacy and southern defeat was "a great deal of pride and of a kind of civilized style and of a desire for fine manners."[41] A certain class of southerner perfected an elaborate Cavalier code and abjured those who attempted a familiarity not deserved by friendship or family connection. Faulkner absorbed this aloof demeanor not only from his family but from his reading of books like *The Virginian* (1902), the Owen Wister novel Damuddy enthusiastically recommended to her grandson. The eponymous hero is always pleasant and courteous but rebuffs all efforts to befriend him from those who dispense with the formalities of introductions and other gestures that protect the privacy of his person. His character depends on his detachment, as it did for Faulkner. While still a young boy, Faulkner liked to dress as a gentleman and to cut a figure, even asking his mother to tailor his clothes tightly to his body, which became another way of shaping his life as the art of William Faulkner. At seven, he went over Sunday school lessons with Damuddy, who reported what Billy said in answer to her question, which her daughter Maud wrote up in the family Bible: "'William, what would you rather have than anything else?' He answered, after a moment's thought, 'I'd rather have honor and do what's right.' Saturday—Oct. 1–1904." Wister's novel in Faulkner's library is signed by his father, Faulkner, and his grandmother (Damuddy) with what is probably her comment pointing out that the characters are sketchy, but that gave "one the more leisure to adore the Virginian."[42]

Grandfather J. W. T. Falkner epitomized the southern gentleman: all in white, topped with a Panama hat, adorned with vest, gold watch chain, and

cigar, swinging a gold-headed walking stick, to command a young boy's attention and emulation.[43] He was salty, wise, and relaxed, slow-spoken and drawl-
ing, although "everything he had to say had a fine edge to it," one observer
recalled.[44] The family considered him their best storyteller.[45] When an interviewer spotted a worn copy of a Dumas novel in William Faulkner's hotel
room, the writer said that he joined his grandfather in reading a paperbound
set of Dumas every year.[46] A romanticized version of the gentleman-hero, a
sort of surrogate for Faulkner's grandfather, appears in *The Reivers*. J. W. T.,
called the "young Colonel," assembled reunions of the old Colonel's Partisan
Rangers, gatherings Faulkner would later remember for the stories, the uniforms, and the flags that inspired games with his brothers playing Jeb Stuart
and their great-grandfather riding out to engage the Yankees. The Falkner
boys would sit on the gallery and listen to their grandfather talk about a time
that was "still a close and intimate thing."[47]

Jack Falkner remembered one especially vivid reunion when the veterans,
fed by the ladies of the family

> gathered together in the parlor, . . . fell to drinking good whiskey and
> telling tales of "The War," there being of course only one. Bill and John
> and I were allowed in the room to listen, indeed we asked for nothing
> more. Finally the speeches became quite serious . . . talking of those who
> had not returned from the war. Then a period of silence came upon the
> group and we saw a slender, white haired old soldier rise and wave his
> Confederate flag for attention. His was the shortest speech of all, but Bill
> and I never forgot it. He said, "What AIR (for are) more noble than to lie
> in the field of battle with YORE (for your) carcase (for carcass) filled with
> CANYION (for cannon) balls." It was, of course, deadly serious at the time
> but, like most everything else, mellowed with the passing of the years. I
> can see Bill now when, in later years, he would remember this phrase. He
> would begin with a sort of wry grin, then . . . a low but hearty chuckle and
> he would once again repeat what the old soldier had said, phonetically
> just as I have tried to give it here.

J. W. T. spoke of the old Colonel's exploits in the Mexican War and how the
family had to cope on its own during the old Colonel's days in Virginia fighting the Yankees, just as Bayard reports his father John Sartoris's war exploits
away from home in *The Unvanquished*. And the Falkner boys had relics to
cherish: the old Colonel's cane, watch, and books, items of a tangible past
that reappear in *Flags in the Dust*. Jack Falkner would later say his brother
patterned his life after the old Colonel's, but that claim is belied by a life and
fiction that seem, in many ways, antithetical to his great-grandfather's. And

if Faulkner's grandfather delighted him with re-creations of the Civil War, J. W. T. also became, like his counterpart old Bayard in *Flags in the Dust,* a relic of a bygone age retreating into deafness, sitting on his front porch in the inner sanctum of his memories.[48]

FATHER AND MOTHER

Faulkner's acute sense of his family's and his region's decline played itself out in the lives of his parents. Murry seemed a sorry attenuation of his forebears. He had not gone to war, built a railroad, or written a best-selling novel that had gone through thirty-five editions and sold something like 160,000 copies. After dropping out of Ole Miss, Murry depended on his father. Murry's passion had been for the railroad J. W. T. managed. Murry worked his way up to ever-more-important positions until his father sold the business without providing for his son's continuing employment in it. Then J. W. T. installed Murry in a livery stable even as automobiles were making that business obsolete.

A frustrated Murry went from one enterprise to another. There was a hardware store, where Billy spent his time at the gun counter.[49] Asked about how often her son worked in the store, Maud said, "Not any more than his father could help—Billy wasn't cut out to be a clerk."[50] An oil-delivery business also failed. Unlike Maud, Murry did not have the redeeming feature of being well-read or well-spoken. He confined his reading to comics and western adventure stories and sulked in silence, forbidding conversation at the dinner table when he was not picking on Billy, calling him "Snake Lips," a nasty dismissal of his thin-lipped, bookish son. Perhaps, though, Murry showed less of himself than was actually there. He kept a scrapbook that included a "short humorous essay in typescript and a series of diary entries that revealed something of a poetic sensibility if not poetic practice."[51]

Murry also had a violent temper. He knocked a man through a plate-glass window in one fight, and in another clash he knocked down a Pontotoc merchant named Elias Walker who had insulted Murry's girlfriend, Martha "Pattie" Fontaine. The irascible Pattie had also insulted Walter's sister Mollie, a seamstress, over a dress. Murry defended Pattti's honor, and Elias walked up to Murry at a drugstore counter and fired a shotgun hitting, Murry just above the right kidney. Murry's fall prevented him from being hit by a second blast. Standing over Murry's body, Elias fired a pistol at point blank range into Murry's mouth.[52] Called to the scene, Murry's mother got him to throw up the bullet lodged in his throat, and the survivor would later show family members the hole (the size of two fists) in his back.[53] As Faulkner would say, the Mississippi of his father's time was not far removed from the ferocity of the frontier. It was not an "old place, so naturally there's more violence and death in it. In a backwoods culture people have a way of settling disputes without recourse to the law."[54]

The one time Murry attempted a bold departure turned into another failure. He proposed to Maud that they move west and pursue a brand-new life. His plan followed the plot of *The Virginian,* which ends with the coming of the railroad to the West. But what had appealed to Damuddy and to Murry as a good, exciting read turned into Maud's scorn when her own husband wanted to turn fiction into fact. She adamantly refused to move, and Murry retreated to the front porch, to his cigars, and to his drinking. Faulkner's niece, Dean Faulkner Wells, observed that "Murry, unfortunately (for him) did not 'belong' to Maud. Marriage, for Maud Butler, could not possibly be equated with blood kinship, which referred solely to one's parents or children."[55]

On one rare occasion Murry tried to share a front-porch confidence with his son. Murry was a big cigar smoker. "He always had one in his mouth," according to Estelle Faulkner. When Murry offered his son a cigar, Billy broke it and jammed one half in his pipe. Faulkner said his father never offered him another cigar. For a historian of material culture this scene resonates, since the cigar symbolized "financial power and social status" in the New South.[56] It is the prop old Bayard sports in *Flags in the Dust.* Faulkner's preference for a pipe associates him with an earlier age, that of his great-grandfather, on whom Colonel John Sartoris is modeled. His pipe becomes one of old Bayard's treasured relics.

And yet there had to be more to Murry than this recitation of failure and diminishment. Why had Maud married a man so obviously unsuited to her temperament and interests? She read the classics and had introduced her twelve-year-old son to Joseph Conrad. She had friends with similar literary and artistic interests. Her mother had opposed the marriage to Murry—an oaf, really, when you consider what was expected of a southern gentleman. What could this brawler have to offer that offset his liabilities?

Murry had Holland, his sister and Maud's confidant, who could well have been a factor. She was only slightly taller than Maud, and the hard-riding Holland had spirit, which set her apart from other women of her time. And Maud was not in a favorable position. Her father, Charlie Butler, Oxford's law enforcement officer, tax collector, and town manager, had run off with the tax receipts and was never heard of again. He had apparently decamped with an octoroon mistress. Charlie Butler, a consummate insider, had bolted for parts unknown, arranging for himself a life that outraged his community, making him a pariah. But he left behind mixed-race children, William Faulkner's aunts and uncles, some of whom became prominent members in the Oxford community.[57] Faulkner's cousin Sallie Murry supposed that he was "probably shy over his mother's background" and all that business about the octoroon mistress.

Maud, after some college secretarial education, had supported herself and her mother, a burden to bear for a young woman, no matter how independent and resilient. Life was not a novel. She could not bring herself to leave home and start anew as New Englander Molly Stark Wood does in *The Virginian,* trusting to fate to find her a mate. Murry Falkner was at hand, and his family name still meant something. Men of few words can also be appealing, especially when they are tall and imposing and seem poised for success. As Gary Cooper demonstrated, taciturnity can be sexy in a garrulous world. Certainly Murry's public persona invited admiration: "Mr. Murry Falkner, the handsome son of J. W. T. Falkner, Pres't of the G & C RR, came in last week and we understand is preparing himself to take charge of one of the trains as conductor," reported the *Ripley (MS) Sentinel* on March 12, 1890.

Murry might be a catch who could be lost to another woman. He looked like a man you could lean on. However halting his talk, he might make a promising project. Reticence can be mistaken for hidden depths. Unlike Maud's renegade father, Murry remained tied to the railroad, which then sounded in its beckoning whistle the romance of yearning that Thomas Wolfe so memorably depicts in *Look Homeward, Angel.* On a Sunday afternoon, Murry took Maud out for either a ride or a walk, and the couple returned to announce they had married, "to the delight of all the Falkners."[58] As the *Oxford Eagle* decorously put it on November 12, 1896: "Mr. Murry Falkner and Miss Maud Butler were married Sunday night [November 8] at the parsonage by Rev. J. W. Forman. . . . The young couple took their relatives and friends somewhat by surprise, but their congratulations and good wishes were nonetheless sincere for their future happiness and prosperity."

Murry apparently knew how to court a woman. One Oxford resident, W. H. Hutchinson, a member of a Boy Scout troop that Faulkner later headed, claimed much worse for Murry—that he "would lay a snake if he had its head in a forked stick." Hutchinson's Aunt Claire "used to tell how Mrs. Falkner would bring Billy, a little boy, over to Grandmother H's house and visit in the consolatory manner of southern gentlewomen with a cross."[59] But the first five years in Ripley, where the couple settled, seemed to go well with the births of William (in New Albany, September 25, 1897), Murry (June 26, 1899), and John (September 24, 1901).

In 1902, five-year-old Willie became Billy when the family moved from Ripley to Oxford. In the coal age, it took the better part of two days, with cinders flying through the train's open windows, making for a sooty arrival in their new hometown, much larger than Ripley. Jack (Murry) remembered the wonder of it all: the people, the horses, the carriages, their grandfather's bank, the courthouse square, the post office, and most of all "the lights—arc lights! The first we had ever seen."[60]

In town, around the courthouse square, the ground floors of faded red-brick buildings, all the same, were the shops, while above, on the second floor, the professional class—the doctors and lawyers—had their offices with balconies facing the street, so that they could walk out and sit in chairs and talk. Here the world congregated in a compact space. As a boy, Billy would not have seen any American flags, except on the federal building. Nothing seemed to change until the First World War. For years, Old Man Stephens (Richard Lane Stephens) remained mayor. Elections were "just a formality because nobody ever thought of running against him," Faulkner recalled.[61]

J. W. T. Falkner, on hand to meet his grandchildren, now dominated his son's every important move. Jack's portrayal of his hard-of-hearing grandfather is reminiscent of the scenes in *Flags in the Dust* with old Bayard, who grew up in Reconstruction when, Jack adds, he saw his "beloved country devastated even more by the carpetbaggers in peace than it had been by the enemy soldiers in war." That view of the "iron heel of Reconstruction" receives remarkably little attention in Faulkner's fiction,[62] which dwells instead on John Sartoris's bloody-minded, exhausted state. It is not what the carpetbaggers have done to him that is the point, but what he has done to himself. In this respect the old Colonel and his fictional counterpart coincide: "Falkner ended as he had so often lived, a man alienated by his own acts from the community of which he was undeniably a part."[63] The symmetry of the life made for the same symmetry in fiction. For all her father's adventures and daring, he was, in Aunt Bama's words, "very lonely and tragic. He had no peer with whom he could exchange ideas and with whom he could share his dreams."[64]

The boys soon had a new playmate, their cousin Sallie Murry, who became like a sister—resembling the intrepid Caddy of *The Sound and the Fury*—joining them in kite flying, shooting marbles, skating, and their own version of hockey. Billy liked to play dolls with Sallie Murry. Damuddy had carved a doll for him, a policeman named Patrick O'Leary. She made a uniform for this eight- or nine-inch wooden figure with a police helmet made of felt.[65] Why did she fashion this urban and Irish character rather than a cowboy, which is what, after all, the Virginian had become? Williamson supposes she had in mind the figure of her renegade husband, Charlie Butler, the town cop, so to speak, who kept the order that the Falkners disrupted in their violent clashes with their rivals. But how could Butler serve as any kind of antidote to Murry—no matter how much Damuddy despised him? The young Colonel didn't blame Charlie Butler for running off. Charlie could not stand his wife, and she, in turn, made Murry's life miserable.[66] Damuddy understood that Billy liked uniforms and always would.[67]

Half the time boys, even in a western setting, prefer policeman dolls, as Erik Erikson reports in *Childhood and Society*. Perhaps playing with Patrick O'Leary imposed a sense of order in a contentious household. The doll may have expressed Billy's solidarity with Damuddy and rebellion against his father's taste for shoot-em-up Westerns. Faulkner would later refer to the composition of *The Sound and the Fury* as a form of play, trotting along after his characters, with very little to do until the "policeman in the back of the head" insisted on "unity and coherence and emphasis in telling it."[68]

Faulkner's New Orleans sketch "The Cop" provides a suggestive insight into his playtime preferences:

> Fellows there were who intended to be pirates, some would go west and kill Indians gallantly from loping horses, others would sit in the cabs of locomotives, blowing derisive whistle blasts at lesser adventurous mortals. But I, I would be a patrolman; in a blue coat and swinging a casual stick and with a silver shield on my breast, I would pace the streets away with the measured beat of my footsteps.
>
> What to compare with this grandeur? To be the idol and fear of the lads, to be looked upon with respect by even grown people; to be the personification of bravery and the despair of criminals; to have a real pistol in my pocket!

Above all, this boy wanted to assert his authority, to be in charge, as he often did by taking command as the eldest brother. Murry's favored westerns and his railroading had to be spurned for the singularity of the cop on the beat. "The Cop" concludes: "Anyway, I prefer to believe that this creature fronting the world bravely in a blue coat and a silver shield is quite a fellow, after all."[69] Sally Murry remembered that Billy played with his policeman doll until he was a rather "big child."[70]

The firstborn son in each generation of the Falkner family had to contend with an aloof and dictatorial father. Billy would fare no better with his father than his father had fared with his going, all the way back to the old Colonel. This depletion of the family's energies in the entropy of their enterprises was reaching a kind of crisis in the lives of Billy and his brothers that each of them would try to resolve in disharmonious ways as soon as the camaraderie of boyhood dissipated. This sense of decay and dependency that called out for a family elder to take command, policing and providing for a whole clan, would gradually envelop Jason Compson in *The Sound and the Fury* and, even more notably, William Faulkner.

LOVE AT FIRST SIGHT

By the fall of 1903, Estelle, the daughter of Lemuel E. Oldham, clerk of the United States Circuit Court and a member of an old southern family of soldiers and politicians, had moved to Oxford and, according to her own account, spotted Billy on a Shetland pony leading a procession of Falkners. "Nolia," she said to her black nursemaid, "see that little boy? I'm going to marry him when I grow up." So Mrs. William Faulkner—using all of her husband's name as women were expected and accustomed to do—expressed her pride of possession.[71] And who knows? She might even have been remembering aright. Given her pedigree, and her schooling in southern womanhood, she may already have been on the lookout for her Virginian, the gentleman who would ride into her life, ahead of all the rest, and he lived just three doors down from her in a house dating back to Oxford's rich antebellum period, complete with a large backyard, a barn, and a pasture—in short, with plenty of room for the Falkner boys to play and to entertain their friends.

The love-at-first-sight anecdote has been repeated with varying degrees of acceptance without lingering to consider Nolia's rejoinder: "Folks what say they goin' to get married while they little is sho to grow up to be ol' maids." Estelle did not reply to Nolia's rebuff but just kept watching the Falkner parade. Nolia not only attended Estelle; she also kept the young lady in her place. Nolia normalized the patriarchal paradigm of the southern white lady, a graceful decoration to any home, a charming hostess, and demure damsel awaiting her gentleman's proposal. Not replying to her minder reflected one kind of dissent; writing would eventually be another avenue of protest that Estelle would take in the mid-1920s, just before Faulkner began to make his great breakthroughs in fiction. If Estelle gave consummate performances as a southern belle, what she thought and how she behaved in private, especially with Billy, was another matter: Estelle was "as much an outsider as Faulkner," playing the budding belle as well as anyone and entertaining the boys at dances and in conversations, but she also withheld from them an intellect and sensibility that only Billy Faulkner could truly appreciate.

In Estelle's fiction, she mocked the pretensions of the Mayflower Old-hams. She found it as difficult to earn her conventional mother's approval as Billy found it to please his father. If Estelle could confide more freely in Nolia, as Billy did in Callie, neither black servant could surmount the hierarchical edifice that enclosed them. Both Nolia and Callie perforce had to wear masks as well, performing roles that both Estelle and William Faulkner would eventually explore in their fiction. With Callie and Nolia, Billy and Estelle moved between black and white worlds, in which a black person could be boss but also just the help.

Unlike many belles, Estelle, thanks to her grandfather Judge Henry C. Niles, was well-read at an early age in the classics. Papa Niles, as she called him, provided explanations and, by the time she was twelve, had her reading Voltaire. Already at eight, she may have been better-read than Billy, who had just started school.[72] By the age of ten, when he began reading Conrad, Shakespeare, and Balzac, he had nearly caught up to her. And, according to Estelle, they were already talking marriage.[73] They did make a stylish couple: Estelle in her laces and bows and frills, and Billy sporting a straw hat when he played croquet.[74] She might have said, early on, what Molly Stark Wood in *The Virginian* says to her southern lover: "I have made one discovery. . . . You are fonder of good clothes than I am." Estelle knew her clothes. One neighbor noted that her father wore a Chesterfield, a long tailored coat, even after hard times when he could not afford groceries. Lem's granddaughter said he wore a white linen suit when working with his gardener.[75] To begin with, the Oldhams enjoyed a grand life on Lem's high salary of six thousand dollars a year, entertaining Oxford's prominent citizens in their impressive two-story house.[76]

Estelle's exceptional family, Republicans in a Democratic bastion, may have seemed remarkably stable and appealing to a boy who had an upsetting relationship with his father and had to watch his beloved, uncomplaining Damuddy slowly die. In Jack's memoir, he makes only the briefest mention that his mother, Maud, and her brother, Sherwood, had been "left without a father," a deft way of avoiding the admission that Charlie Butler, whom Jack did not even name, had abandoned his family. Maud had always relied on her husband's sister—Aunt Holland to the boys, an indomitable woman, as good on a horse, perhaps, as Drusilla in *The Unvanquished,* and as opinionated as Miss Jenny in *Flags in the Dust.* Holland was the first in Oxford to wear a divided skirt, also called culottes, a popular choice for horseback riding. "She didn't know what fright was," said one family member. Holland would later fly with Faulkner's youngest brother, Dean, when his mother, Maud, refused to do so.[77] In *The Falkners of Mississippi,* brother Jack wrote about an unreconstructed Auntee who seemed to the boys a rebel who would have beaten all the Yankees no matter how much they outnumbered her. Aunt Holland had known the Oldhams for two generations, having been present at the wedding of Estelle's parents.

William could never have written his brother Jack's sentence: "How kind they were, those years of long ago, how gentle the life and how pleasant the memories of it." Jack provides a Dickensian scene of father with his paper, mother sewing, Mammy Callie in her rocking chair relating stories about the war, taking possession of the room, so to speak, by referring to "mah white folks." Missing from Jack's account is the impact on their eldest son of the conflicts between Murry and Maud Falkner. To a Freudian, the son's closeness to his mother, resulting in the oedipal wish to supplant his father, made Murry's coldness toward Billy all that more exacerbating. It is tempting to see in the father-son contest one reason why Faulkner later took on the role of patriarch, even at the cost of thwarting his sense of himself as a loner dedicated to his art. It isn't clear how soon—perhaps very soon—Murry took against his firstborn, who was said by so many in the family to look like and take after the Butlers. Billy, almost from the start, then, may actually have increased the animosity between husband and wife. As Erik Erikson observes:

> Parents who are faced with the development of a number of children must constantly live up to a challenge. They must develop with them. We distort the situation if we abstract it in such a way that we consider the parent as "having" such and such a personality when the child is born and then, remaining static, impinging upon a poor little thing. For this weak and changing little being moves the whole family along. Babies control and bring up their families as much as they are controlled by them; in fact, we may say that the family brings up a baby by being brought up by him.[78]

Brother Jack would have us believe otherwise, presenting his Billy as well-adjusted and the leader of various Tom Sawyer–like projects: building a dam and trying to build and fly an airplane with the inevitable crackup. According to another witness, Billy launched the aircraft with the help of a disabled coachman and a yard man with only one arm. They took hold of the wing tips and heaved it up "before an admiring crowd." Of course, the plane abruptly crashed and broke up. Billy removed himself from the wreckage, dignity intact, looking straight ahead. After the discovery of an old rusty pistol, Billy took charge, loading the chambers with gunpowder from a firecracker, and lighting its fuse so that all the chambers exploded. Yet another incident involved a "home-made vehicle" that Billy and his boys "pretended was an automobile. They drove it at night using lanterns as light, with Billy steering until, again, the adventure ended in a crash.[79]

Some of the closest observers of Billy Falkner were black people, accustomed to carefully marking the mannerisms of white people, especially the ones who stood out. For all his adventures, Billy seemed to stand apart, his mind elsewhere, "thinking about Egypt or some other place," said Walter Johnson, who worked for a white family near the Falkner home. "William Faulkner even as a child walked slowly like an old man," recalled Johnson, who could not remember the boy ever skipping and running. Perfectly pleasant, Billy nevertheless seemed "withdrawn."[80]

Jack's passages about the railroad—describing its "heart-stirring," rushing, whoo-oo and then the locomotive pounding into view, the smoking, swirling exhaust of an engine on the track—offer all we need to know about why Murry felt really alive in his railroad work. In Oxford, that life was over. Murry was derailed, his toy taken away when his father sold the railroad. Murry lived in the home his father had vacated for a much larger establishment. Meanwhile, in church with Damuddy, hymnal in hand, Billy deposited in the good book his depiction of a locomotive.[81] If Jack ever sensed that his brother Billy was set apart from his family in a remarkable way, he never said so in print or to other Faulkner biographers. Yet it strains our modern sense of childhood development not to suppose that Faulkner, like most precocious children, did not experience "relative isolation" and a "disquieting imbalance."[82]

The frustrated father and his eldest son were never close, although Faulkner rewrote his past for Malcolm Cowley: "I escaped my mother's influence pretty easy, since my father thought it was fine for me to apprentice the [livery stable] business."[83] His eldest son liked to draw pictures of the horses, especially of their heads.[84] He had a calming influence on horses. "A horse get out there and act a little contrary or something, he'd talk to him just as nice, you know, and go right on," said Earl Wortham, an African American blacksmith who worked in the livery stable. "Mr. Faulkner's temper was just as quiet from, you might say, the time I know him up till the last."[85]

Handling horses put Billy into a masculine world that otherwise "mocked or questioned what he was trying to do."[86] It is a tempting analysis, given what Stark Young, for example, said about his own quest to be an author: "Only in after years did I realize that in our social scheme, as with county families in England, from whom we drew our standards, your son could be a planter, a lawyer, a senator or a doctor—in sum, a man—but a musician, a painter, a poet were likely to be effeminate, weaklings, certainly no credit to our class." Did Billy feel embarrassed about his interest in art? He felt unappreciated, certainly. And his grandfather grumbled that he wanted no artists in the family.[87] But Billy, the leader of his brothers—even a surrogate father since Murry was aloof with all his sons except Dean, the youngest—does not seem to have had any significant concerns about his masculinity or his art. It bothered him from time to time that he was small, as his wife, Estelle, and others testified, but that hardly seemed to matter in the larger schemes of his boyhood and manhood. He was rugged and dogged from the start. As John Cullen, a childhood playmate, asserted, no one ever called William Faulkner a sissy.[88] A later friend, Hubert Starr, insisted: "Bill Faulkner had 'guts' but not the physical strength to fight yokels on their ground."[89] Billy did not get into scuffles or fights. He did "sometimes tease the other children verbally," but he remained an "onlooker."[90]

Faulkner's comment about escaping the influence of his mother, while patently untrue, is also, in a way, a tribute to a father he found so hard to like: "However profane and disparaging his father might be, the boy still felt something for him, for his world of horses and hunting and trains."[91] Faulkner adjusted to all aspects of his upbringing, which he would then transform into his fiction. Father and son, by the way, shared the same soft voice.[92]

Faulkner seemed to revel in growing up, like an unnamed character in an unpublished story "impregnated with the violent ammoniac odor of horses. At ten he could stand on a box and harness a horse and put it between runabout shafts almost as quickly as a grown man, darting beneath its belly like a cricket to buckle the straps, cursing it in his shrill cricket voice."[93] John Faulkner remembered how all three brothers followed their father into the woods: "Dad was a good storyteller. We all remembered the stories he told us on those walks, perhaps Bill best of all, for a number of them, or parts of them, appeared in his stories of the woods and hunting in later years."[94] Not in general given to holding forth, Father Falkner came alive on these expeditions.

Maud could be aloof, and at least one of Faulkner's doctors felt he suffered from a lack of mother love, no matter how much she supported him.[95] A Faulkner relative also suggested as much.[96] But Maud's independence helped more than it hindered. She was "no Southern princess"[97] deferring to her husband's sovereignty. Faulkner's "relations with the women in and outside of his family, rather than his connections with a tenuous and questionable masculine ideal, shaped both his understanding of what it meant to love and his vision of what an artist and a man could be."[98]

Books were another shaping force, of course. It has been said that Faulkner never forgot anything he read. *The Virginian* concerns a southerner who falls in love with a New England schoolteacher who gives him great literature to read at his request as part of his courtship of her. The southerner, no scholar, nevertheless in his rough-hewn way turns out to be a shrewd literary critic who challenges his better-educated beloved's interpretations of Shakespeare. It is not so much what he says, though, as that the talk of books is an integral part of the story, of how this couple falls in love, and it is a story that Faulkner would recast in his own life in his bookish offerings to Estelle, Helen Baird, Meta Carpenter, and Joan Williams. Like the Virginian, William Faulkner wrote and spoke and dressed and rode horses and hunted exactly as he wished and not to prove anything about his choices. This is what his mother communicated to him in her "don't complain, don't explain" mode.

Billy did not complain when his mother put him in shoulder braces designed to perfect the remarkably correct posture he maintained all his life. Were the braces also part of a desire to make him look taller?[99] Perhaps, although his cousin Sallie Murry wore the braces too and rebelled, saying it "hurt like anything," and took the appliance off whenever she could.[100] Faulkner, on the other hand, did not share any similar grievances, leading commentators in the Freudian Age to suppose he suppressed his resentment. Possibly so, but surely the overriding point is that Faulkner just went on without a gripe. His brother Jack, when asked about the braces, could just barely remember them.[101]

Much has also been written about Faulkner's upset over the birth of his brother Dean on August 15, 1907. Now, supposedly, Billy no longer had his mother's devotion. But he already had two brothers who claimed their mother's attention—and Mammy Callie's, as both Jack and John attested. And Dean, as the baby, seemed to be cherished by everyone in the family even as he developed a gregarious personality that seemed to delight everyone. If anything, Dean was received as a surprise gift, especially since his birth occurred just over two months after Damuddy's death.

LYNCHING

On September 8, 1908, when Billy was not quite eleven years old, newspapers across the country reported: "One of the coldest blooded murders and most brutal crimes known to the criminal world was perpetrated one mile north of town yesterday morning about ten o'clock, when a black brute of unsavory reputation by the name of Nelse Patton attacked Mrs. Mattie McMullen, a respected white woman, with a razor, cutting her throat from ear to ear and causing almost instant death."[102] In the *Oxford Eagle,* a six-sentence article, "Negro Lynched by Mob," supplied only a few more details. The town had no telephones then, and Patton had been sent to deliver a message from Mr. McMillan to Mrs. McMillan (different accounts give different spellings of their last name) telling her he was in jail for drunkenness.[103] According to William Faulkner's nephew Jimmy, who seems to have heard the story from his mother, Patton went through the McMillans' front door, considered an outrage then. Another Oxford inhabitant said Patton took himself seriously. His manner of dressing up and the independent way he carried himself reminded her of Faulkner's Lucas Beauchamp.[104] What could this mean, except that Patton acted like a white man, like Joe Christmas in *Light in August*? Patton refused to leave Mrs. McMillan's home and purportedly accosted her. When she tried to defend herself with a revolver, Patton attacked her. One scholar notes how much the newspaper account left out. What was in the message? Why was Patton, with his so-called unsavory reputation, entrusted with this errand? Were there witnesses who could corroborate what happened to Mrs. McMillan? Why did Patton act so rashly and violently? Of course such questions would not be asked because the lynching was about asserting white supremacy, or, as it is put in *Intruder in the Dust,* the "white man's high estate." The black man becomes an "ideological figure," "an object of erasure."[105]

In fact, more than a hundred men pursued Patton, who fled several miles over fences and fields, eluding barking dogs and gunshots, until John Cullen, a thirteen-year-old boy, spotted the fugitive crossing a railroad track and brought him down with two shotgun blasts.[106] Bloodied but alive, Patton was taken to the county jail, where a huge mob had gathered, according to eyewitness John Cullen.[107]

Judge W. A. Roane, Sheriff Hartsfield, and other county officials attempted to disperse the vigilantes with calls to respect the law, behave decently, show Christian compassion, and preserve the honor of the community. Such appeals to a gentlemanly code sometimes did dissuade lynchings.[108] Perhaps in this case the pleas for due process and humanity might have prevailed, but then William V. Sullivan, an attorney and former U.S. senator, intervened, telling the crowd to do its duty. As he told a reporter for the *Jackson Clarion-Ledger* two days later: "I led the mob which lynched Nelse Patton and I am proud of it. I directed every movement of the mob, and I did everything I could to see that he was lynched."[109] It would take more than a hundred years for Congress to finally pass an antilynching law.

The mob broke down the jail's front door, sending in young boys first because, as John Cullen put it, everyone knew the deputies would not shoot boys.[110] The sheriff refused to relinquish the keys to Patton's cell but apparently put up no significant resistance. Cullen remembered grabbing a deputy, his own father, "not very hard to hold anyway."[111] The steel and brick structure, well built to withstand a prisoner's effort to break out, resisted five hours of sledgehammering and chiseling through walls and stairs blocking the way to Patton's second-floor lockup. Outside on ladders extending to the second story the avengers swung pickaxes to strike off the brick facade before their battering ram broke through the remaining twelve-inch-thick log walls and a four-inch metal lining. Patton, a "big powerful man," John Cullen said, confronted the surging gang with an iron coal-shovel handle and managed to seriously injure three men before he went down in gunfire.[112] In a memoir, published while Faulkner was still alive, Cullen described the aftermath: "Someone (I don't know who) cut his ears off, scalped him, tied a rope around his neck, tied him to a car, and dragged his body around the streets. Then they hanged him to a walnut-tree limb just outside the south entrance to the courthouse." This kind of barbaric mutilation often occurred in lynchings. Cullen did not publish all of what he saw and felt, but vouchsafed details to scholar Floyd Watkins: "I was proud. Somebody cut his balls off. . . . I don't know who done that. I was just a bystander. I was just a kid. . . . What they want is intermarriage with white people. Other rights he's got. They will sacrifice their lives for a white woman. We are not going to let them rape white women. That's my real sentiments. I hope you got that and I don't give a darn who heard it."[113] He does not add that the victim's body parts, especially small bones, fingers, toes, and ears, were used as watch fobs or displayed in service stations and general stores.[114]

Cullen concluded: "Nelse Patton's crime and the lynching of Nelse are more widely known than anything else of this kind that ever happened in Lafayette County." Faulkner "must have heard numerous stories about the Patton case," Cullen noted while enumerating examples of how Patton's fate provided material for *Light in August* and *Sanctuary.* "Must have heard" is an odd choice of words coming from someone so closely implicated in the lynching story, especially since, in an Author's Note, Cullen affirms that "William Faulkner and I have been friends since we were little boys." Cullen's younger brother Hal was in the same grade as Faulkner, who joined the Cullens in swimming, bullfrogging, shooting cottonmouths, and in listening to hunting stories. Didn't John or Hal Cullen confide to William Faulkner any part of the Patton lynching, which also included their twenty-one-year-old brother, Jenks? Joseph Blotner reports: "When Miss Kate Kimmons' fifth-grade class was organized that September of 1908, if the boys standing around the playground wanted to know more about what had happened, Hal Cullen, the brother of the boy who had fired the first shot, could tell them."

Joel Williamson estimates that on the night of the lynching Faulkner slept in a bed "not more than a thousand yards from both the jail and the square." How could he not hear the commotion and not want to know what was happening when sounds of gunfire and the demolition of steel doors disturbed the peace? Sallie Burns, Faulkner's cousin who frequented the Falkner household, recalled "hearing the hammers the mob used all the way from the jail up to the campus where she was living."[115]

It is difficult for Williamson to believe that Faulkner did not witness some part of the lynching. Jimmy Faulkner said that his mother, then five, lived two blocks or so east of the jail, and she could hear the "pecking and chipping at the brick wall outside Patton's cell." The next day, Patton's hanging body was on display. "This must have made a real lasting impression on Brother Will, because so much of it is in *Light in August,*" Jimmy concluded, although like Cullen, he apparently never mentioned the lynching to Faulkner, who treated Jimmy more like a brother than a nephew.[116] In discussing Faulkner's lynching story "Dry September," Estelle said that both of them had heard as children a story of Oxford events much like those in the story, and her husband obviously remembered it better than she did.[117]

In his memoir, Cullen describes the gruesome details of the lynching without comment, saying only that his father was certain of Patton's guilt, since he was caught with part of the razor blade that was also stuck in Mattie McMillan's throat. Aspects of the lynching would infiltrate Faulkner's story "Dry September." Cullen reports, for example, that when Patton fell from the shotgun blast, he said to Cullen's older brother:

> "Mr. Jenks, you knows I'se a good nigger."
> "I know you're a good nigger," my brother said, "but get your hands up."

To be a "good nigger" meant to know your place, and until whatever happened in that house with Mattie McMillan, Nelse Patton had known his place, although after his death accounts began to backdate his uppityness. Indeed, what is unspoken in all the lynching stories is the horror that a "good nigger" should go so abominably wrong. And what troubled Cullen—it seems for his entire life—is that even on the point of capture Patton no longer was a "good nigger," no matter what he said. You can almost hear the wonder—or is it regret?—in Cullen's comment, "But Nelse never did put his hands up."

Nelse Patton was well-known to the Oxford community. At the time of Mattie McMillan's murder, he was a prison "trusty," jailed for bootlegging but allowed out of prison to deliver messages. In one account, it is said that Patton had delivered many messages to Mrs. McMillan "without incident."[118] This meant he had observed all the protocols of black behavior, which forbid so much as smiling at a white woman because a "careless gesture might result in the charge of attempted assault, often not distinguished from that of rape itself."[119] Patton, whatever his crimes, was not regarded as a violent threat to the town, and his illegal business prospered. Even more revealing is that the lawyer on the bootlegging charges had been William Sullivan, who took so much pride in directing the lynching, declaring in an Associated Press report: "I wouldn't mind standing the consequences any time for lynching a man who cut a white woman's throat. I will lead a mob in such a case any time." The defense of southern womanhood, in other words, became the whole story.

But that was not the whole story. Several reports claimed a drunken Patton had made advances to Mattie McMillan. Alcohol abuse, as Williamson discovered, had become such a public problem that law enforcement efforts had been renewed to shut down operations like Nelse Patton's, even though it is likely that he had many customers, white and black, which is why Williamson concludes:

> It is not surprising that he should have been treated as a "trustee" in Lafayette County's penal system. Nor would it be vastly surprising to find that Nelse had been well acquainted with both Mr. and Mrs. McMillan before they all gained such signal public attention and that their familiarity was not unrelated to the reasons for Mr. McMillan's incarceration. In brief, it is likely that the whole affair was not so coincidental, and that white parties of both sexes were not as innocent as they might, at first blush, seem.
>
> Somehow in the Patton case the community found itself confronting the alarming results of a commingling of race and sex with the disinhibiting effects of alcohol.

This suggestive passage overturns the official story, which had reduced Patton to the subhuman. To those repulsed by the commingling of white and black, what actually happened between Patton and McMillan did not matter. They narrowed on the penetration of the razor, when the brute could not have his way with the mother, and perhaps with her daughter. In short, the "good nigger" had reverted to his African savagery—like scenes in *The Clansman* in which black people, no longer held in check by the discipline of slavery, succumb to bestiality, including rape. A month after the lynching, on October 8, 1908, the Oxford Opera House announced in the *Oxford Eagle* the coming of *The Klansman,* featuring a cast of forty, "a carload of effects," a "troop of cavalry horse," and "dazzling scenery." Tickets were priced at fifty cents, seventy-five cents, and $1.50.

It would take William Faulkner nearly twenty years to sort out the implications of the Nelse Patton lynching and others that occurred across the South. In 1935, four years after the publication of "Dry September," Faulkner rejected a national magazine's request to write about a lynching, saying he had never seen one and could not describe one. But that very year, in Oxford, on September 18, the *New York Times* reported that a "screaming, terrified Negro was seized in the county jail by a crowd of between 100 and 150 persons and hanged from a tree two and a half miles from town." Faulkner's eight-year-old nephew Jimmy watched the hanging and was warned "fiercely to tell no one what he saw." For decades Jimmy did just that, and he did not divulge what he had witnessed until the mid-1990s during an interview with Faulkner scholar Arthur F. Kinney.

The 1935 lynching may have been, according to the Mississippi archives in Jackson, the "last formal ritual lynching in the state's history." But twenty-five years earlier, the death count resulting from such horrifying misadventures was mounting. Between 1889 and 1909, "at least 293 blacks were lynched there [in Mississippi], more than in any other state in the nation." Mississippi from 1890 onward was deemed the "darkest section of the South for a colored man," and the "South at its worst." The period between 1889 and 1919 has been called the "most repressive in Mississippi history." Just a year before the Nelse Patton lynching, the state's governor, James K. Vardaman, declared, "If it is necessary every Negro in the state will be lynched; it will be done to maintain white supremacy." His vehemence occurred at a time when black people constituted 60 percent of Mississippi's population.[120]

This brutal history of atrocity, the lynching stories, had to be part of what William Faulkner knew and continued to write about into the 1940s in *Go Down, Moses* and in *Intruder in the Dust*.[121] The latter, in particular, enacts the formula of "dependency and disavowal,"[122] in which Lucas Beauchamp, a well-known figure in Jefferson, is turned into a "nigger" who deserves to be lynched for allegedly murdering a white man even as he demands that Chick Mallison, a sixteen-year-old white boy, establish his innocence. An especially vivid scene in the film adaptation of the novel shows that Chick Mallison's family depends on the black woman who serves them even as Chick's father refuses to see why she is upset about Lucas since she is not "related" to him. Lynching promotes the "white fantasy of uncorrupted racial boundaries."[123]

On the only occasion when William Faulkner made lynching the focal point of a short story, he transformed the details of the Nelse Patton lynching to reflect certain latent truths that no newspaper account or historical record could reveal. "Dry September" begins by establishing the season and the psychology that results in lynching: "Through the bloody September twilight, aftermath of sixty-two rainless days, it had gone like a fire in dry grass—the rumor, the story, whatever it was. Something about Miss Minnie Cooper and a Negro." Passions ignite after a parching summer. In fact, lynchings often occurred in September, as if such eruptions were part of a communal outpouring of emotion. And like many of Faulkner's fellow townsmen, the details of who did what to whom, and never mind why, are overwhelmed in the story by those who feel "attacked, insulted, frightened" in the stale atmosphere—in this case of a barbershop's "vitiated air." It is as if in this close or closed environment no one can properly breathe or think. The barbershop, also one of the focal points of *Intruder in the Dust,* is, like the pool hall, one of the gathering centers of community lore and rumor, and the starting point for many of the lynchers.

Before anyone else speaks, a mild-faced, middle-aged barber asserts: "Except it wasn't Will Mayes. . . . I know Will Mayes. He's a good nigger. And I know Miss Minnie Cooper, too." It is a simple statement, but it reflects the complex reality that William Faulkner had to negotiate every day of his life in Oxford. Segregation would seem to mean a white barber could not possibly "know" a black person in any significant sense, but, in fact, "in private homes—not to mention other territories devoted to commerce (such as Murry Falkner's livery stable)—whites and blacks shared social space."[124] The barber realizes how quickly this incendiary climate of stifled emotions will ignite in violence. When he tries to explain that forty-year-old Minnie Cooper is a spinster and "that is why I don't believe," he is interrupted by a "hulking youth": "Believe, hell! . . . Wont you take a white woman's word before a nigger's?" Immediately the barber is called a "damn nigger lover." The barber says that Minnie Cooper is one of "them ladies that get old without getting married" and have "notions" that amount to sexual fantasies, although he never is given a chance to explain himself. The mild but persistent barber does not believe "anything happened," and that very idea infuriates another customer, who says, "Do you accuse a white woman of lying?" The barber of course does no such thing, but to say more—and he is constantly interrupted—would be to reveal the subtext of the story: Like everyone else, Minnie Cooper has been looking for an outlet for her pent-up emotions. Then another barbershop patron turns the psychology of the season away from Minnie Cooper and toward Mayes by making a sick joke: "It's this durn weather. . . . It's enough to make a man do anything. Even to her." No one dares to say, as well, that it is enough to make a woman do anything. In short, the mild barber's call to "find out the truth first" is overwhelmed by outrage that a white man would consider, even for a moment, excusing a "nigger attacking a white woman." Like the guards in the Oxford county jail subdued by Patton's lynch mob, the barber's voice is silenced, although at least two others have their doubts. "Did it really happen?" one of them asks, to which McLendon, who becomes the leader of the lynch mob, says: "What the hell difference does it make? Are you going to let the black sons [of bitches] get away with it until one really does it?" He might as well be called Senator Sullivan, who intervened to make sure Patton, at one time viewed by white people as a "good nigger," was lynched before he received a proper defense. Faulkner learned early on, to his dismay, how the decent and rational voices of his community could be suppressed in the desperate desire to reinforce a racist ideology.

The mild barber makes one more effort to save Will Mayes, going to the site where the lynchers have gathered and not only insisting on Mayes's innocence but also appealing to the community's conception of race relations and sexual mores: "Why, you know as well as I do there ain't any town where they got better niggers than us. And you know how a lady will kind of think things about men when there ain't any reason to, and Miss Minnie anyway—" But he is interrupted again and ignored even as a group of women whisper, "Do you suppose anything really happened?" They are titillated, their eyes "darkly aglitter, secret and passionate." They call her "poor Minnie." Their skepticism seems the result of her having "fallen into erotic irrelevance." Her claim to defilement, then, rehabilitates the "sexual cachet" of a woman who notices that men "did not even follow her with their eyes anymore."[125] And her longing for the "beautiful, passionate and sad" has been stimulated by the "silver dreams" of the cinema that she shares with other women friends in fantasies that would begin to occupy William Faulkner's Hollywood working days shortly after the publication of this story.[126]

Minnie is not the only poor one. McLendon, the mob leader, returns home after the lynching to physically abuse his wife when he finds her sitting up at midnight waiting for him to come in. Even in the framework of marriage, Faulkner suggests, there may be no way for women to freely express themselves. In a deleted passage, he made his point explicit: "Life in such places is terrible for women. Life in all places is terrible for women."[127] The lynching is of a piece with McLendon, the ex-soldier who knows no peace and projects his frustration onto others, including one of the very white women, his wife, he supposedly champions, in a futile attempt to purge his passions. He is bound to Minnie Cooper in a curious way, experiencing the heat of a long drought that makes her hair swirl "crisp and crackling under the comb." Both Cooper and McLendon seem to have used Mayes as a scapegoat to be found in the "primitive and classical patterns" James Frazer traced in *The Golden Bough,* demanding a sacrifice in a futile effort to restore the community's sense of well-being.[128] In "Dry September," the black scapegoat is made the "source of perverse regeneration, that is, the black beast has made Minnie desirable and the white men now wish to partake of her. The white community is again thought to be safe from fear and drought. But conversely, the core of the black community is stricken with fear and terror."[129] The lynching, Faulkner shows, solves nothing. No black people dare appear in public during the lynching, and after it is over, McLendon discovers he has not escaped his despair. He remains in a sweat as he lies bleakly under a "cold moon" and "lidless stars." He is another displaced World War I veteran, like young Bayard Sartoris in *Flags in the Dust,* who looks out on a bleak world, and Percy Grimm in *Light in August,* missing out on the war but seeking to assert his masculinity by depriving a "nigger" of his.

The constant interruptions of the mild barber and the half-finished sentences in this story reveal a culture that cannot express itself except in stereotypical language and abortive thinking. At a very early age, Faulkner learned the costs of speaking out but also the costs of silence that could be broken only through his fiction, which seemed so much more real than the limited facts at the community's disposal. Only through story, through the transmogrification of facts, could he get at the central truths that even male friends like John Cullen either did not recognize or did not dare to articulate.

If Faulkner did not actually witness the lynching, "Dry September" takes on an even more resonant biographical significance. The absences are critical: we are never shown a scene of Will Mayes's lynching, nor are we given a scene either of Minnie Cooper's being accosted by a black man or of her inventing a story to that effect. Nevertheless, "critics almost invariably conclude that some of these at least are 'facts.'"[130] In other words, Faulkner conceived a story in which his readers replicate what he heard but perhaps did not see. Both the narrator and readers are, in certain crucial respects, outsiders who have to imagine what actually happened, watching as McLendon leads the community in creating a fiction, just as we don't know, for a fact, that the mildmannered barber is right about Minnie Cooper. He seems right precisely because he is not all het up about her putative rape, and because the women who know her wonder if anything at all actually happened to Minnie. As soon as the story about her and Mayes is in circulation, however, it becomes "real." For McLendon and his followers, the story has to be subsumed in their white supremacist ideology.[131] To speak out, as the barber does, is to risk ridicule and to be deemed irrelevant, a risk the barber backs away from when he joins the lynching party. If eight-year-old Jimmy Faulkner was admonished not to talk about a lynching in 1935, think of the imperative for Billy Falkner to remain silent in 1908, to observe and listen but not comment on what he could not, in so many words, articulate. Only later in a story could he expose a community that could obliterate or transmute the identities of its own inhabitants, black and white.

ESTELLE

Cullen noticed that as a boy Faulkner did not say much, although he could become animated about hunting and other country pursuits. What, after all, could be said, and who could he say it to? The Virginian rarely shares his thoughts with his fellow cowboys, but he opens up to his beloved, as did Faulkner to Estelle Oldham, who could appreciate sides of him that his male counterparts would not have valued or perhaps even noticed. The sylph-like Estelle played the piano well and enchanted the compact, sturdy boy. They became an audience for one another as he began to draw and write poems and stories for her, which she did not merely accept as is. "You're a damn good literary critic," her teenage admirer told her. They were forming a dual commitment, founded, in part, in their recalcitrant reactions to families with ambitions for their children—for her, a well-made marriage, and for him, a respected profession—that neither of them put as a priority. Entering his teens, it is not surprising that Faulkner was drawn to Estelle as a muse. She came to represent more than "home, Oxford, or Yoknapatawpha. She represented the word itself."[132]

No other young woman would seem to do for a young man who probably resembled the unnamed protagonist of the unpublished "And Now What's to Do," who was "changed by his changing body. Before and during puberty he learned about women from the negro hostlers and the white night-man, by listening to their talk. Now, on the street, he looked after the same girls he had once taken to school in his father's hack, watching their forming legs, imagining their blossoming thighs, with a feeling of defiant inferiority. There was a giant in him, but the giant was muscle-bound."[133] That feeling of being bound up within himself became the theme of his first published book, *The Marble Faun*.

For the suicidal Quentin Compson, 1910 was a year he could not get beyond, and it seemed just as decisive for thirteen-year-old William Faulkner. If his family was not in quite the decline that the Compsons suffered, Billy already realized he was as unsuited as Quentin to fulfill and father the line that the old Colonel had founded. *The White Rose of Memphis*, so superficial and even ludicrous in its pretensions to southern gentility, offered no viable model for an ambitious writer who would seek honor in his chosen profession in ways that would seem to defy the gentlemanly code even as his novels and stories reinvented it. And for all that, William Faulkner needed a lady, a consort, who would always be at and on his side. That is the romantic world, at any rate, that he began to project beginning in his teens. Quentin Compson would be shaken to his core when he realized he could not measure up to the old chivalric code—and his sense of failure was all the worse because he felt what Faulkner would later make explicit in the "Compson Appendix": the code was moribund, and Quentin was not strong enough to replace it after he failed to redeem it.

Change was coming to Oxford, now well lighted and paved, and to William Faulkner, both beset by and proud of his heritage, beginning anew through his deep absorption in literature, now encouraged and enriched by his association with Phil Stone, whose character and sensibility would suffuse so much of Faulkner's Yoknapatawpha fiction.

2

Apprenticeships

1911–1921

~

The Tramp

Billy did his chores, carried coal to fireplaces, performed well in the sixth grade, wore shoulder braces to improve his posture, and listened to Estelle play the piano. By the seventh grade school began to bore him, although he continued to do well, winning a seventh-grade spelling contest, an "important part of the school program." The "teachers and administrators made a great deal out of it," a classmate remembered. She said that William Falkner "knew more about the mythology of Greece and Rome than the entire rest of the school."[1] He amused himself and his friends with pen-and-ink sketches. He had more fun hanging around his father's livery stable. Sometimes he dressed up to suit Estelle.

He also went to the movies with his brothers on Friday nights, the only "free night" during the school term.[2] His brother Jack (Murry) remembered their excitement, how in the dim Opera House theater a projector shot out a "cone of light," accompanied by a thundering piano and the screening of a hoofbeating western. But comedies and melodramas were featured as well. Beginning in 1914, Charlie Chaplin, that small, scruffy, and yet gentlemanly figure, had an enormous following and seems a presence in Faulkner's evocation of himself as a "tramp, a harmless, possessionless vagabond." Decades later, a New Yorker spotted Faulkner in Washington Square Park: "his face reminded me of Charlie Chaplin, and the way he was inserted rather than seated on the bench had the touch of a Chaplin comedy."[3] There was more to it than that: the posing, the elaborate courtesies and compliments, the

37

courtships were all part of the silent, bittersweet comedy of William Faulkner's life.

The movies spread out a "vast new field of incredibly attractive entertainment," Jack recalled. Here was a "newness" with an appeal that "comes seldom in a lifetime. . . . [P]ractically anyone who could walk and possessed a nickel had but one idea—to be entertained."[4] At the same time, the pre-1919 Hollywood dramatized for Billy Falkner the sentimentality of late-Victorian culture. Hollywood itself, not yet built up, remained rural with certain southern values epitomized by Kentuckian D. W. Griffith (1875–1948) and his star Lillian Gish (1893–1993), another ethereal beauty, like Estelle, delicate and yet enduring, as she demonstrated in her first film for him, *An Unseen Enemy* (1912). In *Birth of a Nation* (1915), she became the epitome of white southern womanhood.

In the fall of 1913, Estelle's parents sent her to board in Staunton, Virginia, at Mary Baldwin College, situated right in the heart of the South's leading state, even if the Republican Oldhams had to put up with the legacy of Woodrow Wilson, a Democrat, who had been the college's president and now occupied the White House. At least the school was Presbyterian, an important feature to her father, and it had a college preparatory program—although why a belle destined for early marriage should be treated to this extra educational privilege is not clear, unless that, too, seemed appropriate for her status as the acculturated consort of an accomplished southern gentleman. Estelle, for her part, confided to Billy that her visit to dreary old Woodrow Wilson's house had not impressed her.[5] Even the spunky Tallulah Bankhead, who later played the rebellious Regina, holding her own among the society of her predatory brothers in *The Little Foxes,* did not excite Estelle's interest. She said Bankhead and her sister Eugenia were "loud."[6]

Could it be that a year at the paternalistic Mary Baldwin might keep Estelle in line and away from the decidedly wayward Billy Falkner, already becoming a truant not only from school but from the accustomed pseudo-aristocratic manners of a family looking to marry up? Did Billy already detect a certain pretentiousness in the Oldham establishment? Phil Stone said his friend referred to the family as "the bucolic ducal house of Oldham."[7] Estelle's sister Dorothy suggested that Billy courted the Oldhams as much as he did Estelle, driving the couple around and greeting Mrs. Oldham by kissing her hand.[8]

One longtime resident of Oxford called Estelle's father "high-strung and proud." He could not get along with others.[9] Lem Oldham may also have been touchy about his good fortune as a Republican federal appointee, riding high, it was said, only because he allied himself to a political party that exacted a

2 to 5 percent kickback on his annual salary. Perry Howard, a black lawyer who ran the state's Republican Party, would have been the one to collect from Lem, so that, as one of Faulkner's grade-school classmates put it, Lem "had to pay a Negro (or people thought he had) for his job. People were quiet about the Oldhams, but they didn't think much of Lem."[10] Joseph Blotner's Oxford informants said that Lem was not much of a lawyer. The young Colonel said that "Lem Oldham never tried a case—he wouldn't know how."[11] He handled divorces, but he did not have much business. The Falkners, however, were not much better situated. They did not socialize, Estelle recalled. They occasionally visited the Oldhams, but Miss Maud "did little entertaining because she could never be sure what shape Mr. Murry would be in."[12] And Lem Oldham was a "night drinker" too.[13]

It has been said Estelle's mother and father always disliked Faulkner.[14] Yet others report that Billy Falkner was always welcome at the Oldhams and apparently liked to visit them, but then perhaps that became a problem. Billy saw Estelle nearly every day, and that much company might curtail her marriageable prospects, especially since she matured quickly. She was fast, petite like a partridge, with a "beautiful figure, teeth, and hair, with charm too. She had everything"—and was not the first southern girl to be sent away from home in the hope that she would develop interests that helped her outgrow a certain boy, charming enough, but still not quite suitable for a conventionally successful marriage and career.[15]

The Oldhams, working fast, lined up Cornell Franklin, a promising young attorney seven years older than Estelle, and certainly a world apart from Billy Falkner, a high school student who had just lost, by one vote, an election to become president of the local Boy Scout troop. Lem Oldham cared deeply about position and place. Long after he held public office, the left-hand corner of his stationery included the printed legend: "United States Attorney, Northern District of Mississippi, 1921–1925." Nearly twenty years later he wrote to his granddaughter Victoria about her brother: "am anxious that Cornell will view Malcolm through our spectacles with the result of seeing his first son developed into a refined, cultured gentleman, a reflection of his ancestors, and I might add to a marked degree, the Franklin side."[16]

Cornell Franklin seemed to take no notice of Estelle until she "served his purposes."[17] She did not care much for Cornell's father, the domineering Judge Franklin, but she felt close to Cornell's mother. Cornell seemed to first broach the idea of marriage just as Estelle completed her year at Mary Baldwin, and she assented, although without thinking carefully about the consequences. She continued to see Billy and did not behave as though she had committed herself to another. But then Estelle welcomed the attention of so many others—at dances, for one thing, while Billy looked on. No one can say, of course, how he looked, whether he glowered or smiled or assumed a stoical demeanor. It is tempting, though, after reading *Sanctuary,* to suspect that even at this early stage he saw this old southern world as a rodomontade, the sort of glittering, superficial masquerade his great-grandfather portrayed in *The White Rose of Memphis.* At the very least, he wasn't one of those young gentlemen who beseech Scarlett O'Hara in *Gone with the Wind.* He might have been willing to play Estelle's cavalier, but not in the conventional terms that the other suitors professed like *Sanctuary*'s hapless Gowan Stevens, who proves unable to defend Temple Drake's honor after she is raped.

During Estelle's absence from Oxford, a restless Billy would sometimes catch the train for Memphis and turn up at the home of Falkner friends. "May I spend the night?" he would ask Mrs. Parks, who had a room for him, although he sometimes slept on the porch. Maud Falkner would call, looking for her wayward son, saying she would pay for his return ticket home—on one occasion specifying that he should not be given money but instead be presented with a ticket home to Oxford.

The Poet's Impresarios

Maud regretted that she pushed Billy too hard to be an artist because of her own interest in painting. When she began to realize that he "wanted most to be a writer, and quite early was determined to be nothing else,"[18] she called on Phil Stone (1893–1967), Ole Miss and Yale graduate, a brilliant student with high academic honors, and now studying law to make a living but living, it seemed, on literature. Phil's father, General James Stone, was a prominent lawyer, and on a par with families like the Falkners and the Oldhams. The Stones and Falkners were friends, although Phil seemed to take no notice of Billy until Maud Falkner mentioned to Phil's mother that Billy wrote poetry and might need some guidance and advice. Stone, an avid reader of cutting-edge literary journals such as *Poetry* and the *Little Review,* seemed to be on the lookout for talent. This was a time when there was much talk of the new poetry and the new history, when writers were in search of what they deemed modern. And Phil Stone yearned, it seems, to find a genius in his own environs before the world brought down the shades of the prison house that Wordsworth lamented. Stone later wrote to the curator of the Modern Poetry Library at the University of Chicago: "In 1925 (I think that was the year) I was in Chicago, went around to see Miss Monroe [the editor of *Poetry*], and lunched with her, told her that the literary star in America was passing from the Midwest to the South, and tried to get her to publish free in

POETRY some parts of Bill's 'Marble Faun.' She wouldn't do this but she later wrote a little editorial about what I had told her."[19]

In his copy of the groundbreaking *Some Imagist Poets* (1915), Stone underlined passages from Richard Aldington's poem "Childhood" that spoke, apparently, to Stone's own sense of confinement, and the punishment of "Cruel local gods / Who seared my childhood," his chrysalis shut in a matchbox, and his "shrivelled wings" beaten. The poem may have expressed Stone's grief over his Wordsworthian sense of loss: "the beautiful things" the child "learns before its birth, / Were shed, like moth-scales, from me," and bitterness set in in "that damned little town." Stone's isolation and alienation are palpably expressed later in the poem: "I wanted to be alone, although I was so little, / Alone, away from . . . the dingyness, the dullness / Away somewhere else." How true these lines are to Stone's actual experience is impossible to tell, but the poem resonated.

Stone sought out this young talent, before it, too, might be stifled. In the Falkner home Stone read several promising, if not brilliant, poems. Stone never described the contents or style of this early work. Faulkner later identified Swinburne as a captivating influence, "springing from some tortured undergrowth of my adolescence, like a highway-man, making me his slave." Swinburne's lyrical intensity, his frank sensuousness in rebellion against conservative values that had once seduced undergraduates at Oxford and Cambridge, now became a bulwark for a provincial young man afraid that he was only superficially sincere. Faulkner claimed he had facilitated his "various philanderings" with poetry as well as "completing a gesture I was then making, of being 'different' in a small town." In Swinburne's "Sapphics," in poetic expression he discovered "a marvel, / Made of perfect sound and exceeding passion."

Meanwhile, Stone talked and talked and talked—like Horace Benbow and Gavin Stevens, the two Yoknapatawpha champion speechifiers, and his protégé listened. Stone did not have the discipline or the capacity to write, except for letters and articles that tended toward the dogmatic, but in conversation with an appreciative audience, the tall Stone unbent himself, sharing his knowledge not only of literature and Oxford but of that great world north of Oxford. Stone was a product of the Old South, steeped in the history of the Civil War. He had talked with General Longstreet and had a store of stories from his extensive reading about the subject. Stone claimed that Faulkner's own interest in the Civil War only became a passion after their colloquies: "Bill never seemed interested in the history of the Confederacy at all until I began pumping him full of it around 1919 and 1920 and showed him what splendid romantic material it was for a writer."[20] Even then, it would be another five years or so before Faulkner began to write it down.

Stone was also responding to the New South, to the rise of the rednecks that Faulkner would chart in his stories and novels as he developed his Snopes saga. Stone stimulated Faulkner's need to dispel that "atmosphere with which four generations of cold-blooded men clinging to their outworn tradition of human behavior had imbued the very soil on which they had lived," as he wrote in the original text of *Sanctuary*.[21] Stone, a Greek and Latin scholar, a devotee of English, French, and Russian authors, stood for a kind of southern gentleman nowhere else available in Oxford. And even better, he had befriended Stark Young, who had made a literary career out of being bookish, exposing Stone to the realization that the Ole Miss academics only offered the "usual veneer of thin pedagogical aestheticism."[22]

Stone has been called a "surrogate father," which seems a stretch, since he was not that much older than Faulkner, and as Faulkner's brother John insisted, Billy remained very much his own person.[23] If Stone's letters and articles reflect the man, then Billy may well have bridled at some of his mentor's pronouncements even as he emulated Stone's dogmatic tone, which is on display in William Falkner's dismissive book reviews published while he attended Ole Miss.

Stark Young, urbane and homosexual, provided an alternative to the "swaggering models for male behavior" that Faulkner may have found "stifling." Young is said to have commented that Faulkner had "an interesting face."[24] The aesthetic of the dandy exemplified in Young, Oscar Wilde, and others made its appearance in Faulkner's drawings and poems, and in the mannerisms and other social graces that both Stone and Faulkner affected.[25] Although Phil Stone later married and produced a son and daughter, some in Oxford believed he was a closet homosexual.[26] An aspect of gay culture often commented on is a tendency to perform, to create personae and masks—a very appealing activity to Bill Falkner. To one witness of the budding writer's behavior, Joseph Blotner wrote: "I enjoyed your letter enormously, particularly, of course, its vivid and affectionate picture of Bill, put-on airs and all."[27] How much of an act did William Falkner put on for two older men, one of them certainly gay, who saw so much promise and allure in this literary young man?

In *The Torches Flare* (1928), Young modeled a seventeen-year-old character on a young William Falkner.[28] Eugene Oliver, small and slender but well-muscled, enters a train compartment. His "shy and wandering" eyes evince a "maturity that comes of poetic temperament." He is tense and taut with a bearing typical of a "Southern boy of his class, who has usually been taught a certain show of ease at least and an air of being at home in company." He strikes the novel's narrator (Hal Boardman), a character like Stark Young who periodically returned home from New York City, as restless, even though Oliver is remarkably still and "if anything too steady." He is, as Faulkner was, a paradox. Hal, who is returning home to teach at Clearwater (modeled on Ole Miss), grapples with his impression of Eugene: "He was not restless, then; it was something about him that suggested flight and unrest," like the figure of Aldington's poem "Childhood." Hal guesses correctly that Eugene has written poetry. "I've tried some poetry," Eugene admits, "though father'd rather I didn't." Eugene does not know where to turn and comes to see Hal, who describes Eugene as "all confused with the life rising in him, all lost in his thoughts and desires, bewildered, hurt, exalted. He was in a world that he could not understand but could not get used to. Older men get used to it or blind to it; what made this boy so tragic and so pure was that he could do neither." Young describes a Eugene who resembles Quentin Compson, overtaken by a passion that "lives in all the parts and faculties of his body and is part of his soul; they complete themselves only through passion; and it completes itself through them, and takes on the force of divinity and innocence." Hal is thirty and thinks, "But already I would gladly take his place for him, if I could only help him and could know the things he knows." William Falkner was not suicidal, but it was not difficult to imagine a sensitive young man like Falkner, who had an intensity that men heading toward middle age like Phil Stone and Stark Young envied and wanted to protect and embrace, especially when Eugene confesses: "I just feel so alone. I'm so alone all the time." Hal consoles Eugene: "You'll have to try to think of what the great poets have felt. I mean you're less lonely knowing them and what they said sometimes." Eugene replies to an approving Hal that he has been reading Shakespeare's sonnets: "I just read around, I've always read a lot. Father says I read too much. . . . My grandfather was a writer; he used to publish treatises, but he fought a duel with some statesman and got killed, though that was because he was drunk." Eugene has fallen in love with a Clearwater-born actress, Eleanor Dandridge, who has left a successful career in New York City to accompany her beloved, Arthur Lane, who is teaching for the year at Clearwater. She has shown Eugene kindness, calling him a darling and kissing his brow. Hal comments ominously: "A boy like that at seventeen has wonderful things in him, and you have to be careful. A touch may bring death. For these things of his must be perfections, complete, shining. These ideals cannot bear imperfection or chance fact or disillusion; and how should I know what his soul asks of desire?" Unlike Bill, Eugene has no mother, no woman in his life to temper his devotion to Eleanor Dandridge. Eugene has shown her his scrapbook of poetry, an approximation of the handmade books that Bill would design for his beloveds.

Whatever differences separate Eugene Oliver and William Falkner dissolve in certain sentences that describe the paradox of character: "His movement was curiously certain, full of wayward directness. At seventeen he was grown up, not into a man but into himself, complete in himself like an animal. He was headlong and set, but he was tender and lonely like a child." Hal counsels the depressed Eugene: "The killing yourself you've got from all the newspaper stuff about college-student suicides. Don't you think so? They've played up college-suicide till it's got to be a commonplace," but an unconvinced Eugene replies, "I don't see how death could be that." Like Quentin, Eugene cannot bear to see the love of his life physically defiled. His suicide is the direct result of his witnessing the romantic embraces of Eleanor and Arthur. "Hal, she looked sad and lost," Eugene says—as lost as Caddy Compson, or Estelle Oldham. Eugene implies that he has seen Eleanor and Arthur make love. Eugene blurts out: "I mean I thought they were going to marry. But I didn't know that—you see I stayed on." He had been afraid to move lest the lovers detect his presence. Actually seeing the lovemaking drives Eugene to say, "It's just rotten." Hal tells him, "Well, that's life," but the inconsolable Eugene exclaims: "But what have they done to me now! . . . I just can't bear it. I couldn't ever believe anything again." Hal, sounding a little like Mr. Compson in *The Sound and the Fury,* reads Plato with Eugene, trying to show that "We have to take life all together, not in parts." But the inconsolable Eugene says: "I just can't. Not now, not any more, can't you see?" Hal can only advise Eugene to wait out his feeling and to go home, but as Eugene departs, Hal senses his failure: "When he was gone I should rather have had him there at the table crying and cursing."

Eugene returns home and commits suicide in a novel published the very year that epidemiological reports of the suicide of college students first appeared in medical literature.[29] Written the year before Quentin Compson commits suicide in *The Sound and the Fury, The Torches Flare* resonates with the impress of William Faulkner almost arrived at his first great work of fiction and still troubled by an aesthetic ambition that had no outlet in his own community, which, for all its depreciation of him, was home, the locus of his life and death, as he wrote in "Mississippi Hills: My Epitaph":

> Where is there the death
> While in these blue hills slumbrous overhead
> I'm rooted like a tree? Though I be dead,
> This soil that holds me fast will find me breath.

From Young, Faulkner would have learned that New York City or, for that matter, anyplace outside of Oxford was not necessarily a solution to his dilemma. In *The Torches Flare,* the city is full of "painters and authors, and derelicts" drifting in a "vague artistic Bohemia, most of them failures and ingrates." At the same time, Young had little respect for Ole Miss and its president, cast in the novel as an anti-intellectual autocrat. The students were "like students everywhere; there were those who had worked to get the money for college and whose attitude was at least laborious, others who had some degree of taste for learning, or science, or arts or raw information, and others who came because their parents had sent them." Eugene's isolation is similar to the young Falkner's: "Clearwater seems to have few if any talented, worthwhile young persons."[30] Most Ole Miss graduates were expected to become lawyers or doctors or politicians—professions that did not appeal to Faulkner.

Yet Young's novel shows a devotion to his upbringing that resonated with Faulkner. So Hal Boardman reflects that "it's only natural, of course, that a people who had lost their cause and had a hard time afterward and were so poor and had their pride hurt so, and saw a thing they had been born to dying away from them in a new age, should have created a defense in some sort of beautiful tradition." This tender and critical fealty to the fatherland became crucial to Faulkner's fiction. Young's depiction of older southern women comports with Faulkner's creation of grandes dames like Miss Jenny in *Flags in the Dust.* Young's Cousin Cornelia, for example, relishes reading newspaper accounts of murders and is a stickler for social norms and customs. Along with Miss Bessie, she represents the "standards of Southern tradition"[31] that Faulkner revered and reviled.

Young's art went only so far. His topography is local color, devoid of the grandeur and symbolic heft that distinguishes Faulkner's earliest treatment of his native land. Farley's Mountain in *The Torches Flare* is described as "only a hill of a few hundred feet: from the top of which can be seen the spires of Clearwater, the town clock in the court-house cupola and the water tank, all looking very peaceful through the blowing gale around us." In "The Hill," Faulkner's first prose piece clearly modeled on Oxford's topography, the tobacco-stained courthouse is etched in history, not, as it was for Young, merely a feature against which his characters are posed. The integrative role that black people play even in Faulkner's earliest drawings and first novel is absent in Miss Bessie's remark, "Nothing like the darkies for sweet music." Her vague question about what they are singing is not merely a reflection of her sensibility. No greater understanding of black culture appears in *The Torches Flare.*

Faulkner and Stone, hunters and poker players, had some reservations about Young. Young read D'Anunzio to Stone and Faulkner, telling them D'Anunzio had a following. Stone and Faulkner laughed and thought it a strange way to judge literature. A miffed Young would later vent his ambivalence about Faulkner's success. Stone showed that all kinds of so-called manly pursuits were easily compatible with a literary sensibility. At the very time Faulkner absorbed what Stone and Young had to tell and show him, he quarterbacked a football team. One of Bill's teammates called him a "scrappy player." B. O. Daniel remembered a game with Holly Springs: "I intercepted a pass and was running the wrong way. William was safety man and he was the only one left for me to get by, he tackled me and saved the game but in the tackle he fractured his nose, but we won the game."[32] His second serve, as hard as his first, typified his athletic behavior.[33]

Stone tutored his young charge in Keats and Swinburne but also Sherwood Anderson and other contemporary novelists. In effect, Stone acted the part of an imposing critic like F. R. Leavis, instilling a sense of literature as part of a great tradition that had to be mastered, which also meant the writer had first to be mastered by it. Robert Coughlan, who interviewed Phil Stone, extolled "an oral gift, and a memory that enables him to recite whole pages verbatim."[34]

No one who has not put in the time between the crucial years of sixteen and eighteen can quite grasp what it means to be an instrument of literature. Dr. Johnson said the writer's most important reading has to occur by the age of eighteen. By then, the literary foundation is in place.[35] So the two men walked together along University Avenue with Phil Stone reciting Greek poetry to Billy Falkner and explaining the hard work of a literary career. One of Faulkner's contemporaries presents an attractive two-shot of Stone and Faulkner, a ready-made for the camera: "Phil Stone, a dignified, highly educated lawyer appeared to us, a much older man than he really was, a southern gentleman in every sense of the word. He was a medium built, well dressed individual, compared to Bill at that time, a brunette, rather nice looking, and he had a delightful personality. He was looked upon as being, eccentric, a dreamer, an intellectual, sensitive, kind and thoughtful person."[36]

LOVE AND WAR

In the fall of 1915, Estelle enrolled as a special student at the University of Mississippi, studying English, philosophy, and psychology. This highly intelligent young woman was remembered more for her chic appearance and for the dances she never seemed to miss. The friendly Estelle had the "happy ability to remember names." She adored pretty shoes, and when she changed shoes at a charity event, which featured bidding on the shoes the coeds had worn, she switched her pair with someone else's. The winning bidder was quite disappointed when he discovered Estelle would not be his prize for the evening.[37] Billy Falkner watched Estelle more than he danced with her. He seemed in no hurry to pursue a job, a career, or more schooling, although he read the law books in his uncle's office and brain charts in a doctor's medical books.[38] His grandfather put him to work as a bookkeeper in the First National Bank of Oxford. Billy's brother Jack said, "I bet he didn't do much." Billy told Estelle that making money was contemptible, expressing an attitude appropriate for an eighteenth-century gentleman or movie fan bent on looking like the suave and debonair noblemen in silent films or like the elegant dancing partner giving a fashionable girl a turn on the dance floor in one of his Ole Miss yearbook drawings.[39] Billy became the first of his contemporaries to sport a twenty-five-dollar "Styleplus" dress suit.[40] His pretentious, aristocratic airs earned him a scornful title, "The Count." But he preferred to accentuate his roguish side when reminiscing about this period: "Quit school and went to work in Grandfather's bank. Learned the medicinal value of his liquor. Grandfather thought it was the janitor. Hard on janitor." Heavy drinking had already become a habit.

Dances and banking hardly suited an adventurous young man avidly reading newspaper headlines about the war: "Throbbing thunder and heavy guns mark World's mightiest struggle." Already enamored with flying, an enthusiasm abetted by newspapers that touted the latest advances in aviation, Billy Falkner's war was in the air. But the United States remained neutral, and his poetry expressed the longings of an adolescent steeped in Swinburne and Housman. Estelle, who gave her attention, if not her heart, to so many boys, inspired his early poetry:

> I give the world to love you:
> Now, cross your heart and say—
> By moon and stars above,
> You'll be true for aye.

The Scottish archaism "for aye" suggests the young poet's deep immersion in a poetic tradition that favored fealty and saw love as its uniting force. But so much of that first verse remained stilted, a projection of how a poet ought to express himself. He abjured pungent metaphors and images grounded in his own land. His precious, affected poetry seems a repudiation of his native ground in favor of lofty sentiments that set him apart from his community. He was not quite alone in his poetic bower. Besides Estelle, he had sixteen-year-old Ben Wasson, now on the Ole Miss campus. Ben could outdo Billy when it came to flowery sentiments—so much so that Ben remembered one of his friend's rejoinders: "Ah, we seem to have a young Sir Galahad on a rocking horse come to our college campus." Not offended, Ben said that Billy, most of the time, was kind, gentle, and entertaining in a self-dramatizing way. Wasson fondly remembered his friend's wandering through cemeteries, perhaps because of their quiet and tranquil atmosphere.

Billy affected Britishness, always calling Phil Stone "Stone." Ben knew that Stone took Billy to Memphis whorehouses. Ben thought Bill, a "randy little man," probably did go upstairs with the whores, subscribing to the "cliché of the prostitute with the heart of gold," a figure that appears as Everbe Corinthia in *The Reivers*.[41] Faulkner writes with authority about brothels, but Wasson may have been taken in by his friend's stories. Phil Stone called Faulkner perfectly normal sexually but not an active participant.[42] Dorothy Ware, who operated several brothels and first met Faulkner before World War I, said she never saw him with "one of the girls."[43]

Billy's carefully nurtured reverie in verse came to a halt on April 6, 1917, when the United States declared war on Germany. Three days later, the *Oxford Independent* ran the headline: "War has been declared. America's sweet liberty is at stake."[44] Ben Wasson said the "war in Europe was far removed from our own placid lives, too distant to have reality," but he remembered stories about "diabolical Huns bayoneting Belgian and French babies and ravishing the helpless, holy nuns in French convents." Movie-house newsreels provided silent but graphic horrors of war.

Billy and his brothers John and Jack were eager to do their part. Billy wanted to be an officer, an unlikely outcome for a high school dropout not yet twenty-one.[45] He continued to see Estelle, who still wore a gold ring with the initial *F* he had given her. By the end of the year, it became public knowledge that Estelle was about to marry Cornell Franklin. Yet she consigned her double-diamond engagement ring to a drawer, claiming that John Henry, a black servant, had stolen it, but Estelle's suspicious mother forced her to tell the truth.[46]

In a panic, Estelle wavered, saying she would elope with Billy. Ever the gentleman, William Falkner could not see his way to marriage without obtaining the consent of Estelle's parents, which they would not give—so intent were they on capturing the prize, a handsome assistant district attorney in Honolulu, a major in the National Guard, and judge advocate general of the Hawaiian Territorial Forces. As a gentleman, Billy could not afford Estelle and could not compromise his principles. He represented to himself and to Estelle something altogether opposed to his community's mercantile values, and yet without money he was no man. His principles came into conflict with his lack of principal.[47]

Stone feared that Billy's qualms notwithstanding, he would elope with Estelle, whom Stone treated as a distraction.[48] Stone may have been jealous of Estelle and possessive about his protégé, but he could certainly contend that she did not have the commitment to Faulkner, or the strength of purpose required to sustain a young, vulnerable writer. In short, marrying Estelle would have narrowed Faulkner's world at precisely the time Stone thought it should be enlarged, which is why he coaxed the downcast troubadour to Yale, where Stone studied law.[49]

NORTHERN EXPOSURE

On April 4, 1918, two weeks before Estelle Oldham married Cornell Franklin, Billy Falkner arrived in New Haven. He described his journey by train in a letter to his father, full of appealing technical terms for an aficionado of steam engines: "big locomotives as I have seen since I came, compounds and double compounds."[50] Even as a child, "Bill knew the principle that made the engines run, and built a steam engine," his brother John remembered.[51] On sharp curves Billy, as he signed himself, could see the engines at work: "We lost lots of time. Had to stop at Atkins, Va. and they drew the fires in the engine and put in a new base."[52] Billy knew his father would enjoy these details: every turn of the route—from the Southern (Memphis to Bristol), the Norfolk and Western to Lynchburg, Va., the Southern again to Washington, and then the Pennsylvania through to Jersey City, where he was switched to an electric train that took him under the Hudson tubes into Penn Station. And he followed up this itinerary by saying, "I am terribly home sick and hope to hear from home by Sunday [April 7]." This yearning for home, and the language of family matters, set a pattern. How much he missed home, how much he suffered over Estelle, is hard to say. He did not confide in his family or in Stone when it came to his most intimate feelings. Notice how his brother John characterizes Faulkner's state of mind: "He must have gone through torment in that strange land with his whole world gone to pot."[53] The telltale "must have" reveals how little John actually knew about his brother's feelings. Billy's letters seem designed to reassure his parents that he is doing well away from home. The change of scene also seems to have excited his desire to share his discoveries with his parents. His letters to his parents rarely mention Stone, who may have exaggerated his importance as much as Faulkner minimized it.

To his mother, sometimes addressed as "Lady," Billy wrote, "I am here safely and am about to freeze." He had no idea just how different Connecticut's temperatures were from Mississippi's. It was April, and the heat was not on. "Phil and I went straight to bed" as a consequence. Here, then, began his experience of the cold, iron New England dark described in *Absalom, Absalom!* In New York City, he watched wounded and maimed soldiers walking on Fifth Avenue with their "service stripes and wings and game legs and sticks." These casualties of war were figures of fascination, much like Faulkner himself, who reported, "These people are always saying things to me to hear me talk." They made him lonesome for home and sometimes withdrawn in ways reminiscent of Quentin Compson in *The Sound and the Fury,* who carries his homeland with him everywhere. Carl Cline, who shared Faulkner's company in New Haven, said that Faulkner seemed "nutty" to some people—"not because of his talk but because of his walking in such mental abstraction that he was almost hit by streetcars."[54]

Perhaps this deracinated young man who said he felt "cold all the time" felt a kinship with "furriners," as they are called in *The Sound and the Fury.* Billy consorted not only with English and Scottish soldiers but also with a German veteran who drank and sang with British officers. "Tell Mammy [Caroline Barr], that I have lunch every day with two niggers. They are Hindoos, but dont tell her that," he cautioned his mother. Not many black people presented themselves in New Haven, and so he had to make up some to feel more at home: "It's funny to walk the streets and look at these people—Poles, Russians, Italian communists, all with American flags in their lapels." By the end of April, adjusted enough, he had "broken into poetry again."

In less than three months (April to June 1918), Billy Falkner had thrust himself into a world far greater than he had imagined, compounded and double compounded, separating and mixing together as never before. To Hubert Starr, a Californian studying law at Yale, and a friend of Phil Stone's, this William Falkner suffered culture shock. Starr remembered Falkner's reply to someone who said, "You Southerners don't know that the Civil War is over." Falkner said, "Well, is it?"[55] Starr believed that "Bill started life with a sense of defeat. The feeling has been inculcated in him that his people, himself included, had been mauled, impoverished, and what was worse, humiliated. It was an internal feeling, not a beggar's tin cup, which he was too proud to express."[56] But identification with the South went only so far, Starr admitted: "He wouldn't even tolerate from me an agreement with him regarding that war. When I said that the South was right, he gave me a dirty look. At that age, and travel, he knew that the South was wrong, or at least criminally unwise, but to that opinion he came by an intellectual process. What he lived by was the conditioning of childhood: the heart's reason."[57] Was Starr, the Californian, playing the part of Shreve, the Canadian, the outlander who tries to take over Quentin's narrative of the South? Mention of the Civil War appears only once in Billy's surviving letters from Yale to his parents, when he describes DeLacey, a Brick Row Book Shop employee, saying during a parade of black Civil War veterans: "Well, Billy, you ought to salute the old boys. It was your grandfather and his friends that put him that way." Billy replied that the veterans should salute him, "for had it not been for my grandfather and his friends they would not have had any war to go to."

The callow Billy, as put forth by Starr, resembles the earnest Henry Sutpen of *Absalom, Absalom!*: "At New Haven, Bill, younger than his friends there, first time out of Oxford (except for participating in excursions to Memphis), almost gaped in wonder at us." Henry Sutpen speaks very few words in the novel, almost stupefied as he encounters ideas and customs outside his ken. Another witness to Billy's Yale residence remembered his subdued presence, shyness, and silences.[58] "He was patronized a bit," Starr wrote, "but . . . Bill was learning. . . . Bill always felt that he had missed something great in not having had those leisurely years of 'college life.' A lot of true 'Southern tradition' is but the magnification of status symbols and the minimization of 'brains.'"[59] If Starr is exaggerating, it is nevertheless an exaggeration that Faulkner put to good use in *Absalom, Absalom!* Henry Sutpen's world is shaken when he consorts with the worldly Charles Bon from New Orleans, and Starr sounds a bit like Shreve in his crass characterization of the southern mentality.

Starr's contention that Faulkner did not want to join the Yankee army is not part of the customary biographical narrative, although Faulkner did tell a group of English friends that his grandfather did not want him to join what he still considered the northern army.[60] Faulkner told a Clarksdale, Mississippi, friend that the U.S. Armed Services had rejected him because he was underweight and not quite tall enough, and that was the story told to Joseph Blotner. But it seems just as likely that until Faulkner's sojourn in New Haven, he hung fire, awaiting the denouement with Estelle. "A search of the records of the Army Air Service in the National Archives failed to establish whether William Cuthbert Falkner attempted to enlist in the U.S. Army for pilot training prior to April 1918," a government official wrote to Blotner. Complicating the story further is this message noting a statement from the Office of the Chief Signal Officer entitled "The Present Practices of Accepting and Training Aviators," dated September 18, 1917: candidates "may be light in weight and youthful in appearance." In other words, as the government official observed: "Faulkner's height (5'5") and his weight (115 pounds or less) would not have been serious obstacles to his acceptance for pilot training." The only other specific requirement contained in this document is that the candidate "must be at least nineteen years old and preferably not over thirty."[61]

In letters to his parents, Faulkner expresses his fascination with British officers, imitating their accents and fraternizing with them. He seems bent on joining the Royal Air Corps as an officer, and he believes the quickest way to become an officer and a flyer is through enlistment in the British armed forces. His brothers John and Jack showed no reluctance, however, to join up with Yankees, and no one in the Falkner family seems to have expressed any qualms about joining the American armed forces.

Billy wrote on June 7, 1918: "The chances of advancement in the English Army are very good; I'll perhaps be a major at the end of a year's service. I've thought about it constantly. . . . I shall probably have to enlist in the line and take my chances of promotion, which I'd rather do than get in the U.S. Army and be sent into action under an inexperienced officer. The English officers are the best yet, take better care of their men and weigh all chances for them." Was he putting a good face on the British war effort to appease his anxious mother? She did not want him to serve. Or did he, at this point, believe this propaganda, ignoring the huge British losses during the war? Compared to the British, however, Americans would enter the war less prepared than the Allied forces.

The war seemed a way to grow up and earn self-respect. "I say let Jack go by all means," Billy wrote to his mother:

> He is doing nothing there, will continue to if you keep him there. I know how he feels about it. Some times I used to feel that if I didn't get to go that I could never forgive you for not letting me go and drive an ambulance when I wanted to so much. If he goes in the Q.M. Corps he can make something of him self, when as it is now, he'll keep on until they catch him playing cards, or a similar brand of assininity. He can get things there now that he'll not be able to later.

Biographers have whizzed past the reference to driving ambulances—an odd choice for a young man seeking glory in the air. Still, going to war seemed a sort of deliverance: "At the rate I am living now, I'll never be able to make anything of myself, but with this business [enlistment] I will be fixed up after the war is over." It would not be so easy, of course. What the South came to mean after the war changed in Faulkner's imagination, and part of that change would be due to his interactions outside the South, as Quentin Compson's views of the South are changed by the hectoring of his roommate Shreve in *Absalom, Absalom!* That novel would reveal a South that both is, and is not, outside the Union and the rest of the world.

So far away from home, Billy sends letters that are affectionate, newsy, hopeful, and vivid. He reports on the Yale-Harvard boat race, a Yale-Harvard baseball game, a plane that "stood perfectly motionless on its tail for several seconds at about two thousand feet; then dived nose first, looped three times and finished about three hundred feet up, lying on its back." This acrobatic display is told in precise and intimate terms: "And we could see the pilot's face, pink as a peach blossom, as though we were looking down on him," he writes to "My dear Lady," as though reporting a joust to his queen. "Before he left," Billy continues, "another came and they had a mimic battle, dipping and darting at each other, so low we could see the smoke from the exhausts." This feat was followed by his report of a man who "climbed the face of the Woolworth building this afternoon—here—, with a liberty Bond on his back." Just so he turns his epistolary world into a tournament and feats of daring. He does not dwell on his troubles. "Tell me about Estelle's wedding," he writes three days after the event in the only mention of her. His mother's side of the correspondence has not survived. Did she know then that Estelle's great-aunt offered to intercede with Lem Oldham to call the wedding off? "It's too late," Estelle replied, even though she was not sure that she loved Cornell Franklin or wanted to marry him.[62]

Employed on an eight-hour shift in the Winchester arms factory as a ledger clerk, punching a time clock, Billy called himself a "full fledged working man now" earning twenty dollars a week. He did not tell his parents that he had added a *u* to the family name. He played bridge almost every night. In striking contrast to his ornate poetry, his letters are full of simple, if striking similes: "The fruit trees are in blossom and they looked as though myriads of white and coral butterflies were resting upon them, and the dog wood like bits of silk upon green velvet, and wisps of clouds upon the mountains like flags." This loosened form of imagist verse would later make its way into the Benjy section of *The Sound and the Fury*. Walking in East Haven with Phil Stone, Faulkner could see the "harbor and the ships on the Sound. It was just clear enough to see Long Island, like a pale blue strip of paint on a sheet of glass. We could see the ships going down to New York and the tiny power- and sail-boats darting about like water bugs." He thought the sea "the most wonderful thing I've ever seen."

Billy missed eleven-year-old Dean, the only Falkner brother remaining at home. "Give Dean a kiss for brother Bill," he wrote to his parents. He drew a picture of his "awfully nice" factory badge and wished he could send it to "Sweet," his term of endearment for Dean. He wanted Dean to write about the candy Billy sent to him. Evidently the candy went missing: "Give Dean this gum, but dont tell him about his candy, just so he'll not be disappointed twice." Billy wished Dean had seen the cheerleaders at the Yale-Harvard baseball game. What is missing in all of these sprightly letters is any expression of sorrow. No sign of the melancholy poet who had written after Estelle's marriage to Cornell Franklin seemed a certainty:

> Even though she choose to ignore me,
> > And all love of me to deny,
> There is nought then behind or before me—
> > I can die.

Billy's longing for Estelle, if not eclipsed by Yale, seems to have abated, as Phil Stone hoped. Phil continued to mentor Billy, supplying him with reading from Balzac, Yeats, and others, which Billy took with him to the factory.

The transformation of Oxford dandy to English gentleman is told in two photographs. The first, taken just before the departure for Yale, shows Faulkner decked out in a dark suit, bright vest, and long walking stick. He strikes an angular pose, hands in his pockets, head tilted downward, and somewhat, perhaps, sullen—a rejected suitor? In New Haven, ready for enlistment, he appears subdued, understated, in a somber suit, neat but not too formal with his loosened tie and arms folded—less sporty and ready for business. Shortly after arriving in Yale, he had written to his mother: "I wish some of the boys at the University of Mississippi could see these men. Tight clothes and pink and yellow shirts are as rare here as negroes."[63]

CADET FAULKNER

By July 9, 1918, after a three-week return to Oxford, William Faulkner, adding that *u*, successfully enlisted in the Royal Air Force and was in "an English place," Toronto. He was billeted in Wycliffe College at the University of Toronto, and trained on a back campus field, "the first place to catch the sunlight on the breakup of winter," novelist Morley Callaghan remembered. "The snow and ice on the level ground are like a target for the sun slanting over Whitney Hall. Soon there are pools of water, then patches of muddy earth."[64] Writing shortly after he arrived, Faulkner told his mother, "These people are wonderful to me." His "certification of service" in the Royal Air Force (issued December 31, 1918) stated he had been "born in the parish of Finchley in Middlesex, England," a member of the Church of England—part of a ruse concocted with Phil Stone that presaged much of Faulkner's prevarication about his participation in the war. Faulkner had a performative personality that went well beyond just his fictions of flying. In Toronto, he also pretended to be a French Canadian. He enjoyed having others take him for what he was not. If he ever felt guilty about his deceptions, he never let on. On the contrary, creating such fictions was to become a way of life, providing him with every advantage his falsehoods could contrive. His penchant for fantasizing did not go unnoticed by a fellow cadet: This serious, "retiring, overly introspective loner" who kept "mostly to himself" also "had a tough time separating reality from reverie."[65]

From July to December 1918, Faulkner presented to his parents a constant record of achievement, passing mental and physical tests that proved he could maintain his equilibrium in a spinning chair and that he excelled in plotting the geography of flight. He liked uniforms and drills, although he admitted training began with "mopping floors and such, so when I get through I'll more than likely make some one a nice wife." In his complete outfit, he seemed to enjoy learning how to salute. "The British are great sticklers for this. And it must be done right," as he would show Joseph Blotner forty years later in Charlottesville, Virginia. "To morrow we have church parade—fancy my going to church. The British army is going to reform me after all," wrote the erstwhile Oxford renegade to "Mother darling." He may not have been kidding. There is a certain relief in obeying orders. He was learning Morse code. "It's a great life. I dont even have time to read." The disenchantment that can overcome a volunteer seems never to have bothered him. He treated the military as a kind of fashion show: "I wish you could see some of these flight sergeants and mechanics—fierce mustaches and waists like corset models and tiny caps and swagger sticks." The regalia of regimentation never ceased to beguile him. Even his lapses, like forgetting to shave on parade and having a missing button on his uniform, were reported cheerfully as part of his cadet's mission to become an officer. Here was the dutiful recruit who prudently had himself inoculated during a flu epidemic, the Spanish influenza that killed millions. "I think I'm doing very well," he assured his mother. "I'm having such a hurried life that all my letters sound disjointed. However!" What did his parents make of this suddenly subordinate son, this surrender of his stubborn singularity? Writing at least twice a week, he made them part of the action. Noticing how much mail Faulkner received from home, one of his tent mates said: "Gee, Faulkner, some one is certainly in love with you. And I told him that some one was, two for that matter."

In the end, he could not abide the grounding of his dreams, and so announced: "Unless something happens I shall make a flight tomorrow morning." He never did take off, and his training remained incomplete at the end of the war. He gave a more accurate reflection of his plight in an anecdote Emily Stone relayed to Carvel Collins. The cadets spent much of their days "digging trenches for practice." A visiting officer on an inspection tour observed a cadet "digging a trench busily and with great concentration and care and energy." The officer, addressing the cadet who had been ordered out of the trench to stand at attention, said, "What are you doing there?" The cadet, with a very snappy reply, said, "Learning to fly, Sir." William Faulkner, too, liked to look snappy, even when his war record amounted to very little.

Still, "Billy" wrote about his camp on the banks of Lake Ontario, taking in the pretty sight of big lake steamers and "gulls like blown bits of dirty paper," the trees rustling in the wind and the lake sounding like "tearing tissue paper." He was "eating like a horse." At 127 pounds, he was a good ten pounds heavier than his enlistment weight. He made it sound like an athletic tournament, with racing shells on the lake and track meets. "This is a wonderful place," he assured both his parents at the end of July. "I am going to the lake to swim this afternoon." The tents, according to one of Faulkner's fellow cadets, were a response to the flu epidemic. Dormitories posed too great a risk of spreading infection. He did not tell his parents that the tent, "pitched outside the hedge bordering the grounds[,] was very convenient for coming and going without passing the sentries."[66]

The writing that Faulkner could not accomplish came out in his lyrical letters: "The night here was wonderful. There are lots of trees, that looked like poured ink, with stiff, sharp pine trees, as though they had been cut from paper and stuck upon the sky." He watched wild geese flying in the sunset and mused over what "this old lake carried upon it. The Hurons and the Iroquois fought all about here," in a history-soaked land that perhaps recalled his childhood reading of Francis Parkman. In a sense, he had gone stylishly native: "I am acquiring the prettiest mahogany color you ever saw. I'll look like a pair of fashionable shoes soon." He drew pictures of himself and camp life—many, many pictures making book on his military service. "I look just like a kodak negative now. All brown my self, and my hair is burned rope color," he wrote, illustrating himself in dark face with light hair. Such were the poses of the young man who had intrigued Ben Wasson, who never could tell where the performances began and ended.[67]

For all the garrulity of Billy's letters, thanking his parents for money and boxes of food, he apparently preserved the aloof demeanor for which he would later become famous: "This crowd hangs about like a crowd of vultures, waiting until some one to get a box from home. If I were not naturally rather unapproachable, they'd take it away from me." This view from the ground—he kept reporting sightings of planes in the air—got him no closer to piloting his own plane, or to the exploits he wrote about in "The Ace," a poem he enclosed in a letter to his mother:

The sunlight
Paints him as he stalks, huge through the morning

In his fleece and leather, and golds his bright
Hair. The first lark hovers, singing, where
He flashes through the shining gates of day.

So he wrote in a tent by lantern light: "Cosy and much warmer than you'd think," he told his parents. More like it was this ditty he appended to the end of a letter: "I might be ragged and full of fleas / But my pants, thank God, dont bag at the knees." The neatness of military life appealed to him. A man always had to be in good order.

In September, it seemed to rain every day, and the soggy cadet signed off (you can almost hear the sigh), "so I must carry on." He spent his time in lectures, classes, map reading, artillery observation, aerial navigation interrupted by the scary thrill of learning how to "crank an aero motor by swinging the propeller" until the plane roared. In class, he drew the components of airplanes and took meticulous notes. He could take apart an airplane, which accounts for the precise details in his stories about war pilots. But most of the time it was drill in the morning for more than two hours and ten miles of marching. He went to bed with tired legs and a sore neck—but also in the knowledge that he could be as rugged as the next man. During the flu epidemic a quarantine restricted outings. "My hair is so long," he told his mother, "that I am going to powder it and put a black satin ribbon on it." In mid-October, with really nothing much new to do, he was beginning to long for home again, observing: "for only he whose heart and soul is wrapped about his home can see beyond the utterly worthless but human emotions such as selfishness, and know that home is the thing worth having above everything, and it is well known that what is not worth fighting for is not worth having."

The dreams that never came true had a date put on them when Faulkner wrote his mother on November 7, 1918: "It looks like the whole thing is over." Now he was all talk about railroad fares home. He pretended to have mastered four solo hours of flight. "Glad I've gotten in what I have." On December 9 he sent a telegram from Cincinnati, Ohio: "LEFT TORONTO YESTERDAY HOME TOMORROW NIGHT OR NEXT DAY BILLY."

The Count

The return home seemed no more than a default option. "Nothing in the world would suit me better than to cut off to N.Y.," he wrote to Hubert Starr in early January 1919, "my late experiences in His Majesty's Imperial Royal Flying Corps having made me perfectly competent to be a chauffeur or to hold a job with any bunch of Wops or a Dept of Streets, besides having given me all the necessary attributes to make any one a damned good wife. And besides that, almost all any one needs to make himself in any city is a line of bull and a soap box. And it would be worth working like hell for the privilege of running around New York City with you." He called Oxford a "God-forsaken place." His mother, in poor health, he claimed, held him back, saying he had to wait until his brother Jack returned from his service in the Marine Corps. He was sticking around a while for his kid brother, too, who treated Bill like a hero. He was quite aware of the complex and paradoxical family dynamics that would forever keep him in Oxford yearning to depart: "It all goes to show how ones parents always manœuvre to take one at a disadvantage, and, after chiding one about ones weaknesses and preach the decline of civility and strength, proceed to work upon that same weakness, regarding one who subdues his weakness, with something resembling honor." It would be another three or four months, at least, before he could be on his way.[68]

Faulkner's certificate of service, issued at the end of 1918, noted that after 179 days: "Discharged in consequence of being Surplus to R.A.F. requirements. (Not having suffered impairment since entry into service)." He was due $89.93 for pay, ration allowance, clothing.[69] He bought a smart-looking officer's uniform and a swagger stick, and looking the part, he turned up all turned out in Oxford and thereabouts as the man he wanted people to take him to be. The scar on the back of his neck and another on the inside of his left knee had nothing to do with the war, so he had to make do, showing up in Memphis at the Peabody hotel "noticeably bandaged"—the result of a plane crash, he told a friend, George Bean Jr.[70] Heroes returned from wars with damaged bodies. The old Colonel had three fingers shot off during the Mexican War.[71] So, too, William Faulkner had to arrive home after his trials of strength and courage, a Coriolanus reluctantly baring his wounds in the public forum while maintaining a truculent taciturnity.

With his brothers, Billy Falkner (he still dropped the *u* in some of his early writing), as usual, took the lead, or so he is presented in John's *My Brother Bill*. The memoir reveals that John, a novelist too, declined to destroy the fiction. "I remember how quickly Bill learned," John writes. "He was the first who did. I think it was his sense of balance that helped him live through flying Camels in the First War, for there never was a more tricky airplane built than a Sopwith Camel."[72] John describes how his brothers and father drove to the Oxford train depot to greet the returning hero: "He had on what was called an overseas cap . . . [t]he only one issued to our men if they had served overseas." Bill got off the train limping, the result of having "flown his Camel halfway through the top of a hangar. The tail of his ship was still outside, and they got Bill down from inside the hangar with a ladder." Such was his elder brother's air of authority that John "liked to walk around the Square with Bill on account of all the salutes he received. I was only seventeen at the time."[73] Jack, two years older than John, acknowledged how little action Bill had experienced, although Jack still believed that Bill was a commissioned officer and had learned to fly.[74]

"None of us who listened to his [Bill's] purported experiences believed them," Ben Wasson wrote. "We particularly doubted his account of receiving a leg injury that caused him to limp." They said: "That's the Count for you. Even a war doesn't stop him from telling tall stories."[75] Phil Stone, even more adamant, declared, "It is certainly not generally accepted in Oxford that Bill saw active war service." Stone told Carvel Collins that Faulkner's war exploits were fabrications. He sent Collins to John Faulkner, who just laughed at the very idea of his brother Bill's stories, and then John took Collins to Maud Falkner, who joined in the laughter. To Stone, Faulkner's inventions were part of the Falkner tendency to romanticize their lives,[76] although he does not seem to have realized that they were quite aware of their own penchant for self-aggrandizement and found humor in it—as does the old Colonel in *Rapid Ramblings in Europe,* who treats his own feats with self-deprecating humor. *Flags in the Dust,* with its oscillations between celebrating and disparaging the Civil War exploits of the Sartorises, seems suffused with the Falkner sensibility.

H. Edward Richardson tried to get John Faulkner to comment on his brother's World War I record, and John replied, "Twenty-five or thirty years ago my brother and I made an agreement not to discuss our work or each other." Phil Stone told Richardson: "There was some talk about a silver plate in his head, but I never believed it. . . . As far as I could see he wasn't injured at all." According to Stone, Faulkner never discussed his terms of military service with Stone.[77]

The uniformed William Faulkner who paraded around town had not changed much as a poet. One poem, written sometime in 1919, serves as the prologue for his first published volume, *The Marble Faun* (1924), a work of disenchantment reflecting the aspirant's fear that he will be forever an onlooker, and not part of the main action: "The whole world breathes and calls to me / Who marble-bound must ever be." It is tempting to see the book as a "self-portrait of the artist," an allegory of the southern poet's plight: "Faulkner seems to have been examining himself and finding that he was as different from his fellow townsmen as the faun from the living creatures that surround it." Faulkner was "'saturated with' the past just as the faun was 'sun steep with the memory of all things.'"[78] Faulkner's silence and immobility attracted attention. He was spotted standing still as a statue, and when he moved, a townsman commented, "Damned if it ain't alive."[79] Thomas Moser notes, "Clearly, *something happened* to turn the faun to marble—but that even is not in the poem sequence." Moser's speculation is that Faulkner's loss of Estelle brought on this stasis.[80]

But *The Marble Faun* is the kind of book, full of doubt and dread, that struggling poets, unsure of their gifts, produce—whatever their sex or actual experience. So it is not so surprising that Faulkner's work should resemble Amy Lowell's first tentative and troubled collection, *A Dome of Many-Coloured Glass* (1912), similar in its fealty to nineteenth-century English verse. A Keatsian melancholy pervades both books, as does their penchant for poeticisms about the moon. Stone and Faulkner, resuming their colloquies, discussed Lowell and other contemporary poets, with Stone voicing the common criticism that she played too much to the "grandstand." Faulkner replied that he had his eye on Babe Ruth, a comment Stone would include in his preface to *The Marble Faun*. The new poetry championed by Lowell and others was then in the news, discussed even in regional and local newspapers. Circumspect modernists like T. S. Eliot and Ezra Pound commanded Faulkner's respect, even though this dandy turned war hero turned war-weary and love-worn poet hardly disdained public attention.

"L'apres-midi d'un faune," Faulkner's first and last poem in a national publication, appeared on August 6, 1919, in the *New Republic*. This work reveals a poet drunk with the sounds of words:

> I follow through the singing trees
> Her streaming clouded hair and face
> And lascivious dreaming knees
> Like gleaming water from some place
> Of sleeping streams, or autumn leaves

Like the sonorous doom-minded Poe, Faulkner's poet's reverie is broken by "A sound like some great deep bell stroke." The simpler, simile-strewn letters from Toronto are more touching. He could be thinking of Estelle, as some biographers suppose, in lines about the nymph whirling and dancing through the trees, but those "lascivious dreaming knees" belong on the page and nowhere else. The magazine paid fifteen dollars for this forty-line ode but rejected other submissions. Undaunted, or perhaps just putting on a good show, Faulkner wrote to an acquaintance, "I am sending you a drawing which, when I have become famous, will doubtless be quite valuable."[81]

More promising than his poetry is Faulkner's early fiction, especially the prophetic and taut "Landing in Luck" that appeared in a November 1919 Ole Miss publication. The cadet pilot is inept, a crash-landing artist, so to speak, who escapes death as an improbable hero. He damages his landing gear, as

Faulkner would later do when he did learn to fly a plane. The story is striking for the pilot's persistence—much like Faulkner's own. Later, the writer continued to fly and to ride horses even though he never became a proficient pilot or horseman.

Faulkner believed the war would make a momentous change in his life. Yet here he was in Oxford, play-acting that change but not really sure of what to do next. He had to compete with his brother Jack, a real war hero wounded and invalided home. It took some doing, then, to maintain the guise of a man of action. Biographer Fred Karl notes the Gatsby-like remaking of the past, and the desire to win back the woman Faulkner lost.[82] Estelle had returned to Oxford in the spring of 1919, shortly after the death of her younger sister, who had succumbed to the Spanish influenza. Estelle told her trusted biographer, Joseph Blotner, that on her return to Oxford, Faulkner wrote such a passionate inscription on the Swinburne he gave to her that she tore it out when she departed for Hawaii with her husband in late September 1919. That she belonged to another may have made her all the more desirable, like a lady out of Arthurian legend.

With Estelle gone, William Faulkner visited whorehouses in Memphis and Clarksdale and played golf in Oxford, managing to offend his father and community standards: "To circumvent the Blue laws concerning activity on the Sabbath Bill, Bill's brother Jack, and I [one of their friends] would play the back seven on the golf course. One Sunday as we approached #6 green, having already played our drives, here came Bill's father in a rage. Shaking a big walking stick and uttering all sorts of threats he came toward us. Jack and I picked up our balls and turned tail. Not Bill. He carefully selected an iron—cried "fore" and addressed the ball directly toward his father." Bill's accomplices were too far down the road to assess the damage.[83]

At a Methodist church ice-cream social, Bill decided to take Dean to Beale Street in Memphis, where an amazed Dean realized how comfortable and familiar the brothel was to his brother. Bill knew the "lady who owned the house," and Dean was pleased to be introduced to her just like a grown-up. He remembered that he was permitted to sit in the front parlor and watch "all the pretty ladies" parade by him. "Then he was sent outside to wait for William and the long and exciting ride back to Oxford after dark." They sang Methodist hymns together.[84]

William Faulkner did not pursue a profession. He worked fitfully at various jobs. He also played at being drunk, if his brother John is to be believed. Drinking, or the appearance of it, gave him a certain license to act out and to evade responsibility, or to dramatize the despair of the returning veteran and the lovesick poet. He got waited on and indulged by family members, especially his mother, although she knew when her boy malingered. During one of his drunks she diluted his whiskey with iced tea and gradually reduced the alcohol content to zero. John overheard her say, "Billy, don't you think it's about time you got up and went to work?" He mumbled: "I can't. I'm drunk." She then told him: "If you are, you're drunk on iced tea. That's all you've had for the last twelve hours." He sat up, "as pleasant as you please," John reported, and said, "Well I believe I'll get up and go to work then." Which he did.

As a veteran, Faulkner was eligible to attend the University of Mississippi as a "special student," even though he had not completed high school. It has never been explained why a young man, now in his early twenties, returned to school, although biographers have speculated: He wanted to please his mother and placate his father, or he was making a "gesture toward orthodoxy."[85] Other biographers just ignore the question, assuming that the aimless Faulkner had nothing better to do.[86] Ben Wasson, a witness to his friend's appearance on campus in the fall of 1919, provides no explanation, except to note that both Bill and his brother Jack joined the Sigma Alpha Epsilon fraternity: "The Faulkner men were members of this national organization, and I suspect it was largely because of family loyalty that Bill agreed to join."[87] One of his fraternity brothers remembered he was quiet, kept to himself, dressed in tweeds, and in their large common room painted landscapes, local scenes, and perhaps some depictions of university buildings. He occasionally joined in a game, "Truth or Consequences," in which you had to say "what was true about your feelings concerning other people in the group." Here he voiced a complaint about Gid Montjoy, who either had banged a door loudly or had failed to close a door—Gid could not remember which.[88] Either way the memory suggests a concern for privacy and politeness. Most students had only the slightest acquaintance with him. "I knew him when in the University of Mississippi," Jim Breyealle recalled, in what is probably a typical response: "He came back to the university from foreign service in World War I in 1919. He was not a very popular personality among students, but he was from an outstanding family of Mississippians."[89]

Biographers have ignored another possibility: fraternal rivalry. The real wounded hero, Jack, returned from the trenches in France to enroll at Ole Miss, to study law. The older brother, a dropout, had to compete. Jack had even dared to date Estelle. And what to make of John driving Estelle to the railroad station, where she departed for her honeymoon with Cornell Franklin? Jack and John, in their memoirs, say nothing about strains between them and their eldest brother, but Faulkner's fiction is full of "fraternal fury": the "story of brothers who love and yet hate each other" in *Flags in the Dust*, *The Sound and the Fury*, *As I Lay Dying*, and *Absalom, Absalom!* Jack describes not so much an estrangement but a lack of interest between them: "I had no ideas about the nature of his writing and, since he apparently felt no inclination to talk to me about it, I had even less to inquire about it. . . . Even in later years . . . [w]e never sat down and talked about his work."[90] The high drama of the novels is absent from the Faulkner brotherhood, but there is no telling what tensions might have been unspoken.

Faulkner, as a "special student," was able to avoid the requirements degree students had to fulfill, and he simply took the courses that interested him (in French, Spanish, and Shakespeare). He proved to be a desultory student, attending classes infrequently and rarely saying much, even when called upon. Perhaps more important, the university offered a venue for publication and an "acceptable status." He could concentrate on writing and avoid "constant and considerable external pressures to conform."[91] As rejections of his poetry in national publications mounted, Faulkner's pictures and poems appeared in the Ole Miss yearbook and the *Mississippian,* where he could try out his talent for drawings inspired by Aubrey Beardsley and indulge a "need for a stylized world of sensual beauty," so different from the "gray reality of the economically and culturally undeveloped South." On a university campus, away from the utilitarians, Faulkner did not have to justify his art. He could join others who practiced and appreciated a similarly elegant art nouveau style. The title page of the Ole Miss 1921–22 yearbook, for example, featured M. B. Howorth's pen-and-ink rendition of a French eighteenth-century park scene: a seated court lady with high-toqued hair and a fan obstructs the amorous advance of a cavalier who leans toward her. As in Faulkner's drawings, nature is simplified and abstracted into arabesque shapes and organic patterns. Howorth, like Faulkner, is fond of the rococo. French was Faulkner's best subject. He earned an A and eventually acquired a passable fluency in the language. In Faulkner's pictures, a graceful social life in formal evening clothes or in the latest fashions predominates. This kind of refinement even appeared in a department store advertisement in the Ole Miss yearbook (1919–20). The shop touts "The Best Styles, The Best Quality, The Best Values," with an ornamental arrangement weaving "organic forms into arabesques without neglecting their symmetrical order." The lettering is part of the artistic and commercial display, "coupling beauty in design and commercial intentions."[92] In short, Ole Miss offered a level of sophistication, at least in certain departments, that Faulkner could not find elsewhere near home.

Inspired by William Morris's arts and crafts movement, Faulkner designed his own books for Estelle and others to give his work not merely a personal but a tactile feel. For the famous *Some Imagist Poets* anthology (1915), featuring the work of Amy Lowell, Richard Aldington, H. D., and others, Faulkner designed his own white paper labels for the cover and spine. The rigid, tightly spaced vertical Roman letters on the cover make the title *SomeImagistPoets,* a kind of enjambment that makes palpable the Imagist ambition to make the image itself the cynosure of poetry. Faulkner did not have copies of Amy Lowell's first editions in his library, but it seems likely that he would have seen them in New Haven's Brick Row Book Shop, for example, her beautifully crafted pocket-sized editions with their paper labels, which were, in turn, imitating the look of John Keats's books of poems. Faulkner went beyond such imitations in binding and hand-lettering *Some Imagist Poets,* making the work talismanic, the total work of art as envisioned by William Blake.[93] The young writer who did not want to work at a conventional job, or make money, or serve a machine-driven commercial world found his outlet in hand-crafted creations. He was practicing the hands-on approach to art that William Morris advocated.

One scholar deems Faulkner's graphic work talented but the work of an amateur deriving much of his subject matter and style from Beardsley and more contemporary illustrators. True, although one drawing clearly presages the themes and styles of a great novelist. For the 1920–21 Ole Miss yearbook, he drew an elegant couple so entwined in the sweeping sound of the black jazz sextet that they are the music and the moment. The couple is in front of a black piano to which they seem attached. It is as if the music touches them, and they cannot make a move that is not in sync with what they hear. Canted slightly to the left of center, these swingers are fully integrated into the black band tableau. Each musician is given a distinctive gesture: on the far left the seated ecstatic drummer is caught with his drumstick raised like a salute; the mellow trombonist stands erect with his slide projecting out and up to the left; and upright, leaning on the right side of the piano, the clarinetist in profile fingers his cool, reedy instrument. Below him the seated guitarist looks out, open-mouthed, forming part of a diagonal line that starts with the seated drummer, while below the clarinetist the crouching trumpeter, with his head down, completes another horizontal line directly across from the drummer. Amplifying this intricate composition is the bassist on the far right, whose bow extends across the seated guitarist and above the trumpeter, while the bassist's body throbs with the music, which is emphasized in the double lines that flank his figure and his instrument. This scene is a new and original way of suggesting the wholeness of art, and the miracle of jazz, which depends both on individual and group performances. Like the white couple, the black musicians are stylized, with few facial features other than their exaggerated white mouths, which express their joy and power. This dynamic scene is thrilling—even more so when compared with M. B. Howorth's similar depiction in the 1921–22 Ole Miss yearbook. Once again a blackface sextet plays for a white couple dancing. But the musicians have the big noses and, in general, the darky looks expected in such illustrations. And the couple is naturalistically drawn, without the sharp, distinctive facial planes that make Faulkner's couple cohere. The music in Howorth's scene is just accompaniment to the dancing couple, who are not bonded to the musicians. These black performers are just the background and not an integral part of the configuration. Faulkner's couple grip one another in an all-consuming powerful diagonal posture. Howorth's dancers sedately hold one another in place in a strictly vertical pose, part of a static picture. The "astonishing versatile" artist revealed in Faulkner's drawing is worthy of the novelist he would become. The Faulkner who missed seeing black people when he went north to New Haven, the Faulkner who could not imagine much of his fiction without the presence of black people, the Faulkner whose very life was sustained by black men and women, began to show, in drawings like this one, an integrated world so many of his own people relied on but denied.

Louis Cochran, editor of the *Mississippian* in 1920, who later wrote one of the earliest biographical sketches of Faulkner, commissioned many of his friend's drawings and written works. He regarded Faulkner's reserve as shyness—not arrogance but a form of self-protection against students who did not like him. On November 12, 1920, the *Mississippian* published "Cathay," and the poem also appeared in the *Oxford Eagle* the next day, at a time when regional and local papers regularly published verse. The Shelleyan lament over the vanquishing of vainglory is evident in lines that would certainly strike home:

> Where once thy splendors rose,
> And cast their banners bright against the sky,
> Now go the empty years infinitely
> Rich with thy ghosts.[94]

The lines seems to presage certain passages in *Flags in the Dust*. One commentator, craving more biography, goes further: "It seems to be the poem of a young Southerner looking out of the narrow confines of his own frustration and conflicts, and finding, perhaps unconsciously, his own region's past in the past of Cathay and his own individuation in the pattern of an older rise and fall." The idea of the unconscious, apparently irresistible to certain biographers, proves nothing, of course. It seems enough to say that Faulkner's absorption of post–Civil War lore led to the creation of poems like "Cathay," just as he was drawn as a teenager to Henryk Sienkiewicz's depiction of Pan

Michael, the brave "little knight" in a defeated and occupied Poland, with a nobility reminiscent of southern planters.[95]

Two weeks later the *Mississippian* published "Sapphics," a condensed version of Swinburne's poem but without that poet's reveling in the new spirit in poetry that Sappho represented by speaking of other kinds of love. On the contrary, "Sapphics" portrays a stern white Aphrodite, blind to the "lesbians kissing mouth / To mouth." Their cryings and lamentations make no impression on the goddess. Most Faulkner biographers slight the poem, and only Judith Sensibar has treated it as a sign of Faulkner's uneasiness about same-sex love and his own sexuality. Perhaps, although Ben Wasson remembered Faulkner mentioning his reading of Havelock Ellis, as he supplied "an explanation of the condition."[96] Faulkner may also have been following a nineteenth-century convention, which, in one critic's words, associates the "fruitless love" of lesbians with "an image for the socially ineffective and sacrificial role of the artist." After all, it is the cruelty of the goddess of love that is paramount.[97] Aphrodite is unmoved by the sounds of the lesbians "drunken with singing" and by the sight of the Oceanides, the goddesses of fresh water, "shining and unsandalled." Aphrodite does not acknowledge a world built on art: "The nine crowned muses about Apollo" who "Stand like nine Corinthian columns singing / In clear evening." Surely she is a stand-in for the world around him who similarly saw none of the art that gave meaning to his life that had been damaged with Estelle's departure. She had been a critical part of his idealized world of art. Her disappearance made life seem harsh, insensitive, and unresponsive.

Swinburne's Sappho did not fit into the chivalric tradition that enraptured Faulkner—so caught up was he in his devotion to Estelle, or to what she had always represented. "Fifty Years After," his next poem published in the *Mississippian,* suggests a devotion he could not shake off, even though the poem is cast in the guise of remembering a woman who, now old, can no longer weave a web of enchantment with her "blind bent fingers." Like Faulkner, who could not reconcile himself to the change in Estelle as a married, mature woman, the poem's speaker "with his bound heart and his young eyes bent / And blind . . . feels her presence like shed scent, / Holding him body and life within its snare." Estelle, no longer a young woman caressing "men's arms who rose up to her" (think of them asking her to dance), the vision of her as she once was enthralls and, you might say, blinds him. The poem seems a reverie over what both lover and his beloved have lost.

With Swinburne and T. S. Eliot as important influences, Faulkner searched for a way to combine his mourning for a love lost with the emptiness occasioned by the war, and his feeling that his art did not matter in the postwar world. In "The Lilacs," a poem he hand-lettered and bound as a booklet, which later became the first poem in *A Green Bough* (1933), the setting is reminiscent of "The Love Song of J. Alfred Prufrock": Three at tea sit comfortably on a summer afternoon in "diffident contentedness," although, as in "Prufrock," the dialogue actually seems to occur as an interior monologue, in the mind of the "Poor chap, his mind / . . . Doctors say . . . Hoping rest will bring—." The truncated phrases and ellipses suggest what the poem's speaker overhears as he keeps company with the characters of his own imagination: talking to his past and present selves. In search of a "white woman, a white wanton near a brake," the speaker, a fighter pilot, imagines stalking her in "my little pointed-eared machine"—an image that recalls the pointed-eared satyrs chasing women in Faulkner's drawings. A bullet strikes the pilot's left breast, but it is also the bullet that kills his "pointed-eared machine," making plane and pilot one: "Ah, science is a dangerous mouth to kiss." He longs to fall from some "Etruscan dart / In meadows where the Oceanides / Flower the wanton grass with dancing." As in "Sapphics," what seems lost is a world in which poetry was possible and now is dead, like the pilot himself, experiencing a living death. "And, on such a day as this," he could "Become a tall wreathed column" In the art-built world that is rejected in "Sapphics" and that is killed in "The Lilacs" with "a bullet through my heart." Buried in this poem is Faulkner's own anguish over losing a home that once included the "serene / Of Living and work and joy that was our heritage / And, best of all, of age." As if addressing Estelle as well as his separate selves, he cries, "we were too young." This poem, like "Sapphics," seems a displacement of Faulkner's grief, of a dialogue that, like the speaker's words, he can have only with himself. "One should not die like this," the poem's refrain, is the pilot's lament, but it is also Faulkner's. He imagines the lilacs, so often associated with commemoration of the dead, saying, "Old man . . . How did you die?" He answers, "I—I am not dead," and he overhears "voices as from a great distance—Not dead / He's not dead, poor chap; he didn't die—" Faulkner survived the war with his sense of loss intact but his will to go on troubled by his place in a world that seemed to offer no welcome for his art, as he walked the Ole Miss campus. He was on a campus where it was customary to speak even to those you did not know.[98] But he remained in communication with himself as others wondered about him or rejected this isolated figure, a Quentin Compson, world-weary when he should be just beginning his life. Faulkner faked his war wounds, but he was wounded nonetheless, and writing about themes of "erotic longing, inhibition, and death" that would culminate in *The Sound and the Fury*.[99]

He was not alone in his feelings of displacement. He recognized a kindred spirit in his November 20, 1920, *Mississippian* review of W. A. Percy's *In April*

Once: "Mr. Percy—like alas! how many of us—suffered the misfortune of having been born out of his time. He should have lived in Victorian England and gone to Italy with Swinburne, for like Swinburne, he is a mixture of passionate adoration of beauty and as passionate a despair and disgust with its manifestations and accessories in the human race." Faulkner's own poems said as much, as he brooded over the same dilemma that afflicted Percy: "the dark of modernity which threatens the bright simplicity and the colorful romantic pageantry of the middle ages with which his eyes are full."[100]

The poems in the *Mississippian* right after "The Lilacs," between February and May 1920, are mostly homages to Paul Verlaine, featuring the persona of an old man with vision dimmed by stardust from the wings of women he has loved, "lost ladies—Si vraiment charmant, charmant ("Une ballade des femmes perdue"); reveries of the sorrowful and the disheartened ("Naiads' Song"); scenes of stealthy lovers evading parental prohibitions ("Fantoches"); love songs that melt in the silver moon while "Slim fountains sob in silver ecstasies" ("Clair de Lune"); a lover once charmed by his beloved's "dainty airs . . . now to her my heart is deaf and blind" because "She broke the coin and gave it half to me" ("Streets"); a poplar imagined as a young girl, shivering even in the sunlight, as though her clothes have been taken from her ("A Poplar"); a woman beloved as nature itself, "A nimbus that dances / In my heart and entrances, / So shall it ever be / Through infinity" ("A Clymène"); the longueurs of time and work, the desire to dwell only on the golden beloved ("Study"). Even the last poem, "Alma Mater," becomes a lover's tribute: "Holding, and held by her in fond embrace— / At parting, her kind calmly dreaming face."[101] Was this last, quite conventional poem reflective of his need for the temporary refuge he had found on the Ole Miss campus? He was, after all, in the anxious, brooding phase of a career with promise but as yet no payoff. It rankled him to be the object of several parodies in the *Mississippian* aimed at ridiculing his translations and adaptations and the affectations of "Count No 'Count." The Freshman Literary Class Roll even listed him as "Count Falkner."[102] He loftily dismissed his detractors, pointing out how futile it was to imitate his imitations of other poets.[103]

For support he continued to turn to Phil Stone, spending weekends in the older man's company talking poetry.[104] Stone said Faulkner remained the "black sheep" of the family, greeted by the family's friends with "polite, derisive smiles."[105] Faulkner seemed to court as much as he resented his status as "resident alien."[106] For company, he also had Ben Wasson, whose poetry Faulkner would read and comment on, even though, as Wasson later put it, "I was completely the dilettante and he a serious poet who studied the techniques and forms of poetry."[107] Wasson made the rounds with Faulkner. They often wound up at the courthouse square, where Confederate veterans liked to congregate, and men liked to pitch washers at a line.[108] "You think they're talking about Shiloh or Gettysburg or the siege of Vicksburg?" Bill asked Ben, replying to his own question, "Well, they're probably bragging about how much 'stuff' they got during the war." Wasson said his friend used what was for him a rare "vulgar expression."[109] Apparently the "stuff" alluded not to cupidity but concupiscence.

Faulkner ended the 1919–20 academic year with an A in French, a B in Spanish, and D in English. He also won a poetry prize awarded by Professor Calvin Brown, one of the few faculty members not among the "broken down preachers: head full of dogma and intolerance and a belly full of big meaningless words," if *Mosquitoes* is to be credited. And yet Faulkner decided to return for a second year, perhaps because, as his second published novel revealed, he "kind of got interested in learning things." Perhaps, too, Hubert Starr was right all along, and his friend did feel, back in 1918, that he had missed something by not going to college. At any rate, he now had a home on the campus, where his father served as assistant secretary (business manager) of the university. This impressive three-story structure had a conical roof, a circular stairway to the second floor, and a small room in a tower that suited Faulkner's medieval tastes and in which he could indulge both his drinking and his writing—much to his father's chagrin.

During the summer of 1920, Faulkner made a little money painting houses but mainly spent his time perfecting his tennis game, winning his matches with drop shots and tenacious returns. "With him it was all or nothing. He was the best of the Faulkner boys, quick and fast and persevering for his size. He had good power," one of his competitors observed.[110] Faulkner also continued to play games, hunt, and tell campfire stories of supernatural horror laced with comical touches that amused his companions, teenage boys, including his brother Dean, with whom Faulkner seemed more comfortable than with his college contemporaries and elders. As in his later stories, it is children and younger men who seem capable of imagining a world different from the one grown-ups rigidly enforce. Rejection by the college literary society may have rankled him, but it also comported with his lifelong scorn of the literary world.

Faulkner gave up on college in that second year, officially withdrawing from classes on November 5, 1920, even as he became absorbed on campus working for a theater group, the Marionettes, headed by Ben Wasson. Drama had been a center of interest on campus since 1905 during Stark Young's two years there as a professor. The group included Katrina Carter, already a Faulkner friend; Lucy Somerville, a childhood friend of Ben's who attended

Methodist Sunday school in Greenville with him; and Lucy's cousin Ella, a friend of Estelle's and a subscriber to the *Theatre Arts Magazine,* where she read Young's reviews.[111] Ella, the daughter of the law school's dean, used her sandwich shop as a literary salon and "held the social reins in Oxford," said novelist Elizabeth Spencer. Katrina, Ella, and Estelle were all considered "fast" because they smoked cigarettes. Ella remembered that Bill "didn't go with girls very much."[112]

In 1922, Lucy Somerville became one of two women enrolled in the Ole Miss law school, which started admitting a few women in 1885, even though the profession was still considered not fit for a lady. She found her place at Ole Miss after Columbia University rejected her. Lucy, two years older than Faulkner, had been involved in suffragist campaigns and labor organizing.[113] New York had stripped Lucy of southern prejudices about race: "It was in New York that I learned to be a whole human being," she declared.[114] She had come from a "long line of strong women," including a formidable Aunt Bama–like great-grandmother: "She could have ruled Great Britain," a family member said. Lucy had also grown up with a harrowing sense of how the Civil War had devastated her family, but she disparaged the southern view of Reconstruction as destroying the good old days of antebellum life. She had no romantic illusions about the Lost Cause. She stood apart from aristocratic families like the "Percy crowd" she called "stiff and boring." Faulkner would twit a Percy scion on a tennis court and in a book review for the column "Books and Things," which Lucy started in the *Mississippian.* She had spent the summer of 1917 "trying to be a lady," and it did not take. A few years later New York City, she said, broke "the spell of the South."[115]

For two years she had roamed the length of Manhattan from Greenwich Village to Morningside Heights and seen nearly every play that had run for more than a week. William Faulkner, Lucy reported, had an avid interest in all aspects of the theater. They first met in the scorching days of September 1920, gathering under the shade of the giant oaks that remain a beautiful feature of the Ole Miss campus. Ben told Lucy that Bill, shy and reserved, wanted to write plays. Faulkner didn't like to attend meetings regularly, Ben explained, but the group could count on this budding playwright. He did not like to sit through entire rehearsals or keep to a schedule, but, in Lucy's words, he "lifted the level of production."[116]

Faulkner was also fortunate to have arrived at just the time Ole Miss students were looking for a creative outlet. As Lucy Somerville put it, they were "sullen and depressed," especially over the "abolition of fraternities, the interference with their lives as they called it, by the Legislature and the consequent withdrawal of support by many prominent alumni. In a few weeks this sullenness erupted into a near riot, the Governor was burned in effigy on the campus, politicians rushed to the barricades, denounced the University, the students and University officials for allowing such goings on and threatened to cut off all appropriations; for awhile there was excitement aplenty." With Wasson as president, the group named itself after *A Book of Marionettes* by Helen Haiman, at a time when puppet shows and the figure of Pierrot had become popular on campuses and in the theater world. Faulkner worked with the actors on character development and helped to stage their first play, *The Arrival of Kitty,* performed at a movie house off campus. Lucy remembered how much he hated routine and that he would never argue but took the route of passive resistance. Faulkner's authority, even then, was impressive: "Ben and I respected his feelings and took him on his own terms," Lucy recalled. She did not say what impact she might have had on Faulkner. She was a Mississippi-raised woman who had been to the North before he began his own trek, and a feminist long before anyone else in his circle of acquaintance could have expressed such beliefs. Biographers have downplayed her presence at this crucial moment in Faulkner's life. Judith Sensibar reports: "People in Oxford made it clear that only girls like plain little Lucy Somerville, who excelled in their studies, might be among the two or three women in a class who went on to male bastions of professionalism like law or medical school."[117] Only by the standards of the southern belle and beauties like Estelle Oldham could Lucy be considered plain. Blotner calls her "lively and attractive." In Greenville, where she grew up, she excited some male interest but did not care to dress up and cater to their desires. She disliked "primping" and simply didn't care about male adulation.

Lucy Somerville stood out as the kind of woman Faulkner would grow to admire and even date in New York and later re-create in the radical figure of Linda Snopes in *The Mansion.* Lucy grew up in a home full of newspapers in which her mother, an activist, campaigned for women's rights. Around the dinner table the family would discuss public issues, not local gossip. William Faulkner could not have ignored her independence. She struggled with men of limited imagination who could not conceive of full citizenship for women,[118] and though William Faulkner described himself as old-fashioned, he nevertheless admired outspoken women—not only in his own family but in fiction—like Anita Loos's Dorothy in *Gentlemen Prefer Blondes.* By 1922 Lucy Somerville would have already participated in various activities that would have challenged her contemporaries' provincial prejudices. Lucy said Faulkner "never showed the slightest interest in what made me tick," and yet it is difficult to imagine a man of such acute perceptions not learning something from Lucy Somerville in the conversations they had about literature.[119]

Did she never share her interest in the law with the writer who would later make so much of the law in his fiction?

Bill (through Ben Wasson) also brought an important resource to Lucy's life: Phil Stone. "It was not long before I began to feel the shortage of current books," she later wrote. Lucy discovered that the nearest bookstore was in Memphis, and "not much of one there." No one on the Ole Miss campus expected the library to have a browsing room with current books. Once again, Ben Wasson "came to the rescue," telling Lucy about Stone's private collection that he passed around to Bill and Ben. "On the promise not to tell the source of the books, Ben cut me into the reading circle," Lucy confessed. That sharing of Stone's books led to Lucy's column "Books and Things": "I made no effort to hold Bill to a deadline," Lucy said, "and if I reminded him that he had promised something I did it softly. I have no recollection of his leaving me stranded when a piece was due. His writing was obviously of a much better quality than anything else that appeared in the column. He was beginning to have a professional touch. I have thought since those days that he valued the opportunity to publish his work much more than I then understood and he cooperated not only in writing but in supplying me with books." She never saw William Faulkner after they parted company in 1922, but her parting words about him suggest her identification with his ambition: "a man of talent struggling to find himself."[120]

Part of that struggle is a comic play Faulkner apparently never showed to Lucy. The work suggests he paid more attention to her world than he let on. 'Twixt Cup and Lip features a nineteen-year-old cigarette-smoking liberated woman, Ruth, who is supposed to be saved from herself by Jim, who tells his friend Francis that he intends to marry her and that Francis can conceal himself in Jim's apartment while Jim proposes to Ruth. She arrives, a Prohibition flapper who says she has thrown away her corset and refers to herself as "flat as a boy." A shocked, condescending Jim exclaims: "Ruth! Why do you persist in saying things like that? Would you talk that way before your mother, or any other innocent child?" He upsets her, she upsets him. They are both upset! Jim is not as worldly as he supposes, and she is not as insouciant as she pleases. Francis ducks out while the couple is quarreling and then reappears at the door, announcing that Ruth has already promised herself to him. She explains: "Why, I can't marry you both, can I? And he asked me first, Jim! Why didn't you ask before he did? You would have if you loved me." But when Francis collects a hundred dollars from Jim on a bet that Jim could not get Ruth to marry him, Ruth is outraged: "Do you mean to tell me that you bet money on me just as if I were a racehorse? Oh you beast! You unspeakable cad!" She returns Francis's ring to him. She is none too happy with Jim either until he agrees that she can do anything she wants. "Oh, everything?" she asks. "Can I smoke and drink highballs and do everything I please?" He says yes. The play ends with her throwing her arms around him and with this exchange:

> *Ruth:* Do you know why I love you so much?
> *Jim:* No, why?
> *Ruth:* Because you're so masterful.[121]

Lucy Somerville was no Ruth, but she came from a world that intrigued Faulkner, especially since it revealed how foolish men could behave in their roles as the defenders of female chastity. Is Ruth merely amusing or cynical and ironic? Faulkner would return to these questions of female psychology in *Sanctuary.*

The play is too much of a sketch to reveal much of Faulkner's own actual attitudes, which he explored quite differently in *The Marionettes,* an extension of his derivative poetry and not a precursor of his innovative prose. This dream play, like those "brought into vogue by Strindberg and Maeterlinck late in the nineteenth century and firmly established in American by 1920 . . . belongs also to the tradition of the harlequin play, featuring the clown-lover Pierrot as main actor."[122] As symbolist drama, *The Marionettes* is "determinedly antirealistic," which is to say it frustrates efforts to link characters to specific settings and defies the desire to empathize with them. "Enraptured contemplation" reflected in stylized movements, and decorative motifs (part of Faulkner's illustrations for the play) establish the mise-en-scène. The play is "not about love so much as it is about aesthetics—Faulkner's chief passion at the time."[123]

In the end, the Marionettes decided not to stage the play, and Wasson convinced Faulkner to let him sell copies of the play booklet for five dollars each. Always in need of money, a grateful Faulkner was happy to engage Wasson as his first literary agent.[124] *The Marionettes,* a kind of Yeatsian closet drama, came delivered in a handmade booklet with ten drawings in the Beardsley tradition of stylish, elongated, effete-looking melancholic figures. Faulkner originally produced six copies of the play for the actors who would play the six characters: Pierrot, Marietta, Pierrot's Shade, A Grey Figure, A Lilac Figure, and Spirit of Autumn. Pierrot is an unfulfilled poet, the "paradigm Symbolist poet-*isole,* who appears in the poetry of T. S. Eliot, Conrad Aiken, Wallace Stevens, and others."[125] In *The Marionettes,* Pierrot's Shade engages in what the poet cannot, including an invitation to a dance of love that his beloved, Marietta, declines to perform. Pierrot's Shade sounds a little like one of Amy Lowell's liquefied lovers, crying out: "You are a trembling pool, / Love! . . . And I am a flame that only you can quench." The copy Faulkner presented to Estelle's daughter was surely meant to entice her mother. Marietta's "eyes are fastened upon Pierrot, she is like a sleep walker while Pierrot continues to sing, weaving his song like net about her."

One aspect of the play retains interest for the student of Faulkner's mature work, especially of his interior monologues, since like the speaker of "The Lilacs," Pierrot seems in dialogue with himself, which is to say he is split into different selves, watching himself—like Prufrock or the female protagonist in Amy Lowell's "Patterns." Marietta, however, is a kind of femme fatale: "Nothing save death is as beautiful as I am, and I shall wear a jade gown, and walk on the gravel paths in my garden." In her walled garden, Pierrot makes himself her captive, so to speak, at her service as Faulkner was for Estelle. Marietta in a jade gown and Chinese brocaded scarf is drawn in face, figure, and haircut to resemble photographs of Estelle. Marietta is defined by an obsessive series of similes that suggest her all-consuming fascination for two choral figures, one of whom declares that her hair "is like sunlight combed through maple leaves, and her eyes are like pools in the depths of a forest at night, like twin pools in which are caught scraps of evening sky; her eyes are like windflowers sown across a meadow." The other replies: "Yes, her eyes are like pools in which one could drown oneself, her breast is a narrow white pool, and her breast points are the twin reflections of stars. Her breasts are like ivory crusted jewels for which men have died, for which armies have slain one another and brother has murdered brother." Such romantic and fratricidal passages faintly presage major works like *Absalom, Absalom!*

Faulkner's Pierrot seems, like his counterparts, thwarted, and, as such, a stand-in for Faulkner himself, who was not yet ready to display his dilemma, or that of his characters, in a recognizable Mississippi setting. "Only in a play, a fantasy, could he reveal that he saw himself as a Pierrot or a dandy of the imagination," Fred Karl supposes, drawing on Faulkner's feelings of dislocation,[126] which not even a small campus group that supported him could imagine presenting to the public. Pierrot is a poet "in love with dreams," not with real women, states one authority on the Pierrot figure in literature, which suggests the Estelle whom Faulkner dreamed of was never the real woman, who was bound to disappoint him. This disturbing clash between the ideal and real operated on several different fronts, so to speak, in dramas that were "dream visions. Faulkner was drawn to the mask of Pierrot, as he was drawn to the uniform of a World War I Canadian Royal Air Force officer. And these two costumes—one assumed in writing, the other in life—give graphic evidence of the ambivalence of Faulkner's self-expectations and idealization during his apprenticeship years."[127]

Sensibar suggests that only Estelle could have detected how the play perpetuated the roles she and Bill had played for one another, dressing up and dramatizing their love, and masking themselves in ways that are reminiscent of a Eugene O'Neill play. Pierrot in his drunken dream state, for anyone interested enough to buy the book from Wasson, could be seen as Faulkner's alter ego. This Freudian sense of the repressed self acting out, a puppet of the unconscious, so to speak, was in the cultural air—at least for those like Faulkner, Wasson, and their contemporaries searching for outlets and expressions of their frustrations and ambitions. The immobilized Pierrot, like Faulkner's passive marble faun, is on the Freudian couch, supine with suffering and yearning. The poems Faulkner was writing in 1919–20, collected as *The Marble Faun* (1924), express the "conflict between dreaming and acting" and eventuate in the "theme of a person so imprisoned in his fantasies that he fails to live a creative life and ultimately destroy himself and others in his mature novels."[128]

The Marionettes and *The Marble Faun* are both examples of Faulkner's dead-end neo-Romantic, effete poetry, already antiquated in the early 1920s, and only fitfully freshened with the sensibility Phil Stone promoted as "steeped in the soil of his native land."[129] Even the best passages seem sedate for a poet untouched by Whitman's barbaric yawp:

Sunset stains the western sky;
Night comes soon, and now I
Follow toward the evening star.
A sheep bell tinkles faint and far,
Then drips in silence as the sheep
Move like clouds across the deep,
Still dusky meadows wet with dew.
I stretch and roll and draw through
The fresh sweet grass, and the air
Is softer than my own soft hair.
I lift my eyes; the green
West is a lake on which has been
Cast a single lily.—See!
In meadows stretching over me
Are humming stars as thick as bees,
And the reaching inky trees
Sweep the sky. I lie and hear
The voices of the fecund year,
While the dark grows dim and deep,
And I glide into dreamless sleep.

Faulkner lapses into formulaic phrases: leafy shade, inky trees, dusky meadows, and the like. The relentless decorum of such lines is deflating.

It is as if Faulkner's hand stiffened when he penned his stilted verse. His prose, even at this early stage, is limber and recognizably Faulknerian—even in a trifling story, "Moonlight," about an adolescent's bungling attempt at seduction. He is encouraged by a note: "My dear Forgive my gardian he is old he does not realise that I am yours. See Skeet fix it for him to call me for a date tonight you meat us somewhere and I will be yours tonight even if tomorrow not goodbye but farewell forever. Destroy this. S." But S, Susan, simply wants to go to the movies. His arousal and anticipation are neatly conveyed in a sentence: "Then he heard her—the sweet high whinnying reasonless giggling which turned his bowels to water—the pale dress, the body reed-thin as she and Skeet came across the lawn toward the magnolia." Skeet has been promised a bottle of corn liquor if he delivers Susan to her seducer. The seduction ends abruptly when a shocked Susan demurs and her seducer capitulates: "He felt like wood—the carcass from which sense, sensibility, sentience, had fled along with the sweet wild fires of hope; he thought in quiet amazement: *I wouldn't have hurt her. All I wanted was just to seduce somebody.*" If it is not much of a story, it at least has the pungent, and sometimes eloquent, sensibility that suffuses the interior monologues of *As I Lay Dying:*

> There was a fatality in it—the empty house, the fact that he had gained the veranda unseen. It was as though by gaining the porch unchallenged he had cast the augury, bled the bird, and this was fortune, luck: that instant when desire and circumstance coincide. It was as though they not only coincided, circumstance not only condoned desire, but were actually and suavely coercing it: he thought how, if he should miss out now, if it should not be tonight, if something occurred at this hour to betray and frustrate him, that he would be automatically absolved of all allegiance to conduct, order and even breathing.

The story ably handles the grandiosity and desperation of adolescence, the search for portents of success, the desire to have some absolute outcome, no matter what, and the abrupt shattering of romantic illusions—"All right, fish face," Skeet says, expecting the promised bottle of corn liquor for bringing Susan to the romantic rendezvous. "Where's it?" This comic story ends in bathos: "He felt nothing at all now, no despair, no regret, not even surprise. He was thinking of himself and Skeet in the country, lying on a hill somewhere under the moon with the bottle between them, not even talking."

The Marble Faun and *The Marionettes* seem worlds away from "Moonlight" and from *The White Rose of Memphis,* the old Colonel's Mississippi riverboat melodrama about a cast of characters who in Dickensian fashion are separated from their true loves only to be reunited, after much suffering, in the end. But the old Colonel's confection of a shipboard masquerade, in which no one is what he or she seems, is suffused with the same lovelorn sensibility that governs his great-grandson's verse. What is missing in the old Colonel's potboiler, however, is his great-grandson's sense of tragedy and the fraught consciousness of the artist. The romantic conflicts that are externalized in *The White Rose of Memphis* through long speeches are turned into interior monologues in *The Marionettes* and in so much of Faulkner's mature work. No wonder that his father, a connoisseur of western melodramas, found his brooding son so baffling. What William wrote seemed to have no outlet in *action* any more than Quentin Compson's lucubrations lead to *results.* And at this point, Faulkner himself seemed enmeshed in writing about his own inability to break out of his romantic reveries.

A cryptic, marginal gloss in William Stanley Braithwaite's *Anthology of Magazine Verse for 1920 and Year Book of American Poetry,* a gift from Ben Wasson to Faulkner, provides a brief glimpse into Faulkner's literary sensibility. American writers were just beginning to make serious use of indigenous Native American and "Negro" materials, Braithwaite noted, although "no one who matters actually thinks that a national literature can be founded on such alien bases." Faulkner drew an arrow directed at this assertion and wrote above it: "Good God." If only he had expatiated. Was he deploring, as Henry James did, that America did not have Europe's deep historical roots? Or was William Faulkner, southerner, aghast that Braithwaite made no exception for the South when the anthologist regretted that his nation lacked the "deep soil of memory"? What but its memories had made the South what it was?[130]

In the summer of 1921, Estelle returned to Oxford from Honolulu for a second visit home. Was she wearing Marietta's "jade gown and Chinese brocaded scarf"? Faulkner presented her with another handcrafted book, *Vision in Spring.* Critics have detected various influences, including Verlaine, Conrad Aiken (Faulkner's favorite contemporary poet), Kipling, and Yeats.[131] The first parts of this long poem sequence are not so different from the decadent feel of *The Marble Faun,* but the later and stronger parts of *Vision in Spring* are profoundly Prufrockian, bleak and forlorn: "How all our cherished labors time will crumble, change: / We build our houses, block by block, in pain / For our children to pull down, then build them up again."[132] Like the ineffectual Prufrock, the poet addresses himself but inescapably the reader as well:

"Dust you rose, as dust you someday fall" is one of the poem's refrains. The Poe of death and melancholy appears in passages that lament "How all our life is futile, thwarted dream; / Like that Light, beating frail wings on the dark, / Like these waves that on this dark sand stream." Perhaps just a faint echo of "Dover Beach" resounds in, "For some day all of us, light, waves and all / Will feel the sea of darkness softly touch us, / And one by one in darkness we will fall." The stymied Pierrot gives way to querulous Prufrock in lines that picture the poet seated among "careful cups of tea," trying to smooth his "mental hair," and wondering, "Now, do I dare / Who sees the light gleam on her intricate hair?"

Faulkner visited Estelle often at the Oldham home so that the impertinent biographer has to wonder if he said as much to her over tea, or did he, like the speaker in *Vision in Spring*, "withdraw, retreat, / Conscious of the glances on my feet / And feel as if I trod in sand"? What kind of impression was he making on Estelle? And how did she react to such dispiriting poetry? *Vision in Spring* seems the work of a man who doubted he would ever consummate his love. And what could Estelle do with *that*? Or with yet another parody of Prufrock:

> I grow old, I grow old
> Submerged in the firelight's solemn gold
> I sit, watching the restless shadows, red and brown,
> Float till I disturb them, then they drown.

The poem is a work of great passion—so much so that Estelle removed an inscription that apparently compromised a married woman. No matter what, William Faulkner had asserted his claim on her.

This beautifully crafted book is an ambivalent tribute. Estelle, like the subject of "The Dancer"—the most intriguing poem in *Vision in Spring*—stands for

> Youth, so swift, so white and slim
> Who haunts you, tempts you, bids you fly
> Across this floor of polished porphyry,
> To raise your arms, to try and clasp my knees.

The mixup of "you" and "my" reads like Faulkner channeling Estelle channeling Faulkner. The second stanza begins, "You are Youth?"—as if the poet's vision is in doubt, since the dancer

> cannot appease
> This flame that, like a music from your hair,

Sheds through me as though I were but air,
That strips me bare, my sudden life reveals.

It is difficult not to read such lines as Faulkner's disturbed psyche coming once again into contact with his lost beloved, this vision in spring, which was, in fact, the season of her return. The Estelle who reappears, if this is indeed an allegory of an actual love, is dangerous: "Yes, I will hurt you, as my tiny heels . . . Have mazed your life against your will." To the poet, she is all the more alarming because she is "The phantom that I thought was you," an evanescent image "flown like music" and "like water, wrinkled back where your face mirrored was."

The poem shifts point of view yet again—this time to the third person— picturing the poet watching what is only a reflection of what once was: "Watching her plastic shadow on the wall." These taunting images projected in firelight on the ceiling are part of a steadily humming, wheeling, "Until his brain, stretched and tattered, suddenly cracks." The music she is playing— what was it that Estelle played for William?—is so disturbing that she is asked to "Play something else," while "he tries to keep his tone / Lightly natural" as he "sees his brain disintegrate, spark by spark." Fixated on her figure, the poet watches her out of reach mount a stair. Is he dying or in some kind of sexual ecstasy? And what is the difference? The dancer, now adrift, detached from her youth, realizes that about her is "a shattered spring that, softly playing / She sought to build into a whole again."

What were Estelle's motivations? Perhaps they were a mystery to William Faulkner, too. Perhaps the two never directly addressed their feelings for one another, while in poetry he tried to imagine what the dancer feels as the poet stands by, still watching her "mount the stair / Step by step / with her subtle suppleness / This nervous strength that was ever his surprise" as he notes the "thin crisp swirl of dress / Like a ripple of naked muscles before his eyes." A "bursting moon" is his world falling apart as "wheels spin in his brain / Shrieking against sharp walls of sanity," until "The Dancer" comes to a devastating conclusion: "At the turn she stops, and shivers there, / And hates him as he steadily mounts the stair." If the dancer and her partner are fated to consummate their love, she also appears, in the poet's view, to react with rage—at what is not clear, and perhaps was never clear to William Faulkner. At this early stage, he seems already to have encased himself and his beloved in a myth expressed in the next poem, "Orpheus":

I am she who, one among numberless faces,
Bent to you, to the music you softly played,
Who walked with you, hand in hand, in many places
And followed you through forests unafraid.

In a valedictory, the lover, like Orpheus seeking Eurydice, goes "softly where together we walked and dreamed" and now walks in "memoried spring," for there is no way back to the world the lovers once shared. Although *Vision in Spring* continues with "Philosophy" and "April," they seem anticlimactic and incapable of standing up against the despair reflected in yearning for lost youth, which is also an attack on that yearning.

Did this young poet, proud of what he had written, no matter how dour, offer his work not only to his beloved but to the woman he had once said was a good critic? Did he think *Vision in Spring* was some kind of breakthrough? He offered it for publication to the Four Seas Company, which turned the book down. It seems too much to say the book was a turning point, even if the experimentation with point of view presages the innovative novels. The "ramshackle" *Vision in Spring* is hardly a finished work. Faulkner does not seem fully in control of the "constantly shifting voices and identities" that "trace out a world of masks and mirrors in which nothing is certain or stable—least of all, the self."[133] The poem, in other words, seems as much a product of his personal confusion as of his ambitious art.

Thirty-five years later, Faulkner spoke at the University of Virginia as though he had *Vision in Spring* in mind: "I don't know whether . . . any writer could say just how he identifies himself with his characters. Quite often the young man will write about himself simply because himself is what he knows best. That he is using himself as the standard of measure, and to simplify things, he writes about himself as perhaps he presumes himself to be, maybe he hopes himself to be, or maybe as he hates himself for being." All these possibilities seem to be on offer in the poem he presented to Estelle, working from what he knew, or thought he knew, to what he hoped still might be—against all probabilities—to what he and she may also have detested in themselves. At any rate, in the fall of 1921, Cornell Franklin had to return to Oxford to claim Estelle again on his way to assume a new post in Shanghai. Faulkner turned to Phil Stone and Stark Young, in town in September, as a refuge. Young, who had also confronted a southern community that did not understand his literary sensibility, commiserated with the frustrated Faulkner and proposed that the young writer consider working in New York while he figured out what he wanted to do.

The Catcher in the Rye

As in 1918, when Estelle married and departed from Oxford, so now Faulkner left for New Haven (without Phil Stone) to resume old acquaintances and to await word from Stark Young about that job in New York City. The young artist was drawing (several pictures of undergraduates) and writing short stories and sending them off for publication (without success). He roomed in a Yale dormitory with three others at a cost, he reported to his mother on October 6, of only two dollars per week.[134] He shared with her his delight in traveling by train through the West Virginia mountains and New England villages and the "queer feeling" that came over him watching the "slow magnificent ocean, like something you have heard, or smelled, and forgotten." Sounding like Eugene O'Neill, he found the sea "an utter relief," as if he had found "someone who loved me years and years ago." What an expression coming from the author of *Vision in Spring* in letters that are nothing like the verse of that melancholy poet.

To his mother, Faulkner sounded exactly like the unreconstructed southerner that Hubert Starr remembered: "You cant tell me these niggers are as happy and contented as ours are, all this freedom does is to make them miserable because they are not white, so that they hate the white people more than ever, and the whites are afraid of them." Such callow generalizations contrast with the simple lyrical descriptions of "hills all misted over with azure and gold, grey stone fences half covered by copses of flame colored berry bushes, round yellow pumpkins in fields of shocked corn, and maple forests, yellow and red beside soft blue water, and all against sombre black pines and purple hills." He composed these pictures after walking in the afternoons in breaks from writing in the morning and reading at night.

An acute awareness of fame—even if Faulkner presents that obsession as a comedy—is already apparent. "Oh, yes. I have already stopped traffic in the streets," he wrote his mother: "fame, in fact, has lighted early upon my furrowed brow." Fame, in fact, took him unawares as a traffic cop lectured him for failing to heed a stop sign and escaping one car that almost ran over his feet while another brushed the skirts of his coat, while a trolley nearly clipped his hat brim. The sense of timing in this letter is cinematic. Faulkner could be writing a scene for a Charlie Chaplin or Buster Keaton movie. To Dean, he described the cadet cheerleaders at a Yale–West Point football game, starting at the top row of seats and rolling one of their own "like a log over their heads" all the way down to the grandstand and then rolling him up again.

By early November, Faulkner had accepted an offer to become the Ole Miss postmaster, not wishing to forgo the $1,800 per year salary, but he was able to spend a month in New York City, a stay that began by his losing all his ready cash—exactly how he did not say, although his pocket may have been picked. He washed dishes in a Greek restaurant and was "looked down on" because the Greek and Irish dishwashers thought he was a "wop," a valuable experience for the novelist who would have Quentin Compson spend part of the day with a little Italian girl who is herself looked down on as a "furriner." Faulkner had made two brief trips to New York City during his first Yale visit, and this longer one, which ended up with a stay in Greenwich Village, beginning with a night in Stark Young's basement apartment, "lulled to sleep by the passing of the subway trains."

Faulkner's letters home say little about his conversations with Stark Young, even though the forty-year-old writer had established himself as an important theater critic, calling upon his deep scholarly background in Greek, Roman, English, Italian, and French literature. Faulkner never had any desire to turn critic, but his forthcoming erudite articles in the *Mississippian* emulate Young's authoritative musings in the *New Republic, Theatre Arts Magazine,* and *Vanity Fair.* Young befriended Eugene O'Neill, who would become one of Faulkner's subjects, and Sherwood Anderson, soon to become a promoter of Faulkner's work. Young took a special interest in *The Emperor Jones,* published in *Theatre Arts Magazine* (January 1921),[135] a play that Faulkner would single out for commendation.

The next day (perhaps November 10) he went out looking for his own room, discovering what remains true: living in the city was expensive. A room costing less than fifteen dollars per week would be a find. Faulkner preferred the smaller scale of New Haven, but he did enjoy meeting all sorts of different people, and he looked forward to working in the Doubleday Doran Bookstore, managed by Elizabeth Prall, who would soon marry Sherwood Anderson. She seemed an exotic in her bobbed hair, horn-rimmed glasses, and smock, smoking through dinner while he discussed art. She had agreed to hire him during the busy holiday season. At their first meeting he wore a suit, which she thought made him look "very elegant and distinguished. He fitted perfectly into the genteel atmosphere of the Doubleday Doran Bookstore."[136]

Then occurred one of those chance encounters in New York that can make a young writer believe he has come to the right place. In an uptown bookshop, Faulkner watched the entrance of a "slender man," about forty with black hair and a mustache and a "thin gentle face and glasses, and an almost indistinguishable suggestion of indecision in his manner." Faulkner recognized him from his photographs: It was Edwin Arlington Robinson (1869–1935), an "honest-to-God poet." Robinson, who had come in to autograph books, gave Faulkner a second look, which is perhaps why Faulkner spoke to him. "I didn't gain anything from him, as I probably startled him, but he was too gentle to put me off abruptly," Faulkner told his mother. Did he ever recall this poignant encounter during the many times he became the object of similar gazes and approaches? At the very least, he was learning what it was like to be such an object of attention.

Faulkner described his first subway trip—the crowds cramming into the train, the tremendous velocity of the cars that came to a sudden shocking stop: "Its like being shot through a long piece of garden hose." The hectic, pell-mell pace of getting around, day and night, by "subway, surface cars, elevated trains, and taxicabs" put him off and made "walking a snare and a delusion." He did not believe people really had a destination: "I don't think they know themselves." But was Faulkner any better off? Perhaps New York City troubled him because he became just like everyone else: "It's grab your hat and get on, and then get off and run a block and get on again." He did enjoy the Fifth Avenue bus, which he boarded at Washington Square, riding on top with "poets and country people up to the end of the avenue, along Riverside drive, then back again to the arch. That's the whole length of Manhattan Island and back, but very expensive: costs 20¢." Although he did appreciate the maneuverable urbanity of the city that allowed him to take in so many different places in one day, the crowds annoyed him. Bookshops became a refuge.

Faulkner finally had to settle for a five-dollar-per-week garret four flights up near Central Park (655 Lexington Avenue) and "those big insolent apartment houses where all the wealthy people from Texas and St Louis live," because it was cheaper than his preferred abode in the Village. He visited the Metropolitan Museum in Manhattan and an exhibition in Brooklyn, crowded with art students copying "pictures of dead fish, and baskets of fruit, and colored parrots." He did not seem much taken but hoped to learn more about line drawing for pictures Elizabeth Prall Anderson said he could sell.

Just a few days later (by November 16), Faulkner was on the move again after two days of no heat in his apartment. He alighted at 35 Vandam Street in the Village for a surprising rent of $3.50 per week. To Elizabeth Prall Anderson, he claimed he drank himself to sleep every night and started the morning with White Mule, his favorite corn liquor. Stark Young, alarmed at the heavy drinking, seemed relieved that Faulkner had found his own place to live. He did well selling books, exuding the aristocratic air of the southern gentleman that attracted women who bought whatever he recommended. He could be rude and intimidating, but they seemed to enjoy it when he said, "'Don't read that trash. Here's the book you should have.' They went off with great stacks of books, absolutely thrilled with the young, English-looking man, with his chin tucked down into his tie, very English-looking and charming." He deferred to Prall as "Miss Elizabeth" when her customers consulted him. "It was certainly not a New York way of addressing people and the customers were either greatly impressed or they thought he was crazy—or that I was," Prall wrote. She grew to distrust lurid tales about his life, and with "hurt innocence" he would respond, "Would I lie to you, Miss Elizabeth?" She thought so, not believing his account of his best friend who had married a girl Faulkner had impregnated. She regarded such stories, including his sorrowful one about a girl who had broken his heart at a beach resort, as so much "literary plunder."[137]

On occasion, Faulkner continued to impersonate a wounded war hero—this time in the company of a southern lumber company owner, John Joice, who brought Faulkner home to converse with Joice's French wife. "He was just back from the war," she remembered, and had a "cane and walked with a limp." He told her in French that he had just been released from the hospital with a metal disk near his hip. He also had the mystique of a struggling young writer until he began asking John Joice for a loan, saying he was awaiting funds from the family plantation. Mrs. Joice, finally fed up, shut her door on him after an unannounced visit and never saw him again. This was a curious performance for a young man who, like Holden Caulfield, deplored a city full of phonies. New York had its attractions and opportunities, but it also contained so many pretenders. Faulkner, sooner or later, always wanted to return home, which had its own brand of fakery, to be sure, but also an authenticity he could not live without. And for all his feeling that Oxford did not appreciate his literary efforts, he was a much-indulged firstborn son, and he appreciated it, sending letters home thanking his parents for food and clothing. On the way out of New York, he bought some paints for his mother, urging her to continue her portrait painting.[138] Even at twenty-four, he knew he had a home with his parents, even if his father and grandfather showed not the slightest confidence that he would ever amount to anything.

3

Postings

1922–1924

POSTMASTER AND BOHEMIAN POET

He was a small fellow. . . . And he didn't look like he had ever done much work, but he was a tough one. . . . Those old wide-door 800's were killers too. No automatic foot pedals in those days to let that door close between shovelfuls. You swung that fire door open with a chain, latched it, and put in a big fire in all that heat. When we got in, that boy had blisters on his hands and arms and was pretty well cooked.

The next trip he talked a little more about himself, and I learned that he was to be the next postmaster at the University. I asked him what he wants with a job firing on the railroad. He said, well, his folks all thought he wasn't worth a damn and wouldn't work and he just wanted to show them . . . he picked the hardest job he could find close by.

He stayed with us three round trips. . . . He shook hands with all of us. . . . And I handed his old bag down to him from the gangway and he left us happy as a kid.

—Unidentified interview with Joseph Blotner, February 10, 1964

The railroad that his great-grandfather built, the railroad that his father cherished, never meant that much to William Faulkner. Even though the family entered Oxford by train for the first time, *The Reivers* reveres horses and automobiles, and *Flags in the Dust* pays homage to mules and airplanes. The railroad snakes through *Go Down, Moses* as a harbinger of the future that will whittle away the wilderness, but that train, like the woods it invades, is nevertheless a relic of the old world. Young Bayard arrives home on a train, but his grandfather dies in the fast car that his grandson rams through the land. As needed, to prove himself and to make money, William Faulkner shoveled coal on a train and in a power plant and got his hands dirty like any other workman. But a world elsewhere always beckoned, no matter what temporary postings, no matter what scorn, he had to endure at home or in Hollywood.

Faulkner's grandfather, J. W. T. Falkner, "the loneliest man I've ever known," wrote his grandson John, died on March 13, 1922. He had been a trial to his son Murry, and skeptical of his grandson's literary efforts. J. W. T. had lost control of his bank and had retreated into deafness, retaining his air of command but, in the end, in charge of nothing. His death now made it possible for William Faulkner to begin, in just a few years, to create the old Bayard of *Flags in the Dust,* a moribund and yet still formidable figure, capable of knocking down one of his black retainers but also incapable of restraining his grandson's recklessness. Young Bayard proves no more biddable than his creator. Both the character and his creator never quite feel at home.

Murry Falkner never found much of a place in his son's fiction—in part because his life did not lend itself to the dramatic, legendary saga of the Sartoris clan and, as well, Murry scoffed at the literature his son wanted to write and instead sought to discipline him. On April 13, 1922, he wrote to the Ole Miss chancellor: "I am in receipt of information that my son William Falkner was one of the ones violating the Campus Rule concerning Drinking. I wish to say so long as My Self and Family remain on the Campus we are subject to the same rules as govern the others and anything you see proper to do in reference to this matter will be satisfactory to me."[1] What the chancellor did, if anything, has not been discovered. The stolid Murry never impressed his eldest son. "Dad's square," Faulkner told Phil Stone.[2]

Postmaster on the Ole Miss campus, a job Phil Stone and Major Oldham helped Faulkner to acquire,[3] never meant more to him than a holding action while he figured out what to do next. Unlike his success in that bookshop business, where books were his business, he never cared to exert himself in sorting the mail, summing up his contempt for the job in that famous statement about being at the beck and call of every son of a bitch who had the price of a stamp. In fact, to do the job properly would have meant acting like any other functionary. William Faulkner had to show that the job was beneath him. Getting the mail acknowledges a world that demands your attention. And Faulkner famously liked to throw his own mail away without reading it—unless it arrived in response to his own solicitation, or looked like it might have a check in it. To sit in that post office day after day doing his duty depressed him, and he reacted, by and large, like the most famous passive-aggressive character in American literature, saying, "I prefer not to." Like Bartleby, Faulkner was a scrivener, although in Faulkner's case, he altered what he copied on the way to finding his own writer's voice. So he read the magazines sent to others, delivering them only after he had read what appealed to him. He did not take the measure of each day by obeying the tyranny of time, so the mail was never late on his watch because "late" had no relevance to his way of thinking.

One customer who also wanted to be a writer and had heard about the postmaster's own ambition went to buy stamps in the hope of getting into a conversation about writing. The postmaster was reading *Liberty* magazine, just one of several publications like *Poetry,* the *Little Review,* the *Dial, American Mercury,* the *Nation,* and the *New Republic* that advanced his education in contemporary literature. He "did not look up. . . . William Faulkner put aside the magazine, came over, opened the drawer, flipped the book of stamps onto the counter, swept the coins into the drawer, shut the drawer and, without having looked at Ben Lumpkin, went back and picked up his magazine and started reading."[4] Faulkner would get tired of people coming and calling through the slot when the windows weren't open to say, "Is the mail up yet?" He solved the problem by closing the lobby doors.[5] Patrons at the post office window waited and waited while Faulkner, sitting in a rocking chair with a writing arm, wrote and wrote. Like other writers with a day job, he concentrated on short pieces he could probably get done in a day—in this case, book reviews for the *Mississippian* in January and February 1922.

Edna St. Vincent Millay's one-act play *Aria Da Capo* interested him, no doubt because her use of Pierrot and his beloved Columbine parallels his own verse play *The Marionettes.* As theater criticism or reviewing, the piece is nugatory—annoying for its sense of superiority and condescending in its compliments to the poet's language. One of Pierrot's lines may have registered deeply with Faulkner, who preferred to compose symbolist poetry set apart from his native land and time: "all beauty and romance are fled from the world." It is also not surprising that Millay's use of classical tropes to address her contemporaries appealed to Faulkner, although another side of him surfaced in his March *Mississippian* review of Eugene O'Neill's plays when he noted, "Nowhere today, saving in parts of Ireland, is the English language spoken with the same earthy strength as it is in the United States; though we are, as a nation, still inarticulate." So far, Faulkner had not capitalized on this "earthy strength" in his own work.

However, in "The Hill" the landscape poet of Faulkner's letters home and the symbolist poet, obsessed with states of mind, coalesced in a prose cameo of a laborer climbing a hill for a perspective:[6]

> From the hilltop the valley was a motionless mosaic of tree and house; from the hilltop were to be seen no cluttered barren lots sodden with spring rain and churned and torn by hoof of horse and cattle, no piles of winter ashes and rusting tin cans, no dingy hoardings covered with the tattered insanities of posted salacities and advertisements. There was no suggestion of striving, of whipped vanities, of ambition and lusts, of the drying spittle of religious controversy; he could not see that the sonorous simplicity of the court house columns was discolored and stained with casual tobacco. In the valley there was no movement save the thin spiraling of smoke and the heart-tightening grace of the poplars, no sound save the measured faint reverberation of an anvil.

Here the detritus and the distractions, the messy business of competition and fanaticism, secular and religious, supplied in such vivid detail, is superseded by the calm of nature, barely disturbed by the blows of civilization. In the "sonorous simplicity of the court house columns . . . discolored and stained with casual tobacco" we get one of the first glimpses of Jefferson, Mississippi. "For the first time in any piece of Faulkner's work," as one critic puts it, "the stuff of regional realism" overcomes the "lyricism, although still strong."[7] Another suggests a Wordsworthian influence: "the end of day, the quiet, the sense of peace and detachment."[8]

How to do both—render the real and the symbolic, the land in terms of a new, innovative language—remained to be achieved. The post office at least offered an independent living, even if that living had been arranged by those on whom the young writer still depended. Erik Erikson might as well have had Faulkner and his family in mind when he wrote of the importance of the founding forebear, a "railroad builder . . . or an unreconstructed Southerner . . . [t]he last representatives of a more homogeneous world, masterly and cruel," builders of "bigger and better machinery like gigantic playthings which were not expected to challenge the social value of the men who made them. Their mastery persists in their grandsons as a stubborn, and angry sense of superiority."[9] Several generations out from the old Colonel, William Faulkner felt "disinherited in American life," to borrow Erikson's words, and on his way to creating one of his most exquisitely dispossessed characters, Quentin Compson.

In "The Hill" the laborer, bearing none of Quentin's burden, is reprieved, for a brief moment, from his physical exhaustion, from the damage done to "bodily tissues." Faulkner had suffered as much feeding a steam engine boiler. Accompanying the walker is his shadow, getting out ahead of him, "springing far out," a "monstrous shadow" that "lay like a portent upon the church" he sees from a distance. Suddenly the laborer is the dominant force, and "for a moment he had almost grasped something alien to him." Looking down at the hamlet where daily toil numbered the "days of his existence," the laborer "worked out the devastating unimportance of his destiny, with a mind heretofore untroubled by moral quibbles and principles, shaken at last by the faint resistless force of spring in a valley at sunset." This melding of the land and a character's consciousness in a setting so palpably present is like nothing Faulkner had written heretofore. The trope of life as a Shakespearean walking shadow that bedevils Quentin Compson makes its first appearance, although a tragic sensibility gives way in "The Hill" to a notion that the laborer released from his labor has become something like a Faulknerian poet as he stares at the sunset:

> Here, in the dusk, nymphs and fauns might riot to a shrilling of thin pipes, to a shivering and hissing of cymbals in a sharp volcanic abasement beneath a tall icy star. * * * Behind him was the motionless conflagration of sunset, before him was the opposite valley rim upon the changing sky. For a while he stood on one horizon and stared across at the other, far above a world of endless toil and troubled slumber; untouched, untouchable; forgetting, for a space, that he must return. * * * He slowly descended the hill.

This Promethean moment is predicated on a return, which is a descent into civilization. If this piece is overly portentous, it also is predictive of the kind of writer, with Shakespearean ambitions, that Faulkner would become, beginning with his weekend trips to New Orleans.

In a loft party of editors and writers, James K. Feibleman, then seventeen and an aspiring poet, watched "a little man with a well-shaped head, a small mustache and a slightly receding chin" nursing himself with a whiskey bottle. When discussion turned to Shakespeare's most famous play, the little man, sitting in a corner, spoke his only line of the evening: "I could write a play like *Hamlet* if I wanted to." Anyone who spoke like that, Feibleman believed, would never become a great writer.

Perhaps the excursions to New Orleans turned Faulkner into more of a bohemian than a dandy, for now he was seen around Oxford wearing old clothes and barefooting it. Stories began to be told that placed him without shoes in a Memphis hotel, a taxicab, New Orleans apartments, and elsewhere. Phil Stone, who continued to badger and cajole Faulkner to get on with his writing, said: "The Faulkners aren't conceited, they just have supreme self-assurance. That's the reason for Bill's eccentricity. If he wants to go barefoot, he does, because the opinions of others simply don't matter to him."[10] Stone did more than talk and chafe Faulkner; he also promoted him, writing to a friend at the Brick Row Book Shop, "Bill is getting along fine and is turning out some very good stuff." They had plans to put together some booklets. He wrote Edwin Arlington Robinson, perhaps because Faulkner told Stone about a chance meeting with the poet. Robinson replied, "I am glad to infer from your note that you and your friend have found something in my work that you remember."[11]

Stone promoted the poet, and the postmaster perturbed his customers, playing cards in the post office backroom, or he could be seen on the nine-hole golf course. Lucy Somerville remembered that the "rolling hills made a beautiful natural layout for the course." Occasionally she spotted Bill in his plus fours "playing along by himself." Sometimes he teamed up with Lucy and other friends, stopping at the seventh and eighth holes, which provided a beautiful vista of the countryside and the railroad trestle as they watched a train "come through the cut. This was the time when his troubles at the post office were rolling up. He never mentioned that subject to us but we do recall his brooding melancholy. As of the spring of 1922 his playing was lackadaisical. Few played golf and the course was ideal for leisurely exercise and day dreaming."[12]

A different view of Faulkner and his course emphasized the "poor scrawny fairways" that had once been a cotton field. The nine holes "wound around clumps of trees and across three little branches. Some of the fairways ranged down sidling slopes, and others went over steep hogbacks [steep slopes and narrow ridges]." This was golf as improvisation: "It was hard to tell at times where fairways ended and rough began—it was all rough." Thomas D. Clark, then a groundskeeper, remembered that the "greens were stomped out clay hardpans which had small mud embankments around to keep the sand from being washed away every time it rained. Periodically we placed a new coat of sand on the hardpans and dampened it down with spent motor oil." Bill sometimes helped Clark, enjoying the exercise and the opportunity to improve the course but also, Clark suspected, to look for lost golf balls in the three big water holes to "replenish his own slender stock." In a good humor Bill might be loquacious; otherwise he might remain silent, in "a deep brown study." He never talked about writing, but Clark recognized "a man who had certain qualities about him which did not seem present in any of my other customers. He had a certain kind of sophistication about him which belied the general regard with which most people seem to hold him." He seemed careless and irresponsible and with no sense of time. He might play early in the morning all by himself or show up later in the afternoon. To Clark he talked about "scrubby grass" and other matters related to the state of play. "Bill was a good golf player when he tightened up his game and got down to brass tacks," Clark recalled. "He knew every gully, stump hole, and clump of weeds on the course."[13] This single-minded attention on golf balls and the relentless following of the same course day after day over the three-year period Clark golfed with Faulkner would have its culmination in the obsessive, single-minded caddying in the Benjy section of *The Sound and the Fury*.

Clark later provided a different, perhaps more candid impression in a letter to a Faulkner scholar: "When I knew him he was eccentric, when he was a student in Freshman English he was eccentric, and when he put two sentences in the English language together he was still eccentric. The whole Faulkner tribe was strange. I knew Mr. Murry Faulkner quite well. He was exceedingly kind to me, and sometimes I think that the brooding look on his face was caused by four obstreperous boys." Or perhaps by a wife who took a "queenly attitude," according to Clark, who concluded: "I did know William Faulkner and I did see him away from his public and away from his poses. When a man loses a golf ball in high grass, he sheds a tremendous amount of facade."[14]

Friends enjoyed Bill's stories, although Phil Stone tended to dominate social occasions with his commentary and anecdotes. He rebuffed those outside this tight orbit who assumed they could have a conversation. The formal Faulkner insisted on proper introductions—quite a startling demand to issue from a man who sometimes looked like he was wearing cast-off clothing. He could not abide small talk or the everyday vanities that are abjured in "The Hill." The irksome post office job reminded him every day of the "tattered insanities of posted salacities and advertisements." Thomas Clark concluded that Faulkner was, "it seemed to me, disjointedly in love with his fellow men collectively and blithely indifferent to them as individuals."[15]

Faulkner's art announced the presence of an Oxford native who claimed to have been abroad and to have returned as a cosmopolite. His drawings published in Ole Miss yearbooks (1919–20 and 1921–22) featured a stylish world rarely on display in the streets of Oxford, Mississippi. One campus-related drawing, *Classes,* depicts four men decked out in fashionable array: a cheerleader dressed in beanie and sweater; a dandy wearing a fedora, a double-breasted, belted, and cinched jacket, and bell-bottom trousers; a country gentleman in buttoned-up vest; a townie conservatively dressed, pipe in hand. How many men on campus actually wore such clothes and adopted the different stances of these men, hands in the pockets, arms akimbo, striking attitudes from the informal to the flamboyant to the casual and the respectable? The drawings seem reflective, instead, of the artist himself, who enjoyed the clothes and the roles that suited his performative personality. His drawing for the "Organizations" section is a witty composition of a couple walking in the wind, accentuating their angular elegance. A well-observed and amusing drawing of a military figure in overseas cap and jodhpurs asking a lady of fashion if she speaks English is indicative of a young artist whose mind was elsewhere—anywhere but Oxford, Mississippi. The "Social Activities" section could have been titled "Aubrey Beardsley Comes to Campus," complete with candelabra and a trio of masqueraded figures not out of place in a French drawing room. Another vignette shows three stylish women boarding a train, one in a checked gown, followed by another in a horizontally striped ensemble, and a third in a sleek black gown, with two male figures in pinstripes and plaid. The Red & Blue dancing couple swing in symmetrical abandon, inseparable as figures molded to one another. His two presentations of military figures are distinctive in their regalia, reflecting a sensibility entirely saturated in the sartorial. A sophistication of taste and perception is reflected in the virtuosity and range of these drawings.

A few of the drawings include captions in French. For example, a couple on a ship deck stands against a railing. The woman is stylishly dressed and turned away from the man. It looks like she has just given him the brush-off. And he is just looking at her. Below this drawing is a caption in French:

C'est horrible!—Quel donc?—Le mal de mer de ma fiancée.
La, pourquoi ne trouvez-vous pas une amie qui est orphaline?

(It's terrible. What? The sea sickness of my fiancée.
Why don't you find a girlfriend who is an orphan?)

In *Early Prose and Poetry,* Carvel Collins calls the drawing a joke but does not explain what it is. It seems a play on words with "mer" (sea) and "mere" (mother). Perhaps the woman asking the question in the second line pretends that the man in the first line was saying that his fiancée had a bad mother. French scholars are familiar with this kind of interplay between these words that sound exactly the same when pronounced aloud. In all likelihood, the man's fiancée is down in the cabin being seasick. He is up on deck moaning, and the other woman does not want to be chatted up and rebuffs him with a pun. Faulkner is being too clever by half.[16] Did he care if readers got the joke? Probably not, since he cultivated the mystique of the aesthete.

In one story, "Adolescence," undated and unpublished but written perhaps as early as 1922, Juliet Bunden is the first Faulkner female character to live for herself and to break out of the social and psychological restraints that diminish the male voices in his poetry. She rises above "a background of faintly sentimental decadence, of formal ease among rites of tea and graceful pointless activities," even as she lives under the tyranny of a prudish and sour grandmother. Juliet discovers the innocent pleasures of swimming and lying beside a boy, both unclothed, sharing a friendship unbound by convention or a sense of propriety. She is in the Eden that Ike McCaslin will experience in "The Bear," and the presocietal pleasure that Rousseau said was the birthright of every human being. She is the first character whom Faulkner employs to measure the constrictions and intolerance of his own community. Even better, the setting for this friendship is evoked in a rising action that has visceral and palpable power:

> They lay together, wrapped in the horse blanket beneath the high bright October noon, dozing and waking; almost too warm in the generated heat of their two young bodies to be perfectly comfortable. The heat, the scratchy roughness of the blanket made Juliet restless: she turned and changed the position of her limbs, and changed again. The sun beat on their faces in a slow succession of blows, too blinding to allow them to open their eyes.
> "Lee," she spoke at last.
> "Huh?" drowsily.
> "Lee, what you goin' to do when you get to be a man?"
> "Aint goin' to do nothin'."
> "Nothin'? How you goin' to get along without doin' nothin'?"
> "Dunno."
> She raised herself on her elbow. Lee's tousled round head was burrowed into the hot sand. She shook him. "Lee! Wake up."

Juliet senses that their idyll must come to an end. She realizes, in the narrator's words announcing the supreme Faulkner theme, "that nothing is changeless save change." They are discovered by her censorious grandmother, who wags "her mask of a face above them." The grandmother calls Juliet a slut and arranges for her to be married off to avoid the scandal the grandmother herself has created. Juliet, undaunted, rebels against the "old bitch." The story is explicit, pointing at its theme: "So she sat in the dark, watching her childhood leaving her."

The turn to prose, begun sometime in 1919, did not dissuade Faulkner from submitting in June 1923 a revised version of *Vision in Spring* to the Four Seas Company. The book was publishable, the company reported four months later, but not without a subvention from the author, who was in no position to finance his own work. Still primarily a poet and a postmaster, Faulkner also took on the duties of scoutmaster. "As my then 9-year old mind remembers him, he was patient, also caustic when needed, and by our inept standards he was wonderfully competent in the woods, especially on overnight hikes," one of his charges testified, who also served as Faulkner's caddy: "He wore plus-fours and played golf. Two things that were enough to make him suspect of homosexuality and Yankeeness in Oxford."[17] Another scout recalled enjoying nature study and a scoutmaster who asked and did not tell the boys what to do.[18]

Faulkner told the scouts stories and continued to compose poetry. "Re-reading some of the things," he wrote the Four Seas Company on November 23, 1923, "I see they aren't particularly significant. And one may obtain no end of poor verse at a dollar and twenty-five cents per volume."[19] Over the next several months, Stone and Faulkner recorded his rejections on a suit-box lid. After several conversations Stone agreed to raise the money the publisher required, and Faulkner decided to submit *The Marble Faun* to the Four Seas. With his friend's help, Faulkner agreed to put up four hundred dollars to cover the publisher's initial costs of printing one thousand copies. Almost all of the first edition would have to be sold before Stone and Faulkner recouped their investment. After some hesitation, Faulkner agreed to send two publicity photographs and a brief biography. The photographs, taken in Memphis, were meant, Stone said, to look Byronic, but Stone's wife later said the pose "looked just like what it was—the collar of a scrawny young man who had ridden eighty miles to Memphis through the dust of traveled roads and his own sweat with his tie on (in those days young men did not go to Memphis with open collars; they wore ties), and then had jerked it off and had his picture made with all the sweat and dust still in the hot collar." In a letter to Ben Wasson, Faulkner amused his friend with the expectation that the Sunday newspaper would soon feature a photograph of the poet.[20] A photograph of the author in profile, pipe in hand, with his eyes cast down, made him look professorial and contemplative, perhaps even melancholic, which suited the pensive mood of *The Marble Faun*.

It was the summer of 1924, and William Faulkner does not seem to have been attending to business. Robert Farley remembered that Faulkner produced from his mother's house a bottle of white lightning and a glass concealed under his shirt. Farley introduced Ridley Willis, who wanted to meet Faulkner, and soon the two men were discussing religion. "If you could be anything you wanted to, what would you rather be?" Willis asked. "A lay reader in the Episcopal Church," Faulkner replied. "Oh," Willis said. "You're a real Christian. You want to go to heaven." A solemn Faulkner said, "Sure."

Willis said, "You want to be an angel. What would you do until you got to be a full-fledged angel?" Faulkner answered, "I'd manicure the wings of the other angels." Willis protested, "That's no goal!" Faulkner clapped him on the back and remarked, "My boy, you don't have the true Rotary spirit."[21]

On September 17, Stone wired the publishers that the author "TELLS ME TO AUTHORIZE YOU TO USE ANY FACTS REAL OR IMAGINARY THAT YOU DESIRE TO USE IN THE BOOK OR ADVERTISING MATTER." Faulkner finally did deliver a terse recitation of his life. He mentioned his great-grandfather and his two important books, *The White Rose of Memphis* and *Rapid Ramblings in Europe*. After a boyhood and youth in Mississippi, Faulkner had been an undergraduate, house painter, tramp, day laborer, "dishwasher in various New England cities," a bookstore clerk in New York City, a bank and postal clerk. He had served in the British Royal Air Force during the war and was a member of Sigma Alpha Epsilon fraternity.[22]

In early September, Mark Webster, a postal inspector, delivered to Stone three pages of complaints about the postmaster, including failure to deliver mail, mishandling stamp money, and failure to attend promptly to customers at the post office window. The charges did not disturb Faulkner, who was thinking of quitting, and with Stone's help, the poet eased out of his job by resigning at the end of October 1924. Webster had taken it easy on Faulkner, and the young poet later inscribed a copy of *The Marble Faun* to him: "To whose friendship I owe extrication / From a very unpleasant situation."

FAME AND FORTUNE

Stone and Faulkner took great care with the *Marble Faun* proofs, and with the look of the book, inside and out. They specified no more than twenty lines on a page and the breaks between poems more clearly demarcated. Faulkner wanted the book to be "bound in very pale green boards" with "straw-colored label[s]" on the cover and spine—and the publisher complied. Stone and Faulkner then went to work on lists of friends and family who might purchase and promote the book, and on book review outlets: local newspapers in northern Mississippi and the *Memphis Commercial Appeal,* the *Double Dealer* and the *New Orleans Times-Picayune,* the *New York Evening Post,* and New York bookstores (Doubleday and Brentano's). Stone sent an announcement to the *Yale Alumni Weekly,* repeating parts of his preface about Faulkner's great promise, and then taking a proprietorial tone: "This poet is my personal property and I urge all my friends and classmates to buy his book."[23]

Faulkner relaxed and played more golf, coming near to setting a record, as reported in the *Jackson Clarion-Ledger* on October 6. A week earlier a freshman shot a record 32 on the Ole Miss nine-hole golf course while "William Faulkner made the rounds in 33 the same afternoon."[24] Some biographers picture this period, while Faulkner awaited publication of *The Marble Faun,* as dispiriting: "To be published by a vanity press, at his friend's expense, could not have pleased a proud William Faulkner."[25] But this is the same press that had issued the work of Conrad Aiken, the contemporary poet Faulkner respected more than any other, except for T. S. Eliot. And Ben Wasson, who saw much of Faulkner at this time, remembered his friend at his happiest.

The buoyant mood that Wasson conveys in his memoir is reflected in a letter Faulkner wrote to Mrs. Homer K. Jones of Memphis, Tennessee. The letter begins, "I seem to recall, when Mr Kelly and I were with you one evening last week, giving you a copy of one of my poems." How could he not remember? Was he drunk? "Mr Kelly and I were having such a grand time that I dont know what I wrote; whatever it was, I am sure it is undecipherable, so I am taking the liberty of sending you a correct copy of the verse, as you are interested in literature." The careful phrasing could have been the work of Samuel Johnson. Mrs. Jones, at forty and some thirteen years older than the poet, was widely read in modern fiction and poetry. Her interest demanded, he implied, that he rectify any impropriety or imprecision for which he was responsible. Ben Wasson said that Faulkner, among friends, loved to recite his own words and those of other writers, and on the occasion with Mrs. Jones, he had disappointed her and himself: "Also, this was [the] poem which I tried so unsuccessfully to recite," he wrote, enclosing a copy of his work. He apologized for annoying her about a pipe and scarf he thought he had left behind at her home: "The muffler I had after we left you, I am reliably informed. What I am asking pardon for, is failing to call you again as I should." But he had an excuse: "Almost immediately after calling you that morning I was arrested on a moral charge, and by the time I was a free agent again, I had forgotten it. Please forgive me, and thank you for the whisky-and-soda." No record has been found of an arrest, but it seems likely Faulkner had been detained by police for public drunkenness. Or was this just a story to ameliorate any slight to Mrs. Jones? The moral charge is mentioned the way one might refer to a traffic ticket or some other interruption of a journey. He seems certain of his audience, of a lady who would be amused by his performance, by a letter that, in fact, gave good value, transforming an otherwise messy or sordid situation in a gallant recompense for any inconvenience he may have caused. He ended the letter with a compliment about the drink she had offered him: "I dont know whether I drank it or not, but it was a beautiful tipple." He conveyed his regards to Mr. Jones and signed himself as "Sincerely yours, William Faulkner." What a performance. L. D.

Brodsky brilliantly sums up the letter: "a sense of the youthful Faulkner in all his recklessness, his brash and dashing bravura and pretentiousness, the poet pursuing his own image of the Bohemian artist, the absent-minded genius whose main concerns are for his Art. Withal, there is still the lingering hint that its author is a sensitive Mississippi gentleman aware of his social responsibilities, propriety, and good breeding."[26] Aware of it all, while violating it all, while restoring it all in a letter.

"Pregnacy,"[27] the poem Faulkner wrote out for Mrs. Jones, partly in ink and partly in pencil, proceeds with a grandeur, a showing off of iambic meter, interrupted by spondées, trochées, and dactyls, and demanding a resounding public reading, as the first stanza demonstrates:

> As to an ancient music's hidden fall
> Her seed in the huddled dark was warm and wet,
> And three cold stars were riven in the wall,
> Rain and dark and earth above her door were set.

Imagine a drunken poet negotiating the intricacies of such lines, getting the stresses right in order to prove his prowess. Not to be able to do justice to his own words was mortifying, at least in retrospect, but writing that letter served as a form of redemption.

Faulkner had first presented the poem to his childhood friend Myrtle Ramey, "easily the most popular girl on campus," according to one of her contemporaries and a classmate of Faulkner's.[28] The poem, included in *A Green Bough,* portrays pregnancy in a foreboding tone and is a curious choice to present to a female of any age, given its portrayal of a "harried / Body wrung to a strange and tortured lyre / Whose music once was pure strings simply married." Often it seems that Faulkner, like Poe, reveled in the pose of the melancholy poet.

Ben Wasson remembered that "Bill had arrived [in Greenville, Wasson's hometown] in high spirits, still elated *The Marble Faun* would now be published. He firmly believed the book would become a great success both critically and in sales." The optimistic Wasson also thought they were seeing the "beginning of fame and fortune for him."[29] But a disappointed Wasson, who sent one of Faulkner's photographs to the *Record,* the Sigma Alpha Epsilon national magazine, admitted the "little book was received with indifference by the 'brothers' as well as the public at large."

Wasson also remembered that in his prepublication period Faulkner liked to play the barefoot bard. He showed up at the very proper Wasson household without shoes or socks, a jug of corn liquor in his valise. Wasson, now a member of his father's law firm, delighted in his mother's reaction. She liked

Bill and handed him a mint and observed, "Aren't you and Ben going to play tennis?":

> "Yessum," he said.
> "You've forgotten your shoes, haven't you?"
> "No'm, I just like to play tennis barefooted."
> "Oh," Mother said, "I see," and paused. "Don't you want another mint to take with you."

Mother Wasson knew Faulkner was drunk, Ben was sure. But she would never mention it. "Can't anybody fool Mrs. Wasson," Faulkner said. "I don't try," Ben answered. After playing a few points on the tennis court at the home of William Alexander Percy, whom Faulkner had hatcheted in the *Mississippian,* the dipsomaniacal poet plotzed. "I don't feel very well," he confessed. "My bad leg is hurting a lot," a reference, Wasson noted, to the "flying injury he claimed to have received in Canada."

Wasson liked to watch the "light banter" that often made up the exchanges between this very proper lady and the young poet who "bore an air of superior courtesy." She liked to tease him, and he liked her playfulness. When she successfully maneuvered a reluctant Faulkner into taking a date to a dance, he commented, "You outfoxed me, Mrs. Wasson, and I reckon since you went to so much trouble, I had better mind you." She had even found him a proper suit to wear, and he behaved himself, exhibiting the chivalric manner characteristic of his approach to women, "regardless of age." With Rosamund Watkins Alston Stone, Phil's mother, he liked to play the pliable, accommodating young man, even with a hypochondriac, "always expecting the worst," a model for the querulous Mrs. Compson. On visits to the Stone home, Faulkner would say, "'Miss Rosie, did you see about that terrible fire in Texas where those folks got killed?' And Miss Rosie would blossom. 'I declare,' she'd say, 'that little Billy Faulkner is the politest boy I ever saw.'"[30]

Wasson had a precocious and loquacious four-year-old baby sister, Ruth, who engaged Faulkner in "long serious conversations." In his memoirs, Wasson could not help but think of Caddy and the little Italian girl in *The Sound and the Fury.* When she took two pairs of silver and gold evening slippers to show Faulkner in his bedroom, Ben overheard him tell her about the adventures of the slippers, including encounters with princes and princesses, and magical happenings in forests with silver and gold trees as they laughed together. A poem he wrote for Ruth was lost in a fire, but Ben remembered two lines: "Your eyes are brown and grave, / And gay is your laughter."

But Faulkner was beginning to consider the possibilities of prose. He read aloud Sherwood Anderson's story "I'm a Fool" and exclaimed: "By God, that's a man. I'd sho' like to meet him and know him." Wasson urged him to do so.[31] Anderson's exhilarating style arose out of a palpable environment. His easy, colloquial but elegant treatment of characters and situations delighted Faulkner as he read about horse racing and a Huckleberry Finn–like character whose whoppers make him out to be fool, but a fool all the more admirable for reckoning with his own foolishness:

> Sometimes now I think that boys who are raised regular in houses, and never have a fine nigger like Burt for best friend, and go to high schools and college, and never steal anything, or get drunk a little, or learn to swear from fellows who know how, or come walking up in front of a grandstand in their shirt sleeves and with dirty horsey pants on when the races are going on and the grandstand is full of people all dressed up— what's the use of talking about it? Such fellows don't know nothing at all. They've never had no opportunity.

Anderson was not a southerner, but his way of presenting Burt had to strike Faulkner with considerable force: "I liked Burt fine. We got along splendid together. He was a big nigger with a lazy sprawling body and soft, kind eyes, and when it came to a fight he could hit like Jack Johnson." The young writer who had grown up in his father's livery stable, hanging out with black hostlers, drinking and swearing and getting dirty, naturally gravitated to Anderson, a literary father, a man unlike Murry, who had denigrated his son's belletristic aspirations.

Anderson's sensitivity to nature and to character appealed to a writer who was just beginning to work out a similar nexus in "The Hill" and "Adolescence." Anderson's narrator is a poet by nature: "Gee whizz, gosh amighty, the nice hickorynut and beechnut and oaks and other kinds of trees along the roads, all brown and red, and the good smells, and Burt singing a song that was called 'Deep River,' and the country girls at the windows of houses and everything. You can stick your colleges up your nose for all me. I guess I know where I got my education." And Faulkner knew where he was going to get his.

He headed for New Orleans, to see Elizabeth Prall Anderson, his erstwhile bookstore boss, and Sherwood Anderson, her new husband, now living there. Leaving Oxford near the end of the year marked a new beginning, which seemed all the more to the point after his resignation as scoutmaster, fed up with a local preacher's campaign to oust this misfit drinker and carouser. New Orleans he could use as a staging center for his announced Wanderjahr in Europe.

4

New Orleans

Fall 1924–June 1925

❧

NORTH MEETS SOUTH

Spanish moss, rumbling streetcars, honking automobiles, street vendors, artists, prostitutes, nuns, tourists, speakeasies, restaurants, and bars—that was the New Orleans French Quarter in the 1920s, when Sherwood Anderson and his wife, Elizabeth Prall Anderson, arrived, settling into the Pontalba building, actually two four-story buildings on two sides of Jackson Square, built in the late 1840s by the Baroness Micaela Almonester Pontalba. Restaurants and shops on the ground floors and apartments above formed a kind of complex now commonplace in modern cities. By the 1920s, the buildings, fallen into disrepair, began to be restored. This was not gentrification, exactly, but certainly part of a movement in New Orleans to honor its past and attract tourists and new residents to a city steeped in history. New Orleans was also a good place for a young writer to discover himself among other writers and artists, and for an older artist to renew himself.

From their high-ceilinged apartment in the Pontalba building, the delighted Andersons could see Jackson Square, St. Louis Cathedral, and a sizeable sweep of the city. Faulkner, still a synesthetic poet and painter in *Mosquitoes,* described the conjunction of apartment building and cathedral as "cut from black paper and pasted flat on a green sky; above them taller palms were fixed in black and soundless explosions." The images and metaphors, which perhaps owe something to Ezra Pound, a poet William Spratling said Faulkner revered, also testify to the powerful and lasting impact of New Orleans on a still-developing writer.

Climbing two flights of steep stairs to get a panoramic view, and to Sherwood Anderson, came all sorts, including William Faulkner. "Sherwood made friends with everyone, quickly and easily, and we soon knew all of New Orleans," his wife wrote. "Anderson possessed an ineffable openness and sweetness that made him attractive to nearly everyone"—even the sour Theodore Dreiser.[1] Anderson, with his penchant for dressing like a riverboat gambler, did not look like a literary man. He could connect you to the *Double Dealer* trio, Julius Friend, James Feibleman, and John McClure, who made the city a literary cynosure. You could cast a play, or write a novel like *Mosquitoes,* with characters resembling artist William Spratling, a Tulane architecture professor with a defiant squint; another Tulane anthropologist, Frans Blom, staring at you in bright-eyed amazement; and the writers Roark Bradford, harassed with news items to edit in the *Times-Picayune;* Hamilton Basso flashing a handsome grin; and Lyle Saxon, journalist and bon vivant,[2] somewhat aloof in his immaculate seersucker suit. In the background hovered lesser lights such as George Marion O'Donnell, who would write one of the first significant feature articles about Faulkner. Hamilton Basso likened the French Quarter to "Paris in my own backyard."[3] Others congregated in the city after stays in Greenwich Village. But unlike bustling commercial Manhattan that encroached on Bohemia, New Orleans, surrounded by river, lake, and swamp, was an island of the mind, cosmopolitan but not industrial or conformist.

Anthropologist and novelist Oliver La Farge, a New England brahmin, "all head and thick glasses," deserves honorable mention. He developed a camaraderie with Faulkner that foreshadowed the disruptive antics of Shreve McCannon in *Absalom, Absalom!* La Farge enjoyed getting drunk and indulging in racy talk with women nothing like Boston girls, who would not have dared to damage their prim personas: "I felt deliriously light, I seemed to be someone I had never been." La Farge had first entered New Orleans during Mardi Gras time, which made the city the equivalent of sailing off on *The White Rose of Memphis* in costume, so to speak, masquerading as someone you were not but making what you were not a part of what you were. La Farge, handsome and outgoing, had many affairs with women, according to Harold Dempsey, another French Quarter regular. This was not the case with Faulkner, Dempsey said. He remembered La Farge showing up at party fully dressed in armor. A woman wanted to go upstairs and make love, but La Farge, even with Dempsey's help, could not get off his equipment. But he went upstairs with the woman anyway.[4]

Although reared in the abolitionist tradition, La Farge, like a good anthropologist, absorbed the ethos of southern life and decided not to protest racism but to probe the origins of his friends' thinking. He estimated the arts colony as no more than fifty people, a small enough number that made him feel certain of his ground. "I don't remember anyone cherishing the idea that he was an as yet unrecognized genius in our midst," La Farge wrote, apparently unaware or having forgotten that Faulkner did sometimes present himself as such. La Farge did, however, corroborate the commonly held view of the community's solidarity: "When one of us achieved anything at all, however slight, the other workers were delighted, and I think everyone took new courage." What La Farge said of himself could be applied to Faulkner: "I made more lasting friendships than I had made in the rest of my life."[5]

John McClure remembered watching Faulkner and La Farge saunter down a street boisterously singing a dirty ditty, "Christopher Columbo," parts of which are worth quoting because they capture the flavor of Shreve's slavering over the sexually charged Sutpen saga, and the homoerotic overtones of coupling Shreve and Quentin around a northern-southern axis:

> Columbo went to the Queen of Spain
> And asked for ships and cargo.
> He said he'd kiss the royal ass
> If he didn't bring back Chicago.
>
> Columbo had a first mate,
> He loved him like a brother,
> And every night they went to bed
> And buggered one another.[6]

Who is to say what impact this properly bred and yet randy Bostonian behaving with his pants down, so to speak, had on Faulkner? Here, in New Orleans, a member of New England's founding Puritan class consorted with a Creole, mixed-race culture and would later campaign as a champion of American Indian rights, appearing on television opposing legislation that might deprive Native Americans of their ancestral land.[7] His Pulitzer Prize–winning novel, *Laughing Boy* (1929), reflected a literary sensibility that put him in league with William Faulkner. La Farge's anthropological sensibility became part of the ethos that suffuses Faulkner's Indian stories. At parties La Farge, sporting an Indian headband, dramatized his research and entertained the company by doing an eagle dance on a table.[8] That dance, almost universal among North American Indians, portrays, as one source puts it,

> the life cycle of the eagle from birth to death, showing how it learns to walk and eventually to hunt and feed itself and its family. There is usually a chorus of male dancers, often wearing feathered war bonnets,

who provide a singing and drumming accompaniment, and two central dancers who are dressed to resemble a male and a female eagle, with yellow paint on their lower legs, white on their upper legs, and dark blue bodies. Short white feathers are attached to their chests, which are also painted yellow, and they often wear wig-like caps with white feathers and a projecting yellow beak. Bands of eagle feathers run the length of their arms, and they imitate the movements of the eagle with turning, flapping, and swaying motions.[9]

How much of the dance La Farge enacted, and what Faulkner made of it, cannot be recovered, but without question La Farge brought the immediate and palpable impact of indigenous America to the table.

Photographs of the bespectacled La Farge could easily be used as illustrations for the myopic Shreve. *Sherwood Anderson and Other Famous Creoles* includes a satiric quasi-anthropological caption for Spratling's caricature: "OLIVER LAFARGE OF HARVARD, A KIND OF SCHOOL NEAR BOSTON." Spratling thought Faulkner's words showed his "lack of respect for Yankee culture."[10] Perhaps, but La Farge himself would not have been offended. He reveled in the glory of a fresh start and that, in New Orleans, "Harvard was nothing" to his friends.[11] At any rate, Faulkner seemed fond of Harvard graduates. He could hear plenty about Harvard from Harold Levy (1915), another Harvard alumnus, who collaborated with Faulkner on a sonnet, and from John Dos Passos, one of Levy's friends, when they dined at Victor's. Spratling also remembers Dos and Bill dining every night at Tuchi's, "a grandiose Italian joint in the French Quarter, where Tuchi and his wife gave resounding interpretations of arias from *Pagliacci* and other Italian operas. . . . At that time, we all considered him [Dos Passos] one of the top guys, certainly better than Hemingway was at that particular date." Like Faulkner, Dos was "a little shy," but with Faulkner and Spratling, he "talked endlessly and also drank."[12] Dos Passos, Harvard 1916, wore thick glasses and, like Faulkner, had a gift for the graphic arts. *Three Soldiers* (1921), like *Soldiers' Pay,* Faulkner's first published novel, is not about the war itself but its impact on the men who are trained to fight it. Like Faulkner, Dos Passos had an "artist's eye," as one of his biographers puts it. Dos and Bill rambled down "streets and streets of scaling crumbling houses with broad wrought iron verandas painted in Caribbean blues and greens." They reveled in this tropical city, redolent with the smells of vegetation and molasses produced in sugar refineries, and rife with the characters who populate Faulkner's New Orleans sketches and whom Dos Passos also noticed: "old geezers in decrepit frock coats, . . . [t]all negresses with green and magenta bandanas on their heads, . . . [a]nd whores and racingmen and South Americans and Central Americans in all colors and shapes." Both men found the city conducive to writing.[13] Faulkner would have added, as he does in *Mosquitoes:* "About them, streets: narrow, shallow canyons of shadow rich with decay and laced with delicate ironwork, scarcely seen."

Harold Levy, a Jew; Dos Passos, part-Portuguese; and La Farge, lapsed Puritan, contributed to the multicultural making of *Absalom, Absalom!*, parts of which center on New Orleans as the amalgamation of different cultures, which shaped one another into a kind of mutuality. Newcomers like Faulkner "did not color" the French Quarter. On the contrary, the Quarter "colored them."[14] The novel includes five mentions of Shreve's moon-shaped spectacles, and one reference to his working on the figures of Judith Sutpen and Charles Bon, figures of the past he treats like an anthropologist and an artist: a "meddling guy with ten-power spectacles came and dug them up and strained, warped and kneaded them," making them his creation. Like La Farge, Shreve goes native and takes over Quentin's story, fully immersing himself in the lives of the indigenous inhabitants of his research. What brings Quentin and Shreve together, in the greatest novel ever written about dorm-room bonding, is, in part, their displacement from their homelands, an uprooting that forces them back upon themselves in a form of brotherhood. Faulkner, in many ways a loner, nevertheless discovered in New Orleans, in the experience of rooming and crewing with several men, his Ishmael's tale.

Raffish Sherwood Anderson also came to New Orleans looking for an unbordered America that crossed racial lines and ethnic boundaries. To an old-school New Orleans stalwart like Lillian Friend Marcus, one of the managers of the *Double Dealer,* and the sister of Julius Weis Friend, one of the magazine's founders, Anderson seemed "sweet, simple, and overflowing with the joy of life. He was very nice then—I remember the first time he had ever danced—we all went to a night spot and as everyone else was dancing, Sherwood couldn't resist—well he was exactly like a nice brown little bear—if you have ever seen a bear perform. His tweed suit, his too, too gaudy scarfs which he used instead of neckties and so on—his long hair that always looked as though it needed washing, but just a grand person to be with."[15]

Anderson presided at the head of what might be called the Algonquin Round Table South. Faulkner first met him in the fall of 1924, shortly after he resigned as Ole Miss postmaster. On a visit to Elizabeth Prall Anderson, Faulkner and Anderson "talked and we liked one another from the start." These two short men, sensitive and brooding, also had a flamboyant side that expressed itself in various kinds of costumery. Faulkner remembered Anderson's "bright blue racetrack shirt and vermilion-mottled Bohemian Windsor tie." Anderson, a veteran of the Spanish-American War, had twenty years on Faulkner and a fund of stories about knocking around raffish resorts, especially whorehouses. Anderson, a down-home sort of man, had grown up in his father's livery stable. He was "solid, not 'arty.'"[16] But he was also sensitive, writing about those "grotesques" in *Winesburg, Ohio,* characters deserving of empathy and respect for their plight in a small town that did not value and sometimes scorned their failings and eccentricities in a sort of community intolerance familiar to Faulkner. What Faulkner said about Anderson might be applied to himself: "I think that he maybe would like to have been more imposing-looking."

In his memoirs, Anderson presented Faulkner as a character out of a history book—like Abraham Lincoln meeting Alexander Stephens, vice president of the Confederacy, a small man in a "huge overcoat." Lincoln said to a friend, "Did you ever see so much shuck for so little nubbin?" Faulkner showed up at Anderson's Pontalba apartment in a bulky big overcoat. "I thought he must be in some queer way deformed," Anderson recollected. Faulkner was looking for an apartment and asked if he could leave some things, which turned out to be "some six or eight half gallon jars of moon liquor" stuffed into the big coat.[17]

Faulkner did not immediately take up residence in New Orleans. Elizabeth Prall Anderson recalled that he showed up again—this time in early January with Phil Stone, who spent a week in the city. With Anderson then on a lecture tour, the visitors spent an "uproarious week" with Elizabeth, taking their meals with her but living in a "funny little hotel [The Lafayette] with rickety rooms that opened into a ramshackle courtyard." They liked to go to bistros and to movie theaters frequented by "colored people," as they were called then.

One Faulkner persona was already in place: "I had a feeling at times that Bill Faulkner's studied courtesies and Southern mannerisms were a pose," Prall observed. Joyce McClure, John's wife, had a different impression: "I just thought of him as a nice, pleasant Southern boy who wanted to be a writer and didn't have any money." If he saw her coming home with groceries, he would carry them upstairs for her.[18] Faulkner, Anita Loos said, was then like her: a nobody and a no-gooder, "loafing around in New Orleans."[19]

To Sherwood Anderson, Faulkner presented yet another persona, best evoked in the portrayal of David in "A Meeting South": "He told me the story of his ill fortune—a crack-up in an airplane—with a very gentlemanly little smile on his very sensitive, rather thin, lips. Such things happened. He might well have been speaking of another. I liked his tone and I liked him." Of course what Faulkner described had happened to "another." The almost demure lack of self-pity and the refined manners beguiled the older writer. The pretense that did not fool Phil Stone, Ben Wasson, and other college classmates worked wonders on Anderson, a susceptible writer looking for a good story: "The slight limp, the look of pain that occasionally drifted across his face, the little laugh that was intended to be jolly, but did not quite achieve its purpose, all these things began at once to tell me the story I have now set myself to write." No longer a homeboy looking to impress the locals, a liberated William Faulkner came into his own as Anderson's David.

Was Anderson fooled? Ben Wasson thought so, writing to Monte Cooper at the *Memphis Commercial Appeal:* "I regret that poor old Sherwood was taken in by him. . . . He's all right but not to be taken too seriously."[20] Like Faulkner, the older writer loved costumery and role-playing. It may be that he enjoyed perpetuating Faulkner's ruse. "Sherwood Anderson said we must treat him very, very carefully," Anita Loos said, "because he had a silver plate in his head which he'd gotten from being in some kind of war casuality [*sic*]." Ben Wasson cracked that "Faulkner was so poor that if he had had a silver plate in his head he would have got it out and borrowed on it to buy some more whiskey."[21] Anderson told Loos and others they were supposed to cater to this "little guy" who rose late in the morning. Was Anderson serious? In a sense, Faulkner had bestowed David on Anderson, who took everything Faulkner said in the service of a good story.

"I would go to his [Faulkner's] bedside with a glassful of corn liquor," Loos said. She laughed. "That's the way he started the day." Every day also meant a trip to the cathedral, with Loos and Faulkner climbing seemingly endless stairs to see a priest in the steeple who supplied Faulkner with bootleg liquor. Loos's *Gentlemen Prefer Blondes,* first serialized in a women's magazine, *Harper's Bazaar,* in 1924, stimulated the magazine's popularity with male readers. Then Liveright published the novel to wide acclaim and huge sales. Faulkner wrote home to mother to say this nice small woman who dressed like a flapper earned fifty thousand dollars for photoplays, as screenplays were then called. She hired a big car and took Faulkner along on a tour "almost every day."

In "A Meeting South," David produces a huge bottle out of a pocket that functions like a pouch on a marsupial. And he does it all with a delightful delicacy of a piece with his frangible figure. He appears to Anderson almost like a new species of Americanus: "I went along thinking of Darwin and the marvels of Prohibition. 'We are a wonderful people, we Americans,' I thought." David plies Anderson with drink and a story about the plantation family's "nigger," whose only employment is the making of the family liquor. David treats this drinking as a way of life, as something that has to be "built up." They speak of Shelley and Keats, "the two English poets all good Southern men love." Part of the southerner's charm, Anderson admits, is that those like David are projections of northerners like Anderson himself. Down by the

Mississippi River, David's story flows, swept along by their drinking and the romance of the night that bonds them: "In the darkness the river, very deep and very powerful off New Orleans, was creeping away to the gulf. The whole river seemed to move away from us and then to slip noiselessly into the darkness like a vast moving sidewalk." This scene is as much a mental state as a description of an actual place, a kind of spell. Through stories like this one, Anderson was showing Faulkner another way to that supernal beauty that Shelley and Keats aroused.

David tells the story of going over to England, becoming a first-rate flyer in the war, then crashing and breaking both legs and several bones in his face. He recuperates, but the pain remains because he leaves the hospital abruptly, fed up with the pervasive malingering he witnesses in others. His drinking soothes his "throbbing nerves." So convincing is David's story that the empathetic Anderson wants only to become part of the story: "No wonder he carried his drinks so well. When I understood, I wanted to keep on drinking with him, wanted to stay with him until he got tired of me as he had of the man who lay beside him in the base hospital over there somewhere in France." If ever someone made an art out of drinking it was William Faulkner, if Anderson, or at least his story, is to be believed. The wounded warrior fable is so moving and captivating because the warrior risks the death that eventually comes to everyone in a narrative of fatality that is expressed in the song of three sailors that Anderson hears when he brings David to Aunt Sally's: "I've got to get it, You've got to get it, We've all got to get it in our own good time." Of course, the men could be referring to sex as well as death, but that, too, is part of the romantic appeal of David's story. David has been brought to Aunt Sally, a character based on an Anderson acquaintance, the motherly madam Aunt Rose Arnold, as to a kindred soul, who produces her own liquor bottle: "She, it seemed, had understood him at once, had understood without unnecessary words that the little Southern man lived always in the black house of pain, that whisky was good to him, that it quieted his throbbing nerves, temporarily at least. 'Everything is temporary, when you come to that,' I can fancy Aunt Sally saying."

Part of Aunt Sally's charm, like David's, is old world. Like Anderson, she is a northerner who has moved south and left intact her old French Quarter gambling house (never identified as a brothel) rather than cutting it up in the modern way. She has made her business of sin into an attractive affair, intriguing and charming, with "winding broad old stairways . . . dim high-ceilinged old rooms, soft-colored old marble mantels." She is a "motherly soul," akin to the maternal whores who will grace Faulkner's later fiction. An ex-madam now, at sixty-five she reminisces about the "old river days," a way of life Faulkner would later help to re-create for Hollywood in *Banjo on My Knee.* Just as that river world has disappeared, so has the plantation world out of which David emerges, a world now shrunken to a few hundred acres his family owns—all sold off or otherwise lost, perhaps, like the Compson domain in *The Sound and the Fury.* David's world is now poetry. He drinks to sleep, mainly outdoors, where the world still seems wonderful, even with his bones pressing on his nerves, he tells Aunt Sally: "The little pain makes a kind of rhythm for the great pain—like poetry." Whatever Faulkner actually told Anderson, what comes through in this story is the immense importance of the black people he watches making molasses, singing, shouting, dancing, and laughing—a celebration of life that Anderson embellishes in his novel *Dark Laughter.* David hears their lovemaking rattles. Faulkner, to Anderson, was the exotic who had grown up with black people. It was Anderson, after all, who said apropos of his days in New Orleans that "maybe I'll go whole hog and be a nigger."[22]

David falls asleep on a happy Aunt Sally's brick patio as she comments: "We used to have some good men come here in the old days too." David is happy too in the repose of this perfect setting for his story. Anderson refers to himself again as a northern man. He has, in effect, made David/Faulkner into a pastoral figure, an embodiment of the southern past that is, of course, a literary conceit as much as or more than it is a reality. Anderson gives the game away, saying at the end of the story, "I went along enjoying my thoughts."

Faulkner wrote his mother to tell her about "A Meeting South," emphasizing: "It is not documentary—that is true incident. I just kind of cranked him up. What really happens, you know, never makes a good story. You have got to get an impulse from somewhere and then embroider it. And that is what Sherwood did in this case." Then, expressing the caution and circumspection he would often exhibit when discussing his work, he confided in Maud: "I am now giving away the secrets of our profession, so be sure not to divulge them. It would be kind of like a Elk or a Mason or a Beaver or something giving away the pass word."

Faulkner put in print (*Dallas Morning News,* April 26, 1925) his understanding of the kind of writer he would become by treating Anderson as an organic outgrowth of his environment, as Anderson would regard him, saying: "All you know is that little patch up there in Mississippi where you started from. But that's all right too. It's America too; pull it out, as little and unknown as it is, and the whole thing will collapse, like when you prize a brick out of a wall." Anderson could have described his own book, *Winesburg, Ohio,* in similar terms, as do critics who point to how Anderson employed a localism so intense and vivid as to make it universal. Faulkner also seemed to be drawing on the ideas of Hippolyte Taine in Willard Huntington Wright's *The Creative Will: Studies in the Philosophy and the Syntax of Aesthetics,* a book Phil Stone pressed upon his protégé.[23] Taine argued that artists were the products of their environments. Putting aside comparisons to the Russians, Faulkner declared, "I prefer to think of Mr. Anderson as a lusty corn field in his native Ohio."

What mattered most to Faulkner was Anderson's "helping around livery stables and race tracks." Anderson had written the best short story in America, "I'm a Fool." Faulkner's account of the story presaged his own stories of boys and horses that would culminate in *The Reivers.* He describes it as

> the tale of a lad's adolescent pride in his profession (horse racing) and his body, of his belief in a world beautiful and passionate created for the chosen to race horses on, of his youthful pagan desire to preen in his lady's eyes that brings him low at last. Here is a personal emotion that does strike the elemental chord in mankind.
>
> Horses! What an evocative word in the history of man. Poets have used the horse as a symbol, kingdoms have been won by him; throughout history he has been a part of the kings of sports from the days when he thundered with quadrigae, to modern polo. His history and the history of man are intermingled beyond any unraveling; separate both are mortal, as one body they partake of the immortality of the gods. No other living thing holds the same place in the life of man as he does.

You can almost hear Faulkner talking, getting carried away as he describes the boy getting carried away by his horse.

Anderson and New Orleans liberated Faulkner in a way that New York could not. Anderson proved to be the maestro that both Stone and Wright believed a young writer needed to succeed. Anderson became all the more important to Faulkner because Stark Young had proven to be a master manqué. "Phil was resentful that Stark Young had done nothing to bring Faulkner's work to the attention of a publisher," Stone's biographer reports.[24] Young, in turn, resented Stone's niggardly acknowledgment of Young's efforts on Faulkner's behalf. Certainly Faulkner's work owes far more to Anderson than to Young, who does not seem to have understood Faulkner's genius. He called Faulkner "a great liar," with "no mind," who wrote good stories but also novels that were "too complicated."[25]

The concatenation of Sherwood Anderson and New Orleans was the making of William Faulkner. Anderson pointed the way by elevating the city as a counter to the materialism that dominated American life: "When the fact is made secondary to the desire to live, to love, and to understand life, it may be that we will have in more American cities a charm of place such as one finds in the older parts of New Orleans now."[26] Ten years later, in 1935, Anderson had not changed his mind: "Stark Young and his sort ignore" the "beaten, ignorant, Bible-ridden, white South" of Huey Long, but "Faulkner occasionally really touches it."[27] Carvel Collins identified a *Double Dealer* editorial, first published in 1921 and reprinted in 1924, that seemed to prophesy the arrival of William Faulkner:

> It is high time, we believe, for some doughty, clear-visioned penman to emerge from the sodden marshes of Southern literature. . . . It is no idle conceit to hazard that some Southern Sherwood Anderson, some less tedious Sinclair Lewis, lurks even now in our midst. . . . There are hundreds of little towns in Alabama, Mississippi and Louisiana fairly bubbling with the stuff of stories. . . . The old Southern pot-boiler must go out—the lynching-bee, little Eva, Kentucky Colonel, beautiful Quadroon stuff—a surer, saner, more virile, less sentimental literature must come in.

Unlike New York City, which had no urgent need to acclaim William Faulkner, New Orleans, you might say, was just waiting for him to show up. Even if Faulkner exaggerated his following to hearten his worried mother, he sensed that New Orleans had conferred upon him its special favor. Even though Anderson and Faulkner were to have a falling out, especially after Faulkner parodied Anderson's style, Anderson continued to honor the man and his work, writing near the end of his life: "The man is what they mean in the South when they use the word 'gentle.' He is always that. Life may be at times infinitely vulgar. Bill never is."[28]

New Orleans and the Marble Faulkner

Faulkner's January 6, 1925, letter to his mother reveals that New Orleans was supposed to be the embarkation point for his voyage to Europe, an adventure his mother deemed "foolish." He wanted her to visit New Orleans before he departed, although in his next letter he announced he might depart any day if a ship came available and he was on hand. His reports were all about good meals, golfing, horseback riding, watching the fishing boats, the wheeling gulls, and walking along "long piers black as ink against the west." It was a lush, green-grass world, with "palms everywhere." He recommended the Gulf Coast as a home for his parents, although he could do without all the rain and foul oyster smell. Sounding like a good son, he wrote: "Mrs. Anderson has taken me in to live with them. She is so nice to me—mothers me, and looks after me, and gets things to eat which I like." He spent late mornings writing and the afternoons exploring, part of his work on sketches for the *Times-Picayune,* five dollars per column. Good money since he could live on one dollar a day. But writing to deadline drained him, and so he paced himself with five-hundred-word pieces when he felt like writing them.

By January 22, he had reached one of his high points, telling his mother: "Everyone here is grand to me—painters and writers, etc. . . . Last night I had dinner with John McClure, a poet and literary editor of the Times-Picayune—by the way he reviewed my book, next Sunday it will appear [January 25]. . . . And we talked and sipped hot whiskey punch until daylight, then walked down to the river to see the sun rise." When he sent the review home, he made no mention of his reaction. He probably knew that McClure almost always treated local authors gently.[29] Sherwood Anderson wrote that McClure was the "real thing—one of the most fundamentally sweet men I've seen." McClure, the grandson of a Confederate captain, had taken a year off to tramp through Germany and France and also through the Southwest as a kind of vagabond poet who published more poems in H. L. Mencken's *Smart Set* than any other author.[30] To get McClure's attention, Faulkner knew, was important. McClure's insightful reviews appeared in the *Double Dealer.* He published a column, "Literature and Less," in the *Times-Picayune,* "outstanding among American newspapers which published book pages." H. L. Mencken wrote in the *Smart Set* that "The Double Dealer was delivering the South from a cultural swamp."[31] Ernest Hemingway, Ezra Pound, Hart Crane, Edmund Wilson, and many other emerging literary figures appeared in a magazine concerned with the important aesthetic and intellectual issues of the 1920s. Dedicated to wiping out southern sentimentality, the magazine editorialized: "We mean to deal double, to show the other side, to throw open the back windows stuck in their sills from disuse, shuttered over long since against even a dim beam's penetration. To myopics we desire to indicate the hills, to visionaries the unwashed dishes." Many of the magazine's early covers featured "nymphs and satyrs aplenty done in the Beardsley manner" that matched Faulkner's own drawings and poems in the *Mississippian* and the Ole Miss yearbook.[32] In fact, Faulkner had visited New Orleans in 1922 and introduced himself to the magazine's editors, who published a Faulkner poem in June of that year.

"It is doubtful if there are a dozen thoroughly successful long poems in English," McClure's review of *The Marble Faun* began, and for a young poet to attempt one, "even if his name is Keats, is to fail with honor." Making this link to the famous poet whose early effort, the lengthy *Endymion,* had been greeted with scorn, put Faulkner in league with greatness. He had failed with "real honor," McClure concluded, signaling a way of looking at literature that Faulkner would often adopt when speaking of his splendid failures. McClure singled out "The candled flames of roses here / Gutter gold in this still air" as "a couplet of fine poetry if this reviewer ever saw one." He could cite other "charming couplets" while regretting "stretches of creditable but not remarkable verse." He looked forward to a second book of shorter poems with "some genuinely excellent sustained productions." At present, though, Faulkner's "creative impulse in diction and a keen sense of rhythm and form" could not overcome his "diffuseness and over-exuberance, impatient simile and metaphor," marks of an immature writer. McClure quoted at length from Stone's preface, which emphasizes the importance of *The Marble Faun* as a work of promise. McClure mentioned Faulkner's impending trip to Europe and his résumé—undergraduate, house painter, tramp, day laborer, dishwasher in various New England cities, clerk in a New York bookshop, bank and postal clerk—as if to interest readers in the World War I pilot, who "has taken a flier at nearly everything in his time." Clearly, McClure, like Anderson, did everything he could to promote Faulkner's career.

The brief review in the *Saturday Review of Literature* (March 7, 1925) also focused on the figure Faulkner cut: "An attractively-made book by a young poet who has led a varied and venturesome life." His verse was "fluent and meditative, with an occasional phrase of beauty and an occasional flaw in the rhythm game. . . . His sensitiveness to the poetic possibilities of the language is not sufficiently developed." Faulkner's concern with the aesthetics of book production—the green boards and pale paper labels—elicited the compliment "attractively-made."

Monte Cooper, in a long review in the *Memphis Commercial Appeal* (April 5, 1925), called Faulkner's faun "splendidly atavistic" but tiresome with "outworn phrases such as 'leafy glade' and its like." Taking up Faulkner's allegiance to Swinburne, the reviewer found the young poet lacked the "sweep and the swing of the best of Swinburne's verse." Faulkner was faulted for a "silvery daintiness" that evoked the "image of a kitten stepping fastidiously through wet leaves." But the reviewer also lauded Faulkner at his best in a passage that strips out the tired tropes of post-Victorian poetry:

Upon a wood's dim shade edge
Stands a dusty hawthorn hedge
Beside a road from which I pass
To cool my feet in deep rich grass.
I pause to listen to the song
Of a brook spilling along.

Behind a patchy willow screen
Whose lazy evening shadows lean
Their scattered gold upon a glade
Through which the staring daisies wade.
And the resilient poplar trees,
Slowly turning in the breeze,
Flash their facets in the sun,
Swaying in slow unison.

The reviewer astutely noted that Faulkner might learn much from the "irregular cadences" of his contemporaries from "whose contamination he had so definitely withdrawn." Put off by Faulkner's "sneering" essays on his contemporaries, Cooper concluded, "It seems that Mr. Faulkner, in his splendid isolation from his American fellows is somewhat embittered—almost angry."

This review comes with a backstory: Phil Stone had cultivated Cooper, who "fancied herself the arbiter of Memphis literary culture generally." Stone coerced a recalcitrant Faulkner to one of her parties, saying, "You damn sure *are* going; both of us are going up there and see if we can't sell some of these books; we want to get our money back." As she "sailed across the room like a frigate," Faulkner maintained his position in the corner of a crowded room. Cooper had to do all the work, trying to draw out the young poet about his reading and getting one-syllable answers, "no," to her queries. Finally, she said: "Well, Mr. Faulkner, I've been told you were one of our coming young Southern writers. You mean to say you haven't read any of these people?" Faulkner then apparently spoke his first complete sentence: "Have you ever heard of a prostitute who makes love for fun?"[33]

Stone also set up a literary lunch for Cooper and Faulkner, which the poet failed to attend.[34] In her review, she deplored his "half baked and raw" view of women that was sometimes "evil smelling." She had in mind his comment in "Verse Old and Nascent": "Ah, women, with their hungry snatching little souls!" Even so, Cooper concluded by extolling the "pensive charm about some of the verses" in a first book that, after all, was not making great claims for itself. Faulkner wrote to the reviewer that he had sold forty-three copies of the book to "bootleggers, poets, whores, taxi-drivers, merchants, etc. of my acquaintance. . . . My ambition is to have a copy on the 'parlor' table of every sporting house and gambling den in the south."[35] He relished this kind of claim, promoting his propinquity to prostitutes, criminals of all kinds, bootleggers, professors, and artists to be found in the speakeasies of the French Quarter and other southern pockets of illicit confabulation.

Outside of his own region, Faulkner's first book excited little attention. Phil Stone's letter-writing campaign and other promotional efforts had not yielded much in return. In a roundup of ten new books of poetry, the *Brooklyn Daily Eagle* (February 6, 1925) in "New Books Received" mentioned: "A slender volume of verse by a poet who has been both day laborer and a pilot." In the same newspaper (May 2, 1925), Katherine Renwick treated the book in one sentence: "The Marble Faun is rather melancholy, but pleasantly thoughtful and musical." Under the heading "Belles Lettres," the *St. Louis Post-Dispatch* (February 7, 1925) announced: "A first book of poems by a young man from Mississippi and proud of it."[36] Faulkner continued to work on his poetry, projecting a volume titled "The Greening Bough," but now the poetry became fitful and the prose constant.

Between January and July, Faulkner continued to write his mother and publish local-color sketches in the *Times-Picayune*. Near the end of January, he had turned in five, each one taking him about three hours to write. He estimated he could make twenty-five dollars per week "in my spare time. Grand, isn't it?" (He began repeating one of Anderson's favorite words.) Faulkner found a ready market in "one of the hottest competitive newspaper towns in the country," according to *Time*.[37] He hoped to continue to write while in Europe, earning perhaps ten dollars per week while he traveled. He wanted his anxious mother to know he was doing well and wrote her, "All right, I'll come home about the middle of Feb, for a while." An editor at the newspaper "thinks the trip abroad will be the making of me," he assured Maud, also telling her that when his photograph appeared in the paper, headlined "Southern Poet in New Orleans," he received letters from "strange females," mentioning one "about 40, gushing, you know; and the other about 14— on pink paper and terrible spelling," according to this former seventh-grade spelling-contest winner.

The *Double Dealer* for January–February 1925 published eleven sketches, titled "New Orleans," the product of his forays in the city. Called "gimmicky," with "trick endings and contrived surprises,"[38] these were pieces priced to sell. No one in New Orleans was doing much to "get beneath the colorful surface of south Louisiana's life and landscape. It was too easy to write local color instead."[39] Faulkner showed versatility as reporter and artist in "Wealthy Jew," "The Priest," "Frankie and Johnny," "The Sailor," "The Cobbler," "The Long Shoreman," "The Cop," "The Beggar," "The Artist," "Magdalen," and "The Tourist." Like Stephen Crane's New York City sketches, Faulkner's emanate from an enthusiastic young writer exploring new subject matter and experimenting with point of view and many different characters. The Jew, for example, is defined by his history: "ye took Destiny from the hands of my people, and your sons and my sons lay together in the mud at Passchendaele and sleep side by side beneath foreign soil. Foreign? What soil is foreign to me? Your Alexanders and Caesars and Napoleons rise in blood and gold, shrieking briefly of home, and then are gone as waves hiss curling on the beach, and die." The simile-sodden poet appears as the priest declaims: "EVENING LIKE A NUN shod with silence, evening like a girl slipping along the wall to meet her lover. . . . The twilight is like the breath of contented kine, stirring among the lilacs and shaking spikes of bloom, ringing the soundless bells of hyacinths dreaming briefly of Lesbos, whispering among the pale and fronded palms." Sometimes a sketch descends into the demotic: "LISTEN, BABY, before I seen you it was like I was one of them ferry boats yonder, crossing and crossing a dark river or something by myself; acrossing and acrossing and never getting nowheres and not knowing it and thinking I was all the time." A nautical Eugene O'Neill impersonator surfaces: "A sound footing is good, and wine and women and fighting; but soon the fighting's done and the wine is drunk and women's mouths dont taste as sweet as a man had thought, and then he'll sicken for the surge and the sound of the sea, and the salt smell of it again." The artist, no surprise, is a driven man: "A DREAM AND A FIRE which I cannot control." And New Orleans itself, the den of sin where the young Henry Sutpen in *Absalom, Absalom!* discovers the world as an elsewhere that corrupts his provincial innocence, is enclosed in a paragraph that signals Faulkner's own desire to leave and return, as to the site of an initiation: "New Orleans . . . a courtesan whose hold is strong upon the mature, to whose charm the young must respond. And all who leave her, seeking the virgin's unbrown, ungold hair and her blanched and icy breast where no lover has died, return to her when she smiles across her languid fan . . . New Orleans." An elated Faulkner told his mother: "The funny thing is, I am gaining quite a reputation here. People call to see me, and invite me out, and I sit and look grand and make wise remarks. Another local paper has my picture today. I am sending it along to you." He wanted her to save all his stories for a scrapbook they would make together. His thank-yous for checks indicate that his family still subsidized him, although he likened himself to John Rockefeller because money was always available as long as he wrote sketches: "They know someday I'll be a 'big gun.'" And Elizabeth Prall Anderson kept feeding him grandly.

With this attention and success, Faulkner decided to put off his trip abroad and begin a novel. By early March he was collaborating with Sherwood Anderson on tall tales known as the "Al Jackson Letters"—never published but incorporated, in part, in *Mosquitoes*. He still liked to play the backwoods boy: taking his shoes off at parties and sitting cross-legged on the floor. "He was vain of his small feet," one witness recalled.[40] He had an unusual "elfin quality," John McClure recalled, and also supreme self-confidence. When McClure said, "We can't all be Shakespeare," Faulkner replied, "I don't think I'm so bad myself."[41] He liked to climb porches and balconies for exercise and to argue about writing, flying, and everything else. He could get quite indignant about impropriety and injustice.[42] It was hard to know what Faulkner thought because he might take the opposite side in an argument to rag you, John McClure said.[43] He liked to shock people with "wild theories," Elizabeth Prall Anderson said, "that mulatto girls could not have children."[44] Sherwood thought Faulkner was serious in contending that the "cross between the white man and the negro woman always resulted, after the first crossing, in sterility";[45] Elizabeth was not so sure. When she heard Faulkner claim that mulattos could not bear children, she replied, "Why Bill Faulkner, I had always been told that was the way you crossed over the line and got to be white." She remembered that he was "shocked, and then he burst into laughter."[46]

Although Faulkner sometimes bragged about fathering bastards, one acquaintance said flatly that Faulkner did not have affairs with women.[47] One of Anderson's friends observed that "everyone probably believed in 'free love,'" and "certainly talked about it a lot," but "there was less than one might have expected" from men who "drank a lot and talked a lot and then drank a lot." One French Quarter inhabitant counted seventy-four bars in a nine-block radius.[48] Faulkner continued to elaborate his own legend, saying he had "flown a plane for some bootleggers in New Orleans, bringing in liquor from the Caribbean."[49] His wartime stories provoked jocular jibes from the more skeptical among his acquaintances.[50]

Faulkner's letters to his mother depict him as the life of the party. The artist Carolyn Durieux, the one Creole among the French Quarter bohemians, said Faulkner mainly listened and seemed to be "soaking it all up." James K. Feibleman, an aspiring poet from a New Orleans mercantile family,[51] called Faulkner a "dull fellow" compared to Sherwood Anderson and Roark Bradford.[52] Elizabeth Prall Anderson admitted that Faulkner could sometimes be "difficult at parties. He loved to put things over on people and sometimes his audience never would realize they had been duped. He was also very sure of his own knowledge about certain things and was flatly outspoken about saying so." He could be quite rude and insulting, treating, for example, Ferdinand Schevill, a University of Chicago historian and a world authority on Greek and Roman history, dismissively when the professor tried to correct one of Bill's "more improbable expositions." Bill had been "eyeing Ferdinand suspiciously. His attack rendered speechless the professor, unused to such hostility in academic life."[53] An aghast Elizabeth respected Bill's "wide range of knowledge," but even "if he had been accurate," she emphasized, "I would have been angry at him for having insulted our guest, and for having been rude to an older man . . . startled by the free-wheeling talk and easy laughter of our friends."

Faulkner disliked the "promiscuous mixing of the worlds of art and fashion" that William Spratling, soon to become Faulkner's roommate, enjoyed. In one instance, Faulkner expressed his disdain for mixing Society and Bohemia by showing up barefoot at a party hosted by Elizebeth Werlein, a businessman's widow known as the "czarina," who banned him from her house.[54] Faulkner nevertheless acclimated to the style of New Orleans bohemians, who seemed to avoid the nasty rivalries rife in Greenwich Village and Paris. William Odiorne, who later photographed Faulkner in Paris, recalled that "with us, in New Orleans, jealousy did not exist. If anyone had a small success . . . a story printed . . . the rest were delighted. We probably celebrated with a dinner party . . . with *vino pinto,* made by our Italian neighbors." Oliver La Farge and Hamilton Basso seconded Odiorne's sentiments.[55] Another observer noted that Faulkner had "plenty of acquaintances but no friends." He was "introverted and secretive. Disliked having to write for money"[56]—a claim that contradicts what he told his mother in letters home reflecting his desire to impress her, alleviate her concerns, but also to express his pride in making his words pay. He seemed excited by his earning powers. Lillian Friend Marcus remembered him saying, "If a *Hamlet* was wanted now, I would write *Hamlet.*"

WILLIAM SPRATLING AND OTHER FAMOUS CREOLES

In early March, Faulkner moved into the artist William Spratling's apartment at the suggestion of Sherwood Anderson, irked that Faulkner had overstayed his welcome. The move to Spratling's apartment situated Faulkner pleasantly behind the St. Louis Cathedral garden, the dutiful son reported to his mother, and right in the center of French Quarter Bohemia, since "only Sherwood and Elizabeth Anderson rivaled Spratling and [Lyle] Saxon as hosts and organizers." Spratling, a professor of architecture at Tulane, fond of storytelling, drinking, and collecting and telling dirty jokes, had plantation Alabama roots. It was said he had "very nearly the same voice and delivery as Faulkner." And like Faulkner, he could play the southern gentleman when he was not in bohemian mode.[57] Spratling formed a nexus between town and gown, exemplifying as a gay man the gregarious attributes associated with arts communities. It has been estimated that at least a third of the French Quarter bohemians were homosexual, although many, like Spratling, remained discrete and were careful to appear in public as heterosexuals in the company of women. In none of the accounts that Carvel Collins and Joseph Blotner gathered is there the suggestion that Faulkner and Spratling were lovers, but Faulkner's openness to gay-inspired culture is notable—as were his sympathies with Italian immigrants, who created a relaxed European ambiance, a "live-and-let live" ethos that blended in well with the Creole, mixed-race, Spanish, and French history that later proved crucial to the making of *Absalom, Absalom!* In the largest southern city—small by New York City standards but "three times the size of Nashville and roughly seven times as large as Charleston . . . New Orleans just offered more *room* for communities of every sort." The architecture, the university—no other southern metropolis came anywhere near in scope a port city that also served as an embarkation point for Europe.[58]

From Spratling's digs, Faulkner liked watching the priests, "nice men," and nuns come out of their convent and little choir boys "in their purple robes and white supplices" play leap frog in the garden, "yelling and cursing each other, then go back inside and sing like angels." He did not tell his mother about the free-flowing gin at Spratling's parties, where Faulkner played the good host. He does not seem, however, to have been conspicuously drunk. Elizabeth Prall Anderson said that while drinking certainly went on, drunkenness was not a common experience, although other witnesses undermine her assertion. The dutiful son did not describe Spratling's bathroom full of "large nude figures painted in such a way as to incorporate various parts of the bathroom fixtures as anatomical parts of the nude figures."[59] One visitor to the Spratling establishment called the artist "a real screwball" who had "a very unpleasant habit . . . of standing well inside his room and shooting the sisters with an air rifle."[60] Another account has Faulkner dropping ball bearings on a priest.[61]

Spratling's and Faulkner's juvenile antics jibe with accounts of a "concentration of young men, nearly all unmarried" and living in a "boyish and boisterous atmosphere."[62] When Anderson's teenage son showed up, he took over the shooting, much to Faulkner's annoyance when he was writing. Spratling recalled that they grabbed Bob, "took his pants off, painted his peter green and pushed him out on the street, locking the door."[63] Faulkner made only one reference (pleasant) to Bob in his letters to his mother. Bob seemed no longer to have been a problem, and perhaps the green peter episode is fanciful.

Faulkner would later miss this sort of life, coming and going as he pleased and sleeping as long as he liked. Spratling had done a portrait of him, a "good drawing," Faulkner told his mother, but the "face has more force and character than I have, I think." He was meeting "wealthy Jews," like Margery Gumbel, the wife of a securities broker who backed the *Double Dealer*. She was "quite nice," but she later told Carvel Collins that Faulkner then was "a bit of a joke." She did not elaborate but remembered that he told her, "I am a genius."[64] She did not believe his plate-in-the-head story or that he had fathered illegitimate children. She took him to her mother's for dinner. He did not say a word and then nodded off, holding one of Mrs. Gumbel's fine china cups so precariously that she wanted to reach out for it. But as she watched him, she concluded it was a performance, since he never lowered his hand the way a person falling asleep would do. He was a "humbug," Margery's mother concluded.[65]

Faulkner's encounters with a wide-ranging set, some of whom he met aboard a yacht that Sherwood Anderson chartered, would later provide material for *Mosquitoes*. He enjoyed that trip through the dark water of swamps and lagoons, full of "big yellow wild honeysuckle blooms," and the dancing aboard ship, and fishing and swimming. And always the good food and the alligators sounding like "dragging a heavy plank across the top of an empty barrel." Anderson and Faulkner continued to entertain themselves with stories about Al Jackson, whom Faulkner compared to Sut Lovingood, the bawdy prankster George Washington Harris (1814–1869) popularized. Faulkner rattled off summaries of the Al Jackson tales for his mother, including one about the web-footed hero, a descendant of Andrew Jackson, working on a frog ranch, swimming out to the fish, herding them, and notching their tails: "Whenever you see a fish with a notched tail, Al Jackson once owned him." In one letter to Anderson, Faulkner elaborated the story of sheep Jackson raised in the water so that, he thought, their wool would be silky. But the sheep took to the water and developed scales and other fishy attributes in a speeded-up Lamarckism version of acquired characteristics. Faulkner supplied Anderson with a Jackson family history: a mother who had increased church attendance "three hundred percent with some sort of a secret recipe for communion wine, including among other things, grain alcohol," and a father who at eight learned "by heart one thousand verses from the new testament, bringing on an attack resembling brain fever," a malady that often afflicts the characters in *The White Rose of Memphis*. Al's brother, Herman, "read Sir Walter Scott's complete works in twelve and one half days. For two days afterward he seemed to be dazed—could not remember who he was."[66]

A measure of Faulkner's growing sense of importance is his April 12 sketch "Out of Nazareth," in which he appears along with Spratling as a character: "I remarked to Spratling how no one since Cezanne had really dipped his brush in light."[67] Not only did Faulkner and his artist friend discuss art and go to galleries, they were using the city as their own canvas. Spratling spots the Christ like face of a young tramp, David, who appeals to the pair because he is so self-contained. The Faulkner who thanked "Moms" for her largesse is captivated by a young man who expects nothing from no one. "He reminded one of a pregnant woman in his calm belief that nature, the earth which had spawned him, would care for him," Faulkner notes, describing a character that would later metamorphose into Lena Grove in *Light in August.* This young man seems, indeed, an invention—too good to be true—because he just happens to be carrying with him a copy of Housman's *A Shropshire Lad,* the very volume Faulkner kept with him on his own tramps. David has never heard of Elizabeth Barrett Browning or Robert Frost, a sign, evidently, that his taste for Housman is not a taste for poetry itself but for the sensibility of a "man that . . . felt that way, and didn't care who knew it." The unlettered tramp, reminiscent of John Clare (1793–1864), son of a farm laborer, and a working-class, peasant poet, consigns to Faulkner a writing sample full of misspellings that reflect an unschooled but authentic contact with nature, a bond that Faulkner himself experienced and that increasingly distanced him from what he took to be the overly literary concerns of his contemporaries: "With a pack on my back (consisting of necessary articles rolled in two blankets) I trudge along. The smell of farm house fires drifts down the wind to me. Pure air fills my lungs and gives an exhileration unlike any other that I know. The morning sun casts long shadows accross the fields. The dew of early morning glitters and the tall grass overhanging the side of the road is heavy with it. . . . I seem to be in true communion with nature." Faulkner concedes that David's writing is "blundering and childish and 'arty,' and yet with something back of it, some impulse which caused him to want to write it out on paper." A paradox is at work here: a work of art that aspires to be artless, insofar as it is not motivated by the desire to produce art. The early Faulkner, Faulkner the poet, qualifies as "arty," and through such sketches he seems to be tramping out his affectations.[68]

Faulkner was drawing nearer to the subjects and characters of his novels, including the April 25 sketch "The Kingdom of God," featuring an idiot, a precursor of Benjy Compson, and on May 24, "Sunset," depicting a black character called "insane" in a newspaper account whose actions are in fact understandable as his deluded effort to find his home in Africa. Certain entrancing passages recall *The Emperor Jones,* a play Faulkner knew well: "Dozing and waking, he passed the long day, crawling at intervals to sip the muddy, stinking water in the ditch. At last he waked to night, and lanterns and fires, and men walking in the firelight and talking." The ironical juxtaposition of the crude newspaper account of the man's life and the narrative that explores his consciousness is Faulkner's first foray into the inner lives of black people that grace his work in *Go Down, Moses,* especially in his depiction of Ryder in "Pantaloon in Black" and the white deputy who interprets Ryder's grief-stricken behavior as simple savagery.

Faulkner had yet to reckon seriously with racial themes, and the writers in his environs were no help. "The trick is to write nigger stories," Sherwood Anderson advised. "The North likes them. They are so amusing." Roark Bradford, a Faulkner friend, specialized in dozens of comic black-dialect stories.[69] Faulkner liked to train street urchins to perform in impromptu minstrel shows, getting them to clap their hands and sing in unison. He would then "toss them some coins to pay them for their trouble." He also liked to watch black and white children playing baseball together, a pastime that other people, including the police, enjoyed in an open space near the cathedral.[70]

An unpublished story, "Peter," set in New Orleans, reveals a sensibility not yet fully engaged with the reality of black lives. The tradition of the tragic mulatto informs a description of Peter: "his face round and yellow as a new penny, brooded briefly. What does he see? I wondered, thinking of him as an incidental coin minted between the severed yet similar despairs of two races." Outside a brothel, Peter has come to the attention of William Spratling, who is drawing the boy, the son of a prostitute. Peter is her doorman, so to speak: "I have to sit here and tell 'em when mamma's busy talking to some body. And the others, too. I got to watch out for 'em," Peter explains. His touching sense of responsibility plays out against the shouts of johns and whores, brutal and urgent. In this scene of violent, almost homicidal sex, Spratling and Peter form an aesthetic accord that Peter's mother interrupts:

> "Peter," said his mother.
> "He's drawing me in a picture, mamma. He'll draw you too, if you will stay."
> She came languorous as a decayed lily and looked at the sketch.
> "Huh," she said. "You come on with me," she told Peter.
> Peter wept. "But he's drawing me in a picture," he told her.
> "Haven't I told you about hanging around down here?"

The story's narrator, sympathetic to Peter, treats him almost like an equal and Peter's mother as the victim of a history she cannot resist:

> "But he's drawing me," Peter crooking his arm about his face wept from some mature reserve of masculine vanity, seeing his life temporarily disrupted by a woman. But she took his hand and led him up the salmon stairs. At the turn she paused like a languorous damaged lily, and her dark eyes in which was all the despair of a subject race and a thinned blood become sterile except in the knowledge of the ancient sorrows of white and black, as a dog can see and hear things we cant, looked at us a moment. Then she was gone, and Peter's weeping soon died away.

The phrase "a thinned blood become sterile" is reminiscent of Faulkner's claim to Elizabeth Prall Anderson that mulattos could not get pregnant. An overriding sense of fatalism, and even acquiescence and corruption ("decayed lily"), pervades this moment, so different from Faulkner's mature sense of race and history. In this world of "art and vice," as the narrator describes it, he hears the "broken phrases of a race answering quickly to the compulsions of the flesh and then going away, temporarily freed from the body, to sweat and labor and sing; doomed again to repair to a temporary satisfaction; fleeting, that cannot last. The world: death and despair, hunger and sleep. Hunger that tolls the body along until life becomes tired of the burden." This bleak, repetitive cycle, reflected in the story's weary tone at this point, is relieved by an exuberant Peter, no longer crying, but thinking about his friend's toy, a kind of yo-yo: he "can spin one end and pick it up on the string." As Spratling and the narrator depart, Peter calls down from a window, "When you come next time I bet I can spin that top." The sketch has the makings of the race and history and scenes that Faulkner will learn to layer in his later work.[71] Even the difference between "decayed" and "damaged" lily reflects a subtle shift in perspective, away from corruption and toward a sense of injury that the fiction seeks to redress. The fatalistic tone is also mitigated by Faulkner's clear-eyed portrayal of a "working mother come to retrieve her child at the end of her labors."[72]

Novel writing overlapped with sketches. By early April, Faulkner reported to his mother, "my novel is going splendidly." One friend remembered Faulkner locking himself up for a day or two of uninterrupted writing.[73] Anderson mentioned hearing Faulkner's typewriter whenever he visited Spratling, and Spratling wrote: "By the time I would be up, say at seven, Bill would already be out on the little balcony over the garden tapping away on his portable, an invariable glass of alcohol-and-water at hand."[74] He put in full eight-hour days on it and showed a chapter to Anderson, who called it "good stuff" and promised to help in getting Boni & Liveright, Anderson's publishers, to take it. Liveright, then at its apogee, published Hemingway's *In Our Time,* Dreiser's *An American Tragedy,* and works by Eugene O'Neill, T. S. Eliot, and Sigmund Freud. In Faulkner's account, Anderson is compliant and encouraging. Harold Dempsey told Carvel Collins a different story. While interviewing Anderson, Dempsey "looked up to see a small, rather thin and as he remembers it ragged man slithering under the door with a typewritten manuscript in his hand which he presented to Anderson. Dempsey remembers that Anderson's response was that Faulkner who this happened to be was bothering him too much with these writings and at this point Anderson said, 'Well if I read this and try to get it published for you will you promise to go back to

Oxford and leave me alone?'" Dempsey could not remember what happened next, or whether Faulkner acceded to Anderson's demands.[75]

For his mother's gratification, Faulkner always presented himself as popular and successful. Lewis Piper, a shy young salesman working in the advertising department of the *New Orleans Item,* seemed enthralled with Faulkner and Spratling and supplied them with food and drink while they conversed.[76] "He tells me about his mother," Faulkner wrote to his mother, "and how old he is, and how he likes New Orleans. . . . Funny kind of a boy. He has the strangest admiration for me. Makes me feel like I ought to do something quite grand for his sake. Like saving the child in the burning building, or capturing a burglar, or going into the movies. Or maybe I should be a fireman in a red shirt and a two gallon oil-cloth hat." Faulkner was twenty-seven and still an apprentice himself, but he liked to strike the sardonic note: "Anyway, I know I am not doing what he thinks I ought to. But then the law-breaking and heroic market is so crowded these days." Quite an attitude to strike for a man still young, in thrall to William Spratling, and grateful for care packages from home. But he could also feel in command, having Piper type part of *Soldiers' Pay,* and telling his mother, "I am drafting every man woman and child who can use a typewriter into service."

Did Piper's hero worship of Faulkner, if that is what it was, stem from Faulkner's tales about his wartime service? The reality, of course, produced far different results. With fellow writer Samuel Louis Gilmore, described as "exuding an air of ineffectuality and dilettantism," Faulkner tried his hand at sailing, but the twosome only managed to "go around in circles."[77]

The outcome was better with Hamilton Basso, who noted that he bonded with Faulkner when they went together to see the Gates Flying Circus. Basso had been assigned to do a story for the *Times-Picayune:* "Nobody else in our crowd had gone looping-the-loop in a bucket seat and open cockpit over the Mississippi River," a fun-filled adventure that made them feel it was "something to be 'in' on."[78] Faulkner always treasured that sense of exclusivity, which appeals to the Reporter in *Pylon* when he goes up in a plane with Roger Shuman. To be in the know even motivated Faulkner to accept a onetime ten-dollar offer to become a French Quarter tour guide. His employer, Marc Antony, one of those caricatured in the Spratling-Faulkner production of *Sherwood Anderson and Other Famous Creoles,* said the author captivated his auditors with horror stories he made up about the history of the Quarter's buildings.[79]

Carvel Collins collected other reactions to Faulkner. Harold Levy, a musician and Pontalba building tenant who seemed to know everybody and "turned up everywhere"[80] as a kind of "Zelig figure,"[81] remembered that

Faulkner had a British accent and told Levy he was British. Faulkner's talk about his wounds left the impression of a neurotic and "war-shocked" veteran "deracinated or uprooted by the war. It seemed to have thrown him off balance." The "nervous, insecure young man" Levy described seemed "very different from the self-possessed figure others describe," Collins noted. Levy helped a grateful Faulkner complete a sonnet, published in the *Double Dealer* and dedicated "To H. L." Their proximity in the Pontalba building and Levy's knack for collaboration foreshadow the Quentin-Shreve dorm-room duo.

Yet another witness recounted Faulkner wearing a habitual "heavy sport coat and a pair of trousers that did not match." He sported a cane that resembled Charlie Chaplin's. Sometimes, "out of exuberance," Faulkner would "bounce his cane down onto the street or sidewalk on its tip and catch it when it flew up in the air."[82] Joyce McClure, John McClure's wife, remembered Faulkner's filthy old raincoat, which he habitually wore to breakfast as a dressing gown.[83] He seemed indifferent to what others thought of such behavior.

Almost all the stories about Faulkner in New Orleans concern his activities with men. James Feibleman declared that Faulkner seemed awkward with women. Flo Field, a French Quarter stalwart caricatured in *Sherwood Anderson and Other Creoles,* recalled Faulkner backing away from her as she was introduced to him. Invited to address a women's book club, Faulkner, it was said, behaved rudely and refused the invitation. Genevieve Pitot, a pianist and composer, remembered an uncommunicative Faulkner sitting in a corner and drinking.[84] So it came as quite a surprise—even cause for amusement— when Faulkner and another male friend, Keith Temple, urged her not to give up her baby for adoption, saying that they would raise the child for her. "Fifty years later, she was still laughing about that offer."[85]

Temple, a *Times-Picayune* editorial cartoonist, in the thick of the Creole crowd, shared a French Quarter flat with another Faulkner pal, Oliver La Farge. To Faulkner, Temple would have been a specimen to study and admire. He had fought in France and returned home wounded. His brother had been killed in the war. In Temple's estimation, Faulkner was not imposing but rather the "sort of person you wouldn't have looked at twice," a "silent member of every gathering, saying very little and drinking very much."[86]

Faulkner's letters in the spring of 1925 are full of New Orleans local color as he describes a Catholic church: candles, incense, people in pews kneeling and praying, dipping their fingers in holy water, crossing themselves, bowing to the altar, a service in Latin, with no preaching but plenty of music: "Grand to watch, and how those little boys can sing!" New Orleans, to this Mississippi youth, was not so different in its exotic ways from the city Henry

Sutpen sees in the company of Charles Bon in *Absalom, Absalom!* Faulkner wrote more stories and half his novel while evading a woman of about thirty, an "empress of stormy emotions. But then a man's life is never a bed of roses. If it ain't mosquitoes its something else." The panoply of personalities and customs that would move him toward writing a second, socially engaged novel, *Mosquitoes,* began to congregate in his letters home.

To Faulkner, at least, the interest that Sherwood and Elizabeth had taken in him amounted to a familial feeling: "They have taken me in charge," he wrote to his mother on April 23, and would not let him "read anything" until he had finished his "dog-gone good novel." He was aiming to finish what would be titled *Soldiers' Pay* by June and gave his mother a précis:

> It has the war for a background. Two men who didn't get overseas, and for whom the war stopped too soon, and one man who was missing in action, his father gave him up, and then he turns up at home so badly hurt that he dies. The war didn't stop soon enough for him, you see. His father has to go through the whole thing twice. Mother is dead. There are two women, one who helped him get home—he is going blind and his mind is deranged, and the one he was engaged to who sees his scarred face and throws him down.

Faulkner in embryo emerges in this passage, in the proclivity for counterpointed stories, for characters who miss out or are incapable of decisive action, and those who are maimed by proactivity. New Orleans, as cosmopolitan in its own way as New York City, but functioning on a much smaller scale, galvanized Faulkner's genius and made him a magnet for those wanting to discover a new talent and relaxed him to a degree, with new companions (writers and artists) with outrageous stories he shared in his correspondence.

Faulkner had his first contact with Hollywood in the guise of a "terrible man" from the Palmer Institute, a company that claimed to teach screenwriting, "the new road to authorship." He said, "You are the one." Faulkner plied this "bland and blithe" huckster with enough liquor to foil any efforts at instruction. Faulkner remained the same son his mother fussed over, he assured her: "You see, when I have worked all morning my back is so cramped that I get out and rear back almost as much as grandfather, and walk six or eight miles. I expect I am straighter than I was at home." The only difference? "I fear I am getting fat." So he continued his walking regimen. And his mother continued to supply him with money orders, golf clubs, several cakes, cheese, and even soap, toothpaste, towels, sheets, and a pillow case—not to mention various items of clothing, including "linen knickers" and a "lounging robe." How Murry reacted to this pampering is not apparent, but his son later acknowledged his father's parental support, his "unfailing kindness, which supplied me with bread at need despite the outrage to his principles of having been of a bum progenitive."[87]

By the middle of May, Faulkner had a complete draft of the novel, finishing up in a flurry of ten thousand words and wondering if he would ever have quite so much fun again. But he was already thinking about another one, although it is not certain if he meant the abortive *Elmer* or *Mosquitoes*. He took time off to get good and brown on an oyster lugger, fending off mosquitoes "big as sparrows and vicious as tigers." Most of the time, though, he worked at revisions of his first novel. On June 1, 1925, Sherwood Anderson wrote to Horace Liveright: "That young Bill Faulkner I told you about down here as the one writer here of promise has finished a novel. . . . Do you want to see it? I think he is going to be a real writer."[88] Faulkner announced to his mother: "Sherwood Anderson is all blowed up over the novel. He has written Liveright two letters about it and Liveright has written asking me to send it on to him. Sherwood thinks it is going to be a sensation. I hope so." But Anderson, now absorbed in writing his memoirs, began to tire of an importunate Faulkner. "I'll do anything for him," Anderson told his wife, "so long as I don't have to read his damn manuscript." Estelle told Joseph Blotner that "Bill remembered those words," but he did nothing then to express his resentment.

Helen

On Faulkner's return to New Orleans from Pascagoula, where he enjoyed a brief holiday, he met twenty-one-year-old Helen Baird. Described as "elfin"—a word also applied to Faulkner—she had a "don't give a damn look," which also fit him. They did not so much couple as flit. Helen's aunt said Faulkner appeared like "a bird who just flew in from the trees." He arrived barefooted, a nature boy.[89] This female Faulkner could be not only aloof but downright recalcitrant, as Carvel Collins discovered in one of his frustrating interviews with her. Faulkner liked to recall "a sullen-jawed yellow-eyed belligerent humorless gal in a linen dress and sunburned bare legs sitting on Spratling's balcony and not thinking even a hell of a little bit of me that afternoon, maybe already decided not to."[90] He did not exaggerate. She called the scruffy, short writer "a fuzzy little animal." And yet she would become a kind of counter to Estelle, whom Faulkner had recently seen again on one of her periodic returns to Oxford. Perhaps Faulkner found Helen appealing precisely because she was not "very interested in him."[91] He could pursue her, like one of those figures on a Grecian urn, without ever worrying that she would let him catch up.

Faulkner sailed and swam in Pascagoula with Helen. Often dressed in a painter's smock, she had an artist's eye: "Look, the moon looks like a fingernail in the sky," she said to Faulkner, who asked, "May I use that?"[92] She treated him as he sometimes treated others. She failed to show up. She had the boyish, tramp-like flair he had celebrated in his sketch about David in "Out of Nazareth." She abjured the southern lady courtesies and cared nothing for the gentlemanly code that he sometimes profaned in his barefoot performances. He worked on a sequence of poems that he would present to her in June 1926. Her remarkable personality informed the portrayal of Myrtle Monson in *Elmer*—"a Dianalike girl dark and fierce and proud with an impregnable virginity"—Patricia Robyn in *Mosquitoes,* and Charlotte Rittenmeyer in *The Wild Palms,*[93] and he would see her occasionally after she married. Something about her independence forever intrigued him. She did more than rebuff him and later told Carvel Collins that Faulkner was "one grand person to know and be with—a truly great companion like the ones you read about but never meet."[94] If Helen could not reciprocate Faulkner's romantic interest, perhaps her presence bolstered him. Helen may have reminded Faulkner of his diminutive self-contained mother, who also painted.[95]

During a short trip home to say his good-byes before sailing off to Europe, he conferred with his Aunt Bama, the old Colonel's daughter and Faulkner's closest link to his great-grandfather. Faulkner decided that he would support his travels by writing for various newspapers, perhaps in emulation of *Rapid Ramblings in Europe,* first published as reports to the *Ripley Southern Sentinel.* Phil Stone wrote to the Four Seas Company, hoping to get a second contract, asking for $250 for the published travel articles in book form.[96] The contract never materialized, and Faulkner never wrote the articles.

He came aboard the *West Ivis* on July 7, 1925. He had taken aboard five hundred sheets of paper, promising to write his mother and to keep a diary. He sailed with Bill Spratling and had a list of people to look up abroad. "Quite a gang are coming down to see us off," said the literary hopeful whose favorite word in his letters home was how "grand" the world seemed in New Orleans, the place where so many have come to find a new future. And now: "If Europe just stands by me, I'll do her up brown and come home." He believed he would find a receptive audience in France by introducing himself, "Je suis un poete."[97] The last New Orleans letter to his mother on July 6 sounds the familiar note of the boy who always thought he could go home again: "I wont hesitate to sing out if I need any cash, in plenty of time. . . . I got my hair brushes alright. Thank you. Love, Billy[.]"

5

Wanderjahr

July–December 1925

Faulkner said little about his four weeks at sea except that he wrote a good deal. He also destroyed much of what he wrote, if William Spratling's memory is accurate: "When we were some two days out in the blue of the Gulf Stream, one morning Faulkner appeared on deck with a mass of MS about four inches thick. This he laid on the deck and proceeded to dispose of by tearing it in batches and dropping it overboard. . . . [H]e was not yet sure of an acceptance on *Soldiers' Pay*."[1] Short stories that may have been a part of his shipboard work and published later reveal that he absorbed a good deal of naval nomenclature that is almost as impressive as his pilot's vocabulary. If it has often been supposed that Faulkner actually experienced what he wrote about, it is because he immersed himself so thoroughly in the way ships and boats, sailors and aviators functioned and talked. And he was writing on the spot, hefting a typewriter and several hundred pages of paper as he soldiered on in search of material. He would take aboard their experiences, so to speak, and own them.

Faulkner was already cultivating his image as a tramp abroad, although after debarking at Genoa on August 2, Spratling had the first adventure. In a Genoa nightclub brawl, the artist had stomped on, or perhaps spit on, Italian bank notes with the king's image. He was arrested and released in the afternoon of the next day. In Spratling's account, Faulkner appeared as an innocent abroad, an envious sidekick wishing it had been his lot to be locked up. If Spratling, who liked to tell stories, has been believed, it is probably because Faulkner passed off the incident as his own to Ben Wasson and because the incident itself made it into three Genoa newspapers.[2] He would later incorporate Spratling's tale in an abortive novel, *Elmer,* and in a story, "Divorce in Naples," without noting that these events occurred in Mussolini's Italy under the headlines "Exploits of a Drunken Foreigner" and "Foreign Rabble," reflecting fascist xenophobia.

Spratling's antics made no appearance in Faulkner's letters home, which present pictures of a welcoming populace positively embracing his presence. He did not mention spending time in Spratling's company of prostitutes and pimps who appear in Faulkner's short stories. On August 6, on his way to Ezra Pound in Rapallo, with a letter of introduction from Phil Stone. Faulkner wrote to his mother, enclosing a drawing of a locomotive—no doubt for his father's enjoyment, putting him in the cab with the engineer and fireman who "stand all the time. That's because they will be wherever they are going in 20 minutes."[3] He may have wanted to be on his own, but in his drawings and letters he took his home along with him. The romance of the expatriate life never seems to have seduced him. He wanted to know about his nephew Jimmy (John's son) and "Whiz," the name given to his athletic younger brother Dean. Faulkner never contacted Pound, known to promote young writers. Faulkner simply said, "I went my way."[4] He contented himself with a glimpse of Joyce in a Paris cafe.[5]

Spratling remembered that the good food and drink made Faulkner a tiresome and talkative traveling companion who interrupted Spratling's efforts to draw a bridge in Pavia, for example, with "loud and rambling" meditations. Perhaps Spratling's lack of interest convinced Faulkner not to emulate his forebear's rapid ramblings in print. Keep it to yourself, Spratling advised him. They decided to part company and rendezvous in Paris. Faulkner's stories about this period featuring two young Americans discovering and dilating on their European adventures seem, then, a kind of recompense for the departure of his artist brother.

And so Faulkner walked on his own. He watched women doing their washing in a river, slapping clothes with wooden paddles. He stayed at a small country hotel with cobblestones and a vine-covered courtyard. It was all "grand—so old and quiet." The leisurely pace exuded "calm pleasure." He joined river boatmen at dinner, laughing and talking about politics and music. They did not gulp down their food and run back to work. His letters home provide a meticulous account of how much he spent on various items and meals like a good steward of his sojourn: "People in Italy all think I am English. Which is good, because Americans are charged two prices for everything." His meal of spaghetti, salad, beans, a bowl of peaches, apples, plums, plus coffee and a bottle of wine cost fifty cents.

A visit to Milan stimulated an effusion: "This Cathedral! Can you imagine stone lace? Or frozen music?" He reveled in sculpted "mailed knights" and "mitred cardinals." But he also liked the repose of mountainsides and lakes, where "people eat and sleep . . . [w]atching the world pass, and that's all." He disliked tourists. On a postcard of Lake Maggiore he wrote, "Full of Americans—terrible." In mountain villages in the Italian Alps he got by using a system of signs. Sometimes he worked beside villagers cutting grass and gathering hay. After he stayed four days in one village, everyone turned out to say good-bye.

In mid-August, Faulkner and Spratling rendezvoused in Stresa on the way to Paris, taking a train to Montreux. Faulkner described Switzerland as a land of mountains, tunnels, "rushing rivers," chalets, churches, cattle, and sheep. The word for the weather was cold. Arriving in Paris by August 13, he settled in at a hotel near the Luxembourg Gardens and tried to work on travel articles—none of which were ever published and do not seem to have survived. He composed a sonnet sequence he would present to Helen Baird when he returned to the States. Referring to the four-inch pile of paper he had pitched overboard, he said the disposal made him "feel clean."[6]

For the rest of the month, Faulkner visited Versailles, Fontainebleau, the Arc de Triomphe, and walked along the Champs-Elysées to the Place de la Concorde. He enjoyed itemizing his meals: lunching on an omelette, lettuce, cream cheese, coffee, and a bottle of wine and practicing his improving French. He took the metro to the Bastille, then went to see Oscar Wilde's tomb and Jacob Epstein's bas-relief. He compared Notre Dame with Milan's cathedral, noting, especially, the "sardonic mirth" of its gargoyles. He liked the Louvre's treasures—the Winged Victory, Venus de Milo, the *Mona Lisa,* and "more-or-less moderns" like Degas and Manet and Cezanne—but, honestly, he preferred watching children in the Luxembourg Gardens sailing boats. He asked his mother not to faint. He was growing a beard and awaiting word on the fate of his novel at Liveright.

By late August, Faulkner had begun work on his second novel, *Mosquitoes,* but then put it aside for *Elmer,* a "grand one . . . New altogether. I just thought of it day before yesterday," he told his mother. *Elmer* explored the consciousness of an artist, whereas *Mosquitoes* dealt much more with the social reality of other people, and that gave him pause: "I dont think I am quite old enough to write it as it should be written—dont know quite enough about people." He had found a cheaper room to write in, enumerating for Maud his moderate expenses for food and lodging. He spent mornings in French cafes and returned to his room to write for about three hours, from nine to twelve. On rainy afternoons he frequented museums and galleries.

Parisian culture had a unity of effect that beguiled him. Young and old, for example, sailed finely crafted miniature boats. In the Luxembourg Gardens he watched an old man in a blue yachting cap launch his toy steam yacht to the accompaniment of advice from half a dozen bystanders: "Think of a country where an old man, if he wants to, can spend his whole time with toy ships, and no one to call him crazy or make fun of him! In America they laugh at him if he drives a car even if he does anything except play checkers and sleep in the courthouse yard." The desire to play, a part of the aesthetic impulse, created a society that deeply appealed to this young novelist. His own art, in his own land, would always be a thing apart.

"I have come to think of the Luxembourg as my garden now," Faulkner wrote his mother in early September. "I sit and write there, and walk around to watch the children, and the croquet games. I always carry a piece of bread to feed to the sparrows." He was working rapidly, erecting twenty thousand words of *Elmer* by September 6. But he seemed even more excited by a two-thousand-word piece—"such a beautiful thing that I am about to bust": "Luxembourg gardens and death," with a "thin thread of plot, about a young woman." He had worked on it for "two whole days and every word is perfect." He considered it "poetry in prose form" and had not slept for two nights "thinking about it, comparing words, accepting and rejecting them, then changing them again" until it had become a "jewel." Perhaps he had Helen Baird in mind. He met Helen and her mother in Paris, but he did not make a good impression on his beloved: "He was an oddball. Others traveled in autos, he on foot. He knew he was a genius." Her mother called him a "screwball."

So much seemed to coalesce in what would become *Sanctuary* six years later, begun in what was, in effect, his own garden sanctuary. The young woman became Temple Drake, and his words about himself, written to his Aunt Bama on September 10, reflected his growing appreciation of what literature meant to a proud man who, like Temple Drake, had yet to fully mature: "Did that ugly ratty-looking face, that mixture of childishness and unreliability and sublime vanity, imagine that? But I did. And the hand doesn't hold blood to improve on it."

Faulkner's brooding on death arose out of the evidence of what war had wrought. He visited the Pantheon, "where the unknown soldier's grave is. There is also in the Pantheon, on a blank panel of wall, a wreath to Guynemer, the aviator. . . . And so many young men on the streets, bitter and grey-faced, on crutches or with empty sleeves and scarred faces." In *Soldiers' Pay,* written in New Orleans, Faulkner had anticipated the fate of a returning war hero, Donald Mahon, who is, in effect, any soldier who loses his identity in war. He comes home as a kind of relic and wreck, one of the living dead, a ruin.

Mahon's scarred face and impending death is what Faulkner found in France in churches, "no matter how small," with "long long lists of names." France was a war museum: "Full of relics: crashed aeroplanes and guns and tanks and alarm klaxons." In late September, on a walking tour, he saw rolls of wire, shell cases, and a rusting tank in a farmyard. No sign of trenches, but trees with their tops blasted off and "cemeteries everywhere."

Faulkner continued to write, but what he should settle on seemed to elude him. Still, he seemed exhilarated by the possibilities that led him from the beginning draft of *Mosquitoes* to *Elmer,* and now to "a sort of fairy tale," the "book of my youth" that would eventually become a novella, *Mayday.* The symbolist, allegorical, and realist impulses that would eventually culminate in his mature work remained in an unresolved tension and disambiguated in these separate writing projects.

A visit to the Moulin Rouge, "a vaudeville, where ladies come out clothed principally in lip stick," actually was more art than a girlie show. The songs and dances were "set to real music," including compositions by Rimsky-Korsakov and Sibelius. "It was beautiful," Faulkner told his mother, and so much finer than plays—"Nasty things"—put on for Americans: "After having observed Americans in Europe I believe more than ever that sex with us has become a national disease. The way we get it into our politics and religion, where it does not belong any more than digestion belongs there. All our paintings, our novels, our music, is concerned with it, sort of leering and winking and rubbing hands on it. But Latin people keep it where it belongs, in a secondary place. Their painting and music and literature has nothing to do with sex. Far more healthy than our way." Faulkner's own sexual needs—not a subject for letters home—are opaque.

In "Divorce in Naples," the innocent, virginal Carl does not realize he has become involved with a prostitute: "Maybe I got her into trouble." Carl's male lover, George, has to explain the facts of life and asks Carl if the woman showed Carl her "petite," which is a prostitute's license but also an allusion to her private parts. When George explains what a prostitute does, Carl, according to the story's anonymous narrator, seems about to cry, but then George realizes that "he was just trying to not puke. So I knew what the trouble was, what had been worrying him. I remember the first time it come as a surprise to me. 'Oh,' I says, 'the smell. It don't mean nothing,' I says; you don't want to let that worry you. It ain't that they smell bad,' I says, 'that's just the Italian national air.'" This reference to a prostitute's raunchy pudenda is just the kind of remark a seaman like George might make.

Stories like "Divorce in Naples" and "The Leg" explore the homoeroticism and coupling of men that Faulkner observed in New Orleans and elsewhere.

He traveled comfortably in William Spratling's company and, in Paris, consorted with another gay artist, William Odiorne. Did Faulkner's visit to Oscar Wilde's tomb acknowledge the artist's affinity for all kinds of sexual experience? Seamen had easy commerce with women and men, no matter the circumstances, language, or sexual orientation, as the beginning of "Divorce in Naples" displays:

> We were sitting at a table inside: Monckton and the bosun and Carl and George and me and the women, the three women of that abject glittering kind that seamen know or that know seamen. We were talking English and they were not talking at all. By that means they could speak constantly to us above and below the sound of our voices in a tongue older than recorded speech and time too. Older than the thirty-four days of sea time which we had but completed, anyway. Now and then they spoke to one another in Italian. The women in Italian, the men in English, as if language might be the sex difference, the functioning of the vocal cords the inner biding until the dark pairing time. The men in English, the women in Italian: a decorum as of two parallel streams separated by a levee for a little while.

The setting is France, but it might as well be New Orleans in the reference to "levee." The passage evokes the image of an embankment between men and women that overflows in the "dark pairing time" of sexual intercourse, a union of otherwise two different but "parallel streams." The story practically oozes in sexual emissions. Seamen? Semen?

ELMER AND OTHER ERECTIONS

Faulkner seemed to work out his awakening desire to reconcile the erotic and the aesthetic in his portrait of Elmer, the artist:

> Then he would rise, and in his cabin draw forth his new unstained box of paints. To finger lasciviously smooth dull silver tubes virgin yet at the same time pregnant, comfortably heavy to the palm—such an immaculate mating of bulk and weight that it were a shame to violate them, innocent clean brushes slender and bristled to all sizes and interesting chubby bottles of oil . . . Elmer hovered over them with a brooding maternity, taking up one at a time those fat portentous tubes in which was yet wombed his heart's desire, the world itself—thick-bodied and female and at the same time phallic: hermaphroditic. He closed his eyes the better to savour its feel.[7]

Elmer's tactile expectation of creation, the ejaculatory joining of genders that is both a defilement and a fulfillment, a commingling of opposites—smooth and rough, thin and thick—amounts to an expression of a Faulkner full of possibilities and the pent-up energy that stymied his marble faun and Pierrot, who cannot consummate their art or their sexual desires.[8] Elmer is similarly thwarted when a saleswoman in an art supply shop tells him he will need "lots of white": "What would this tube bear? A woman white and soft as the inside of a loaf of bread, heavy-limbed, of a dull inevitable calmness leaning her full breasts on a window-sill, brooding on far things while a lean Harlequin striped like a snake in a slim passionate immaturity plucked his insincere guitar, singing up into a sky larks had emptied, unheard?" Faulkner drew a picture of this kind of unresolved, inauthentic world in *The Marionettes,* and in the Prufrockian figure of *Vision in Spring.* Elmer emerges as their complement aboard a ship to Europe: "He slid the virgin pregnant cylinders each into its proper place, as they had been when he purchased the box, with an old-maidish precision putting the box away beneath his berth." Elmer has all the equipment of the artist, but he cannot generate art. The world that Elmer wants to encompass in his art is so near and yet eludes him, as Estelle and the figures in Faulkner's poems whirled away: "From the bridge he could see the waist of the vessel sweeping forward and upward to the bows, no longer clumsy but graceful as the unconfined body of a dancing girl." The simile, comparing the graceful bodies of a boat and a dancing girl, reflects Elmer's search for form, which is Faulkner's, of course, as well, drawing men and women, as Elmer does, making them "conform to that vague shape somewhere back in his mind, trying to reconcile what is, with what might be."[9]

Faulkner's shipboard voyage, his traveling away from home, engendered in his portrait of Elmer a reckoning with what it meant to be an incipient artist outside his father's hardware store, and outside what was considered normal male behavior:

He had already found that people, family, friends, and just people, were beginning to expect a certain propriety of conduct of him; that it was no longer permitted to stand before the windows of a hardware store and admire shining nickel joints and slim pipes at the end of which shower bath sprays bloomed like imperishable flowers; that before the drugstores he must feign interest in bars of soap or rubber bottles instead of in tall simple glass vases filled deliciously with red and green. . . . He would like to touch them, to stroke them as you might a dog. But he dare not. So he must pass along the street looking as empty as any other adolescent in the fifth grade, sneaking looks at things he once might have stopped and frankly admired.

Now, in Paris, he could stop and admire as much as he liked with no one to urge him on to more practical matters. And yet, what were Faulkner's letters home but an effort to maintain that "propriety of conduct" even as he cultivated his dissent in a beard that could now hold water, as he told his mother, and in a running commentary on how, at so many points, Europe offered a liberating perspective on down-home habits. Seldom did a letter of his reach home without a drawing in it, a constant reminder of the artist in embryo. "I have him half done, and I have put him away temporarily to begin a new one," Faulkner wrote home. "Elmer is quite a boy. He is tall and almost handsome and he wants to paint pictures. He gets everything a man could want— money, a European title, marries the girl he wants—and she gives away his paint box. So Elmer never gets to paint at all." You can have it all, but when you have it all, you have no art, no recompense for what you cannot have. This little parable, which remained "half-done," and which Faulkner never did complete, suggests he was in suspension, somewhere between the boy, the man, and the artist. When Vannye, the daughter of Aunt Bama's elder sister, visited Paris, she laughed at Billy's beard, because—he admitted to his mother—"she could see right through it to the little boy I used to be."

Elmer is portrayed as developing from his innocent attachment to his sister, with whom he shares a bed, to his infatuation with a fourth-grade classmate to his coupling with Ethel, who spurns him for another financially secure suitor. Faulkner's trauma over Estelle seems vaguely in the picture here, as does Elmer's desire to return to Ethel as famous "Elmer Hodge the painter." His "sexual development merges with his development as an artist."[10] But *Elmer,* like its eponymous hero, fails to achieve full growth because its author, still cultivating his beard, could not coalesce a narrative that fully integrated the psycho-sexual-aesthetic dynamic that he explored again in another story, "The Leg," inspired, it seems, by twenty-five-mile-a-day walks through Bretagne, Rouen, Amiens, Artois, Cantigny, where American troops first entered the war.

Faulkner described "The Leg" as a "queer story about a case of reincarnation." It is much more than that, exploring "a profound sense of guilt" and "moral shock that World War I evoked in those who naively believed in human enlightenment and progress." Nothing in Faulkner's previous writing prepares one for the uncanny power of a tale of two men, an American, David, and his British friend, George, who are punting on the Thames just before the war begins. Like a poet in the pastoral tradition, George quotes Milton's *Comus* in a setting that is like a "dream of a prewar paradise,"[11] interrupted when George nearly drowns in a lock and is rescued (pulled out on a fishhook) by Jotham Rust, the brother of George's beloved, Everbe

Corinthia. This prefiguring of death occurs less than a year before David loses his leg in the war and George is killed. David, delirious in hospital, urges George—reincarnated, so to speak—to make certain David's leg is dead and properly buried. The leg, in other words, has a life of its own and is no mere body part but somehow represents to David an independent member liable to wreak havoc. What follows is a scene in which Jotham attacks David in hospital, claiming to a chaplain that David deserves death. David also learns that a screaming Everbe Corinthia has committed suicide, notwithstanding Jotham's effort to keep her at home. And then the chaplain shows David a photograph, dated on the day David was in hospital talking to the reincarnated George:

> I sat quite still in the blankets, looking at the photograph, because it was my own face that looked back at me. It had a quality that was not mine: a quality vicious and outrageous and unappalled, and beneath it was written in a bold sprawling hand like that of a child: "To Everbe Corinthia" followed by an unprintable phrase, yet it was my own face, and I sat holding the picture quietly in my hand while the candle flame stood high and steady above the wick and on the wall my huddled shadow held the motionless photograph. In slow and gradual diminishment of cold tears the candle appeared to sink, as though burying itself in its own grief.

What has happened? What could have happened? One explanation—an extrapolation of this passage—is that David "discovers that the leg has been reincarnated in another person, a physical likeness of himself,"[12] a shadow self, but David does not recognize his pernicious visage. The unprintable phrase is almost surely something nasty and lewd, and the implication is that David seduced Everbe Corinthia. This is why her brother, George's savior, has tried to kill David. In the fiction of Robert Louis Stevenson, George would be David's better, redeemable self. In Faulkner's fiction, George is David's conscience, the part of himself that is not in the photograph, the part of himself that cries out: "I told him [George] to find it and kill it. . . . I told him to. I told him." The "it" is clearly that other member, David's penis, the projection of a libido that has a life of its own, or a leg that leads a man to do what he knows he must not do—in this case seducing his friend's beloved and betraying his friend. David and George are brothers as closely bound to one another as Henry Sutpen and Charles Bon will become in *Absalom, Absalom!* David is as surely buried in his own grief as the candle that flames out and gutters. The wick, often a euphemism for penis, subsides as David reacts in horror at the consequences of his desire. "Rather than shaped by war," David's "identity has been torn apart by it, bright self from dark, head from leg."[13]

Even in his prewar idyll with David, George jocularly refers to the Thames as "Thou mighty sewer of an empire!" Such allusions reflect the "coexistence of surface innocence with unseen diabolic forces that will betray the dreams of the naive and unleash the horrors of World War I."[14] Faulkner's Freudian orientation, even if he had not read Freud then—or ever—is palpable and could have been absorbed from Ford Maddox Ford's *The Good Soldier* (1915), a copy of which was in Faulkner's library, or Rebecca West's *The Return of the Soldier* (1918), which was not. Her novel exposes the return home of the shell-shocked, amnesiac veteran and the prewar paradise of home and family that the war, in fact, reveals to be an illusion. This is why the "structure of the narrative itself is torn between realism and a sort of hallucinatory surrealism."[15] We do not know how David's leg was lost or even if he really did rape Everbe Corinthia. What matters is that he has lost control over himself and what the war has done to him.

Faulkner's letters home reveal nothing of how deeply steeped he was in the war that had dislocated civilization before he set foot in England. By early October he had docked in London, arriving in the "usual fog," a concoction of coal smoke and grease. He walked through streets "full of beggars, mostly young, able-bodied men who simply cannot get work," selling boxes of penny matches, playing music, and drawing with colored chalk on the pavement for "a few coppers." He hit all the highlights: "Westminster, the Tower, all those old coffee houses where Ben Jonson and Addison and Marlowe sat and talked, and Dickens' Bloomsbury, and Hounslow Heath where they robbed the mail coaches, and Piccadilly, and St. Paul's, and Trafalgar and Mayfair," the fog notwithstanding. He was amazed at how much the English ate—five times a day, and "nothing under heaven is allowed to interfere with it." He listed the full menu for his mother, beginning with a small pot of tea and toast brought by a servant while he was still in bed, then eggs and bacon and sausage and marmalade, butter and toast with a "huge pot of tea" in a coffee room, followed by a lunch of "beef or mutton and cabbage and boiled potatoes and ale" in a pub, and, at four, tea wagons rolling down train platforms with tea and muffins and scones. By seven, more "beef or mutton and cabbage and baked potatoes and ale." By eleven or twelve in the evening, the English were still at it with "a smoked herring-and-cheeses sandwich and a tumbler of whiskey and water, or hot rum punch." He did not stay in London long because it was so much more expensive than Paris. The deep-green peaceful countryside pleased him: "No wonder Joseph Conrad could write fine books here." In spite of more complaints about the high cost of living, he bought a hand-woven Harris tweed that had "every possible color in it . . . [c]ut by the swellest West-End tailor—one of those places 'By

Appointment to H.M. The King, H.M. The King of Sweden, H.R.H. The Prince of Wales.'"

By mid-October, Faulkner had returned to France, landing in Dieppe and spending time on a fishing boat and enjoying the food: "A french cook can take an old shoe and make it taste good." Then he claimed to his mother that he had been arrested and turned the incident into a scene in *Elmer*. Although Faulkner had his passport with him, a gendarme seemed to think he was loitering, and for some reason his trips to Switzerland and London were regarded as suspicious. They searched him—"for bombs I guess"—and confiscated his possessions, including his money. When Faulkner announced he was a poet, the police released him. "It takes a lot of stupidity to do anything really well," he told his mother, "but I think it requires more down right dullness to be a cop than anything I know."

Something like this contretemps with the police had happened to Bill Spratling, and this would not be the last time Faulkner would commandeer someone else's experience for his own comic purposes, or invent a persona, as he did in a November 1, 1925, letter to H. L. Mencken. Writing as Ernest V. Simms of the Baptist Young People's Union, he addressed the "magazine orthur," recommending a poem, "Ode to the Louver," by Faulkner, who "wants to get a start at poetry." Simms opines: "I think our Americans poets will be good as any foregner with encouragements and corrections since reading your magazine feel sure you feel the same sentiment."[16] Simms, who includes explanatory footnotes, is the pedantic and parodic equivalent of Ezra Pound, who edited Eliot's *The Waste Land*. Simms tells Mencken, "I onely made corrections in the above poem without changing its sentiments because the poet himself quit schools before learning to write because I have a typewriter." After the poem's title, a footnote explains, "Big house in Paris, France. Near City Hall." The poem begins: "The Louver is on Rivoli street / You can take the cars or go by feet," with a second footnote: "Foot dont rhyme with street." After similar lines about the size and history of the museum (with more footnotes), the poet as tour guide ends with a recommendation: "The Louver is worth going to see / The pictures in it is very pretty."[17]

Faulkner made fun of himself and of the erstwhile artist, Elmer Hodge, and perhaps of Phil Stone as a too officious impresario. Throughout his European expedition, Faulkner had sent Stone letters and postcards, asking his friend to keep in contact with Liveright and check on sales of *The Marble Faun*. The Simms letter reminded Stone's biographer of letters in the Stone office file, mixing his business, literary, and personal concerns just like Simms, who tells Mencken, "my family is long a reader of your magazine until a train reck 2 years ago," which comports well with a Stone letter that begins "Twenty years ago, when my father's bank failed . . ." Faulkner treated all comers as fair game, friend and foe alike. The prevalence of "I" in Faulkner's Simms letter, so much like Stone's practice, "may be the earliest sign that the balance of their heretofore complementary relationship had shifted a degree or two."[18] Very soon, Faulkner would do the same for Sherwood Anderson, putting his mentor behind him by burlesquing his style and writing him into a story that is a companion piece to "A Meeting South."

Early on, Faulkner's poses and guises were for the camera as well. In Paris, he commissioned photographs from William Odiorne, one of the New Orleans set who had left the city before Faulkner arrived. Odiorne shot him in close-up and also posing with full beard and pipe, hat, and trench coat, standing straight and stalwart against the backdrop of a cathedral. The photographs were, in effect, a collaborative enterprise. Faulkner described Odiorne to his mother as "a man here who admires me very much, who kind of looks after me."[19] This mothering, to a notable extent, came from gay men—not only Spratling and Odiorne but also Ben Wasson and others in the French Quarter.[20] Odiorne, Spratling, and Faulkner walked the Seine. Otherwise, Faulkner kept to himself. "I don't think he knew anybody in Paris I didn't introduce him to," Odiorne remembered.[21]

Faulkner sent one of the Odiorne photographs to Estelle and others home to his mother. Faulkner told the photographer: "Nobody reads what I write except my mother. She reads everything I write."[22] Odiorne had trouble remembering what Faulkner said about his work but was sure that at least the rudiments of *The Sound and the Fury* were beginning to emerge. Faulkner seemed to be commemorating a moment in his own portrait of the artist as a young man. He was returning home, it was to be supposed, more assured of success. He had enough of tourists and cities and traveling and tramping. He yearned for the "blue hills and sage fields" of home and to play golf and to eat home cooking. To Odiorne he confided: "I'm goin' back to Mississippi and I'm goin' 'possum huntin' with the niggers. . . . I'll go out to the woods at night. After a while the dogs will tree the 'possum and the niggers will kill it. They'll make a fire to cook the 'possum. I'll make a bed of pine branches and stretch out and smoke my pipe and listen to the niggers talk." What did they talk about? Odiorne asked. "Religion, sex."[23]

Faulkner planned to sail on November 19, spend time in New York on proofs of *Soldiers' Pay*, and be home by mid-December. By the end of November, he had in hand a contract to publish *Soldiers' Pay* and a two-hundred-dollar advance. Liveright had sent a personal check, and for several days Faulkner tried to cash it at the American Express office and elsewhere. No one had ever heard of Boni & Liveright. The exasperated author gave up: "Damn that Jew." He shivered in the cold, hoping to sail on December 2, while repeating "O *damn* that Jew." He did not sail until December 9, arriving in New York on December 19. He sent a telegram to his mother: "WIRE FIFTY DOLLARS CARE HOTEL PENNSYLVANIA. HOME WEDNESDAY."

6

Return

1925–1927

FASCISM AND EVERYTHING

From New York, Faulkner wrote Cicero (Odiorne), taking a tone nowhere evident in the son-to-parents epistles. He reported on his voyage with the "goddamdest group of people," seasick German and Balkan peasants "vomiting, on the floor, each other, and themselves." No one seemed to speak English. He had to threaten one, reaching for the food on Faulkner's plate, with a table knife. He made it through customs, like an unreconstructed southerner, without an inspection: "All serene—I didn't have to open the box—Inspector was a nigger, and I kind of ran it over him."[1]

Faulkner just made it home for the holidays, after a brief visit to the Liveright offices in New York to talk about *Soldiers' Pay* and to mention he had another novel in mind. He arrived in Oxford looking like a tramp with a long beard. His mother said, "What do you do with that thing at night, wear it inside the sheets or out?" He had not cleaned up: "For heaven's sake, Billy, take a bath," Maud scolded. He retreated to a room in the Delta Psi house at Ole Miss, bearded the Oxford square, and on a balmy day was back on the golf course. To a startled friend who watched him tee up, he said, "Did you think I was Jesus Christ?" He worked on stories that evolved out of his European sojourn, especially "Mistral," as well as dating on January 27, 1926, a draft of an allegory, *Mayday*, also begun on his European trek and dedicated to Helen Baird.

Perhaps the most surprising event of his return home was an address he delivered to the Rotary Club. The minutes report that president Alexander

Bondurant introduced "William Falkner who spoke of his recent European trip."[2] Why would the tramp do that? It was more like something the old Colonel would do. Unfortunately, no record remains of what William "Falkner" said. He would hardly have read one of his stories. Perhaps he commented on fascism, an undercurrent in the stories.

A passage in "Mistral" suggests that he wrote or at least completed a draft of the story in Oxford:[3] "We were young: Don, twenty-three; I, twenty-two. And age is so much a part of, so inextricable from, the place where you were born or bred. So that away from home, some distance away—space or time or experience away—you are always both older and eternally younger than yourself, at the same time." At home, Faulkner thought of Europe, and in Europe he thought of home, and both places helped to define his youth as well as his farewell to it. The story is set in an Italian village, probably Sommaruga, in the Alps, and Don is the anonymous narrator's traveling companion, just slightly older and more sexually experienced than the teller of the tale, which is about a young woman, an orphan brought up by a priest who becomes obsessed with her, then arranges for her to be married and perhaps arranges for another of her suitors to be drafted into the army, and then seems undone when the woman's intended dies (possibly murdered) in suspicious circumstances, and the soldier-suitor returns home. The mystery is never solved, but the story is as much about the narrator's bond with Don, which resembles Faulkner's pairing with Spratling that is also reminiscent of the later symbiosis between Quentin and Shreve, as they piece together the enigma of Thomas Sutpen and his brood in *Absalom, Absalom!*

"Mistral" sums up what Faulkner tried to tell the annoyed Spratling during their Italian sojourn: There were "only two basic compulsions on earth, i.e. love and death."[4] Like Quentin and Shreve, the two young men in "Mistral" are passionate about their story and about themselves. The narrator is forever watching Don and describing his actions and what he says. They catch glimpses of a young woman in white in scenes that may allude to the Wilkie Collins classic "The Woman in White" (1859), the story of a troubled and mysterious young woman at the mercy of male duplicity. The young woman also carries just a whiff of Estelle as the "brightest and loudest and most tireless in the dances," a fetching figure promised to two men, one of whom is rich and the other a villager conscripted into the army.

The narrator's white woman is associated with Evelyn Nesbit, who figured in a sensational murder trial. She had been seduced by the architect Stanford White, who was murdered by her husband, Harry Thaw, when Thaw discovered White had defiled her virginity. The overwrought passage is suffused with the narrator's obsession with romance, youth, and loss—the themes of Faulkner's poetry and of *Mayday*—and with a Poesque morbidity of the imagination:

> She was all in white, coatless, walking slender and supple. I didn't feel like anything any more, watching her white dress swift in the twilight, carrying her somewhere or she carrying it somewhere: anyway, it was going too, moving when she moved and because she moved, losing her when she would be lost because it moved when she moved and went with her to the instant of loss. I remember how, when I learned about Thaw and White and Evelyn Nesbit, how I cried. I cried because Evelyn, who was a word, was beautiful and lost or I would never have heard of her. Because she had to be lost for me to find her and I had to find her to lose her.

What is lost is not just the woman, but youth, innocence, and time itself, which is fleeting and elusive as the moment when the woman in white appears and disappears. As in Poe, the narrator's obsession is actually the point of the story. Faulkner channels Poe in providing his narrator with a double, a William Wilson—in this case Don—so that both men share their erotic attachment to the woman in white, who is, in large part, a figment of their imagination, a synecdoche of the beloved:

> We were halfway up the flagged path when a casement beneath the eaves [of a church] opened and somebody in white looked down at us and closed the shutter again. It was done all in one movement. Again we said together, quietly:
> "Beaver." But it was too dark to see much, and the casement was closed again. It had not taken ten seconds.
> "Only we should have said, Beaverette," Don said.

Beaver, or the more common term, pussy, is what is on their minds, and they try to make light of it. "Is that a joke?" the narrator asks Don. "Yes, that's a joke," Don confirms. Well, it is and it isn't. Or rather, as with Quentin and Shreve, they are joking in dead earnest.

The connection to the gloomy, Gothic Poe and the longing for lost youth and its mix-up with sex and courtship and growing up that will mark *The Sound and the Fury* and other novels to come is palpable:

> So I watched the white dress, thinking, She'll be as near me in a second as she'll ever be and then she'll go on away in her white dress forevermore, in the twilight forevermore. Then I felt Don watching her too and then we watched the soldier spring down from the bike. They came together and stopped and for a while they stood there in the street, among the people,

facing one another but not touching. Maybe they were not even talking, and it didn't matter how long; it didn't matter about time.

Forevermore, nevermore. All that is missing is the raven. The boy on the bike is the woman in white's suitor come home from his conscription in Mussolini's army to court his beloved now that her betrothed has died in suspicious circumstances.

From a cafe Don and the narrator watch the couple: "But they were gone now, with her white dress shaping her stride, her girl-white, not for us." Not for us! And she has departed with a soldier, which invites this curious exchange with the waiter: "'You have military in town,' Don said. 'That's right,' the waiter said. 'One.' 'Well, one is enough,' Don said. . . . 'Too many, some say,'" the waiter replies. The story has a running joke, repeated twice, about how happy the travelers are in Italy: "I love Italy. I love Mussolini," the narrator tells Don. The first time this joke is introduced, the two are speculating on why the soldier has returned home. To attend the funeral? Well, how would he know about the funeral? Perhaps the priest wrote to him? "Maybe so," Don says. To which the padrona, who turns out to be the soldier's aunt, says, "It is so." Is it so? Is there a plot against the deceased in favor of the returning soldier? But this is no more than an implication that the two Americans dare not investigate in Mussolini's Italy, which is why the narrator repeats: "No spika. I love Mussolini." They do not want to become involved in the kind of contretemps that put Spratling in prison. The "no spika" is the phrase the Americans have undoubtedly heard when Italians explain they speak no English, but "no spika" has now become code for not wishing to speak the unspeakable: a murder may have been committed. But the pressure against speaking out is so great that we cannot be sure, in fact, that a murder has been committed. This is just how closed up Mussolini's Italy has become. The details of what actually happened can never be determined any more than what precisely happened in the Nelse Patton lynching can be, because both stories occur in societies where the truth cannot be publicly spoken.

"Mistral" is about a girl and about youth, but in the context of becoming a story about something else: "You know: girls: they are not anything, then they are everything. You watch them become everything before your eyes." Girls become everything, including politics, and become everything because of the passion these two young men put into a story about what happens to those who attach themselves to her and the world they make. Don speaks of their youth in the past tense: "Because we were young. And the young seem to be impervious to anything except trifles. We can invest trifles with a tragic profundity, which is the world." Have they invested this village woman in white with an unwarranted tragic profundity, as youth are wont to do? But it is their youth, so important a factor in the success Quentin and Shreve have in breaking open the story of Thomas Sutpen, that allows the male couple in "Mistral" to crack, or at least expose, the code of fascist Italy, and that is no trifling thing.

"Mistral" is, as its title implies, chilling: "The closer they come to the epicenter of the tale they have heard—the priest's passion and anguish—the more intense is the icy wind and the aura of Gothic horror." That the two young men persist in spite of the Mussolinian blackout suggests, "Perhaps a secret of the artistic imagination is that it remains young, capable of enveloping reality plunging through and beyond it, enfolding it in transcendent beauty and transcendent terror."[5] But the story is also a confession of failure, as the wind bites into the two travelers, and the narrator muses on what they have done to themselves as much as on what has been done to them: "For we were young, and night, darkness, is terrible to young people, even icy driving blackness like this. Young people should be so constituted that with sunset they would enter a coma state, by slumber shut safe from the darkness, the secret nostalgic sense of frustration and of objectless and unappeasable desire."

"Mistral" is a symbolic representation of what traveling to Europe meant to Faulkner as a writer in the world: "It is of the first importance in 'Mistral' that the incidents described should be framed by the arrival and departure of the narrator and his companion—thus constituting a stage in a journey—and that they should be seen chiefly in their bearing upon the two transient observers rather than upon those figures directly involved."[6] Coming to terms with another culture, with how its people think and behave, as Quentin and Shreve do in their Harvard dormitory room, which is as frigid as the mountain village in "Mistral," becomes from this point on a constituent part of Faulkner's epistemology. The story is the fruition of all those letters home that reflect on the manners of Europeans and their American counterparts.

Mayday, a playful, anachronistic, prose pastiche of medieval romance, would seem the antithesis of the contemporary ambiguities in "Mistral." But the portrayal of Sir Galwyn setting out to liberate the lady of his dreams with a "bright smooth face wherein naught was as yet written" is another exploration of youth, desire, and disillusionment. Like Faulkner on his European Wanderjahr, Sir Galwyn is far from home, and his "young and hasty youth" shows as the knight encounters not a dragon or a giant but Father Time, who does not appear as old or with a long white beard, and who instructs the knight: "as any standard magazine will inform you, one's appearance depends purely on one's inclination or disinclination to change it."[7] The world is not as stable or predictable as Sir Galwyn has supposed. Like Elmer, Sir Galwyn supposed that "Fame awaits me." But like the struggling artist, Sir Galwyn is taken aback when Father Time asks, "But has it not occurred to you that every young knight who rides into this enchanted wood seeks a maiden whose hair is like bright water and who reminds him of young hyacinths, or perhaps of narcissi, or of cherry bloom?" In short, Sir Galwyn's quest is jejune and as derivative as Faulkner's own poetry. Even worse, Time asks which lady the knight is going to "deliver from captivity." Sir Galwyn is shocked to learn that there is more than one and that he might have to divide his quest, as Faulkner divided his between Estelle and Helen, both of whom, he seems to have realized, were valued as his own romantic projections as much as they were for themselves. "'It occurs to me,' young Sir Galwyn continued profoundly, 'that it is not the thing itself that man wants, so much as the wanting of it.'" Even more discouraging is Time's reporting of gossip—that Princess Aelia, for example, "left some talk behind her in Provence, not all of which was flattering." When he courts Princess Yseult, she responds: "Do you really think I am beautiful? . . . You say it so convincingly that I must believe you have said it before—I am sure you have said that to other girls. Now haven't you?" Faulkner presented his booklets to both Estelle and Helen, and Helen had a direct way of speaking that blasted through Faulkner's fanciful courting of her. Yseult's seasoned and skeptical treatment of Sir Galwyn, as well as her boredom with the "impossible Sir Tristram," sworn to defend her honor but bested in battle by Sir Galwyn, dismays her champion, who "began to be restlessly aware that young hyacinths were no longer fresh, once you had picked them." Hunger, one of Sir Galwyn's companions, anticipates Mr. Compson's defeatist philosophy that weighs down his shadow-haunted, suicidal son Quentin, explaining that life is "a ceaseless fretting to gain shadows to which there is no substance. To my notion man is a buzzing fly blundering through a strange world, seeking something he can neither name nor recognize and probably will not want." Sir Galwyn, no longer full of gall, rejected by yet another princess, Aelia— who scoffs, "how many girls have you told that to, Sir Galwyn?"—confesses he may have "said something like this to Yseult," and Aelia dismisses him with, "Oh, men are such children: any toy for the moment." A disgusted Sir Galwyn then formulates his own succinct Compsonian aphorism: "Man is a buzzing fly beneath the inverted glass tumbler of his illusions." *Mayday* ends with Sir Galwyn's suicide, drowning like Narcissus and Quentin Compson, a victim of his own quest where "there in the water was one all young and white," another woman in white, a reflection of himself he can possess only at the cost of his own life.

What Helen made of this ironic fairy tale cannot be told, and Faulkner's motivations are occluded. She had rebuffed a proposal of marriage, and yet he did not seem daunted, valuing a woman, like a Sir Galwyn princess, who speaks her mind and is not easily fooled and perhaps would enjoy a romantic quest turned into a sardonic sally. This handmade book, illustrated with both drawings and watercolors, reflects the melding of autobiography and a certain aesthetic conceit, which seems to figure Faulkner, in one drawing, as a faun piping his song at a nude slim woman in bobbed hair, her back turned to him, standing indifferent. Her stance recalls Sir Galwyn's preference for Princess Yseult, "seeing her back to front, naked or otherwise." This tongue-in-cheek allegory, which mixes medieval and modern, is the work of an increasingly confident and maturing artist engaging in a self-critique—like his first published novel, *Soldiers' Pay*, which appeared on February 25, 1926.

NATURAL MAN, THE GENTLEMAN, AND WAR

The novel's working title was *Mayday*. It features a kind of returning knight-errant, Donald Mahon, mortally wounded in the war, on the way home to die. The barely conscious Mahon is too far gone to wonder, as does Sir Galwyn, "if his restless seeking through the world had been only a devious unnecessary way of returning to a place he need never have left." The war is never made out to be a good cause, or any cause at all. Like Rebecca West's *The Return of the Soldier*, Faulkner's novel concentrates on the war's disruption of the home front. Like West's shell-shocked protagonist, Chris Baldry, who cannot remember much of his prewar adult experience, Mahon, going blind, does not recognize much of his former life.

This bleak novel sanitized, in some respects, the dirtier humor that English war veterans had patented. For example, Faulkner's unpublished draft includes this ditty:

> Who is lower than the dust,
> Whose arse is mud, whose balls is rust?
> Who sprung to be his land's defence
> And has been sorry ever since?[8]

The published novel:

> Who sprang to be his land's defense
> And has been sorry ever since?
> Cadet!
> Who can't date a single girl

Long as kee-wees run the world?
Kay—det!

Mahon's plight is contrasted with the frustrated Julian Lowe, "a flying cadet," who, like Faulkner, never saw combat: "they had stopped the war on him." The callow, egocentric Lowe, twenty-one at the end of the war, is, like Sir Galwyn, unable to prove himself and win his lady. That is Lowe's wound. The banter of returning soldiers on a train home disguises their anxiety. The sober, ominous, expectant tone of Faulkner's language is like nothing he wrote before: "Caught both in the magic of change they stood feeling the spring in the cold air, as if they had but recently come into a new world, feeling their littleness and believing too that lying in wait for them was something new and strange. They were ashamed of this and silence was unbearable."

An exchange between Cadet Lowe and Joe Gilligan, another returning soldier, arises right out of Faulkner's feelings about home and abroad. Lowe has been complaining that his mother wants him home, and Gilligan says: "Sometimes a man does want to see his family—especially if he don't hafta live with 'em. I ain't criticizing you. I admire you for it, buddy. But say, you can go home any time. What I say is let's have a look at this glorious nation which we have fought for." Lowe replies: "My mother has wired me every day since the armistice to fly low and be careful and come home as soon as I am demobilized. I bet she wired the President to have me excused as soon as possible." Gilligan, who could be speaking for Faulkner, answers: "Why, sure. Of course she did. What can equal a mother's love? Except a good drink of whisky." The brash Irish Gilligan announces, "We are among gentlemen to-day and we aim to act like gentlemen." And for all his bravado and rude behavior, Gilligan will fulfill the gentlemanly ideal, courting his lady and defending the honor and decency of his wounded fellow warrior, Donald Mahon. Gilligan does not seem to have served abroad. He makes no allusions to combat, so that it seems that Mahon is his man, a stand-in who has suffered in Gilligan's stead.

Like Faulkner's letters, the novel contains racial slurs and generalizations—in this instance, a depiction of a porter trying to treat the unruly soldiers correctly and compassionately: "With the instinct of his race the negro knew that his kindness was becoming untactful, yet he ventured again." The black man does his job with finesse and sensitivity. In early Faulkner, black people may be in the background, but they make society work.

The ravages of war rob Donald Mahon of his memories. He is profoundly still as Gilligan and Lowe talk and look at Mahon's face, "young, yet old as the world, beneath the dreadful scar." Like the stories begun on Faulkner's

European promenade, *Soldiers' Pay* depicts the destruction of youth that has marked Mahon and that Gilligan has survived and Lowe has yet to experience.

Gilligan speculates that Mahon has a girl who will give him "the air." When the idealistic Lowe protests, Gilligan declares: "You don't know women. Once the new has wore off it'll be some bird that stayed at home and made money, or some lad that wore shiny leggings and never got nowheres so he could get hurt, like you and me." Gilligan accurately forecasts what awaits Mahon when he returns to his girl. When Mrs. Henderson, a train passenger, stares at Mahon and asks if he is wounded, Gilligan tells her: "he fell off of a chair on to an old woman he was talking to and done that." The outraged matron, reflecting the "ruthless humanity of money," says she will report Gilligan to the conductor. "All right, ma'am," Gilligan says. "But you tell the conductor that if he bothers him [Mahon] now, I'll knock his goddam head off." Gilligan sits beside Mahon "in silent comradeship, the comradeship of those whose lives had become pointless through the sheer equivocation of events, of the sorry jade, Circumstance." There is nothing to be done, Gilligan tells the officious Mrs. Henderson, except to leave Mahon alone.

This opening scene establishes that the soldiers are returning to a world that cannot understand them any more than Faulkner's own family could understand his time in Canada, no matter how many letters he sent home. It is tempting to see Lowe as a former Faulkner self the novelist discards in this novel—except that he continued to play the part of wounded warrior after the publication of *Soldiers' Pay*.

Gilligan, like Shreve, is most emphatically not a southerner, and yet he realizes that Mrs. Margaret Powers, a southerner, does understand that he and Lowe will take care of Mahon "all right." Mrs. Powers says as much to Mrs. Henderson. Margaret Powers emerges out of Faulkner's earlier portrayals of enticing female figures: "She was dark. Had Gilligan and Lowe ever seen an Aubrey Beardsley, they would have known that Beardsley would have sickened for her: he had drawn her so often dressed in peacock hues, white and slim and depraved among meretricious trees and impossible marble fountains." If Mrs. Powers is depraved, she is so only in conventional society. She turns out to be Faulkner's dream of the complete, unattainable woman, so self-contained that she can find no room for the romantic interest that Gilligan will invest in her. She appears in triplicate, a projection of the narrator, Gilligan, and Lowe: "She was young: she probably liked dancing, yet at the same time she seemed not young—as if she knew everything. (She is married, and about twenty-five, thought Gilligan.) (She is about nineteen, and she is not in love, Lowe decided.)"

When the porter appears to check on Mahon, Mrs. Powers says, "He couldn't be in better hands than these gentlemen." An admiring Gilligan thinks: "How keen she is! . . . She has known disappointment." In fact, she has lost her husband, Richard, in France, a man she had known for only three days in the passionate desire of her youth to hold on to something in war. Just before he was killed, she wrote him a letter saying they were "better quit of each other with nothing to mar the memory of their three days together . . . wishing him luck." Her husband did not live to read the letter, and now she must live with the thought that he remained faithful to her. She lives now without illusions, refusing to confuse the exigencies of war with what she really desires.

Gilligan and Mrs. Powers converge in their concern over Mahon. Mrs. Powers asks, "Joe, do you know he's going blind?" He answers: "I know more than that. He's going to die." Gilligan has searched through Mahon's possessions and tells Mrs. Powers: "I got the low down on him, see. He's got a girl at home: folks got 'em engaged when they was young, before he went off to war. And do you know what she's going to do when she sees his face?" Mrs. Powers knows but doesn't want to believe it: "Oh, no, Joe. She wouldn't do that." Joe is unrelenting: "Don't you kid yourself. I've seen her picture. And the last letter he had from her." That letter, written by Cecily Saunders, "one of them flighty-looking pretty ones with lots of hair," is full of "all the old bunk about knights of the air and the romance of battle, that even the fat crying ones outgrow soon as the excitement is over and uniforms and being wounded ain't only not stylish no more, but it is troublesome." Gilligan is not "belittling the chivalry of air combat. He is ruing the fact that no modern woman is attracted to it."[9] Faulkner himself could wear his uniform only so long until it became a joke. The joke in the novel becomes Cadet Lowe, whose absurd love letters to Mrs. Powers are like a refrain that parallels Cecily's knights-of-the-air letter. Aviation is "in Lowe's mind clearly emblematic of sexuality, a badge of masculine achievement, and wings and flying are embroiled in his sexual fantasies about Margaret." But like Faulkner, he does not have the wings or the scar to show how he has been marked by war.[10] Margaret is the one who has a "red scar" of a mouth and has been wounded by war. Lowe's drinking seems a substitute for sex, as it may have been for Faulkner: "He gaped and his vitals coiled coldly in a passionate ecstasy." Frustrated sexual potency appears in his eyes, "like two oysters," when he is drunk and tries to speak with "quenchless optimism."

When Mrs. Powers is troubled that Joe has gone through Mahon's things, he hurries her along: "I mean, you and I know what to do for him, but if you are always letting a gentleman don't do this and a gentleman don't do that interfere, you can't help him. Do you see?" In fact, by doing what is right for Mahon, Gilligan is behaving like a gentleman, abiding by a noble standard of behavior that will replace the stultified, effete gentlemanly code that in later novels will debilitate characters like Gowan Stevens and hamper Horace Benbow and Gavin Stevens, a code that will have to be reformed again by Chick Mallison and V. K. Ratliff. Gilligan and Mrs. Powers agree that it is a rotten world and that they will make the best of it by accompanying Mahon to his Georgia home and helping him die in peace while Cadet Lowe returns to his family in San Francisco. At the same time, Gilligan and Powers are aiding their own rehabilitation. Mrs. Powers's identification of Mahon with her dead husband "becomes representative of her private search for expiation." She can remain faithful to Mahon as she could not be to Richard Powers. Similarly, Gilligan's "incipient relationship with Mrs. Powers opens possibilities for their romantic union" that helps him resume a civilian life.[11] First introduced as Yaphank, or just another type of returning soldier, Gilligan matures into the gentleman she has called him.

The very ideas of a gentleman, of fighting for a cause, of sacrificing self, and of love are subverted in the insidious figure of Januarius Jones, "born of whom he knew and cared not . . . lately a fellow of Latin in a small college." Like a satyr, he haunts the garden of Mahon's father, a kindly but ineffectual rector, a defeatist who has resigned himself to a faithless world, saying, "As I grow older, Mr. Jones, I become more firmly convinced that we learn scarcely anything as we go through this world, and that we learn nothing whatever which can ever help us or be of any particular benefit to us, even." This fatalism will reappear in Mr. Compson's philosophical reflections in *The Sound and the Fury.*

Jones seems ripped right out of *The Marionettes,* his face "a round mirror before which fauns and nymphs might have wantoned when the world was young." Why the rector tolerates Jones's lurking and leering behavior is not clear, especially since Jones looks at a photograph of Donald Mahon and says, "There is death in his face." And death in the tin box that holds Donald Mahon's possessions and a remnant of his passions: "a woman's chemise, a cheap paper-covered 'Shropshire Lad,' a mummied hyacinth bulb. The rector picked up the bulb and it crumbled to dust in his hand." The contents, a reader of Faulkner's life realizes, are what might have been left of him if he had made it to the western front: a copy of Housman, his favorite poet, the hyacinths of Sir Galwyn, and the disintegration of a romantic quest. The bond between Mahon and Faulkner is sealed when his own old mammy Caroline entreats him: "Donald, baby, look at me. Don't you know who dis is? Dis yo' Callie whut use ter put you ter bed, honey. Look here at me. Lawd, de white folks done ruint you, but nummine, yo' mammy gwine look after her baby." The cantankerous and candid Caroline Barr makes her appearance, suddenly churning up the novel's white world, the one that knows better and puts figures like Caroline in their place. Donald Mahon, who rarely speaks or is able to follow conversation, blurts out after Caroline's visit: "I've got to go home, Joe." Mahon is natural man, and closer to the black characters in the novel who escape the "blight of modern skepticism."[12] Mahon was happiest in the woods, sleeping in a sandy ditch where the black characters would find him. His affinity with nature, his "virile, sensitive, and sentimental" side expressed before the war, also makes him a romantic.[13]

Donald Mahon, however, has not always been a gentleman. He has seduced Emmy, although their interlude is treated as a natural occurrence that Emmy does not regret. She tells Mrs. Powers that Mahon told his father about Emmy. He "never lied about nothing he ever did," Emmy asserts. She now attends the rector and becomes the object of Jones's attentions, a warm-up for his pursuit of Cecily Saunders. Like goat-eyed Jones, Cecily seems taken from one of Faulkner's earlier illustrations: "She turned graceful as a flower stalk against the rector's black bulk." Mrs. Powers watches Cecily with the "passionate serene alertness of a faun" as Cecily leans "against the oaken branch of the rector's arm, believing that she is in love with the boy, or his illusion—pretending she is, anyway." As Gilligan predicted, Cecily already has another suitor, George Farr, whom she treats as the parody of a gentleman: "Take me home, kind sir," she says, refusing his embrace. Cecily is like the swaying poplars of Faulkner's love poems, a willowy, pliant creature who cannot sustain his devotion. When Cecily sees Donald Mahon's scarred face, she screams: "The light passing through her fine hair gave her a halo and lent her frail dress a fainting nimbus about her crumpling body like a stricken poplar. Mrs. Powers moving quickly caught her, but not before her head had struck the door jamb." The poplar, associated with the myth of Persephone and with regeneration, casts Cecily in a role she cannot fulfill: restoring Donald Mahon to health.[14]

We are not in Yoknapatawpha yet, but the small Georgia town post office in which the community converges—"embracing the professions with a liberal leavening of those inevitable casuals, cravatless, overalled or unoveralled"—resembles the world that circumscribed William Faulkner, and the world that Donald Mahon abandoned only to return a fatally injured hero. The former postmaster, now novelist, observes: "The mail was in and the window had opened and even those who expected no mail, who had received no mail in months must needs answer one of the most enduring compulsions of the

American nation." A courthouse, like the one in "The Hill" and familiar to readers of Yoknapatawpha fiction, is accorded its first full appearance:

> a simple utilitarian edifice of brick and sixteen beautiful Ionic columns stained with generations of casual tobacco. Elms surrounded the court-house and beneath these trees, on scarred and carved wood benches and chairs the city fathers, progenitors of solid laws and solid citizens who believed in Tom Watson and feared only God and drouth, in black string ties or the faded brushed gray and bronze meaningless medals of the Confederate States of America, no longer having to make any pre-tense toward labor, slept or whittled away the long drowsy days while their juniors of all ages, not yet old enough to frankly slumber in public, played checkers or chewed tobacco and talked. A lawyer, a drug clerk and two nonedescripts tossed iron discs back and forth between two holes in the ground.

A defeated society in sum, unprepared to reckon with Donald Mahon's return, but complete in itself, confronts the reader as it did in all its familiarity to Faulkner, imagining what it would be like to return home, no longer knowing or caring who Tom Watson, the Alabama populist champion of small farm-ers, was. "We have a beautiful town, Mr. Saunders," the rector says to Cecily's father. "These streets, these trees. . . . This quiet is just the thing for Donald." It is wishful thinking, of course, and hardly what Donald wanted for himself when he left town. And politics, so central to southern living, deserves only a mention and will remain on the periphery of Faulkner's Yoknapatawpha, not allowed to usurp the attention of its creator, even as it diverted his southern contemporaries.

Mrs. Powers discovers she has to conduct nothing less than a campaign to coax the revolted Cecily to return to Donald—not to resume their courtship, exactly, but to ease his final days. Extracting a promise from Cecily's father that he will do his best to encourage Cecily, Mrs. Powers runs "across the lawn toward the house before assaulting gray battalions of rain. Her long legs swept her up and onto the veranda as the pursuing rain, foiled, whirled like cavalry with silver lances across the lawn." Her courage is of another order than men like Donald showed in the war, but it is courage that honors his sacrifice.

Emmy, a stronger woman than Cecily, remains true to her memory of Donald and regards their earlier time together as an idyllic prelapsarian romance similar to the one depicted in "Adolescence." Emmy is like Juliet Bunden. Emmy tells Mrs. Powers: "When we was both younger we dammed up a place in a creek and built a swimming hole and we used to go in every day. And then we'd lie in a old blanket we had and sleep until time to get up and go home." As admirable and as serious as Mrs. Powers, Emmy capably fends off the advances of Januarius Jones, giving in once after she realizes Mahon is forever lost to her, but then rebuffing Jones again, who exhausts himself in pursuit of her.

Joe Gilligan continues to pursue Margaret Powers. They share a similar sensibility. Although she cares for him, she cannot reciprocate his love, thinking to herself: "Can nothing at all move me again? Nothing to desire? Nothing to stir me, to move me, save pity?" In a way, she is as dead as Donald Mahon; the war has done her in. Making Mahon's last days comfortable, bringing his life to some resolution, seems all that she can manage to do. She confirms what the reader has already concluded, telling Joe: "It isn't me that made you lose a night's sleep. I just happened to be the first woman you ever knew doing something you thought only a man would do. You had nice fixed ideas about women and I upset them. Wasn't that it?"

The war also stimulated all sorts of posing and pretending familiar to Faulkner and that Margaret is putting a period to, telling Joe:

> You remember how it was then—everybody excited and hysterical, like a big circus.
>
> So every night we went out to dinner and to dance, and after we would sit in my room and smoke and talk until all hours, till daylight. You know how it was: all soldiers talking of dying gloriously in battle without really believing it or knowing very much about it, and how women kind of got the same idea, like the flu—that what you did to-day would not matter to-morrow, that there really wasn't a to-morrow at all.

Soldiers' Pay puts paid to a kind of fantasy that Faulkner himself perpetuated. The war itself is depicted briefly and bitterly in passages that show corruption and confusion. Commissions are given away for political reasons, and during a gas attack a panic-stricken man shoots Richard Powers, an officer, in the face. A captain confesses: "I had to promise the mother of every goddam one of them that I'd look out for him and not let him get hurt. And now there's not a bastard one wouldn't shoot me in the back if he got a chance."

The shock of such gruesome scenes and sentiments is played against the dance that revolves around Cecily Saunders flitting from Donald Mahon to Januarius Jones to the sulking George Farr, tracking her as William Faulkner sometimes tracked Estelle Oldham. "From the outer darkness," George "glowered at her, watching her slim body cut by a masculine arm, watching her head beside another head, seeing her limbs beneath her silver dress anticipating her partner's limbs, seeing the luminous plane of her arm across his black shoulders and her fan drooping from her arched wrist like a willow at evening. He heard the rhythmic troubling obscenities of saxophones, he saw vague shapes in the darkness and he smelled the earth and things growing in it." Faulkner provides a stylized picture, especially in the phrase "watching her slim body cut by a masculine arm," reminiscent of his Ole Miss yearbook drawings. "Once Society drank war," the narrator opines, but now society wanted another beverage and expected something else of men, although the hangover of war makes it hard to see what these men should do. "I wonder where my easy rider's gone," the title of a blues song Faulkner would have heard W. C. Handy sing on the Ole Miss campus, becomes a refrain, expressing longing and loss as well as sexual desire. Readers in 1926 could have supplied more of the chorus: "He never told me he was goin' away / If he was here he'd win the race." There was a merging of black and white in a "period of reverse acculturation. . . . Aspects of the minority culture moved into the dominant one with an accumulative effect of transforming the majority," Thadious M. Davis writes apropos of *Soldiers' Pay*.[15]

Januarius Jones seems impervious to the music, a sure sign of his unnatural or perverted nature. He lounges in "slow and fat belligerence" to the "negro cornetist" who spurs "his men to fiercer endeavor" as "the brass died and a plaintive minor of hushed voices carried the rhythm until the brass, suspiring again, took it." Unmoved by the "fiercer endeavor" that is like a reverberation of the war Jones has not experienced, he sucks his pipe, "thrusting his hands" in a tweed jacket in a gesture familiar to Faulkner. To Jones, Cecily is a "white blur," another woman in white, as he tries to home in on her face for a kiss, and she resists, seeming as "fragile as a captured bird," just barely escaping the smell of wool and tobacco that Faulkner often exuded. *Soldiers' Pay* is not autobiography, but it is an album of the sights and smells and fantasies that filtered through the novelist's sensibilities and imagination.

Unable to hold Cecily, Jones dismisses her: "You are a fast worker, too fast for me. I doubt if I could keep up with the men you kiss and lie to, let alone with what you mean in each case. I don't think you can yourself." Cecily has indeed wavered in her resolution to stand by Donald Mahon, or elope with George Farr, or even submit to Jones's caresses. But to her, as to Estelle, most likely, this male resentment seems obtuse: "So you cannot imagine letting people make love to you and saying things to them without meaning anything by it?" As the rector tells Jones: "Women, women! How charming never to know exactly what you want! While we men are always so sure we do. Dullness, dullness, Mr. Jones. Perhaps that's why we like them, yet cannot stand very much of them. What do you think?" Cecily is a "body created for all men to dream after. A poplar, vain and pliant, trying attitude after attitude, gesture after gesture." Poplars with their soft, light wood and heart-shaped leaves perfectly expressed the novel's vision of a certain kind of woman made not "for maternity, not even for love: a thing for the eye and the mind." Estelle Oldham, Helen Baird, Cecily Saunders are all projections of the same aesthetic impulse, the elusive feminine that Jones cannot catch and crush. Similarly, Gilligan cannot convince Mrs. Powers to marry him, and she brings Donald Mahon's homecoming to a close by marrying the dying man.

An eloquent passage near the end of the novel is a triumph of the imagination but also of Faulkner's own flight training. Donald's last waking moment is also his dying moment, which is also his own triumph, what he has lived for in battle: "Day became afternoon, became dusk and imminent evening: evening like a ship, with twilight-colored sails, dreamed down the world darkly toward darkness. And suddenly he found that he was passing from the dark world in which he had lived for a time he could not remember, again into a day that had long passed, that had already been spent by those who lived and wept and died, and so remembering it, this day was his alone: the one trophy he had reft from Time and Space. Per ardua ad astra." "Through adversity to the stars," the motto of the Royal Air Force, becomes his obituary. He believes he has been on a long mission and is running out of fuel. The "staggered lower wing . . . partly shadowed by the upper one" tells him it is about ten in the morning. In Toronto, Faulkner had drawn a Curtiss JN-4 in his notebook, noting its "stagger."[16] Without ever saying so, Faulkner captures the shocked pilot's discovery of the enemy overhead: "In the moment of realizing this, cursing his stupidity, he dived steeply, slipping to the left. Five threads of vapor passed between the upper and lower planes, each one nearer his body, then he felt two distinct shocks at the base of his skull and vision was reft from him as if a button somewhere had been pressed." The vapor trails are made by magnesium and barium tracer bullets boring in ever closer until Donald feels their impact. Attacked from above and behind, he has no chance of escape. He takes in the near-death blow calmly as many pilots did. The mice that he hears gnawing through the frontal bone of his head are most likely "bullets striking his skull or, possibly, his head hitting the gun sights, which were only inches from the pilot's face."[17] This scene is profoundly shocking because it is so succinct. Donald Mahon has awakened to the climax of his life, and then he dies. Finally, Faulkner had an opportunity in his novel to say what Spratling no longer wanted to hear: "SEX AND DEATH: the front door and the back door of the world. How indissolubly are they associated in us!"

After Donald's death, Mrs. Powers leaves town, and Gilligan runs after her but cannot catch up. He returns to the rector, who may be "obsolete" but is also the symbol of a traditional culture that the war has disrupted. The rector in his carefully cultivated garden offers at least a "remnant of security."[18] That Margaret can only think to leave town reinforces the insight that so many of the characters in *Soldiers' Pay* long "for something beyond reach; each is engaged in the pursuit of the unattainable; each fastens upon some immediate goal"—like Jones pursuing Emmy, then Cecily; Gilligan pursuing Mrs. Powers; Cecily running to and from Mahon and to and from and to George Farr; and even Cecily's younger brother deterred from getting a good look at Mahon's scar, not to mention the thwarted Julian Lowe: "Each character in the novel is like the 'bold lover' on Keats's Grecian urn, who, though ever in pursuit, can never kiss."[19]

All along, underneath or beside the main action has been a black blues chorus that Gilligan hears as he passes cabins: "dark but from them came soft meaningless laughter and slow unemphatic voices cheerful yet somehow filled with all the old despairs of time and breath." The passage could have come out of Sherwood Anderson's novel *Dark Laughter* (1925), which portrays black people as more closely in touch with human elemental emotions and experiences than their white contemporaries. The final tableau brings together the rector, Gilligan, and their black counterparts into one congregation. It is what William Faulkner, returning home, told William Odiorne he wanted to hear: "They stood together in the dust, the rector in his shapeless black, and Gilligan in his new hard serge, listening, seeing the shabby church become beautiful with mellow longing, passionate and sad. Then the singing died, fading away along the mooned land inevitable with to-morrow and sweat, with sex and death and damnation; and they turned townward under the moon, feeling dust in their shoes." The novel's ending that puts the shabby black church in the foreground—a foreshadowing of the Faulkner to come—and the emphasis on "sex and death and damnation" did not endear him to his hometown. His father refused to read *Soldiers' Pay,* and his mother advised him to stay away from Oxford for a while. Billy's book had no appeal for readers of rousing westerns like Murry Falkner, or for those who reveled in the melodrama and sentimentality of *The White Rose of Memphis,* which elevates its female heroines as paragons of virtue. Perhaps most disturbing was the portrayal of Cecily Saunders, an inconstant southern belle who foreshadows the wayward Temple Drake. Faulkner had besmirched southern womanhood. Even the First World War in the defeated old Confederacy deserved a respect that the novelist did not display. Faulkner noted that only with the advent of World War I did the South really rejoin the Union, flying the country's flag from its public buildings. Here begins Faulkner's reputation as a decadent who defiles his native land's traditions and sentiments. Stark Young had just published *Heaven Trees,* a much more sedate and conventional novel, which now seems soporific but then appealed to those lolled into a genteel version of the Old South that Faulkner could not countenance.

Faulkner's outrageous novel came even closer to home for those who recognized that Mahon with his scar reminded them of brother Jack's head wound at a time in the war when his family thought he might be dead, and that Faulkner had given to Mahon's intended the name of Jack's wife. In other respects, the virtually catatonic Mahon is more like Faulkner in his frustrating silences. And what about the bulky, ineffectual, phlegmatic rector? Did gossip point the finger at Murry Falkner, who bore a slight resemblance to the character? Accurate or not, such correspondences get made. And was the novel fair to Estelle, or to Cornell Franklin, who, like George Farr, whisks the belle away from her hometown? Or did townspeople see Faulkner himself in Farr's drunken sprees, worrying that the indecisive Cecily might yet marry Donald Mahon? With fiction striking so close to home, it might not have occurred to Oxonians that a novel is symbolic and that Mahon, pronounced man, stood not for local characters but for a nation of men scarred by war. Certain passages could easily have triggered the community's view of the Oldhams—like that referring to Cecily's parents as Catholic, "almost as sinful as being a republican." But then how many in Oxford actually read the book? Ole Miss's library declined Phil Stone's offer of a free copy, although he managed to get the Gathright-Reed Drugstore to take copies on consignment and asked Liveright for "posters or reviews" to help him tout the book.[20] By May 19, the novel had sold a little over two thousand copies, a modest success.

Soldiers' Pay received a respectable reception for a first novel, although reviewers "tended to see it as an ineffective synthesis of the fictional styles of the time."[21] The word for Faulkner and his novel: "promising."[22] E. Harley Gratton, "A Book of Hatred" (*New York Sun,* April 3, 1926), described characters "thrown together in a fashion rather reminiscent of Dostoevsky. That is to say, haphazard." He found improbabilities in the plot: Why is Mahon on the train alone until he is taken up by Gilligan, Lowe, and Powers? In *Literary Digest* (July 4, 1926), Louis Kronenberger countered that the characters "probably had no real plans: a conventional world had crumbled, in mind and body and soul they were drifting, and to seize this tangible undertaking [returning Mahon to his home] was probably the nearest approach to adjustment they could have found." Gratton's reactions were not so different from those of polite society in Oxford, or perhaps in any small town, or even big city: "The whole passionate strength of his book is derived from his hatred [of sex]." Like so many subsequent reviewers of Faulkner's work, Gratton paid tribute to Faulkner's power, to his "passages of genuine beauty," even as the novelist's attitudes were deplored.

In the *Nashville Tennessean* (April 11, 1926), Donald Davidson, one of the Nashville-based Fugitive poets and later one of the Southern Agrarians, hailed Faulkner's powers of observation, calling him a "sort of poet tuned into prose." Unlike Dreiser, Faulkner did not write "as if he were washing dishes; nor like Sinclair Lewis, who goes at words with a hammer and saw." Davidson quoted this passage to make his point: "Solemnly the clock on the court-house, staring its four bland faces across the town, like a kind and sleepless god, dropped eleven measured golden bells of sound. Silence carried them away, silence and dark that passing along the street like a watchman, snatched scraps of light from windows, palming them as a pickpocket palms snatched handkerchiefs. A belated car passed swiftly." Davidson did not add that the clock, mentioned several times, is a structural device and not just there as a set piece. It not only sets up the rhythm and pace of a small southern town, but it also is marking the time until Donald Mahon's death, so that in a later culminating passage, "The clock went Life. Death. Life. Death." Davidson thought *Soldiers' Pay* superior to the much-celebrated *Three Soldiers* (1921) by John Dos Passos because Faulkner "digs deeper into human nature." Davidson realized that Faulkner had touched a nerve: "His book will baffle and perplex some people who read it. Or at least they will say they are baffled and perplexed, largely because they are disturbed at the very core of their being."

The anonymous reviewer in the *New York Times* (April 11) picked up on the many allusions to Greek mythology to say that the novel "tells an old story—as old as the Greek—and older—as old as war and its folly." Faulkner avoided a "dreary" naturalism, the "piling-up of details" by focusing on sharp contrasts of character with poignant beauty and "penetrating irony." On the contrary, Thomas Boyd, in the *Saturday Review of Literature* (April 24), com-plained about "strange humans" in a story "pitched unnaturally high; and as the tale continues it seems as if the author were struggling to break all con-tacts with the normal world and to vault upward into a sort of esoteric sphere of his own making." He called the disjointed dialogue "suspiciously reminis-cent of the mad dream of Leopold Bloom"—one of the earliest comparisons with James Joyce. Faulkner got high marks for vivid writing, but his prose seemed ungovernable, "slap-dash."

A brief, selling review appeared in four newspapers from the *Palm Beach Post* (West Palm Beach, Florida) to the *Arizona Daily Star*, announcing that the novel "deals brilliantly and ironically with what happened to many a vet-eran once the war had ended. It is the story of the seven years since the war, the tale of one who came out into a changed world and somehow could not

swing into the change. It is extremely well written." A much longer enthusiastic review by H. S. in the *Minneapolis Morning Tribune* positively reveled in Faulkner's iconoclasm, predicting his novel would make enemies of
readers who would throw it in the fire, calling it vile and incomprehensible.
Faulkner "doesn't ease his reader's journey by throwing bridges from episode
to episode." Those who did not want reading to challenge them would want
to smash Faulkner's face for the "insolence of his style, for its disregard of
fictional precedent. The style of *Soldiers' Pay* has a chip on its shoulder and 'I
dare you to read me' in its eye." Words like "insolence" and "disregard" certainly matched up the man and his work. The reviewer admired Faulkner's
irreverence and integrity, refusing to sentimentalize Mahon's death or to tidy
up the lives of his drifting characters. This reviewer anticipated later evalua-
tions of the novel that exposes a "value structure based upon sentimentality,
feminine delicacy, the glory of manhood through battle, rhetoric, and faithful love," which has degenerated into the "anti-values of lechery, selfishness,
and impotence." In this interpretation, Reverend Mahon "wanders confused
in a world which his generation all too clearly has made, his very optimism
the result of ignorance and his faith reduced to futility."[23]

In the *Atlanta Journal,* Margaret Mitchell, ten years before her success with
Gone with the Wind, wrote that *Soldiers' Pay* "strikes an entirely new note
in postwar fiction, for it tells of a different sort of home-coming—a home-
coming that will be especially interesting to southerners." Although she mentioned the novel's "crudities," she held it in high esteem and was untroubled
by its disturbing elements, nailing its foreboding quality in a sentence that
foreshadows much of what Faulkner would go on to write: "The atmosphere
of the small southern town where the duck-legged Confederate monument
ornamented the courthouse square, the red dust of the road settled thick on
the magnolia blossoms in the hot afternoon and the summer somnolence
pervading everything except the hearts of the characters, is perhaps the best
thing in the book."[24]

Like Joe Gilligan at the end of *Soldiers' Pay,* Faulkner could not stay at
home and cultivate his own garden while contending with his neighbors' animosity, or, like Margaret Powers, immediately entrain for elsewhere. According to Ben Wasson, Faulkner became "something of a celebrity, at least in our
immediate part of the South." He had been reviewed in national magazines
like the *New Republic,* and his work had appeared in the *Double Dealer* and
the *Times-Picayune.* The novel's frank treatment of sex shocked locals, and
"Faulkner was delighted at their outrage," Wasson recalled.[25] In fact, when
Faulkner paid a call on Miss Alice Mayer, then head librarian at the University of Mississippi, she said: "William, I never knew such a nice boy could

have so many ugly thoughts in his mind. I don't believe I would have loved you had I known." According to Mrs. J. C. McGehee, who was there, "William threw his head back and laughed more heartily than I believe I ever saw him laugh on any other occasion."[26]

The Decadent Hero

In the end, Faulkner took his mother's advice to get out of town, which also happened to be his inclination, and lit out for New Orleans, where the "reticent" novelist managed to accumulate an "astonishing number of lifelong friends."[27] Faulkner shared another house with Spratling, a dusty domain full of artist's paraphernalia (easels and palettes). Outside a dormer window, Faulkner built a precarious wooden platform, which seemed a kind of death-drop to one visitor who looked down on the alleys. He also climbed the wrought-iron balconies in the Quarter.[28]

Awaiting Faulkner's return was John McClure, who had announced in the *Times Picayune* (April 11, 1926) that Faulkner had written a "corking first novel on this theme of the return of the hero." In New Orleans, Faulkner could think of himself as a hero as he could not do in Oxford. McClure's review heralded one of the newspaper's own, mentioning the tales and sketches and poetry of promise. McClure made light of defects: "incoherent development of the theme, rather random motivation. . . . Dialogue, often delightful, is not always convincing." Even so, "none of the younger novelists, and few of the older" wrote as well as Faulkner. McClure also noted that even when characters spoke as they would not actually express themselves, "there is nevertheless a symbolic truth in the byplay"—an observation that would apply to later novels like *As I Lay Dying*.

No one in decadent New Orleans would be bothered by the subtle pornography in *Soldiers' Pay*. In Oxford, perhaps the impact of certain sentences was only subliminal. When Joe Gilligan tries to make love to Margaret Powers, she demurs, but what he desires is graphic: "Her black hair and her mouth like a pomegranate blossom." Did the fruit's ovary-like appearance and the supposed arousing effect of its juice stimulate libidos in a small southern town? Recalling her lovemaking with Richard Powers, Margaret exclaims: "Kiss me, kiss me through my hair. Dick, Dick." The repetition of "Dick" is followed by her ambivalent, tormented ecstasy entwined and split in two with an aroused member of the male sex: "My body flowing away from me, dividing. How ugly men are, naked. Don't leave me, don't leave me! No, no! we don't love each other! we don't! we don't! Hold me close, close: my body's intimacy is broken, unseeing: thank God my body cannot see. Your body is so ugly, Dick! Dear Dick. Your bones, your mouth hard and shaped as bone: rigid." Margaret is not prepared to go through this kind of intimate encounter with another male, no matter how much she admires Joe. The very idea of writing such scenes would not be discussed in polite Oxford society any more than Narcissa Benbow can discuss with Miss Jenny the pornographic letters Narcissa receives in *Flags in the Dust*. The sex in *Soldiers' Pay* scandalized Maud Falkner, although like many of Faulkner's readers she eventually caught up with him. When she died, a copy of *Lady Chatterley's Lover* was at her bedside.

The Faulkner-Anderson friendship had subsided. On April 29, Anderson wrote to Horace Liveright that Faulkner was "so nasty to me personally that I don't want to write him myself, but would be glad if you were to do it in this indirect way, as I surely think he is a good prospect."[29] Anderson had moved on to Virginia, purchasing a small farm in the southwestern part of the state. There, at least in fiction, Faulkner followed him, writing a story that reads like a companion piece to "A Meeting South" and suggests how the twenty-seven-year-old Faulkner managed to disrupt the equilibrium of Sherwood Anderson's well-established life.

Faulkner and Anderson Finis

An Anderson-like figure, Roger Howes, "fattish" and forty, secludes himself in a house in the "Valley of Virginia." The rural retreat is the writer's antidote to the phoniness of New York literary life, although his years there follow him in the form of mooching writers who turn up to take residence and trash his rustic hideaway. Howes welcomes these spongers, needing their stimulus to write, just as Anderson craved the company of younger writers.

Then Howes promises his put-upon wife, Anne, that he will no longer entertain these "eager and carnivorous tymbesteres of Art," but he succumbs to a persistent young poet, John Blair, who arrives, limping like Faulkner's wounded poet-pilot persona, in a "sky-blue coat," so slight that a local wonders if he will fly rather than walk the four miles to the Howes' house. Blair appears with no baggage—just two shirts and an extra pair of socks, saying to the startled Mrs. Howes, "Your cook can wash, can't she?" For all his threadbare look, he is a dandy and a southern gentleman, convinced of his own importance. Howes tries to mollify Anne, suggesting the house will benefit from the "mellifluous overtones and subtleties" that accompany poets. But what can such a poverty-stricken poet want from a commercially successful writer like Howes except to be fed? Advice? "Not advice," Howes replies to his wife: "You must have gathered at supper what his opinion of my mentality is." Here the haughty Faulkner appears, as does his penchant for consorting with black people. Mrs. Howes observes: "He revealed pretty clearly what his own mentality is. The only thing in the house that really pleased him was Pinkie's colored head-rag." She is the black cook whose company Blair craves. After two weeks, Anne notices he has supped with Pinkie's family and attended their prayer meetings several times: "I am imagining right now that sky-blue dressing-sacque in a wooden church full of seated niggers without any incongruity at all." Blair, in fact, is most comfortable in just such settings, seeing no contradiction in his aesthete's clothing and down-home tastes—so peculiarly different from the behavior of his fellow writers and those who have exploited Howes's hospitality. Faulkner as invading presence in the lives of the Andersons is vividly transformed in this made-up scene: "He enters the room which the children are absolutely forbidden and puts his one finger on that typewriter which Pinkie is not even permitted to touch with a dust-cloth, and writes a poem about freedom and flings it at you to commend and applaud." And, even worse, Blair tosses the poem at Howes "like flinging caviar at an elephant, and he says, 'Will this sell?'" This is the Faulkner who would boast in letters to his mother about making money from writing and used Anderson as a measuring stick and promoter. Blair's crass ambition leads the wife to call him a "Young Shelley [who] has not crashed through yet." Her husband assures her that Blair will: "Give him time." Just when she seems worked up to denounce this interloper, she bursts out: "Damn, Damn. Damn. He doesn't eat enough." Anne, it turns out, has this maternal side, the Elizabeth Prall Anderson side, a woman, as Faulkner reported to Maud, who mothered him. Mrs. Howes joins Mrs. Anderson and Aunt Sally, the madam who mothers David/Faulkner in "A Meeting South."

Like Faulkner and Prall, Blair and Anne become a kind of couple, as Blair, on the days when there are no prayer meetings, dopes along with Anne in the garden, talking about poetry, freedom, and flowers while preparing for "the clinch," a pass that she rebukes: "You damned idiot!" Nothing like this pas de deux seems to have enveloped Prall and Faulkner, but they nevertheless had shared a bond before Anderson had even met Faulkner, and Faulkner had encamped in the Anderson residence before Anderson had an opportunity to discover him. As Faulkner said to his mother, fiction is a reordering of reality. Just so, Blair stands in front of Anne, waiting for her to strike him, "offering her a clean shot." A pass, in his gentlemanly code, must be punished. In similar fashion as a man of honor he tells Roger: "Tonight I kissed your wife. I'm going to again, if I can." Roger, who has Anderson's bluff temperament, tells Blair: "I'm afraid I can't advise you about that. I have written a little poetry, but I never could seduce women." Howes wants

Blair to sleep on it: "We'll talk about this tomorrow." But Blair declares, "I cannot sleep under your roof." After Blair departs, Roger begins typing what becomes, it seems, an account that is, or at least resembles, the story the reader is absorbing even as it is written. Blair returns to court Anne, saying that he has nothing and that she is everything to him. "The only thing he remembers of his mother," she tells Roger, "is the taste of sherbet on Sunday afternoon. He says my mouth tastes like that. He says my mouth is his mother." That kind of need may not have ever been expressed to Elizabeth Prall Anderson, but Faulkner's letters to his mother make clear how much Elizabeth cosseted him. "He's never lived," Anne tells her husband, describing Blair as a kind of love-starved Pierrot or Prufrock. Anne believes the lovesick Blair, who stands outside her house in a downpour, will drown (like Shelley), but he refuses her aid and Roger's. Blair does indeed drown in sorrow and die while Roger continues to type the story about "Him, and Anne, and the poet. Word for word . . . with a few changes here and there because live people do not make good copy."

For Anderson, Faulkner really put himself out, as he did for a select few. And Anderson reciprocated by making Faulkner, as David in "A Meeting South," a figment of Anderson's imagination. Does Howes actually engineer Blair's interest in Anne in order to create material for a story? Are Blair and Howes collaborators or adversaries? It is hard to tell: "We do not know what Roger writes and we do not know what, if anything, he *feels* about Anne and John, whether he feels anything at all about his cuckolding, or whether it is very difficult to control those feelings in order to channel them into his fiction."[30] And the same can be said in the realm of biography. We do not know, and Faulkner and Anderson did not say, how fraught their triangle became, and Elizabeth Prall Anderson did not disclose anything more in her own memoir. Anderson may have felt cuckolded even if, as seems likely, Faulkner did not make love to Elizabeth, since, like Anne, she did not desire sex but to make sure the artist felt at home. In the Faulkner-Anderson New Orleans axis, their imaginations could take them anywhere, as in the Al Jackson tall tales, as in "A Meeting South" and "Artist at Home." The protean nature of their friendship, governed by the need to remain gentlemen and writers, is what bound them together and tore them apart. Lothar Hönnighausen's comment on Roger Howes and John Blair applies as well to Sherwood Anderson and William Faulkner: "Both gentlemen, being artists: the one doesn't want the other to get wet; the other whose conscience won't let him wreck the house from inside."[31] Like Howes acknowledging Blair's promise, Anderson never doubted Faulkner was a "thoroughbred colt" and was even prophetic in predicting Faulkner would need "a race or two before he can do his best." Exactly how Faulkner offended Anderson is not clear, but Mrs. Anderson's memoir makes clear how high-handed and Blair-like Faulkner could be.

Why does Blair have to die for love? John Irwin writes of Faulkner's "troubadouresque" attachments in which the "love object is idealized and often unattainable or is ultimately denied to the lover (because he is rejected), an amorous involvement in which the lover's devotion is absolute, the measure of his life the suffering it causes, and the ultimate form of his love is a consummation that is death, a *Liebestod*." Like Faulkner chez Anderson, Blair can find no place for himself, no home. Similarly, Faulkner had to move out of the Anderson home, and then they moved on to Virginia, leaving Faulkner's affection for them unrequited or perhaps suspended in the imagination of the writer who created "Artist at Home."

So when Faulkner found a new room in Spratling's house, he may have alleviated the buildup of certain tensions in the house of Anderson but also exacerbated his own juvenile resentments. Critic Melvin Bradford notes that Blair's immaturity is a "foil to Roger's mature creative rejuvenation." Anderson was more like an older brother than a father to Faulkner, a Charles Bon to Henry Sutpen in the hothouse of New Orleans. Anderson and Faulkner do not share a sister, as Charles and Henry do, but the Sherwood-Bill bond had been mothered by Elizabeth. Blair is so wrapped up in his love for Anne that she might be called, in Irwin's terms, a "narcissistic love-object"[32] in Blair's love poem, published after his death.

SHERWOOD ANDERSON AND OTHER FAMOUS CREOLES

In December 1926, Pelican Press issued four hundred copies of the Spratling and Faulkner spoof *Sherwood Anderson and Other Famous Creoles,* taking their inspiration from *The Prince of Wales and Other Famous Americans,* which had just appeared. In Spratling's caricatures, the leading lights of the French Quarter, the "artful and crafty ones," Spratling noted, were drawn in presumably customary poses, including a dumpy, burly Sherwood Anderson seated in a chair looking a bit miffed, his legs drawn up and his hands clasped about his knees, a copy of his autobiography, *Tar,* on the floor to his left and a walking stick beneath his legs. He is a potentate suited up in vest and tie, prepared to receive an audience. In another sketch, lanky Oliver La Farge, wearing moon-shaped glasses, is sprawled out in an armchair, pipe in hand reading *Scribner's,* with his right, impossibly long leg curving outward. William Odiorne is seated at a cafe, peeking out from a newspaper, apparently on the lookout for interesting subjects. Spratling included himself and Faulkner in a kind of huddle over a table, Faulkner with a drink, in three-quarter profile, his aquiline nose prominently displayed, a big-nosed man like one of his favorite characters, Cyrano, whom Faulkner would quote when telling Helen Baird, "your name is like a golden bell hung in my heart," a line he also used in *Mosquitoes* and later with other women. Spratling is shown head-on, with ink pot and pen, an air rifle hanging on the wall and Faulkner's corn liquor jugs underneath his chair. In his foreword, Faulkner observed: "One trouble with us American artists is that we take our art and ourselves too seriously. And perhaps seeing ourselves in the eyes of our fellow artists, will enable those who have strayed to establish anew a sound contact with the fountainhead of our American life."

Spratling recalled Anderson's response when they presented the book to him: "He turned it over, looked inside, scowled and said, 'I don't think it is very funny.' Sherwood was taking himself very seriously at that time. He had recently been referred to by a critic as the 'Dean of American Literature.'"[33] Elizabeth Prall Anderson said biographers had made too much of Anderson's "grievously wounded" reaction: "Actually, Sherwood had forgotten all about it in a short time, and no one was radically affected by it in any way."[34]

If Anderson was sore, it was because Faulkner perfectly caught the older writer's blend of pomposity, verbosity, and condescension in the guise of wishing to be helpful and encouraging. In the foreword, Faulkner treated Spratling as Anderson had treated Faulkner: "When this young man, Spratling, came to see me, I did not remember him. Perhaps I had passed him in the street. Perhaps he had been one of the painters at whose easel I had paused, to examine. Perhaps he knew me. Perhaps he had recognized me when I paused, perhaps he had been aware of the fellowship between us and had said to himself, 'I will talk to him about what I wish to do; I will talk my thought out to him. He will understand, for there is a fellowship between us.'" Since Spratling was only three years younger than Faulkner, the joke was even better. Faulkner, hardly the dean of anything, seemed to be twitting his own tendency to assert his authority in the absence of much significant achievement. Still he had declared his independence from Anderson, who no longer felt needed or wanted by this rude young man. To be laughed at is no fun, and yet reading the foreword is fun, and a writer like Anderson would know that, and resent it.

A LABOR OF LOVE

In the early spring of 1926, Faulkner returned to Oxford for Dean's graduation from high school, and perhaps to save expenses, since his novel was not going to make that much for him. He saw a bit of Estelle, home again from the Far East, exhibiting more signs of an estrangement from her husband. Faulkner resumed his rounds on the Ole Miss golf course, but he yearned for a more hospitable and quiet place to write. New Orleans already seemed a passing phase, he wrote to Helen Baird: "I don't come back much because I had more fun there than I ever will have again anywhere now."

On June 4, Faulkner wrote a letter to his publisher asking for fifty dollars to allow him to spend the summer in Pascagoula working on his second novel, *Mosquitoes,* which he said was half-done and better than *Soldiers' Pay,* "better articulated" and "sustained." He thought he could double the sales of his previous novel. Several discerning readers of his manuscript agreed, he told Liveright.[35] At Pascagoula he stayed in the Stone family cottage writing his novel. He dedicated a volume of poems to Helen Baird, *Helen: A Courtship,* but she was not there, having departed with her mother on a European tour. Faulkner shared his feelings with Helen's aunt, Mrs. Martin, a sympathetic, perceptive, and candid woman with an excellent sense of humor and a son, Edward, who became "absolutely devoted" to Faulkner. Mother and son seemed to enjoy the way Faulkner would "take either side of an argument just to see how the person he was talking with really felt and thought."[36] They formed a kind of cordon around Faulkner's feelings and drew him out, as did his devotion to his youngest brother, Dean, who drove his mother to Pascagoula to spend a week with Billy.

In this comforting enclave Faulkner reenacted the drama of his romantic attachment to Helen, as he did more graphically in *Helen: A Courtship.* This hand-lettered Faulkner-bound volume reworked earlier poems and introduced new ones—numbered and centered on re-creating a romance with Helen as he had imagined it during his European summer of 1925. The sequence of sixteen poems identified by place and month shifted from June in Pascagoula to July in Majorca to August in Genoa, Pavia, and Lago Maggiore, and to September in Paris. The first seven poems culminated in his proposal to Helen and its aftermath. In the first poem, he turned his vision of her swimming into an epic event played out in the confines of her body: "Hands of water hush with green regret / The brown and simple music of her knees."[37] In the second poem, "Bill," Helen's presence calms him, and in memory she becomes a refuge for his silence: "Like silver ceaseless wings that breathe and stir / More grave and true than music, or a flame / Of starlight, and he's quiet, being with her." Faulkner once asked Helen's aunt what she thought of her: "She said she didn't quite know. She asked him what he thought of Helen, and he said 'As an amber flame.'"[38] In the fourth poem, he includes her in the pre-Christian satyr/faun nexus of his early poetry and *Soldiers' Pay* as both satyr and faun dream of making love to her. The former "Dreams her body in a moony night / Shortening and shuddering into his," and the faun "bolder than the rest" slides "his hand upon her sudden breast," although his passion "Gutters and faints away" in the cold night and "bitter wanton grass." In "Proposal," the fifth poem, Faulkner likens her "honeyed hips" to "little moons" he would "break" in the "hushed virginity / Of sleep." Sexual desire figures in an image of "her narrow house," where she finds him "drowsing when she came awake." This arousal as in a sexual climax, and the poem's reverie of desire, is abruptly broken by a voice that asks: "Sir, your health, your money: How are they?" The sixth poem identifies the speaker as "Madam"—presumably Helen's mother quizzing Faulkner on his prospects. "My health," Faulkner responds, is a "fevered loud distress," which segues into his query to Madam: "Did your knees ever sing / Like her's in passing with such round caress / And parting, with such sweet reluctance cling?"

What did Helen make of all this passion that seems eighteenth-century pornographic in its portrayal of her spreading knees and maternal chaperoning? Was she supposed to be flattered, amused? Helen later said she did not even bother to read the book of her courtier. Part of the problem is that some of the poems are so opaque, part of a private language that perhaps he shared with Helen alone, or even just with himself. Or perhaps all that mattered was to show her as his inspiration. If not in the flesh, in the word he had possessed her. To her demurrals: "Ah no, ah no: my sleep is mine, mine own / And I'll not share it: I'll not make it twain," he responds at the end of the tenth poem: "So you no virgin are, my sweet unchaste: / Why I've lain lonely nights and nights with you." In his sleep, in his dreams, he had her with him; she was the world to him (eleventh poem). She was the breath of life to him, the flesh of his being (twelfth poem), and he could part with her only in death.

Helen: A Courtship conflates the loss of Helen with the loss of youth: "Somewhere is youth, a grave sweet mouth to kiss— / Still, you fool, lie still: that's not for you." These lines that are followed with the identifier: "PARIS— SEPTEMBER—1925" seem to put a historical period to the courtship, ending in the fifteenth poem: "Knew I love once? Was it love or grief / This young body by where I had lain?" The Romantic and the Realist remain in flux as the poet counts "one by one those years" that "Bell their bitter note," but also clings to "one stubborn leaf that will not die / But restless in the wild and bitter earth, / Gains with each dawn a death, with dusk a birth." In *Helen: A Courtship* Faulkner remained caught in the cycle of sex and figurative death, the reality of the days when her rejection could not be denied, and the birth of that love that came to him at night. *Helen: A Courtship* wrests a literary feat out of a lover's defeat. Unlike Sir Galwyn, Faulkner was not suicidal; his work thrived on unrequited love.

Ben Wasson visited Faulkner in Oxford in the fall of 1926 just as the author received the galleys of *Mosquitoes* and learned that Liveright wanted changes to appease the censors. Faulkner respected his publisher's professional opinion but did not like skirting matters such as lesbianism and incest, and the bit about an outdoor privy that had to be made "less graphic and vivid," thus ruining it, the bitter novelist said. Wasson, reading the galleys, heard Faulkner running up the stairs: "He stared at me from the doorway, his eyes keen, mobile, and birdy. His cheeks were deeply flushed, and there was that fury in his eyes. He held out a letter to me." Liveright had written to say Miss Maud had accused the publisher of withholding royalties from her son. Billy needed the money, and she evidently had taken action because he knew nothing about "financial affairs." Her livid son told Wasson: "All women should be made to do a big tub of washing every day. Maybe that way they'd be too busy to interfere with what other people are doing." Wasson did not know what to say as his worked-up friend declared, "Godamighty, fellow, if there's anything that upsets the world, it's people who do things because they consider it's 'well meaning.'" But almost as soon as he erupted he subsided, freeing a tactful Wasson to say, "After all . . . she is your mother." They went off on a long walk so that Faulkner could calm down. Along the way, he told Wasson about Helen Baird. Wasson had met her at dances in Sewanee, where he went to school with her brother Pete. Faulkner could only say, "It's hell being in love, ain't it?"

Faulkner liked to talk with Wasson's mother, although she only read light romantic novels. She advised him to write love stories that appealed to women who, after all, made up the majority of book readers. "Maybe they do," Faulkner replied, "but I don't write for readers. I write for myself and because I have to." Mrs. Wasson leveled with him. She had not been able to read *Soldiers' Pay:* "It's way over my head, and what I read was ugly." Faulkner grinned and replied: "I never said it was pretty, and anyhow, I couldn't read it now, either. So we're even." True? Perhaps. He was always on to the next book or story, believing he could do better and that he had failed to achieve his ambition.

It may have been during this period that the exotic Estelle returned home for one of her periodic visits. Ben Wasson knew the Oldhams and was there to witness what an event her homecoming became for townfolk "agog with excitement" as Estelle appeared with her young daughter, Victoria, and a Japanese nurse in traditional dress, including an obi around her waist, and a large bow in the back. "I was nearly spellbound by my first sight of her," Wasson admitted. A "constant open house" at the hospitable Oldhams featured an "effervescent and welcoming Estelle" at tea, served by the Japanese nurse. Ben remembered Bill telling him a "ridiculous tale, then current, that oriental women were sexually different from occidental women, being 'made on the bias.'" Like his fanciful stories about mulattos, Faulkner loved to indulge in such lewd nescience. Both Wasson and Faulkner speculated that a few of the local lechers tried to seduce Estelle. On October 29, the other Faulkner, the gentleman, still assembling books of the courtier, bound together a collection of his New Orleans sketches with the dedication: "To Estelle, a Lady, with Respectful Admiration."

Estelle entertained her guests at the piano. During one of her performances, alone with Wasson, he watched as she "rose from the piano stool, put her arms around my shoulders, and we spontaneously kissed." Then Victoria (Cho-Cho) appeared, calling to her mother, as the couple broke from their embrace, and Wasson left the scene "as quickly as I could get away." He worried that Victoria might say something, and he blurted out what had happened to a musing Faulkner, who said: "Watch out, and remember, Bud, that Eve wasn't the only woman who handed out an apple, just the first one."[39] But Estelle returned to her husband.

The return to Cornell Franklin was short-lived. In January 1927, Estelle appeared again in Oxford with her children but no nurse or the other accoutrements that graced her life abroad. The marriage was over, and divorce papers had been filed. It seems that she had never really loved her unfaithful husband. She told a friend, "While Cornell had his lovers in China, you don't think I was sitting at home, do you?"[40] He had his own complaints about Estelle, vouchsafed to an Oxford confidante: "If you could only tell when she's telling the truth. She lies all the time." The couple's life had dissolved into quarreling, gambling, and drinking—"a fast life in a fast set," Estelle noted. She arrived in Oxford on one of her visits with bandaged wrists, provoking talk of a suicide attempt. Yet she had also written a novel, and Faulkner had been encouraging, persuading her, he wrote Horace Liveright on February 18, to give the publisher "first shot at it. I think it is pretty fair."[41] When Liveright rejected the novel, a furious Estelle burned the manuscript.[42] "I wrote one book in my life," she told an interviewer after her husband's death. "I thought it was grand. I sent it to a publisher, but it came back awfully quickly. I was so offended. It was summertime and we lived in an old frame house. I forgot the chimney had been stuffed with paper—we didn't have dampers back then. I sat down with a box of matches and I burned the manuscript page by page. Before I knew it, I had set the house on fire." If true, this was an apocalyptic end to her writing career with repercussions she never seems to have acknowledged.

Copies of her stories survive, revealing a sensitive portrayal of a woman abroad, unafraid of other cultures and foreign lovers. Faulkner worked with her on her stories and submitted at least one of them for publication.[43] How Faulkner regarded these joint efforts is not clear, although a good case can be made that his reading of Estelle's fiction, which dealt with bisexuality and racism, is reflected in a lesbian episode Liveright deleted from *Mosquitoes,* and in Faulkner's subversive treatments of race, sex, and marriage in the work he was about to begin.

Faulkner seemed in no position support Estelle financially, if marriage was then on his mind. The impecunious author made do with manual jobs and small loans from Phil Stone, still quite active in touting Faulkner's work, and predicting a glorious future. On a copy of *The Marble Faun* dated 1927 and inscribed by Faulkner to Estelle's sister Dorothy, Stone added: "Dot, you keep this book. Someday this tramp will be famous." In February, Faulkner wrote twice to the poet and anthologist William Stanley Braithwaite, asking this well-known New England literary figure for advice. The Four Seas Company had not paid eighty-one dollars in royalties, and Faulkner was seeking a way to "collect this money without resorting to legal means," which he could not afford. "It never occurred to me that anyone would rob a poet. It's like robbing a whore or a child"—all dependents on the patronage or the care of others.[44]

THE DARK TWIN OF A MAN

Mosquitoes, published on April 30, 1927, and dedicated to Helen Baird, departed from the tone and style of *Soldiers' Pay.* This second completed novel seemed shadowed by a state of disenchantment. After learning that his beloved Helen intended to marry Guy Lyman, Faulkner wrote to Horace Liveright about the dedication: "I made the promise some time ago, and you can lie to women, you know, but you cant break promises you make 'em. That infringes on their own province." He was writing, after all, in a world where women could still sue for "breach of promise."[45] A woman might be free to change her mind, as Estelle had done, but not the man. He nursed his grievances in literature. As a character says in *Mosquitoes:* "But people do not die of love. . . . You do not commit suicide when you are disappointed in love. You write a book."

The novel also allowed Faulkner to air out ideas about art and artists that were stillborn in *Elmer,* too limited by a "single character and his history."[46] Now he created a dialectical narrative with competing accounts of the literary/artistic life, positioning characters at polar opposites, such as the garrulous novelist Dawson Fairchild and the taciturn sculptor, given only one name: Gordon. Although Gordon has been discussed as Faulkner's stand-in, exposing the futility of arguments about art, many of Fairchild's comments can be cited as similar to Faulkner's own beliefs in the power of words.[47]

Mosquitoes had its origins in a Lake Pontchartrain outing Faulkner had taken with Sherwood Anderson and company, resulting in going aground, sunburns, vicious mosquito bites, and other adventures in a kind of ship of fools rodomontade of bohemian and society types. William Spratling said he had a "fine time and so had Bill." Elizabeth Prall Anderson did not remember anything eventful during the excursion.[48] Onshore, the art crowd might be tolerable in small doses, but to be in the same boat with artists and their patrons and hangers-on could not have entertained Faulkner, except as material for a book. As much as New Orleans had stimulated his genius, the novel also seems a kind of farewell and critique. *The Double Dealer* had suspended publication, signaling an end to an era. Like *Sherwood Anderson and Other Famous Creoles, Mosquitoes* seals up a phase in several lives. Anderson moved on to Virginia, and Spratling headed for Mexico.

New Orleans, now viewed as history, provoked mixed feelings. Visitors from New Orleans to Oxford never knew whether to expect a good or bad reception. "Sometimes he did not seem to remember people or want to see them," Marjorie Gumbel said. She was told about a visitor from the "old days" who reported a rude, cold, and unresponsive Faulkner.[49] Referring to *Mosquitoes,* he told his mother, "This one is going to be the book of my youth." A renovated French Quarter presaged the commercialization of art that Faulkner, the tramp, traduced. Art as an industry of producers and consumers disturbed him, as he makes clear in a scene when Josh, Patricia Robyn's brother (the characters are modeled after Helen Baird and her brother), is working on a pipe that will burn all its tobacco without becoming hot. Josh's invention comes to the attention of Major Ayers, a British entrepreneur who wants to turn Josh's pipe into profits. Josh is an artist-craftsman fixated on his carved/sculptured piece and not on its monetary value.

The novel resembles, in format, Aldous Huxley's dialogic *Chrome Yellow* (1921), one of the novels Phil Stone purchased and that Faulkner probably read, perhaps identifying with the unrequited love of failed poet Denis Stone for Anne, who seems as oblivious of Denis's feelings as Helen Baird was of Faulkner's. Huxley, in turn, borrowed from Thomas Love Peacock (1785–1866), the inventor of the English country house novel, in which an array of characters represent different temperaments and philosophical/esthetic positions while binging on the hospitality of their wealthy host. Like Peacock and Huxley, Faulkner confected a dialectical novel, one that spreads out over several days of a yachting excursion, presided over by the bumptious

Mrs. Maurier, who collects artists: the smug novelist Dawson Fairchild and his interlocutor, the Semitic man Julius Kauffman; the arrogant sculptor Gordon, who has the hawk face of a Sartoris and a Faulkner; the irresolute and unproductive poet Mark Frost, who nevertheless has a bit of Faulkner in him ("I am the best poet in New Orleans"); the love-starved painter Dorothy Jameson; as well as Major Ayers, "the complete stage Englishman,"[50] who has a plan to sell his "salts" to constipated Americans; Mrs. Maurier's feisty niece Patricia Robyn and her besotted lover, David; another feckless southern gentleman, Ernest Talliaferro; the nubile Jenny and her surly suitor, Pete; the shrewdly observant Eva Wiseman; and one swamp-water miscreant who treats this shipboard society with the contempt that Faulkner himself showed in the company of New Orleans patrons of the arts. Much has been made of characters who are supposedly based on the men and women Faulkner knew in New Orleans, and while such resemblances can be detected, in the main the connections to actual people seem beside the point. Dawson Fairchild, supposedly a stand-in for Sherwood Anderson, does talk with Anderson's blithe confidence, but he is really just part of a menagerie and not the main show. Anderson had assembled an excursion on Lake Ponchartrain, but by making him just one of Mrs. Maurier's company, the focus shifts away from Fairchild per se and to the phony world of which he is just a part. By accepting Mrs. Maurier's material help and by supplying her demand to engineer aesthetic discussion for her to consume, the artists risk "turning themselves and their art into commodities."[51]

A kind of shipboard masquerade aboard the *Nausikka*, like *The White Rose of Memphis*, *Mosquitoes* nonetheless has no damsels in distress; no one is in danger of dying from brain fever (one of the old Colonel's favorite fictional maladies); no falsely accused characters are put on trial for murder. *Mosquitoes* is devoid of the Dickensian sentimentality that suffuses the old Colonel's novel. Falkner pulps romance; Faulkner probes sex, or the "sex instinct," as Mr. Talliaferro puts it, fresh from his reading of Freud and his followers. Mr. Talliaferro is confused about how he should uphold tradition, what Mrs. Maurier calls the "chivalry of our southern men." Her concern with chivalry is atavistic and a measure of how far Faulkner was from the old Colonel's antiquated imaginative world. Mrs. Maurier is a "scarred and mutilated victim of the aristocratic system of the New South";[52] her story, the novel's narrator explains, is "that her people forced her to marry old Maurier. He had been overseer on a big plantation before the Civil War."

Mr. Talliaferro may owe more than a little to Faulkner's own plight. Talliaferro has wandered abroad and returned to New Orleans as a displaced man thwarted in his pursuit of women and wondering about his sexual prowess: "It was unbearable to believe that he had never had the power to stir women, that he had been always a firearm unloaded and unaware of it." Not that Talliaferro, any more than Faulkner, gives up: "No, it's something I can do, or say, that I have not yet discovered." When Faulkner later names himself in the novel, he is shown as having no appeal whatsoever to the young woman who meets him.

A curious passage in *Mosquitoes* that derives from Faulkner's Italian sojourn explains a good deal about the decentered world depicted in the novel, a world not dreamt of in *The White Rose of Memphis*, which preserves the code of chivalry and the illusion of a society that can be organized around such ideals. The Semitic man comments on Mr. Talliaferro's gentlemanly code:

> "After all, it doesn't make any difference what you believe. Man is not only nourished by convictions, he is nourished by any conviction. Whatever you believe, you'll always annoy some one, but you yourself will follow and bleed and die for it in the face of law, hell or high water. And those who die for causes will perish for any cause, the more tawdry it is, the quicker they flock to it. And be quite happy at it, too. It's a provision of providence to keep their time occupied. . . .
>
> "Do you know who is the happiest man in the world today? Mussolini, of course. And do you know who are next? The poor devils he will get killed with his Cæsar illusion. Don't pity them, however: were it not Mussolini and his illusion it would be some one else and his cause."

Of course, Mrs. Maurier is no Mussolini, but Patricia resents her aunt's muscling in on everyone: "My Lord, what've we got to do now?" the niece moans. She sighs, "She sure makes life real and earnest for everybody, that woman does."

And yet Mrs. Maurier does not speak simply as a foolish tyrant: "Only he who creates has not lost the art of this: of making his life complete by living within himself. Don't you think so, Mr. Gordon?" He grudgingly assents. She is aware that society is not enough: "But to be a world in oneself, to regard the antics of man as one would a puppet show—ah, Mr. Gordon, how happy you must be." Gordon resembles the Spratling that Faulkner admired in a New Orleans sketch, "Out of Nazareth," as the artist whose "hand has been shaped to a brush as mine has (alas) not." Gordon is the true artist who does not like to talk, the Spratling who tired of Faulkner's words during their Italian trek. Gordon sculpts a powerful depiction of Mrs. Maurier:

> It was clay, yet damp, and from out its dull, dead grayness Mrs. Maurier looked at them. Her chins, harshly, and her flaccid jaw muscles with savage verisimilitude. Her eyes were caverns thumbed with two motions

into the dead familiar astonishment of her face; and yet, behind them, somewhere within those empty sockets, behind all her familiar surprise, there was something else—something that exposed her face for the mask it was, and still more, a mask unaware. "Well, I'm damned," Fairchild said slowly, staring at it. "I've known her for a year, and Gordon comes along after four days . . . Well, I'll be damned," he said again.

Gordon's delineation of character cuts through all the palaver in a novel about how there is too much talk about art and not enough accomplishment. *Mosquitoes* is a work of self-criticism, too, by a writer who confesses in "Out of Nazareth" that "words are my meat and bread and drink." But Faulkner is not rejecting words, his own art, any more than he is simply endorsing Gordon, who may be a promising artist but is also as callow as Stephen Dedalus in *A Portrait of the Artist as a Young Man*. Gordon removes himself from society even as Fairchild plunges in. Neither behavior is, by itself, enough to create great art.

Mosquitoes portrays artists as phonies. Fairchild is happy to imbibe Mrs. Maurier's largesse. His idea of rebellion is refusing to eat the grapefruit served at every meal. He wastes his time making fun of Mr. Talliaferro, a diffident widower trying to seduce Jenny. The surly Gordon despises Mrs. Maurier but seems to have gone along for a few free meals and because of his attraction to Patricia Robyn, whose unpretentious youth is preferable to those who gush about his art.

Perhaps the best scene in the novel occurs when Patricia Robyn is introduced. Like Helen Baird, she does not care for society. But she is not an artist and has no way to channel her rebellion. On a visit with Patricia to persuade the recalcitrant Gordon to join her party, Mrs. Maurier tells Mr. Talliaferro, "I want Patricia to see how genius looks at home." That kind of pretentiousness puts Patricia off: "'Gee, Aunty, I've seen these dives before,' the niece said. 'They're everywhere. I'll wait for you.'" But with a reluctant Patricia in tow, Mrs. Maurier admires Gordon's work and is seconded by Mr. Talliaferro: "'Do you see what he has caught?' he bugled melodiously. 'Do you see? The spirit of youth, of something fine and hard and clean in the world; something we all desire until our mouths are stopped with dust.'" Talliaferro admires the pristine Patricia and later Jenny, the seductive teenager Patricia brings aboard. Faulkner, susceptible to the same sentiments about youth as expressed in the Pierrot and Prufrock figures of his poetry, did put a bit of Helen Baird in Patricia, who apparently preserved much of her youthful insouciance. If Patricia is no artist, she still understands Gordon's art, as her aunt does not. Mrs. Maurier comments:

"How beautiful. What—what does it signify, Mr. Gordon?"

"Nothing, Aunt Pat," the niece snapped. "It doesn't have to."

Gordon is intent on his art, not on what it signifies outside itself. Mr. Talliaferro plays the art critic, mediating between art object and its audience, saying:

> "We must accept it for what it is: pure form untrammeled by any relation to a familiar or utilitarian object."
>
> "Oh, yes: untrammeled." Here was a word Mrs. Maurier knew. "The untrammeled spirit, freedom like the eagle's."
>
> "Shut up, Aunty," the niece told her. "Don't be a fool."
>
> "But it has what Talliaferro calls objective significance," Gordon interrupted brutally. "This is my feminine ideal: a virgin with no legs to leave me, no arms to hold me, no head to talk to me."

Gordon, who wants to be in complete control of his art as he cannot be of an actual woman, has the Faulkner penchant for shutting off talk when it turns to art and he is about to be corralled into the conversation. Such an artist, also a sculptor, serves a similar function in *Chrome Yellow*.[53]

Patricia has iconoclastic possibilities that her society does not allow, and like Helen Baird, Patricia is refreshing. Mr. Talliaferro first observes her as though he is looking at a William Faulkner drawing: "The niece spun slowly and slimly on one high heel: the sweet young curve of her shanks straight and brittle as the legs of a bird and ending in the twin inky splashes of her slippers, entranced him." She has that light elusiveness that made Estelle and Helen Baird so attractive, like a well-turned aesthetic object. The parts of Patricia's anatomy that he inhales and appraises are familiar to readers of Faulkner's poetry and *Soldiers' Pay:* "Mr. Talliaferro was conscious of the clean young odor of her, like that of young trees; and when they passed beneath lights he could see her slim shape and the impersonal revelation of her legs and her bare sexless knees."

Aboard ship, Patricia loses her compass, so to speak, striking out on land after the ship runs aground and she becomes bored with the company. She is beset by mosquitoes that suck the life out of her in a concentrated force that she has not known before in a society that only takes it out of her a few bites at a time. She gets lost in the swamp, having known no other world than society, which has not equipped her to forage on her own. Patricia does not give a damn for her aunt's proprieties, but Patricia has no replacement for them. She would just like to go around with the steward David, her dog-like devotee, "camping" and, like Faulkner, tramping. But no artist, in the end, can be so unattached, as Faulkner himself would soon have to say to himself now that Estelle had returned to Oxford for good. In the mosquito-filled swamp with David, Patricia is nearly done in until a swamp denizen takes them back to the ship in his boat. He calls Patricia an unprintable name. Her return to society suggests how futile her revolt is without having art, or some focus, to counter the vapidity of her upbringing.

A singular passage in *Mosquitoes,* a colloquy between Julius (the Semitic man) and his sister, Eva Wiseman, about Fairchild, seems to explain why Faulkner felt he had to separate from his mentor:

> "His writing seems fumbling, not because life is unclear to him, but because of his innate humorless belief that, though it bewilder him at times, life at bottom is sound and admirable and fine; and because hovering over this American scene into which he has been thrust, the ghosts of the Emersons and Lowells and other exemplifiers of Education with a capital E who, 'seated on chairs in handsomely carpeted parlors' and surrounded by an atmosphere of half calf and security, dominated American letters in its most healthy American phase 'without heat or vulgarity,' simper yet in a sort of ubiquitous watchfulness. A sort of puerile bravado in flouting while he fears," he explained.
>
> "But," his sister said, "for a man like Dawson there is no better American tradition than theirs—if he but knew it. They may have sat among their objects, transcribing their Greek and Latin and holding correspondences across the Atlantic, but they still found time to put out of their New England ports with the Word of God in one hand and a belaying pin in the other and all sails drawing aloft; and whatever they fell foul of was American. And it was American. And is yet." "Yes," her brother agreed again. "But he lacks what they had at command among their shelves of discrete books and their dearth of heat and vulgarity—a standard of literature that is international."

The White Rose of Memphis had followed the conventions of nineteenth-century fiction that Faulkner forsakes in *Mosquitoes,* favoring, instead, a modernistic novel of manners. Whereas the Mississippi riverboat in Colonel Falkner's novel has a destination and a plot resolution, *Mosquitoes* occurs on a ship that literally goes nowhere, getting stuck in the sand for several days in a stasis that reflects the inertia of its passengers.

At times, in this self-reflexive novel, Faulkner peeps out at us—at one point even naming himself as a "little kind of black man" Jenny meets before she boards the boat. "A nigger?" Patricia inquires. No, just a sunburned man who describes himself as a "liar by profession," Jenny explains. Unlike his fellow artists, Faulkner does not proclaim an exalted status, although he may be alluding to Oscar Wilde's essay "The Decay of Lying," which defines the artist as a liar engaging in "rich rhythmic utterance" that is not a "casual inspiration" but rather a practiced perfection.[54]

This unkempt tramp-like figure, one of his cherished personas, identified with being black, is a hard-to-overlook aspect of a writer who believed black people were an integral part of southern life and associated them with his own artistry. He missed them when away from home. The self-description can be dismissed as a joke, but so much in Faulkner's makeup as the dark sheep of his family seems insistently present and prophetic of the "nigger-lover" he would later be called. "Why are you so black?" Patricia Robyn asks Gordon. She does not mean his hair and beard, but insists, "'You are black. I mean . . .' her voice fell and he suggested Soul?" The black Faulkner is also present in this brazen passage about the writer's alter ego: "A book is the writer's secret life, the dark twin of a man: you can't reconcile them. And with you, when the inevitable clash comes, the author's actual self is the one that goes down, for you are of those for whom fact and fallacy gain verisimilitude by being in cold print." Dark could mean impenetrable, and as such the word rebukes biographers. *Mosquitoes* refuses the effort to reconcile the writer and his work, the page and the facts, Jekyll and Hyde. Faulkner has a point, except that the book, a "dark twin of a man," is a reflection of a person in another body just as biography is a life reflected in a book. The match cannot be identical, but much can be learned from a study of twins, and the double lives of writers, which have both a black and white side, like the two Faulkner families Joel Williamson discovered. A white family secret, such as the existence of black Faulkners, fits the Freudian frame as well—the notion of buried origins and relations, a submergence of the self, the artist, in not only his fiction but in the fiction of his family, transforming the "essentially personal element, which would repel strangers, and yield satisfaction to others as well." Freud argued that artists knew how to disguise the origins of their "despised sources."[55]

Toward the end of the novel, the characters disembark and return to their native habitats—Pete, for example, returning to his family's Italian restaurant, rendered with the affection for Italians Faulkner seems to have picked up in New Orleans and that carries the day in *The Sound and the Fury*. Much discussion in *Mosquitoes* concerns a changing, modernizing world, as applied to literature, but in the restaurant scene, Faulkner presages a concern with change in the material conditions of existence that will inform much of his later work:

And where you once got food good and Italian and cheap, you now paid so much for it that you were not required to eat it at all: and platters of spaghetti and roasted whole fowls, borne not by Joe, barearmed and skilful if taciturn, but by dinner-coated waiters with faces ironed and older than sin;—platters which served as stage properties for the oldest and weariest comedy in the world, were served you and later removed by the waiters with a sort of clairvoyant ubiquity and returned to the kitchen practically intact. And from the kitchen there came no longer any odor of cooking at all.

The departure from older, simpler, authentic ways will appear again in *Flags in the Dust* in both serious and comic scenes, an expression of Faulkner's own displacement as he straddles past and present.

In this novel, art is Robert Frost's momentary stay against confusion that an artist can own: "a man can create without any assistance at all: what he does is his," Fairchild declares. It is also a form of restitution: "Art reminds us of our youth, of that age when life don't need to have her face lifted every so often for you to consider her beautiful. That's about all the virtue there is in art: it's a kind of Battle Creek, Michigan, for the spirit. And when it reminds us of youth, we remember grief and forget time. That's something." In the shapes of Patricia and Jenny is that yearning for perfection that thwarts Mr. Talliaferro and that the artists in the novel seek to possess in their art.

Near the end of the novel, Faulkner has Fairchild sum up, in a Keatsian passage, what the experience of art means, both inside and outside of books:

"That's what it is. Genius." He spoke slowly, distinctly, staring into the sky. "People confuse it so, you see. They have got it now to where it signifies only an active state of the mind in which a picture is painted or a poem is written. When it is not that at all. It is that Passion Week of the heart, that instant of timeless beatitude which some never know, which some, I suppose, gain at will, which others gain through an outside agency like alcohol, like to-night—that passive state of the heart with which the mind, the brain, has nothing to do at all, in which the hackneyed accidents which make up this world—love and life and death and sex and sorrow—brought together by chance in perfect proportions, take on a kind of splendid and timeless beauty."

Fairchild is, in this respect, like the Sherwood Anderson Faulkner honored: The older writer could figure for the younger one what it was like to live the aesthetic experience, to inhabit and express it not just as a matter of writing but as a mode of perception. To see the world aesthetically, this novel argues, is to see it apart from what most others see who want to use and manipulate the world. What makes Gordon so mad, what momentarily captures Patricia Robyn in his studio, and what makes Fairchild fitfully insightful, is the art that is sufficient in and of itself and that the world, like Mrs. Maurier, wants to commandeer and thus corrupt. No wonder Faulkner, like Gordon, so often came off as surly and recalcitrant. Talking about art can never be commensurate with the creation of it.

Mosquitoes received a more mixed reception than *Soldiers' Pay*—not an uncommon phenomenon for second novels. For some, like Lillian Hellman in the *New York Herald Tribune* (June 19), the irony worked, and for others, like John McClure in the *Times-Picayune* (July 3), the satire seemed cruel. It is tempting to attribute these two diverse reactions to the temperaments of the reviewers. Hellman became famous for her astringent plays and McClure for his usually gentle and generous critiques. McClure also knew the originals of what he called "composite" characters. Hellman pointed out how much *Mosquitoes* owed to Aldous Huxley's *Antic Hay* and *Those Barren Leaves* in structure and tone. She liked the "swift and lusty writing that comes from a healthy, fresh pen." At the same time, she conceded Faulkner overwrote in a Joycean manner, making some of the novel "heavy and dull with overloaded description." By contrast, McClure almost sounds like a disappointed lover, characterizing Faulkner as a writer with a promise still unfulfilled. To be sure Faulkner wrote with "verve and gusto," but with a brilliance that was not profound. McClure alluded to Faulkner's affront to the "Puritan imagination," a very genteel way of signaling the novel was about sex. In fact, four sexually explicit episodes had been cut from the novel.[56] Just one of the offending sentences struck out reveals how much closer Faulkner was to the pornographic than to the Puritan: "Her [Patricia's] moving hand ceased in the valley beneath the swell of Jenny's thigh and she was quite motionless a moment." A sentence later Jenny is moaning.

Donald Davidson in the *Nashville Tennessean* (July 3), continuing his admiration of Faulkner, ignored the sex, except for a veiled reference to "mixed bathing," and concentrated on Faulkner's "buoyant zest," which seemed to compensate for an otherwise "scornful" novelist pursuing the "principle of the grotesque," dispatching "mayhem, assault and battery upon the bodies of numerous persons with such gracious ease that you almost overlook the savagery." Ruth Suckow in the *New York World* (July 12) came the closest to calling the novel obscene.

Other reviewers called the novel a lot of fun, with the author's "tongue in his cheek" according to the *Cincinnati Enquirer*. The *New York Evening Post* (June 11) praised Faulkner's humor and satire and thought his dialogue as good as Hemingway's—indeed reproducible as a play because of its natural rhythms in scenic exposition. Conrad Aiken deplored the purple passages: "One gets heartily sick of his blanched moons, spreading their boneless hands, on the boneless and ceaseless water." Aiken noticed that Fairchild becomes a more formidable character by the end of the novel, almost contradicting his appearance at the outset. The reviewer accounts for the change by concluding, "The story has the brilliance of improvisation but also it's shapeless."

Faulkner was attracting a core of critics with significant reputations who were committed to promoting his work, whatever their reservations. None of them thought he had yet done his best work, but they seemed as confident as the author himself that he would do so. If he had yet to solidify his literary reputation, he had returned home ready to reckon with his own soil in a novel and stories, he wrote Horace Liveright, "of my townspeople."[57]

7

Coming Home

1927–1929

IMPROVING ON GOD

Although Faulkner wrote to Horace Liveright in late July about publishing a book of poetry, an enthusiastic Phil Stone announced that his friend was at work on a story—"very good indeed." Liveright evidently showed no interest in the poetry, and Stone predicted a short-story sale to the *Saturday Evening Post:* "If anybody with the slightest taste for writing happens to read it they are certain to take it."[1] And yet, there were no takers.

In Stone's papers, a draft of a newspaper article describes Faulkner's work-in-progress on two novels, one a comic masterpiece centering on "typical 'poor white trash'" (the Snopeses) and the other on the "aristocratic, chivalrous and ill-fated Sartoris family."[2] Sherwood Anderson had encouraged Faulkner to write about his native grounds, but Faulkner, until now, resisted writing about home. Why? A few years later he would draft an explanation of how his first two novels had been a kind of "casting about":

All that I really desired was a touchstone simply; a simple word or gesture, but having been these 2 years previously under the curse of words, having known twice before the agony of ink, nothing served but that I try by main strength to recreate between the covers of a book the world as I was already preparing to lose and regret, feeling, with the morbidity of the young, that I was not only on the verge of decrepitude, but that growing old was to be an experience peculiar to myself alone out of the teeming world, and desiring, if not the capture of that world and the feeling of it as you'd preserve a kernel or a leaf to indicate the lost forest, at least to keep the evocative skeleton of the dessicated [*sic*] leaf.

Approaching thirty, William Faulkner was staving off a midlife crisis. Most of the men in his family had died before sixty, and this self-absorbed writer felt the decay setting in before he had an opportunity to memorialize a way of life, his life, as his great-grandfather had done his own, and as his Aunt Bama had preserved her own in the memories she shared especially with her nephew. However, this common, nostalgic impulse that leads others to compose genealogies and write family histories did not appeal to a writer who desired not a commemoration but a creation: "Created, I say, because they are composed partly from what they were in actual life and partly from what they should have been and were not: thus I improved on God who, dramatic though He be, has no sense, no feeling for, theatre."

Between the Sartorises and the Snopeses, between past and present, a bifurcated Faulkner stood. Phil Stone, stocked with white-trash anecdotes, with tales about the "rise of the redneck," urged Faulkner to take on this robust and ribald and conniving clan, responsible for the rise of poor white politicians like Theodore Gilmore Bilbo (1877–1947), a Mississippi governor and U.S. senator. Stone loved talking about Bilbo's corrupt rise to power, and though Faulkner never interested himself much in the details of politics, the maneuvering for position and prestige and the displacement of the old Bourbon governing class, replicated in the fate of his own family, proved an irresistible subject, which he began to probe in an aborted novel, *Father Abraham,* an ironic fable about Flem Snopes's ignominious rise to power.

Before Flem makes his unobtrusive entrance, Faulkner describes the world of Frenchman's Bend and its shadowy English-Irish-Scottish past, now the habitat of poor farmers who go about on their own except at election time, when the campaigning county officers show up. Otherwise, these people "support their own churches and schools, and sow the land and reap it and kill each other occasionally and commit adultery and fear God and hate republicans and niggers." Stone's rise of the redneck is thus compacted into one sentence.

Many of the present-tense passages read like a treatment for a screenplay:

Uncle Billy Varner is the big man of the Frenchman's Bend neighborhood. Beat supervisor, politician, farmer, usurer, present owner of the dead Frenchman's homestead and the legend. Uncle Billy is a tall reddish colored man with bright blue eyes; he looks like a Methodist elder, and is, and a milder mannered man never foreclosed a mortgage or carried a voting precinct. He wears a turnip shaped silver watch on a plaited horsehair chain and his son in law is election commissioner of the precinct and his son owns the store and is postmaster of Frenchman's Bend. The rest of Uncle Billy's family consists of a gray placid wife and a daughter of sixteen or so—a softly ample girl with eyes like cloudy hothouse grapes and mouth always slightly open in a kind of moist unalarmed surprise and a body that, between rare and reluctant movements, falls into attitudes passive and richly disturbing to the male beholder.[3]

If Darryl Zanuck, production chief at Twentieth Century-Fox and also a screenwriter, had read this passage, he might have signed Faulkner to a lucrative contract. Far more than anything else Faulkner had written, this passage makes us *see* his character in situ. Exposition is minimal, the character's mannerisms, affect, and image are immediately fixed, and the wardrobe department already knows how to dress him. And there is a part for a Hollywood starlet, a young Anne Baxter, say, who would later play such a role in *Swamp Water,* set in Georgia. Here is the first sight of Eula Varner, whose serene sexuality is so disruptive to the male sex in *The Hamlet.* Above all, humor and irony, the Methodist with his mind on money, reflect the viewpoint of an author delighted with the details of the mise-en-scène that he will develop in an unexpected and yet apposite vocabulary, as Eula abides in the "placid honey of her being" next to her "chosen swain stiffly arrayed and garnished on the back seat." Men are garnish because Eula is the meal, the prize that Flem Snopes, clan leader, wins.

Faulkner even supplies a soundtrack: "So they sit leashed and savage and loud amid her rich responsive giggles until the shadows merge eastward and night falls upon the land and the crickets raise their dry monotonous voices from the dew, and the frogs quaver and thump from the creek side and whippoorwills are quiring among the trees and the cold remains of dinner have been eaten beneath the moth swirled lamp." This stunning passage is like a Whitmanian catalogue, an imagist concatenation of sense impressions of nature and human arousal. Into this concert of sights and sounds comes the unwinking Flem, his eyes "all surface" and the "color of stagnant water," who springs from a "long line of tenant farmers," tethered to the land and yet rootless—the perfect background for a man "owing nothing to the soil, giving nothing to it and getting nothing of it in return," bent on profiting only himself. In what would become "Spotted Horses," and a vital section of *The Hamlet,* Flem employs Buck, a Texas cowboy auctioneer, to cajole a mob of poor whites to bid on a herd of wild horses. It is hard work, but Buck eventually arouses their competitive natures with the idea that he is offering bargain prices, although the horses are patently ungovernable and can be subdued only by violently striking them with coiled ropes and other objects. The horses are Flem's way not only of making money but of disrupting the conventional order of this still frontier society for his own advantage. When the horses break out of a barn, they are simultaneously shattering not only public order but even domestic peace as one of them rushes a porch and gets inside a home. In effect, they become a disintegrating force: "single atoms whirling and dashing about the lot." Sometimes Faulkner the pictorial artist appears, tracking the horses that slide down a path in "gaudy fluid flashes." Frontier humor emerges as Buck makes his Mark Twain pitch, saying his fractious stock will "outlast four ordinary horses: you cant kill one of them with a axle tree." Each horse has its qualities: "Look at that there shoulder action . . . look at the way he totes his head." And what cinematographer would not want to get this in frame: "Above, the bowl of the sky hushed itself into mysterious ineffable azures, and the apple tree where tethered horses stamped and gnawed was like a candelabra tinged faintly with pink and gold."

Perhaps it would have been a little too much for Hollywood, though—at least in the scene where Henry, a desperate poor white farmer, wants to spend his last five dollars on an untamable horse because he demands something to subdue. He forces his protesting wife to help corral the beast and when she fails to hem in the horse, he strikes her with a coiled rope, just as Buck had struck his horses. Henry says to his wife, "Why didn't you head it?" Then he strikes her again, repeating, "Why didn't you?" The brutality makes the men watching along the fence stand "quietly, brooding on the earth at their feet." Afterward, the somber narrator intones: "In her weathered and fading wagon the woman sat quietly, patient and tragic as a figure out of Sophocles." This tragic note gives way to humor: "Get out of here, you son of a bitch," Mrs. Littlejohn says as she breaks a scrubbing board over a "beast's long evil face" when it invades her hallway. She sees the stupidity and folly but does not have to say much: "I declare, you men." This is as succinct as the convict's summing up in "Old Man": "Women!" The dynamics of a disrupted culture and the very same words that would be employed in describing Sutpen's invasive presence in *Absalom, Absalom!* are already apparent in the wild chase after the horses: "'Whooey. Head 'im, ther.' Strophe and antistrophe; clear and remote; dramatic and sourceless and without meaning."

The "humorous recital" of the spotted horses fiasco by a sewing machine salesman, V. K. Suratt, later to be surnamed Ratliff in the Snopes trilogy, predicts that Flem, the instigator of the mayhem who has made his money off the horses, will evade responsibility and feel no shame. He owes nothing to his community, nothing to its past. He is the perfect foil for Faulkner's exploration of "a fundamental tension between familial, social, and historical forces as they bear down on individual life."

And here this brilliant beginning to the rest of Faulkner's writing life abruptly ends. How could he not go on? It would take time to work out an understanding of the ramifications of Snopesism. "The imperial dimension of his enterprise" may have daunted as well as invigorated Faulkner, putting "stress upon the kingdom he was making," even as he "asserted the power of his verbal art to outdo even the most aggressive social and historical realities. He wanted the world he was creating to possess all the salient features, all the wonderful and threatening qualities, of the world he knew—its grandeur and ruthlessness, its vulgarity and energy—precisely because he wanted to master as well as evoke it."[4] The other novel he had started, *Flags in the Dust,* was even closer to hand and more pressing since it delved into the Falkner legacy, made even more dramatic as the Sartoris saga, which would include the emergence of the Snopes clan in the banking and other businesses of Jefferson, Mississippi, displacing the decaying traditions of the Old South.

A Crossing

In his biography, Joseph Blotner seems certain that Bill and Estelle observed the proprieties, but off the page, he was not quite so sure and quizzed a Faulkner relative, the outspoken Sallie Murry,[5] whose chain-smoking voice hit the lower registers of Falkner family history. She would not have been out of place in a cigarette-lipped rural film noir. She said neither the Oldhams nor the Falkners were eager to see Estelle and Bill married. Major Oldham wanted a proven breadwinner to take care of his daughter, now accustomed to the high life of years abroad. "William had no job and nothing to offer," Sallie Murry said. When Estelle had come home for visits, "both from Honolulu and China, William was always around. There was a lot of talk." And, Sallie continued, "William was down there [at the Oldhams] all the time. Somebody certainly encouraged somebody in the deal."[6] But the gossip that Bill and Estelle were living together seemed impossible to one of their contemporaries, who pointed out to Blotner: "In the first place Oxford is a small community; in the second, would their neighbors accept it; again what would Estelle's mother have said or done, and finally did WF have a house or place where they could live together?"[7] Maud, hardly partial to Estelle, would also have raised objections to cohabiting lovers.

But how could they live apart much longer? Estelle had been taken away from Bill and had returned transformed but still Estelle. And the same might be said of Bill. Her life during her years with Cornell Franklin paralleled his in curious ways, beginning with her three years in Hawaii, a multicultural land something like the Europe and New Orleans that Bill experienced. She had made "a crossing," to borrow the title of a story she later wrote when she moved to Shanghai. She was no longer simply like her heroine, Edna Earl, a pretty girl bound in marriage to a man she did not love. In her fiction, Estelle Oldham (she put E.O. on her typescript)[8] had begun to take charge of her life, like an Earl taking command, awakened in Hawaii by the sea, which she would later depict in her bold, abstract paintings. Judith Sensibar reminds us that William Faulkner had a similar reaction to first seeing the sea on his first journey to New Haven, when he was striking out on his own.[9] In Hawaii, as in New Haven, these Mississippians had to reckon in new ways with their upbringing in a colonial, racist world. Lillian Smith, who worked with missionaries in China, reported: "I saw white supremacy over there.... And the further away from home I was, the worse it looked." Both Estelle and William Faulkner, by virtue of such experiences, were displaced persons.

The cosmopolitan Oahu and later Shanghai, teeming with foreigners, including the French, White Russians, British, Sikhs, and many others, matched Faulkner's cross-cultural forays in New York, Paris, London, and New Orleans. In boozy New Orleans, like boozy Honolulu and Shanghai, Bill and Estelle drank heavily, unhappily away from home, relying on liquor to relax and to buffer the changes in themselves and in their worldviews. Both found themselves among addicts who made addiction a way of life. Estelle, even more than Faulkner in New Orleans, floated in the port city of Shanghai, adrift in an inebriated society, presided over by a fellow Mississippian, Dr. Anne Fearn, who ran a sanatorium for colonials trying to control or break their opium and alcohol habits. Estelle discovered a world that included those drying-out refuges familiar to the Falkner males. From Fearn, Estelle derived an understanding of the damage done not only to colonial subjects but to their masters, since Fearn treated the "diseases of colonialism," which had "replaced those from filth, superstition, and ignorance."[10]

To be sure, Estelle remained in a kind of confinement, subject to the continual rounds of teas and luncheons and dinners and dances and bridge parties and polo tournaments that the wife of a colonial lawyer and judge was expected to attend. But her stories show how much she chafed in the role of the good wife. Estelle Oldham's Edna Earl reflects the author's self-criticism and even self-loathing that is reminiscent of William Faulkner's own dismissive depictions of himself in his fiction as a funny little man and liar, a forgettable figure to the young woman, Jenny, who pays him no more mind than Helen Baird, who said she did not even read the book of poems Faulkner wrote for her and that *Mosquitoes* was a bad book. Edna's masculine last name and title also suggest that she is displaced, a servant of those to whom she is superior—at least in terms of her ability to assess the repressive colonial society she is supposed to grace with her presence. Estelle Oldham's stories, written just before Faulkner began his New Orleans sketches, detail the racism aimed at the Chinese, Jews, and African Americans that William Faulkner was only beginning to factor into his nascent fiction. When he bound his sketches as a gift to her, he was acknowledging not only the critic he had praised much earlier in their relationship but also his beloved and fellow artist. This was a powerful aesthetic and erotic and fraught union of sensibilities that brought out both the noble and ignoble sides of his character. He would soon think of their marriage as a fate he could not forestall, a failure he could not rectify, but also a duty that was his destiny to fulfill.

In her fiction and in many accounts of her character, Estelle is shown to be a consummate role-player. In "A Crossing," as in Faulkner's first two novels, a bisexual aesthetic emerges, with Edna Earl entertaining the advances of male and female alike, including a "feminized, orientalized Jew."[11] Edna Earl, the man-woman, has her counterparts in *Soldiers' Pay* and *Mosquitoes*. Estelle's fiction belies the picture of her as a social butterfly. She held in reserve an acute awareness of her society that matched and enhanced Faulkner's own aloof consciousness. The longer she remained in Hawaii and Shanghai, the more she seemed to detach herself from society, as reflected in the diminishing reports of her attendance at various gatherings. "Months of intense emotional isolation" eventually resulted in the Shanghai stories. It is not clear what Cornell Franklin knew about his wife's disaffection as expressed in her writing, but every trip home to Oxford resulted in a renewal of her intimacy with Faulkner, with whom she had no need to explain herself. Cornell Franklin, an ambitious man who wanted money and position above all, neglected her, did not accompany her home, and treated her as an adjunct to his career, a commodity, really, who retained her value only so long as she contributed to the family store. What a relief then to deal with Billy—not only Cornell's antithesis but also her antidote to boredom with the repetition and regimentation of a business wife. Called a "stuffed shirt" and a "shyster lawyer from Shanghai," Cornell Franklin, to some in Oxford, was no more popular than Bill Faulkner.[12] All told, Estelle spent two years in Oxford away from a husband busily engaged in erotic and business affairs. William Faulkner's many depictions of conflicted southern belles derive a great deal from Estelle Oldham's ambivalence. And Cornell Franklin, now far from the fictional ideal of the dashing southern gentleman, supplied his own contribution to Faulkner's defrocking of the South's male aristocrats.

Estelle Oldham's stories date from her move to Shanghai in 1921, and by 1924, she had work to show to William Faulkner. The extent of her influence on him is debatable but also impossible not to contemplate. Alfred Dashiell, editor of *Scribner's Magazine,* acknowledged a joint submission from Bill and Estelle that he did not publish. Unlike Scott Fitzgerald, who seemed threatened by his wife's writing, Bill encouraged Estelle's fiction and derived at least two of his stories, "Elly" and "Idyll in the Desert," from drafts she had originated. How sympathetic he remained to Estelle's literary efforts, especially after he married her, is unknown.

While Estelle's stories dramatize bold themes like racism and sexism, plotting and characterization need work—requiring the kind of patience and rewriting that Faulkner would have to endure over the next five years before his stories began to be accepted by Dashiell at *Scribner's* and by other editors of major magazines. Nothing in Estelle's character suggests she had this kind of patience and ambition, and that lack of fortitude would have tested Faulkner's own tolerance, no matter how much he loved the woman who now turned to him. Like Patricia Robyn, Estelle Oldham could separate herself from society, but she could not follow through to another identity. Robyn leaves the yacht with her faithful knight, the steward David, but they are not armored against the mosquitoes who swarm them and take the life blood out of her, and they return in defeat, much as a humiliated Estelle arrived in Oxford after her sojourns abroad.

The odds were against Estelle Oldham the author, even if an ambivalent William Faulkner did not say as much. His letter to Anita Loos, written a year earlier, praising *Gentlemen Prefer Blondes,* evinces his atavism: perhaps she had "builded better than you knew. I am still rather Victorian in my prejudices regarding the intelligence of women, despite Elinor Wylie and Willa Cather, and all the balance of them. But I wish I had thought of Dorothy first."[13] The wisecracking Dorothy, reminiscent of the character Eve Arden patented in pictures and of Dorothy Parker puncturing pretensions, is the polar opposite of the Loreleis who live a lie, like southern belles, leading on their male suitors in a charade of ladyhood. If Faulkner was a confessed old-school male, he nevertheless thoroughly enjoyed the company of liberated women like Dorothy Parker and Lillian Hellman who spurned the falsities of the feminine mystique.

In *Mosquitoes,* Eva Wiseman is treated seriously as a poet, although her poem "Hermaphroditus" is actually Faulkner's, a fact that puzzles critics who have wondered what comment he may have been making on his own work as well as on the female imagination. In *Mosquitoes,* Julius Kauffman refers to "Dr [Havelock] Ellis and your Germans," headed indisputably by Freud, who "destabilized traditional delineation between male and female, artist and muse." The result is a "split psyche," the dialogue between the characters forming Faulkner's debate with himself, intensified, in all likelihood, by his reading of Estelle's stories. Two lines in "Hermaphroditus" sum up the half of him that was her: "Weary thy mouth with smiling: canst thou bride / Thyself with thee, or thine own kissing slake?" The pronouns are wedded to one another as surely as William was to Estelle, and yet both are put to a question. Could he ever be satisfied with himself, with her, with his art? Could this brooding man ever slake his desire? And did his desire for Estelle unnerve him? Was she like Fairchild's female spider? When the male goes to her, he goes to his death, Fairchild points out: "she devours him during the act of conception."[14] The writing male is supposed to be the female spider in Fairchild's insect fable: notebook in hand, the writer kills the charming things he observes "for the sake of some problematical something he might or he might not ever use." Estelle Oldham, attractive and dangerous and subject to William Faulkner's desire and his aversion, is transformed into the "male author in the role of devouring female" so as to avoid "being devoured by her."[15]

Estelle challenged Faulkner's "gendered ideology" that "defines creativity as a masculine impulse."[16] Mrs. Maurier exclaims, "Ah, to be a man, with no ties save those of the soul! to create, to create"—a sentiment seconded by Fairchild's contention that art is man's creative offspring: "a man can create without any assistance at all: what he does is his." But are the comments of characters who often seem at least as foolish as they are wise to be taken as Faulkner's settled views? Estelle Oldham's fiction is unsettling, and it is a loss to biography that we do not know what happened when what was hers was appropriated by what William Faulkner considered his. The closest we can come to what Bill thought about Estelle as his other half is Eva Wiseman, who is both Eve and a wise man.[17] That conjunction of male and female, if biographical, also becomes in Fairchild's commentary universal when he describes his process of hermaphroditic creation, giving birth to art out of himself.

Mosquitoes has often been criticized as a confused and indeterminate text, but that may be the point. Men may *say* all sorts of things about women, sex, and creativity, but look at what happens: The sculptor Gordon pursues Patricia Robyn, who resembles his sculpture, his ideal woman, which is to say she is part of himself. In her face, he finds a "grave and sexless replica of his own." He has imagined the woman who has come to him, as Estelle Oldham kept returning to William Faulkner. The sculptor and his model, projections of the artist's imagination, are "double-sexed,"[18] a product of what Fairchild calls "emotional bisexuality," a term that contradicts his otherwise male view of literary creation. It often seems that *Mosquitoes* is an example of what Susan Sontag calls a text's arguing against itself. The dialogues in the novel, as in the debates in *Go Down, Moses,* are meant to be inconclusive and to keep several competing ideas in play, making the characters more than the specific arguments they advance and, in this respect, rather like William Faulkner himself, who would often take up a side of an issue that did not necessarily reflect his opinion but to keep the argument going. Contemporary reviews of the novel had less trouble with seeing the fun of this party of arguments and characters than later critics do.

What happens when Estelle Oldham's fiction is factored into Faulkner's problematic responses to himself and his male and female characters? Did her fiction trouble a latter-day Romantic artist who wanted her to serve mainly as his muse? Or did she liberate him to explore sex and race more persistently than was possible in his earliest poems and sketches? Estelle was a double agent—at once part of the male imperial mission at home and abroad and also its critic. The claim that Estelle Oldham directly influenced William Faulkner is hard to document, since no correspondence between them or testimony from others survives to second such a strong connection. Yet they shared similar sensibilities. She turned to an avant-garde theater group, playing several roles in Honolulu, including a leading role in Susan Glaspell's Freudian farce *Suppressed Desires,* while Faulkner at the same time joined the Marionettes theater group on the Ole Miss campus. "Like Faulkner's Pierrot," Sensibar notes, "Edna Earl drinks herself into a stupor," expressing the libidinal desires that torment Faulkner's poetic figure. She emulates the "Southern white boy's initiation into manhood," escaping her strict upbringing as a southern lady while Faulkner did much the same, simultaneously liberating himself from Oxford while still performing when it suited him the role of southern gentleman. Complicating these mutual influences was Estelle's awareness of all the poetry Faulkner had shown her with his own stylized fantasies of the enticing women his poetic personas pursued. From his point of view, in so many overdetermined ways, Estelle led him quite a dance that would forever be fascinating and infuriating. They, in turn, were acting out of a code of manners dating back to the masquerade aboard *The White Rose of Memphis,* the old Colonel's novel about the differences between appearance and reality, and the masks men and women perforce had to wear as gentlemen and ladies wooing one another even as the gritty true stories of their lives were slowly unmasked in a plot that was pure melodrama, now replaced in the age of the Faulkners with Freud's suppressed desires, erupting in the characters of their stories and novels.

No woman could step out of the pages of *The White Rose of Memphis* and declare her independence, but that is what Estelle Oldham did in her fiction. She understood how she had become the property of a husband and her father who both profited by putting her out for show. Estelle was on the cusp of a consciousness that Lillian Hellman would finally liberate in *The Little Foxes,* when Regina dickers with her brothers, telling them that if they want her cooperation they would have to increase her share of the business. Estelle never went quite that far, but she knew the value of her position, exercised first by absenting herself from Cornell Franklin's business-and-pleasure parties. Then she created her own property by writing—staking out her territory. Although she always seemed willing to give herself to William Faulkner, the very act of conceding his title to her would provoke, from the day they married, a profound misgiving about what she had relinquished. The play of their marriage, which might well have been called "Strange Interlude," involved his awareness of her awareness that he was aware of her bifurcated mentality: at once subservient to the idea of a traditional marriage and yet diurnally disposed to test its integrity. Her alcoholism worsened in Shanghai. She later told her daughter, "I don't think I took a sober breath for three years." Drinking was yet another dissent from her southern lady role, although an especially complex one, since her second husband matched her drink for drink and then some. Why they drank solicits all sorts of explanations, including one by her fictional character Dr. Wohlenski, who declares, "One tosses it down purely for the effect it gives—that of well-being, a lift from care." Estelle's daughter Jill had her own take: "My mother was not a happy person: she was a lot more sophisticated and intelligent than anyone gave her credit for and I think that's why she was unhappy."[19] Drinking abroad or drinking at home also relieved Estelle of those traditional and sometimes demeaning female marital duties. Drama, taking the stage, allowed the expression of suppressed desires—as did those fashion shows she later put on in Oxford.

Estelle and her fictions, what Cornell Franklin called her lying, made a "theater of everyday life." Her stories explored the "roles constructed for women and other minorities. . . . Her portrayals of such theatricality of characters who have a great capacity to disassociate and to watch themselves watching themselves will be of great interest to Faulkner."[20] Januarius Jones acts the seducer, and Joe Gilligan plays a character, "Yaphank," the disorderly veteran returning home. The masquerade, begun in *The White Rose of Memphis,* continues, with all the characters playing parts and watching one another, wondering what is behind the mask, and who it is they are actually addressing. Will Cecily Saunders play the role cast for her by her parents and society, or run off with George Farr? Will Margaret Powers continue playing war widow or give way to Joe Gilligan's proposal of marriage? Can Donald Mahon's father really maintain his delusion that his son will get well? Will he ever break his composure as the tolerant man of the cloth? In *The White Rose of Memphis* characters can engage in a masquerade that does no damage to their psyches, but in the Freudian world of suppressed desires such impersonations risk unraveling the self.

The superficial social/psychological conflicts of southern role-playing in the old Colonel's novel gives way in Estelle and William Faulkner's fiction to a much more troubled and tragic portrayal of their characters' dual natures as they mask and unmask one another. In "Star Spangled Stuff," written a good year or more before Faulkner wrote anything comparable, Estelle Oldham explored the degraded notion of the southern gentleman, the farcical idealization of white southern maidenhead, and the nexus of racial and sexual tensions that would become her husband's province in *Sanctuary, Light in August, Absalom, Absalom!, Go Down, Moses,* the Snopes trilogy, and other novels and stories. While Estelle's contemporaries wrote about the "host country's barbaric practice of buying and selling its women and children, she wrote about her contemporaries' marketing of their own women."[21]

In the ironically titled "Star Spangled Stuff," the female object for sale is Emma Jane, the perfect picture of the Faulknerian slim-figured ingenue—or rather a travesty of the same, since Emma Jane is an outright racist who believes she cannot bear the touch of a "Chink." She adores male attention and enjoys the prospect of men fighting over her. She has plenty of sexual desire but appears to both her white suitors and a Chinese contender as pristine, a shining white thing—*the white woman* who appears in so many Faulkner poems, stories, and novels. Indeed, his fascination with such figures seems a kind of transference, since like Estelle and her fictional heroines, this slimly built man favored tightly tailored clothes and paid close attention to his diet.[22] The implication is clear: What else did Bill Faulkner crave that Estelle and women like her had to offer? In typing Estelle's stories, did he subsume Estelle's imagination, masking himself with another identity as the characters do in *The White Rose of Memphis*?

Chang, sometimes called Lord Chang because he is the scion of a noble family, is an aristocratic figure designed to capture Bill Faulkner's attention. Chang reads Keats, and like Bill, Chang projects into Emma Jane his desire for a woman who is unattainable—his Helen Baird, you might say. Chang is also the quintessential displaced alien figure and lover, *Absalom, Absalom!'s* Charles Bon in the making: "Ah, woe is me that at last and among foreign surroundings have mine eyes beheld the woman I have dreamed after all my life; a woman as far beyond my reach as the evening star, and as shining." Estelle mocks the stilted romanticism of such male suitors, including her own and those of another race, but in such a way as to make Chang, in the rest of the story, the superior to the crass white men who vilify him and vie for Emma Jane's favors. She later created another mixed-race New Orleans native, Harvard- and University of Virginia–educated Paul de Montigny in "Selvage," a story Faulkner rewrote and eventually published as "Elly," featuring another southern belle, like Emma Jane, who struggles with her desire for the forbidden black lover. The story's original title is intriguing since it refers to the edge of a woven fabric manufactured to ensure against unraveling. Estelle had an exquisite taste in clothes, often making her own and her daughter's dresses, and she was aware of how the fabric of a society could unravel as soon as its borders or edges came apart, as they threaten to do in her stories as well as in novels like *Absalom, Absalom!*

Chang, whose first name is Needham, Needy for short, has been named so by a father who thereby endows his son with a cross-cultural appeal, enhanced by Chang's physical features, like a "fine blade," and his impeccable attire. He moves exquisitely and with none of the oafish gestures, manners, and expressions typical of his white "gentlemen" friends. He commands their admiration, but only so long as he observes the color line and does not actually assert the privileges of a white man. Chang, overcome with desire for Emma Jane, carefully manipulates one of the stupid white males into arranging a meeting with her, which must be done casually, as if by accident, so as not to violate the club rules in colonial Shanghai. All the white people want to do business with Chang and so try to oblige him without ever considering him an equal. And Chang is their collaborator, insofar as he maintains an impassive face in public while thinking of Emma Jane as "white jade not yet uncovered to the sun. Pure and untouched." The thought of having to actually meet, let alone dance with Chang revolts Emma Jane, but in person, in the flesh, before she knows it is Chang, she spots a charming man gazing at her and she locks on his dark eyes. Although she cannot deny her attraction to him, her parents, no less racist, nevertheless want the resistant Emma Jane to make nice with Chang since it is good for business. In spite of her cross words, she dances with Chang and is charmed by him. As if to break his spell, she makes one of her suitors, George Taylor, repeat that he loves her, even as another, Marc Monjoy, proposes marriage. By herself, though, she dwells on all the wonderful things Chang has said to her and how beautiful he made her feel "all in one dance." She plans on writing down his endearments for her friends. He was tender. He was deferential. Her language begins to resemble his own, and she believes she is in love.

Chang knows he is playing with "dangerous fire," as he imagines "no pomegranate has ever burst redder than her parted lips, no pearls gleamed whiter than her even little teeth." This scene does not go quite so far as *Soldiers' Pay*, in which the pomegranate suggests the lusciousness of sexual attraction.

Chang plans to return the next day to his betrothed, a Chinese woman his family has picked out for him. But he cannot resist writing a note to Emma Jane: "I go to my father's house after four long, long days and find peace." She eagerly reads his parting romantic gesture and immediately bathes, dresses in chiffon-and-lace, and properly perfumed and coiffed, frothing her hair in "light swirls," she steps next door to Chang's suite, slipping in like she has seen "cinema-queens walk" right into the arms of their lovers, as she does with Chang. They embrace. They kiss. Chang exclaims: "I could die now, Moon-flower, and say that I have lived life to its fullest." His words mock romance stories, although his language is also quite accurate in depicting the way men of all races in this story treat women as undefiled vessels they would treasure with their lives. Emma Jane may want Chang, but she is no romantic. When Chang asks her to sit by him so that he can open his heart to her, she giggles and rearranges her hair. It is all great fun, and she has come to him hoping to receive some great gift she can take back to Toledo, Ohio, with her. But just then this tender interlude is interrupted by Chang's American friends, who have lingered in his rooms sleeping off the night's bender. As in southern lynching episodes like "Dry September," the white people immediately attack the colored man, assuming he has raped, or is about to rape, the white virgin. In fact, even though taken by surprise and susceptible to Emma Jane's kiss, Chang remains the perfect gentleman, although he is denounced as a "yellow cur" who has taken advantage of an innocent girl. Although injured, Chang does not fight back. He maintains his composure and does everything pos-sible to prevent a scandal even as Emma Jane's parents have no idea and are incapable of imagining their daughter's behavior. The white males marvel at how courageously Emma Jane has withstood the assault of the "Chinaman."

The ironic coda to the story is a final scene with old Fairman, a lush modeled after Cornell Franklin's uncle, an officious colonial who believes he enforces club rules and white prerogatives in an impartial manner. But he is a fool and hypocrite, not worth anyone's respect. He stands, like so many such figures in Faulkner's own fiction, for an idiotic status quo. He is the epitome of the star-spangled bunk the story ridicules.

The implications of this story for the author of *Absalom, Absalom!* and *Sanctuary* are stunning. Chang does not have the symbolic heft that propels Charles Bon into Jefferson, Mississippi, but the theme of a foreign gentle-man rejected because of his race, and the role of an uncomprehending racist society provided, at the very least, material that demanded deeper explora-tion. If Faulkner often suggested he had rescued Estelle, it is not too much to say that in some ways she was his salvation. No one else—not Phil Stone, not Sherwood Anderson—had the background or the sensibility to help William

Faulkner move on to the next phase of his career. If no evidence of his gratitude has ever appeared, that may in part be a measure of how much further he
had taken Estelle's story—so far, in fact, that he ultimately went way beyond
what her sensibility and talents could absorb. What started so well did not
end so well.

As Faulkner began to create one major great work of fiction after another,
the debt he owed to Estelle may have receded in importance and have even
been forgotten, like her stories that were never published, but it is hard to
gainsay Judith Sensibar's assessment: "As postcolonial critiques, her stories,
set in a mutually shared culture, were Billy's most emotionally and experien-
tially intimate models." A friend of Estelle's remembered that when Estelle
returned to live in Oxford permanently, she took over a wing of the Oldham house for herself and her children. There she would lock the door and
write, sometimes receiving visits from her friend, and they would talk about
her writing. The friend distinctly remembered that William Faulkner told
Estelle "Star Spangled Stuff" was "junk."[23] Another friend reported that
Estelle "would usually bring her manuscripts to one of their University faculty friends to criticize because, she said, 'Bill thinks they're terrible.'"[24] Was
Faulkner behaving like F. Scott Fitzgerald, declaring, in effect, there could
be only one writer in the family? And yet he tried to publish Estelle's story
"Selvage" with both their names on it, later rewrote the story as "Elly," and
submitted her novel "White Beeches" for publication and was angry when
she destroyed it.[25]

Faulkner's ambivalence about Estelle comes through in an undated letter
he wrote to his Aunt Bama: "I told the family that you had almost promised to drive down [from Memphis] and see us. We all wish you would." He
wanted the approval and the affection of this formidable patriarch, and he
warily announced: "I have something—someone, I mean—to show you, if
you only would." "Of course it's a woman," he adds, without ever giving away
the name. But who else would he dare to show off? "I would like to see you
taken with her utter charm, and intrigued by her utter shallowness." Such
a sentence strikes a certain pose and is certainly unfair to the woman who
wrote "Star Spangled Stuff" and, according to one of her friends, "did a great
deal to shape William Faulkner ... [a]s a result of this sophistication from her
life in the Orient."[26] And yet Estelle's granddaughter, who thought of Estelle
as a wonderful person, admitted the "strain of shallowness and weakness" in
her grandmother.[27]

Faulkner likened Estelle to a "lovely vase. It isn't even empty, but is filled
with something—well, a yeast cake in water is the nearest simile that occurs
to me." Estelle as art object, Estelle as inspiration to a rising talent? Did her

effervescence lift his spirits, even as he worried about a deeper attachment? Was Aunt Bama supposed to disapprove or absolve him of his qualms? He closed with a seemingly offhand comment: "She gets the days passed for me, though. Thank God I've got no money, or I'd marry her. So you see, even Poverty looks after its own." Was it just imprudent to declare his love? Or is this just what seemed necessary when addressing Aunt Bama? He was not exactly acceding to her authority, but he was certainly saying he had his amour that dare not speak its name under control. Or so he thought or wanted to believe.[28]

The bond with Estelle Oldham included her children, whom Faulkner had begun to incorporate into his imaginative universe, as he did with a cousin, Dorothy Falkner, calling her sister and sharing a five-cent box of vanilla wafers and telling her about witches and fairies.[29] He walked in the woods with Cho-Cho (Victoria), called so by an amah (a Chinese nurse) who said she was like a little butterfly.[30] On February 9, 1927, he inscribed a handmade copy of *The Wishing Tree* to Estelle's daughter:

> For his dear friend
>   Victoria
> On her eighth birthday
>   Bill he made
>   this Book

Faulkner's affinity for children, especially girls, is expressed in this charming story about Dulcie, who wakes up to be greeted by a boy, Maurice, who tells her anything is possible on her birthday. She ventures out with him in a gray mist scented with wisteria, that odor of memory and expectation that so powerfully pervades *Absalom, Absalom!* She hears "far voices," as if from the past, calling her to "come down." She descends on a toy ladder that gets longer and bigger as Maurice blows on it. This is a recognizable world that is stretched and enlarged by the human breath and mist of the imagination, reflecting the power of storytelling that Faulkner wanted to bestow upon his beloved's daughter. Awaiting Dulcie are her familiar companions Alice, her black family servant; Dicky, her little brother; and George, a neighbor boy. The mist envelops them all like a big tent. What they wish for becomes their reality, although Alice, like several other black characters Faulkner would create, sounds a skeptical refrain, constantly admonishing the children to beware of what they wish—like the ponies (the spotted horses of *Father Abraham*):

> "Well," he [Maurice] said, "how shall we go? walk, or in a motorcar, or on ponies?"

"Ponies! Ponies!" Dulcie and George shouted, and Dicky said, "Pony! Pony! Want to wide pony!"

But Alice didn't want to. "Naw, suh," Alice said, "me and Dicky ain't goin' to ride on no hawss, and, Dulcie, you ain't got no business with no hawss, neither."

"Oh, Alice!"

"Naw, suh," Alice repeated, "you knows your mommer don't allow you to ride no hawss."

Back of this dialogue is Billy Falkner, superintended by Callie and other black people, drawing his pictures and dreaming his stories, and now beginning a lifelong conspiracy with children to preserve the wonders of the world they can create with their own toys and stories. The ponies, like the ladder, are miniatures that Maurice can blow up with his breath, as Billy blew up his own stories and adventures. Maurice is simply irresistible, no matter how hard Alice tries to check him. They ride as Billy Falkner rode on ponies with his brothers. They journey to the Wishing Tree, meeting along the way a gentle old man whittling wood who tells them the Wishing Tree is far off—like, you might say, the desires of our dreams. Like the children with Alice, the old man is saddled with a hectoring adult, his wife, who throws at him a rolling pin, a flat iron, and an alarm clock—all the mundane objects of workaday life and time that the children and the old man wish to transcend. The old man is childlike in his simple desires and his decision to accompany them to the Wishing Tree. When the wife slams the door on them, Alice calls her "white trash." The wife, it is tempting to say, is the world that turned its back on William Faulkner and on what children like to imagine: there is more to life than chores and more to be learned beyond what they are told not to do. On their way they try to figure out what the old man is carving. He doesn't know himself. It is not a puppy or a lizard or a dragon. The old man does not know for sure, but he thinks he has created a "gillypus," although he can't tell the children what it looks like. He is, in short, the artist creating the world anew. Not that this imaginative world is without its cost. Wishing can lead to surfeit, like too much of the strawberries and chocolate cake that make George "terribly sick." The hazards of the creative journey cause Alice to rebel. She flops "around on the seat. 'We's goin' right straight home: you tell that redheaded boy [Maurice] to pick out the first road. I'se had about all of this goin' on I can stand.'" And yet they persist, coming to a gray castle with soldiers. Alice's husband, Exodus, turns up and becomes part of a dialogue about war:

"I was in a war," the little old man said to Alice's husband.
"Which one?" Alice's husband asked.

"I never did know," the little old man answered. "There was a lot of folks in it, I remember."

"Sound like the one I was at," Alice's husband said.

"They're all about alike, I reckon," the little old man said.

"I 'speck you's right," Alice's husband agreed. "Was it across the water?"

"Across the water?" the little old man repeated.

"Across the big up and down water," Alice's husband explained.

These white and black veterans of the Civil War and World War I agree that "wars don't change." And Alice's husband adds: "I never seed a soldier yet that ever won anything in a war. But then, whitefolks' wars is always run funny. Next time the whitefolks has a war, I think I ain't goin'. I think I'll jes' stay in the army instead." This wry black-on-white commentary will occur again— off to the side in *Flags in the Dust,* which Faulkner was commencing to write even as he welcomed Estelle and her children back to Oxford. The nostalgia for war gets the better of the old man as he sets off on a charging horse like those Civil War veterans who entertained Billy and his brothers, but the old man is halted by the astringent Alice, who warns him, "I'll tear your head clean off and unravel your backbone down to your belt." Caroline Barr could probably not have said it better. Saint Francis appears, as in *Mayday,* to state the moral of the tale, that wishing can be reckless and has to be done with the welfare of others in mind: "if you are kind to helpless things, you don't need a Wishing Tree to make things come true." When Dulcie returns home, she is greeted with her mother's gift of a bluebird in a cage. It is a delicate moment that seems to be an evocation of Bill's love for Estelle: "Dulcie's mother was beautiful, so slim and tall, with her grave unhappy eyes changeable as seawater and her slender hands that came so softly about you when you were sick." What you could wish for might be elsewhere, but it could also be right there at home. Unhappy? Estelle's impending divorce hovers over this story.

Quite aside from what Estelle meant to him, William Faulkner felt bound to her progeny as his own, blood kin or not, whether it was the children he knew or those he imagined. The intrepid Dulcie, climbing out of a window and caring for her younger brother, has been called a "kind of first draft of Faulkner's 'heart's darling.'"[31] Caddy and Dulcie and Cho-Cho have to be protected and nurtured and encouraged beyond what their everyday world could offer, just as he needed that Irish cop doll who could police the world William Faulkner wanted to create, a world that expanded like Maurice's miniatures and surpassed the nostalgia of Civil War veterans whose spell only went so far in commanding William Faulkner's allegiance. Children, ungoverned by the prejudices of their parents, minders, and other adults, were open to experience but also vulnerable, and Faulkner could use them to "level a critique at those in power who have controlled history's course and made violent and often selfish choices that impact the future." The old man gets carried away at one point, reenacting his cavalry charge, vowing to slice the enemy in two with his sword, and Dicky wants to do the same and does so, slicing the gillypus in two. The result is that Dicky is reduced to the size of a lead soldier, and his companions shrink in solidarity,[32] repeating, in effect, what happens in the pell-mell of violence that Bayard Sartoris will later halt in "An Odor of Verbena." It is as if in *The Wishing Tree* Faulkner wanted to rewrite his childhood as a gift to Cho-Cho, who could be shown a way out of the past that pervaded his own consciousness. But she had to be aware of it in order to obviate it.

That the story meant more to William Faulkner than just a momentary diversion and part of his attachment to Estelle Oldham is reflected in his assembling another version of the story as a Christmas gift to Phil Stone's son.[33] In fact, the story had been first created for Margaret Brown, a dying child. In the Brown version of the story, it is Daphne who returns home to her sad mother, who is not Estelle but Mrs. Brown, who knows her child will soon die. The act of writing for a child, before Faulkner had completed his first Yoknapatawpha novel, began the process of liberating his own imagination from the precedents of the past.[34] Certainly this story for a child shattered the shibboleths of Faulkner's upbringing, introducing the subjects of war and race in a new voice. In the Victoria (Cho-Cho) version, he cut more than a thousand words, eliminating some dialogue so that the characters spoke more directly and succinctly:

> "It's just my pony," the red-haired boy explained. "But he will come on home by himself: he always does that." [Brown]

> "It's just my pony," the red-haired boy explained. "He knows the way home, all right." [Victoria]

Even more impressive is Faulkner's move away from minstrel show dialect:[35]

> "You have something else, honey. Here, gimme yo' candy. You don't want no old candy, does you?" Alice took the candy out of Dicky's hand. [Brown]

> "You better have something else. Here, give me yo' candy." Alice took the candy out of his hand. [Victoria]

Alice appears in sharper relief as custodian and authority figure, and the voices of Yoknapatawpha begin to emerge in words and rhythms familiar to readers of stories like "That Evening Sun" and novels like *The Sound and the Fury.* Personal energy now poured into new work, beginning with *Flags in the Dust,* a departure from the "sardonic detachment" of *Soldiers' Pay* and *Mosquitoes.*[36] Helen Baird had married in May 1927, and though William Faulkner could not forget her, his energies turned once more toward Estelle Oldham and Oxford.

A Breakthrough

During the summer of 1927, Faulkner wrote from early morning to noon, then golfed and drank and gambled. He remained devoted to his younger brother Dean, now twenty, who had been writing his own stories for at least two years. Brother Billy encouraged and examined the work, providing Dean with word lists. Dean had a talent for drawing too, producing pictures of horses and cowboys. Ben Wasson remembered that Bill was always patient with his younger brother, and judging by a playful letter Bill wrote to Dean, the brothers liked to think of themselves as hick writers in the Ernest V. Trueblood vein: "I b3en P*acti)cin-on m7 typx%iter c'vever? Day and 7 h(VF, takcn afwe lexxon$ and onwards 7 a5 grtt7ng petted %!rrgkgoOD."[37] Their mother preserved hundreds of pages of Dean's handwritten stories (with corrections by Bill) that reveal a penchant for folk humor and hunting.

Estelle took her children to Columbus, Mississippi, where Bill visited during a relaxed period away from prying Oxford. Estelle's mother-in-law remained sympathetic to Estelle and fond of Bill.[38] Back home, he was on his own, painting signs and trying to cobble together enough to get by while he wrote. With Sallie Simpson typing stories in Phil Stone's law office, Faulkner sent out work to high-paying publications like *Collier's* and the *Saturday Evening Post,* and their rejection slips began to fill up a drawer in Stone's desk.[39] Faulkner asked Horace Liveright for a two-hundred-dollar draft on the writer's future work, promising a new novel by the fall. Liveright, who subsidized other writers (including Dreiser and Anderson),[40] complied but did not like the impromptu request. Something about Faulkner put off Liveright, who confessed to Anderson, "Hang it all, he's not the man that I can write to frankly and intimately and wholeheartedly."

Faulkner seemed to go out of his way to make his tales taller, telling his publisher that a "nigger" had dug up the whisky the impecunious novelist had planted in the family garden and sold it.[41] The writer presented himself to his publisher as like so many Mississippians, strapped for cash in an economy devastated by the great flood of 1927, which would later become a motive force of *The Wild Palms.* Estelle's sister Dorothy remembered the sight of

Faulkner on the golf course in white duck pants pursuing a nickel-and-dime business selling Nehi bottled beverages stored in a barrel lined with sawdust and filled with ice and covered with tow sacks.

When it turned really hot, he decamped for Pascagoula, visiting Helen Baird and her family, entertaining her Aunt Martha's delighted children, and taking at least one side trip to New Orleans—although nothing seemed to keep William Faulkner from writing. By the end of September he announced to Liveright: "I have written THE book, of which those other things were but foals. I believe it is the damndest best book you'll look at this year, and any other publisher."[42] What made this new book a breakthrough? The first three paragraphs provide virtually a template for so much of what he would write about in the next three decades: Old Man Falls walking into town from the poor farm, "fetching, like an odor, like the clean dusty smell of his faded overalls," the spirit of Colonel John Sartoris, which unites the pauper and old Bayard, the banker. As the two old men shout at one another, the old Colonel is a "far more palpable"[43] presence, even though he is long gone, because old deaf Bayard, propped against the corner of a cold hearth, seems enveloped by the dead man's breathing, which he hears in his "citadel of silence." The old Colonel is treated like a mastodon from prehistoric time, ineradicable and "too grandly conceived and executed either to exist very long or to vanish utterly when dead from an earth shaped and furnished for punier things." The past is archaeological: Old Bayard bites on a pipe with prints of his father's teeth. These vivid three paragraphs provided Faulkner with a mastery over his material that defined his family and community and history.

But there was something more: the sheer flamboyance of his heritage, of the black characters who provide the color commentary, so to speak, the chorus—here represented by the family retainer, old Simon, who arranges the carriage for old Bayard: "With his race's fine feeling for potential theatrics he drew himself up and arranged the limp folds of the duster, communicating by some means the histrionic moment to the horses so that they too flicked their glittering coats and tossed their leashed heads, and into Simon's wizened black face there came an expression indescribably majestic as he touched his whiphand to his hat brim. Bayard got into the carriage and Simon clucked to the horses, and the onlookers, halted to admire the momentary drama of the departure, fell behind." Notice the deft economy of Simon's action built into the language itself: "touched his whiphand to his hat brim." If in New Orleans and elsewhere Faulkner seemed to be performing the part of southern gentleman, he now put that performance into scenes that showed how everyone: pauper, banker, and black factotum—and even the horses—contributed to the spectacle of southern living. At this point, however, black people are still part of the minstrelsy of Faulkner's Yoknapatawpha, designed to exhibit their "race's fine feeling for potential theatrics." The novelist is just beginning to see Simon and other black people in their own right by recognizing their "self-serving manipulation of spectacle." Simon is, after all, acting as a banker himself, as the custodian of his church's funds. He is part of a trend in black businesses that steadily increased between 1918 and 1929—many of them, like Simon's, "fly by night" and prone to failure. The irony was not lost on William Faulkner. As one family banker to another, old Bayard has to bail Simon out. When church members come calling for the money that Simon has lost, crotchety old Bayard advances Simon the funds, partly, at least, out of "paternalistic pride."[44]

That black people could also stand apart and act in their own right is only an incipient element in *Flags in the Dust* when the recalcitrant Caspey demands to be treated as an equal after serving in the war. When old Simon wheedles old Bayard into paying his debts, old Bayard shouts, "Why in hell cant you niggers tell me the truth about things?" The subversion of white hegemony in Faulkner's fiction has just begun. The enormity of the black contribution to American forces in World War I is played for laughs, really, with Caspey cast as the uppity "nigger." In fact, the presence of black troops abroad, often welcomed into French homes, disturbed white southerners, who rightly worried about the repercussions back home, where black people might claim equal rights denied them in a segregated culture. Politicians like James K. Vardaman (1861–1930), a Mississippi governor and then senator, had resisted America's entry into the war in part because they believed black participation in the war threatened the white power structure.

Young Bayard returns from the war without displaying the uniform that Faulkner exhibited on his return to Oxford, and without a reverence for the past, even though he is bedeviled by the vainglorious behavior of his twin. Young Bayard never acknowledges his bitterness about a family defined by defeat, exemplified in the figure of Miss Jenny, Colonel John Sartoris's sister: "a slender woman with a delicate replica of the Sartoris nose and that expression of indomitable and utter weariness which all Southern women had learned to wear." Like Aunt Bama, who exulted in her father, Colonel Falkner, Miss Jenny is the repository of stories about Colonel Sartoris, the Carolina Bayard, and a version of the "gallant and finely tragical" South. But her stories undermine the chivalric myth. When Jeb Stuart is intent on playing the part of a Sir Walter Scott hero, a union officer tells him: "No gentleman has any business in this war. . . . There is no place for him here. He is an anachronism." The very war she upholds as the splendid display of an aristocratic culture is shown never to have been that at all.

Young Bayard is fixated on the moment his reckless twin brother died. "I tried to keep him from going up there on that goddam little popgun," he tells old Bayard, describing his brother as a fool for relying on the notoriously unreliable Sopwith Camel, a single-seater that made a sort of popping noise, although young Bayard may also have in mind a child's popgun, a toy that used berries as ammunition in an early version of paintball. In effect, Johnny has been as childish as the Carolina Bayard. Johnny even shoots at young Bayard, who tries to ward off his brother from a futile engagement "full of Fokkers," one of the most feared German planes on the western front.[45] Young Bayard's trauma is that he has lost part of himself, of their "violent complementing days."

The novel is hardly all gloom and doom, though, with scenes between old Bayard, Miss Jenny, and Simon that are like comic interludes in a Hollywood film. Simon admonishes Miss Jenny: "You ain't never yit planted nothin' what hit ought ter be planted." She retorts: "And whose business is that? . . . Yours, or Colonel's? Either one of you can loaf on this porch and tell me where a plant will grow best or look best, but if either of you ever grew as much as a weed out of the ground yourselves, I'd like to see it." The down-to-earth Jenny rebukes the sedentary authority of these old males even as she abets their right to lord it over others.

While *Flags in the Dust* was well under way, Oxford progressed by paving its streets, removing the muddy mire of the past, pleasing merchants with sidewalks and new housing that subdivided the land with the promise of more customers. The novel treated such changes with mixed emotions. No doubt the world was becoming cleaner and more antiseptic, like Dr. Alford's immaculate facilities, but also impersonal in the professionalism and specialization that displaced patients from their communities and detached them from their traditional ties to men like Old Man Falls, who painstakingly removes a wen from old Bayard's face with a salve based on a secret formula. The old-fashioned cure, delivered not in a pristine doctor's office but at old Bayard's bank, takes time, defying the quick, efficient methods of the surgical Dr. Alford. Old Man Falls's home remedy resembles the gunpowder/snuff concoction Buck Collins used to sell in a store Faulkner frequented. The Collins treatment had a harsh outcome, taking off not just the growth but a part of the patient too.[46] In *Flags in the Dust* the old cure is much neater; the growth, after a course of treatment, falls off, leaving unblemished skin as rosy as a baby's.

World War I has speeded up the pace of change, enabling young Bayard to race around the countryside in his car, seeking his doom after the fatal separation from his ebullient twin, John, whose foolhardy self-destructive aerial exploits are reminiscent of the Carolina Bayard on horseback rounding up a Yankee encampment on the strength of his bravado. The air war is supposed to have supplanted the glories of the cavalry charge, but young Bayard suffers from survivor guilt and a postwar climate that suffocates him with its demands for him to settle down, marry, father children, and pursue a conventional career like his stodgy old grandfather. Young Bayard's trauma is what William Faulkner affected in his own person and employed in his fiction to highlight the plight of a South still recovering from the Civil War even as it participated in the new patriotic war and peacetime progress. Faulkner was caught somewhere in the in-between, evoking the romantic power of the past that in reality could never be perpetuated, and yet could not be relinquished in favor of a mundane present providing little opportunity for a new generation to distinguish or ennoble itself. Bayard, a popular southern name with chivalric connotations—Robert E. Lee was called the "Bayard of the Confederate Army"[47]—is an ironic appellation for a young man who cannot cope with or overcome the expectations of his family and culture. It is fitting that Old Man Falls informs old Bayard about young Bayard speeding in a "low gray car." Old Man Falls, with eyes as "blue and innocent as a boy's," is reminiscent of the childlike old man in *The Wishing Tree*. Old Man Falls tells old Bayard: "Seems like everybody knows how fast he runs hit except you." Old Bayard, who employs Byron Snopes in the bank, and thus unwittingly advances the clan that will ultimately supplant the Sartorises in power, believes he can still control his grandson and assert his authority—as he does by striking down Caspey to end an incipient rebellion. Old Bayard's blow hardly settles the matter in a constantly changing world. The Sartorises and the Snopeses are not opposing but overlapping forces.[48]

Young Bayard also offends Narcissa Benbow's sense of propriety, but she is attracted to his reckless behavior, so antithetical to that of her effete brother Horace, a YMCA noncombatant during the war, whose untidy involvement with every woman he meets is in "stark contrast with Bayard's cold and rigid independence."[49] Narcissa Benbow lacks Estelle Oldham's flirtatious flair, but Narcissa, like Estelle, remains a proper lady while entertaining an alarmingly unconventional man. Narcissa watching young Bayard calls to mind an image of William Faulkner—"he appeared as usual at the time—a lean fixture in casual easy clothes unpressed and a little comfortably shabby"—although young Bayard's "air of smoldering abrupt violence" is the kind of drama Faulkner liked to add to fiction when reality would not quite do. Young Bayard is aloof and arrogant—traits familiar to William Faulkner. But young Bayard's chain smoking, "a sign of his incessant need and its eternal lack of fulfillment,"[50] did not dog William Faulkner, who seems to have pacified himself with a pipe.

Young Bayard is scary but also attractive because he is trying to break out of the impasse of an older generation. Aunt Jenny is thrilled by rides in his speeding car. And Narcissa wants part of that action even as she fears it. Old Bayard, on the contrary, opposes change even if it kills him—as it does on one of his harrowing drives with his grandson. Horace Benbow seems suspended in his own urn, returning from the war to practice law, complacently Keatsian, apostrophizing the "quietude of peace." Horace is a caricature of the Roman poet, his namesake, and perhaps also of friends like Ben Wasson, who feared he might be a model for Horace, and like Phil Stone, trained in the classics and an artist manqué. Both Wasson and Stone played their part in encouraging the daring young man who welcomed their help and then went way beyond what they could accomplish. Horace has come home with an elaborate collection of glassblowing equipment, which requires considerable skill. But the intricacy of his hobby does not yield much art. His work has reminded one critic of Faulkner's dismissal of Amy Lowell's polyphonic prose: "in spite of the fact that she has created some delightful statuettes of perfectly blown glass . . . it has left her, reed in hand, staring in naive surprise at the air whence her bubbles have burst." Another interprets the glassblowing as the "effeminate nature of his pursuit." Horace's idealization of Narcissa that verges on incest, and her anger over his affair with a married woman, Belle Mitchell, reflect Horace's stalemated personality. Horace's connection to Wasson is strengthened in a scene when Belle rises from her piano to embrace Horace just as Estelle enveloped Ben, although Frederick Karl links the "sexually ambiguous" Horace to Phil Stone—and even to "reverse sides" of an author who pursues a married woman (although Belle Mitchell hardly resembles Estelle) and simultaneously engages in an unmanly occupation (writing) and manly expeditions (war and hunting).[51]

Horace has his Byronic moments, when he emerges from his sooty artistic labors "a little mad, passionate and fine and austere"—if not exactly the Byron whom Caroline Lamb called "mad, bad, and dangerous to know." He "resists the parochial moral pronouncements with which his sister attempts to control him" and the cant that Byron despised. "He is not passive like Old Bayard; he is not reckless or desperate like young Bayard. He does not maniacally work to own things as does Harry [Mitchell]," Belle's husband. Horace wants to make things that accord with the images in his own head, not with those dictated by the values of "commodity fetishism."[52] Unlike Narcissa, who calls Belle dirty, Horace does not need to maintain the presence of pristine gentlemanliness. But he still succumbs to Belle, and to that fatalism that ultimately drives him dejectedly to the spring in *Sanctuary,* where he is an easy mark for Popeye.

Narcissa is a focal point for three marginal males: young Bayard, Horace, and Byron Snopes, whose pornographic notes simultaneously shame and titillate her—or so Miss Jenny supposes because Narcissa holds on to Byron's effusions. When he writes, "I think of you at night the way you walk," the allusion to Byron's "She Walks in Beauty Like the Night" is unmistakable. Byron will eventually abscond with bank money, becoming even more of a marginal man,[53] like the self-exiled poet. Narcissa rebuffs all three men even as she advances toward them, although only young Bayard has the strength of purpose to actually, physically, command her presence, pulling her down to him on his sickbed, and eventually marrying her. She becomes, in a sense, a pivot point in the plot since she attracts males of such different temperament and outlook. She is a sedate version of Temple Drake and Eula Varner, who bewitch a passel of suitors. Faulkner found the seductions of femininity, by turns, fascinating, disturbing, and amusing. In *Mosquitoes,* the well-endowed Jenny reports his observation that "if the straps of my dress was to break I'd devastate the country."

The abiding memories of the Civil War, the disruptions of World War I, the heightened, Freudian consciousness of sex, the changing nature of race relations, the internal contradictions of the Sartoris and Benbow families, and the growing impact of the usurping Snopes clan overtaking the commercial life of a Jefferson that looks a lot like Oxford without a university—all contribute to a sense of everything in flux. Much has been made of young Bayard's inability to adjust to postwar society, but what is there to adjust to? What role would suit this returning veteran? At one point, he takes refuge with a country family, the MacCallums, who resemble the Cullen clan with whom Faulkner hunted as a boy. The MacCallums are off the grid, so to speak. Although Buddy MacCallum has been to war, that experience is not what defines him and determines his family's behavior. Buddy is not another Bayard and has no slotted role in family history. He does not have to reckon with the expectations of generations. The unromantic MacCallum country life can momentarily soothe young Bayard, but it cannot suffice any more than Faulkner's own yearning to be a tramp and an artist unbound by family fealty. What rankles young Bayard is the claim that others put upon him and that he, however grudgingly, puts upon himself. And the same could be said for Faulkner, although he had his art that could transcend family and community entreaties.

Dr. Peabody, the Sartoris family physician, positioned between the ultramodern Dr. Alford and the folk healer Old Man Falls, is a kind of bridging figure between past and present. He tells Dr. Alford: "Folks got along with cancer a long time before they invented knives." Peabody has none of Alford's arrogance, even if he does not exactly endorse the old ways: "Will has done some curious things with that salve of his," Peabody reports. Better just to leave the growth alone, he concludes. Peabody treats the whole man and recognizes that what ails Bayard is not on his face but in his heart. Peabody knows his man—and his woman—in ways that Alford could never divine. When Peabody teases Miss Jenny about courting her when they were young, she calls him an "old gray-headed liar." But he rejoins that her blushing belies her protestations. Like Faulkner's Aunt Bama, Miss Jenny is, in her contradictory way, the family's standard-bearer. Her blushing cheeks are "like banners, and her head was still high amid the jibing laughter." Faulkner's own paradoxical view of past and present, of the flags in the dust that were nevertheless held high in his family's posture, is replicated in Miss Jenny's erect figure. If the Falkner code invited ridicule, it still commanded respect. Young Bayard, who refers to the Civil War as a "two-bit war," nevertheless cannot escape the consequences of his actions. He is, for all his rejections of the Sartoris ethos, a gentleman, living by standards that Faulkner never forsook, restating them in *The Reivers:* "A gentleman accepts the responsibility of his actions and bears the burden of their consequences."

Young Bayard runs away from his dead grandfather, leaving behind the engine of what has become not his salvation but his destruction. He takes refuge with the premodern MacCallums, who see he is in a bad way. Bayard tries to blame his grandfather's death on a "bum heart," but he sees his months of "headlong and heedless wastefulness" swiftly unroll like a film, and he incriminates himself: *"You made a nigger sneak your horse out to you. You, who deliberately do things your judgment tells you may not be successful, even possible, are afraid to face the consequences of your own acts."* He has deserted the gentleman's code. His realization is also a prophecy of his own death when he flies an experimental plane that is bound to crash. And that crash is also foreshadowed in his effort to master a stallion, "a symbol of the old order,"[54] that throws him to the ground, where Faulkner would often find himself after his mount rebuffed his desire to take command. If Faulkner was no runaway, and kept returning home, he nevertheless understood the urge to flee.

Young Bayard's fate is counterpointed in Horace's romantically decadent letters to his sister Narcissa. Horace is an attenuated Byron, sad that "all the spring couldn't be one spring, like Byron's ladies' mouths," an allusion to the Byronic desire to make of all his women one mouth to kiss. These are words that have no outlet and are sort of like the young Faulkner mooning over the ladies he could not have. Horace is as out of place as young Bayard: "At home I always found myself remembering apple trees or green lanes or the color of the sea in other places, and I'd be sad that I couldn't be every-where at once," he writes to Narcissa, who has the thankless role of serving as Horace's muse and young Bayard's wife. In their different ways, both young Bayard and Horace are failures as southern gentleman. In *Sanctuary*, Horace will try to redeem the code of the southern gentleman by defending a man wrongly accused of murder. He should amount to more than the spots made by the dripping, stinking shrimp that he carries for the delectation of Belle Mitchell, who is the doom of his gentlemanly pretensions. She is the wife of a cotton speculator, one of the nouveau riche who displace the old moneyed Sartorises. In *Flags,* she is "repeatedly associated with rank sexuality: filth, unpleasant smells, heat, flesh, and rottenness"—all of which revolt Narcissa, the lady, and undermine Horace's own delicate glassblowing aesthetic.[55] Even as Horace walks toward his fate with Belle Mitchell, young Bayard runs away from home, ending with the wingtips of his plane buckling, then coming off and driving into his tail, a perfect image of a man who has, like Horace, undone himself.

Young Bayard's death took on "a terrifying sense of prophecy when Faulk-ner's own brother Dean died in a plane crash six years after the novel was published, to be buried under a tombstone with the same inscription as John Sartoris's: 'I bare him on eagles' wings and brought him unto me.'"[56] Fiction, fact, history, and the Bible coalesced for Faulkner in an epitaph that derives from Exodus 19:4 and that is on the RAF memorial in London.

John's "warm radiance" and his "sweet and merry and wild" temperament are reminiscent of Dean, "one of the sweetest people" Cho-Cho "ever knew. He taught her to drive on the Old Taylor Road in a Buick touring car. She thought of him as a kind of beau. At camp, she delighted in his letters."[57] But Dean, according to others, was reckless and, according to one contemporary, "a loud mouthed fellow."[58] Estelle said, "It was good he went when he did. He had practically become an alcoholic. He was wild, he had a self-destructive streak in him, almost like a wish for death."[59] Dean's death seemed the out-come of the very fatality Faulkner invokes at the end of *Flags in the Dust.* It is tempting to see young Bayard's inability to adjust to family life, to an attentive wife and an expected child, as deriving from "his years in his own strife-ridden household" and as an "exaggerated psychological self-portrait of the author himself."[60] Dean Faulkner (he added the *u*), Murry Falkner's favorite son, is transformed into the nexus of Bayard and John Sartoris, both of whom die, even as Faulkner eliminates from the novel their father, who, like Faulkner's father, has no story worth telling. *Flags in the Dust* is a kind of clearing out of the House of Falkner. If brother Jack seems not to have minded his brother's Bill's creative ascendancy, brother John did. He told a friend, "'Mama always said I had more talent in my little finger than Bill had in his whole body.' He was serious."[61]

Narcissa attempts to deflect the doom that devastates the Sartorises by naming her child by young Bayard, Benbow Sartoris. "Do you think," Miss Jenny says, "that because his name is Benbow he'll be any less a Sartoris and a scoundrel and a fool?" Narcissa does not seem to listen to this retort, and she is oblivious to the concerns of the narrator, who depicts the Sartorises as pawns in the Player's game, "a game outmoded and played with pawns shaped too late and to an old dead pattern and of which the Player Himself is a little wearied." The medieval, chivalric ethos mocked in *Mayday* is sounded again in the Sartoris legend: "For there is death in the sound of it, and a glamorous fatality, like silver pennons downrushing at sunset, or a dying fall of horns along the road to Roncevaux." The irony and the allure of glamorous fatality are unmistakable, even as the serene Narcissa is enveloped in an evening like a "windless lilac dream, foster-dam of quietude and peace." The novel's ending yields neither the truth nor beauty of "Ode on a Grecian Urn." Benbow Sartoris, mentioned a few times in the Yoknapatawpha saga, does not bear out Miss Jenny's prediction. That a new pattern has to emerge seems evident, even if young Bayard and Horace are powerless to effect one.

Flags in the Dust, as the title suggests, is a "commentary on the moribund society of Jefferson and on the twilight of civilization itself" in prose that evokes a medieval sensibility right out of *Piers Ploughman* and its "fair field full of folk." The past in this novel, "swollen with the experience of the generations and romanticized into legends of things that really never were, still gnaws into the present and rearranges the future."[62] The hallowed Confederate flag has its counterpart in the "gay flapping of an orange pennon from the nose of John's Camel," as he goes down to death in the First World War.

RISORGIMENTO IN YOKNAPATAWPHA

In November, Faulkner received the devastating news: *Flags* was a failure, Liveright announced. It had no plot and disintegrated into a "thousand loose ends." Faulkner knew better and told the publisher so: "I still believe it is the book which will make my name for me as a writer."[63] The protean nature of the novel eluded the publisher, and so Faulkner asked for its return so he could try it out on other houses. Liveright would charge the advance for *Flags* against the next book Faulkner submitted. In the meantime he worked on short fiction that extended the implications of his first Yoknapatawpha novel, and drew yet again on his family's experience of the change beginning to overtake the Falkners and the South.

One piece, intended as a story, would develop into a novel, first titled "Twilight," and then *The Sound and the Fury*.[64] Two others, "That Evening Sun" and "A Justice," involving all the Compson children except Benjy, extended the range of Yoknapatawpha in stories of initiation and race and gender that would fuel and unify Faulkner's fictional universe. No one has been able to determine which story came first, or the sequence of composition—or even if Faulkner worked on them one at a time or in conjunction with one another.[65] Only the fragment "Twilight" includes Benjy and the essence of what became the first section of *The Sound and the Fury*, which suggests that "Twilight" is the culmination, or perhaps the concomitant, of Faulkner's thinking about historical process in "That Evening Sun" and "A Justice," as well as of his references to twilight in the New Orleans sketches *Soldiers' Pay*, "Mistral," and "Dry September." The title on the first manuscript page of *The Sound and the Fury* is "Twilight," a word that Faulkner employed to suggest how the decline of day into night is the optimum moment in which to assess what is fast becoming the past, a degeneration of the present, an in-between phase in which what has been fades before what is to be has been born. An earlier title for the story, "That Evening Sun Go Down," made the allusion to W. C. Handy's "St. Louis Blues" more explicit, especially the evocation of the song's first four lines:

> I hate to see that evening sun go down
> I hate to see that evening sun go down
> Cause my baby, he gone lef' this town,
> Feelin' tomorrow like I feel today

Twilight is not only the intersection of past and present and a premonition of the future, but it also marks the transition, in Faulkner's stories and in *The Sound and the Fury*, from childhood to adulthood as the Compson children, except for Benjy, segue from innocence to experience, each of them already evincing a good part of their adult selves—like Jason, who is already threatening in "That Evening Sun" to tell on his siblings to his parents, already trying to dominate Caddy, as he tries to do in *The Sound and the Fury*.

In "A Justice," Quentin refers to "that strange, faintly sinister suspension of twilight," a phrase that occurs at the very end of a sinister story in which Sam Fathers—part black and part Choctaw—has told Quentin about Doom (Ikkemotubbe) aka "the Man," who took power by poisoning his rivals and then adjudicating the conflict between Sam's "pappy" and his black challenger, the slave whose wife pappy coveted. Faulkner knew, of course, what it meant to love another man's wife, and later on he enjoyed his status as his family's "pappy." Estelle's children, especially Malcolm, treated him as "the Man."

Sam's name was once "had two fathers," he tells Quentin. Sam embodies his native land's race mixing. Quentin describes Sam talking about "the old days" and how Sam "talked like a nigger—that is, he said his words like niggers do, but he didn't say the same words—and his hair was nigger hair. But his skin wasn't quite the color of a light nigger and his nose and his mouth and chin were not nigger nose and mouth and chin. And his shape was not like the shape of a nigger when he gets old. He was straight in the back, not tall, a little broad, and his face was still all the time, like he might be somewhere else all the while he was working or when people, even white people, talked to him, or while he talked to me." Sam is both here and somewhere else, in the past but also in the present, living like a black person but not exactly like one either. He straddles time and race just as Faulkner does in his fiction, creating characters of and beyond their times and places—like Doom, who returns from New Orleans having won six black slaves on a riverboat, and later in *Absalom, Absalom!* like Charles Bon, whose New Orleans sensibility intrigues and disturbs the Sutpens.

"That Evening Sun" begins with a paragraph suffused with an awareness of historical change:

> MONDAY IS NO DIFFERENT from any other weekday in Jefferson now. The streets are paved now, and the telephone and electric companies are cutting down more and more of the shade trees—the water oaks, the maples and locusts and elms—to make room for iron poles bearing clusters of bloated and ghostly and bloodless grapes, and we have a city laundry which makes the rounds on Monday morning, gathering the bundles of clothes into bright-colored, specially-made motor cars: the soiled wearing of a whole week now flees apparitionlike behind alert and irritable electric horns, with a long diminishing noise of rubber and asphalt like tearing silk, and even the Negro women who still take in white people's washing after the old custom, fetch and deliver it in automobiles.

The "now" is monotonous, predictable, inorganic, denatured, and corporate (the city laundry). Oxford's civic improvements troubled Faulkner, although he had no illusions about the exploited labor involved in sustaining the old times and old customs. But like Quentin, he regretted the quickening pace and impatience he heard in those "irritable electric horns" and the heating up of human activity. Gone was the time when Quentin, or Faulkner, could walk in the shade of city streets. The rubber and asphalt were noisily and gratingly tearing up the silk of an earlier age. The evocation of now inevitably leads to the memory of then, when what one heard had nothing to do with the telephone, always an interruption that Faulkner never liked answering. Even the evidence of life, when what you soiled was more of a public spectacle, "flees apparitionlike." Even the vestiges of the past, like the "Negro women" taking in white people's washing, is "after the old custom," which is to say a way of life is actually over, its very fabric rent apart by "progress."

Quentin is "repelled by the barren world in which he finds himself"[66] and seeks solace in the past: "But fifteen years ago, on Monday morning the quiet, dusty, shady streets would be full of Negro women with, balanced on their steady, turbaned heads, bundles of clothes tied up in sheets, almost as large as cotton bales, carried so without touch of hand between the kitchen door of the white house and the blackened washpot beside a cabin door in Negro Hollow." Quentin's dismay over historical change is muted but still evident. Cotton bales weighed as much as five hundred pounds, an impossible load for these black women, but an exaggeration that emphasizes how large they loom in Quentin's memory. Similarly the streetlights, invidiously compared to "bloated and ghostly and bloodless grapes," contrast with the oil-lamp glow of his reminiscence, and "Negro Hollow," the section of town to which Nancy will take the children. The changing scene as described by Quentin Compson is one of Faulkner's first forays into a consciousness that is displaced, held in suspension, so to speak, by a fealty to the past, to how it used to be done. Walking the streets of Cambridge in *The Sound and the Fury* is a constant reminder to Quentin that he cannot remain in childhood, in the past, and removed from the remorseless movement of time, which he can stop only by putting an end to his life.

At first these opening passages in "That Evening Sun" are a puzzle. Are they really necessary? Ostensibly, this is the story of a black woman, Nancy, haunted by a black lover (husband?) named Jesus who is out to slash her throat because she has betrayed him with another man and gotten herself pregnant. She is, however, a laundress who has toted the white man's burden, not to mention his dirty clothes, and you might say, his dirty everything. Nancy has served the family faithfully, but she is also a whore who demands her recompense from a white Baptist deacon, Mr. Stovall, a putative moral example to his community but also a bank cashier, part of the cash nexus she has contracted: "When you going to pay me, white man?"[67] Mr. Stovall kicks in her teeth as she makes a public spectacle of herself that puts her in jail laughing and singing like the condemned black man in *Sanctuary* whose songs greet Horace Benbow on his way to defend Lee Goodwin, a white man accused of a murder actually committed by Popeye and described as a "black man" in spite of his whiteness. Who is truly black and who white, if you take those terms as moral categories of good and evil?

The time and racial shifting in Faulkner's work begins in these first mature stories with Nancy's yelling. Why she carries on in jail is never explained, but that she carries on is the point: the black impress on Quentin's consciousness is indelible, and the force with which black people enter white lives is profound and disturbing—so much so that Quentin's brother Jason obsessively repeats, "I ain't a nigger," which is a kind of call-and-response to Nancy's compulsion to say, "I ain't nothing but a nigger." She is not supposed to count for anything, but she counts, in the end, for everything. Mr. Compson, the children's father, would like to rid himself of responsibility for Nancy, who is immobilized by the menacing Jesus, but the white master, in spite of his wife's complaints, is compelled to escort the terrified Nancy to her home and reassure her constantly that Jesus will not be her doom even as Doom (Ikkemotubbe) in "A Justice," written around the same time as "That Evening Sun," is out to convince his tribe that he is "the Man" and their fate. In "That Evening Sun," "the man" is Mr. Compson, the gentleman-knight charged with defending his family, black and white. To his wife's demand that he stay home and protect his family rather than escorting the terrified Nancy to her home, he declares, "You know that I am not lying outside with a razor," even though Mr. Compson prefers to believe that Nancy is imagining her doom. At the story's conclusion Mr. Compson abandons Nancy to her terrors, to her black Jesus. Or, as Faulkner himself said, he created a black Jesus "not so much to shock but to emphasize the point I was making, which was that this—this Negro woman who had given devotion to the white family knew that when—when the crisis of her need came, the white family wouldn't be there."[68]

Faulkner saw the futility of white paternalism firsthand in his own family. His cousin Sallie Burns remembered a black cook whose husband beat her mercilessly. She would complain to her employers, the Falkners, and they would report the husband to the police. But he would deny the charge and after release would beat his wife again. Sallie Burns recalled this cook, called Nancy Snowball by the Falkner boys because she was so black. She was just as lean as the Nancy in "That Evening Sun."[69]

The irony of an avenging black Jesus suggests there is no deliverance in these stories. We don't even learn whether or not Jesus does slit Nancy's throat, but then that is the point: This is a world that cannot be saved and that is bound to perish, a world that is very upsetting to Jason, Caddy, and Quentin, who asks, "Who will do our washing now, Father?" It is a twelve-year-old's reaction but also reflective of how much the family relies on the labor of black people, whose lives the white family can comprehend only fitfully and never fully. No one is prepared to understand why Nancy tried to commit suicide in her jail cell, but readers of *The Sound and the Fury* may note that this is

Quentin's early exposure to a self-destructiveness that eventually overtakes him. Caddy, who has been taunting Jason that he is "scairder than a nigger," overhears Jesus talking to Nancy, referring to her pregnancy as a watermelon under her dress and threatening to cut off the vine that gave it to her. Caddy, who will be unfaithful to Quentin when she becomes pregnant in *The Sound and the Fury,* asks, "Off of what vine?" Caddy's words to Quentin innocently convey Nancy's fear that she will not be saved in a faithless world:

> "Maybe she's waiting for Jesus to come and take her home," Caddy said.
> "Jesus is gone," I said. Nancy told us how one morning she woke up and Jesus was gone.
> "He quit me."

She means her lover, but the allusion to Jesus as savior is inescapable. "Jesus is a nigger," Jason says. And so he is because like Nancy's nemesis, Jesus, "the other one," never does show up for his redemption scene. Instead, she dreads the appearance of her black Jesus, "intimidated by the power of the whites," Edmond Volpe writes, and intent on avenging himself on her, the "living symbol of his humiliation by the whites. Nancy becomes the sacrificial victim. The menacing violent black Jesus, ironically, is the creation of the white culture whose God is the gentle, loving 'other Jesus.'"[70]

Coming to "That Evening Sun" from a reading of *The Sound and the Fury* suggests that the story, which depends so much on Quentin's evolving consciousness, is as much about his "isolation and unhappiness," his living in the shadows or the twilight of a decaying family, which cannot cope with Nancy's "unbearable misery" any more than it can with Quentin's.[71] It is impossible to say how far Faulkner's own identification with Quentin extended, but he certainly shared the plight of a sensitive young man whose family provided few resources for understanding the common fate they shared with the very black people who served them and were even thought of as family while so many other black people were being driven away. As John T. Matthews observes:

> The South's violent Jim Crow regime was scaring black people out of the region in unprecedented numbers in the first decades of the twentieth century. Who would do the washing—and the tilling, planting, tending, picking, hauling, stacking, feeding, fixing, cooking, serving, cleaning—turns out to be a question many white people were asking. Quentin sees his world at twilight, when the sun dropping below the horizon creates a virtual image, an object visible but already gone. What Quentin is truly grieving for is not Nancy and the setting sun of black terrorization, but himself, a dying son of the plantation South.

Faulkner's return in story and novel to the scene of a black singing behind bars signifies the "barred expression" his own fiction seeks to liberate.[72]

HARK: A COMING MAN

The powerful new stories as well the support of Ben Wasson, acting as Faulkner's agent, buoyed the young writer, who sounded cocky in a story submission to the *Saturday Evening Post*: "And hark in your ear. I am a coming man, so take warning."[73] Nevertheless, the magazine did not accept his story, and Wasson had a hard time interesting publishers in *Flags*. Finally, Wasson's friend Hal Smith, an editor at Harcourt, Brace, wrote a favorable report on *Flags*, although the diffuse book needed cutting, said the firm's head, Alfred Harcourt. Smith thought that Wasson, rather than the author, ought to do the surgery. Accepting the fifty-dollar cutting job and a three-hundred-dollar advance for Faulkner, Wasson also coaxed his friend to New York City. Faulkner arrived wearing a raincoat, carrying a satchel and a bag of his golf clubs. As he climbed the stairs of Pennsylvania Station, Wasson wondered where his friend expected to play: "In Central Park?" Already rattled by the noise, Faulkner said, "Bud, I sho am glad you met me at the dee-po."[74]

On one of their New York adventures they went to Harlem to watch Carl Van Vechten's latest discovery. The author of the novel *Nigger Heaven* (1926), a superb photographer and cultural impresario, wanted them to see the performance of a cross-dressing female in a tuxedo swaying through a lewd performance of "Sweet Violets," which began something like this:

> There once was a farmer who took a young miss
> In back of the barn where he gave her a . . .
> Lecture on horses and chickens and eggs
> And told her that she had such beautiful . . .
> Manners that suited a girl.[75]

Wasson remembered that Faulkner found it all too decadent, although he spent the evening making "obvious passes" at Wasson's fiancé, which Wasson leaves out of his published memoir, preferring instead to make his friend seem more of a prig, thanking Van Vechten for the experience but also saying it was too much for a "countryman" and that he did not want to indulge in such faddish activities.[76]

The novel Faulkner intended to publish as *Flags in the Dust* is, in one sense, irrecoverable. Two versions by two different editors attempt to reconstruct from a manuscript and typescript what Faulkner originally wrote, but there is no telling what else Faulkner might have done to the book if a publisher had accepted the full-length *Flags*. Faulkner tried different beginnings, each time approaching history in a different way. One version began in World War I France with the Sartoris great-grandsons named Bayard and Evelyn; another introduced the Colonel's son (old Bayard) in Mississippi musing on the family's history, an approach Faulkner would later employ in *The Unvanquished;* yet a third option cast the Sartoris saga in the reminiscences of Old Man Falls, emphasizing, as a result, the many filtering layers of memory that gave history its texture, resonance, and complexity. Beginning with Horace Benbow was yet another choice Faulkner seems to have considered, and one that he began with in the original draft of *Sanctuary*. *Flags in the Dust* had gone through several stages of composition before Ben Wasson worked on it, with Faulkner revising and rewriting many passages, changing time sequences, the placement of scenes, and first- and third-person points of view. All these modifications reveal the "ongoing creative ferment out of which Yoknapatawpha came."[77]

Although it pained Faulkner to see Wasson remove scenes with Horace and Narcissa and Byron Snopes while trimming other passages making the story *Sartoris,* the novelist acquiesced—in part, perhaps, because he found a new ally in Hal Smith, who wanted him as a Harcourt author. One of Smith's friends called him Faulkner's "uncle-confessor." Smith, born in 1888, nearly a decade older with already graying hair, "looked on the world with sort of a gentle, ironical look, as if he found it all very amusing."[78] Urbane, handsome, debonair, and a charming raconteur, he was a Yale man of a type Faulkner had already encountered in Phil Stone's company. Smith had worked as a textbook salesman and a reporter.[79] He was worldly in a way that appealed to Faulkner, who knew little about business. Faulkner's new champion "did everything in a stylish way." Smith could infuriate authors with his "extremely vague and rather unpredictable behavior," as their mutual friend Eric Devine said. Some thought Smith took advantage of Faulkner, offering him advances below market rates, but Faulkner remained fond of Smith long after their business relationship ceased and never expressed any qualms about how Smith had handled his work. Smith appeared at just the right time as the risk taker who rejuvenated Faulkner after his dispiriting dealings with Horace Liveright.[80]

By the fall of 1928, Harcourt accepted the cut-up version of *Flags*. Faulkner had extricated himself from the Liveright contract, announcing to Aunt Bama, "Well, I'm going to be published by white folks now." That sentence sums up a world in 1928 in which Jews were not considered white, and writers like Faulkner could indulge in slurs. As to *The Sound and the Fury*, he did not believe that "anyone will publish it for 10 years. Harcourt swear they will, but I dont believe it."[81] In fact, Harcourt had made no commitment, but Hal Smith had, a man like no other in the publishing business, so far as Faulkner was concerned, a man whom Faulkner later called his only friend in New York—not to mention his confidant, editor, banker, and, soon, publisher.[82]

From New York, Faulkner wrote to Aunt Bama: "Having a rotten time, as usual. I hate this place." But the city seemed tolerable so long as the unbusinesslike Hal Smith was around to shepherd Faulkner through the commerce of authorship. Smith "published books because he liked them, thinking that if he did, the audience would follow in time."[83] The casual Smith seems to have been the perfect foil for the elaborately courteous southerner, who could show up at the door of Louise Bonino's Sheridan Square apartment, swaying, and ask, "Miss Louise, could I, right now, take a short nap?" She was one of the many women working in publishers' offices and later in movie studios who would be treated to this gentlemanly behavior. In her case, he later followed up with, "Miss Louise, can I sleep with you tonight?" And then he graciously accepted her refusal.

When Faulkner met Leane Zugsmith, then twenty-five and an aspiring author who had not yet published novels and short-story collections, he encountered a friend of Lillian Hellman, Louis Kronenberger, Saxe Commins, and other Liveright lights. She was a talker, and though Faulkner is often depicted as shying away from the voluble, he made exceptions for erotic and spirited women. Dark-haired, intense, and exotic, she could play Lamia to Faulkner's Keats. Her biographer calls her incendiary. She was a keen antifascist, and Faulkner had seen enough of how fascists operated during his sojourn in Italy to appreciate her political fervor. She was also a pilgrim from Louisville, Kentucky, and perhaps southern enough, to begin with. In Faulkner, she would have observed a man like her father, holding himself powerfully erect, a gentleman, and yet sometimes appearing with the louche air of the dandy, decked out to impress. Both understood the virtues and vices of a patrician household. Like Faulkner, she began writing early and appeared in school and local publications in Louisville. As a Jew, she was hyperconscious of caste and class, and like Lillian Hellman and Faulkner, she rejected what college had to offer. When Faulkner met her in 1928, she had been in New York City for four years, working for pulps like *Western Story* and *Detective Story*. But she was poorly paid, and Liveright represented a step up, especially with its appealing line of important writers. She said she had no time for dates, but for Faulkner she made an exception, and he for her. But their time together seems to have been brief.[84]

Faulkner made lifelong friends in New York City—like Eric (also called Jim) Devine, a man with a literary bent who had attended college in

Louisiana and had worked for Doubleday Doran. Devine remembered first meeting Faulkner at the apartment of their mutual New Orleans friend Lyle Saxon. Faulkner wore a handsome Harris tweed with stylish raglan sleeves and inside pockets that held two bottles of bootleg gin. A quiet Faulkner only warmed up after a few drinks. Unlike other southerners, Faulkner never asked where the women were. Devine and Faulkner used to frequent a beer joint in Hoboken. Their visits were commemorated in Faulkner's inscription in the first edition of *As I Lay Dying:*

> To Jim Devine
> Baron of Hoboken
> from his friend Bill Faulkner
> Earl of Beerinstein[85]

Devine had the duty of picking Faulkner off the floor during drinking bouts in Village speakeasies. At midnight, in front of the Fourteenth Street subway entrance off Union Square, a wobbly Faulkner sat down on a curb, holding his head, and said: "Don't make me go up to your place. I have never been upstate on the subway." Laughing, Devine and his friend Leon Scales managed to get the writer through the turnstiles and onto the uptown express anyway. Sometimes he comforted himself visiting with New Orleans friends, including Lyle Saxon and William Spratling. Faulkner also met another Louisiana native, Owen Crump, with whom the writer lived in a building at the corner of Mac-Dougal and Sixth Avenue. Faulkner would write with diligence and concentration in cheap notebooks purchased at Woolworth's and sip bootleg gin. He visited magazine offices, still trying unsuccessfully to sell short stories. At parties out would come in conversation stories about the spotted horses or instead the silent, moody, aloof, and lonely, if well-turned-out, figure. Crump remembered their going to the theater, attending performances of *The Cherry Orchard* and *Peter Pan,* both starring Eve Le Gallienne at the Civic Repertory Theatre on Fourteenth Street.

From Crump's apartment, located close to Ben Wasson's office at 146 Mac-Dougal Street, Faulkner came to consult with Wasson on his shaping of *Sartoris.* How the two men worked together will probably never be known in any precise way. Fifty years after the fact, Wasson said it was "hard for him to remember exactly what each of two young men in New York . . . had cut or added to the *Flags* material."[86] Wasson's role is intriguing, and no one, it seems, ever pressed him on what the novel meant to him *personally,* or pointed out that Wasson cut the Horace bits that arguably pertained to Wasson's own personality as a figure off to the side of Faulkner's life and yet indispensable, as indispensable as Horace Benbow is to *Flags in the Dust.*

Faulkner sometimes suggested that he just abandoned the novel to Wasson, but that could not have happened. As he wrote his Aunt Bama, "Every day or so I burn some of it and I think I shall put it away for a while and forget it."[87] And Wasson just as adamantly emphasized that he had done none of the new writing that appeared in *Sartoris*. He subtracted. In some cases, the subtractions and reshaping resulted in more powerful passages as statement turned into action, so that what went on for a few pages in *Flags* became a paragraph in *Sartoris*.[88] Standing over the text like two surgeons, Wasson removed passages and then Faulkner restored parts of them with vivid interpolations, so that, for example, Byron Snopes's "mind coiled and coiled upon itself, tormenting him with feeling obscene images in which she [Narcissa] moved with another," became in *Sartoris*: "he bent over his ledgers, watching his hand pen the neat figures into the ruled columns with a sort of astonishment. After his sleepless night he labored in a kind of stupor, his mind too spent even to contemplate the coiling images of his lust." That brief period when Faulkner worked in his grandfather's bank paid off. He knew what it meant to bind yourself to a ledger, to, in fact, be ruled by it as your own imagination sought a way out. Byron is bent over and neat as a banker even as his pornographic imagination is out of control. In the end, according to Wasson, Faulkner said, "You've done a good job, and it ought to suit them." Hal Smith concurred, and the book went to the printers and was published on January 31, 1929, with this dedication: "To Sherwood Anderson, through whose kindness I was first published, with the belief that this book will give him no reason to regret that fact."

That Horace Liveright had made a colossal mistake became apparent in the reviews. Henry Nash Smith (*Dallas Morning News*, February 17) heralded William Faulkner's work, putting it in the vanguard of the novels now coming out of the South. "One of the most promising talents for fiction in contemporary America," Smith declared. The excited reviewer watched Faulkner learning his trade and broadening his thought "almost visibly from chapter to chapter," confronting "post war pessimism without falling into the sophomoric pose of his New York compères, or the epicene dreaming indolence of Sherwood Anderson." Smith predicted, "From such a man one might well expect the definitive utterance of the generation who went to the war and came back when it was over."

In the Age of Dreiser, Faulkner wrote with a majesty resembling blank verse, only occasionally overdoing his eloquence—"too long for modern ears." Smith even detected the counterpoint that had been damaged when so much of the Benbow material had been cut from the novel. This prophetic reviewer noted perceptions "Keats-like in their delicacy and richness." His vivid prose put the "best efforts of the imagist to insipid shame, and his range includes smells and sounds even more keen sensed and regarded than his pictures." Smith picked out a passage as an example of Faulkner's palpable prose: "The negroes gathered the puppies up one by one and tumbled them into a smaller box behind the stove, where they continued to move about with sundry scratching and bumping and an occasional smothered protest. From time to time during the meal a head would appear, staring above the rim of the box with blinking and solemn curiosity, then vanish with an abrupt scuffling thump and more protests, and the moiling, infant-like noises rose again." This passage conveys the sheer delight Faulkner took in capturing a world in two sentences, complete in itself, and a counterpoint to the angst and violence of the Sartoris-Benbow story.

Smith understood exactly what Liveright had missed: "But here more than usually the plot is unimportant." What mattered, as Donald Davidson argued in a *Nashville Tennessean* review (April 14), was that southern writers like Faulkner were "bringing back a sense of style that almost vanished in the experimentalism of the post-war period." He saw the humor that kept breaking through the fatality and despair that read like a medieval allegory, and quoted Miss Jenny: "It always does me good to see all those fool pompous men lying there with their marble mottoes and things. . . . I reckon the Lord knows his business, but I declare, sometimes . . ." J. Dana Tasker in *Outlook and Independent* (February 20) went so far as to claim Faulkner did better with the women grappling with the "man's point of view. . . . Although the personalities of each of the men are strong in their different ways, the reader's sympathy remains with the women in almost every situation."

For Mary Ellen Chase (*Commonweal*, June 5), Faulkner's eloquence was too dear to him and sometimes became intrusive, but she remembered what was said of Robert Louis Stevenson: "His faults are so much more lovable than other people's virtues." She, too, mentioned the charming space black people occupied in Faulkner's fiction and the sensory pleasure of young frogs piping "like endless, silver, small bubbles rising."

In spite of the promising good reviews, plenty of others deplored the novel as disjointed. They could have been written by Horace Liveright himself. Even more disappointing, Harcourt did little to promote *Sartoris,* and with far fewer reviews than the two previous novels, it sold fewer than two thousand copies. Faulkner told his publisher he wanted to see the reviews but had no ideas about selling the novel, except for stocking it at the Gathright Drugstore in Oxford, where his friend Mac Reed took his books on a consignment basis. By the time reviews appeared, Faulkner had already completed *The Sound and the Fury.* He did not seem disconsolate that Harcourt had already decided not to publish the new novel.[89]

Hal Smith was leaving the firm and planned to publish the novel under the imprint of Cape and Smith. Thirty years later, Smith told biographer Tom Dardis: "When I first saw a section of the manuscript of *The Sound and the Fury* and confronted that tiny, tiny script of his, line after line of it, I thought immediately that this is a man who believes absolutely in the importance of what he is doing—it's just *got* to be published!"[90] What did the "tiny, tiny script" have to do with it? Smith did not explain, or Dardis did not ask. For anyone who has tried to decipher Faulkner's handwriting, which looks like it has been scratched out of stone and somehow transferred to paper, Smith's reaction is understandable. Reading Faulkner in the raw is a mining operation requiring an intensity of focus and dedication that has to match his own inimitable devotion to the text. Smith did not tamper much with Faulkner's work but rather performed what might be called an archaeological recovery of the artist's chirography.

Smith worked out of a brownstone on Forty-Sixth Street off of Lexington Avenue. Lenore Marshal, looking for a job, remembered walking into "absolute chaos." Smith interviewed her without saying he was head of the firm. The intimate scale of Smith's operation, as Evelyn Harper Glick recalled, was a new, inviting, and exhilarating home:

> In a small house like ours—I don't suppose we had more than fifteen people there, counting the salesmen. But everyone knew each other. The place vibrated with enthusiasm and energy. In this old brownstone house of four floors, my office was in the basement, in what used to be the kitchen. . . . On the main floor where you came in, there was a reception room. The telephone operator was right there in the hall. The salesmen were on that floor, too. On the next one up—you went up these curving wooden stairs—Louise Bonino and Harrison Smith had their offices. On the top floor, that is the third floor, Ben Wasson lived. When I came, he was already living there. He was doing proofreading and other chores and he was right in residence there.

The firm had been established at the beginning of the Depression, but no one was depressed. They ran up and down the stairs. A "very businesslike" Faulkner sat in the "kitchen" beside Glick's desk, always courteous and "agreeable about everything." At publishing parties, he remained silent most of the time, squatting with his glass of bourbon, although sometimes rising for talk with Hal Smith.

Faulkner needed a new lease in publishing. In spite of discerning reviews, the poor reception of his third published novel only strengthened his own battered sense of vocation—that he would never again turn out a work "as youngly glamorous as 'Soldiers' Pay' nor as trashily smart as 'Mosquitoes.'"[91] Although Faulkner had sometimes vowed to quit writing, Phil Stone encouraged him to "write anything he wanted to, any way he pleased, and perhaps he would get prestige and later could make money." About his own doubts, Stone said, "I didn't dare tell Bill because I was the only one who believed he could do anything, and I was afraid if I told him he would lose heart." Well, Stone was not the only one so long as Faulkner had Hal Smith and Ben Wasson to support him. But Stone realized: "I should have known better. You can no more stop a professional from writing than you can stop a dope fiend from taking dope."[92]

Stone believed nothing should deter Faulkner from writing. For him, then, Faulkner's marriage to Estelle Oldham Franklin on June 20, 1929, was nothing less than a catastrophe. And Stone was not the only one.

8

Married

June 1929

The Prince and the Pauper

Estelle divorced Cornell Franklin on April 29, 1929. Estelle's sister Dorothy had given Bill an ultimatum: He had to marry Estelle. He said the ultimatum came from Lem Oldham.[1] The couple married on June 20 and honeymooned in Pascagoula.

Estelle wrote her worried parents, "I wish with all my heart that this leave-taking, for you, had been as joyous a one as the other." Over a decade earlier, she had left Oxford for Hawaii with Cornell Franklin, a bona fide gentleman and a coming man, the very epitome of what the grand Oldhams had wanted for their daughter. The world—and Estelle—had been different then. On April 17, 1920, she had written to her "dearest Daddy" describing a scene right out of *Gentlemen Prefer Blondes* when the Prince of Wales asks Lorelei Lee for a dance. A week earlier "Mrs. Cornell Franklin" had been the only one with whom the Prince of Wales had danced twice. She had been dancing at a ball with Cornell when an aide came over to say that the Prince "wanted to meet and dance with the young lady with a blue and silver gown on and would I be good enough to come over to be presented." Estelle was wearing the "most fetching blue taffeta dress" her mama had made for her. "I was dying to tell him to say to Edward that if he would come to me I'd be very glad to meet him," she told her Anglophobe father. But instead she "meekly went over, was presented and we danced off. . . . I was the first one outside of the Governor's party with whom he danced (He first asked Mrs Rothmell, the Gov's daughter—then Miss Parker and then me!)" Afterward, the prince introduced her to Lord Mountbatten, the Duke of Battenberg's younger brother, with whom she also danced: "Two dances passed and H.R.H. again sent to ask if I would dance with him. The second time he was quite human and pleasant and said when we started off 'I've discovered you haven't I, but you're the young lady whose red hat gave me such a start this morning?'" He was referring to an incident when his car had stopped abruptly in front of Estelle as she was crossing a street. Mississippi did not seem so far away after all: "He is really as nice as any well-bred boy and I just imagined that I was at a University dance . . . my experience with College boys furnished me with such a 'line of conversation' that I was asked for a 'second dance.'" This was the world Estelle had been dressed for. Of course, all the girls wanted to know about her conversation with the prince. "I would like for all the girls at home to hear about it. Everybody in fact because they would think it wonderful I'm sure," Estelle wrote, signing herself "Your devoted little girl."[2]

Now she had married quite another kind of gentleman: "the best and only thing for me to do." She could not ask for forgiveness, but she prayed that her parents realized that she honestly loved Bill. She wanted to be a "loving and loyal daughter." The couple wanted to live in Oxford, where she could see her parents every day. She pleaded, "Please don't shut your hearts and minds against me." She wanted her share of joy—and for Bill, whom, she reiterated, she loved and respected—and she wanted happy lives for her children that included, she insisted, her parents.[3]

William Faulkner had written a confidential letter to Hal Smith explaining his decision to marry Estelle Franklin: "Both want and have to . . . For my honor and the sanity—I believe life—of a woman." He did not explain that Estelle had gone against everyone, family and community—virtually anyone who had an opinion on marrying William Faulkner. In dissolving her first marriage and returning to her first and only choice, she had shown a strength of character that her granddaughter, Vicki, greatly admired.[4] Faulkner was not under duress, he assured his publisher, or duped: "We grew up together and I don't think she could fool me in this way; that is, make me believe that her mental condition, her nerves, are this far gone." Estelle was not pregnant; that alone, Faulkner assured Smith, would not have been a deciding factor. Rumors of an abortion abounded and were later picked up by Joseph Blotner and Carvel Collins. But other than hearsay, evidence for such a drastic measure has not been found.[5] Consider also how Faulkner would have reacted to the idea of aborting his own child, or even that of another man's, given the warm way he took to Estelle's children and the huge risks he would be taking with a beloved already in a debilitated condition. Putting Estelle in this kind of peril is reminiscent, of course, of Harry Wilbourne's botched abortion in

The Wild Palms. Faulkner could almost be said to swagger when he implied to Smith that he was experienced in dealing with bastards, although his fathering children outside of marriage seems unlikely. Estelle's parlous state had nothing to do with any promise of his own, and yet he had created a situation that he "permitted to ripen" and become "unbearable, and I am tired of running from the devilment I bring about." Presumably he referred to his constant visits to the Oldham home, which had provoked a lot of gossip. It all sounded "insane," he admitted, a revealing word choice, since he had begun the letter worrying about Estelle's sanity. Who was truly the insane one? he seemed to inadvertently wonder. In truth, the marriage seemed inevitable and fraught to both parties. Faulkner asked Smith for five hundred dollars, which Smith did not have.

Pairing Estelle's letter to her parents with Faulkner's to Smith shows, in Judith Sensibar's words, a couple working in tandem, perfecting rhetorical performances to "create the best possible conditions for making their marriage a success."[6] They needed both their families and his publisher's support.[7] Smith had advanced Faulkner monies even before contracts were signed.[8]

Quite aside from Lem Oldham's concern that William Faulkner could not support his daughter in anywhere near the style she had enjoyed with Cornell Franklin, Estelle's involvement with Bill Faulkner threatened to become a scandal that did not please his mother or father, who did not want him involved with a divorced woman who was a risk in other ways as well. Scornful of his son's ability to make a living by writing, Murry Falkner did not see how his son would support a family. Others suspicions might well have been in play. When Fred Karl questioned Dean Faulkner Wells and her mother, Louise, he recorded in a handwritten note: "Feeling is Estelle & F consummated the relat[ionship] before she married Cornell Franklin. Although this was ag[ainst] the core, they all felt Estelle was quite capable of doing it. That reinforces my pt [point] of their 'drinking' together." Karl did not elaborate, but the drinking together is suggestive of a couple that sinned together. In a separate interview with Dean, Karl also learned that "Estelle was not only an alcoholic, but on heavy drugs when Faulkner married her—Dean said cocaine; later Seconal, and other heavy sedatives."[9] "It was said," Robert Coughlan noted, "that when E came back from the Orient she was on some sort of dope, an opium derivative."[10]

Faulkner's prospects hardly seemed to have improved over the last decade. He had very little income and did not expect much from *The Sound and the Fury,* which he had just completed. His brother Jack, working at the Memphis airport, suggested putting off the marriage. "I got what I deserved," Jack recalled, "no reply at all." Bill then told Lem Oldham, "Stelle and I are going to be married." Lem said: "Billy, I've always been fond of you as a friend, but I don't want you marrying my daughter. But if you're determined, I won't stand in your way."

Phil Stone did try to stand in the way. Estelle said he was violently jealous of her, and he told Bill that she would be the "ruination of him. He wanted W all to himself and to take the credit for everything," she told Joseph Blotner. The biographer speculated, "W apparently got fed up with Phil's possessiveness-advances?"[11] Advances? This was Estelle's conviction: that Stone, whose friendships were all with men, had an amatory interest in her husband.

Mr. Bill, Billy, and Pappy

There were mediating factors: Cornell Franklin paid child support for Cho-Cho and Malcolm. And the children had already become attached to William Faulkner the year before he married their mother. Malcolm remembered that he was about five when he first caught sight of William Faulkner at Cho-Cho's piano recital. He showed up in cap, cane, and uniform. Malcolm, often called Mac, took the small man for a policeman. In his experience, only policemen wore caps—like Patrick O'Leary, Faulkner's doll. The scene seems almost too pat, like the children in *The Sound and the Fury,* on the outside looking in. Mac could not believe that Faulkner was just "standing outside the window listening intently to this childish piano recital, featuring pieces by Mozart, Chopin, and Liszt—the things that old ladies like to have young children play." Mac just wanted to eat ice cream in the kitchen—anything to get away from the old ladies and children. He had been made to dress up in "little short white pants, with coat and tie to boot" in as formal a fashion as Faulkner, who held a bouquet. Then he came into the kitchen and said, "These are for Miss Cho-Cho because she played so wonderfully." Cho-Cho, now in the kitchen, accepted her tribute from the "gentleman in uniform." Mac's nurse told him that it was the uniform of a "foreign army" because Faulkner had been rejected by the American army as underage and too small. Mac did not say what it meant to him to suddenly see this undersized adult and be told by his nurse, "You know, Mr. Malcolm, Mr. Bill is courtin' your mother." But it was like Mr. Bill was courting the children. Mr. Bill took Mac to Chilton's Drugstore for chocolate ice cream while Mr. Bill drank corn whiskey, "as did most men around the Square," and asked Mac to call him Billy. The boys, for that is what Billy and Mac now were, went on picnics, and Billy, like an older brother, showed Mac how to light a fire on a rainy day with kindling from an abandoned squirrel's nest while Estelle stayed in the car, out of the rain, "awaiting Billy's signal to bring the lunch." Hot dogs on sticks, asparagus sandwiches, chocolate cake and roasted marshmallows, and learning the lore of the woods completely enthralled and exhausted Mac, who remembered other trips with Billy and Dr. Calvin Brown, a botanist and anthropologist who showed Mac a colored people's graveyard and the tombstones mentioning a yellow fever epidemic. Mac learned the names for the plants and trees, which delighted Estelle, a dedicated gardener. Soon after Billy and Estelle were married, he became "Pappy" to Mac. Pappy gathered "pockets full of wild flowers—roots and all," digging them out with a "big old Barlow pocket knife," now considered an antique, beautifully shaped with a teardrop handle, a prized gift to Tom Sawyer, who went into a "convulsion of delight that swept his system and shook him to his foundations. . . . [T]here was inconceivable grandeur in that." Pappy spotted Mac's fascination with snakes, like a beautiful black one, called a blue racer, climbing a tree. Explaining that some snakes were poisonous and others not, Pappy said both kinds could be vicious, but with gentle handling they became docile. Herpetology became Mac's passion and eventually his profession. Mac claimed he spent more "man-hours with Faulkner than any other man has."[12]

When Mac and Cho-Cho enrolled in school, Faulkner showed up at recess with candy. One of their schoolmates remembers the Franklin children were always dressed up. Estelle appeared a glamorous figure, a "divorcee whose children had an amah. She was like a visiting movie star, beautiful, with beautiful clothes, gowns out of *Vogue*. People liked and admired her." Faulkner seemed just as glamorous to the children because he had been a wartime pilot. He seemed "free, not tied down like others. He was handsome and an idol to the children. Cho-Cho and Malcolm adored him. He would take the children for walks, along with Cho-Cho's friends."[13]

Estelle had the support of Cornell's family, a crucial factor. Cho-Cho and Malcolm's Franklin-side grandmother, "a charming and admittedly romantic woman, approved and applauded my marriage to Bill," Estelle wrote in her son Malcolm's memoir, *Bitterweeds*. "She also unhesitatingly upbraided my father for coldly insisting that I'd married a wastrel." And yet the bond between Lem and Billy, as Lem always called him, was stronger than the words exchanged about the marriage would suggest. In some ways, Lem had a sensibility closely attuned to that of his son-in-law, who had so little in common with his own father. Lem was not much of a lawyer, according to the Falkners and others. "Grandfather said, 'Lem Oldham never tried a case—he wouldn't know how,'" Sallie Murry told Joseph Blotner.[14] Lem Oldham, "high-strung and proud" like his ex-postmaster son-in-law,[15] had relied on family connections to help secure his position in the community. He wrote poetry, later addressing his wife:

Seventy to day—but not to me,
Though your hair be silver white,
You're the radiant maiden of the long ago,
My boyhood's vision bright.

Lem knew what it meant for Billy to marry the woman who had been his "vision bright."[16]

As a divorced woman, Estelle could not be married in the Episcopal Church, a regretful Reverend McCready told her. But he encouraged her to return for services after a year's "probation." How the rest of Oxford took the marriage is not certain, but years later Phil Stone expressed his contempt to Robert Coughlan, writing for *Life:* "They ran off to get married like two children."[17] David Hedleston, a University of Mississippi professor of philosophy and ethics, performed the marriage ceremony at the College Hill Presbyterian Church without any apparent fuss. "At times I've wondered if Dr. Hedleston welcomed us to the church and married us out of pure Godly love and understanding, or was he thumbing his nose at the Pharisaical laws imposed upon divorce by the Episcopal Church? I'll never know the answer," Estelle wrote.[18] According to Hedleston's daughter, who was present at the wedding, the service was actually performed in the Hedleston home.[19]

THE STRANGEST OF HONEYMOONS

Pascagoula, not yet a fashionable Gulf resort, had been the site of the Helen Baird courtship. A Pascagoula resident, Mrs. Leatherbury, said, "Faulkner liked very much to be away from large crowds." The beach had a rough, unkempt, open look, a "tiny quiet place," she called it.[20] Faulkner wore a red bandanna in his pocket and attracted the attention of an admiring younger boy, who also began wearing a bandanna. Faulkner sometimes wore the handkerchief around his neck and put it on his face when driving an open car over dusty roads. The Faulkners stood out. "They look like such strange people," Mrs. Shepherd, a neighbor, said to her husband, Martin. Mrs. Leatherbury remembered that Estelle dressed for dinner in "Asiatic silks and extremely fine dresses" but also walked about in "fashionable and aesthetic dresses" in waist-high weeds on the beach.[21] She made a spectacle of herself—rather like Edna Earl, her heroine aboard ship in "A Crossing": "Every day before tiffin she had come out on deck for a promenade, but she'd always had the feeling that she was a beautiful actress playing her part on the stage. Clothed in strange luxurious fabrics and furs and looked upon with mingled admiration and envy, she had gloated over her masquerade. And in the evenings, in smart, exquisitely beautiful dinner gowns, she had come out on this very deck to the dances."[22]

In her son's memoir, *Bitterweeds,* Estelle glossed over a trying time, mentioning her father's disapproval but abruptly going on: "And this now brings me to what I'll wager was the strangest of honeymoons—one even a novelist would hesitate to invent: the groom a bachelor, the bride a divorcee with two children, and all of us having a gay, carefree time in a tumble-down old house on the Gulf of Mexico, with a colored cook loaned to us by my first husband's mother." In retrospect, did she only remember the happier moments? She suggests that Faulkner did his best to overlook difficulties. When they arrived to pick up Malcolm at the Oldham home for the journey to Pascagoula, they discovered that the nurse, Ethel Ruth, had not attended to the "dirty, grass-stained, and generally unkempt" boy. That would not have upset William Faulkner, who would appear unkempt on the unkempt Pascagoula beach. Mac had an "intense dislike for bathing." Estelle recalled that Bill laughed and "thrust Malcolm into the car, stowed our bags and headed east toward Columbus [Mississippi]," where they would pick up Cho-Cho, staying with grandmother Franklin.

Estelle did not say what happened next. Drinking and brooding? In the *Sanctuary* urtext, Horace Benbow drinks "a lot ... talking again, glibly, about love and death and how a man's soul is the scoriation of his individual disasters upon the primary putty." Such passages align with Faulkner's fraught and obsessive love for Estelle, even as Horace resumes "talking about love with a glibness which even then could not quite obscure the fundamental truth and tragedy which the word evoked." To love is to suffer tragedy and a kind of death, as Estelle would shortly demonstrate.

And yet Pascagoula presented, to begin with, a happy family frolic. It started well enough. Malcolm Franklin remembered how much fun he had swimming and seeing the ocean for the first time.[23] Faulkner went crabbing with Cho-Cho. Mrs. Shepherd watched Estelle come out in her "gorgeous clothes." Estelle never went swimming, and Mrs. Shepherd concluded she did not know how to swim, although Jill Faulkner says her mother could do a sidestroke but disliked swimming. An "extremely gallant" William Faulkner bowed to Mrs. Shepherd and said: "Madame, would you permit me to use your phone? I'm William Faulkner but just call me Bill." He wanted to order groceries. He then invited the couple for a visit in the honeymoon cottage.[24] To Ben Wasson, he wrote: "We have a very pleasant place on the beach here. I swim and fish and we row a little. Estelle sends love."[25]

Bill and Estelle walked the beach and drank openly. He was the same old Billy: punctual and deliberate and never in a rush. They did not discuss politics;

the divide between Democratic and Republican families was just too deep. Although he would dress elegantly for dinner, he also went about unshaven and barefoot. "Why does a man of your education dress that way?" Mrs. Shepherd inquired. "I prefer to dress like this," he curtly replied. Faulkner knew the word was out that the marriage could not possibly last. He told a Pascagoula friend, "It is gonna stick." Besides fishing and playing with the children, he worked on the proofs for *The Sound and the Fury,* which he had turned in to Hal Smith, now in charge of his own firm, several months earlier after several futile attempts to attract interest from other publishers. Ben Wasson had made changes in the Benjy section, taking out the italics and introducing more spacing between passages to indicate time shifts. Faulkner restored the italics, not wishing to make every time shift apparent but rather to show the simultaneity of every moment in an idiot's life. Although he had expressed some irritation with Wasson, that quickly faded as Faulkner acknowledged that his friend was "more interested in the book than anyone there." Faulkner's short stories remained unpublished as the rejections continued.

Mrs. Hairston, Cornell's mother, visited, and Bill took them on drives in a touring car he had purchased. As soon as Mrs. Hairston departed with her grandchildren, Estelle's sister Dorothy visited. Then Bill and Estelle drove to New Orleans—all this happening in a month of family outings. The couple seemed to be quickly integrating into worlds they had enjoyed apart from one another. But certain fissures began to open by late summer of 1929. Mrs. Shepherd watched Estelle, in silk and satin, submerge herself in the sea. Bill shouted at Martin Shepherd, "She's going to drown herself!" Shepherd caught up with her just before she dropped into the deepwater channel. She resisted. But he dragged her back to shore, and a doctor gave her an injection. Soon Estelle recovered. But what to make of Faulkner's behavior? Why had Martin Shepherd retrieved another man's wife, as Bill had saved Cornell Franklin's? Was Faulkner too drunk to rescue her once again?

Was Estelle really attempting suicide when she walked about a half mile to that channel, allowing for plenty of time for someone to catch up with her? Jill believed the suicide attempt a "pure fake" and that her mother would have chosen something "cleaner and quicker."[26] Was this, then, one of the recurrent dramas the couple would stage for themselves and others? Jill had been present at many of those performances and thought so. Estelle, drinking heavily, had certainly chosen the most theatrical way to drown her sorrows in a scene right out of a movie like *A Star Is Born.* Did the days with a preoccupied writer, working on *The Sound and the Fury* galleys, shut her out, prove too much for such a sociable woman, a woman who had dreamed of a very different beach scene in her poem "White Beaches"?

White beaches and starlight,
The sea was beckoning me
To a place that man might
call lonely
But it means all heaven to me
To my beach—with its surf and

Its wind-swept palms
And the feel of your loveliness
In my arms
With the God of true-lovers to
stay with us always
On my white beach neath
The low tropic stars.[27]

Cho-Cho's daughter, Vicki, always believed the poem—more of a song Estelle used to sing at the piano—was written for William Faulkner, luring him to that beach of beauty she had first seen in Hawaii.[28] And yet, as Cho-Cho said of her stepfather, "He could say things that cut you to the heart."[29] What had he said to Estelle? And was it something like what he had written in *Sanctuary*?

Did the horrifying tale of Temple Drake's rape shake up the marriage at its very start? On May 25, less than a month before his marriage, Faulkner completed a draft of the novel. It infuriated Estelle. She called it horrible. "It's meant to be," he said. "It will sell."[30] Horace Benbow imagines marrying Belle Mitchell, a divorcee, in a ceremony that "neither promised nor meant any new emotional experience." She wears her second husband "like a garment whose sole charm for her lay in the belief that no other woman had one exactly like it." The novel nudged even closer to Estelle in having Temple wear a one-hundred-dollar imported "Chinee robe."[31] Marriage itself seems second-best: "Any woman makes a better mistress than she does a wife." The passage most hostile to Estelle occurs in Horace's letter to his sister Narcissa, when he expatiates on the "unfailing aptitude of women for coinciding with the emotional periphery of a man at the exact moment when it reaches top dead center, at the exact moment when the fates have prized his jaws for the regurgitated bit." Marriage had bridled Faulkner, notwithstanding his efforts to avoid it. Was that his point?

The shocked women in Hal's Smith office—all of whom had supported Faulkner's work—argued against publication. Smith concurred, telling Faulkner: "Good God, I cant publish this. We'd both be in jail."[32] Faulkner said he forgot about the book until the galleys arrived in November

1930, which is hard to believe, given Estelle's reaction and what they both knew about her own stories. She had created Edna Earl, who forsakes her southern belle imposture for a forthright sexual desire and then, ironically, is defended by white men, representatives of a corrupt society, who think that a foreigner, Chang, has defiled her. So what angered Estelle about her husband's work? The graphic nature of Temple's rape, the raw desire Temple expresses for sex with another lover, Red? "I cant wait. You've got to. I'm on fire, I tell you," Temple cries as she clings to Red. Is it the intense carnality of the novel that went beyond Estelle's notions of proper literature? Whatever the trouble between the newly married couple, it is hard to suppress the thought that the quarantined *Sanctuary* continued to ferment in Faulkner's imagination, especially since Smith intended to publish the novel all along—no matter how risky that might seem. Faulkner told an interviewer in the summer of 1931, "Hal Smith said this [*Sanctuary*] was too tough and he held it up until I had written *As I Lay Dying*."[33] Smith apparently felt that *Sanctuary* should not be the immediate sequel to *The Sound and the Fury.*

Somehow the couple overcame Estelle's death walk. What Estelle thought remains a mystery, although it is doubtful that she looked back and regretted her parting from Cornell Franklin. Later her daughter Cho-Cho thought so, but judging by Estelle Franklin's short fiction, she had developed a distaste for the colonial life, especially its smugness and racism. She was well quit of it. She indulged in her love of finery and liked high living, to be sure, but not the society that seemed to go along with it. Estelle told her granddaughter, Vicki, that "during the entire time of her [first] marriage" she had been "homesick for her parents and friends and Pappy [Faulkner], too."[34] Jill Faulkner added another explanation: Cornell Franklin was predictable and dull, "despite all the places he'd been and things he'd done. . . . I think that, as much as anything, caused the problems between them, because Mama didn't care for the pedestrian aspects of any life." Estelle's divorce revealed an intrepid nature that buoyed William Faulkner even if he rarely said as much. "I stood a little bit in awe of her," one of Estelle's relatives recalled. "She was one of the first in the family to get a divorce. It was an event in the family history."[35] And Billy Faulkner provided the antidote to the stuffy, corrupt, and complacent society Estelle had put up with for over a decade.

FAMILY MAN

Faulkner returned with Estelle to Oxford, where she set up a household on the first floor of Elma Meek's home at 803 University Avenue. Elma was related to the Oldhams, and her claim to fame had been winning the contest that selected "Ole Miss" as the university's nickname. Her grand house, including front porch, balcony, drawing room, two bedrooms, dining room, bath, and kitchen, provided ample space for Estelle's Honolulu furniture. Estelle sent her children to school and collected child-support payments from Cornell Franklin. She employed a young woman to do the cleaning up, and Estelle did the cooking, including hot curry meals her husband enjoyed. He worked at a night job in the university's power plant and afterward had breakfast coffee with his mother and visited the Delta Psi house on campus. This was the housebroken Faulkner, the one Phil Stone seemed to resent. Miss Maud, with a son disposed to drinking sprees since his teens, looked askance at a daughter-in-law who had the same proclivities. No biographer has apparently asked why Faulkner chose a wife who drank, perhaps because there is no answer, except to ask another question: What would his life have been like with a teetotaler? The last thing William Faulkner would have wanted, it seems safe to say, is a woman who wanted to reform him. He never gave the slightest indication that he wanted to quit drinking, no matter the dire consequences. Miss Maud, who had no success in curbing her own husband's drinking, nevertheless seemed to hold it against Estelle that she did nothing to restrain and perhaps even encouraged Billy's bibulousness.

William Faulkner got married at the height of his powers, with *The Sound and the Fury* already in his creative bank, *Sanctuary* still accumulating assets, several superb short stories that he would soon publish, and now *As I Lay Dying* in the last months of 1929 humming along as steadily as the dynamo in the power plant where he sat, doing his business, collecting a regular salary and supervising two black men who fed the boiler. Marriage to Estelle did not slow him down and perhaps even spurred his creativity. Even Phil Stone had come around a bit, and they resumed their chats at the Gathright Drug-store or at the post office,[36] where so many in Oxford gathered for local news. Estelle and Bill were also working on her stories as well as his. He showed her his novel-in-progress.[37] Maybe he was able to put the bitterness of *Sanctuary* aside for a time. Faulkner never said in so many words that he was happy or contented while writing *As I Lay Dying,* but it sure looks like it.[38]

The old Colonel, William C. Falkner (1825–1889), the model for
John Sartoris in *Flags in the Dust* and *The Unvanquished*.

Marble statue of Colonel William C. Falkner in the Ripley, Mississippi, cemetery. Faulkner pictured his great ancestor riding through the country "like a living force."

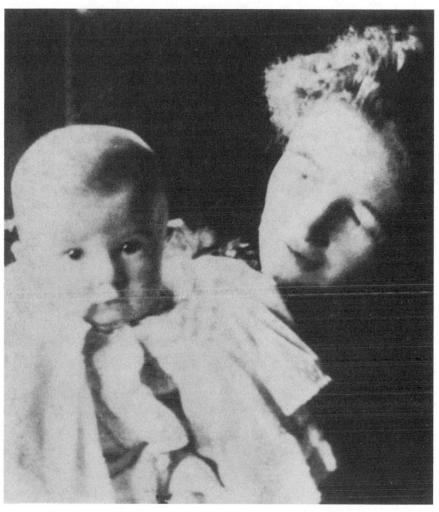

Maud Falkner and her baby William. Later, while in Oxford, Faulkner visited his mother nearly every day. Her motto: "Don't complain. Don't explain."

Faulkner's birth house in New Albany, Mississippi.

Murry Falkner, William Faulkner's father. Murry indulged
William, his firstborn, but preferred reading westerns.

Uncle Ned Barnett, the Falkner family servant. He wore the old
Colonel's clothes and performed well in a theatrical household.

The courthouse in Oxford, Mississippi, with Confederate soldier statue,
on the city's downtown square, where Faulkner imbibed history.

Faulkner's childhood drawing of Abraham Lincoln. Already
he is making his own material out of history.

Caroline Barr and Dean Faulkner.

Faulkner as a young boy.

M. B. Howorth drawing in Ole Miss yearbook, illustrating
the conventional approach Faulkner eschewed.

Faulkner drawing in Ole Miss yearbook. The couple
is in sync with the music they hear.

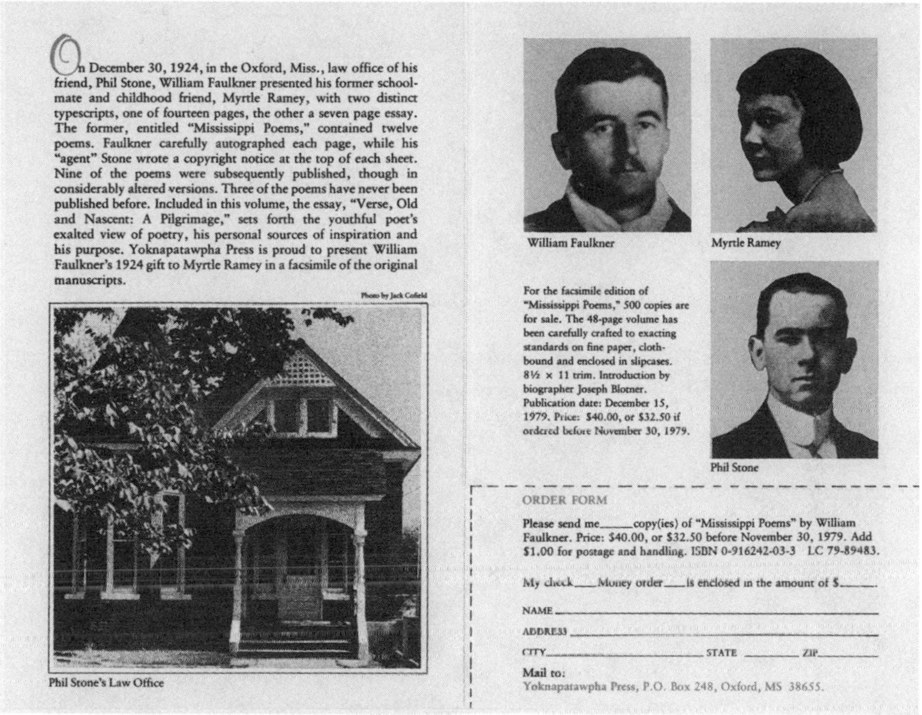

On December 30, 1924, in the Oxford, Miss., law office of his friend, Phil Stone, William Faulkner presented his former school-mate and childhood friend, Myrtle Ramey, with two distinct typescripts, one of fourteen pages, the other a seven page essay. The former, entitled "Mississippi Poems," contained twelve poems. Faulkner carefully autographed each page, while his "agent" Stone wrote a copyright notice at the top of each sheet. Nine of the poems were subsequently published, though in considerably altered versions. Three of the poems have never been published before. Included in this volume, the essay, "Verse, Old and Nascent: A Pilgrimage," sets forth the youthful poet's exalted view of poetry, his personal sources of inspiration and his purpose. Yoknapatawpha Press is proud to present William Faulkner's 1924 gift to Myrtle Ramey in a facsimile of the original manuscripts.

Photo by Jack Cofield

Phil Stone's Law Office

William Faulkner   Myrtle Ramey

Phil Stone

For the facsimile edition of "Mississippi Poems," 500 copies are for sale. The 48-page volume has been carefully crafted to exacting standards on fine paper, cloth-bound and enclosed in slipcases. 8½ × 11 trim. Introduction by biographer Joseph Blotner. Publication date: December 15, 1979. Price: $40.00, or $32.50 if ordered before November 30, 1979.

ORDER FORM

Please send me_____copy(ies) of "Mississippi Poems" by William Faulkner. Price: $40.00, or $32.50 before November 30, 1979. Add $1.00 for postage and handling. ISBN 0-916242-03-3 LC 79-89483.

My check____ Money order____ is enclosed in the amount of $_____

NAME _____

ADDRESS _____

CITY_____ STATE _____ ZIP_____

Mail to:
Yoknapatawpha Press, P.O. Box 248, Oxford, MS 38655.

Yoknapatawpha Press brochure with photographs of Faulkner's mentor Phil Stone, Stone's law office, Faulkner himself, and Myrtle Ramey, Faulkner's childhood friend to whom he presented his drawings and later his books.

Faulkner in the World War I RAF uniform in which he paraded around Oxford.

Faulkner in Paris, 1925.

Estelle Oldham and her daughter Cho-Cho (Victoria),
photographed by Estelle's first husband, Cornell Franklin.

Faulkner in the early 1930s.

Faulkner's home, Rowan Oak: "One has the feeling of walking back in time, into a different world," said a town resident. The shift from present to past, from the modern neighborhood on the boundary of Rowan Oak to that cedar-lined lane occurs as quickly as the time shifts in Faulkner's fiction. (Library of Congress)

Miriam Hopkins, in *The Story of Temple Drake* (1933), portrays with "perfect understanding the complexities of literature's most spirited character . . . a strange composite of good and evil forces, a curious mixture of conventional attributes and uncontrollable desires," wrote the *Jackson (MS) Clarion-Ledger* reviewer.

9

All in the Family

The Sound and the Fury, October 1929

~

Published on October 7, 1929, *The Sound and the Fury* follows the fortunes of the Compsons, a southern family in decline: Mr. Compson, the father, is a world-weary dipsomaniac, and his wife a neurasthenic, self-pitying whiner. Their children all suffer a want of love: The oldest son, Quentin, tries to hold on to his sister, Caddy, the only source of deep affection available to this sensitive and troubled young man no longer sure of what it means to be a southern gentleman. He commits suicide in an unbearable state of agony over the futility of his efforts to defend an outmoded code that only confirms his anomalous existence. Caddy is just as crucial to Benjy, her idiot brother, who has been three years old for thirty years and the butt of cruel treatment by virtually everyone, except for Caddy and the family's black servant, Dilsey. Benjy troubles every Compson except Caddy because his very existence mocks the family's pretensions to distinction and achievement. He is castrated when it is mistakenly assumed he has tried to rape a group of girls. His loss of manhood ironically reflects on all the Compson males, who in a variety of ways cannot perform the traditional male function of procreating, preserving, and protecting the family. The remaining brother, Jason, named after his father, is an embittered bachelor who satisfies his sex drive by consorting with prostitutes. He is outraged by his family's failure and tries to get ahead by cheating Caddy's daughter, named after her brother Quentin. Caddy sends money home that Jason pockets, all the while blaming everyone, except himself, for his lack of success. So fractured are the Compsons by their own frailties and misfortunes that, in the end, they, and their story, can only be repaired by Dilsey, who is presented by a third-person narrator who enters the novel in order to bring some perspective to the skewed projections of Benjy, Quentin, and Jason. The novel goes to Dilsey, so to speak, as Faulkner turned to Caroline Barr, a momentary stay against the confusion and conflict engendered by his warring parents and the pervading sense that the family has seen better days. The hard-boiled Jason, working in a hardware store, is reminiscent of Faulkner's father, Murry, selling equipment and reduced to the nuts and bolts of a mundane existence, or of Faulkner himself clerking in that same store. The age of chivalry was dead, and just making a living made for resentment, palpable in Jason and just as prominent in Faulkner. If the novelist was no Quentin in distress at Harvard, the writer was nevertheless the errant scion. He had a sort of sabbatical at Yale and had sulked about the South he missed, even though he had not won his lady except on the rebound as a Caddy who had come home if not in disgrace, than at least in humiliation, having spoiled her prospects. Southern manhood, as it had been created by the obstreperous old Colonel and his cohort, had collapsed.

To Henry Nash Smith (*Southwest Review*, Autumn), *The Sound and the Fury* portrayed the "spectacle of a civilization uprooted and left to die. Scope such as this is not usual in American novels." This epic note set the novel at odds with the prevailing sentimentality about the Old South, the nostalgia for the antebellum aristocracy, now replaced by the "decadence of an American family"—an unpardonable insult to his region's pride, as many of Faulkner's contemporaries saw it. Smith, like other reviewers, was quick to detect Joyce's influence in Quentin's stream-of-consciousness section, although Smith insisted on Faulkner's original use of it. Others, like Walter Just (*Philadelphia Public Ledger*, October 4), suspected the author of playing a tricky game that made it difficult to tell the two Quentins, boy and girl, apart. This "arty" novel was a "stunt."

For every exasperated reviewer there was an exhilarated one, like Ted Robinson (*Cleveland Plain Dealer*, October 18), who proclaimed Faulkner's technique "strikingly original and hauntingly effective." A first reading of the Benjy section confused him until he realized that in the "idiot's consciousness there is no sense of time, and any chance smell, sound, or other physical stimulus will take him back to some past event that impressed him." Recounting Quentin's suicide, Jason's cupidity, and his niece Quentin's promiscuity, Robinson deemed the novel a "sordid and revolting story" with a "tragic dignity" reminiscent of *The Brothers Karamazov*—a comparison other reviewers also made. Robinson hailed a work of genius.

In the *Providence Journal* (October 20) and the *Nation* (January 15, 1930), Winfield Townley Scott and Clifton Fadiman were not impressed, believing Faulkner's modernism amounted to obscurantism and, in Fadiman's words, that the "characters are trivial, unworthy of the enormous and complex craftsmanship expended on them." Julia K. W. Baker (*New Orleans Times-Picayune,* June 29, 1930) hailed "one of the finest works in the tragic mood yet to appear in America." She singled out Caddy as a "beautiful character. There is something uncanny in Faulkner's penetration of the feminine heart. Ask women how true his rendering is. They know it, men can merely sense it." Baker caught an aspect of Faulkner's treatment of race that escaped most reviewers: "The benevolent tyranny of negroes over any Southern household is charmingly reflected in *The Sound and the Fury.* Faulkner knows and loves the negro." If he read this review, one can imagine him thinking about how true this was of his own experience with Caroline Barr. The reviewer in the *New York Times* (November 10) noted the "efforts of the Negro servants, a peculiarly sane chorus to the insane tragedy."

Evelyn Scott's pamphlet-length endorsement—she was a highly respected southern poet and novelist—irritated reviewers like Clifton Fadiman even as others welcomed an eloquent guide to a difficult work. Scott's involvement, suggested by Wasson, gave the novel a "blue ribbon" sendoff that Faulkner deeply appreciated.[1] She had no doubt of the novel's permanence and wanted to be the first to say so. She countered the impression of Faulkner as a morbid writer. Pessimism and despair certainly informed his fiction, but so too did his "reassertion of humanity in defeat that is, in the subjective sense, a triumph." She regarded the novel as refuting materialists, whom she does not name, although Jason Compson would certainly be numbered among them. Benjy she saw as a kind of Adam before the fall, an innocent who cannot experience the full descent into human consciousness. Describing Quentin as an "over-sensitive introvert, pathologically devoted to his sister, and his determination to commit suicide in his protest against her disgrace," Scott did not apparently see how both Quentin and Benjy are Caddy-driven, so to speak, with Quentin representing Adam after the fall. Scott realizes that Jason, in his own way, is as mad as Quentin and as easily riled as Benjy. Jason dreads, like Quentin, the moment when his world will collapse, when his investments will fail, when his family will let him down—again. Scott summed up Dilsey and the last section of the novel in a sentence: "She is the conscious human accepting the limitations of herself, the iron boundaries of circumstance, and still, to the best of her ability, achieving a holy compromise for aspiration." Scott calls Jason, with his scorn for "outworn tradition," the "young South," or he might be called the "New South" that Henry Grady championed, scornful of tradition and hospitable to industrialization and new business but also full of the connivery that Lillian Hellman dramatized so cannily in *The Little Foxes*. He is the "dollars and cents" man, "completely rational" and also completely deluded, like an Edgar Allan Poe ratiocinating character. For Scott, Dilsey embodies wholeness, while her white folks "accept their fragmentary state, disintegrate. And she recovers for us the spirit of tragedy which the patter of cynicism has often made seem lost."

Few reviewers were able to view the novel's subject matter and its form together or to understand the role style played in Faulkner's exquisite sense of structure. On the contrary, they chided him for lack of control and sensationalism, for dwelling on disease for its own sake. However, the *New York Times* reviewer ended with a succinct paragraph that does lead the way into a full consideration of the novel: "The author has chosen an unusual medium for his story in not one but four styles. Yet the four are welded together in perfect unity. The objective quality of the novel saves it from complete morbidity." Faulkner may well have been building on "The Book of the Grotesque" in Sherwood Anderson's *Winesburg, Ohio,* which dramatizes how truth gets distorted in the minds and manners of individuals.[2] Each narrator has a truth to tell, but in the telling, the truth itself buckles under the psyche's pressure.

Many critics have sought the source of the genius displayed in Faulkner's fourth novel, the one that set him apart from his earlier work. Many of the characters, scenes, and techniques in *The Sound and the Fury* have their analogues in his poems, sketches, and novels. The novelist "revisited his past, saw it afresh, and reworked it into his future."[3] Benjy is not the first idiot in Faulkner's fiction, Quentin is not alone in his obsession with a sister lost or unattainable, Mrs. Compson is not the first mother to be emotionally absent from her children's suffering, and the ending in Dilsey's church is not the first time that Faulkner finds a sense of salvation without which his white characters are doomed. But no totting up of precedents and influences can account for the sudden aesthetic discovery that amazed Faulkner himself.

BENJY

The first paragraph of *The Sound and the Fury* is a work of wonder, a precise capturing of a moment, a scene, a perception fused in a sensibility akin to the imagist poets, seeking direct treatment of the "thing":

> Through the fence, between the curling flower spaces, I could see them hitting. They were coming toward where the flag was and I went along the fence. Luster was hunting in the grass by the flower tree. They took

the flag out, and they were hitting. Then they put the flag back and they went to the table, and he hit and the other hit. Then they went on, and I went along the fence. Luster came away from the flower tree and we went along the fence and they stopped and we stopped and I looked through the fence while Luster was hunting in the grass. [April 7, 1928]

Faulkner's language is a verbal representation of what Benjy sees, "at the precise moment of seeing."[4] No other character can remain so bereft of language, so innocent of nouns like "golf" to describe what he sees. No imagist in Faulkner's time was likely to describe the absence of flowers. It is April and the flowers have not yet bloomed, but in summer Benjy has seen them there in the spaces where the flowers are now not yet there. The "curling flower spaces" may also represent the fragmented visual pattern of what Benjy perceives in the floral design of a cast-iron fence like the one behind which Edwin Chandler played, the severely retarded brother of Faulkner's first-grade teacher, Annie Chandler.[5]

Why go to all this trouble? Clifton Fadiman might have asked. John T. Matthews has an answer: "It is as if Faulkner wants to convey the immediacy of life—the most direct sensations of what constitutes reality—prior to the intrusions of ideas, beliefs, even language itself. And what constitutes Benjy's reality, as Faulkner imagines this cradle of human consciousness, is the experience of loss, lack, pain. Consciousness of self is born in the twilight of an awful rupture—in a separation from the ambient nurture of the mother-world."[6] Benjy is bereft of his loving sister, Caddy, and his existence isolates him dreadfully from what others take for granted.

Faulkner spent many days on the roughly made Oxford golf course looking for lost balls and losing his composure, as a fellow golfer had observed. And looking for what is lost absorbs Benjy all day and every day as he cries for the departed Caddy as the golfers, in the next paragraph, cry for their caddies. Life, for those moments, becomes fixated on what is lost. The golf course is the lost greener pastures of the Compson family, which has sold the land, piece by piece, to maintain its position and to send Quentin to Harvard. Caddy is the lost southern belle, the lost cause of happiness that Benjy yearns to recover, that Quentin wants to redeem, and that Jason seeks to renounce by tormenting Caddy's daughter, Quentin. The flag is the Compson standard brought low in a hole, now part of a pointless and yet obsessive game, with Luster (Benjy's black minder) on the other side of the fence as intent on finding his lost quarter as Jason will later be on the money he steals from his niece Quentin. "They went along the fence and they stopped and we stopped" is a perfect representation of the parallel universe Benjy inhabits alongside the one that suits Luster, sounding like Jason fixated on money and scornful of "niggers." Luster tells Benjy: "Aint you something, thirty three years old, going on that way. After I done went all the way to town to buy you that cake. Hush up that moaning. Aint you going to help me find that quarter so I can go to the show tonight."

Like Quentin following his shadow in his section of the novel, Benjy is measured by the shadow of himself he sees on the garden fence near the broken place where he always gets snagged on a nail. This ritualistic action, occurring on April 7, 1928, repeated evidently many times, goes all the way back to Benjy's childhood, to the day (December 23, 1908) when Caddy "uncaught" him, freed him as no other has done since her flight from a confinement on ancestral ground that Benjy and Quentin can never escape, no matter the distance between Jefferson and Cambridge, the golf course and the Compson home. Caddy is the only Compson who speaks in a loving manner to Benjy. She comes home from school and runs to him (spring or early summer 1908): "'Hello, Benjy.' Caddy said. She opened the gate and came in and stooped down. Caddy smelled like leaves. 'Did you come to meet me.' she said. 'Did you come to meet Caddy. What did you let him get his hands so cold for, Versh [Luster's predecessor].'" She mothers Benjy, rubbing his hands on a winter day just before Christmas, while her own mother bemoans her Benjamin as "a judgment on me." Caddy is natural woman, unsullied, trying to speak a language Benjy understands: "You're not a poor baby. Are you. Are you. You've got your Caddy. Haven't you got your Caddy." Every boy, every man, needs a Caddy. She is not just the sister Faulkner never had. She represents the love he never found enough of from his own mother, although she was nothing like the self-pitying Mrs. Compson, except that both women find it difficult to express love. Mrs. Compson will not hold the five-year-old Benjy, which is the way to quiet him, Caddy tells her. Always the lady, Mrs. Compson calls her daughter Candace, pointing out that "only common people" use nicknames. Caddy understands quite well that her mother's job is to evade responsibility, telling her, "You go up stairs and lay down, so you can be sick."

Benjy's laments are constantly and harshly interrupted, which is the way children, not only idiots, experience their world: *"Cant you shut up that moaning and slobbering, Luster said. Aint you shamed of yourself, making all this racket."* The italics signify a time shift, a return to Benjy's cruel present (April 7, 1928), where slave and master, so to speak, Luster and Jason, see in Benjy only a weakness to be deplored, not a soul to be salved, as Dilsey ministers to Benjy in Caddy's absence, although even Dilsey expresses her impatience when she shoves him into a carriage. Accept no substitutes for Caddy; they are of no avail.

Benjy is in a position to see everything without the ability to comment, but we are hardly at a loss in understanding that his Uncle Maury is an alcoholic. Benjy notices all his trips to the sideboard. We also can figure out that Uncle Maury is having an affair with Mrs. Patterson, when Mr. Patterson comes running up to the fence on their property to intercept Maury's love note that he has entrusted to Benjy. Earlier Caddy is scolded by Mrs. Patterson, who is put out because she told her lover not to *"send you alone."* Mrs. Patterson snags herself on the fence, like Benjy, with only an irate husband to unsnag her. Caddy's fate is to be snagged on the hypocrisy and duplicity of family life. She is used by the very adults who will condemn her promiscuity. To Jason, named after his father, the family is, even as a boy, a burden he would shirk but for his own greed still tied to a Compson brand, a business from which the grown-up Jason still hopes to profit. Benjy has to keep his hands in his pockets to keep warm; Jason, as a boy, keeps his hands in his pockets as a sign of keeping to himself just as he will later pocket the money Caddy sends for the support of her daughter, Quentin. All these detrimental behaviors, the Benjy section intimates, began in childhood in the fraught world of Sigmund Freud, notwithstanding Faulkner's claim not to have read the alienist. Benjy shows us; he cannot tell us. He is constantly sending out alarms that no one but Caddy can interpret. Benjy is Wordsworth's child, abandoned, the child who never becomes the father of the man but whose proximity to nature and his sister who smells like trees brings life back to its first principles, its grounding in the earth.

The unladylike seven-year-old Caddy takes off her dress when it gets wet while her older brother Quentin berates her for impropriety, slapping her while she splashes him in the branch they have been playing in. Caddy's spontaneity riles the rule- and convention-bound Quentin and his jealous, calculating brother Jason. Quentin predicts they will get a whipping, but Caddy is already vowing to run away from home. The sense of crime and punishment (whipping is mentioned twenty-five times in the novel) spoils the Edenic world of Benjy's senses and corrupts the Compson childhood as Jason continually threatens to tell on the children for their transgressions.

Back home, Jason begins crying because he cannot sleep with his grandmother (Damuddy), although the children do not realize that she is more than sick. They are excluded from the funereal gathering upstairs and think it is a party. Only Caddy climbs the tree that gives her a glimpse of the death scene. She is grounded in a reality that her blinkered brothers have trouble registering. She is not afraid, as they are, of being her own person. Benjy, like the others, sees the bottom of her muddy drawers, and when his memory is triggered again, he sees her at fourteen in a veil and what Jason calls a "prissy dress" that makes Benjy cry because she no longer smells like trees. Caddy, who is the most insistent on finding out what is happening in the adult world, and on her prerogatives to boss around the children, upsets Benjy because she is no longer natural and pure but adulterated and no more acceptable to Quentin than to Benjy, both brothers wishing to idealize her, as Faulkner so wanted to idealize his beloved, in a kind of tyranny of love that Caddy tries to appease when she washes herself for Benjy so that she can smell like trees again. She intuits what undoes him, giving her bottle of perfume to Dilsey, because the smell interferes with his experience of her. "We don't like perfume ourselves," Caddy tells Dilsey, as though for Benjy's benefit. Her powerful love and empathy have no complement in this dysfunctional family, save for Dilsey, who, of necessity, is like Callie Barr, a disciplinarian, the one whom the children really do have to mind. With a feckless father and a languishing mother, it is no wonder that Caddy wants to be the minder, to feel in control, even though at every juncture Jason, child and man, opposes her. If every time is the same time for Benjy, his mode of perception equals anyone else's because the family does go around and around, compulsively repeating the same behaviors as if time has not progressed. When Quentin in his section smashes his watch to stop time, his action is futile because he already acts as if time does not exist, as if what happened in childhood is happening now, as it does for Benjy.

QUENTIN

If Benjy is a wailing imagist poet manqué, Quentin is an abject symbolist, the defeated southern gentleman. Both brothers are powerless to protect Caddy, which means they cannot honor their love for her. Quentin is as fixated on restoring Caddy's purity as Benjy, who wants her to smell like trees. For Quentin, she is associated with the smell of honeysuckle that seems to exude from her face and throat like a "carnal secretion."[7] The brothers cannot freshen her, and their lament is for a world that has been corrupted and dirtied like Caddy's muddy drawers and like the Italian immigrant girl in her dirty dress whom Quentin takes in hand only to be accused of defiling her during his suicidal walk in Cambridge, Massachusetts. For all their differences, Quentin and Benjy treat time the same way, with incidents in Quentin's Harvard day (June 2, 1910) triggering his obsession with Caddy and his family's degeneration. Both brothers are cases of arrested development.[8]

Quentin labors under the heavy burden of his father's futility, a frame of mind alien to the long line of Compsons who have fought for and settled the land. Mr. Compson tells his son: "no battle is ever won. . . . They are not even fought. The field only reveals to man his own folly and despair, and victory is an illusion of philosophers and fools." Mr. Compson is a walking dead man, as ineffectual as Faulkner's own father, but with the additional liability of a Spenglerian pessimism propounding the decline of Western civilization. His demoralizing speeches make any effort to rectify folly seem foolish. The son is shadowed by the father and his absent sister throughout his Cambridge day. Father and sister are often coupled in Quentin's thoughts: "Father said that. That Christ was not crucified: he was worn away by a minute clicking of little wheels. That had no sister." What Quentin's obsession with time amounts to is the defeat of the heroic by the mundane. It is not the crucifixion that is the tragedy but rather the human inability to live by a heroic code day in and day out. Every day is a defeat just as it is for Benjy and maddeningly so for Jason. Not until the novel reaches Dilsey in the fourth section do we find a character capable of enduring, which is to say triumphing, day by day with the tensile strength demanded of a servant not simply of the Compsons but of human-kind. She is, as apparently Caroline Barr was, indomitable, to use a favorite Faulknerian word, unbowed by her servitude and in fact ennobled by it. Like Caroline Barr, Dilsey serves with a purpose and without the pretensions of aristocracy or the aggrieved sense of entitlement that torments Jason.

Quentin is mortified that Caddy has lost her virginity before he forsakes his own, which is a blow to southern boys like Quentin who brag about their sexual initiations: "In the South you are ashamed of being a virgin. Boys. Men. They lie about it. Because it means less to women, Father said. He said it was men invented virginity not women." Even worse, Quentin has been bullied and treated as less than a man by a Harvard classmate who calls Shreve, Quentin's roommate, Quentin's husband. What is it about Quentin that invites such ridicule? It seems to be his sense of decorum, his earnest effort to play the gentleman in full regalia. He simply cannot unwind like Spoade, a South Carolina senior, who never makes it to "chapel or first lecture with a shirt on his back and socks on his feet."

To his jaded father, Quentin, seeking some dramatic reaction, some rec-ognition that what he feels *counts,* has to claim the worst: *"I have commit-ted incest I said Father it was I it was not Dalton Ames."* Like a gentleman, Quentin strives to protect Caddy's honor, even if it means impugning his own integrity. But Mr. Compson rejects the role of outraged father. He will not even concede that any transgression ultimately makes a difference. He tells Quentin that people "cannot even remember tomorrow what seemed dreadful today." Life is not a heroic struggle. It has no meaning. And to this nihilism Quentin has no counter. He thinks of drowning himself in an act so definitive that there will be no resurrection.

All that is left for Quentin to do is behave as a meticulous gentleman dressing and carefully stacking the books he has brought from home and those he borrowed from the library while recalling his father's jaundiced observation: *"it used to be a gentleman was known by his books; nowadays he is known by the ones he has not returned."* Quentin resorts to "primping," to use Shreve's word. He is wearing his best suit for the day of his death, doing the gentleman in style, so to speak, since he cannot fulfill his role alive and every day. Like Benjy, Quentin is mesmerized by watching Caddy in the mirror on her wedding day. Benjy is bellowing as Quentin remembers *the smells roses roses the voice that breathed o'er Eden.* Her loss is of biblical proportions, and Benjy, whom Mrs. Compson always calls Benjamin, the son of her pain, voices the primordial agony of paradise lost, which Quentin feels just as acutely—with the death of their grandmother (Damuddy) breaking in upon them as mortality came to Adam and Eve in the garden. The consciousness of sex and death that comes together in the Garden of Eden is reenacted in the Adamic fall of the Compsons. Shreve's question to the suited-up Quentin, "Is it a wedding or a wake," is, as usual, perceptive, since Quentin is remembering Caddy's wedding—*"the floating shadow of the veil running across the grass"*—and preparing for his funeral. The grass, the golf course, the rounds that Benjy and William Faulkner regularly made on the made-over pasture, the pasture that is sold to fund Quentin's Harvard year, are part of the repetition-compulsion cycle that envelops not merely the Compsons but the fate of humankind's post-Edenic existence.

A curious exchange between Shreve and Quentin reveals the repercussions of his family's and region's history. Quentin thinks of what his roommate has said about the "Deacon," a black man always present on Decoration Day, first established to decorate the graves of Confederate soldiers before becoming Memorial Day. The Deacon dresses up in a G.A.R. (Grand Army of the Republic) uniform, on all birthdays commemorating liberators like Garibaldi, even carrying an Italian flag. The Deacon is in the street-sweepers section that cleans up after the paraders' horses, prompting Shreve to say to Quentin:

> "There now. Just look at what your grandpa did to that poor old nigger."
> "Yes," I said. "Now he can spend day after day marching in parades. If it hadn't been for my grandfather, he'd have to work like whitefolks."

Faulkner quoted virtually the same exchange in a letter home from New Haven at a time when he was no more prepared than Quentin to deal with family and southern history. Quentin tries to make light of the history that will later haunt him in *Absalom, Absalom!* So why does Quentin want to see the Deacon before dying, even though Quentin makes a wry Jason-like comment: "But I never knew even a working nigger that you could find when you wanted him, let alone one that lived off the fat of the land." What would Quentin or his brother Jason do without their "niggers," who become catch-all factotums for virtually any mood their white masters care to express? Is the irony intended? Here is a racism so ingrained that Quentin does not seem to see how it arises out of his own nugatory existence. Yet he is hardly Jason and even realizes "a nigger is not a person so much as a form of behavior; a sort of obverse reflection of the white people he lives among." This perception arises also out of Faulkner's own conflicted experience at Yale, when he wrote home to his mother about how black people behaved in New Haven, where he doubted they were better off than in the South. Quentin's comment makes out black people to be no more than conformers to white expectations, and yet, ironically, his statement also reveals how agile black people can be in performing as their white masters wish. Like Faulkner, Quentin sees black people as not only serving but buoying white people: "a fond and unflagging tolerance for whitefolks' vagaries like that of a grandparent for unpredictable and troublesome children." The Deacon, though, is a sort of con man, picking out southerners, naming their states, and putting on a kind of minstrel show for them, engaging in servile behavior, as Quentin tells it, even as the Deacon becomes a familiar, calling those same southerners by their first names, as he does Quentin while confiding, "you and me's the same folks, come long and short," as Dilsey will say Luster has Compson devilment in him. When Quentin vouchsafed his suicide note to the Deacon, enjoining him not to deliver it to Shreve until the next day, the Deacon affirms his role in a patronizing fashion: "I'll confer to your wishes, my boy." The Deacon is like Dilsey and like Caroline Barr insofar as he defers to white people and yet puts them in their place.

Quentin sees Gerald Bland rowing along the Charles, a figure in Oxford (England) flannels, a Kentuckian version of the gentleman scholar, done up in the smartest clothes that are a rebuke to Spoade, the scruffy South Carolinian. The sight of the impeccably dressed Bland triggers memories of Dalton Ames, who refused to accept Quentin's challenge. Quentin's effort to defend Caddy's honor becomes a charade and then a deep humiliation, compounded by his chagrin at Bland's misogyny: *they're all bitches,* confirming what Jason will say in his own section. Bland, Spoade, Ames, and Herbert Head (Caddy's betrothed) are all an affront to Quentin, whose aborted heroic quest mocks Sir Walter Scott's eponymous hero Quentin Durward, intent on restoring the age of chivalry, and Lochinvar in Scott's *Marmion,* who rides off with his lady love before she is forced into marriage with another. Quentin fails to intervene to redeem Caddy or his family and is dogged by the shadow of himself that he cannot shake any more than he can arrest the movement of time that is constantly alerting him in watches and clocks and chimes to his ineffectual actions, recalling Faulkner's own botched effort to run away with Estelle, the sister-bride of his childhood.

Like Benjy, Quentin lives in a world of absolutes—one that offers Caddy no reprieve because of its rigid distinctions, enforced by her own mother, who declares her shame over her daughter's promiscuous behavior in disjointed, self-interrupted complaints expressive of the outmoded, truncated southern lady code that has become nearly inarticulate: "I was taught that there is no halfway ground that a woman is either a lady or not but I never dreamed when I held her in my arms that any daughter of mine could let herself dont you know I can look at her eyes and tell you may think she'd tell you but she doesn't tell things she is secretive you dont know her I know things she's done that I'd die before I'd have you know." Of course Caddy is secretive. How else can she maintain her own independence and integrity? Mrs. Compson is married to a man who looks down upon her family, the Bascombs, who do not have a distinguished pedigree, a line of governors and soldiers that the Compsons, Falkners, and Oldhams treasure. She berates her husband for indulging Caddy and refusing to see the worst of her behavior. Her favorite is Jason, who is more like a Bascomb in her opinion, and like her brother Maury, whom, she believes, her husband treats with condescension. She even seeks permission to separate from her husband and take Jason to where they can start again, which means she has abandoned her daughter. That renunciation of Caddy bedevils Quentin, whose own father could not defend her, prompting Quentin to imagine shooting Dalton Ames and Herbert Head, and those southern gentleman at Harvard who have no sisters and no desire to preserve feminine chastity. Gerald Bland is an especially disturbing presence because of his beauty, wasted on a male it is said as he is accompanied by an overly protective mother who does for him what Mrs. Compson would not do for Caddy. No wonder then that Quentin bloodies himself in a fight with Bland. Just as Quentin relives the past in the present, so Faulkner seems to have drawn on his attachment to the elusive Estelle, home from the Orient and transmogrified in the moment Quentin watches Bland and thinks of Caddy and their lost childhood Eden: "'What a shame that you should have a mouth like that it should be on a girl's face' and can you imagine *the curtains leaning in on the twilight upon the odor of the apple tree her head against the twilight her arms behind her head kimono-winged the voice that breathed o'er eden clothes upon the bed by the nose seen above the apple.*" William Faulkner had come to the rescue by marrying kimono-winged Estelle, recovering the idyll of their youth, yet knowing full well, like Quentin, that such bliss could not come again, with the knowledge that accompanies the biting of the apple, the knowledge that leads to the awareness of sin. Unlike Faulkner, Quentin cannot bear to live beyond knowledge of the fall. Grief was better than nothing, Faulkner would say, inside and outside his fiction, but nothingness is precisely the condition Quentin craves—at least it is so after his own quest to give and receive love has failed.

Quentin takes himself all too seriously, like Scott's Quentin Durward, and cannot come to terms with the absurdity of his absoluteness that demands that Caddy and the rest of the world conform to his courtly behavior. Quentin's uncompromising idealization of the gentlemanly code is the obverse of his father's renunciation of his role as patriarch and paladin. Shreve sees the absurdity of Quentin's position but plays along, even casting himself as Quentin's beloved. Shreve, getting a start on the mock-heroic southern gentleman palaver that he will perfect in *Absalom, Absalom!,* reports to Quentin that Mrs. Bland has sought to have the "fat Canadian youth" removed as a roommate unworthy of Quentin, as though the two men are lovers. Shreve, taking the part of damsel in distress, exclaims: "Cruel fate may part us, but I will never love another. Never." Shreve's parodies Quentin's quasi-romantic affectations, but Quentin should not be regarded as simply living in a world of his own. His feelings have been reciprocated, as Herbert Head reports in telling Quentin how much Caddy has told him about her brother: "I dont mind telling you it never occurred to me it was her brother she kept talking about she couldn't have talked about you any more if you'd been the only man in the world." Quentin feels betrayed as her defender, brother, and lover. In a household where both parents abnegate their responsibilities, Quentin, like Caddy, has taken on more roles than he can possibly fulfill, as the worldly Herbert Head tells him when explaining his marriage to the pregnant Caddy: "I dont give a damn whether you tell or not understand that a thing like that unfortunate but no police crime I wasn't the first or the last I was just unlucky you might have been luckier." In Head's words, Caddy becomes common and not worth the outrage over the loss of her virginity. The not telling, who gets to tell, which is to say who has the power, is part of the struggle that Quentin, Caddy, and Jason have in a family that no longer has a central authority, a reason for being, a purpose to fulfill. What Quentin does is inconsequential not only to Herbert Head but to everyone else, and his powerlessness makes a mockery of the sacrifice of the pasture to send him to Harvard. What Mrs. Bland wants to defend in banishing Shreve as Quentin's roommate has turned to farce in Shreve's burlesquing of her uncivil treatment of him: "I make it a point never to speak harshly of females . . . but that woman has got more ways like a bitch than any lady in these sovereign states and dominions."

Ladyhood, as practiced by Mrs. Bland and Mrs. Compson, has become bitch-ery, a chronic nagging about propriety and decorum that has driven Caddy and her daughter away from home and society and made Quentin a stooge. Without Caddy's presence and belief in him, Quentin is quashed and rele-gated to refusing Herbert Head's expensive Cuban cigar, a petty instance of independence that has only the kind of symbolic value that Faulkner apparently found in refusing his father's offer of a cigar. Quentin refuses to be manly on those transactional terms even if the world, like Herbert Head, calls him a "half-baked Galahad," or just as easily in Faulkner's case, a "Count No 'Count."

Quentin obsessively repeats to himself Caddy's question, Will he take care of Benjy and father? Here, too, Quentin has failed, since Benjy will be sent to Jackson and castrated, and Mr. Compson will continue drinking himself to death. The pregnant Caddy cannot stay home. She must marry someone, she tells Quentin. Mr. Compson, unlike so many southern patriarchs, has not imposed ladyhood on his daughter, but like Quentin, he can do nothing pos-itive. She is on her own. Mr. Compson's main contribution to her upbring-ing has been his aloof and sardonic attitude toward the entire enterprise of rearing a southern belle. As he tells the resistant Quentin: "Women are never virgins. Purity is a negative state and therefore contrary to nature. It's nature is hurting you not Caddy and I said That's just words and he said So is virginity and I said you dont know. You cant know and he said Yes. On the instant when we come to realise that tragedy is second-hand." If Mr. Compson can-not know what virginity means to a woman and to Caddy specifically, then neither can Quentin, his father rejoins. They are arguing about words, yes, the playful patriarch-rhetorician concedes, but both men, in this instance, cannot know what Caddy experiences. Tragedy, however each man chooses to define it, is secondhand. And this is Quentin's tragedy: He cannot share his sister's plight no matter how intensely he longs for their commingling or to redeem her errant reputation by virtue of his errant knighthood, symbol-ized by his Harvard hegira. His "lady" of cohabitation is Shreve. Any other is the hell he imagines for himself and Caddy: *the clean flame the two of us more than dead. Then you will have only me then only me then the two of us amid the pointing and the horror beyond the clean flame.*

Quentin's profound displacement is subject to yet another irony when he talks to a group of boys fishing who say he talks "like a colored man," like the language they hear in minstrel shows, like, in other words, the Deacon. Quentin has become marginal to boys arguing, one calling the other a mam-ma's boy who will get licked if he get his clothes wet—thus recalling the quar-reling Compson children and especially Caddy, who will get whipped if she submerges herself in the branch and returns home wet and dirty. Quentin has all along regretted that Mrs. Compson has been such an absent parent that he feels he has had no mother. But like his mother he yearns for escape, pleading with Caddy that they and Benjy can go away where no one knows them. Well, Cambridge is such an away place, and the deracinated Quentin, observing a little Italian girl in a bakery shop, thinks, "Land of the kike home of the wop." Quentin is not without his prejudices, but his parody of "land of the free and home of the brave" seems ironic, especially given his reaction to the skeletal-looking woman at the counter who complains about foreigners, advising Quentin to "stay clear" of them. But Quentin addresses the silent Italian girl as "sister," a common form of address that also calls Caddy to mind and Quentin's desire to die with his female counterpart. He refers to the girl as a "lady who wants something," but the woman calls her a wretch who only wants to steal, a foreshadowing of Quentin's own predicament when he is accused of abducting the Italian girl. Her face "like a cup of milk dashed with coffee," makes her colored, like Quentin, and also comforting, like Quentin's and Faulkner's warm feeling for black people. For the first time in his fiction, Faulkner is here working out a complex of emotions linking races and peoples that first erupted in his visits to New Haven. The shop woman wonders how the girl got into the shop without ringing the bell, so Quentin explains, "It rang once for both of us." Quentin treats the girl like a sister, as if he knows what she is thinking and feeling:

"You going to give her that bun?" the woman said.
"Yessum," I said. "I expect your cooking smells as good to her as it does to me."

The girl is now attached to Quentin, and he cannot shake her off any more than he can forget his earliest exposure to sex with a girl named Natalie, an episode like others with women that reveal his wariness of the opposite sex. He even tries to run away from the Italian girl, unable to speak her language in every sense of the word. "She looked at me, black and secret and friendly," Quentin reports, just as the black people in Quentin's life have done. The Italian girl takes possession of Quentin just as Caddy intervened with Natalie, keeping Quentin for herself. He remembers his confused rage when he smeared Caddy's body with mud, making her dark, in some sort of sexual play, it seems, but he can no more possess his sister (*"her wet hard turning body"*) than he can possess or understand the Italian girl. The boys earlier seen fishing are now swimming naked and try to splash Quentin and the girl as interlopers, defiling an Edenic refuge, as Quentin once saw his own childhood paradise corrupted. This time his bond with the Italian girl is shattered as her brother Julio catches up with them, attacking Quentin for stealing his sister. Quentin is arrested by a marshal as Julio threatens his sister with a beating, doing an injury to her that he had attributed to Quentin.

Quentin's friends vouch for him, and he is released, paying fines for the time taken to apprehend him. Quentin Compson is a chevalier manqué once again. He never does manage to have a single conversation with the little Italian girl. Females simply do not speak to him and are beyond his understanding and a part of his humiliating sexual inexperience, as he himself notes: In Mrs. Bland's automobile sit "Miss Holmes and Miss Daingerfield and they quit listening to her and looked at me again with that delicate and curious horror, their veils turned back upon their little white noses and their eyes fleeing and mysterious beneath the veils."

As these Cambridge concurrences reach their crescendo, Quentin relives a conversation with Caddy on the eve of her wedding. He vows to kill Herbert Head. She calls him "poor Quentin" because he cannot understand the force of sexual desire, of how she can be with a man she hates but also craves, hates but would also die for. She knows he is lying when he says he has had sex "lots of times with lots of girls." Quentin is as castrated as Benjy. With a phallic knife at Caddy's throat he offers to kill her and then himself, and she consents, telling him to stop crying as he puts his hand on her "damp hard breast" and hears her heart "going firm and slow now not hammering." She is comforting him, like a mother, and he drops the knife, and his effort to penetrate her, apparently aware that she does not share his self-destructive urge or his sexual passion, no matter how much she empathizes with him. As with Benjy, Caddy's love, her fearlessness, and, above all, her magnificent selflessness in such moments put her out of reach of Quentin's tormented desire to possess her for eternity and to deny the depredations of his rivals. Like Benjy, he can think only of *his* Caddy. Quentin, Benjy, and even Jason all manifest "a clan in love with itself."[9]

Caddy's pity is unbearable, and Quentin remembers trying to salvage his honor by confronting Dalton Ames—even uttering the cliché, "I'll give you until sundown to leave town." Has Quentin been reading *The Virginian*? Ames, acting very much like the Virginian, kindly tells Quentin: "no good taking it so hard its not your fault kid it would have been some other fellow." When Quentin takes a swing at Caddy's seducer, Ames catches the shaking Quentin by the wrists, and after showing Quentin how good he is with a gun, he offers it to Quentin, who instead tries to hit Ames again but then finds himself on the ground. He asks Ames if Ames has struck him, and Ames says yes, but as Ames leaves, after offering Quentin his horse, Quentin realizes he has passed out "like a girl." Ames has been the gallant one, lying for Caddy's sake.

This memory, reflecting Quentin's deep humiliation and unquenchable desire to redeem himself, drives him to attack Gerald Bland, "blowing off" about his women, as Shreve puts it. Quentin, again in a daze, asks if he has at least bloodied Bland, but no one saw him land a punch on Bland, a trained boxer, whom Quentin accosts with his perpetual question, "Did you ever have a sister?"

For the rest, Quentin withdraws into himself, remembering his father's unbearable words about Caddy: "even she was not quite worth despair"—a conclusion that Quentin will come to in time, Mr. Compson assures him, but that Quentin forestalls by ending time, so to speak, with his own suicide.

JASON

Jason's words (April 6, 1928) come hard upon Quentin's thwarted chivalry: "Once a bitch always a bitch," the very words that Gerald Bland and Shreve have used to undercut the idealization of women. Jason's words apply to Miss Quentin and are addressed to his mother, wailing away over her inability to make her granddaughter stay in school and behave like a lady. Jason calls for drastic measures: "When people act like niggers, no matter who they are the only thing to do is treat them like a nigger." Jason's problem with Miss Quentin is a crude version of his brother Quentin's concerns over Caddy: Both brothers, wary of women, are rigidly intent on enforcing a stultifying standard of behavior, which is what the whining Mrs. Compson wants but cannot accomplish. Jason whips Miss Quentin around so that her kimono opens and she is "dam near naked," recalling her "kimono-winged" mother. Like Caddy, her daughter eludes male authority. Jason accuses her of hiding out in the woods with "dam slick-headed jellybeans." He gets out his belt, threatening to beat her, but Mrs. Compson appears, as Jason has to know will happen, while he fixates on Miss Quentin's closed kimono, her sexuality shut against him in this sadomasochistic scene. Relying on Dilsey, who is ready to take Jason's blows and referee between her white family members, Miss Quentin cries out, "Dilsey, I want my mother." With no one else to turn to, this third-generation Compson woman is just looking for a way out.

Jason's fear of female sexuality and his disgust with women rule virtually every aspect of his behavior when he is not blaming his plight on freeloading "niggers." In fact, Caddy writes a businesslike letter demanding to know what Jason does with the money she sent him for her daughter's clothes. Jason's nonsensical racism is given full comic treatment in this duo with a drummer:

"I give every man his due, regardless of religion or anything else. I have nothing against jews as an individual," I says. "It's just the race. You'll admit that they produce nothing. They follow the pioneers into a new country and sell them clothes."

"You're thinking of Armenians," he says, "aren't you. A pioneer wouldn't have any use for new clothes."

The Jason section has a startling contemporary ring to it: "I'm an American," the drummer emphasizes. "My folks have some French blood, why I have a nose like this. I'm an American, all right." To which Jason assents: "So am I. . . . Not many of us left."

In Cambridge or Jefferson, the result is the same: fear of foreigners and a projection of hostility onto a class, gender, ethnicity, or race. The severe insecurity that shadows Quentin is replicated in Jason's repetitious chauvinism. This acutely ironic novel is constantly showing how all the characters are bound to one another be they black or white, Christian or Jew, French or Italian—it hardly matters the distinction because it makes no difference. Faulkner simply cannot let his characters get away with their inhumanity. We know who Jason voted for when he says: "But I'll be damned if it hasn't come to a pretty pass when any dam foreigner that cant make a living in the country where God put him, can come to this one and take money right out of an American's pockets."

Jason often sounds like he has been reading too many pulp novels: "I never promise a woman anything nor let her know what I'm going to give her. That's the only way to manage them. Always keep them guessing. If you cant think of any other way to surprise them, give them a bust in the jaw." The up-to-date Jason, monitoring by the minute his losses in the stock market, is just as deluded about women as Quentin, even though Jason shares none of his brother's chivalric conceit. Caddy returns disguised with a veil, like the veiled women who observe her brother Quentin in Cambridge, and like her mother, who appears at crucial instances in a veil. Caddy has promised not to visit, but she offers Jason a hundred dollars if he will arrange for Caddy to see her daughter. All she gets for her money is a quick drive-by look as Miss Quentin is rushed past her in a carriage—Jason's revenge, he says, for not getting the job that Herbert Head, now estranged from Caddy, promised Jason. Jason cannot acknowledge his inner turmoil as his brother Quentin does and can only speak of "feeling funny" when he remembers his childhood. Caddy's return, after he thinks he has the household to himself, upsets him. He worries that Caddy will take it all away from him: "Somebody's got to hold on to what little we have left, I reckon."

Jason desperately wants to believe he is in command. He is convinced that "he alone has a firm grasp on reality. He cannot imagine that there might be other facts, other aspects of the situation, than the ones that directly affect him."[10] When Dilsey disobeys and makes sure that Caddy sees Benjy on her surreptitious visits home, Jason complains: "That's the trouble with nigger servants, when they've been with you for a long time they get so full of self importance that they're not worth a dam. Think they run the whole family." Did any of the Falkners ever grouse about Caroline Barr? Their nostalgic reminiscences say otherwise, but was there really no uneasiness in a family where the boys had two mothers to mind? John and Jack never raised the issue of race where Caroline Barr was concerned, which is perhaps why it becomes one of the focal points of *The Sound and the Fury*. Race remained the unspoken tension between them and their older brother, who defied not only their conventional racism but his mother's as well.

Dilsey knows her place but speaks out when it is a question of character, as most likely Caroline Barr did too: "You's a cold man, Jason, if man you is," she says. "I thank de Lawd I got mo heart dan dat, even ef hit is black." Not until he writes the "Compson Appendix" does Faulkner reveal why Caddy feels she cannot have her daughter live with her instead of sending checks for Quentin's support that Jason appropriates. Caddy simply confesses it would be "crazy" to take Quentin with her. Caddy cannot provide Quentin with a stable home and desperately hopes that Jason will take her offers of money to provide her daughter with a proper upbringing. Caddy's is a futile gesture in a family that includes Uncle Maury, Mrs. Compson's brother, a character straight out of Dickens, a Macawber who always misses the main chance but speaks the language of a gentleman, referring to Mrs. Compson as Jason's "lady mother" and drawing on Mrs. Compson's bank account for one of Maury's promised bonanza investments that never materialize while advising Jason: "And knowing your Mother's delicate health and that timorousness which such delicately nurtured Southern ladies would naturally feel regarding matters of business, and their charming proneness to divulge unwittingly such matters in conversation, I would suggest that you do not mention it to her at all."

Jason, no gentleman, has withdrawn Mrs. Compson's one-thousand-dollar investment in the hardware store where Jason works and bought an automobile. His boss, Earl, knows as much but refrains from telling Mrs. Compson, since Earl also abides by the gentlemanly custom of not troubling a lady with worldly matters. To Jason, the Compson code is a farce and has been taken to the grave by his brother and father, releasing Jason, in his own mind, from any compunction about collecting what he feels is due to him. Not that Jason will not pull a Compson when he feels like it, telling Earl: "I says my people owned slaves here when you all were running little shirt tail country stores and farming land no nigger would look at on shares." He is as tied to the family as any other member, no matter how much he ridicules his heritage.

Jason pretends to be all Compson in defending the family honor, which means preventing Miss Quentin from running around with one of the show-men: "Like I say it's not that I object to so much; maybe she cant help that, it's because she hasn't even got enough consideration for her own family to have any discretion. I'm afraid all the time I'll run into them right in the middle of the street or under a wagon on the square, like a couple of dogs." Yet, like his father and brother, Jason is derelict, showing up to work late, leaving early, or interrupting the workday while chasing after Miss Quentin even as he accuses the "niggers" and others of not doing their jobs. The superior tone he takes with Earl and with everyone else has not been earned but simply inherited as a result of the Compson position as a founding family. Jason's throbbing headache—a reaction to the gasoline fumes of the car he drives around in a chase to catch the promiscuous Miss Quentin—is an expression of his inability to adapt to the present any better than his brother did. Both are self-defeated, as old Job, one of the "niggers" Jason jeers at, tells him: "'You fools a man whut so smart he cant even keep up wid hisself,' he says, getting in the wagon and unwrapping the reins. 'Who's that?' I says. 'Dat's Mr Jason Compson,'" old Job rejoins.

Jason shares his brother Quentin's anachronistic attitudes. One brother's behavior is as futile as the other's, with Jason's plight especially comic, as he gets tangled up in lice, twigs, and poison oak while following Miss Quentin's trail of transgression. Both brothers claim to be acting in the family's interests even as their actions drive the Compsons apart, providing no place whatsoever for Caddy and her daughter to exist. Both brothers indulge in melodramatics that render their principles absurd. The time for acting like the Virginian is long gone, but the Compsons clutch at their decadent, stifling gentility so that Caddy and her daughter are forced to look for an escape.

If the Compsons are not the Falkners by a long shot, the families neverthe-less share a proud, if now attenuated, fealty to a family heritage that requires them to act as an upper caste, even though their authority and record of accomplishment has eroded. As the eldest, the scion, Faulkner felt the pres-sure, rejected a good deal of Falkner precedent, and yet sought, especially beginning with his marriage, to continue some sort of family tradition. If he could be as sarcastic as Jason, he could also be as reverential as Quentin, and yet not take entirely seriously the very models of gentlemanly behavior that his characters so manifestly fail to perform. As with Quentin, Jason never manages a showdown—a duel, a fight, *something* that would justify his big talk. He has some inkling that he has been acting like a fool, but he ascribes the outcome of his bootless chase to Miss Quentin's desire to make him a laughingstock. In other words, like his brother Quentin, Jason turns virtually every situation into a reflection of himself: the wayward Miss Quentin acts only to thwart him, not to express her own wish to act independently of the Compson prerogative. To not be your own person, which is the fate these women face, was familiar to William Faulkner, who saw his intended taken away from him in what was in effect a family decision Estelle felt powerless to prevent and that he could not, or would not, try to stop.

By the time Faulkner married Estelle, the Oldham fortunes were beginning to take a turn for the worse. Faulkner would do his best by them, but the bitterness Jason feels about having to be the one to pick up the pieces has its origins in Faulkner's own experience, one that he would go on to complain about in the next decade, sometimes in the sardonic tone that Jason takes at the end of his monologue, coming full circle in his persecution of Miss Quentin and in reiteration of his credo: "Once a bitch always a bitch."

DILSEY

The first paragraph of the final section, rendered in the third person, is a rebuke not only to Jason's crudity but to the tortured interior landscape of all the narrators. The length of line, the sobering dignity of the principal figure, who is built to weather service and punishment, reflect a new sensibility, with a power to envision an enduring response to existence that is absent from the Compson lexicon. Much has been made of Faulkner's reluctance to directly enter the minds of his black characters, but in this case Dilsey's magnificence can only be rendered from on high, so to speak, and not in her dialect or even in her thoughts.

Ben Wasson, whose own novel *The Devil Beats His Wife* was published the same year as *The Sound and the Fury*, realized he would never be able to compete with his friend's genius. Aunt Ana, the Dilsey figure in Wasson's novel, declares: "'White folks is white folks an niggers is niggers, an dats de way it always was an dats de way it always gwineter be. I was barn, by de Lawd, belongin' to yo' family, an if dats de way de Lawd put me in de worl, ain't no Yankee gonna undo de work of de Almighty.' She said this with an air of triumph." This stalwart, faithful "darkie," rendered in painfully phonetic detail, is a figure out of the tradition Wasson and Faulkner shared, but she is utterly transformed in Dilsey, whose menial work is never menial and whose independent spirit makes her part of the family in a sort of paradoxical dependency that drives Jason mad. Unlike Aunt Ana, Dilsey can stand outside of the very world that subjugates her, very much as William Faulkner believed his Callie did. It is how Dilsey stands, outside in the elements, so to speak, that makes her a cynosure, wearing the worn mantle of her authority:

> The day dawned bleak and chill, a moving wall of gray light out of the northeast which, instead of dissolving into moisture, seemed to disintegrate into minute and venomous particles, like dust that, when Dilsey opened the door of the cabin and emerged, needled laterally into her flesh, precipitating not so much a moisture as a substance partaking of the quality of thin, not quite congealed oil. She wore a stiff black straw hat perched upon her turban, and a maroon velvet cape with a border of mangy and anonymous fur above a dress of purple silk, and she stood in the door for a while with her myriad and sunken face lifted to the weather, and one gaunt hand flac-soled as the belly of a fish, then she moved the cape aside and examined the bosom of her gown.

In her person, Dilsey represents an aged network of associations, a history that the Compsons have failed to maintain. While Jason has been grousing about supporting his family, she is the one who actually brings the meal to the table and provides for Miss Quentin the sole means of psychic and social support, saying to Jason that the girl has to be let alone to be herself—something that not only Jason but also his brother Quentin and Mrs. Compson and the insatiable Benjy could not permit in regard to Caddy, and that Mr. Compson could only acknowledge by abnegating his responsibility as head of the family. In the Falkner home, a battleground of warring parents with conflicting expectations, the eldest son had recourse to Mammy Callie, Dilsey's progenitor. Only in Caroline Barr's care could William Faulkner escape his role as the object of his parents' contradictory purposes; only in Dilsey can the knotted history of the Compsons be straightened out, the tangle of their perceptions unwound. In purple silk, Dilsey rules as surely as a Roman emperor over his domain, in spite of the chaos the Compsons foment in a threadbare kingdom, her person insubstantial, her very body exposed like the pale belly of a fish, "flac-soled," in Faulkner's compressed expression of a woman exposed and yet with her soul intact. She is at once a symbol or abstraction and a palpable person. We see the "loose palm-skin, the flaccid sole not of a foot but an aged hand, pale and convex as a fish belly."[11] She is as powerfully present in Faulkner's coinage as she is absent in Jason's dismissal of her importance.

Unlike the novel's first-person narrator, the voice in this section has a sense of history that breaks through the Compsons' repetitive-obsessive, self-defeating cycles of experience. Dilsey's presence is the work of time and her own industry, a maturing of a role that is beyond the Compson ken:

> She had been a big woman once but now her skeleton rose, draped loosely in unpadded skin that tightened again upon a paunch almost dropsical, as though muscle and tissue had been courage or fortitude which the days or the years had consumed until only the indomitable skeleton was left rising like a ruin or a landmark above the somnolent and impervious guts, and above that the collapsed face that gave the impression of the bones themselves being outside the flesh, lifted into the driving day with an expression at once fatalistic and of a child's astonished disappointment, until she turned and entered the house again and closed the door.

Only such a long sentence can gather up and display Dilsey's full humanity that encompasses all of life from childhood to old age in a range of activity, grounded in the earth and flesh that no other Compson can understand let alone rival. She seems without illusions and yet as spontaneous as a child. Without her, the novel would degenerate, which is to say the Compsons cannot be left to their own devices. Which is also to say that Faulkner, reflecting on his own family's history, could not let it be as it was. The family's history had to mean more than itself, point to some other outcome than the old Colonel's brief moments of glory and the family's subsequent decline. That history had to be redeemed in fiction, in truths larger than any assemblage of fact.

Everywhere you look in this last section, there is history, seen for the first time and recounted not as tales in *Flags in the Dust* or even in the mementos that old Bayard treasures but in the texture and detail of the material world: "The earth immediately about the door was bare. It had a patina, as though from the soles of bare feet in generations, like old silver or the walls of Mexican houses which have been plastered by hand." Was Faulkner thinking of the Mexican jewelry and furnishings William Spratling first worked on beginning in the summer of 1926? These opening passages of the novel's fourth section are saturated with an anthropological and architectural sensibility unlike anything Faulkner had written before and with a wide-angle perspective unavailable to the novel's other narrators. Dilsey is a ruin, a landmark, and a figure of the past, a skeleton paradoxically alive while in a seeming state of collapse—in short, a death-defying figure, the very antidote to Compson defeatism. Quentin, Jason, Benjy, Mrs. Compson, and Mr. Compson are all defined by their sense of loss and their inability to recover their equilibrium. Dilsey stands even though she seems built to fall. Bones seeming to break outside of flesh ought to signal the onset of structural failure, and yet Dilsey looks up into the driving day, without illusions and yet prepared to be let down by life again. She knows the history that is fated to happen, and yet she perseveres.

On this particular day (April 8, 1928), Dilsey has to do everything for herself as well as dealing with the fretful Mrs. Compson because Luster has overslept after the show that Dilsey has given him the money to attend after Jason has burned his free passes in front of the tormented black boy. Luster is slow to do his chores, and Dilsey rightly suspects he is up to something in the cellar, telling him he has "jes es much Compson devilment in you es any of em." She watches over Benjy in the kitchen, where we get our first good look at him, at his hairless, dead-white skin and bear-like shambling gait but also his "sweet vague gaze." Jason also gets his close-up: "close-thatched brown hair curled into two stubborn hooks, one on either side of his forehead like a bartender in caricature, and hazel eyes with black-ringed irises like marbles," and Mrs. Compson: "cold and querulous, with perfectly white hair and eyes pouched and baffled and so dark as to appear to be all pupil or all iris." Anything Jason cannot catch, like his niece, eludes his understanding; almost anything that obtrudes on Mrs. Compson's consciousness is cause for concern because she cannot focus on whatever task is at hand.

In a brilliant stroke, Faulkner conjoins mother and son in their blindness to Miss Quentin's escape. Jason only realizes what has happened when his mother says, "I cant understand it. . . . It's just as if somebody had tried to break into the house," at which point he springs up to discover Miss Quentin has taken the money Caddy had sent to her and that Jason has hoarded. Miss Quentin has broken a window into his room, raided his metal box bank, and then departed out the window and onto the pear tree of knowledge, where Caddy had climbed to observe Damuddy's funeral. Mrs. Compson supposes that Miss Quentin has committed suicide like her namesake because this "lady mother" cannot imagine any other outcome than a repetition of the past, which Jason fulfills, in a way, by setting off to capture Miss Quentin. As Luster reports, Quentin has been seen using that pear tree to go out every night, exercising an initiative that the misogynist Jason, so dismissive of her, cannot imagine. In such plot details and characterization, in which even a minor character like Luster is fully integrated into the story and never functions as just local color, Faulkner advances beyond *Flags in the Dust,* where certain characters, black and white, appear in vivid vignettes but do not coalesce around the action as they do in *The Sound and the Fury.*

Benjy, aroused by the family crisis, wails, smelling trouble, as Dilsey puts it. She allays his instinctual response by smoothing his brow and telling him they are setting forth from the House of Compson to church. "We be gone in a minute," she soothes him. How many times, it has to be wondered, did Faulkner seek similar refuge with Caroline Barr, when the tension of his parents' set-tos became unbearable? White and black worlds converge in responses to Benjy, as Frony tells her mother that people are complaining about Benjy's presence in church. Dilsey, as much a Compson as she is her own person, retorts: "And I knows whut kind of folks. . . . Trash white folks. Dat's who it is. Thinks he aint good enough fer white church, but nigger church aint good enough fer him." The racial divide that this society so painstakingly observes and that is a part of the everyday speech of everyone—no matter whether it is Quentin or Jason Compson—is simultaneously reified and rejected in Dilsey's complex character that derived from William Faulkner's keen attachment to Caroline Barr. Both in dialogue and description, Faulkner escorts the reader through the refuse of discarded "broken things" and up the embankment to the rickety, weathered black church where human hurts are healed, where Reverend Shegog will provide "de comfort en de unburdenin" in the first tableau of the novel: "Toward the church they thronged with slow sabbath deliberation, the women and children went on in, the men stopped outside and talked in quiet groups until the bell ceased ringing. Then they too entered."

That Shegog is an outsider, a guest preacher from St. Louis, is crucial to understanding how this last section of the novel obliterates the confident provincialism not only of the Compsons but also of their black counterparts: "The black church was local, but it also transcended the local in that black ministers belonged to denominational organizations that were national, and it was usual for black ministers, like white, to move from church to church over the years."[12] Faulkner's revolutionary use of black culture to define, by contrast, his white characters is both a breakthrough in terms of his creative powers and also a magnificent recognition of how the color line had divided the white characters—all but Benjy, ironically—from the impact of African American life, "perpetually evolving," in Joel Williamson's words, and "never white":

> Sometimes elements in black culture were deliberate borrowings from whites, sometimes they were deliberate rejections of whiteness, most often they evolved from perceptions by black people of their own needs without a focused regard to color. Most of all, black people simply struggled, as everyone does, to create meaningful lives for themselves. White people, however, saw black culture as a more or less crude imitation of their own. Blacks might sing and dance differently, but most whites could not imagine that black people could have a life that was not complimentary in some way to their own.

And of course this is exactly how Jason treats Dilsey: as an adjunct. Yet she can traverse the color line, although she, too, gets grief for taking Benjy across it. That she does so against both white and black objections explains why she is such a crucial focal point for Faulkner as he moves away from the self-absorbed perspective of the Compsons. He seems to have taken his cue from Caroline Barr, who stood out among her black brethren. Faulkner watched Barr's "transformations as she moved between these two worlds," and he learned that "race, like culture, was performative and that its performance changed in response to place and audience."[13]

Shegog's appearance surprises the congregation. He is "undersized, in a shabby alpaca coat. He had a wizened black face like a small, aged monkey." Frony whispers: "En dey brung dat all de way fum Saint Looey." Shegog is, in short, as unprepossessing as Dilsey herself, but all the more impressive because he is a small conduit of tremendous import. His monkey-like features are mentioned several times—apparently to dramatize the incongruity of his appearance and the power of his delivery, which is not just a matter of words well expressed but of his style, posture, and sound: "His arm lay yet across the desk, and he still held that pose while the voice died in sonorous echoes between the walls. It was as different as day and dark from his former tone, with a sad, timbrous quality like an alto horn, sinking into their hearts and speaking there again when it had ceased in fading and cumulate echoes." He has become an instrument of his sermon the way an actor makes an instrument of his body: "He was like a worn small rock whelmed by the successive waves of his voice. With his body he seemed to feed the voice that, succubus like, had fleshed its teeth in him." This depiction of a spirit speaking through a corporeal vessel runs counter to the interior monologues of the novel, in which all human hurt is focused on the self, which recoils in Benjy's sobbing, Mrs. Compson's whining, Quentin's agonizing, and Jason's rages. The sermon serves as an analgesic, a remedy Dilsey has often applied to Benjy by bringing him to church. The penetrating music Shegog makes with his voice is also reminiscent of the jazz ensembles Faulkner depicted in his drawings in which the players are presented as a congregation of sound, their instruments swinging high and low in space even as the preacher's words inspire and then sink resonantly into the hearts of his flock.

Jazz democracy reigns: "their hearts were speaking to one another in chanting measures beyond the need for words." The only other voices that speak from the heart have been the isolated Caddy and the abused Dilsey taking care of heartbroken Benjy. Placing him in the church, after all of Jason's jokes about him as the Great American Gelding, is a powerful rebuke and also a powerful premonition of the world to come in just a few years, when the Nazis would begin to cull the mentally deficient from the nation—a procedure well within the parameters of Jason's fulminations and those of his fellow travelers in Cambridge muttering about those damn furriners. The world to come, the "land of the kike home of the wop," is more than Quentin can bear, however sensitive and un-Jason-like he may seem. Faulkner had a further irony in store for Caddy when he mentions in the "Compson Appendix," written fifteen years later, that she has become mistress to a German staff general during World War II. Latent in *The Sound and the Fury,* to be explored later, is a historical dimension that Faulkner himself may only have fully appreciated after his work with Malcolm Cowley on *The Portable Faulkner* and after Faulkner's war years in Hollywood.

Placed against the depredations of history is Dilsey herself, responding to the sermon of salvation. "Yes, Jesus!," one congregant cries out, as Dilsey sits "bolt upright, her hand on Ben's knee. Two tears slid down her fallen cheeks, in and out of the myriad coruscations of immolation and abnegation and time." For Dilsey and her people, suffering has a divine meaning and an end that none of the other Compsons can even contemplate. The reality of that faith is what made Faulkner's own early home life supportable. How else to explain the Falkners' indulgence of Callie Barr, who would sometimes leave them for husbands and lovers and then called the Falkner home so that Mr. Murry could come for her and return her to a place that no one else could occupy. The tributes that not only Faulkner but his brothers made to her reflect no mere sentimentality or nostalgia. In a family that often did not seem like a family and could not pull together, Callie Barr prevailed. Dilsey does the same. Her "determination to make something of her circumstances leads to her aura of triumph."[14]

In Reverend Shegog's sermon the story of Christ's crucifixion becomes a lynching, and Mary's cry a mother's lament for her murdered son, although the analogy is never explicitly enunciated. The swaying congregation does not seem to notice the moment when the preacher's "intonation, his pronunciation, became negroid." This is a jazz performance, with Shegog presenting the resurrection accompanied by "de golden horns shoutin." Amid the vibrant sounds of this joyous assembly Benjy sits "rapt in his sweet blue gaze," delivered from the acrimony of the Compson household. Peace on earth, and the very idea of redemption, seems attainable in such moments. Belief here seems to arise out of a surrendering of the self to the group gathered around the word that conveys more than just meaning, like the words that were Faulkner's feelings, his reasons for being.

Approaching the Compson home, Benjy begins to whimper. He has always signaled the Compson dysphoria, not needing the self-serving words to which Quentin and Jason and the rest resort. Dilsey is silent except for her declaration that she has seen the first and the last and understands the doom she witnesses in the disintegration of the Compson family. And of course the same routine ensues, with a moaning Mrs. Compson asking for her Bible and wondering why as a lady she has been made to suffer. While she is expecting Jason home for supper, Dilsey knows better—that he is off on a futile chase after Miss Quentin. The sheriff, whom Jason calls on to catch his niece and restore the three thousand dollars she has stolen, knows the score: "You drove that girl into running off, Jason. . . . And I have some suspicions about who that money belongs to that I dont reckon I'll ever know for certain." Jason, who has run his own version of a police state, tells the sheriff: "This is not Russia, where just because he wears a little metal badge, a man is immune to law." Of course, Jason does not realize that this is exactly what the sheriff has just told him: this is not Russia. In fact, Jason follows up with his fantasy of a fascist state: "I'm Jason Compson. See if you can stop me. See if you can elect a man to office that can stop me," he said, thinking of himself entering the courthouse with a file of soldiers and dragging the sheriff out.

As much as any Compson, Jason is saturated with the mentality of the Lost Cause: "The air brightened, the running shadow patches were now the obverse, and it seemed to him that the fact that the day was clearing was another cunning stroke on the part of the foe, the fresh battle toward which he was carrying ancient wounds." Jason might as well be setting out from the battle of Culloden like the first of his fated-to-fail family in the "Compson Appendix." In fact, the weather on the day of that decisive battle was poor, with sleet and rain—the kind of storm that Jason is still expecting in his pursuit of Miss Quentin. Jason pictures himself on the losing side in a battlefield. Driving in his car to catch up with his niece, he passes "unpainted frame buildings with sheet iron steeples, surrounded by tethered teams and shabby motorcars, and it seemed to him that each of them was a picket-post where the rear guards of Circumstance peeped fleetingly back at him." He is also reminiscent of Milton's Satan with his "file of soldiers with the manacled sheriff in the rear, dragging Omnipotence down from his throne, if necessary; of the embattled legions of both hell and heaven through which he tore his way and put his hands at last on his fleeing niece." Jason is the last Compson in Faulkner's version of *Paradise Lost,* and it has all been a long time coming, ever since Caddy climbed up that tree.

Gagging on gasoline fumes and as unfit as any Compson to cope with the modern world, his misogyny becomes just another contribution to his defeat and chagrin: "that he had been outwitted by a woman, a girl. If he could just believe it was the man who had robbed him." The showdown Jason is anticipating with Miss Quentin and the red-tied carnival man she has run off with suddenly turns the novel into a thriller as Jason nears the town where the next show will open. Jason himself seems determined to make this a scene from a pulp novel as he pulls up to a train station, where he thinks he will find his niece in one of the two "gaudily painted" Pullman cars:

> Now I'll have to take him by surprise, before he can warn them, he thought. It never occurred to him that they might not be there, in the car. That they should not be there, that the whole result should not hinge on whether he saw them first or they saw him first, would be opposed to all nature and contrary to the whole rhythm of events. And more than that: he must see them first, get the money back, then what they did would be of no importance to him, while otherwise the whole world would know that he, Jason Compson, had been robbed by Quentin, his niece, a bitch.

Pulp fiction turns to low comedy as Jason barges into a railroad car, assaulting an old man as if he is part of the plot and knows where the absconding couple have alighted. Quentin's botched duels with Dalton Ames and Gerald Bland come to mind when Jason is hit in the back of the head and passes out, only to awaken and go into a fright because he is bleeding. "What were you trying to do? commit suicide?" says a bystander who has seen Jason accost the old man. Jason has hit his head on a rail, the bystander tells him; in other words, Jason has not even landed a blow. The bystander is the owner of the show, who tells Jason he has fired Miss Quentin's lover. "I run a respectable show," he adds, making it all the more ironic that Jason, who has been disparaging the show, now has become a foolish spectacle, reaffirming old Job's wry observation that Jason gets ahead of himself. Disabled by a massive headache, he is reduced to paying a black man four dollars to drive him home. Like his mother, like virtually everyone in the Compson family, he cannot function without the very black support he scorns. Mrs. Compson constantly refers to him as the head of the house, but he lords it over no one—not even himself.

The story of the hapless Compsons is a stunning rebuke to a society built on segregation and on the ideology of white supremacy. Quite aside from the attacks on Faulkner for showing a decadent South and the seamier side of society is his crucial subversion of the ruling class, of the very foundations on which his own family prospered. A more insulting, subversive indictment of the status quo can hardly be imagined and seemed intolerable to many of Faulkner's contemporaries, who dismissed *The Sound and the Fury* because of the disrespect shown to prevailing conventions and pieties. That he was just as hard on the provincialism and xenophobia in Cambridge, Massachusetts, escaped the notice of southern chauvinists.

As the novel's ending shows, its author had more in mind than simply exposing southern and northern provincialism and prejudice. Luster resumes tormenting Benjy, who bellows outside the fence that separates him from the golfers' cries of "caddie." Knowing full well that Luster has made Benjy worse (Luster has been calling Caddy), Dilsey coddles the suffering man-child, who expresses "the grave hopeless sound of all voiceless misery under the sun." A family, a society, is judged by how it treats the unfortunate, and most societies fail every time, just as the Compsons do. The Compsons may fail more than others, but failure is a constant no matter the instances of triumph. This unnerving novel exposes the family as a farce but also deserving of Dilsey's compassion because without her it is at a loss, beyond even the concept of redemption. Dilsey does not falter because her faith actually has for her a historical basis in the crucifixion of Christ. "'Dis long time, O Jesus,' she said. 'Dis long time.'" Humanity works out its salvation in time, in thousands of years of suffering. So why would it be any different for the Compsons, or for Dilsey? She rocks back and forth like a pendulum as she comforts Benjy and restores some sense of equilibrium. Time for Dilsey is no scourge as it is for Quentin, who smashes his watch, and running late is not for her an affliction, as it is for Jason, who wants his meals on time and arrives late for work. Dilsey performs all her tasks in her own good time, refusing to be hurried by anyone.

As Dilsey, with misgivings, allows Luster to drive Benjy in a wagon through the town square to the graveyard, a journey that will have a calming effect, she wants to be sure that Luster knows the way. Her question is, of course, two-sided, since it involves knowing the physical and moral route to Benjy's place of peace. She takes the whip away from this unruly black boy, knowing full well he is likely to show up and raise a ruckus: "En ef you hurts Benjy, nigger boy, I dont know whut I do. You bound fer de chain gang, but I'll send you dar fo even chain gang ready fer you." With a flower in his fist, his eyes "serene and ineffable," Benjy is in the very heaven of his journey. Fashioning a switch from a hedge, Luster beats the horse as he enters the square and says, "Les show dem niggers how quality does, Benjy." Luster is, as Dilsey said earlier, a Compson too, which is to say vainglorious and proud of his own supposed superiority. And so he swerves to the left instead of to the right, reversing Benjy's accustomed route. Benjy, in a voice mounting to an "unbelievable crescendo," calls to mind Macbeth's agonized cry resulting from the disorder his own actions have caused in a world of sound and fury signifying nothing. Benjy's cry, however, is a protest against the misdirection of life as he knows it, a misdirection that the Compsons have compounded, going the wrong way now for generations. Jason, whose car is now in the square, intervenes, knocks Luster off the wagon, and wrenches the vehicle around so that it goes to the right again, telling Luster: "Get to hell on home with him." Home is hell, as Caddy and Quentin knew, a hell that Jason perpetuates. The order Jason restores is, of course, as temporary as Benjy's own bliss: "The broken flower drooped over Ben's fist and his eyes were empty and blue and serene again as cornice and façade flowed smoothly once more from left to right, post and tree, window and doorway and signboard each in its ordered place."

ESTELLE

Faulkner later wrote that he began *The Sound and the Fury* with no plan at all. One part grew out of another, one voice responding to a previous voice, in a Hegelian process beginning with *Flags in the Dust,* in which the Sartoris and Benbow stories serve as counterpoints to one another even as the MacCallums and Snopeses provide the minor accompaniment to the full unfolding of Yoknapatawpha history, with only its aboriginal inhabitants missing. Just as Faulkner refashioned the history of his own family, his characters rework the past and their part in it. It is no longer just a matter of how characters like old Bayard and young Bayard react to the past, for example, but how in concert and in conflict Quentin and Jason and Caddy and their parents obsessively go over their memories, which form a collective archive, so to speak, of their experience. Their impressions and recollections are like palimpsests, requiring the reader to become a scholar of what they report and redact. *The White Rose of Memphis* tells just as many intricate stories of family relationships, stories that withhold vital details and keep readers in suspense, but William Faulkner, a devotee of the delayed and occluded revelations that occur so often in Joseph Conrad's novels, disliked the superficial way the old Colonel solved all mysteries and resolved all conflicts, putting "each in its ordered place." However many stories Faulkner heard about his great-grandfather, he realized so much had been left out, unsaid, or, at best, implied. The real story, in other words, is in the gaps and erasures, the silences and suppressions, which generations of biographers have tried to rectify in William Faulkner's own biography.

Faulkner told his French translator about writing the novel during a struggle with "difficulties of an intimate nature," which is enough for one biographer to say the novelist meant primarily sexual problems. That kind of presumption, buttressed by references to Faulkner's waiting for Estelle to get divorced while he wrote the novel, leads nowhere in particular.[15] That Oxford had a doctor with a retarded son who may have been the model for Benjy also seems a dead end. That Faulkner had three brothers also does not illuminate that much about the novel. To be sure, both Faulkner and Quentin shared the burden of birth order and experienced the disruptions of family life. But the novel is so much more than biography, so that it might well be called the artist's triumph over his own experience, although it is hard for a biographer to leave it at that. Much has been made of Faulkner's observation that "Ishmael is the witness in *Moby Dick* as I am Quentin in *The Sound and the Fury*" so as to presume a "close relationship between author and protagonist." Yes, to be sure, but as *witnesses,* not necessarily as suffering the same problems.[16]

More intriguing is the alignment of Caddy and Estelle as sister-lovers. Faulkner was deprived of Estelle while still quite young. He could not protect her any more than Quentin can defend Caddy. Faulkner's ecstasy while writing the novel may have derived from having Caddy all to himself, so to speak, in a way that he could not have Estelle. After losing Estelle, the blow to Faulkner's self-esteem and place in the world is reflected in his poetry, yet he moved along to other interests, including other women, whereas Quentin has only Shreve, who is mocked as Quentin's beloved. In literary terms, Quentin and Shreve are like Ishmael and Queequeg, bicultural, if not quite bisexual, brothers, roommates and traveling companions on the same voyage, so to speak, as were Faulkner and Spratling, and the other male partners in Faulkner's short fiction.

Faulkner moved along, but he did not abandon Estelle, not only as sister-lover but also sister-creator. She shared the novel's cross-cultural consciousness reflected in her own short stories, which Faulkner helped to revise. In her extant fiction, Estelle Oldham remained fascinated with other races and nationalities—for example, with Dr. Wohlenski, a Pole and the eponymous hero of her unpublished short story, set in antebellum Mississippi, and which Faulkner first read and typed in December 1924, when Estelle was still married to Cornell Franklin but at home in Oxford.[17] Wohlenski is on his way to Kosciusko, a trading center, where he hopes to find employment as a veterinarian. Like Quentin Compson in Cambridge, and Faulkner in New Haven, Wohlenski finds himself a curious object of study for the locals. Felix Jackson, a plantation owner, who is none too polite to begin with, changes his hostile tone when Wohlenski mentions his academic degrees and shows by his manners that he is a gentleman. Jackson generously extends his hospitality to accommodate Wohlenski and his team of horses for the night, taken care of by a gregarious and attentive slave, Isaiah, who is curious about this "forin gemmun" who has a hard time making out the slave's dialect. Isaiah knows right away that Wohlenski is not "white trash" because he does not "holla 'hey nigger, come git my baggige an unharness my hawses.' Us niggers got feelins lots er White Folks don't have, an us can tell Quality sooner dan Quality kin theyselfs."

Except for Wohlenski's style of dress, he could pass for a Mississippi gentleman, Isaiah tells him. "The mark of a gentleman," Jackson declares when Wohlenski, after his bath, appears at precisely the appointed time. Jackson introduces Pompey, body servant and butler: "A gentleman even though our skins differ a bit in colouration." Pompey bows "with the grace of a courtier." The interactions between black and white put the story in familiar Faulkner territory, although without the irony of *The Sound and the Fury* and the psychological complexity he brought to the presentation of the Deacon and Quentin's dealings with him. But Wohlenski is as displaced as Quentin, calling himself a fugitive from his own family, rejecting the sycophantic example of his older brother married to a grande dame. Wohlenski is, in fact, an assumed name he has chosen in pursuing his fortune in America, reinventing himself as certain Faulkner characters like Thomas Sutpen are wont to do. Wohlenski is a superb surgeon. He saves the life of Jackson's foaling mare and is persuaded to stay on by the importunate Mrs. Jackson, who is fearful of her husband's increasing involvement in the events leading to the Civil War.

Then the story abruptly shifts to 1904, and from third to first person, a reversal of the shift from first to third person in *The Sound and the Fury*. The first-person narrator reveals that Wohlenski is the only survivor, the Jacksons all having perished in the war. Wohlenski's interlocutor during reminiscences about Reconstruction is Judge Niles, a character named after Estelle's grandfather, also a judge. The story now identifies the first-person narrator as a character named Estelle. This Estelle is attended, as the author was, by Nolia, who treats the narrator, Estelle, with a Dilsey-like firmness and affection, cautioning her young charge to sit up "like a lady." Judge Niles is upset when he discovers that Estelle's playground is near a privy, an impure place for a lady-in-training who comes perilously close here to Caddy with her muddy bottom. And like Caddy, Estelle is unrepentant. Nolia, akin to Callie Barr, keeps her charges in line, including Estelle, who voices an independence reminiscent of Caddy's when Estelle has the temerity to air her complaints to God in a prayer that elicits Nolia's rebuke. All pretense of fiction seems to drop when we are told that this story is the "tangled skein" of the Oldhams. Estelle loves the "sounds of big words" and has a sister Victoria, nicknamed "Tochie," just as Estelle, the author, does. The Oldhams treat Wohlenski as a member of the family, and he tends to their ailments and forms a link to the past that fascinates Estelle. It is a world remarkably intact, like the Falkners', with black servants carrying on the services rendered by slaves that stayed with their masters, even after the devastation of war. Like William Faulkner, Estelle's namesake loves to listen to the stories of grown-ups, "white and coloured," and does not care much for her younger contemporaries. Wohlenski's death becomes a family matter, and his will a remembrance of the black people like Isaiah who cared for him and of his woman in New Orleans. For Estelle, too, the bond with black people is as important as her connections with her family and other white people.

Estelle's story is sentimental and stereotypical and yet suffused with a sensibility akin to Faulkner's, if not as searing as his own insights into the fraught nature of race relations and family history. The tensions and strains of characters like Quentin and Jason are absent in her anodyne story, which is not nearly as challenging as "Star Spangled Stuff" and "A Crossing." Even so, in Estelle Oldham, Faulkner had a partner who approached, even if she could not ascend to, the heights that his fiction had now attained. As children, they had both chafed at the conventional aspects of their upbringings and formed a bond partly based on their precocity. In "Dr. Wohlenski," Estelle Oldham "privileges the imagination and sees herself as, therefore, different." The story is set just before the Oldhams move from Kosciusko to Oxford, an abrupt change in Estelle's life akin to the startling passage of the Falkner boys from Ripley to Oxford that Murry (Jack) Falkner describes in his memoir. What is more, "'Dr. Wohlenski' is important because of what it tells us about Estelle's understanding of how hard it was to be an independently minded white girl-child in a small Mississippi town at the turn of the century."[18] Wohlenski, who is apparently not drawn from an actual person, enters the South as a foreign body, so to speak, like Charles Bon, a wish fulfillment. And like Henry Sutpen, Wohlenski is a ghost of the past, serving both as a memory of the antebellum South that has helped to shape Estelle's upbringing and providing her with a perspective on her heritage, much as Faulkner's characters reckon with their patrimony in his major novels. In a closing scene, the dead doctor appears clutching one of Estelle's dolls he had brought home from New Orleans, the "Great Southern Babylon," Sensibar reminds us, where Wohlenski keeps a woman, where the races mix, and the firm categories that restrict Estelle are relaxed. Wohlenski is the one character in the story free to come and go, unhindered by the rigid categories of black and white. The doll he presents to Estelle is a token of her "desiring self."[19] Unlike Quentin Compson in *Absalom, Absalom!*, who reluctantly confronts Henry Sutpen, the ghost of a man come home to die, Estelle seeks Wohlenski in the very spot where his coffin rested in the Oldham home. Wohlenski is, then, the ghost of her childhood, the memory of her time as a child when she mixed freely with this foreigner and with black people, learning from them as William Faulkner learned. Wohlenski returns as a reminder of the childhood that has shaped her singular, aggressive sensibility, which, it may have seemed to Faulkner, she had betrayed in marrying Cornell Franklin, the proper consort for a lady but not a fitting match for a young woman who had stood out intellectually and sexually from her peers, a renegade Caddy sacrificed on the altar of southern propriety. The Billy-Estelle nexus, if not exactly the bond that Quentin and Caddy share, nonetheless became an integral part of what might be called a joint identity, a pact, a coalescence, however, that he never seemed to acknowledge and yet could not do without.

The world that Billy and Estelle created for themselves cut them off from their coevals and the older generation, making the couple a mystery to their parents and siblings, especially to those with temperaments like Jason in *The Sound and the Fury*. Faulkner's own mother testified that Jason spoke like Murry Faulkner in the hardware store giving a hard time to his black employee, old Jobus—"same words and same style," she told an interviewer. Presumably, Murry's bitterness about his failed career and the sense that he was robbed of something did give an impetus to Jason's character, although, again, the implications of Jason's behavior go so far beyond Faulkner family history that to dwell on the parallels does the novel injustice. But if Jason's grievances also sound like Faulkner's later sardonic complaints about his own role in supporting and keeping his extended family together, Faulkner, as Pappy, proved a damn sight better than his mean-spirited character.

MAUD

Like her son, Maud Falkner felt compelled to affix Caroline Barr to a work of art. James Dahl, a college student visiting Oxford in 1953, had the good fortune to speak with Maud, who showed him a painting of Barr, noting how Barr had served the family for three generations and used to sit right by Maud in a rocking chair to keep her company, just as Maud portrayed her in a painting. Her account of Barr is strikingly in line with Dilsey's view of herself as a "nigrah," a member of the family but one, Maud insisted, who was proud to be a "nigrah," which in effect meant she knew her place and was not about to challenge white hegemony. Dahl learned that Maud, like her son, was intensely interested in black people and wanted to know how they behaved at the University of Minnesota. No problems there, Dahl said. Not so in Mississippi, Maud wanted him to know. Integration had made southern "Negroes" rude, she reported: "Why, just the other day a white woman on the Square was shoved right off the sidewalk by a group of 'nigrah' boys." She took a proprietorial tone: "These of ours don't want equality, they want to trample us down." This was a view that could have come right out of Margaret Mitchell's depiction of Reconstruction in *Gone with the Wind,* which voices a grievance about a privileged status now imperiled. Complaining about both integration and high taxes in the "so-called 'Land of the Free,'" and sounding like a combination of Quentin and Jason Compson, Maud Falkner declared, "I sometimes think life in Russia would be preferable." Revolutionary Russia became in the minds of some white southerners a way of decrying their own limited freedom of action and could be used as handy shorthand for their uneasy awareness of a changing world that would make their own predominance insupportable.[20]

THE LOST CAUSE

Faulkner told Ben Wasson he understood readers would feel defeated by *The Sound and the Fury,* especially by the first section, which he supposed might be clearer with the use of colored inks to indicate the time shifts. But the novel could never have been popular even in a more conventional form because it exposed how rooted his characters were in the Lost Cause, white privilege, and the remains of an antebellum myth of heroism and gentility. *The White Rose of Memphis* could never command his respect because it pandered to a faux aristocratic ethos that he makes sure John Sartoris scorns in *Flags in the Dust.* Yet Faulkner remained, in important respects, the courtly southern gentleman, and his mother's son, almost in spite of himself, so that when James Dahl, a northern intruder, tried to engage him in conversation, the writer did not respond, but then, as if he could not help what his upbringing had taught him to do, Faulkner spoke: "I hope you have a nice summer in Oxford; it ain't a bad town if you ain't used to a city."[21] In Jason's monologue, the city is quite a far-off place, the haunt of Wall Street traders, mostly Jews, who are fixers of the economy—for themselves. Neither Jason, nor the South, can compete with a rigged system, a world, really, that is set against the last male Compson. And being a Falkner, as Phil Stone kept telling anyone who asked, meant you regarded yourself as a cut above others, whom you cut off with impunity. This went for Dean Faulkner as well, who added a *u* to his last name and could abide no criticism of his brother, especially after the publication of *The Sound and the Fury.* To Faulkner's detractors, Dean would steadily maintain that his brother would write the "great American novel."[22]

If Faulkner often expressed an exhilaration over the writing of *The Sound and the Fury,* it is not so much because he found a way to deal with his private demons (after all, they would continue to dog him) but because in the novel he had found a way out of just being Faulkner, adding not just the *u* to his name but creating an iconoclastic novel that put to bed once and for all the soppy sentimentalism about the South so prevalent in popular fiction and film and in his own family. Southern historian Joel Williamson reveals what the novelist had to contend with: "Southern culture developed ingenious devices for preserving its image of itself as a whole, harmonious organism. One of these was an amazing capacity for not seeing what was clearly before its eyes." The startling imagery of the novel, beginning with the Benjy section, made it impossible to look away, unless the reader simply refused to read.

ALONE

Fred Karl points out that no one was clamoring for a novel like *The Sound and the Fury,* and Horace Liveright had in effect dismissed not merely *Flags in the Dust* but Faulkner's whole career.[23] He shattered a culture's view of itself in a novel of great originality, neatly summed up by John T. Matthews, who recalls that Ben Wasson predicted it would take a hundred years for the novel to be published because, presumably, it would take that long for readers to catch up with the novel's "quick cuts, fades, and flashbacks; its uncanny voice-over narrations (how can Benjy narrate if he can't use words, and how can Quentin if he's apparently already dead?). Today's readers may nearly have caught up with Faulkner, after experiencing a vast aesthetic revolution he helped orchestrate. Few of Faulkner's narrative tricks surprise viewers familiar with the films of David Lynch or Quentin Tarantino."[24] What Faulkner wrought set him apart from friends, family, and, for a long time, from many readers as well. And he did all this virtually *alone.*

10

Desire and Death

As I Lay Dying, 1929–1930

> The novels written during those years, especially *The Sound and the Fury* and *As I Lay Dying,* are novels about lack and loss, in which desire is always intimately bound up with grief and death. And it is clear too that they have sprung out of a deep sense of lack and loss—texts spun around a primal gap.
>
> —André Bleikasten, *The Ink of Melancholy*

FAMILY DISASTERS

The primal gap is occasioned by the curiosity of three brothers about sex and dying "prompting their common desire to see."[1] Caddy climbing the tree of knowledge to witness her grandmother's death scene as her brothers fixate on the bottom of her muddy drawers also associates the awareness of sex with filth and shame and the punishment that Quentin and Jason threaten to visit on their sister. The children never do actually see their dead grandmother, who is as locked away from them as Addie Bundren is in the coffin her son Cash constructs for her in the opening pages of *As I Lay Dying.* "A Rose for Emily," written in the wake of *As I Lay Dying,* intensifies the nexus between sex and desire and death, with Miss Emily Grierson lying beside the dead and rotting Homer Barron, her lover, in bed. She lives with her grief, as Faulkner would often say he lived with his, no matter how life corrupted his desire, no matter how many times he denounced his own wife, he could not look away, and he could not forsake the object of his desire, his awareness of death, or his anguish over what his life lacked and what he had lost, or of the "delicate equilibrium of periodical filth" Quentin associates with women but also with the desire for women as the originators of the male prerogative that women still somehow flout.

What happened in Faulkner's marriage, especially in the first three months during which *As I Lay Dying* was conceived? Sorting through Faulkner's motivations and influences yields several options open to him. He could continue his study of a family adrift and disintegrating—this time turning to poor whites, the Bundrens, to fill in the social structure of Yoknapatawpha County adumbrated in *Father Abraham,* his Balzacian quest to populate his fictional universe. But the Bundrens do not appear in *Father Abraham,* and much of the Snopes material did not make its way into a novel until nearly a decade later in *The Hamlet.* That long gestation period suggests the intricacy of the Snopes saga that Faulkner turned away from to make good on a promise he made to Hal Smith shortly before the marriage to Estelle. In exchange for five hundred dollars, Faulkner promised to deliver a new novel by March 1, 1930. With only nine months to complete and deliver a new work, the idea for a compact narrative focused upon a family and a journey with a mission seems to have galvanized Faulkner's professional drive. He would prove himself by deliberately writing what he would later call a "tour-de-force," a book by which he could stand or fall if "I never touch ink again." The Bundren wagon could serve as the ship of fools equivalent of the *Nausikka* in *Mosquitoes.*

Faulkner was under tremendous pressure to produce for Hal Smith, who had taken a chance on him—as Evelyn Harper Glick, Smith's book designer, testified: "Faulkner wouldn't have gone on writing during those years that were so tough if Hal Smith hadn't given him advance after advance which was never earned; if Hal hadn't spent his nights roaming around and talking to him. I think Hal kept him going." In effect, *As I Lay Dying* was Faulkner's "personal rededication to his craft and his career." Faulkner would hammer away at his new novel as deliberately and precisely as Cash Bundren made a coffin, and no matter that their handiwork would go underground. "I dont think it'll sell, either [referring to *The Sound and the Fury*]. Dont think I'll ever crash though with a book," Faulkner told Smith.[2] To those around him his persistence may have seemed absurd, but, like the Bundrens honoring their mother's last wish to be buried with her folks in Jefferson, he went on, having made a promise to Hal Smith and to himself. And he struck out boldly, creating a novel quite different from *The Sound and the Fury,* even though these two works are often paired because they both employ interior monologues and focus on a disintegrating family.

The Sound and the Fury is stationary, introverted, and centripetal even when Quentin roams Cambridge, and Jason chases Miss Quentin in his automobile, whereas *As I Lay Dying* is mobile, extroverted, and centrifugal. The Bundrens are cantilevered out into a larger world, put on the road with their mother inside her homemade coffin on the way to her desired resting place forty miles away in Jefferson, Mississippi. Although the novel's heightened language and interior monologues deviate from the standards of social realism, the characters are nevertheless products of their environment, recognizable to Faulkner friends like John Cullen, who describes the novelist's familiarity with country people and their land that is featured in *As I Lay Dying,* the first published novel to name Yoknapatawpha.[3] Cullen evokes the atmosphere of the "steep hills and valleys and forests in Lafayette County," where the boys played along the Yocona River, with its virgin forests, great trees, and swift-running water that would flood the ground, making it a habitat for bullfrogs, turtles, and water moccasins. Death in this devastated Depression-era land touched nearly everyone, Cullen suggests: "Cash's building his mother's coffin while she was still alive, for example, would not have been thought a terrible thing in those days. Some country people built their own coffins before they died."[4] Carpentry was second nature to William Faulkner, who had been busy with his hands even before entering school. Writing was shaping and fitting together piecework, you might say, and that is also what a reader does assembling the parts of the story each narrator has to tell in *As I Lay Dying.*

Each Bundren, like each Compson, is distinctive, and yet all are concerned with the same questions: How do you mourn? How do you cope with what you have lost? How do you go on? Did marrying Estelle assuage Faulkner's grief over having lost her? Or did life with her only aggravate his sense of the years they had forfeited? Cornell Franklin visited Oxford in the fall of 1929. At the Faulkner home on University Avenue, Estelle spoke with Cornell in the parlor while Bill conversed with Cornell's new wife, Dallas Lee, in the garden. Did William Faulkner feel displaced in his own home? His eldest step-granddaughter, Vicki, who lived with him during World War II, said that he "realized early on that Cornell Franklin was not at fault for having whisked his [Faulkner's] sweetheart away. He [Cornell] was almost as much of a victim of the arrangement as Estelle was." For Cornell Franklin's part, he was "grateful to Pappy for his care and concern for Malcolm and my mother," Vicki recalled.[5] It is difficult, though, not to suppose that Faulkner harbored resentment over how he had been left behind, to begin with. While he maintained cordial relations with Estelle's parents, he never again entered their home.[6] Another sore point: The Oldhams held on to Malcolm Franklin and pocketed the child support Cornell sent to them and which they used, Faulkner suspected, for their own purposes. Sometime during the Franklin visit,

Faulkner began to drink and then departed for Memphis, keeping his reactions to Cornell's incursion, apparently, to himself. So no definitive account is possible. He honored marriage and family, but the decade-long separation of William Faulkner from Estelle Oldham had done its damage.

The night shift in the power plant with the dynamo humming along seems to have given the writer the satisfactions of a workman in a world without interruptions. The actual composition of *As I Lay Dying* went smoothly, even if, as with all his work, Faulkner meticulously revised the wording. Philip Weinstein believes in the organic relationship between *The Sound and the Fury* and *As I Lay Dying,* that the difficult gestation of the former prepared for the easier birth of the latter: "Both novels trace the helpless dependency of children on their parents and the frustration that occurs when that dependency is betrayed. *As I Lay Dying* turns the screw yet further, capturing the children's anguish when the mother dies and their dependency is ruptured altogether."[7]

Like the journey of the Bundrens, which, in a sense, suspends their daily lives and takes them on an adventure, the novel performed the same function for its author, relying entirely on his inner dynamo. None of his other novels ever proceeded as quickly and smoothly, but then none of them had the kind of insulation and protection extended to *As I Lay Dying.* The novel is a reverie with its monologues emitted from Faulkner's power plant of an imagination, the constant humming becoming the very pulse of his prose, the heartbeat of his imagination. He called the novel a tour de force, otherwise known as a stroke of genius, for that is how it seemed to him: He had perfected his stroke—clichés like hitting the nail on the head keep coming to mind. Cash grieves for his mother even as his meticulous coffin creation is an expression of love and of his carpentry, which is the man in all his pride and satisfaction.

At the center of the action, in both the novel and in Faulkner's biography, is the mother. The Bundren sons seek to please their mother, the formidable Addie Bundren. Like Maud Falkner, Addie is estranged from her husband, but even more importantly, she is aloof from her family. *As I Lay Dying* can be interpreted as an act of appeasement, the eldest son's conflicted tribute to a mother who never did approve of his marriage. Did Faulkner consider his marriage a betrayal of his mother's expectations? That possibility intrigues the psychologically minded biographer since it helps to explain Faulkner's ambivalent treatment of his wife. Marriage is supposed to be part of settling down, but for Faulkner it became an unsettling experience. Estelle had been his Eurydice, but unlike Caddy, Estelle could not remain forever as his heart's darling. Unlike Caddy, Estelle could not be made to disappear into the shadows and the moonlight that make Caddy an evanescent figure.

Caddy could be simultaneously everywhere and nowhere in the memories of her brothers.[8] Estelle, on the other hand, no longer eluded her Bill. She had, however fitfully, taken possession of him and robbed him of his illusions just as surely as Miss Quentin stole Jason's hoard. Every morning, after doing his shift in the boiler room and writing *As I Lay Dying,* William Faulkner walked a short distance to his mother's home for morning coffee.

Faulkner, a creature of routine, understood how disturbing it was to break the familial pattern, as the Bundrens have to do, risking fire and flood to bury their mother in her stipulated resting place. If she is their organizing principle, what happens as they confront her loss? Told in the present tense, the novel is an existential journey but also a remarkable social document. Darl begins *As I Lay Dying* describing the family's world: the "baked, brick-hard" straight-as-a-plumb-line path to the cotton house built of rough logs that have lost their chinking. Darl is good with words that make his world concrete and precise, which is also the way his brother Cash wants to see things:[9] "Square, with a broken roof set at a single pitch, it leans in empty and shimmering dilapidation in the sunlight, a single broad window in two opposite walls giving onto the approaches of the path." The worn-down world these characters inhabit is palpable. Their deterioration is both physical and mental, and intensely so in Darl himself, who will end up laughing hysterically like Nancy in jail in "That Evening Sun" or the condemned black man in *Sanctuary.* Like these earlier characters, the Bundrens are all broken. They are also a class acutely aware of their marginality: "We are country people, not as good as town people," Dewey Dell thinks. Bicycles are for town boys, Vardaman is told. A Bundren cannot even afford a horse—just two mules to pull a wagon or plow, and Jewel has to work all night over several months, clearing forty acres, to get his prized mount.

The temptation to quote Darl is overwhelming because he is so precise and poetical, with the perceptiveness of a novelist establishing his characters, as with his brother Jewel: "Still staring straight ahead, his pale eyes like wood set into his wooden face, he crosses the floor in four strides with the rigid gravity of a cigar store Indian dressed in patched overalls and endued with life from the hips down, and steps in a single stride through the opposite window and into the path again just as I come around the corner." We learn that Jewel is a head taller than Darl, that Cash, the eldest son who has the workmanlike discipline of William Faulkner, is sawing away at the boards that he will fit together as his mother's coffin. "A good carpenter, Cash is," Darl affirms: "Addie Bundren could not want a better one, a better box to lie in." Not saying "Mother" but rather her full name is the first sign of Darl's estrangement.

Jewel is just as estranged as Darl, if not as eloquent. Jewel shapes himself to a horse, Darl observes, in a violent caress that at the same time repudiates his family even as he affirms his affinity with his mother: "It would just be me and her on a high hill and me rolling the rocks down the hill at their faces, picking them up and throwing them down the hill faces and teeth and all by God." He feels as isolated as the mother who has favored him, "lonely with her pride, trying to make folks believe different," says Cora, a neighbor who comments on the futility of taking Addie, as soon as she dies, to Jefferson to be with her people, even though alive she has not been willing to join them.

Cora's is a powerful feminine voice not previously heard in Faulkner's fiction, except, perhaps, in Miss Jenny's diatribes against men. Cora dismisses the Bundrens as "those men not worrying about anything except if there was time to earn another three dollars before the rain come and the river got too high to get across it." Later her criticism is seconded by another outraged female witness to the male Bundrens. Rachel tells her husband, Samson: "I just wish that you and him [Anse] and all the men in the world that torture us alive and flout us dead, dragging us up and down the country—" When Samson interrupts, trying to calm Rachel, saying she has upset herself, she rejoins, "Don't you touch me!" Her baffled husband reflects: "A man cant tell nothing about them. I lived with the same one fifteen years and I be durn if I can." The Bundren journey brings out the tensions in other families that have been suppressed or simply ignored. "And I imagined a lot of things coming up between us," Samson says, "but I be durn if I ever thought it would be a body four days dead and that a woman." As absurd as the Bundren men are, Samson remains their collaborator, shifting the problem, as he sees it, to his wife and her sex—"But they make life hard on them, not taking it as it comes up, like a man does"—like the unfaithful Agamemnon does in *The Odyssey*, returning home to his forsaken wife, Clytemnestra, whose hostility to him and his male enterprises is perpetuated in the women in *As I Lay Dying*, who protest the male economy that demands of them their consent to whatever "comes up." Faulkner told Saxe Commins that his novel's title derived from the Homeric lines: "As I lay dying the woman with the dog's eyes would not close mine eyelids on mine eyes as I descended into the abode [of Hades]."[10] Plenty of women in this novel wish their men would go to hell.

Anse makes a show of abiding by Addie's wishes, saying he is beholden to no one, but he leaves it up to everyone else to honor her deathbed demand, refusing to stir himself for fear that sweating will kill him as it almost did when he was twenty-two and working in the sun. He is inertia personified and the feckless father of sons teeming with conflicting feelings about how to function in a family while remaining themselves.

Dr. Peabody, last seen examining the wen on old Bayard's face in *Flags in the Dust,* shows up to treat Addie. He is again a witness but to a dying way of life, reflecting later on the deforestation of the land that leads to the flash floods that inundate families like the Bundrens. This environmental depredation later surges up in the log like the Christ arisen in a judgmental Second Coming, breaking Cash's leg and submerging Addie's coffin. Peabody arrives late because Anse has not wanted to pay the doctor's ten-dollar fee— suggesting not so much Anse's meanness but instead this family's proximity to penury. Peabody realizes it is too late to do much for Addie, too late, really, for the economy of this family's life built on the exploitation of the mother: "She watches me: I can feel her eyes. It's like she was shoving at me with them. I have seen it before in women. Seen them drive from the room them coming with sympathy and pity, with actual help, and clinging to some trifling animal to whom they never were more than pack-horses." She sits up one more time, calls to Cash, who shows her the boards he is fitting together for her coffin, and she dies, creating in her youngest son, Vardaman, a void, "his mouth full open and all color draining from his face into his mouth" as he backs out of the room. Or so Darl imagines the scene, since he is actually on the road with Jewel, finishing one last haul to earn the three dollars this lowly cotton-picking family needs so badly. As Tull, a Bundren neighbor, later says about Darl: "It's like he had got into the inside of you, someway. Like somehow you was looking at yourself and your doings outen his eyes."

Darl has also divined that Dewey Dell is pregnant. She silently beseeches Dr. Peabody: *"You could do so much for me if you just would."* No one feels more abandoned, more alone than Dewey Dell, whose pullulating agony culminates in her cry, "I feel like a wet seed wild in the hot blind earth." The words cannot be hers, and yet they make her passionate sense of abandon and abandonment palpable.

Cash's response to his mother's death is to make her coffin on the bevel, arguing in thirteen numbered statements that the slanting of the coffin surface makes the structure sturdier and the job neater. His carpentry organizes his existence just as Jewel's shaping himself to his horse does, so that they obviate Darl's existential agony: *"In a strange room you must empty yourself for sleep. And before you are emptied for sleep, what are you. And when you are emptied for sleep, you are not. And when you are filled with sleep, you never were. I dont know what I am. I dont know if I am or not."* This terror of not knowing, of moving from conscious to unconscious states, and from life to death, presages Vardaman's disturbing discovery that his mother's death deprives her of an identity. She can be put into a box and buried just as the dead fish can be "cooked and et": "My mother is a fish," he declares.

Anse presents himself as the paragon of propriety—the only way, it seems, that he can maintain the illusion that he is the head of the family. He calls out Jewel for riding his own horse, "prancing on a durn circus animal," rather than accompanying the family in the wagon. To Jewel, Anse declares it is a "reflection on your ma." Anse has "some regard for what folks says about my flesh and blood even if you haven't." The sanctimony of this shiftless father is too much for Darl, who cannot help laughing at the irony of Anse as a moral example. That Anse is impervious to the absurdity of his pharisaical sentiments only makes Darl laugh even more.

Without Addie, the Bundrens lack any sense of perspective and proportion, of what they can accomplish in the flood that is about to overwhelm them, but then isn't that Faulkner's point about humanity? We are too self-absorbed to see how absurd our behavior is as the world crashes down on us in death and destruction, ruining our complacent climate of opinion. Tull, Cora's husband, is the sensible one, constantly making suggestions to the Bundrens that they stubbornly ignore, as most people do when dealing with an onlooker's advice. Like so much of his fiction, *As I Lay Dying* is prophetic: In just a few years Faulkner would become the patriarch of an extended family that relied on him as their sole support even as he veered from bouts of inaction and insobriety to steady, salaried jobs in California. To Faulkner himself, his family obligations and misfortunes would come to seem absurd and yet inevitable, just like the journey of the Bundrens.

Darl captures these divergent family members in remarkably few sentences: "Cash looks up the road quietly, his head turning as we pass it [the coffin] like an owl's head, his face composed. Pa looks straight ahead, humped. Dewey Dell looks at the road too, then she looks back at me, her eyes watchful and repudiant, not like that question which was in those of Cash, for a smoldering while." Jewel rides ahead, not even looking at his family while his horse's hooves fling back a clot of dirt onto Addie's coffin, which the fastidious Cash scours with a tree branch and dead leaves. Faulkner's characters move so as to define themselves, except for the "humped," immobile Anse.

Faulkner is not known as a socially or politically engaged writer, and yet his creations suggest otherwise: "Nowhere in this sinful world can a honest, hardworking man profit. It takes them that runs the stores in the towns, doing no sweating, living off of them that sweats," Anse declares. We have to wonder if he has ever done business at Jason Compson's hardware store or Will Varner's company store. Such thoughts occur because Samson observes that Jewel is riding "one of them Snopes horses," the spotted horses first auctioned off in *Father Abraham* and that will appear again in *The Hamlet*. The horses have been a swindle that ultimately will help to bankroll Flem's takeover of the Varner store, marking an end to his days of sweated labor, and the beginning of a change in the Yoknapatawpha economy.

Darl, the most disoriented Bundren, captures how the family's journey has upended their world, as though their plunge into the water current (the bridge has been washed away) makes their coffin-bearing wagon a submersible: "Above the ceaseless surface they stand—trees, cane, vines—rootless, severed from the earth, spectral above a scene of immense yet circumscribed desolation filled with the voice of the waste and mournful water." He is describing his state of mind but also how the mourning of a family flows into natural devastation. Confronting this elemental catastrophe they sit in the wagon "talking quietly of old security and old trivial things." Only Darl, recognized by everyone as the odd man out, registers and absorbs their peril while Anse retreats into his pathetic piety, Cash into his precisely measured perceptions, Jewel into just his grim go-ahead gallop, Dewey Dell into her desperate search for how to resolve her pregnancy. Vardaman experiences a sheer terror that no one in the family is equipped to allay.

When Addie's voice suddenly is heard midway through the novel, it is the aloof, unsentimental voice of Maud Falkner, a Maud even more embittered about a family of Bundrens she simply cannot hold close to herself: "In the afternoon when school was out and the last one had left with his little dirty snuffling nose, instead of going home I would go down the hill to the spring where I could be quiet and hate them." She whips her students to wrest from them the identity they have taken from her, but which she wants to impress on them: "Now you are aware of me! Now I am something in your secret and selfish life, who have marked your blood with my own for ever and ever." It is said that Maud Falkner would paint family portraits, and as the mood struck her, she would change the color of their clothing and silently wait to see how long anyone, especially her estranged husband, would notice.[11]

More than eight days since her death the smell of Addie's rotting body has become so intolerable that Darl sets fire to the barn that houses his mother's coffin for the night. What ensues is a tableau out of a Greek epic, but also a scene similar to a staged nineteenth-century melodrama, or a Hollywood spectacular. Jewel, desperate to rescue his mother's coffin, struggles with Mack Gillespie, who is trying to save his father's animals: "They are like two figures in a Greek frieze, isolated out of all reality by the red glare. . . . The sound of it [the fire] has become quite peaceful now, like the sound of the river did. We watch through the dissolving proscenium of the doorway as Jewel runs crouching to the far end of the coffin and stoops to it. For an instant he looks up and out at us through the rain of burning hay like a portière of flaming beads." The theater arch, the curtain, are the backdrop for Jewel's miraculous escape virtually riding atop the coffin he had knocked off its sawhorse. Realism and symbolism conjoin in Faulkner's effort to make this particular story topical and timeless. "I took these people of—of the kind which I know, and simply subjected them to—to the two fiercest natural cataclysms, which are flood and fire," he told his University of Virginia audience. Only Faulkner could see a Bundren like Jewel as a figure on a frieze, both himself but also part of a tragic time and a tragic literature—yet also a comic one, since he never loses sight of his characters' absurdity, of the "very fact that these people endured for a reason that on the face of it was foolish, that is, to carry their mother that far just to bury her, but it was noble in that they had promised her to do that, and so they were—they had dropped their own baseness, their own pettiness, to follow out this simple wish of the mother, which was—was noble, even though it was foolish."[12]

The fire has further marginalized the Bundrens, as Vardaman acknowledges by calling his brothers "niggers," after observing Cash's blackened foot (the result of encasing his broken leg in concrete to "steady it") and Jewel's burned back. The irony would not be lost on Mississippi readers, knowing that James K. Vardaman (1861–1930) was popular with small farmers because they thought he protected them from the lower-waged black labor. Faulkner's words at the University of Virginia describe how politicians like Vardaman ingratiated themselves with poor whites: "I'm one of you all," he would say, shaking hands, "even if I do have a white shirt every day. I'm just—you're just as good as I am and I'm one of you, and so they name their children after the successful politicians."[13] Back on the road, passing three black men and a white man in the lead, the Bundrens hear one of the black men say, "what they got in that wagon?" Jewel, as if blind (Darl notes), turns on the white man and swings at him only to be restrained by Darl: "'Thinks because he's a goddamn town fellow,' Jewel says, panting, wrenching at me. 'Son of a bitch, he says." As Darl calms down Jewel, he tells the white man, who has his knife out, that Jewel did not mean it (the assault):

> "I thought he said something," Jewel says. "Just because he's—"
> "Hush," I say. "Tell him you didn't mean it."
> "I didn't mean it," Jewel says.
> "He better not," the man says. "Calling me a—"
> "Do you think he's afraid to call you that?" I say.
> The man looks at me.
> "I never said that," he said.
> "Dont think it, neither," Jewel says.
> "Shut up," I say. "Come on. Drive on, pa."

Family honor and dignity are preserved even in this nonsensical confrontation, with Vardaman's desire to proclaim victory: "Jewel would a whipped him." As alienated as Darl can seem from the family, he remains a Bundren, taking on the role of his inept father, who helplessly repeats "fore God" as his only reaction to the impending violence.

And yet the family must forsake Darl, not Anse, because Gillespie has figured out that Darl has set fire to the barn. "It wasn't nothing else to do. It was either send him to Jackson, or have Gillespie sue us," Cash relates matter-of-factly. But he is also uneasy and knows that it is not so simple to declare Darl crazy: "Sometimes I aint so sho who's got ere a right to say when a man is crazy and when he aint. Sometimes I think it aint none of us pure crazy and aint none of us pure sane until the balance of us talks him that-a-way. It's like it aint so much what a fellow does, but it's the way the majority of folks is looking at him when he does it." All the Bundrens feel societal pressure, especially Darl, who has always stood apart and yet is one of them. Darl, Cash realizes, has done what others in the family have wished all along: to relieve themselves of the burden they have been carrying. Even so, Cash continues: "I dont reckon nothing excuses setting fire to a man's barn and endangering his stock and destroying his property. That's how I reckon a man is crazy." The reckless disregard of others is what troubles Cash, who cannot resist the subsidiary concern that undergirds a good deal of the novel's awareness of social inequity: "It's like some folks has the smooth, pretty boards to build a courthouse with and others dont have no more than rough lumber fitten to build a chicken coop." Cash can only console himself with the idea of building well: better a solid chicken coop than a shoddy courthouse, he concludes.

Dewey Dell is the first to attack Darl when the fellows come to take him away to the asylum, confirming Cash's suspicion that somehow through her Darl's barn burning has been revealed even as he has kept the secret that torments her. Darl resists and then capitulates to his defeat. Cash, never admitting the agony of his broken leg caked with the concrete chunks that have been pounded off of him, calls it all "bad" but better for Darl: "Down there it'll be quiet, with none of the bothering and such." Darl laughs, troubling the straight-ahead Cash, who nevertheless understands Darl's dissociation of sensibility: "But I aint so sho that ere a man has the right to say what is crazy and what aint. It's like there was a fellow in every man that's done a-past the sanity or the insanity, that watches the sane and the insane doings of that man with the same horror and the same astonishment."

Out of how much of his own pain and estrangement did William Faulkner, also a queer man to his contemporaries, create Darl Bundren? Darl has T. S. Eliot's notion of a detached intellectuality. He is part of the action but also apart from it, observing himself and others in much the same way that Bill behaved among his kin and kind. Cash has some inkling of Darl's predicament, but like Faulkner's townspeople, Cash has to go on, fixated on doing a good job, as good a job as he can no matter the horror that Darl is especially attuned to experience and articulate. Cash cannot bear to describe the details of Darl's apprehension, having to watch them "throw that poor devil down in the public street and handcuff him like a damn murderer," as an onlooker reports. This shocking scene precipitates Vardaman's obsessive refrain: "Darl is my brother." He knows that in this disintegrating family he has to hold on to his sanity: *Lots of people didn't go crazy. Pa and Cash and Jewel and Dewey Dell and me didn't go crazy. We never did go crazy. We didn't go to Jackson either.*" On the train, Darl's dissociation of sensibility is complete when he refers to himself in the third person: "Darl has gone to Jackson. They put him on the train, laughing, down the long car laughing, the heads turning like the heads of owls when he passed." Only when Darl is on the train do we learn, in his own words in one sentence, that he has been to war and has come home a different man: "Darl had a little spy-glass he got in France at the war." He has returned home a displaced person, as alienated as the Faulkner who went abroad and brought the rest of the world home with him. But Darl is now a double agent, subject to both the impact of nature and of the economy that will soon displace his family as it has dispossessed him: "I can hear the rain shaping the wagon that is ours, the load that is no longer theirs that felled and sawed it nor yet theirs that bought it and which is not ours either." Some critics find in the flooding river scenes that muddy the novel an allusion to the disaster of 1927, the culmination of 938 natural catastrophes occurring between 1881 and 1928, which are also likened to the trench war muck that Darl presumably suffered. Darl's worlds, at home and abroad, erode as precipitously as his own identity. The biblical, Hellenic, historical, and psychological inundation of this family and of its chief emissary are all dying in a manner of speaking, or of the kind of thinking that sends Darl to the madhouse.[14]

If the novel has one sort of culmination in Addie's burial, accomplished with two spades Anse has to borrow, and Darl's incarceration, another kind of climax delivers to Dewey Dell her own defeat, when MacGowan, the drugstore clerk, exploits the ignorance of this "pretty hot mama, for a country girl." She is only a type to him: "Them country people. Half the time they dont know what they want, and the balance of the time they cant tell it to you." He gives her a bogus remedy for her pregnancy (six talcum-powder capsules) and explains that the hair of the dog (she has had it before, he tells her) will help to cure her. Such is the way of this world and of his way with her. She has no other way out and submits to the clerk's desire, even though she knows, as she tells Vardaman, "it won't work." Her final defeat and the novel's denouement comes when her father takes the ten dollars her lover Lafe has given her. Anse purchases a set of false teeth, and to the astonishment of his family, introduces a new wife toting a portable graphophone,[15] signaling the fulfillment of a modern pleasure that Cash has desired. Cash's final words about Darl, in this context, are both tragic and comic: "This world is not his world; this life his life." How Darl would laugh if he could see them now. Cash's final verdict on Darl makes it conceivable to suppose that his real purpose had been greater than setting fire to the barn as a way of immolating his rotting mother. If this is not his world, he would just as soon be rid of it: burning "the whole structure down, and the old South along with it."[16]

The Technics of Art and History

In terms of typography and use of white space, *As I Lay Dying* is one of Faulkner's most innovative novels.[17] The italics often signal a language that conveys what the characters, in their speaking voices, could not express. The white spaces are the wordless areas of life, or the moments when a thought, once expressed, simply opens a void or an expanse that cannot be filled with any other thought or action, as when Vardaman announces his mother is a fish, leaving the rest of the page a blank. An object like Addie's coffin is drawn on the page in manuscript and typescript and published novel, as if to suggest only a picture will do. Such instances derive from Faulkner's earliest sketches of objects, like the totemic locomotive he drew in a hymn book in church to express the power of the engine that drove his father's life and his family's fate. So it is with the coffin-shape, so precisely beveled and fitted to Cash's notion of what can be made perfect in an imperfect, mercenary world. "To make a beautiful object intended never to pass into economic circulation constitutes the idealism of Cash's artistry, and it makes a stand against the capitalization of all labor," writes John T. Matthews, who emphasizes that the Bundrens are part of a failing cotton crop economy in the 1920s even as they are attracted to what the town has to offer in the way of a toy train for Vardaman, and a graphophone Cash covets.[18]

Even as the advent of certain technological advances like the telephone annoyed Faulkner, he craved his own airplane. Even though he said he wrote novels like *The Sound and the Fury* for himself, he dreamed of the cash he could leaven with *Sanctuary,* which he compared to dough rising. The complexities and contradictions of his own complicity in the modern economy, in other words, have their outcome in *As I Lay Dying.* Faulkner identified with country people who felt the lack of respect for their way of life, a plight he shared with them insofar as his own dedication to writing was deemed an affectation and inconsequential. At this point he was as much a subsistence writer as the Bundrens were subsistence farmers. He had an upbringing quite different from theirs, of course, but he had many of the hands-on skills like carpentry associated with country people, and he never looked down upon them. In fact, he listened to them, and he liked what he heard on the Oxford square, in the stores, on the farms, and while he hunted. *As I Lay Dying* is a tribute to the folk, but without sentimentality, treating them with a dignity and respect they deserved. By endowing them, at times, with a vocabulary and style that surpasses the demotic, he demonstrates that they are more than types, that each of them deserves a separate monologue, a declaration of self in and against the world. These characters are "transformed into process rather than product" and seen in "a state of perpetual becoming."[19] As in so much of Faulkner's work, his characters in *As I Lay Dying* may be rooted in their culture, but they are also dislocated, like Jason and Quentin, who cannot depend on an inheritance or their inherited status as Compsons to give them a perch in life.

Cash's growing consciousness seems an outgrowth of the family's journey, which reinforces their keen awareness of how society enforces their class status and creates in their meager circumstance the desire for more goods (toys, teeth, and graphophone). Cash expands from a "somewhat narrow sensibility and limited moral horizons into a fully conscious, sympathetic participant in the sorrows and struggles of his fellow man" that is comparable to Faulkner's own "growth in perceptive sympathy through his commitment to family and artistic responsibility."[20]

Byronic with a Touch of Mark Twain

Faulkner exuberantly turned in the typescript of *As I Lay Dying* to Hal Smith, declaring in the language of the novel's characters, it was "a son bitch sho enough."[21] Book production proceeded quickly, with Faulkner correcting a few errors and noting that the proofs were "quite clean."[22] On October 6, 1930, some nine months after Faulkner began writing the work, Smith published *As I Lay Dying* with a dedication to him, perhaps reflecting the novelist's gratitude that he now had a firm that would print what he wrote straightaway without cavil or qualms.

The reviewers did their job, telling readers what it was like to read the novel. Margaret Cheney (*New York Herald Tribune,* October 5) called it "photographic mysticism," by which I suppose she meant to evoke Faulkner's vivid realism modified by intense figurative language. She thought the method hit-and-miss and exasperating when some of Vardaman's thoughts seemed to stray much too far from what he could actually express. But she also quoted passages exemplifying the author's amazing "fecundity of imagination." Like Cheney, an excited Ted Robinson (*Cleveland Plain Dealer,* October 12), a great admirer of *The Sound and the Fury,* found the new novel its equal and concluded that Faulkner was "one of the two or three original geniuses of our generation." Julia K. W. Baker (*New Orleans Times-Picayune,* October 26) was even more emphatic, suggesting Faulkner had surpassed Hemingway as the most important writer of their generation. The novel was sure to "scandalize the squeamish," Baker predicted, since it "unrolled with sordid horror." Her condescension materialized in her reference to "primitive types" whom she matter-of-factly calls "white trash." Clifton Fadiman (*Nation,* November 5) blithely referred to the "phosphorescent rottenness of the family." The anonymous reviewer in the *New York Times* (October 19) deplored the "witch's brew of a family." In effect, the characters were unworthy of their author.

Social attitudes of the time, of which the Bundrens themselves are aware, infected the negative reviews, especially in the comment that the Bundrens reflect "inbreeding of the sort that undoubtedly weakens the stock in certain of our backward country districts." This was the kind of eugenic thinking quite acceptable at the time and that made it impossible to see the obvious: The Bundrens are about as diverse a family as can be imagined. All of them are distinctly individual and original. James Burnham, writing in *Symposium* (January 1931), delivered a one-sentence rebuke to eugenic criticism: "The excitement of his [Faulkner's] books depends on gradual dramatic disclosures of relations between persons, the imaginative complexity with which so many of his characters are developed, the strained handling of emotional situations, the sometimes passionate intensity of his style." In a certain sense, as Burnham understood, Faulkner's characters were not to be taken literally, as representative of a class or region. On the contrary, Burnham argued, he is "using the data of observation only as material in the construction of his own world. It is to be judged not as imitation but as creation, by the emotional integrity with which it is formed."

Henry Nash Smith (*Southwest Review,* Winter 1931) singled out Faulkner's affinity for the Elizabethans in his attraction to "unusual mental states, morbid compulsions, and lurid, Gothic intensity." Smith praised Faulkner's eloquence and regretted his lack of "cheerfulness and restraint." As John Bassett observes, "almost no one recognized the book's humor or the comic vision behind the most bizarre and catastrophic events in the journey."[23] In passing, Basil Davenport (*Saturday Review of Literature,* November 22) referred to

Faulkner's "sardonic humor," but no reviewer seemed to grasp Anse as a comic character, presenting himself as a figure of probity, piety, and then declaring his relief, which becomes a refrain, that now he can get "them teeth." The mordant humor of the commentary on the Bundrens as they made their disruptive way through the county escaped notice.

One discerning reader expressed admiration in one sentence, published on October 12, 1930, in the *Oakland Tribune* and *Indianapolis Star*: "A beautifully written novel in which perverse beauty is created out of the starkest elements." The *Central New Jersey Home News* in New Brunswick recommended the novel by a "young Southerner who has learned his lesson from James Joyce . . . a swell story about the death and funeral of an old woman . . . very effective." "A swell story" might seem an inappropriate response, and yet it is not so different from Faulkner's. When asked to comment on Malcolm Cowley's statement that Faulkner's "characters carry a sense of submission to their fate," the novelist replied:

> That is his opinion. I would say that some of them do and some of them don't, like everybody else's characters. . . . The Bundren family in *As I Lay Dying* pretty well coped with theirs. The Father having lost his wife would naturally need another one, so he got one. At one blow he not only replaced the family cook, he acquired a gramophone to give them all pleasure while they were resting. The pregnant daughter failed this time to undo her condition, but she was not discouraged. She intended to try again and even if they all failed right up to the last, it wasn't anything but just another baby.

Darl is left out of Faulkner's equation, and yet he is right: The family may be disintegrating, as all families sooner or later do, but they also carry on, as people tend to do, against all reason.

The *Jackson (MS) Clarion-Ledger* (December 7) was curiously terse and noncommittal, erroneously noting that Faulkner had "a greater following in England than in the United States" and had produced "a unique piece of writing." In a preface to the British edition of *Soldiers' Pay*, published in June 1930, Richard Hughes, the highly regarded author of *A High Wind in Jamaica*, observed that Faulkner was largely unknown in both his native land and in England but that he was the "most interesting novelist in America." Hughes went out of his way to present the man as well as his work, noting that the "young and prolific" author from Mississippi was "short in stature; but he is hardily constructed." He made Faulkner seem Byronic, noble, intense, and with a touch of Mark Twain: "His hair and eyes are very black. His nose, broken once, is aquiline, and his expression sharp and keen. He has a ready wit,

and is a brilliant and sure conversationalist, with the talent for inventing spontaneously extraordinary and imaginative stories." Hughes had met Faulkner
in the company of Ben Wasson and Hal Smith, and they had gone to work
on the British novelist, supplying him with Faulkner's work. An enthusiastic
Hughes then offered to write introductions for the British editions.

A Faulkner persona was emerging, one that Anthony Buttita, a year later,
helped to solidify with his report on walking with Faulkner during a visit to
Oxford: "He takes it slow, quiet, absorbed in himself. He may even tell you a
story, outlandish and incoherent, and if you question him for an explanation
you won't get any satisfaction. He goes right on telling the story in his own
way." Faulkner maintained the mystique of an author who would never quite
explain himself—reveal his trade secrets, as he called them in that letter to
his mother—while giving the reporter just enough to tantalize him: "'That's
the bridge that washed away. Made it tough for Anse and his sons so they
couldn't cross with Addie's body.' . . . He pointed to a stream. 'That's where
the folks dropped the coffin in *As I Lay Dying.*'" Was it, really? Did it matter?
Already, Faulkner was laying down the path for the pilgrims intent on visiting
the origins of Yoknapatawpha.[24] He had put to good use his brief stint as a
tour guide in New Orleans.

The English during the American Civil War had expressed some partial-
ity to the South, especially its planters, and Hughes laid it on thick, saying
Faulkner came from an "aristocratic family," inferring that the young novelist's avoidance of the "swirl of literary fashions and . . . literary people" was
beneath him even as Faulkner followed the "solid calling of a house-painter:
producing at the same time, out of the natural fecundity of his spirt, novel
after novel to be dropped by hesitant publishers into an ungrateful world."[25]
No wonder the *Jackson Clarion-Ledger* decided it might not be the time to
demystify a native, especially since Hughes heralded novels to come that
revealed even more of a writer who wrote "tragic, fascinating, and beautiful" novels. An even more distinguished novelist, Arnold Bennett, amplified
Hughes, calling Faulkner "the coming man. He has inexhaustible invention,
powerful imagination, a wondrous gift of characterization, a finished skill in
dialogue; and he writes, generally, like an angel."[26]

The praise and recognition far outweighed the negatives, and yet Faulkner's books did not sell. What to do?

11

Old Days and New Ways

1930

~

Short stories paid more than novels. And Faulkner was prepared to write for the market, responding promptly to an editor's suggestions and revising when necessary, as his correspondence with the *Saturday Evening Post* reveals.[1] That magazine paid the highest rates on acceptance—a boon to writers who often had to wait as long as two years before seeing print and a check. But the *Post* rejected many more stories than it accepted. Between 1930 and 1932, Faulkner sold twenty stories out of more than forty submitted—a "remarkable achievement."[2] Even at the low end of two hundred dollars, this was good money in the 1930s and went a long way in the Depression-era economy of Mississippi. It was never enough because his family responsibilities continued to expand, as did his desire for land and a home. "At present I am living on corn field peas," he told a *Post* editor.[3] A letter to *Scribner's Magazine* reflects a desperation couched in a kind of backwoods palaver typical of a persona that he used to distance himself from the very literary establishment he courted: "So here's another story ['Red Leaves']. Few people know that Miss. Indians owned slaves; that's why I suggest that you buy it. Not because it is a good story, you can find lots of good stories. It's because I need the money. The other time I wrote one of these Indian stories, it got bought again by Blackwood's in England, for 125 guineas. And that's why magazines get published, is it not? To get bought and re-bought?"[4] "Few know," but Faulkner was in the know. In fact, his story of Chickasaws executing a slave as part of the ritualized reaction to their chief's death had no precedent in the lives of the Chickasaws he depicted.[5] He made it up, although he certainly would have heard tales about the tribe, displaced from their lands in the 1830s. He knew Chickasaw descendants who had mixed with both the black and white races.[6] The British sale was bogus, the casual, offhand commentary misleading, the faux-naïf frankness disingenuous and humorous—like his biographical sketch for the *Forum* (April 1930), which concluded: "Own and operate own typewriter."[7] Did Faulkner think this rustication of himself made him a more intriguing figure to sell to northern sophisticates? At any rate, *Scribner's* did not buy the story, but the *Saturday Evening Post* did, for $750, publishing it on October 25, 1930.

Faulkner wrote stories for money, but they also had to be the best he could create, including three masterpieces of the genre he would publish in the next two years: "A Rose for Emily," "Red Leaves," and "Dry September." Similarly, the purchase of a home involved a meticulous study of a property suited to a sensibility steeped in the lore of the "old days," as Three Basket puts it in "Red Leaves." Faulkner, as always, was looking to make his own world, even as the world pressed upon him with financial obligations. He would live, nevertheless, as much as possible on his own terms, longing for a time when, as Three Basket claims: "A man's time was his own then. He had time." This is a perennial complaint, made at just about the same time by Wordsworth: "the world is too much with us." The getting and spending he deplores had also become part of this Native American community.

Faulkner was not so foolish as to suppose he could actually return to the past: "In the old days, there was the good way. But not now," Three Basket tells his skeptical Chickasaw interlocutor, who counters, "You do not remember the old way either." Three Basket answers, as Faulkner could have done, "I have listened to them who do." The two Chickasaws are discussing Three Basket's dislike of slavery and his rejection of black people who like to sweat. "Man was not made to sweat," Three Basket says, aligning himself with Anse Bundren, who says he does not want to be beholden to any man even as every man Anse encounters enslaves himself in an effort to help the hapless Anse, who complains about his burdens. This is where the Chickasaws chime in. "Damn that Negro," one of them says, referring to the slave who runs off rather than acquiesce to his own murder as part of the tribe's ritualized burial of their chief and his black factotum. "When have they ever been anything but a trial and a care to us?" This "grim vision of paternalism" makes the slave hunters sound like housewives sighing over their domestic servants or employers over labor.[8] The words are also akin to Faulkner's own laments about the family and servants he would have to support.

Faulkner, like Moketubbe after Issetibbeha's death in "Red Leaves," had become "the Man," responsible for his clan—for Estelle and her two children, but for many more, including black dependents he foresaw as part of the establishment he was about to acquire on land a Chicksaw, E-Ah-Nah-Yea, occupied and sold in 1836, when he was removed along with other Native Americans as part of President Jackson's resettlement policy.[9] Faulkner, with his keen understanding of frontier Mississippi, began sometime in the spring or summer of 1930 to think about a people who had been dispossessed and displaced, a theme that would grow in importance and culminate in *Go Down, Moses* (1942). With an anthropological perspective he probably first absorbed in the company of Oliver La Farge, he set about imagining the home the Chickasaws were not able to retain. Or to put it another way, what had been their home became his home.

In "Red Leaves," the Chickasaws set themselves up like white slaveholders. Contrary to all expectations, they own a plantation and have not been forced to move. The Founding Fathers "gambled that no Indian community would become 'civilized' as they defined the term in the late eighteenth and early nineteenth centuries." Faulkner, in effect, created a civilization of Chickasaws who would play the white man's game and win,[10] performing as extraordinary assimilationists. They ought not, according to the racial ideology of the time, exist: "They were both squat men, a little solid, burgher-like; paunchy, with big heads, big, broad, dust-colored faces of a certain blurred serenity like carved heads on a ruined wall in Siam or Sumatra, looming out of a mist." They are, in short, a William Faulkner European-Asian-American fantasy that upends history. They are, indeed, part of a history that did not happen, and for precisely that reason they are fascinating. In their Faulknerian world they get to stay because they are slave owners: "It is a 'new way' for these Indians to live, perhaps no better than the 'new way' of the Indians removed to the west or the Indians who went underground (like the Poarch Band of Creeks or the Florida Seminoles) or even the Indians who died, but it is their 'new way.'" Native Americans did not assimilate as slave owners but as Christians who did their best at staying put and accommodating to the white world, which in Faulkner's fictional land includes slavery.

"Red Leaves" is prophetic: "Have modern Indian tribes not started up bingo halls and slot machine palaces? How are they different—really—from the Indians in 'Red Leaves'?"[11] How different, really, Faulkner might have asked himself, was he?—about to set up his establishment, purchasing it from a burgher, and living, at least in some respects, like one?

"Red Leaves" is also a story about succession, which often means displacing what has come before and founding a new order, a new way that paradoxically derives from the old one. Moketubbe has been wearing, on the sly, Issetibbeha's red-heeled shoes, but now he can openly walk in the shoes of his predecessor much as Faulkner meant to do as he set himself up as a property owner in an antebellum home. Doom, Issetibbeha's father, salvages a sunken steamboat and has his slaves haul it for five months on cypress rollers over twelve miles "home overland." Faulkner would single-handedly jack up an abandoned mansion in its "faint splendor" akin to that steamboat with its flaking paint and chipped, gilded moldings. Where do these Chickasaws acquire their cosmopolitan tastes? In New Orleans, of course, where Faulkner acculturated himself. The red heels are procured when Issetibbeha makes it all the way to Paris and returns with his souvenirs, including a pair of girandoles, which are perhaps like a pair shown online with figures of Native Americans forming their base.[12] Issetibbeha's airs, his insouciance, are reminiscent of a young Faulkner, home from abroad, establishing his authority and his mystique. The Issetibbeha-Moketubbe father-son dynamic is as fraught as the Falkners' generational strains. The short, obese Moketubbe is not William Faulkner, but he is the heir of a tall father who distrusts his inert, lazy son.

Issetibbeha dies suddenly, apparently poisoned by Moketubbe just as Issetibbeha poisoned his father, Doom. Did Faulkner know, in creating this treacherous saga of succession, that poisoning was often the preferred way to end European reigns? Just as Doom's personal slave ran off to avoid the ritual death accompanying his master's demise, Issetibbeha's slave has escaped. It will take, the tribe estimates, three days to capture him. Like Egyptian pharaohs, these chiefs must leave this world with their prized possessions. As with most white slaveholders, black slaves remain with their Native American masters in perpetuity.

As Issetibbeha's body rots in the moldy, decomposing steamboat, with "gutted windows . . . like cataracted eyes," the Chickasaws complain about a "world going to the dogs"—surely Faulkner's comic sendup of the sentimental lamentations over the loss of the Old South, the Dixie portrayed in the films and stories of his upbringing, except, in an ironic twist, the Native Americans blame their decline on the advent of the white man and his slaves, which has occasioned their own slaveholding as a way to maintain their status in a changing world. The rundown condition of the steamboat—the dust and the animal droppings—is not that far removed from the leaky-roofed home Faulkner would have to rehabilitate, restoring the past, in a sense, but also wiring it, as he promised to do when first proposing a rental while he worked on raising the purchase price.[13] The $750 he received from the *Saturday Evening Post* for "Red Leaves" would pay for installing electricity in his new home and for the electric stove Estelle wanted. The writer who had been a tramp, who had once proclaimed he could not wait to decamp from Oxford, reluctantly and yet determinedly, like the immobile Moketubbe, took up the offices of his heritage. As in "Red Leaves," it was all coming to a head for William Faulkner. He would have to take the lead just as the recalcitrant Moketubbe finally does in pursuit of his father's body slave.

When "Red Leaves" shifts to Issetibbeha's black man and his flight from his fate, the story becomes centered on a struggle with the atavistic, with what is expected of this slave to the past. He runs away from his fate as William Faulkner tried to tramp away from his, as the Emperor Jones runs to the sound of the drums that reminded the black man of his first capture and the horrendous Middle Passage. The drums beat out a destiny that pursued William Faulkner as well, as he resisted but also claimed his heritage. Although the slave wants to live, he understands he is also part of a mythos that requires his death: "the Negro, the quarry, looked quietly down upon his irrevocable doom with an expression as profound as Moketubbe's own." In fact, the story's narrator digresses, like a biographer, seeking a way inside his subject, who, it is supposed, also feels the call of his destiny: "To Moketubbe it must have been as though, himself immortal, he were being carried rapidly through hell by doomed spirits which, alive, had contemplated his disaster, and, dead, were obviously partners to his damnation." Even as Faulkner resisted and remained on the run for a while, he realized he could not escape home or history. Even as a cottonmouth slashes the black man's arm with its poisonous fangs, the slave touches its head, salutes it ("Olé, grandfather"),[14] and when the snake strikes again, he repeats twice, as if speaking to fate or death itself: "It's that I do not wish to die." The snake is the man's "totem ancestor" and "actually prepares" the slave for death. In "Red Leaves," the slaves retain vestiges of African snake cults but also the mentality of voodoo ceremonies still performed in William Faulkner's time.[15]

The slave is young and strong, and for six days he outlasts his pursuers as Issetibbeha's body "began to smell; they could smell him for a long way up and down the bottom when it got hot toward noon and the wind blew." The corrupted body adds to the absurdity of fulfilling what is required of Moketubbe, every bit as indolent as Anse Bundren, and as fainéant as Faulkner could be during periods of inebriation when he simply could not be roused. No one can say for certain what this drinking meant, or what its cause, but the fiction seems to say that, like the running slave, Faulkner could resist only so long before giving way to resignation and inertia. To the fugitive slave, now delirious, his Chickasaw captor says in tender tribute: "Come... You ran well. Do not be ashamed." To Faulkner it was the running, even if it meant failing, that mattered, just as he prized his "most splendid failure," *The Sound and the Fury*. His ideal love was life itself, symbolized in the deathless bond between the Phoenix and the turtledove in Shakespeare's poem, which Faulkner liked to recite in the grips of his dipsomania. The last word spoken to the slave in "Red Leaves" is "Come," which is an invitation to death, the welcome Faulkner never wanted to hear. Edmond L. Volpe reads "Red Leaves" as articulating Faulkner's "feeling that his own civilized culture had failed him by making him incapable of accepting death."[16] The story, on the other hand, represents the masters partaking in the "antique virtue" the slave represents.[17]

Although so much has been written about Faulkner's obsession with the past, it is remarkable how much of his fiction is a projection of the future—his and ours. In 1930, his first order of business was to secure his home by writing stories about home and heritage. Miss Emily Grierson, in "A Rose for Emily," is in every sense of the word homebound and resisting death as fiercely as that slave in "Red Leaves," holding on to her decaying lover. And when she dies, the town attends her funeral in "respectful affection for a fallen monument. . . . Miss Emily had gone to join the representatives of those august names where they lay in the cedar-bemused cemetery among the ranked and anonymous graves of Union and Confederate soldiers who fell at the battle of Jefferson. Alive, Miss Emily had been a tradition, a duty, and a care; a sort of hereditary obligation upon the town." It is this sense of respect and obligation that went into the purchase of the home that came to be called Rowan Oak.[18]

Built circa 1848 by Robert B. Sheegog,[19] the house and property, located on eight city lots, made an impressive but not opulent or original abode for a prosperous Oxford merchant prince. When he died in 1860, he owned six thousand acres in four counties, and ninety slaves.[20] Slaves built a kiln to make the bricks for its foundation. The entrance hall made your arrival into an event. Large rooms on each side of the hall made you aware of the owner's character. In Faulkner's day, and still on display, the room on your left (the library) featured family portraits, including one of the old Colonel. On the right (the sunlit parlor), you might dine at a table, or relax in armchairs, in an atmosphere of restrained elegance. At the end of the first-floor hall, a rudimentary pantry and kitchen reflected the minimal amenities afforded to the home's occupants. Upstairs, you could walk onto a porch supported by Greek-inspired columns soaring to the roof and look out on the lane that led to this height. Again on either side of the second floor were large rooms where the master and his mistress slept, with smaller rooms in the back, with a wraparound back porch, a carriage house, smokehouse, and barn—built, Faulkner told his stepson Malcolm, by E-Ah-Nah-Yea—out of "thick hand-hewn logs of cypress," like those, it can be imagined, that were used to transport the steamboat to the Chickasaw plantation. On these native grounds a formal garden completed the template of an estate that backed onto wooded land that buffered this refuge from what is now part of the Ole Miss campus.

The original house, even with later alterations, enforced a sense of order, hierarchy, and serenity that abided the advent of each new owner.

This antebellum relic acquired romantic and even occult associations. That second-story porch, it might be pointed out to you, is where Robert Sheegog's daughter, Judith, fell to her death while trying to elope with a Yankee lieutenant who helplessly watched her plunge earthward. On moonlit nights to the sound of baying hounds in the woods and the wind in the trees, she is said to have haunted the premises. Faulkner would later tell scary stories to his stepchildren, his daughter Jill, and their friends about Judith's descent down the Rowan Oak stairs on the anniversary of her death. Faulkner's niece Dean never outgrew a belief in spirits and sensed in the home Maud Falkner had willed to her the presence of her grandmother and her uncle William Faulkner.[21]

Known for fifty-three years as the Old Bailey Place, the house William Faulkner wanted sat on the edge of town, just off Old Taylor Road, situated in exactly the right spot for an observer of the action, secluded, and yet within walking distance to the Oxford square. As one town resident testifies, walking along the Rowan Oak lane sided by towering cedars toward the Greek Revival house, "one has a feeling of walking back in time, into a different world."[22] Then, as now, the shift from present to past, from the modern neighborhood on the boundary of Rowan Oak to that cedar-lined lane, occurs as quickly as the time shifts in Faulkner's fiction.

Like the ghost that haunted the Old Bailey Place, Faulkner became obsessed with it and would not let go, writing to the property's owner, William Bryant, on March 22, 1930: "I will never give up hoping to own this place until you sell to someone else, and probably not then." Bryant, like William Faulkner, had stories to tell. He had enjoyed a colorful and lucrative period in Paris, Texas, and Denver, Colorado, befriending Wyatt Earp and other Wild West types. Then he had come home and married Sallie Bailey on May 1, 1887. He took his bride to Paris, Texas, living out the frontier dream that had captivated William Faulkner's frustrated father. Sallie did not take to the West and the shoot-outs in the streets any more than Maud supposed she would, and the Bryants returned to Mississippi, settling in Coffeeville, thirty miles from Oxford. The Baileys, the Oldhams, and the Falkners all knew one another. Sallie remembered William Faulkner as "quiet child, artistic and different, and no one was surprised that he grew up wanting to be a writer like his great-grandfather."[23] Ellen Bailey, Sallie's sister, well known for her paintings on porcelain plates, considered Maud Falkner one of her most talented students.

When William Faulkner first expressed interest in the Old Bailey Place, it had been on the market for several years. Ellen Bailey, the house's occupant, had died in 1922, and Will Bryant did not wish to move that far from his plantation and other holdings near Coffeeville. Renters had left the neglected property in a sorry condition. The very sight of the house alarmed Cho-Cho when she first saw it: "tumbled down, surrounded by brush, outdoor privy, snakes, no electricity, plumbing."[24] The city had refused to extend services to what was then the end of the line on Old Taylor Road. So the house remained fixed in its original time, with oil lamps, fireplaces, and a cast-iron stove in the kitchen.[25]

Malcolm Franklin remembered his "first visual recollection of the house I was to grow up in and love was of the most dilapidated dwellings I had ever seen." In fact, his account reads like a gloss on "A Rose for Emily," with Oxford despairing at the folly of attaching a family to this necrotic commorancy occupied by tenants, the Andersons, on a month-to-month lease: "The only time that my mother's father, Judge Oldham, and Mr. Murry, Billy's father, saw eye to eye was when they got together in an effort to try and stop the sale of this place. . . . It looked as if it was going to collapse with the next rainstorm or wind." The driveway defeated automobile traffic, which meant it was passable only with a wagon and mules. Up close, Malcolm observed "raw, unpainted and weathered boards, many of which had rotted through."[26]

But thirty-two-year-old William Faulkner saw something else. This was the land the black slave in "Red Leaves" had run on, the hare to the Chickasaw's hounds. In his twenties, Faulkner had still played games with teenagers like Calvin Brown, running in their hare-and-hounds races over four-mile stretches, including half-mile sprints, "giving no quarter" and matching the pace with boys half his age rampaging through Bailey's Woods.[27] What Faulkner wanted, right from the start, was not just that particular home but a nature preserve that would include the woods as soon as he could afford the purchase price.

Taking possession of the Old Bailey Place and its environs was a point of pride, the same pride Faulkner exhibited in those races, which Brown describes as feats of perseverance and exaltation driven by the "feeling of having gone to the limits of endurance and beyond—first with straining lungs and leaden feet, and then with a vague, light-headed feeling of an almost effortless running with no remembered beginning or foreseeable end. Sometimes I wondered if I was about to collapse, but pride kept me going." The man who created the runaway slave was bound to create his Rowan Oak. Faulkner had played the fugitive, making his own trail like his teenage playmate Calvin Brown, doubling back, hiding, and climbing trees to gauge the pursuit.

Against the opposition of the Oldhams and the Falkners, William Faulkner persisted, fortified by his wife. As his letters reveal, she took the lead, and he deferred to her, moving quickly to secure their dream home. They had played, as did other neighborhood children, near the house and in Bailey's Woods.[28] This couple, always on the edge of Oxford in so many ways, symbolized their ramshackle and yet enduring union in this decrepit and yet durable home, their paradise regained.

Faulkner visited Coffeeville in late March to speak with Sallie Bailey. She owned the property but put her husband, William C. Bryant, in charge of negotiations. On that very day Bryant decided he wanted to sell the house to a man who "wanted a lovely home to care for." Within two days Bryant had agreed to Faulkner's proposition that he could have the house and about eight acres for between seventy-five and one hundred dollars per month, as both rental and partial house payment. The very next day (March 25), a thrilled Faulkner admitted, "I was afraid the only proposition which I could make you was so hare-brained that you wouldn't consider it." What, after all, did Faulkner have to offer? Certainly not steady employment or even family backing. But he had something far more important in Bryant: a man who respected him, admired him, and even liked him.

Although Faulkner had a reputation as lazy and unreliable, Bryant saw another man, one that Phil Stone explained to Louis Cochran, who wrote an early profile: "He is the most normal, the sanest man I have ever known. He has less tendency to any sort of excess—either physical, mental or emotional—and has more practical common sense than any man I have ever known. He can make almost anything on Earth with his hands and is a good carpenter and a good housepainter. When he is not practical about the things other people are practical about it is not that he doesn't realize it but that he doesn't think it worth the trouble sometimes to be practical about such things. And this, I think, is the very apex of practical common sense."[29]

An excited Faulkner revealed to Bryant how much he relied on his wife: "Estelle says the next thing to do is to examine the house." Perhaps because Bryant wanted them to keep the sale a secret, Faulkner proposed that Bryant escort them as a carpenter checked the joists, walls, and foundation, and they figured out what to do about "wiring, piping, etc." By March 29, with Bryant's reply in hand, Faulkner wrote: "on behalf of Estelle, I extend to you and Mrs. Bryant our invitation to spend as much of the day you plan to come to Oxford with us as you will. We will kill the fatted calf as soon as we hear from you again." He reiterated his offer of seventy-five dollars and "whatever amount above that which we can make . . . [d]epending upon what improvements etc which we must make to the house as it now stands." He was hoping to raise his payment to one hundred dollars per month but thought it prudent to begin at the lower figure.

Faulkner spoke for Estelle in these letters, but what did she think? "It was a shabby place," Cho-Cho later told her daughter Vicki, who said: "My mother told me how when they arrived, she sat on the front steps and cried. And I'm sure it must have been a shock to Grandmama as well. However, you must understand, she was very much in love with Pappy, so I don't think it was as bad to her as it appeared to have been for my mother." Then a child, Cho-Cho could only think how the decrepit place would look to her friends. Estelle, her granddaughter remembered, found Rowan Oak a relief from the intense social world of Shanghai, at first diverting and then overwhelming with the drinking and gambling and—Vicki did not add—the sexual raffishness rampant in her stories. This new home, "on the fringes of Oxford" in soothing solitude, meant a new start.[30]

All told, the property would cost William and Estelle Faulkner six thousand dollars. In April 1930 the Bryants signed over a warranty deed to the new owners. Faulkner and Bryant discussed a new name for the house, Rowan Oak. "My grandfather," Sally Stone Trotter recalled, "applauded the selection, persuaded by their chat about the religious connections of the Rowan tree, and the sturdiness and long, sheltering life of the oak tree. A piece of Rowan wood over the door was to bring peace and happiness therein." This was sacred ground.

But moving in was another story, a William Faulkner story, in fact. "Our tenants are disinclined to vacate," Faulkner wrote to Bryant on May 12. "Disinclined" expresses the gentlemanly way William Faulkner went about taking possession of his domain.[31] This talk of vacating and taking possession by dispossession inevitably recalls the fate of Faulkner's Chickasaws. He had counted on the Andersons vacating by June 1. But they had said Bryant had given them until September. Bryant quickly responded, telling the Andersons: "This is Mr Falkner's property and you must make your arrangements with him. He has the right to take possession June 1, 1930." Anderson reluctantly relented, recounting the "severity of his loss and inconvenience it would cause." To which Bryant said, "You [Anderson] must absolutely depend on him [Faulkner] for favor in the matter." Bryant was more than businesslike in his dealings with William Faulkner. The two men obviously had grown close. "Will say I admire your leniency in the matter," Bryant wrote Faulkner on May 31.

Faulkner secured Anderson's agreement to vacate by July 1, and a good thing, too, since Faulkner had trouble containing Estelle's outrage over her husband's forbearance—as he confided to Bryant on May 30: "I have tried to be just and fair with him, at no little cost to my domestic peace, since Estelle counted on the place for the first of June, and when I told her that I would not turn Mr Anderson out neck and crop and that I had given him until July 1,

I might as well have told her that I had set fire to the place. But then, women seem to be like that." Except they were not. Sallie Bailey Bryant, who was also fond of Faulkner, wrote to him on June 7: "Dear William . . . I thank you for being lenient with them [the Andersons]."

The Novelist

In mid-May, in the midst of the Rowan Oak ructions, the galleys of *Sanctuary* began to arrive. This is the moment, Faulkner wrote in his March 1932 Modern Library introduction to the novel, that he decided to rewrite his cheap idea so that it did not shame *The Sound and the Fury* and *As I Lay Dying*. His claim is baffling because the rewritten novel does not remove any of what then would have been deemed its sensationalistic elements. So what was the point of this misdirection? Actually, it is a misunderstanding. His introduction states that he received the book in galley form in the spring of 1930 and discovered "it was so terrible that there were but two things to do: tear it up or rewrite it. I thought again, 'It might sell, maybe 10,000 of them will buy it.' So I tore the galleys down and rewrote the book." Many readers of the introduction assume that Faulkner found the sensationalism terrible. But he does not say what he found terrible. Judging by his revisions, he was reacting to a novel that could be made to move more quickly and dramatically, focused not so much on Horace Benbow but on the gangster Popeye, a familiar type to readers of pulp fiction and of celebrated authors such as Dashiell Hammett and W. R. Burnett specializing in the seamier side of urban and small-town life.[32] The first gangster movies began to make Warner Brothers popular and profitable in 1931, putting *Sanctuary*, published February 9, 1931, in line right after *Little Caesar* (January 25, 1931) and before *The Public Enemy* (May 15, 1931). Faulkner could not have timed his novel's appearance any better than that or set his novel in a better location: near and in Memphis, then the U.S. murder capital and said to be even more saturated with bootleg whiskey than New York City. This was a murky world Faulkner knew from talks with prostitutes and the proprietors of gambling establishments.[33]

Compare the movie-like opening of *Sanctuary* 2 with *Sanctuary* 1:

[S2] From beyond the screen of bushes which surrounded the spring, Popeye watched the man drinking.

[S1] Each time he passed the jail he would look up at the barred window, usually to see a small, pale, patient, tragic blob lying in one of the grimy interstices, or perhaps a blue wisp of tobacco smoke combing raggedly away along the spring sunshine.

In S2, Popeye is immediately present in all his anomie, set apart watching, never partaking in society. Impotent, he cannot experience what he craves when he sees Temple, who becomes the novel's Clara Bow, the It girl, who is designed for male attention and invites it. "Popeye is Faulkner's grotesque portrait of the moviegoer," John T. Matthews suggests. "No character in fiction is as compulsively watched as Temple Drake."[34]

Popeye is the prurient epitome of other characters like Clarence Snopes, who will later observe Temple through a whorehouse keyhole. Our vision is quickly centered on "the man," who happens to be Horace Benbow, so that in one sentence the story, its theme, and two central characters are, as in film, immediately established. In S1, it will take some time to figure out that this is the jail where first a black murderer and then Lee Goodwin await their executions, the latter accused of a murder Popeye has committed but that will be pinned on Lee unless Horace gets him off. In S1, the pace is leisurely, weighed down with clauses. We have to wait quite a while in S1 to find anything like this description of Popeye's face, which occurs on the first page of S2: "vicious depthless quality of stamped tin." The metallic, inhuman, flatness of Popeye's appearance and affect, which will unnerve nearly everyone beginning with Horace, is what makes S2 so unsettling with its depiction of implacable evil.

S1 includes twelve flashbacks, including a flashback within a flashback, as Horace pieces together what happened to Temple and how she is connected to Popeye's murder of the retarded Tommy, who ironically is Temple's gentlemanly protector during Gowan Stevens's dereliction of duty. Gowan passes out and gets clobbered when he tries to assert himself. By constantly delaying the forward progress of the novel and having its most dramatic scenes filtered through Horace, Faulkner would have frustrated those ten thousand readers he wanted to reach. As Howard Hawks would later tell him in Hollywood: No flashbacks. Nothing should impede the story's rapid development. In effect, Faulkner went to work on himself, in the way a Hollywood studio writer would take apart another's screenplay and reassemble it, experimenting with "scene and structure . . . character against character, chapter against chapter," switching passages as necessary for maximum dramatic impact.[35]

In the summer and fall of 1930, in the sanctuary that had become Rowan Oak, Faulkner deepened the sense of violation that pervades the first version of the novel that became vulnerable to his penetrating stylist's eye. He took the story away from Horace, who was not someone who could help him sell ten thousand copies, and gave it to Popeye. And though this was a commercial move, it was not a crass one. As Faulkner said in his introduction, he thought his revision a "fair job" and wanted people to read it. "Tore the galleys down" is a kind of rape, and the bloody-minded Faulkner, determined to show he could sell, spent $270 that he could hardly afford to pay for the job. He went at his book with relish. In this brutal mood he performed brilliantly, willing, as he said in his introduction, to pay the price for resetting the book. He chose to be more provocative, not less. He did not tone down the so-called salacious parts but made them, instead, even more dramatic and insidious, inspired, it seems, by his reading of Shakespeare's *Measure for Measure,* which is best evoked in the question Angelo poses concerning his "conflict between his desire for Isabella and his sense of virtue and justice": "Shall we desire to raze the sanctuary / And pitch our evils there?"[36] The "sanctuary" is, of course, the virtue of southern white womanhood, which is like a glass vase in the mind of Horace Benbow in *Flags in the Dust/Sartoris* but is vulnerable to corruption in the body of *Sanctuary*'s Temple Drake. The split sensibility of Angelo, torn between preserving and despoiling what he desires, becomes, in Popeye, a demented rape of Temple that nevertheless results in his perverse and paradoxical effort to succor and immure her in a whorehouse. That she is destined for Popeye's purpose, and put into his "doll-like hands," is signaled in Ruby's rejection of Temple as a "doll-faced slut." Ruby remains faithful to her bootlegger-lover Lee Goodwin, even as flighty Temple does not know her own mind.

Faulkner's conflicted sensibility contended with his desire to please Estelle, to find for her a home, a sanctuary, and at the same time to treat her with suspicion, puzzlement, and sometimes even contempt. He could not just tell Bryant about Estelle's fury when told she could not move into Rowan Oak on June 1. He could not leave it at that. He had to add: "But then, women seem to be like that." Yet Estelle Oldham had been a temple for William Faulkner. Cleanth Brooks suggests that Conrad's Marlow in *Chance* sounds like Horace Benbow describing Temple Drake: "you pass by and wonder what mysterious rites are going on there, what prayers, what visions?"[37] Faulkner's own vision in spring had atrophied. Observing Estelle, like the superlative observer Marlow, Faulkner lamented the "withered brightness of youth, a spirit neither made cringing nor yet dulled but as if bewildered in quivering hopelessness by gratuitous cruelty; self-confidence destroyed and, instead, a resigned recklessness, a mournful callousness." Estelle had not done all this to herself. "The privileged man," Marlow observes, "the lover, the husband, who are given the key of the sanctuary do not always know how to use it." As Miss Myrtle says in Miss Reba's brothel: "Men just cant seem to take us and leave us for what we are. They make us what we are, then they expect us to be different. Expect us not to never look at another man, while they come and go as they please." What to make of Estelle, what to make of Temple, is one of the central mysteries in Faulkner biography, captured in Richard Gray's formulation of Temple's behavior: "She is pure mobility, a creature who may sometimes seem like an automaton and sometimes like a trapped animal but who, whatever the details of her associations, never manages to stay still."[38] Estelle's distracted behavior, like Temple Drake's "swirling glitter," would puzzle journalist Robert Cantwell on a later visit to Rowan Oak and is reminiscent of Temple's discomposed personality.

Sanctuary was revised at exactly the time that Faulkner was settling down in a land that had been acquired through dispossession and a house built on the corruption of slavery and refurbished in an era of high crime and Depression and Prohibition garishly depicted in the pulps and motion pictures in characters like Popeye, a pulpish movie villain, half man and squinting like the cartoon character. He functions as an affront to both Horace Benbow and Gowan Stevens, neither of whom can defend the honor of the women in their charge. The impotent Popeye sees half as much as other people, although his deadly aim with a gun compensates for his physical impairment and his lack of dexterity in other respects. Faulkner heard about the Memphis gangster Neil Karens Pumphrey, aka Popeye, who made the news. Pumphrey's parents, a wealthy cotton merchant and real estate entrepreneur and the daughter of Arkansas's attorney general,[39] have no place in *Sanctuary,* since Faulkner wishes to emphasize his character's impoverished background in stark contrast to the genteel world and rule of law that Horace Benbow tries to uphold. John Foley, who knew the "handsome and well fed" Popeye, said he did not look like Faulkner's sinister character.[40]

But why did Faulkner *need* Popeye? For the same reason he so often liked to casually mention his dealings with bootleggers. Only a few years before marrying Estelle he had presented himself in New Orleans as a "barefoot and shaggy vagabond, criminal bootlegger, bohemian extraordinaire."[41] When he arrived in Charlottesville for the first time in 1931, he asked a reporter, "Know where I can get a drink?" and was promptly taken to the local bootlegger. In respectable company, he liked to pitch in with Prohibition stories about rum-running in New Orleans—as he did to students at the University of Virginia, explaining that he worked with a bootlegger and his Italian mother, "a nice little old lady, and she was the expert. . . . We had the labels, the bottles, everything—it was quite a business."[42] At home it was a business with black people who brought him his liquor or absconded with it, as he claimed to Horace Liveright. A visit to the local bootlegger was on the itinerary of screenwriter Buzz Bezzerides when he visited Faulkner at Rowan Oak. If you wanted to drink in Oxford, especially on a regular basis, you went to the bootlegger. When Faulkner said in his Modern Library introduction that he wanted to write a shocking story to sell, part of the shock had to do with the connections between the underworld and polite society. "My father's a judge," Temple repeatedly whines in the company of bootleggers and a Virginia "gentleman" who cannot make it home without a drink. And when bootlegging Bill got home, he might encounter an inebriated Estelle and perhaps remember how she had been cosseted by Judge Niles. One friend of the Faulkners said that a drunken Estelle would embarrass her husband by propositioning anyone, including her doctors, although she never seems to have actually had an extra-marital affair.[43]

In contrast to Temple and Estelle, Narcissa Benbow is the embodiment of the propriety and conventional morality that the Falkners and Oldhams struggled to maintain. Narcissa does not want her brother to have anything to do with this case of bootlegger Lee Goodwin and his fallen woman, Ruby. The pressures on Faulkner, family man, to conform increased and chafed him. Similar pressure is too much for Horace, and he walks out on his wife. He needs to prove a point about himself: he does have the courage and stamina to stand by his principles. For Faulkner, however, what dooms Horace is his reluctance to see that the worlds of Popeye, Temple Drake, and Narcissa are consanguineous. They are of the same kind, if not of the same class or milieu. Leaving your wife does not alter matters much. After all, Horace, like Gowan Stevens and like the drinkers of Oxford, traffics with moonshiners like Nelse Patton. Ruby, a former prostitute, bears a last name, Lamar, that recalls L. Q. C. Lamar (1825–1893), a Mississippi congressman, senator, and associate justice of the Supreme Court. Maud's home was located on South Lamar, and Good-win's first name, Lee, evokes the fabled Robert E. Lee. The coupling of Lamar and Lee in a common-law marriage, and their devotion to one another, coun-terpoints Narcissa's false sense of propriety that she tries to impose on her brother Horace, telling her brother to have nothing to do with them. That Ruby takes care of Lee's blind, deaf-mute father with tenderness and without complaint reinforces her basic decency in an indecent society. Unlike Tem-ple, Ruby does not abide by the strictures of conventional morality. But she is, paradoxically, her own woman in a way Temple cannot imagine. The tough-talking Ruby is Faulkner's version of Dorothy, the character he admired in *Gentlemen Prefer Blondes,* who constantly punctures pretensions and male posturing. Ruby knows that Horace's effort to play Sir Galahad is doomed. She will do what it takes to protect her lover, whereas Temple, a fallen Lorelei, will do only what is required from someone of her class and sex, or try to hide those instances where her lapses lower her status as a lady. Miss Reba parodies propriety when she sets her own standards as queen of her brothel, enunciat-ing her own principles in taking care of Temple. Neither Miss Reba nor Ruby is respectable, but they remain preferable—more empathetic—than Narcissa and Temple, although Temple by virtue of her exposure to an underworld that Narcissa dares not contemplate let alone enter experiences a disquieting dissociation of identity that ultimately drove Faulkner to imagine her redemption in *Requiem for a Nun,* in a post-Prohibition society.

So far as is known Faulkner never carried stinking shrimp home to Estelle as Horace does to Belle, whose daughter calls Horace a shrimp. But Faulkner was clearly put out when Estelle took charge of the Rowan Oak move-in and he had to write that complaining letter to Will Bryant. But at least Faulkner did not have to deal with banks, arranging his own face-saving mortgage with Bryant, whereas Horace decries the "flat and foul land" that has been so commodified "you wouldn't be surprised to find that you could turn in the leaves off the trees, into the banks for cash." What he wants is a hill like the mounds, "bumps of dirt the Indians made to stand on when the River overflowed." This fleeting reference to the world of the Chickasaws and their proximity to nature occurs even as Popeye flinches at the approach of a dog as if he thought it was a cottonmouth moccasin. Horace has walked away from a corrupt world only to find himself in another with Popeye, whom Tommy says is the "skeeriest durn white man I ever see," meaning not only how frightening Popeye is but also how terrified he is of natural surroundings. The leaves of trees would be valuable to Popeye only if they could serve as bank notes.

Slippers, Moketubbe's fetish item, perform a similar function in *Sanctuary,* as status symbols. Several references to slippers suggest Temple's quasi-royal status (her pair have "glittering buckles"). Horace uses slippers to indicate a fall from status when he chastises Little Belle for bringing home a man she met on the train: "you dont bring them home, you know. You just step over them and go on. You dont soil your slippers, you know." Temple takes off her slippers when they sink in the sand on the way to Lee Goodwin's, suggesting her diminished status as a depraved Cinderella. Tommy, her guide to Goodwin's, remarks: "Durn ef I could git ere two of my fingers into one of them things. . . . Durn my hide." He shows the same fascination that Moketubbe does in the royal slippers that he cannot fit on his feet. Tommy's cursing of himself is a kind of comic abasement to the lady he escorts to a gin den. As soon as she arrives, Temple puts her slippers back on, but now she is reduced to no more than an object of desire as one of the men watches her lifted thigh as the slippers slide on and she jerks down her skirt. She keeps her slippers beside her head, as if they were a crown, when she lies on one of Miss Reba's beds. Later the pair of slippers get separated, and she finds one in the fireplace in a scene suggestive of how she is becoming estranged from her former self and is no longer the well-put-together Temple, daughter of a judge.

The rape, never actually described, deprives Temple of all her protections of class, sex, and self—it all vanishes during the moments she exclaims: "Something is going to happen to me. . . . Something is happening to me!" Ruby, who had once sold her body to help get Lee out of prison and has never enjoyed the advantages Temple takes for granted, is incapable of fully empathizing with Temple's self-estrangement since Ruby has always remained her own person. Identity is circumstantial, the novel implies, which is perhaps a more disturbing thought than the rape scene or even Popeye's evil. Miss Reba trudges heavily up the stairs in worsted slippers, a coarse, textured fabric that is of a piece with her establishment, although the solicitous madam has a softer side expressed in her other pair of flowered felt slippers, a sign of her own high standing—at least in her own house of prostitution and among the city officials who patronize her business. Miss Reba, perhaps approximating the size of Moketubbe, commands a boy to fetch her slippers. The worlds within worlds of *Sanctuary* all have their ranks and hierarchies, making the novel as anthropological as "Red Leaves." Miss Reba's brothel is as separate a compound as the Chickasaw preserve, a world unto itself, a Rowan Oak, a sanctuary, especially compared to Lee Goodwin's place, where Ruby Lamar, angry over Temple's privileged life and worried that Temple will disrupt Ruby's bond with Lee, treats Temple as a sexual tease fearful of intercourse with a real man. Ruby is resigned to her fate, telling Horace that he ought not to associate with her because his community would condemn him: "There's no use fighting it," she tells him. In this respect, she is like the black murderer who will be hanged without "pomp, buried without circumstance." Low-status lives, without a sanctuary, the novelist implies, will not be recorded or recognized. Hostile community opinion, as William Faulkner well knew, required a more robust response than Horace is able to sustain.

The Memphis whorehouse, like the novel itself, is a permissive refuge from the cant and censorship of conventional society. Miss Reba names one of her dogs after her former lover/pimp Mr. Binford, which also happened to be the name of a Memphis censor, Lloyd Y. Binford, notorious for his exiguous standards of what was proper and decent. In a parody of propriety, Miss Reba wears a "widow's bonnet with a veil," already out of fashion by 1927 but indicative of the decorum she observes in her own establishment.[44] Miss Reba has her standards, objecting to Popeye's use of Red to bed Temple: "I aint going to have my house turned into no French joint."

The whorehouse is just one of several segregated domains in *Sanctuary* that Faulkner seems at pains to expose. Horace Benbow enters a train compartment, where a seated passenger "leaned forward and spat tobacco juice between his knees." Horace departs for the smoking car but cannot find a seat, as a door swings open on the "jim crow car. . . . Standing in the aisle he could look forward into a diminishing corridor of green plush seat-backs topped by hatted cannonballs swaying in unison, while gusts of talk and laughter blew back and kept in steady motion the blue acrid air in which white men sat, spitting into the aisle." Anyone then familiar with these cars would know they did not have luggage racks and that suitcases would be jammed into any available space. The bathroom would be smaller and not as well equipped as in the whites-only cars. Black people traveling from the North would have to switch to Jim Crow cars at border states like Kentucky or in Washington, D.C.[45] On the same train, Horace meets state senator Clarence Snopes, who calls him "Judge," endowing him with a honorific title, implying that they are on the same high level and can therefore do business, which in this case means that in a later phone call Snopes wants one hundred dollars for telling Horace Temple's whereabouts so Horace can interview her about Goodwin's role in Tommy's murder. Forgoing this traffic in corruption, Horace loses an opportunity to turn Temple into his witness.

Goodwin is burned to death by a mob on the strength of Temple's testimony incriminating him. She has lied rather than tell the true story of her own degradation and Popeye's role in it. Horace is fortunate to escape the mob that has tortured Goodwin. As Horace walks away from the murder scene, he hears: "Do to the lawyer what we did to him. What he did to her. Only we never used a cob. We made him wish we had used a cob." The defeated Horace returns home to his wife, driven from the train station in a taxi owned by a bankrupt planter, still sporting the waxed mustache of his heyday but no longer wearing a top hat, now replaced by a cap, or a Prince Albert coat, now disowned for his "suit of gray striped with red made by Jews in the New York tenement district." This curious combination of old and new, past and present, gentile and Jew, seems the perfect ironic accompaniment to the social, psychological, racial, ethnic, religious, and political stratifications summed up by Senator Clarence Snopes, aggrieved that he has not been able to get more than ten dollars out of the Memphis lawyer who also wanted to know Temple's whereabouts: The "lowest, cheapest thing on this earth aint a nigger: it's a jew," Snopes declares, sounding like Jason Compson: "We need laws against them. Drastic laws. When a durn lowlife jew can come to a free country like this and just because he's got a law degree, it's time to put a stop to things. A jew is the lowest thing on this creation. And the lowest kind of jew is a jew lawyer. And the lowest kind of jew lawyer is a Memphis jew lawyer." No one escapes Faulkner's scorn in a novel full of sarcastic references to white Baptists. Clarence Snopes declares himself a decent Baptist before going on his anti-Semitic tirade. As Horace notes, these Baptists have kept Goodwin in business:

"They knew what he was doing, but they waited until he was down. Then they all jumped on him. The good customers, that had been buying whiskey from him and drinking all that he would give them free and maybe trying to make love to his wife behind his back. You should hear them down town. This morning the Baptist minister took him for a text. Not only as a murderer, but as an adulterer; a polluter of the free Democratico-Protestant atmosphere of Yoknapatawpha county. I gathered that his idea was that Goodwin and the woman should both be burned as a sole example to that child; the child to be reared and taught the English language for the sole end of being taught that it was begot in sin by two people who suffered by fire for having begot it. Good God, can a man, a civilized man, seriously. . . ."

"They're just Baptists," Miss Jenny said.

In Miss Jenny's hierarchy, Baptists don't count, so their hypocrisy hardly troubles her. After such passages, however, the only place for Faulkner was on the edge of town.

Sanctuary stands out as Faulkner's most uncompromising attack on his community and a body politic riven by segregation and prejudice from top to bottom. Even Popeye has a sense of position and propriety. When he is convicted of a murder he did not commit and is on the way to execution, his chagrin is apparent: "to have it hung on you by a small-time j.p."

This novel, so full of disaffection, becomes unusually personal when Faulkner returns to the Luxembourg Gardens, his favorite Paris haunt, where he situates the alienated Temple, seated beside her father, the judge, "sullen, and discontented and sad."[46] Estelle's father had not taken her off to Europe, but Cornell Franklin had taken her even farther away but surrounded her with Europeans and Americans. And like Temple, Estelle did not flourish in the change of scene. In effect, she was immobilized and reacted by returning home again and again. She would not stay put, any more than Temple could, reappearing in *Requiem for a Nun* to take command of her own story and fight over it with Gavin Stevens, another male protector/persecutor who supplants Horace Benbow. In *Sanctuary,* it is a shock to see Temple stabilized in the Luxembourg Gardens, the Temple who, as Ruby Lamar complains, "wouldn't stay anywhere. She'd just dash out one door, and in a minute she'd come running in from the other direction," constantly attracting the male gaze. So it was with Estelle.

Faulkner had written a version of the Luxembourg Gardens passage in 1925, before his marriage to Estelle, before his purchase of Rowan Oak, before he quite knew how these two paragraphs he was so proud of would fit into his future. It is a bleak, if beautifully drawn autumnal picture of a jaded woman in twilight juxtaposed against the European past and its present, played out in a concert of "dying brasses, across the pool and the opposite semicircle of trees where at sombre intervals the dead tranquil queens in stained marble mused, and on into the sky lying prone and vanquished in the embrace of the season of rain and death." The last words are lifted from Eliot's *The Wasteland*. Something happened to Faulkner during his stay in Paris that helped to put his upbringing and society into the larger perspective of European history. Temple is no longer the southern belle. She is already moving toward the figure she will become in *Requiem for a Nun*, haunted by her immoral, criminal behavior. She seems on the verge of articulating another Eliot concern: "After such knowledge, what forgiveness?" This line from "Gerontion" seems to reflect the novel's corruption of justice, and the poem's vision of decay. The novel's last scene comes full circle to the first scene when Popeye confronts Horace across the spring in a wasteland reminiscent of the "depraved May" in "Gerontion."[47] They are in the vicinity of a "gutted ruin" with a garden gone wild—a decaying plantation world something like what Faulkner found when he began to repair Rowan Oak. The queens in the Luxembourg Gardens are stained like Temple, who no longer can be regarded as a sanctuary of womanhood and for whom the world holds no sanctuary. And her father, the judge, has not wrought justice but just a cover-up. The "tragedy is the more terrible because it is not Temple's but man's."[48]

Rebuilding and Revising

During the process of taking apart *Sanctuary* and rebuilding it, Faulkner was doing the same to Rowan Oak. Dean pitched in, bringing along quail from his hunting trips.[49] Brother John would visit, watch his brother saw logs into firewood lengths: "I'd take a hand at the saw and then help him split the bolts and tote the wood to the house." John always got a thank-you but not much more. He knew his brother was worried about money. "I guess he had just too many other things on his mind," John concluded.[50]

"Will you please make my excuses to Miss Sallie for having failed to answer her kind letter last month," Faulkner wrote to Will Bryant on September 13. "I must plead work, if that be an excuse. I have just finished roofing the house, and we are now putting in a bath room, and what with the cleaning of the grounds and such, I have been putting in about ten hours a day with saw, hammer, and axe. Hence my laxity." Estelle sent her thanks for the cornices Miss Sallie was going to send them, and he wanted Bryant to know they had cleaned and painted the chandelier.[51]

Faulkner made his renovation and furnishing of Rowan Oak of a piece with his writing and his life, preferring to set up the simplest form of platform, working on a spindle-legged table belonging to his mother. His brother John thought this delicate item better suited to a lady's parlor, but Faulkner placed his makeshift desk next to a window where the light came in over his left shoulder, and sat in a tall chair that he adapted by sawing off its tall back and placing a cushion on its small seat. "It was the only writing chair he ever used," John claimed.[52] Perhaps Faulkner sat in that chair when he wrote to Will Bryant: "I am glad you liked the story ["Thrift"] in the post." In a few weeks the magazine would publish "Red Leaves," Rowan Oak's new owner reported: "a story about our Mississippi Indians, the scene laid in 1830. I am anxious for you to see that; In fact, I would have sent you the manuscript to read, if I thought you could read my handwriting." Faulkner, so often depicted as secretive about his writing, added: "I believe that I have got into it something of the Choctaw nature: a nature that is peculiar to our Mississippi, slave-holding Indians, and of which the rest of the world knows nothing at all."[53] If, as he said later, he just made up his Indians, here he suggested a closer tie to history, and to a certain pride very different from the sarcastic letter he wrote to *Scribner's* when first submitting the story for publication

Visits and letters between Faulkner and the Bryants continued to the end of the year as they worked out various details, including how the house was to be insured and what to do with various items the Andersons claimed were theirs and that others had also said they stored on the property before Faulkner took possession. These letters were friendly and mentioned visits. Without much capital to invest in the house, Faulkner turned scavenger: "Not a barn or shed of logs was safe in all of Lafayette County, even if tumbled-down," for he wanted to use the old logs to patch the dependencies already on the place. Eventually he found enough to add a house or two, which he placed on the old garden lot.[54] Scholars familiar with Faulkner's method of composition and his reuse of old materials can appreciate how much Rowan Oak resembled his compositional methods. He always found new ways to deal with the work of old days.

In the fall of 1930, work on Rowan Oak went apace while Estelle experienced an apparently uneventful pregnancy, although childbirth had been difficult for her, and she suffered from persistent anemia. Then this brief, calm, hopeful period came to an abrupt, shocking end.

12

Sorrow and Scandal

Sanctuary, January–August 1931

To me the very title *Sanctuary* has such connotations of brooding peace
that I think all those who care for sweet and sentimental books should be
warned what a terrific experience awaits them within its covers.
        —Alexander Woollcott, "Up from the South," *McCalls,* June 1931

A Death in the Family

On Tuesday, January 13, 1931, Faulkner wired his aunt in Memphis: "Alabama Faulkner born Sunday both well.[1] But the baby, two months
premature, and her mother, weakened after a fourteen-hour delivery, were
not so well. For the first few days, Faulkner continued to hope, announcing
on January 15 the birth of his child to the editors at the *Saturday Evening Post,*
even joking about her three-pound weight. A farmer had told him: "Well
dont feel bad about that. What with this Hoover prosperity and the drouth
last summer, a fellow does well to get his seed back." Already worried about
finances, and about the magazine's eight consecutive rejections, he sent a letter in the third person referring to "this Faulkner" with one *Post* story that
had won an O. Henry Award, another reprinted in England, and to fourteen
letters praising this work. He warned the *Post* that it risked "falling from that
high place in letters to which these fourteen people (including the aforesaid
Faulkner) raised it."[2]

Estelle had been anemic to begin with, and the baby began to struggle
for breath and bubble at the mouth. An alarmed Mammy Callie had awakened Mr. Bill at dawn. Faulkner told Ben Wasson he had called the doctor,

who told him there was "nothing he or anyone else could do." The local hospital had no incubator, and Faulkner decided to bring mother and child home to be attended by two nurses and Mammy Callie. Dr. John Culley visited every day, concerned with the infant's poor metabolism reflected in what was commonly called "locked bowels." Near the end of the week Faulkner and his brother Dean drove to Memphis to obtain an incubator. On January 20, Faulkner's aunt, Holland Wilkins, sent a telegram to Bama: "WILLIAMS BABY DIED THIS MORNING." She was nine days old, and on her death certificate Dr. Culley put the cause as "prematurity." Faulkner carried the little casket on the trip to the cemetery. It was the first time Estelle had seen him cry.

Did Estelle's heavy drinking contribute to Alabama's death?[3] Perhaps, although the infant apparently did not exhibit physical signs of fetal alcohol syndrome such as a smaller-than-usual head, drooping upper eyelids, a thin upper lip, smaller-than-normal eyes, a short, upturned nose, and flattened cheeks. To her parents, she looked perfect. Estelle's heavy drug use may have also been a factor, but we do not know if Estelle's addictions continued throughout her pregnancy, or even if stopping her substance abuse would have changed the outcome. Since the child died so quickly, it is hard to say what other symptoms might have developed, and the diagnosis of fetal alcohol syndrome only began to appear in the early 1970s.[4]

Faulkner did not seem to blame Estelle, but he did feel the need to lash out at Dr. Culley, who had a good reputation, although Faulkner did not care for his dogmatic personality, which is perhaps reflected in Dr. Alford's pretentious professionalism in *Flags in the Dust/Sartoris.* But Faulkner, creating a scene that belonged in *Sanctuary,* claimed to have confronted the doctor, shooting him in the shoulder, in one version, and missing the shot in another. "The bastard deserved to die," Bill told Ben Wasson, and the town tacitly agreed. "A true story?" Wasson asked in his memoir. "A fabrication? The latter I have come to believe."[5] Faulkner's grief, for a time, seemed unbearable, and perhaps the doctor's manner put the grieving, weeping father into a murderous mood. Estelle and Culley's wife, Nina, were friends. With no need to fictionalize her life, Estelle did not share her husband's anger at Culley, believing he had done his best. Estelle remained anemic, and it would take her the good part of a year to recover. During this same period her husband drove his car into a tree, continued his bouts of heavy drinking, and brooded on his daughter's death. In an introduction to *The Sound and the Fury,* written in 1933, Faulkner recognized how his life had been foretold in his own fiction: "So I who never had a sister . . . and was fated to lose my daughter in infancy, set out to make myself a beautiful and tragic little girl."

The death of a child, especially in the early days of a marriage, sometimes tears a couple apart. Even if husband and wife do not engage in recriminations, they grieve differently, and tensions that might already exist can become magnified. A man as distant as Faulkner could be, a woman as sociable as Estelle had always been, struggled with their natures and their fraught union. She had danced while he had held back, watching. She desperately wanted the approval of her parents, and he went off to abide by his mother. Alabama's death stopped time in a way, as it does for the couple in "The Brooch," a story written about this time, with links to *Sanctuary*. A husband like Gowan Stevens, a University of Virginia gentleman, will not leave his mother, and his wife is as unmoored as Temple Drake and will not stay home.[6] The wife wants her husband to forsake the home his mother presides over, and though he has defied his mother to marry, he relapses into a fealty to her that he vows not to break until she dies. The couple has lost an infant, and their future seems foreclosed until his mother, catching her daughter-in-law coming home late from a party on a cold night, issues a command to leave the house. The wife welcomes this interdict, which has been a long time coming, and tells her husband they have been liberated and are lucky. They can now leave and start a new life. The trouble, however, is not just with the marriage and the mother but with the husband's distrust of women:

> She turned now, facing him, as if she had only been waiting until she became warm, the rich coat open upon the fragile glitter of her dress; there was a quality actually beautiful about her now—not of the face whose impeccable replica looks out from the covers of a thousand magazines each month, nor of the figure, the shape of deliberately epicene provocation into which the miles of celluloid film have constricted the female body of an entire race; but a quality completely female in the old eternal fashion, primitive assured and ruthless as she approached him, already raising her arms. "Yes! I say luck too!" she said, putting her arms around him, her upper body leaned back to look into his face, her own face triumphant, the smell now warm woman-odor where the frosty fragrance had thawed. "She said at once, now. So we can go. You see? Do you understand? We can leave now. Give her the money, let her have it all. We won't care. You can find work; I won't care how and where we will have to live. You don't have to stay here now, with her now. She has—what do you call it? absolved you herself."

The husband refuses his stylish wife's proposal, turning her into a type to be found on magazine covers, a constricted celluloid Estelle, and declares that his mother has them "beat." The couple's inability to begin a new life suddenly makes the wife think of her lost child: "Then she began to cry. It was as quiet now as the way she had spoken. 'My little baby,' she said. 'My dear little baby.'" The infantilized husband begins to drink from a two-gallon jug of corn whiskey in the bathroom, thinking of his father, who abandoned the family only six months after his son was born. The son, now a father grieving over his own lost child, capitulates to his conflicted view of women and of his own maternal imprisonment, as he prepares to commit suicide:

> *Like your father, you cannot seem to live with either of them, but unlike your father you cannot seem to live without them;* telling himself quietly, "Yes, it seems that it was right. It seems to have known us better than I did," and he shut the bathroom door again and stuffed the towels carefully about and beneath it. But he did not hang the coverlet this time. He drew it over himself, squatting, huddling into it, the muzzle of the pistol between his teeth like a pipe, wadding the thick soft coverlet about his head, hurrying, moving swiftly now because he was already beginning to suffocate.

Like a suffocating infant, life itself—"it"—is too much for him. The man with a "pistol between his teeth like a pipe," shooting rather than drinking himself to death, is how the story ends, a case of arrested development in every sense of the word. How does one carry on after the death of a child and the rupture of a marriage? Some can't. Others, like the Faulkners, work through the grief without ever giving it up.

Writing Like a Devil

A week after Alabama's death, Rowan Oak helped to steady the couple as Faulkner continued to build a future for his family. On January 27, he had recovered enough to write a letter to "Miss Sallie and Mr. Will" expressing his intention to purchase more property from them to create a proper garden and orchard to "make of the whole place the pleasing spectacle which it once was." He vowed to keep the property intact, emphasizing he had no "secret subdivision and building plan." He addressed them as a caretaker of his property and theirs. He was quite aware that the city would in a few years be paving streets and encroaching on his land, but he was determined to retain and even enhance its original character.

Faulkner was counting on *Sanctuary*, published on February 9, to support his family and his renovation of Rowan Oak. He knew enough about publishing to realize that the novel would attract more attention than his other work. He already had a small, devoted following at home and abroad. Hal

Smith had gone into business with Jonathan Cape to assure Faulkner's publication in England. A French professor at Princeton, Maurice Coindreau, was at work on a translation of *As I Lay Dying* and an article that would appear in June in *Nouvelle revue française*. But right now Faulkner needed something that would *sell*. He needed reviews that made the book a cause célèbre, one that he would continue to foment in his Modern Library introduction the next year.

Paul H. Bixler in the *Cleveland Plain Dealer* (February 7) began the tumult and tributes by taking on Arnold Bennett's often-quoted declaration that Faulkner wrote like an angel: "the young American is better described as writing like a devil."[7] The novel depicted "evil unadulterated." The reviewer could find only one character who approached "the normal." In perversion heaped on perversion, with characters "psychically wrong," this "one long tattoo of horror" left the reader "stunned and insensible from too many blows." And yet, Bixler hastened to express the hope that his remarks "will not prevent anyone from reading the book" by the "most gifted novelist writing in the United States." Faulkner had taken an old genre, the "tale of terror," and replaced the ghosts, sliding panels, and shrieks in the night with an absorption in abnormal psychology. Bixler could have added that Faulkner had caught the crest of interest just then in the "new psychology," exploring psychosexual behavior and early childhood development in the coda to the novel that described Popeye's deprived childhood.[8] Bixler astutely drew readers' attention to "A Rose for Emily," which combined Poe's penchant for "horrible detail" with local color, in which the "credibility of the horror comes directly from the setting"—unlike Poe's tales that occurred "in a vacuum." This was a writer, Bixler concluded, who could not be ignored.

The very next day in the same newspaper, Ted Robinson, another critic who had closely followed Faulkner's career, asserted, "I am fairly hard-boiled, but *Sanctuary* nauseated me." This "unutterably violent" and "obscenely diabolical" story was not for the squeamish: "Its central point is an unthinkable act of degenerate outrage; its final catastrophe is an orgiastic lynching." The words again reflect the psychosexual dynamic that was also playing out just then in Hollywood's pre-Code films—not yet restrained by what came to be known as the "Production Code," designed to prohibit even sexual innuendo, let alone degenerate outrages. Prohibition remained in force, and Robinson treated this bootlegging novel as practically an illegal product: "Jonathan Cape and Harrison Smith risk much in publishing this frenetic thing."

B. K. H. (*Providence Journal*, February 17) treated Faulkner as a phenomenon: "a tremendous probability, and very nearly an enormous fact." The reviewer, already a Faulkner admirer, "suspected nothing like this": "Some will have the chills, some the creeps, some nightmares." The Depression had driven the nation into hibernation, and *Sanctuary,* "huge and terrific and upsetting," could not be ignored. "One of the most terrifying books I have ever read. And it is one of the most extraordinary," concluded Edwin Seaver in the *New York Sun* (February 13): "Mr. Faulkner is a superb movie director." Popeye is called a "Dr Caligari of the novel." John Chamberlain in the *New York Times Book Review* (February 15) finished the novel in "that limp state which follows a frightening encounter in the dark or the sudden sickening realization that one has just escaped sudden death." The same day in *New York Herald Tribune Books,* Margaret Cheney Dawson admonished, "And no one should read 'Sanctuary' who is not willing to bear the scars." "This is not the novel to send your maiden aunt on her birthday," advised Frank Daniel in the *Atlanta Journal* (March 1).

In the *Saturday Review of Literature* (March 21), Henry Seidel Canby praised the novel's inexorable narrative, calling it "as vivid as modern caricature and as accurate as Dutch painting." With silent films having just come to an end, Canby speculated that Faulkner "seems to be trying to write a 'talky,' where the dialogue gives the situation while the continuity is left to the pictures." Canby was one of only a few reviewers who actually mentioned Temple's rape only to see it as an example of sadism that deformed Faulkner's otherwise brilliant work. Similarly, Alan Reynolds Thompson in *Bookman* (April 1931) deplored the novelist's "sadistic cruelty" but praised his "cinematic scene-shifting of expressionism, the almost obscure brevity and vision sensationalism of the imagists, and the intense exploration of momentary experience characteristic of writers like Conrad, with the classic formal beauty of an intricate plot skillfully implicated, rigorously unified, and implacable in its advance to a fore-designed end."

In the *New Orleans Times-Picayune* (April 26), Julia K. W. Baker announced that Faulkner was already a "scandal in Mississippi," but that was beside the point: "He is more a son of a Confederate veteran than he is a Rotarian." He belonged instead with Euripides and John Webster, in Greece and London, because of a "tragic sense" as fine as "any writer of fiction of his time." She realized how much the novel owed to its own times, saying it "could not have been conceived or executed except under prohibition." She ranked the novel below *The Sound and the Fury* and *As I Lay Dying,* but even so, Faulkner remained "probably the best living novelist in America." Robert Sherwood ended his review in the April 1931 *Scribner's Magazine* with the verdict: "a great novel."⁹

The concentration of rave and overwrought reviews and notices propelled William Faulkner forward as a public figure for the first time. "William Faulkner Rakes up Human Garbage to Fashion a Powerful Magnum Opus," ran the headline in the *Brooklyn Daily Eagle* on April 1, 1931. The reviewer sold the book in the first paragraph, announcing the author had "assembled the gloomiest elements of social decay to be found in the South, but with a masterful restraint has whipped them into one of the most powerful heartrending novels of the past ten years." A *New Yorker* column labeled the novel "melodramatic" and "gruesome" and then added, "but maybe you like things like that."[10] A *Brooklyn Daily Eagle* story (May 31) about a cruise to France reported that a "hard boiled newspaperman . . . shuddering and feeling degraded" threw *Sanctuary* into the sea. Even Clifton Fadiman, who rarely missed an opportunity to deflate Faulkner's reputation, admitted in the *Nation* (April 15): "Mr. Faulkner has an almost Joycean power of exteriorizing his horror-obsession. . . . By virtue of this book alone he at once takes his place among the foremost of the younger generation of American novelists. He is an original." Alexander Woollcott, Algonquin Round Table stalwart, a popular radio raconteur who became the model for Sheridan Whiteside in *The Man Who Came to Dinner,* promoted the novel on his radio show.

Few reviewers caught the novel's flashes of sardonic humor, as Roscoe Fleming put it in the *Pittsburgh Press* (February 15). But the "Literary Lantern" columnist in the *Wichita Daily Times* (April 26) did, pointing out Faulkner's "sure and cutting humor" exemplified in Senator Clarence Snopes's bogus befriending of Horace Benbow: "Let's see, you're in Kinston now, ain't you? I know your senators. Fine men, both of them. But I just cain't call their names."

In England, the reviews fluctuated from somewhat squeamish high praise to outright condemnation. He did not "cushion keyholes or soliloquize in boudoir talk." You had to swallow his "bootlegger prose" whole. "*Sanctuary* is hard to read, difficult to like, and impossible to forget," declared Helen Fletcher in *Time and Tide* (September 19). The *Times Literary Supplement* (September 24) dismissed the novel as having no "moral or aesthetic purpose." It seemed misanthropic and sordid to R. McNair Scott in the *English Review* (October). Faulkner had outdone Jonathan Swift. The *Illustrated London News* review (October 3) deemed the book "painful and disagreeable" but also "a terrifying story, and the art with which it is written makes it doubly so." The verdict from Rebecca West, a writer of formidable reputation, took on this mounting crest of interest and encomium in order to turn it back, announcing in the *Daily Telegraph* (October 2) that Faulkner had told his story "badly" and with "inherent improbabilities." This coarse mishmash of André Gide, Bret Harte, Sherwood Anderson, and Richard Hughes exemplified an art that had "lost its sense of values."

Outside the realm of professional reviewers and critics, *Sanctuary* received a different reception. A notice of the novel in the University of Illinois student-run newspaper the *Daily Illini* referred to J. B. Priestley's on-campus lecture-diagnosis that Faulkner was "in need of medical attention. Personally, I cannot see that this objection, even if true, is anything against his work. Do we object to Dostoieveski on the ground that the morals of a dementia praecox are detrimental to our youth?" The paper published a review of *Sanctuary* written by a female undergraduate, Mary Morris, on March 15:

> Do you recall how often you have begun to read a book which so fascinated you that you plunged through the intricacies of its plot to an unknown but magnetic ending? And when late at night you closed the last cover as you breathed a sigh of relief that the heroine was saved from a perilous attack? I have done just that. But, this time, when I finished *Sanctuary,* it was different. I didn't have a feeling of relief because the heroine had not been saved. I didn't have a feeling of assurance. Rather, I closed the last cover slowly as I realized that the book contained more than the mere words of black print on white pages, that the book contained a potent drug for the imagination—that the book would never be finished by reading the final word but would require a tallying of events before finding out just exactly what had occurred. *Sanctuary* is different. I read bits of it aloud to my roommate and we were both caught in the whirlwind of its spell and swept along. I couldn't cease reading—she couldn't cease listening. My throat became dry; my eyes blurred; before I knew it, I had read 50 many pages aloud.

We might as well be in that dormitory room in *Absalom, Absalom!* with Quentin and Shreve energized over figuring out what happened to Thomas Sutpen and his family. This coed's response to *Sanctuary* suggests that Faulkner attracted a much broader and more understanding audience of readers than the professional reviewers had the capacity to imagine. This undergraduate is familiar with conventional popular stories and is aware of how far Faulkner departs from women's domestic fiction. She does not call Faulkner gruesome, sordid, or crazy. Instead she welcomes his deviation from the norms established by the mainstream print media. She has no concern with the morality of the novel over which critics fretted. What captures her, instead, is the work's compelling style. Her reading may be outside the range of most early responses to the text and to Faulkner, but it is just as likely that he was beginning to attract readers whose experience of fiction was not represented in the public prints. At the same time, she shows why the novel became a bestseller—not simply because it was sensationalistic in its treatment of sex and crime but because it was gripping in a way the readers of popular fiction demanded. If reviewers recoiled from certain scenes in

Sanctuary, they might have been having the kind of visceral reaction that this coed valued for its own sake.[11]

THE HOME TOUCH OF INTEREST

Most people in Oxford did not read the novel. Some who did were disgusted. "Now you know you weren't raised that way," his cousin Sallie Murry told him.[12] "Do you think up that material when you're drunk?" she asked. Faulkner gave her a sober look and said, "Sallie Murry, I get a lot of it when I'm drunk." An outraged Murry Falkner who spotted a coed with the book in her hand said, "It isn't fit for a nice girl to read." To a university secretary, Murry said: "It's trash. Don't waste your time on it."[13] Bill's brother Dean seemed to get some amusement out of mocking Murry, solemnly saying he could not procure a copy for a female friend because it was "not fit for a young girl." Maud Falkner told people to leave her son alone about his work. She shut them up: "My Billy writes what he has to write." To her husband, she said the same thing, adding, "Let him alone."[14] Professor Calvin Brown, a Faulkner friend, said to his wife, "Now, why would *anybody* write a book like *that*?" The Oldhams were aghast, and Faulkner had some explaining to do, saying to Estelle's sister Dorothy that he "had to do it" to make money. He advised her not to read the book and that he would bring her one that would suit her.[15] Lem Oldham said, "If he writes another book like that, I'll have to get him out of the penitentiary or put him deeper in."[16]

John Faulkner believed that his brother, "a tender man," placed a shell around himself to protect his feelings: "Bill could not stand the hurt of adverse criticism. He simply refused to hear it. Except on rare occasions, he wouldn't even talk to anyone about his writing. . . . When I first started writing, he told me never to read a review. He did not explain why. I know now." William Faulkner stood alone with his writing, John wrote: "A criticism of it is a criticism of him."[17]

But there was another Oxford and another William Faulkner, seemingly separate from the author of *Sanctuary,* who nevertheless could probably not have written the novel without certain sources of hometown support. Perhaps only one reader in Oxford, Phil Stone, one of the inspirations for the "lawyer-artist manqué" Horace Benbow,[18] was qualified to judge Faulkner's treatment of the source material for *Sanctuary.* Stone did not seem to resent his likeness to the ineffectual Benbow, perhaps because he knew himself well: "I'm like an elaborate intricate piece of machinery which doesn't quite work."[19] To scholar Robert Daniel, Stone wrote: "I really suspect that I am the original of Horace Benbow. It is so much trouble getting details out of Faulkner in oral conversation that I long ago gave up trying to find out." Even with a friend, the author maintained his trade secrets.[20] Phil and Bill had visited whorehouses together, although Stone said Faulkner, like Popeye, did not partake. Phil remembered a prostitute propositioning Bill, who replied, "No, thank you, ma'am; I'm on my vacation," an amusing conceit implying he had come to a whorehouse for a holiday from sex.[21] Stone had no harrowing stories to relate about those visits to brothels, making it all seem more like Faulkner's later mellow rendition of the rendezvous with Miss Reba in *The Reivers,* insisting that the women looked like "middle-aged Baptist Sunday School teachers," although conceding that the madam was "fat and flamboyant."[22]

Oxford had no bookstore, but the local druggist, Mac Reed, a Faulkner friend, sold the books on consignment. Faulkner deemed it a great favor since "anything without pictures, selling for more than 50 cents is indeed a drug here." The "book-author," as some referred to him, supposed that a few might buy copies of his book, but "I'd not like to deprive them of their Tanlac and Pinkham's Compound by tying Mr Reed's capital up in books."[23] Jimmy Faulkner called Mac "the epitome of a southern gentleman," and a "real close friend" of Jimmy's uncle: "Real close. I don't believe the man ever had a bad thought in his mind." Reed had been an artillery officer in World War I. Sergeant Reed had attained local fame celebrating Armistice Day in 1918 by shooting an anvil: putting two anvils together, one upside down on top of the other to form a hole into which packed gunpowder exploded with a cannon-like sound "loud enough to make stock break out of the lot."[24] When Congress passed the Soldiers' Bonus Bill, Reed refused his award, saying it had been enough of an honor to serve his country.[25]

Reed had come to work at the Gathright Drugstore on Sunday, July 1, 1923, and first met William Faulkner a few days later in the company of Phil Stone, Reed's schoolmate. Reed remembered Faulkner as "wholesome. He spoke as if he were interested in knowing me." Sincere, loyal, and gracious are the words that came to mind, said Reed, "just a home touch of interest there that I thought was appealing from the very beginning." Reed had lost a brother who wanted to be a writer, and he quickly identified with the Stone-Faulkner duo. Even better, Reed, a diplomat by nature, never judged Faulkner or his friends. Mac "only needed to be fitted for wings to fly up to heaven," Phil Stone said.[26] Over the years Reed watched Stone, who had always done so well in school, answer Faulkner's questions, and "if he couldn't find the answer immediately he would give him a reference almost without having to look it up himself." And when it came to points of law, no one could outdo Phil Stone, Reed believed.

Reed had vivid memories of what it was like during the Depression: "it was just so dead. . . . We just went right from bad to even worse as time went on. Faulkner arrived at the drugstore with a gold piece asking Reed for ten dollars, without saying when he could redeem the coin. Reed went to the cash register and gave Faulkner the money. People were utterly desperate back then," and Faulkner felt for them in quiet, unobtrusive ways. After a death in a family known to him "he would come by the house where the people lived. . . . I don't believe I ever heard him offer a word of sympathy to anybody but he had a way of shaking hands with people maybe putting his hand on somebody's shoulder, and if there were great sorrow why he would somehow or other be close by. He might just go over . . . put his arm around somebody and use the words, old friend." On the square, Reed noticed, "the only thing that moved about him that anybody ever saw was his head. He would turn from right to left," also shifting from one side of the square to another, as if to get a better angle or to see someone he knew. "He just liked to see people moving," Reed said. Sometimes he would just look off into space thinking no one knew what, but sometimes you could see him greeting someone with a sign of pleasure. Reed liked to think his friend was wondering how that person "tied in with one of his characters."

Reed saw Faulkner in the mornings around seven, when the drugstore opened, coming in for his copy of the *Memphis Commercial Appeal* and maybe to get something to smoke. He rarely stayed long unless he had a prescription to fill. Then he would stand erect with his arms folded. Sometimes when the wait was as much as thirty minutes, he would walk over to the magazine stand, mainly looking for a new paperback mystery. He said little and just stood outside the drugstore watching human traffic. People who knew him—farmers and hunters, for example—adjusted their schedules to his if they wanted a word with him. At around eight he would head over to the post office.

Along with other Ole Miss authors, Faulkner's work was part of a drug-store display, which people liked, Reed said. "It was refreshing to them to have some literary activity with a local color," although some customers did not "get on to what William was trying to do or understand some of his writing." Even so, they had a "good business," especially with *Sanctuary*, he recalled. Customers wanted to know if Reed had read the book. Not yet, he would say, adding that he believed Faulkner wrote the truth "more vividly than many other people could." Reed disputed stories that the novel had been sold under the counter. It was there out in the open, with the other books. But it was the kind of book you might send one of your servants to purchase.[27]

By the spring of 1931, close to seven thousand copies of *Sanctuary* had been sold, outpacing Faulkner's last two novels combined, and doubling the number of reviews his previous books received.[28] But Faulkner received no royalties because Smith had gone out of business, with debts he could not repay his partner, Jonathan Cape. Faulkner told Reed that he had received no money from his publisher "in over a year . . . due to the hard times."[29] He had yet to receive a payment from an English magazine for a short story, and he had only one other source of income: a forthcoming check from *Scribner's Magazine.* "Our bereavement last month, including the hospital bills, exhausted me financially," Faulkner wrote Sallie Bailey. In short, he could not make the March 1 payment on Rowan Oak. If she could wait until April 1, he believed he could send her $150, a double payment: "This is not business; I know that. By our contract, my failure renders the contract void, and, I believe, voids my title to the house. However, I cannot help myself." He was sorry to have put his claim to Rowan Oak in jeopardy and said he would understand if she wished to enforce the "letter of the contract. . . . You are within your rights, to which I agreed." He signed himself "respectfully and regretfully yours, William Faulkner."[30]

Faulkner's sincere letter expressed his humiliation. On March 2 Miss Sallie replied that she appreciated his situation and acceded to his request: "I know what illness and hospital bills mean too, and sympathize with you very much. I hope Estelle will soon be her sweet self again. . . . Mr. Will asks to be remembered to you both." They knew William Faulkner was as good as his word. He wrote on April 5 to Mr. Will, thanking Miss Sallie for her kindness. But now matters were even worse, so that he requested a delay in payments until September 1. He was going to New York to try to get something out of his publishers and to understand why his short stories had suddenly stopped selling. To save on expenses while in the city he wanted this postponement of payments, expecting that away from home he could arrange a year's income stream: "My troubles appear to have descended upon me all at once, but I believe that with a—call it breathing spell, a chance to get to where my money comes from and see to things myself, I can get into shape again."[31]

Once again, Mr. Will and Miss Sallie assented, prompting, on April 12, an unusual expression not merely of gratitude but of solidarity in their plight as Mississippians: "I still have in the back of my mind THE novel of Mississippi, of the action and reaction upon one another of white and red and black men, the scene to be laid in those days. That was when Mississippi WAS; integral, both its own father and its own son. Since then we have been but the appendage of the damned Yankees who set the price on cotton and force us to raise it—or starve. (You might say, and starve.)" He had not left home yet, still in "a breathing speed in which to gird my loins, as the Book says."[32]

Faulkner never seems to have considered the other way writers made money: publishing reviews and delivering lectures. But then he never wanted to trade on his reputation as a writer, and the thought of subordinating his time to critiquing the work of other writers could not have been appealing. He would never prove to be much of a public speaker, and he did not care for the attention that lecture tours invited, even though income from such extracurricular activities could yield thousands of dollars a year in income. Interviews were the closest he could come to such writing-related labors that would help to promote his own work. When he wrote *Sanctuary,* he hoped not only for huge sales but also expected the requisite attention. As Phil Stone insisted even as Faulkner did his first important interviews: "We have seen so much of the effect of contemporary literary propaganda and have seen stupidity and poor work proclaimed so often that he and I have always been sure that the present furor would arrive in time."

The furor, however, produced little income for Stone or Faulkner. On June 17, Stone wrote to E. Byrne Hackett, owner of the Brick Row Book Shop: "Bill is already one of the leading figures in American literature. He is already established and his reputation is going to grow because the achievement will be forthcoming." Stone, hard-pressed during one of the direst moments of the Depression, was selling four autographed copies of *The Marble Faun,* noting that Faulkner rarely gave autographs, except to family and close friends, and his only book of poetry was bound to appreciate in value, one having just been sold for twenty-five dollars. Stone added that Faulkner, who fondly remembered Hackett from their days in New Haven, wanted the book dealer to have the first opportunity to offer the four signed copies for sale. But Hackett apparently did not purchase any copies, and another Stone letter of July 29 to a book collector also yielded no results, as Stone reported to Faulkner on November 2: "Try your best and see if you can't get up some buyers for 'Marble Faun.' I simply must have some money."[33]

Stone was not exaggerating Faulkner's newfound fame. Faulkner appeared in the *Brooklyn Daily Eagle's* book gossip columns as the master of "frank decadence" (July 22, 1931) and a recluse who rarely ventured among the literati. Fragments of Faulkner's biography filtered through the press: "William Faulkner, who wrote 'Sanctuary,' had a great-grand pappy who wrote fiction about the glorious old south. One such effort was *The White Rose of Memphis,* which some authors rewrite at stated intervals even yet," the Illinois *Daily Alumni* reported on August 7.

On December 14, the first item in a *Daily Eagle* column entitled "Odd and Interesting" announced, "William Faulkner is the newest literary light for whose first editions collectors are scrambling." Not judging by Phil Stone's efforts. He placed an ad in the *New Republic* for those *Marble Faun* copies without success. The boom in Faulkner first editions did not, in fact, begin until the 1950s. And Stone's problem was Faulkner's as well. Stone had lent money to Faulkner over much of the past decade. Faulkner's best hope of paying back the loans, he told Stone, was to sign those editions of *The Marble Faun*.[34] What looked like a success in the public prints seemed an entirely different affair to the author and his associates.

On July 10, the *Memphis Press-Scimitar* published the first extensive interview that began like a Hollywood press release of biblical proportions: "A GREAT VOICE CRYING in the wilderness—the literary wilderness of Mississippi—that is William Faulkner." The novelist had "shot from obscurity to fame in the last few months." Seventy-five miles south of Memphis lived "the man whose praises the New York critics cannot sing too loudly." The rudiments of the Faulkner persona were already intact: "He is dark, small, keenly alive, virile and as he might term it—touched with a little sadness and a mild sense of frustration." Faulkner's novels were quickly introduced, with a few sentences about how he wrote them, and the difficulty of getting published. The reporter, Marshall J. Smith, sketched in his subject's spurious combat record, European sojourn, postmastership, and residence at Rowan Oak. Its antebellum origins and "simple wooden columns lend a gentle dignity" to a self-effacing author who eschewed literary talk for stories about fishing and hunting. Faulkner's marriage is mentioned, but Estelle is otherwise written out of the story.

Faulkner supplied biographical details in a southwestern folk humor vein, saying, "I was born in 1826 of a negro slave and an alligator—both named Gladys Rock." The humor masked his hostility: "About the biography," he wrote Ben Wasson in the spring of 1930, "Don't tell the bastards anything. It cant matter to them. Tell them I was born of an alligator and a nigger slave at the Geneva peace conference two years ago. Or whatever you want to tell them."[35]

A longer version of the Smith interview, published in the *Bookman* in December, added homely details such as an unshaven Faulkner bottling beer in his kitchen even as Smith lauded a "new luminary . . . in the very darkest part of the South." Looking for the dramatic, Smith discovered the mundane, the author of *Sanctuary* "squatting on the floor beside a cracked churn siphoning scummy homebrew out through a piece of hose into second-hand ginger ale bottles." Smith believed this Faulkner was a persona, a "barrier . . . he places about the sensitive part of him" that went into the novels. Smith said they smoked, drank beer, and talked Mississippi politics. Alas, what Faulkner made of Bilbo's state Smith did not relate. The most Faulkner would say about his work was that he had made only a beginning: "Perhaps in five years I can put it over. Perhaps write a *Tom Jones* or a *Clarissa Harlowe*." Anderson and Stark Young were given due credit for their encouragement. No mention of Phil Stone.

Smith displayed Faulkner's version of himself as farmer and common man, a recovering World War I veteran, ridiculing his exploits: "War came. Liked British uniform. Got commission. R.F.C. Pilot. Crashed. Cost British government 2000 pounds. Was still pilot. Crashed. Cost British government 2000 pounds. Quit. Cost British government $84.30. King said, 'Well done.' Returned to Mississippi." To Faulkner's flip résumé, Smith added a sober gloss: "The war hurt Faulkner. It took him time to recover." It may be a mistake to conclude that Smith was naive and took Faulkner's statements "literally."[36] It is in the nature of much profile writing that the price of access to the subject is just this kind of collaboration in make-believe. The journalist and his subject are creating a story together serving their mutual interests. The interview can be a form of play, although Faulkner often did not want to play, but an interview is a performance, one that allowed Faulkner considerable flexibility in self-presentation, which gave him ample room for maneuver—to present contradictory impressions as the occasion and the mood suited him.

The Smith interview in July caught Faulkner in between novels. A month earlier he had written to Ben Wasson about a possible trip to New York City in the fall. "I need a change. I'm stale. Written out."[37] But on August 17, he began work on "Dark House," eventually titled *Light in August*.

13

Fame

September–December 1931

⤳

DOING THE WORK OF GLOBAL HISTORY

In the *Philadelphia Record* (October 4), Edward McDonald sounded the alert almost better than a PR person:

> What, another book by William Faulkner! Yes, just that—his fifth since 1929, the year in which Mr. Hoover became President of these States.
>
> Howsoever things have recently stood with the rest of us, all has been well with Mr. Faulkner. He has in the last three years just about walked off with the literary show. In an amazingly short time he has with breathless speed risen to fame—or, if you will, to notoriety at least.

The country might be suffering through its worst depression, McDonald implied, but not William Faulkner. And McDonald didn't know the half of it—how Faulkner had scraped together a marriage and a home and career in spite of an economy that rewarded very few writers of his caliber. In fact, Faulkner's rise coincided with the rediscovery of Herman Melville, who had spent twenty years in obscurity in a customhouse job without a single salary hike. Faulkner, the ex–postal employee, had, however precariously, prevailed as a *writer*. And next to *Sanctuary*, *These 13* sold better than his earlier books.

Reviewers picked their favorites—most often "Dry September" and "Red Leaves," with "A Rose for Emily" receiving surprisingly little attention. No reviewer considered the book's structure or even supposed the book had one. Some were relieved at the accessibility of the stories, dubbed the "easy-to-read Faulkner" in the *Tennessean* (June 24). But no one seemed to notice that the

325

volume, divided into three parts, presented the range of Faulkner's fiction—from the war (part 1), to Yoknapatawpha (part 2), to the European setting of his travels (part 3):

Part 1: Victory, Ad Astra, All the Dead Pilots, Crevasse
Part 2: Red Leaves, A Rose for Emily, A Justice, Hair, That Evening Sun, Dry September
Part 3: Mistral, Divorce in Naples, Carcassonne

Faulkner would always resist the label of regionalist, and this collection suggests that the heart of his native land, like the middle of his book, can only be fully understood in terms of a wider world, set in England, France, Germany, Italy, and with allusions to Senegal and India. *A Rose for Emily and Other Stories* had been the titular title of his collection, but his ambition, as usual, had gone way beyond his initial proposal to Horace Liveright four years earlier to produce a book of stories about "my townspeople."[1] Now the townspeople were part of a much larger canvas, composed in third- and first-person points of view in a variety of styles that showed Faulkner could write like almost anyone and remain his own man.

The collection's title seemed to announce these were stories Faulkner would stand by. The book's structure mimics its author's trajectory. He had come out of the war and returned home to rediscover his native land and to write fiction about it, but not until he had been abroad did he conceive of putting Yoknapatawpha on the map. The volume's historical and geographical sweep, and its probing of race and class and the sexes, also reveals a capacious sensibility attuned to the provincial and the metropolitan in the experience of a man who had done his time in a small town and in the big city and had brought them together in his prose—in a story like "Hair," in which Hawkshaw moves his life from town to town as the story's never-named narrator, a traveling salesman, follows along, creating a story out of his fascination with Hawkshaw by interviewing townspeople about this laconic, middle-aged barber and his improbable relationship with Susan, a wayward teenager. The anonymous narrator's curiosity about the barber is reminiscent of the colloquies in "Mistral" (part 3) that concern the priest and his passionate attachment to his young ward in the Italian mountain town. It is Susan's hair, neither quite blonde nor brown, that attracts Hawkshaw, who has been faithful to the memory of his betrothed, Sophie, with similar hair, who died before they could marry. Hawkshaw may be a case of arrested development, but he also appeals to the romantic sensibilities of district attorney Gavin Stevens, who enters the story at the end, after the traveling salesman/narrator tells Stevens that Hawkshaw had fulfilled his promise, made many years earlier to Sophie, by making the final payment on her family's mortgage. Now Hawkshaw is free, Stevens suggests, to pursue his romantic dreams: "And he's not much over forty-five. Not so much anyway. Not so much but what, when he wrote 'Paid in full' under that column, time and despair rushed as slow and dark under him as under any garlanded boy or crownless and crestless girl." Not so much separates the barber from the teen-ager, as we learn at the very end of the story when Stevens announces to the returning salesman/narrator that Hawkshaw has just married Susan. The narrator is surprised. This is not where he thought Hawkshaw's story was headed, and this is the point of *These 13*'s sharp juxtapositions between stories that do not fit seamlessly but have to be got at from several different angles before they cohere. Small-town life is the perfect foil for Faulkner, because it is a place where barbers are supposed to talk, where everyone knows everyone else's business, and yet where, as his stories suggest, everyone remains something of a mystery. "Hawkshaw," a bemused storekeeper says the name in wonder in a town where the barber has been known as Henry Stribling until the narrator explains otherwise. "Is that what they call him?" the storekeeper asks. "Well, I'll be durned. Hawkshaw. Well, I'll be durned." The shifting identities of Yok-napatawpha are on a small scale the same as the shifting identities of time and place in the stories that occur outside its postage-stamp boundaries. Shortly after the publication of *These 13,* Faulkner included "Hair" among the stories to which he felt especially close.[2]

In part 1, "Crevasse" transforms a farm into a World War I battleground: "a field which a month ago was sown to wheat and where yet wheatspears thrust and cling stubbornly in the churned soil, among scraps of metal and seething hunks of cloth." This could also be, to begin with, a Civil War scene. The party of British soldiers, mainly Scots, traversing the terrain of war could easily fit into a Stephen Crane story that abruptly turns into an Edgar Allan Poe horror tale as a cave-in plunges them into the shifting ground of a burial pit in a chalky field of skeletons. They find a partly buried rifle dating back to 1914, its stock disintegrating, and then stumble on the remains of "Senegalese troops of the May fighting of 1915, surprised and killed by gas probably in the attitudes in which they had taken refuge in the chalk caverns." The Senega-lese, who were subjected to gas attacks until May 25, 1915, had been first used by the French only two months earlier. In this soiled and corrupted archive of war, the Zouave trousers on corpses also indicate a French presence. Shifting heaps of desiccated bodies and dirt dissolve the distinctions of nationality and race that are so rigidly maintained in the stories in part 2 such as "Red Leaves, "Dry September," and "That Evening Sun."

Michael Millgate was the first to see how Faulkner integrated the stories with a contrapuntal impact, separating in part 2 the Indian stories, "Red

Leaves" and "A Justice," by placing "A Rose for Emily" between them, and, similarly wedging "That Evening Sun" between "Hair" and "Dry September," even though Quentin Compson appears in "A Justice" and "That Evening Sun" and Hawkshaw in "Hair" and "Dry September." In short, Faulkner did not make the obvious choices in grouping his stories together but instead approached Yoknapatawpha by a series of detours with characters who reached across the stories, so to speak, appearing and reappearing at intervals, not in sequence, a method Faulkner would refine in *Light in August*. By avoiding simple linkages, Millgate argues, Faulkner made the reader recollect and configure the resemblance between stories and characters.[3] In effect, by seeking connections between different times and characters and locations, the reader does the work of the global history that fashioned Faulkner's sensibility.[4] Only one writer could have served as Faulkner's model: Joseph Conrad.[5]

By refusing to follow one story immediately with its matching counterpart, Faulkner also accorded full value to each individual story. "A Rose for Emily" ends with "a long strand of iron-gray hair," the sign that she has lain beside her long-dead, decaying lover. Yet Faulkner "resists the beckoning opportunity to follow the shocking conclusion of 'A Rose for Emily'—the last word of which is 'hair'—with the story titled 'Hair.'"[6] Like Miss Emily, Hawkshaw has been so devoted to his beloved that he acts as though he could turn back time, and he succeeds insofar as he secures another opportunity to love, even if it is difficult to imagine Susan acting with the fidelity Hawkshaw has shown to Sophie. "Hair," it might be said, is the comic side of "A Rose for Emily," although both stories are joined in the ironies Faulkner finds in romantic love. This collection of short stories drawn together by its interstices eluded reviewers and even most later critics, who have not seen or at least not been motivated to comment upon the subtle integrity of *These 13*.

THE HOUND DOG UNDER THE WAGON

Faulkner's first short-story collection had sold nearly two thousand copies by the end of September 1931. And he had become unavoidable—one of the new literary lights invited to a conference of southern writers in Charlottesville, Virginia. On September 24, he wrote to Professor James Southall Wilson, accepting an invitation to attend, noting Wilson's "pleasing assurance that loopholes will be supplied to them who have peculiarities about social gambits." This genial tone conveyed a vivid warning as well a prediction: "You have seen a country wagon come into town, with a hound dog under the wagon. It stops on the Square and the folks get out, but that hound never gets very far from that wagon. He might be cajoled or scared out for a short distance, but first thing you know he has scuttled back under the wagon; maybe he growls at you a little. Well, that's me."[7] Faulkner as hound dog would become a staple of his self-characterizations in the months to come. He promised to show up on October 23.

On the train to Charlottesville, he thought of Cho-Cho, about "taking her to New York with me soon. You know: having her at my mercy to talk history to; to tell her how Jackson won this battle here and that battle there," he wrote to Estelle.[8] Cho-Cho (Victoria) regarded Faulkner as her "special friend" and called him Billy. She claimed him for her own and regarded her mother as an "interloper."[9] This bond soothed Faulkner's uneasiness away from home. He had dedicated *These 13* to Estelle and Alabama, signaling that his child's death, however it had disturbed his marriage, had also brought him closer to home and family and the still ailing Estelle: "I dont think that I will need to tell you," he assured his wife, "to give my love to the children, any more than to tell you that you already have about 1,000,000 tons of it yourself. But I do, nevertheless. Get well fast, darling, darling, darling."[10]

The best part of the trip, the "fall coloring . . . Yellow hickory and red gum and sumacs and laurel, with the blue-green pines," was just "grand," Faulkner wrote his wife. Perhaps that favorite word, shared with Sherwood Anderson, prompted him to wire Elizabeth Prall Anderson, who now lived in Marion, Virginia. He got no answer and thought that perhaps "she is still mad at me."[11] He reassured Estelle, "The people here are mighty nice to me." But as Anderson understood, his protégé would feel the pressure:

> I think Faulkner's difficulty is ahead. I saw him at Charlottesville & told him that. They'll make an ass of him if they can, prying into him, boosting him—
> Then dropping him for another new man.
> There's the difficulty—to ride through that & forget it.[12]

In Charlottesville, Faulkner met up with Hal Smith, now in serious financial trouble but intent on holding on to his prized author and funding Faulkner's trip to New York, where, as he had told Will Bryant, he hoped to set up his career on a more lucrative basis.

At the two-day conference, Faulkner showed up with corn liquor and an aviator's cap, a relic from wartime service, he told playwright Paul Green. Before thirty-four writers, Ellen Glasgow rambled on about historical and fictional truth, with an apparently drowsy Faulkner murmuring, "I agree." When the professors took over, the proceedings became especially dull, Sherwood Anderson reported. Most people who met Faulkner remembered him asking where he could get a drink. To various comments addressed to him, he would softly reply, "I dare say." Anderson never saw him sober. Faulkner attended few meetings and skipped the excursion to Monticello. Literary talk made Faulkner feel "unlettered," one biographer suggests.[13] He just didn't seem to give a damn, others thought. Most accounts of his appearances probably describe more than he saw and certainly more than he remembered of the trip. He felt hemmed in and unwilling to share his trade secrets. The notoriety of *Sanctuary,* the awe *The Sound and the Fury* inspired in many of his fellow southerners, made him, as one reporter put it, "beyond doubt, the focal point of every gaze." That alone undid him: "You know that state I seem to get into when people come to see me and I begin to visualise a kind of jail corridor of literary talk," he told Ben Wasson.[14] Faulkner threw up on Ellen Glasgow when introduced to her.

The very idea of a writers' conference in a university setting was then something of a novelty. Most universities did not offer classes in creative writing, and southern literature was just beginning to attract an attention that Faulkner himself hardly thought it deserved. He had said as much to Marshall Smith and repeated the statement in Charlottesville: "Nothing of any real value is likely to come out of it [the South] in the next twenty-five years at least. The outstanding Southern authors of today are only the pioneers; their work is setting the pace, but not very significant in itself."[15] Karl calls the comments "facetious," but who knows?[16] The days when Faulkner might want to exchange ideas and receive encouragement had ended in New Orleans and were tossed overboard in *Mosquitoes.* He did not want to be regarded as part of a movement such as the Southern Agrarians, who had recently published *I'll Take My Stand,* their chauvinistic championing of the South. Faulkner had no significant exchanges with the Agrarians, except for throwing up on the new dress of poet Allen Tate's wife. What Faulkner made of others— like historian Ulrich B. Phillips, an apologist for slavery—is unfortunately unknown.[17]

Faulkner wanted to capitalize on *Sanctuary* even as he kept trying to preserve his privacy, which, he argued to a reporter, was part of an aesthetic of impersonality that would come to dominate the novel: "There will be no straight exposition, but instead, objective presentation, by means of soliloquies or speeches of the characters, those of each character printed in different colored ink. Something of the play technique will thus eliminate much of the author from the story."[18] The reporter seems to have caught Faulkner at the moment his past was turning into his future—the comment about the inks referring back to an edition of *The Sound and the Fury* in which the Benjy section would be inked according to time shifts and recurring scenes, and forward to *Requiem for a Nun,* with its play structure buttressed by a narrative written in a kind of cosmic voice, history objectified. The idea for the latter novel first came to him a year later, judging by a letter he wrote to Hal Smith.[19]

But what about "the personality of the author?" the reporter inquired. "Is not all writing interesting and important only insofar as it express the personality of the author?" Faulkner said, sounding like the T. S. Eliot of "Tradition and the Individual Talent," that the author, "all exclusive of the story . . . is dead weight. What is interesting in Dickens is not the way he takes things, but 'those people he wrote about and what they did.'"[20]

Paul Green, on the way to New York to see a production of his play *The House of Connelly*, invited Smith and Faulkner to accompany him. Away from the crowds, in Green's Buick, a loquacious Faulkner opened up, reciting Joyce's poetry by the ream and even reading from a draft of *Light in August*. What had bothered him at the conference, most likely, had been the expectation that he would perform, and he seemed bound to resist the demands Anderson said would be made. Faulkner's boozing was one way to ban the boosting.

October 26: In New York, the pressure resumed. Publishers like Harold Guinzburg of Viking Press, Alfred Knopf, and the new publishing firm of Random House, headed by Bennett Cerf and Donald Klopfer, hoped to lure the author of *Sanctuary* away from Smith's failing firm. Cerf had written Faulkner in early April, offering to send him several books of his choice and to say he wanted one of Faulkner's novels in the Modern Library series. Faulkner responded on April 15, suggesting *The Sound and the Fury*, with Evelyn's Scott's appreciation of the novel as a preface. Faulkner asked Cerf to send some Dostoevsky. Reviews mentioned the Russian as an influence, but Faulkner claimed not to have read him. "I would like to see the animal," and then he added a teaser postscript: "Also Joyce's PORTRAIT OF THE ARTIST. Is this asking too much?" Was it by accident that Faulkner requested just those two authors, the ones so often cited as influences upon him? He appreciated Cerf's "kind word" about *Sanctuary* and added: "I don't think it will be a choice of title that will hold any agreement among the three of us up."[21] For one hundred dollars, Faulkner wrote the preface to the Modern Library edition of *Sanctuary*, and for another four hundred dollars, he consented to a limited edition of his story "Idyll in the Desert," which Cerf published in early December 1931.

Hal Smith fretted that Faulkner, drinking heavily, had become vulnerable to side deals that Cerf and others might propose, so he paid for Faulkner's brief excursion on the steamer *Henry R. Mallory* to Jacksonville, Florida. Smith's intervention worked—temporarily. On the way back to New York, on a stopover in Chapel Hill, North Carolina, Faulkner, a jug of corn liquor in hand, kept saying to his hosts, "It's time for a jolly spot." He drank himself into Halloween night, confined at his own request to a room. Then he wanted out for a trip to the barber and a shave and, with pants pressed, "emerged rather dapper." Next he said he wanted to see a movie, but after watching Katharine Hepburn for five minutes, he said, "Let's leave, I want to talk."[22] He sobered up to speak with a college writing class in Chapel Hill. Professor Phillips Russell admired his guest's straightforward, unpretentious presentation. Faulkner also promised Anthony Buttita "Once Aboard the Luger," a "bum story," and some poems for his literary magazine, *Contempo*. Faulkner's freelancing—consigning work without consulting his agent or publisher— would continue to complicate his career for some time.

By November 4, a sobered-up Faulkner returned to New York. A *New York World Telegram* reporter was on the scene to hail the conquering novelist: "The mysterious man from Mississippi cat-footed off the coastwise steamer Mallory at dawn today and ducked into a taxi." This profile, "William Faulkner, 'Literary Hope' from Mississippi Likens Himself in City to a 'Houn' Dawg under a Wagon,'" presented an enigma, a man who said he had one friend in the North, one man he liked. The "dog under a wagon" quip, what might be called a sound bite now, got picked up the next few days by more than thirty newspapers, especially in the Northeast and Midwest, but also in the South and as far away as Honolulu.[23] Faulkner had actually used the term "spring wagon," which described "an important vehicle in the late horse-drawn era. Built with two removable seats, its practicality made it popular both in rural areas and in cities and towns where, with a single seat, it served as a business wagon. Many spring-wagons had fringed, canopy tops."[24] In 1931 many readers probably did not need an explanation. At any rate, Faulkner cultivated an image of a down-home country boy who had nothing whatsoever to do with the highfalutin' literary world while at the same time exciting readers with the idea that the stealthy author had been exposed, following the Cary Grant rule of stardom: Always play the role of the pursued, not the pursuer. So he appears in Anthony Buttita's memory of the fall of 1931 after *Sanctuary* became a sensation: "Publishers who had turned him down on previous books were flashing contracts in his face. It made Bill dizzy. He fled south."[25]

In New York, on November 4, Faulkner settled into the Hotel Century on 11 West Forty-Sixth Street, writing Estelle about a movie agent who told him he could make between $500 and $750 a week in Hollywood. A trip west would do "*you* a lot of good," he assured her. "We could live like counts at least on that, and you could dance and go about." Hal Smith was against it, but Faulkner suggested he might as well "hack a little on the side and put the novel off." He did not say how, but he was already $300 to the good and expected to stay in the city for at least another month.[26] On the same day, he sent Will Bryant a note: "The enclosed check pays us up for the balance of the year—that is, until September 1, 1932, as per our talk. Thank you. With kindest regards to Miss Sallie and yourself."[27] The "us" could have referred to Bill and Estelle, but it might just as well have been meant for Will, who seemed less like a creditor and more like a partner in Faulkner's devotion to Rowan Oak.

The next day, he lunched for the first time with his French translator, Maurice Coindreau. Over the next thirty years, Coindreau wrote, Faulkner remained invariably cordial, "consistent with himself: not talkative, I admit, but always courteous, somewhat ceremonious, never giving me what I did not expect of him, but nevertheless surprising me at times by spontaneously telling me what I wanted to know but would not have dared to inquire about." This was not the same Faulkner others experienced, Coindreau noted, but one of "several Faulkners."

One of the other Faulkners showed up for an interview published in the *New York Herald Tribune* (November 14) with the headline "Slavery Better for the Negro, Says Faulkner."[28] This paternalistic parry to the reporter's insistent questions reflected Faulkner's annoyance, it has been suggested. The offended novelist assumed "a tone of deadpan, hostile irony" as a defense against "invasions of his privacy."[29] As the narrator of *Absalom, Absalom!* might say, the observation may be "true enough," but this is also the Faulkner who wrote *Flags in the Dust,* in which the Negro characters, as they would have been called then, are presented with a somewhat paternalistic air not entirely out of keeping with the Faulkner who told the *Herald Tribune* journalist that he pictured "a kind of 'benevolent autocracy' as the ideal condition for the Negroes." Faulkner had been exposed to just this sort of thinking in school: Slaves were better off in slavery than in Africa; slave owners believed they could take better care of slaves than the slaves could take care of themselves. Reconstruction had proved that black people could not govern themselves.[30]

A Faulkner letter in the *Memphis Commercial Appeal* (February 15, 1931) does not seem the product of drinking or of an effort to rile up a reporter. Captioned "Mob May Be Right," and signed "William Falkner," using the family name he had abandoned more than a decade earlier, the letter condemns lynching but adds: "I have yet to hear, outside of a novel or story, of a man of any color, and with a record beyond reproach, suffering violence at the hands of men who knew him." The letter reflects standard Falkner family sentiments as stout defenders of Reconstruction myths that supported vigilante justice and the murder of lawless black people. In his letter, "Falkner" aligns the post–Civil War lynchings with the invasions of New Englanders who had a history of "hanging people whose conduct they did not approve." This is the still unreconstructed southerner whom Hubert Starr met at Yale in 1918. Faulkner drew on myth, not history, for the belief that good black people were not lynched, when, in fact, they were often strung up because of property disputes with white people encroaching on black-owned land, for bad debts, and for even more trivial matters.

If any of his New York friends challenged Faulkner's beliefs, their objections have not been recorded. They all seem to have feted him. As he wrote to Estelle: "I am writing a movie for Tallulah Bankhead. How's that for high?" She had been to school with Tallulah and did not like her. Bankhead was a beauty but too crass and boisterous for Estelle, even though Estelle, too, had a histrionic personality. The actress had made her name first on the London stage in the mid-1920s and just a few years later began to appear in Hollywood films. Faulkner had signed a contract that could bring in as much as ten thousand dollars, he said, for an outline, synopsis, and screenplay. The elated author announced, "I have created quite a sensation." At luncheons and dinner parties hosted by magazine editors and publishers, he had "learned with astonishment that I am now the most important figure in American letters." Sinclair Lewis had touted Faulkner in his 1930 Nobel Prize address, and Theodore Dreiser wanted to meet him. H. L. Mencken had famously declared the South a literary wasteland but had traveled from Baltimore to see Faulkner, who assured Estelle that he remained "level-headed." But he did want to impress Cho-Cho with the fact that he had dined with Jack Oakie and was going to meet Nancy Carroll.[31] Oakie, called "America's Joyboy," appealed to children because he looked like an overgrown kid who flummoxed adults. Adept at sight gags, especially triple takes, he had appeared in the musical *Sweetie* (1929) with Nancy Carroll, an early star of the talkies with a huge fan base. Faulkner mentioned a dinner party with Pauline Lord, the acclaimed actress who starred in the first New York production of Eugene O'Neill's *Anna Christie* (1921). In London, she had received a half-hour ovation for her performance. She had flattered Faulkner, telling him, "I'm famous, too."[32]

In the 1920s and 1930s, writers enjoyed a centrality in American culture that no longer obtains. In 1923, British novelist and critic Rebecca West, the lover of world-famous H. G. Wells, arrived in New York on a luxury liner with the press awaiting her. Joseph Conrad received the same reception. Scott Fitzgerald and Ernest Hemingway and Amy Lowell made the pages of even the smallest regional papers, all of which quoted writers, retailed anecdotes about them, and touted their books. Faulkner enjoyed the same celebrity status. Hollywood's interest in him signaled another "high."

What did Estelle make of her husband's almost gushing letters, revealing a side of himself he carefully concealed in the company of others? He wore his fabled aloofness like a mask reminiscent of Dion Anthony's in *The Great God Brown* (1926). Anthony, an artist called Billy, adopts a cruel and cynical mask that protects a sensitive artist. "O'Neill had the right idea in *The Great God Brown*," Faulkner told an acquaintance in New York, suggesting that the masks "express emotion in a way no human being could express it. Maybe that's the way all plays should be done."[33] Did Estelle suspect that in Billy, aside from those proclamations of success, there lurked a desperate man overwhelmed by sudden fame?

Faulkner took some comfort in making new friends. A great admirer of detective fiction, he enjoyed meeting Dashiell Hammett, another hard drinker who seemed nearly as prolific as Faulkner, publishing *Red Harvest* (1929), *The Dain Curse* (1929), *The Maltese Falcon* (1930), and, in the spring of 1931, *The Glass Key*. Over the previous decade he had published dozens of stories in pulp magazines, but he aspired to the Parnassian heights Faulkner had already scaled. He found Faulkner's claim that *Sanctuary* was written for money deeply upsetting and tried to argue Faulkner out of such a flippant derogation. Hammett looked as spare and hard-boiled as his prose. At over six feet, he towered over Faulkner. These two men of very different styles and looks liked to wear tweeds. They shared powerful feelings about corruption and were relentlessly unsentimental. They were on the same team. Lillian Hellman liked to watch them, "drawn to each other without either having any jealousy of the other as a writer, both respected the other as a writer and as a literary man."[34]

Lionized in literary society, Faulkner and Hammett stood apart, ostentatiously scorning flattery. At a Bennett Cerf party that November in New York, they showed up together and promptly passed out. At another party Faulkner refused to sign the first editions brought to him by Alfred Knopf: "I only sign books for my friends." The emollient Bennett Cerf coaxed the recalcitrant novelist to reconsider. After a moment, Faulkner relented: "Well," he said, "Mrs. Knopf has been very kind to me, so if you want to pick out one of them, I'll inscribe it for you." The reply is telling: only one begrudging autograph and only for the lady. Faulkner never misbehaved except when drunk, said Cerf's business partner, Donald Klopfer: "Faulkner was one of the greatest gentlemen that I've ever met. He was truly a gentleman. He always called my wife 'Miss Pat.' He always behaved himself when she was around. He was punctilious about manners and appearance, everything like that. . . . He was an idiot when he drank. You wouldn't be able to understand him even. He talked sheer nonsense and passed out, and we had to dry him out any number of times."[35] Did drinking disarm the gentlemanly armor that usually protected Faulkner but also burdened him with the wearying obligation to be polite to people who wanted something from him? Self-disgust may also have been involved. Both Faulkner and Hammett wanted to believe that only their writing mattered, not what publishers thought, and certainly not what parties they attended or whom they ought to appease. So they showed up but still registered their passive-aggressive protests. It was not manly to cater to this crowd, but at least they could escape emasculation by drinking man-to-man. Isn't this what Gowan Stevens does? He drinks like a gentleman, he says, but he drinks, in fact, to pass out, so that he does not have to defend Temple or oppose Popeye and his ilk.

Faulkner and Hammett had something else in common: a woman who could drink with them. To be sure, the feisty Lillian Hellman did not resemble Estelle Faulkner. But Hellman was southern born—in New Orleans, no less—even if partly raised and educated in New York City. She had served her apprenticeship in Horace Liveright's shop and beginning with *Mosquitoes* had hailed Faulkner's genius. She went after the men she wanted, not letting her marriage to writer Arthur Kober slow her down. Hammett memorialized his bibulous, contentious liaison with Hellman in *The Thin Man* (1934). In 1931, he was about to begin working over drafts of Lillian Hellman's first produced play, *The Children's Hour* (1934), a rousing success with more than seven hundred performances on Broadway, getting her to tighten her structure and dialogue and toughening her up as a writer beginning to feel comfortable and competitive in the company of powerful male authors. Faulkner took to her even if her politics were far to the left of his. She had an outspoken nature akin to Leane Zugsmith's. Miss Lillian (two syllables please) could play the southern lady as well as Estelle but added zest to the performance with a New York moxie that made men admire and want to bed her. No one has ever adduced that she tempted Faulkner, but her demeanor, by turns flamboyant and decorous, made for compelling theater. She claimed that at this point, before her first fame, she was "shy" and "southern" and that Faulkner liked to call her "Miss Lillian."[36] The threesome spent long liquored nights together, if not as a ménage à trois, then as a trio of copacetic companions never bothered, so far as anyone knows, by the strains of male/female friendship and love that Hellman would so superbly delineate in her film *These Three* (1936).

Faulkner's adherence to Hellman had even stronger sources. In her black nursemaid, Sophronia, Hellman had the equivalent of Faulkner's Callie, a loyal and yet outspoken servant who seemed more like a second mother, providing affection and wonderful stories but also a critical perspective on the biracial world these budding writers had to negotiate. And like Faulkner in his fiction and nonfiction, Hellman in her memoirs and plays felt compelled to offer tributes to her black begetter. Bill and Lillian understood one another without even having to speak, I suspect. And what a comfort that had to be for a man who felt out of his element in New York. Hellman loved the company of men, and she could be as New York or as southern as you please.

Add to the Faulkner-Hammett-Hellman triune novelist Nathanael West, whom Faulkner first met during this heady period in New York. West had managed a New York hotel that accommodated Hellman and Hammett and other friends. Hellman remembered joining conversations almost every night about Thomas Mann, whom Faulkner would continue to extol over the coming years as the greatest living writer.[37] Later, out in Hollywood, Faulkner and West went hunting together. In *The Day of the Locust* (1939), a satirical West portrayed a phantasmagorical Hollywood that reflected a sardonic sense of the absurd that Faulkner shared with Hammett and Hellman as well.

Sometime in early November, Faulkner took his friend Eric Devine to a party at Dorothy Parker's suite in the Algonquin. Ben Wasson had first introduced Faulkner to the hotel. "He loved it," Wasson said, recalling that agent Leland Hayward, Wasson's employer, once told Ben: "I've just met William Faulkner and Popeye was with him." Hayward was referring to Anthony Buttita, "small and dark," who had accompanied Faulkner to the hotel after attending the Southern Literary Festival in Charlottesville.[38] By now, Faulkner had met several members of the Algonquin Round Table, two of whom, Parker and Alexander Woollcott, championed his work in newspaper interviews and on the radio. Devine recalled that Parker was in good form. She nudged a well-built journalist who walked by her and said, "Don't let your body go to your head."[39] Why Faulkner never submitted work to the *New Yorker,* so closely affiliated with Parker and the Round Table, is a mystery.

Woollcott deserves special mention for the way he linked Faulkner to his work. In *McCall's* (June 1931), Woollcott reminded readers of how *Sartoris* ended, with Faulkner's voice merging with the history of the Sartorises, saying there is death in the very sound of the family's name, "and a glamorous fatality like silver pennons downrushing at sunset, or a dying fall of horns along the road to Roncevaux." Woollcott took that image and applied it to his Round Table visitant: "I seem almost to see him—small, darkling, lame—standing quite still (like a soldier while Taps is being played) until the sound of those horns died away; then turning more than a little weary at heart and still, I think, somewhat bemused, to the task of chronicling the harsh new life around him." Isn't this the very image of himself that Faulkner had cultivated?[40]

Robert Lovett, a Royal Navy Service veteran, often invited Faulkner to the Algonquin Round Table. They were fond of Faulkner, Lovett remembered, for a "variety of reasons, including his talent." The impressive Lovett, a Yale man, and like Phil Stone, a Phi Beta Kappa, liked racing fast machines—motorcycles and cars. On one bombing mission during the war, Lovett had to manually dislodge a bomb stuck in his airplane's rack right over the target without getting sucked into the downdraft.[41] It became an incident Faulkner worked into his story "Turnabout," when a sailor unjams a torpedo as his boat drives directly at a German ship. Other details from Lovett appeared in the story finished at Rowan Oak just after the end of the year and published in the *Saturday Evening Post* (March 5, 1932). Lovett described the young men on torpedo boats: "They would go in over the mine fields, prow high, and make their run straight at the target ship." Lovett marveled at "those kids out in their cockle shells in all kinds of foul weather, with no rescue gear. Night after night." These same "kids" would be found drunk in gutters, and the dashing flyers would take care of these seamen who, in turn, found the pilots fascinating. Ben Wasson remembered Faulkner's reaction: "'Great God Almighty, Bud, think of those boys lying in that gutter—doomed.' He was haunted by it." A shaken Faulkner asked Wasson to spend the night with him.[42] Wasson told Blotner he did not stay the night, but in Wasson's memoir, he does remain with Faulkner and even falls asleep on Faulkner's bed.

But why was Faulkner so disturbed by the story that he wanted Wasson beside him? Faulkner, like Julian Lowe in *Soldiers' Pay,* had been left out of the war, feeling cheated at missing his moment of glory, and like other men who missed their war, he made one up for himself. At dinner in a French restaurant with Hilda Nauman, a copy writer introduced to Faulkner in an agent's office, he declared, "I'm a dead man." The war had used him up. Describing all the killing, he lamented: "They took away the only thing I could do." He took her to an Algonquin party, saying he needed her company, and afterward told her was going off to dinner with old war buddies. She went along, but they left early with no war stories to tell. The next day he called and said he had trouble sleeping and wanted to see her. She arrived to meet Ben Wasson and a few others who seemed like courtiers attending to a depleted Faulkner on his bed of woe. He seemed utterly different except for his glittering dark eyes. Apropos of nothing, he suddenly said, "If you will lie with me, it will warm me . . . maybe then, I'll sleep." It seemed biblical to her—like being invited into King David's bed. Taken aback, she said she had to return to work. His mournful gaze rebuked her, and she thought, "I had failed him." She thrust her copy of *Sanctuary* at him for an autograph. He glanced at her, lowered his lids, and turned his head away from her. She was dismissed.[43]

Literary society was for the decadent, and Faulkner apparently had to restore his own hegemony by playing the wounded king. In New York out came his grief, almost panic, of getting nowhere near what those torpedo men had experienced. But there is another kind of courage, a steadfastness that men like Ben Wasson demonstrated. In "Turnabout," Claude strikes the American pilot, Bogard, as not merely boyish but effete and, in short, incapable of the manly action required in war. Included in a bundle of gifts Claude sends to Bogard is a Japanese parasol and a yellow silk sofa cushion—not a manly offering—which Bogard drops off a wharf into the water. It is reminiscent of Faulkner buying the embarrassed Paul Green roses after they had arrived in New York City in Green's car. But Claude, in fact, is the better man, proving his prowess during the aerial bombing run Bogard takes him on, and on the sea in the torpedo boat attacks. Bogard learns a lesson about courage from an unlikely source—from the "girlish" Claude. And it was to the gay Ben Wasson that Faulkner turned on the night he took in Robert Lovett's story. Did Wasson accompany Faulkner and another friend, Owen Crump, in visits to New York restaurants and speakeasies that catered to a gay clientele?[44] Faulkner, it seems, identified with homosexuals as he did with African Americans—not because he was one himself but because they felt, as he did, left out.

Like a soldier, Faulkner traveled with his kit—all the necessities he could carry on his person—arriving in Farmington, Connecticut, at the estate Hal Smith had inherited from his Uncle Winchell. There Smith awaited Faulkner's reaction to the snooty butler, also named William. Faulkner entered without baggage in his trademark trench coat, an article he would wear throughout his life because he could put so much into its deep pockets but also, perhaps, because of its association with World War I. It became a matter of speculation as to how William the Butler would confront this "crisis"—a guest without an equipage. Smith crept up the stairs to peek into Faulkner's room: "William had laid out WF's things: a tooth brush, a razor, and pajamas on the bed—all having been carried in the huge-pocketed coat." All that could be remembered from the weekend was the punch they concocted out of every drinkable beverage in the house.[45]

Faulkner's drinking worsened toward the end of November. Ben Wasson wired Estelle to come to New York, apparently at Faulkner's request. Perhaps she could steady him, and perhaps, as Faulkner told Wasson, Estelle might ease her grieving over Alabama by a change of scene. On November 30, on her way to New York City, Estelle gave her first press interview with Marshall J. Smith for the *Memphis Press-Scimitar,* appearing with aplomb as an "animated, vivid person" with "friendly eyes": "Mrs. Faulkner prides herself in catering to her husband's peculiar relish for rare foods. Her curries and dishes she learned while living in Shanghai are the particular delight of the Mississippi author." One of Estelle's cousins, a close observer of William Faulkner, insisted that Estelle, after she returned from the Orient, never received credit for making Faulkner a more sophisticated man.[46] Now in New York, he needed her poise and savoir faire in social situations.

Estelle would seldom get a reporter, or even a biographer, to concentrate on her, which is a great loss not only to her but to an understanding of her husband. She preferred his novels to his stories, she told the *Press-Scimitar* reporter, asserting that *As I Lay Dying* was his best, although she believed his "greatest novel is yet to come." She said Faulkner had educated her, insisting that she read Joyce's *Ulysses* twice, and that had been a big help to her understanding of *Sanctuary*. She let on that it was not always easy living with a writer: "There are times when Billy will go into his workroom and stay for hours. He hasn't any key, so he takes the door knob off and carries it inside with him. No one can get in and he is quite secure." Faulkner wrote in the early morning in daylight. His room did not even have a lamp. "The reason I'm going to New York," she told Smith, "is to keep people away from him. He has an apartment on the 28th floor of a building and his last letter said that he liked it better, for he could forget the noise and see the sun and sky."[47]

Smith did not detect, or was simply not willing to say, that an enervated Estelle was hardly in a position to help her husband much. Ben Wasson watched her arrival in New York: "She seemed exhausted and her eyes were enormous in her thin face, but she was making every effort to be animated and was even a bit kittenish." Husband and wife eyed each other carefully in the taxi to their hotel.[48] Like Billy, Estelle could put on a good performance for public consumption when it was in her interest to do so. Apparently F. P. A., the columnist Franklin Pierce Adams, an admirer of "Spotted Horses," noticed nothing amiss, reporting in his diary on December 6 about an evening at Robert Lovett's with "Will Faulkner and his wife. . . . [S]he tell[s] us of life in the town of Oxford, in Mississippi [he made it sound a *long* way from New York City], and I found Will a soft-spoken boy, but I would know him for a powerful one at a glance even if I had never read a word ever he had written."[49]

Estelle's role varied depending on the condition and concerns of her husband. She watched and waited and was *there* when he needed her—even if her strength sometimes deserted her. She remembered her husband's sorry expression. Publishers were "pulling at him." He was very relieved to see her. He took her straight to the Algonquin, and when they got there he told her that he had nearly had it with all the pressure. During her week in the hotel, Peter Arno, a *New Yorker* cartoonist, called and invited Estelle to join him in his room for a drink. She declined. Afterward, she could not decide if her husband, in the room at the time of the call, was amused or annoyed. She preferred the bibulous Robert Benchley.[50]

Bennett Cerf watched her shiver as she gazed from an apartment window at the brilliant New York skyline. Estelle had gone into labor on a bitterly cold night. "When I see all this beauty," she said, "I feel just like throwing myself out the window." Cerf expostulated, "Oh, now Estelle, you don't mean that." She gave him a hard look and said: "What do you mean? *Of course I do.*" Estelle reportedly tried to jump out of an Algonquin window after a day of shopping with Dorothy Parker. At the Algonquin, Faulkner told Ben Wasson about the birth and death of Alabama, "a puny, little thing."[51] On this same trip, playwright Marc Connelly saw Faulkner slap a hysterical Estelle, apparently without anger or reproach, as if her behavior, in Blotner's words, was "something with which Bill was obviously familiar." She seemed to settle down immediately and resumed a normal conversation. Faulkner said nothing about it.[52] Set this curious incident beside an earlier draft of "The Brooch," carefully assessed by Edmond Volpe, who notes a different ending in which the husband does not attempt suicide but instead avoids looking at his wife, distraught over losing her child, as he stirs the fire in the fireplace: "This ending, like those of Faulkner's finest stories, creates a feeling that lingers, a feeling of sustained despair, of anguish that will go on and on."[53]

On December 10, at a Bennett Cerf party to celebrate the publication of *Idyll in the Desert,* he put on a record and asked Estelle to dance, and they did so for a long time. The publisher charmed her on that night. Ben Wasson wrote Cerf to tell him how much the Faulkners had enjoyed the party: "both liked you so much and appreciated all you did for them."[54]

On the train trip back to Oxford, husband and wife stopped in Baltimore to see Mencken, who joined them for dinner at their hotel. Estelle didn't like him and called him "crude." The two men went out and "got pretty well loaded." Faulkner saw Mencken the next day before departing for home.[55] How many times was Estelle called on for her support only to be deserted for her husband's male companions?

Back home by December 14, she put a photograph of Cerf on her mantle—to irritate her husband, Malcolm Franklin said. The shivering, the dancing away from Faulkner, are inescapably reminiscent of the estranged couple in "The Brooch." The photograph and the trip to New York signified something else as well. Her Billy was now a public figure in a way he had not been before, and the world was coming to call.

14

Home and Hollywood

1931-1932

Homebody

"Home again now, where it is quiet. The novel is going fine," Faulkner wrote on December 16 to editor Alfred Dashiell at *Scribner's Magazine*.[1] Two days later, Sam Marx at MGM sent a telegram to Leland Hayward, the renowned Hollywood agent and Ben Wasson's boss: "DID YOU MENTION WILLIAM FAULKNER TO ME ON YOUR LAST TRIP HERE, IF SO IS HE AVAILABLE AND HOW MUCH." In spite of Faulkner's initial enthusiasm about a lucrative Hollywood assignment, he hesitated—for several reasons, including, perhaps, doubts about his ability to perform well as a screenwriter. Agent Morton Goldman, an assistant to Ben Wasson, told Faulkner that "Night Birds," a two-page treatment for Tallulah Bankhead, was "very bad." Faulkner agreed he had written trash. He seemed, in Goldman's words, to "believe that movies had to be contrived and maudlin to succeed so he tried to meet that requirement." Goldman said the treatment was about a southern belle "inclined to go around to a lot of nightclubs." It sounded like "The Brooch," Carvel Collins thought.[2]

The risks Faulkner would take away from home—in New York or Hollywood—interrupting his work on *Light in August,* did not then seem worth taking. He put off another journey, explaining his decision to Bennett Cerf on December 27: "Xmas was quiet here. Estelle and the children are with her mother in town, and so I am alone in the house. I passed Christmas with a 3 foot back log on the fire, and a bowl of eggnog and a pipe and Tom Jones. That was a special dispensation, as I have been on the wagon since reaching home, and I shall stay on the wagon until the novel is written. It is going great guns."³ This sober-sided citizen of Oxford gave his second talk, on aviation, to the Rotary Club on January 26, 1932.⁴

At the end of the month, Henry Nash Smith showed up to do a profile for the *Dallas Morning News,* published on February 14. At Rowan Oak he met "a small man in a blue shirt and carpet slippers, standing before a coal fire in a front room." Faulkner sounded a little like Jason, telling Smith "how hard it was to get any work out of a colored boy and girl employed about the place because they would stand for hours, one holding a mop and the other a broom, gazing into one another's eyes"—although Smith saw the comedy in the complaint. Smith delicately noted the difficulty of easing into an interview with his reserved subject. Eventually Faulkner relaxed as he regretted the advent of billboards and electric signs—the blare and glare of modern life he would portray in *Pylon.* He described for Smith the two-story galleries that surrounded the town square: "the lawyers had their offices upstairs overlooking the courthouse and in the afternoons used to sit with their feet on the railing. Sometimes they chewed tobacco," Faulkner said, resting his feet "comfortably on a table." He stroked a smoke-colored kitten on his lap, saying, "Her mother went off and left her and I fed her with a rag soaked in milk."

Smith, understanding that Faulkner did not like intruding reporters, attuned himself to his subject's moods, and Faulkner reciprocated, treating Smith as a guest, telling him what Smith, like Coindreau, did not have to ask but what Faulkner knew the reporter wanted to know. So he showed Smith "a small typewriter table with curving legs, on which rested a sort of metal rack holding a completed page of manuscript." Sheets of "typewriter paper ruled in pencil" were also on the rack, although Faulkner wrote with a fountain pen in a "beautiful and almost illegible hand." Faulkner the craftsman showed Smith the finished product, pointing out, "I bind my own manuscripts."

The two men regrouped around the coal fire that Faulkner built up again as he deflected Smith's questions about Joyce's influence: "But surely you had some idea of modern experimentation with the technique of the novel." Smith knew he was pushing it, getting Faulkner to acknowledge "a sort of pollen of ideas floating in the air, which fertilizes similar minds here and there which have not had direct contact." *The Sound and the Fury* "simply grew from day to day."

Smith could not get Faulkner to talk about his wartime flying. "I just smashed them up," Faulkner commented, already trying to back away from the legend. That Smith had come from Dallas to Jackson in a trimotored cabin plane excited the Faulkner of the Rotary talk: "I'd like to have a chance to fly one. I was looking at the inside of one some time ago. They don't have the old stick—a steering wheel instead. I guess the plane couldn't be steered by one man's strength—they need a wheel with gears." The mechanics of flying fascinated a Faulkner who sounded like the reporter in *Pylon* who could not fly but wanted to go along for the ride.

About his writing, Faulkner said he worked "pretty early in the morning, and by 10:30 or 11 I'm through. But I can sit down and write almost any time. The stories seem to shape themselves as they go along. I'm working on two novels now, and it may take me two years to finish one of them." Two? *Light in August* and? Perhaps it was the Snopes material he was then fashioning into short stories. He summed up his development as a writer by saying he had gone through three stages, regarding "everything and everybody" as good, then in cynical reaction believing "no one is good," and finally that "everyone is capable of almost anything—heroism or cowardice, tenderness or cruelty."

Smith departed, having encountered a man as "unobtrusive" as General Grant, "not very much impressed with himself," and a little amused at the sudden enthusiasm for his work in eastern cities. Smith's last words captured the homebody: "He is much interested in the new draperies which Mrs. Faulkner is planning for the living room of their very fine old house, and he seemed prouder of the hand-hammered locks on the doors than of anything he had written." Smith had met the husband with a wife who could, on a daily basis, intrigue and delight him.[5]

Another caller, Anthony Buttita, came to collect the story and poems Faulkner had promised him for *Contempo*. Faulkner honored his promise but regretted it after Hal Smith objected. "I didn't realize I had a commercial value," Faulkner told Smith, who did not want to dilute Faulkner's stock in the marketplace. Faulkner felt like a hunted animal, he confessed to Ben Wasson, unable to help itself: "I dont know what in hell it is, except I seem to lose all perspective and do things, like a coon in a tree. As long as they dont bother the hand full of leaves in front of his face, they can cut the whole tree down and haul it off."

Faulkner apparently did not mention to his callers that a collection of his poetry, *A Green Bough,* was in production. "I won't bother you about the 'Poems' contract," he wrote Smith. "Give me the best you can, tho, I am going cold-blooded Yankee now; I am not young enough anymore to hell around and earn money at other things as I could once. I have got to make it by writing or quit writing." And his novel was "about finished," he assured Smith, who had now reorganized his firm as Smith & Haas, dissolving the partnership with Jonathan Cape. Chatto & Windus continued to publish Faulkner in Britain.[6]

In March, Random House published the Modern Library edition of *Sanctuary*. A growing sense of his marketability prompted Faulkner to think he could get five thousand dollars for a serialization of *Light in August*. But he did not act like a commercial author, telling Wasson he did not want a word changed: "This may sound not only hard, but a little swell-headed. But I can get along somehow if it is not serialized." It was not. Still, acting like a commodity, he husbanded his autograph, telling Paul Romaine, a bookshop/publisher of a Faulkner story, "Miss Zilphia Gant," in a Texas Book Club edition, that he would sign only a few copies: "I hate to be stingy, but the damned autographs are like cotton down here: the more you make the less it is worth, the less you get for it. And I have got to live on either it or cotton, and I cant make anything farming."

In April, nearing the end of his work on *Light in August,* which would not be published until October, Faulkner signed a six-week contract with MGM for five hundred dollars per week. Screenwriting now became imperative because Faulkner would never see the four thousand dollars owed to him for *Sanctuary*. Cape & Smith went into receivership and was liquidated in May. At the moment he had no income from magazine sales of his stories, and he had a five-hundred-dollar bank overdraft. A train ticket and an advance from MGM sent him west and to the most prestigious Hollywood studio.

SCENARIST

What did Faulkner know about filmmaking? He had a well-developed visual sense that could even be called cinematic in a novel like *Sanctuary*. By 1929 or 1930, he seems to have become a fan of Lynd Ward's woodcut novels, which were inspired, in part, by silent films.[7] Ward explained Harrison Smith's decisive response when the artist brought his portfolio to the publisher's office: "so enthusiastic and so complete that on leaving I seemed more to float than walk down the steps of the brownstone. I was buoyed up by the warmth of his words and the vote of confidence implicit in his promise of a contract in the next mail."[8] Cape and Smith published Ward's first woodcut novel, *Gods' Man,* in 1929, the same year as the appearance of *The Sound and the Fury*. In 1933, Smith published *A Green Bough* with Ward's woodcut illustrations, which Martin Cohen describes in terms that apply to cinema: compositions filled with the tension of "long rays and controlled curves; the cuts' size varies from page to page creating, along with intentional black-white imbalances, the reader's urge to press on rather than to linger with the energetic figures on each page."[9] "Black-white imbalances" is a suggestive phrase for a reader of fraught interracial confrontations in *Absalom, Absalom!,* a novel that in theme and coloration resembles Ward's second novel, *Mad Man's Drum,* which Faulkner pointed out as a favorite.

Gods' Man is like Faulkner's *Elmer,* a portrait of the artist, but even starker in its "depictions of good and evil on a Faustian theme," Art Spiegelman observes: "Our Hero, a destitute artist seeking fame and fortune, accepts a magic brush from a Mysterious Stranger. His rapid rise proves hollow, but he flees the corrupt City, meets a beautiful goatherd, and lives a life of Edenic beatitude until the Mysterious Stranger comes to collect payment and Our Hero dies."[10] The eruptions of the mysterious, dark strangers into the plots of Faulkner's first MGM scenarios may owe something to Ward's fable of the artist and its evocation of eruptive erotic forces.

Faulkner's own intricate sense of a visual text of the kind he had produced in his handmade, handsewn volumes made him particularly susceptible to Ward's drawing and to silent films with their emphasis on scenes and intertitles bound together into an art that some critics, like Rudolph Arnheim, supposed could never be surpassed by the talkies. In Faulkner's first treatments, the very spare use of dialogue that could be put in a sentence or two is reminiscent of silent movies.

"I saw a fine movie," Faulkner wrote to his mother in early April 1925, "'He Who Gets Slapped,' with Lon Chaney. Make Bob Williams get it."[11] Williams, the husband of Faulkner's cousin Sallie Murry, owned Oxford's Lyric Theater, which had originally been Murry Falkner's livery stable. Faulkner saw his first films in the Lyric. The critics concurred with him: "At the Capitol this week there is a picture which defies one to write about it without indulging in superlatives. It is a shadow drama so beautifully told, so flawlessly directed that we imagine that it will be held up as a model by all producers," wrote Mordaunt Hall in the *New York Times* (November 10, 1924). Worthy of Chaplin and Lubitsch, Hall concluded. Shadow drama is what Faulkner had attempted in *The Marionettes.*

The film is about a diminutive scientist, Paul Beaumont, duped by his tall and imposing patron, Baron Regnard, who claims the scientist's discoveries as his own. The Baron slaps Paul in a public meeting, evoking the laughter of their colleagues. Even worse, Paul's beloved has collaborated in the fraud that has led to Paul's humiliation. She tells him he is a fool and a clown, and, in a line that spoke to Faulkner, she scornfully asks what poor Paul has to offer her besides his silly face and books. The duplicitous female is a staple of Faulkner's MGM treatments.

Paul leaves the Baron and his female accomplice and becomes a "common clown," as one intertitle explains, turning his humiliation into a performance of "He Who Gets Slapped." In short, Paul becomes an artist, making art out of his misery. Intermittent shots of a laughing clown spinning a globe—the globe Paul once spun as he dreamed of thrilling the world with his discoveries—depict the mask of the artist having the last laugh. A hundred slaps a night and Paul laughs, becoming famous for his art, as one circus performer puts it. Lon Chaney, the man of a thousand faces, plays Paul as a dedicated, even maniacal artist, mobilized in silent film better than in any other graphic medium. During his act, in his mind's eye, Paul sees the faces of the jeering scientists as he performs in front of the laughing circus audience, amused at the clown who declares he will prove the world is round and gets slapped and slapped again by his fellow clowns when he apologizes and announces the world is flat. Every claim and counterclaim provokes slaps. Then Paul sees the laughing Baron in the audience. Paul has to say no more than "there is" for the slaps to come faster and faster, timed to the tempo of the convulsing audience and clowns. In a final humiliation the heart sewn to Paul's gown is ripped away and buried in the center ring as a mock funeral cortège enters to carry Paul away. The Baron comes backstage but does not recognize Paul in his clown costume or that Paul has divined that the Baron's purpose is to seduce Consuelo (Norma Shearer), Count Mancini's daughter, who has become a circus bareback rider. Consuelo awakens Paul's devotion and then his love, which he declares to her, only to be playfully slapped since she believes he is only joking. Rejected twice, as Faulkner was with Estelle and Helen Baird, Paul intervenes to prevent the Baron from marrying Consuelo, who has been essentially sold by her father, the impecunious Count. In a confrontation scene, the Count stabs Paul, but Paul has locked the doors to the room, where he releases a caged lion that mauls and murders the Count and the Baron. Paul staggers to the circus ring announcing that the world must have love and tragedy as he collapses in death—a "new act," one of his fellow clowns announces. Paul tells Consuelo he will die happy because she will be happy with her male bareback rider partner (John Gilbert). Paul's dying agony is also his joy and his art. It would not be surprising to have Paul repeat Faulkner's later refrain that between grief and nothing he would take grief, since Paul has made art out of his grief. He who gets slapped is the masked tragicomic artist, as Faulkner well knew. He also knew what heights film could attain as art.

On May 7, Faulkner's first day at the studio, he showed up bleeding from a cut on his head, the result, Sam Marx suspected, of drinking. Marx offered to get a doctor, but Faulkner said he had come to work. Dealing with a beginner, Marx wanted Faulkner to familiarize himself with the typical Hollywood product and then submit a treatment—not a fully developed screenplay but more like an idea for a film with scenes and some dialogue and a plot that other writers would perfect. In short, Faulkner, who said he had an idea for a Mickey Mouse film, felt trapped and already shortchanged. MGM could not make a Disney product, obviously. Did Faulkner have to be told this much, or was the Mickey Mouse idea a way of asserting his independence, no matter what? Disney films and newsreels were all he watched, Faulkner told Marx. But that was not true. Did he have in mind the visual inventiveness of cartoons that contrasted sharply with the crude and awkward action of many early talkies—retrograde cinema compared to what Faulkner had admired about *He Who Gets Slapped* seven years earlier?

On Faulkner's first day at MGM, Sam Marx assigned him to *Flesh* (1932), a wrestling picture follow-up to Wallace Beery's success in the prizefighter film *The Champ* (1931), for which he won an Academy Award for best actor. Faulkner said he did not know who Wallace Beery was, so Marx set up a screening of *The Champ*. The actor played crusty, lovable rogues. In the screening room, Faulkner asked the projectionist, "How do you stop this thing?" It is a curious remark, if it is exactly what Faulkner said. He certainly knew about film projectors as early as 1913, when they were cranked in the Oxford opera house. His question, at least in retrospect, seems portentous: How do you stop getting caught up in the mechanism of making movies? Suddenly, it seems, Faulkner realized he had committed himself to a means of production that put him onto the revolving stories of the movie industry, repetitious and utterly predictable, much as Charlie Chaplin's character in *Modern Times* (1936) would be trapped in the turning wheels of machines. At the twenty-minute mark, Faulkner said it was pointless to watch more since he knew how the film would end. He walked out.

After four days, with Faulkner a no-show, Marx wrote to the MGM legal department requesting the cancellation of the writer's contract. Then on May 16, Faulkner reappeared, telling an improbable story about wandering for a week in Death Valley. But in fact the adventure had been proposed by Hubert Starr, then practicing law in Hollywood. Starr decided to get his drunken friend out of Hollywood just as Hal Smith had earlier sent Faulkner to Florida to recover from an alcoholic binge. Along with another friend, Bill Elliott, Starr took Faulkner, then in hot flannels, to a J. C. Penney to get him outfitted for the desert trip. Faulkner emerged in white duck pants, as shown in Starr's photographs. Faulkner, still drunk, wandered away, and the two men had to catch up with him walking a block or so away from them. Then, at a hot spring in Death Valley, they immersed Faulkner, finally sobering him. He said that until his hot spring wake-up he had no memory of their journey. Starr believed that for the rest of the trip he managed to keep his friend away from liquor, but later Faulkner told him, "That's what you think." Starr remembered they stopped at Dante's View for a panoramic look at Death Valley. Starr estimated they covered something like six hundred miles in three days, enjoying the flowers and the quality of the light. It is no wonder that Faulkner could give Marx only the vaguest idea of where he had been during his absence.[12]

By May 19, Marx had reinstated Faulkner with the legal department and settled him into a studio building. Within a week he would begin turning out an impressive number of treatments. Now calmed down, Faulkner made a good impression on Bill Elliott's wife, then his fiancé. She remembered a beach scene when the waves swept her hard against the shore so that the top half of her bathing suit came off. Faulkner, dressed in a sport coat and reading a book, went out to pick her up, saying that when she emerged from the foam she looked like Aphrodite. She thanked him and said his comment reminded her of the dashing Sir Walter Raleigh. Faulkner's conversation, she remembered, often contained literary allusions, which is perhaps why her remarks, he said, interested him. He described himself as an Anglophile. At the beach he became quite animated and talkative. She visited Starr in the evenings at his house in Rustic Canyon and often found Starr and Faulkner playing chess. She called him a "lone wolf" and did not know he was married. Her husband wanted to be a writer, and she said Faulkner would look at Bill Elliott's work and make suggestions that Elliott had trouble understanding. Faulkner showed her a novel in progress (presumably *Light in August*), but she found his handwriting hard to decipher. He complimented her penmanship and seemed impressed with her style, saying to her husband that she should not be so self-deprecating. She found Faulkner penetrating.[13] He would pick up on the way people said things. She had lived in Africa and the Orient, and Faulkner seemed to enjoy her memories,[14] which, in an oblique way, he may have drawn on, along with Estelle's, in his earliest screen treatments of women living abroad.

Faulkner arrived in Hollywood near the end of the pre-Code era, when films began to back away from boldly exploring and exploiting sexuality and violence, capitulating to conventional morality. Films like *Laughing Sinners, Safe in Hell,* and *The Road to Ruin* (all released in 1931) would be impossible to make a year or two later. For a brief period, then, the neophyte scenarist would experience a degree of freedom in his choice and treatment of subject matter, suiting studio assignments to the emerging themes of his novels, even if, in the end, he capitulated to the ruling studio and Production Code stipulations.

From May 7 to June 16, Faulkner worked on four unproduced treatments. "Manservant," sent to the script department on May 25, is set in India but seethes with the cultural tensions that enliven Estelle's stories and the sexual innuendo that suffused pre-Code films. The action begins with Das, a Malay, packing for his master, Major Blynt, who is off to Calcutta to see the "woman in the photograph, whose reputation is well known" as a "high-class demi-mondaine." Already, Faulkner was following Sam Marx's injunction to "write for the camera."[15] In the initial intrigue of the opening scenes, Das is developed as Blynt's colored double: "We learn that between the woman and Das there is a definite affection. Das loves her because his master does. She depends on Das to take care of the man she loves." The following scenes develop the backstory of the woman in the photograph. Judy is an American who cannot cope with the "hysteria and fast living" of white colonials and goes "to pieces" after her husband dies. A year later she appears in Calcutta, recovering from an affair with a "shady" character and the trauma of losing her baby. After another period of promiscuity she meets Major Blynt and becomes as faithful as a wife. Das professes an inability to understand white people, and when he dresses in European clothing he is called "comical," and yet the transference of feeling that animates the Das-Blynt-Judy triangle, with Blynt at the apex, is reminiscent of the Charles Bon–Henry and Judith Sutpen triangle in *Absalom, Absalom!* with Bon at the apogee of a family fraught with racial tension. Faulkner had not yet, in film or fiction, figured out how to fulfill poor Paul's dying declaration in *He Who Gets Slapped* that the world must have love and tragedy. The words "shady" and "fast living" in Faulkner's treatment reflect the pre-Code clichés he drew on. Like Estelle, Judy is under the sway of her family as she tries, back home, to bury her past and recover from the loss of a child. Judy never speaks of her past to her father, who only knows "something tragic happened to her." Blynt, meanwhile, becomes a famous scientist. In a contrivance acceptable in a Hollywood melodrama, Blynt meets Judy's sister, Marcia, and visits her family estate, not realizing that Judy, who refused five years earlier to marry him because of her sullied reputation, is now home. Blynt has to fend off Marcia, who jumps into his bed in an impulsive moment that recalls Emma Jane's bold kissing of Needham Chang in "Star Spangled Stuff," except that the racial mixing of Estelle's story cannot be shown in a Hollywood film, although Das's romantic attachment to both Blynt and his beloved Judy is the subtext. Das knows and sees all, including the machinations of a maid in love with Blynt, who decides to poison him since she cannot have the Major for herself. The vigilant Das maneuvers to reunite Blynt and Judy but takes the fatal poison himself. Tragedy then becomes inept farce in Faulkner's treatment: a "CLOSEUP shows" a bottle "labeled 'Poison.'" The treatment is crude and undeveloped but also suggestive: "Das knows that if he were to tell Blynt the drink is poison, Blynt would not believe him." In the end, serious themes are sentimentalized: "ON SHIP—Judy and Blynt—they are married. They are taking Das' ashes back to the home which he had not seen in fifteen years."

On his first outing, for all his faults, Faulkner did a creditable job, providing many opportunities for the camera to view the action through windows and doorways, creating an intimate, invasive sense of watching and speculating on human behavior. Faulkner deftly deploys photographs and newspapers to heighten curiosity and reflect the passage of time. Using Das as the linking figure—the "whole plot hangs on his accurate guesses"—not only unifies action and theme but also presages the speculative dynamic, the watching and waiting that distinguishes novels like *Absalom, Absalom!* and *The Town*.

The speed and tenacity of Faulkner's work in this new setting is remarkable. The script department received his second treatment the day after he turned in "Manservant." "The College Widow" seems a reworking of "Night Bird," the two-page treatment he wrote for Tallulah Bankhead, in which the heroine goes out with undergraduates as a belle in the manner of Temple Drake and also Estelle, since she (the character is never named) is in love with an undergraduate her parents will not permit her to marry. She becomes involved with a mysterious older man who stalks her. Frightened, she flees and marries her first love, that undergraduate who has "now become successful." The scary older man returns, her husband shoots and kills him, the heroine miscarries, and she divorces her husband and is "now déclassé," like Judy in "Manservant" and a more extreme version of Estelle.

In nearly all of these early treatments, the elements of Faulkner's biography reverberate and reassemble in various combinations—in this case producing a "woman with a past, a dashing widow" who becomes a "night bird," consorting with "equivocal people." The menacing but enticing stranger is a Popeye figure. The death of a baby, the portrayal of a young woman, named Mary Lee in "The College Widow," who does not have "enough character to stick to" in a southern town, is the first time Faulkner sets a treatment in his native land. Another vital element is a dance floor, the scene of Estelle's triumphs, and the rendezvous Mary Lee has with her lover. Like Judy, like Temple, like Estelle, these women are drama queens, although they continually back away from their self-destructive gestures. Like Judy, Mary Lee is afraid to turn to her father, but on her own she is terrified in a scene reminiscent of Temple's terror at Lee Goodwin's place in *Sanctuary:* "Mary Lee is afraid to turn on the light. She is weak with terror; it seems to her she can hear the two men creeping about the dark house seeking one another." But unlike the Judy of "Manservant," Mary Lee is not redeemed, and the grim denouement would have been too much even for a pre-Code movie: "She now lives in an expensive hotel—she must get money to live on somehow, so she is the companion of middle-aged men at night clubs and such."

Faulkner's third treatment, "Absolution," delivered on June 1, seems even more autobiographical in its dealing with two friends, Corwin, the scion of an old southern family, and John, from a family "without social position." At the center of their lives is Evelyn, a young woman from a socially prominent family. John proves the more gallant and chivalrous of the two men, retrieving a ribbon Corwin has snatched from her. As John grows up, he realizes the implications of his low standing in society, which results in Evelyn's family choosing Corwin as her suitor. Like Estelle, Evelyn dares not oppose her family. Hurt and bewildered, John leaves town. In this case, the ostracized hero turns to crime and a "dissolute and vicious life."

In all these treatments, social underpinnings matter for males and females— as they did to the Faulkner who spoke at the Rotary, even if he, too, had to leave town. With time John comes to regard his attachment to Evelyn as "actually . . . an illusion of her from his childhood." And yet he cannot resist the "thought . . . that perhaps he might be worthy of her." These conflicted, ambivalent feelings were certainly familiar to Faulkner. John's attraction to Corwin resumes, even though they have been rivals, and Corwin, realizing Evelyn is unworthy, laments his estrangement from John. In the same squadron during the war, Corwin and John are unable to reconcile, and a drunken Corwin strikes John, who does not fight back. Later, John demands that Corwin repudiate his remarks about Evelyn's unworthiness, but Corwin refuses, and the men agree to an aerial duel, presumably so that John can defend Evelyn's honor. Corwin feels he has been in the wrong and is willing to hazard death in combat with the more experienced pilot. But John, again exercising forbearance, forces Corwin to land. But a determined and self-destructive Corwin ultimately makes John shoot him down in self-defense. John believes he has "slain" Evelyn's happiness, although he is not aware that she never married Corwin or that his death frees her to marry another. Returning home a war hero and no longer troubled by his low social position, John is startled to discover Evelyn has married, and then he intuits that Evelyn and Corwin were only lovers. She begs John not to create a scandal, and he agrees but is sickened: "He gave up the friend he loved for a woman who was not worth it." Returning to France, John draws a pistol from his pocket. "THE END." Bruce Kawin observes that "Absolution" "goes far beyond thirties . . . prototypes in its misogyny. It seems that the only way Faulkner could clarify the lifelong bond between Corwin and John was at the expense of Evelyn."[16] Biography, never an exact fit, nevertheless seems to barge in right at this point when Faulkner's marriage to Estelle began to drive Phil Stone away, who began a lifelong campaign of disparaging comments about Estelle. Faulkner's disenchantment with the feminine mystique provokes Kawin to note that "John judges Evelyn as Quentin judges Caddy, finding her betrayal of his image of female virtue so destructive to his concept of how the world had and ought to run that he is unable to continue living in that world."[17] So, too, does John commit suicide. "There is little difference between an elevated concept of Evelyn's virtue and an outright fear of women," Kawin writes, "and that fear turns quickly into condemnation when it develops that the virgin can be 'touched.'"[18]

Unlike previous treatments, "Flying the Mail," copied in the script department by June 3, is Faulkner's effort to work on a property already developed by other writers. It was supposed to be a Wallace Beery vehicle. "I am a sort of doctor, to repair the flaws in it," he explained in a letter to Estelle, sending home a hundred dollars to pay off debts. "I ran into Lawrence [sic] Stallings, whom I knew before in N.Y. He is a Georgian, author of 'What Price Glory' and he has given me some good advice about keeping my balance with these people," he assured her.[19] Like Starr, the stalwart Stallings, a World War I veteran who had lost his leg at Belleau Wood, provided some sense of continuity in a land that seemed rootless to Faulkner. Stallings often drove Faulkner around Hollywood and remembered his "great delight in recounting the nature and activities of the Snopes's," including the time they had caught and cooked and ate a two-thousand-dollar Pekingese.[20]

In "Flying the Mail," Beery plays an aging pre–World War I flyer, Wally, with a Marie Dressler female counterpart, Min. Dressler and Beery had been a hit in *Min and Bill* (1930). Earlier treatments were not as blunt as Faulkner's. He makes Wally and Min "longtime sexual companions." Min has been unable to get Wally to marry her. In fact, Wally already has a family and an adopted son, Bob, who stows away on Wally's plane, which is the start of their barnstorming lives together. Of course, an ingénue figures in this too, a sort of Caddy who becomes Bob's girl, although he does not know that she is Wally's daughter. When he finds out, he says she is sort of his sister, leading to the inevitable comparison of the Quentin-Caddy bond again, the association of deep passion with brother-and-sister love.[21]

Perhaps a story conference about "Flying the Mail" later filtered into a Budd Schulberg anecdote about Faulkner in Hollywood. A group of writers were told that the movie should open with a boy and girl "very much in love." The audience should know this instantly without it being said. No one seemed to have an idea about what to do. A silent Faulkner then wrote a few words on a piece of paper, folded it, and sent it forward to the writer leading the meeting. He read Faulkner's words aloud: "make them brother and sister."[22]

"Flying the Mail" foreshadows *Pylon* in treating aviation as a liberating force that collides with life on the ground, which does not permit the aviators the "freedom from history that many of Faulkner's characters find only in death."[23] Faulkner craved that sort of freedom, which made his talk on aviation to the Oxford Rotary such a curious gesture, like Wally's appearance before the "gaping crowd. The word precedes him, 'Here comes the aviator.' The people look at him as on some strange beast with awed respect. Little boys appear from everywhere following him," like that boy who followed Faulkner on a Pascagoula beach and like the Scouts in Oxford. Bob is one of those boys, and he fixes on the pilot "an undeviating stare of complete worship." Wally craves that attention, as Faulkner did with children: "Wally is now bursting with swaggering and vain glory," as Bob literally hangs on to a wing of Wally's plane and later learns to be a wing walker. Like young Billy, Wally "once attempted to fly from the barn roof with a pair of home-made wings and lit on his head."

After several complications, including yet another mysterious stranger who has compromised the virtue of Wally's daughter, "Flying the Mail" has the obligatory Hollywood happy ending, with Min and Wally married, and Wally's daughter and Bob constituting a new extended family. The treatment is not exactly a prototype for *Pylon,* but it began Faulkner's conception of a novel that would perhaps turn into a film that he could sell to Hollywood. "Flying the Mail" also confirms Faulkner's reputation as a motion picture doctor, capable of a "masterful compression and rearrangement of many long and inefficient scenes."[24]

Faulkner took pride in his work, even scripts for hire, as screenwriters Daniel Fuchs, Stephen Longstreet, and Budd Schulberg said.[25] He also made almost as much in six weeks as he had in ten years of writing fiction.[26] On June 16, Paramount had taken an option on *Sanctuary.* But it had been a trying time for him. Estelle did her best to keep him abreast of family news, and he was grateful: "So Jack [Oliver] and Josie are married. I reckon we'll have to build a house now—a cabin. I love you and I am homesick as the devil. I think it is because I want to sleep with you, in our bed and our room. That must be it."[27]

Letters home, of course, did not tell the whole story, as Hubert Starr insinuated: "In 1932 whatever his relations with Estelle were, she was no damper or restrictive background music to a not unhappy bachelor." Starr said that Faulkner "didn't write about Hollywood, but you should have heard him talk about it. Some of the conversation of Jean Harlow on the set, which he repeated to me, was worse than anything he implies of a Memphis brothel in his novels." Sometimes he gave way to loathing: "This whole city is made of spit and tissue paper, and one can conceive of an angry God who will rise up disgusted and finish it in a convulsive holocaust."[28]

Faulkner had been about to leave Hollywood a failure, Sam Marx said. None of his scripts had been produced, and his abrupt departure on the day he first reported to work "had become known to producers and directors."[29] Even among his fellow writers, Faulkner did not seem to fit in. One remembered him sitting at a table in the MGM commissary with everybody "bitching." Faulkner said, "there's something immoral about all these writers together here like this."[30] Yet, he could also sit there in silence and "then make one crack that would break everybody up."[31]

Then Howard Hawks appeared. Just a year older than Faulkner, the product of elite schools (Phillips Exeter Academy and Cornell), the director began his career in silent films, working in 1917 for Cecil B. DeMille and directing a film sequence for Mary Pickford. He served for a brief period as a flight instructor during World War I but, like Faulkner, had never seen action. He liked to race cars. His wealthy family's connections ensured that by the end of the silent era he knew virtually every important figure in Hollywood. After several moderately successful social comedies and dramas, his first sound film, *The Dawn Patrol*, about the Royal Flying Corps in France, was a box office success. Hawks had been reading Faulkner since the publication of *Soldiers' Pay* and ranked him as high as Hemingway, another favorite. Hawks wanted to film Faulkner's story "Turnabout," a natural choice for an Anglophile director who loved to do male-bonding pictures and dress in tweeds. A daring American flyer, Bogard, takes a British sailor, Claude Hope, with him on a bombing mission, and then Claude takes Bogard on a torpedo-boat mission with Ronnie, Claude's friend and comrade-in-arms. Bogard, misreading Claude's typical British understatement, had not realized just how dangerous the torpedo missions were: They have to go straight at enemy ships to deliver their bomb and then swerve, opening themselves up to enemy fire. Ronnie and Claude perish on another mission, and the story ends in a "romantic exaltation of heroism."[32]

Hawks offered Faulkner a drink (always a good idea). Faulkner said, "I've seen your name on a check." Not the best beginning. Was Faulkner putting Hawks in his place as just another of those Hollywood paymasters? Hawks, used to bowling over people with his projects, got mad. But he made his pitch. The film would closely follow Faulkner's short story, making it a "formidable companion piece to *The Dawn Patrol*, a terse, compelling look at young soldiers daily risking their lives on highly perilous missions during World War I, complete with a suicidal ending."[33]

A silent Faulkner looked at this big man, over six feet, and said nothing and got up to go. "See you in five days," he said. Hawks said, "It shouldn't take you that long to think about it." Faulkner, employing the clipped words of his characters, said, "I mean to write it." He delivered, and Hawks took the treatment to his brother-in-law, Irving Thalberg, the presiding MGM genius, head of production, and the inspiration for F. Scott's Fitzgerald's Monroe Starr in *The Last Tycoon*. "Shoot it as it is," Thalberg told Hawks. "I feel as if I'd make tracks all over it if I touched it."[34] This was quite a compliment from a producer famous for altering writers' scripts and directors' plans. Did Hawks also tout Faulkner's bogus bona fides, as he did to the *New York Post* (January 21, 1933)?: "Faulkner spent four years in the British air forces and saw service both in the air and behind the lines during some of the heaviest fighting, so he knows what he is writing about. From this basis of real imagery in the author's brain we should be able to produce a result on the screen that will approximate the actual experience." Did Faulkner ever level with Hawks?

When Hawks received word that the film had to include Joan Crawford, a star in high demand who appeared in three or four pictures a year, he watched a silent Faulkner absorb the news and then say in his usual quiet, understated manner, "I don't seem to remember a girl in the story." Hawks, just as curt, did not bother to explain: "That's the picture business, Bill. We get the biggest stars we can, and Joan's a nice girl, too." The spare dialogue Hawks provided in his reminiscence apparently reflected reality. Screenwriter Nunnally Johnson watched them sit for long periods of silence, broken by a word or two, or a few slowly drawn-out sentences.[35] For film scholar Joseph McBride, Hawks supplied this Faulkner reaction to adding Joan Crawford: "Holy smoke!" Ever the master of the two-word cliché.[36]

Faulkner and Hawks liked to drink, smoke pipes, hunt, and fish. They both had stepchildren and were the oldest of three brothers. Hawks had a bar made out of a hogshead cask. "He had made it with his own hands. He had his own forge. He was a very deliberate man,"[37] just what the novelist needed: respect and no inclination to use Hollywood's production line methods. Hawks could not be hurried. He could be haughty, but he treated Faulkner well and seems to have liked to show him off. Producer Robert Buckner called Hawks a snob and a "head hunter." He entertained lavishly as one of the royals of the movie business. "He wouldn't mix and he had a coterie," Buckner said. Hawks introduced Gary Cooper to Ernest Hemingway, and Hemingway to Marlene Dietrich, and Hawks "took pleasure in introducing WF to people—like a Ming vase: 'Have you seen this T'ang?'" Buckner suspected that Faulkner was "paying out his special debt by letting the headhunting go by unnoticed." Certainly Hawks loved to corral Faulkner as one of his discoveries, and Buckner believed Faulkner would avoid Hawksian social gatherings whenever possible, although when it came to business, Faulkner followed the director's lead. Instead of putting the writer in a projection room, the director took the time to explain certain fundamentals and why many of Faulkner's fictional techniques would not work in Hollywood, which required a straightforward approach: no flashbacks, concentrate on the story and the characters. Hawks would figure out where to put the camera and how to shoot the film.

After reading a first draft of the screenplay (now apparently lost) Crawford, according to Hawks, was in tears, upset about barging into an all-male picture. He counseled her: "Now look, I don't think you can get out of this. I don't think I can get out of this. We both have contracts. You can make it absolutely miserable unless you accept this well, and if you start taking it miserably, those are the kind of scenes you're gonna make."[38] Appealing to her self-interest apparently worked, although Hawks's self-serving reminiscences are suspect, since he always emerges as the hero of his own stories and seems a little too facile with remembered dialogue. But, after all, he was a director famous for his deft collaborations with actors and actresses, a man's man also remarkably at ease with strong women and pleased to be working with them. It didn't hurt to tell Crawford the picture depended on her wholehearted participation. Hawks could flatter without seeming to do so.

For sure, getting Crawford's assent was not as easy as Hawks suggested. She had no experience with accents and doubted she would be convincing as an Englishwoman. Donald Spoto, a Crawford biographer, suggests a more likely enticement: "She may have felt more optimistic when she learned that Gary Cooper was among her leading men: at that time, he was a major star at Paramount who had already worked with Marlene Dietrich, Claudette Colbert, Helen Hayes and Tallulah Bankhead."[39] Who worries about accents when Cooper is wooing you? But Franchot Tone is the one she married.

Crawford requested that Faulkner write the same kind of terse dialogue spoken by her male counterparts. Later, she described the film as a product of the Depression, reminding women of the sacrifices and responsibilities of the war, the postwar indulgence and spendthrift behavior that led to the 1929 crash (*Greenwood [MS] Commonwealth,* April 25). Faulkner complied with Crawford's request, although he interrupted his work when Murry Falkner died on August 7. His heart had stopped in the brutally hot season. An unhealthy diet, drinking, and disappointment in himself seemed to be the family verdict on Murry, who did not make it to his sixty-second birthday. Murry had been ailing and bedridden and before that had sat on the porch eating heads of lettuce or walking back forth almost like a demented person.[40] Faulkner told Dorothy Oldham: "He thinks if he eats a bushel of lettuce it will help make up for all that fried fatback he's eaten over the years. It won't."[41]

To his cousin Sallie Murry, Faulkner said: "He just gave up, got tired of living." Estelle liked Murry and felt sorry for him.[42]

Faulkner wanted to return home—as much, probably, out of concern for his family as over the death itself, since father and son had never been close. William Faulkner now headed the clan. Howard Hawks, with his pull, convinced MGM to allow their contract employee to work on "Turn About" at Rowan Oak, a remarkable turnaround for a writer whose contract would not have been renewed without Hawks's intervention. At home, Faulkner awaited word from Hawks about reporting to Hollywood to finish collaborating on the film. In late September, Faulkner wrote to Ben Wasson that he had completed the screenplay and his work on the galleys of *Light in August*. Sam Marx had asked if the novel might be filmable. "I told him I didn't think they could use it," he wrote Wasson, adding his absurdist view of Hollywood: "It would make a good Mickey Mouse picture, though Popeye is the part for Mickey Mouse. The frog could play Clarence Snopes." Anything for another Hollywood payday. "Dad left mother solvent for only about 1 year. Then it is me," Faulkner confided in his agent/friend.[43]

Faulkner's anger provoked by dealing with Hollywood producers exploded in another late September letter to Wasson: "I was too busy and too mad all the time I was in California to write you. But now I am home again, eating watermelon on the back porch and watching it rain." He was wary of David O. Selznick, who approached Faulkner about signing a contract for "all subsequent business." Faulkner believed he had worked out his troubles with Sam Marx: "I certainly made a better contract with those Jews than he seemed able to: I get $250.00 a week for staying in Oxford: he got that for a six months' contract in California. I think I'll send him a bill today."[44] To Hal Smith, he sent word of his satisfaction with *Light in August* while continuing to work on restoring Rowan Oak: "I made enough jack in Hollywood to do a lot of repairs on the house, so all the floors will be out of it next month, and we will be living with kinfolks." He was also looking forward to the publication of his poems, suggesting the title *A Green Bough*.

Faulkner's letters tell one story, his work in Hollywood another. Confronted with a studio's arbitrary decision to throw one of its Hollywood female stars into a picture powerfully focused on men at war in the air and on the sea, based on a superb story under the direction of a consummate filmmaker, a disgusted Faulkner could have simply made Crawford another buddy, a tough-talking dame, and collected his cash. Plenty of movies did just that in the early 1930s heyday of stars like Jean Harlow and Glenda Farrell, not to mention Joan Crawford. Instead, on his home ground, he scripted a new work that returned to the primal scene in *The Sound and the Fury*. In the summer of 1910, three English children are catching crayfish in a brook. Ronnie, 12, "sober, almost dour," is the oldest and is the group leader. Claude, 11, adopted into the Boyce Smith family, is "lively, talkative, vivacious," and Ann, 10, Ronnie's sister, given no epithets, is nevertheless the focus because she is the challenger: "Why do you have to tag along after me all the time?" Ronnie asks. "I'm not tagging after you. I have just as much right here as you have." The assertive Caddy-like Ann not only declares her independence; she also establishes that the film will be about her—her choices, her desires, her way of looking at the world even as her male counterparts indulge in the male illusion that they are protecting her. Even Claude, who adores Ann, tells her: "We're busy. We can't be bothered with girls. Go away."[45]

Nothing in Faulkner's earlier screen treatments, verging on the misogynistic, foreshadows this sudden volte-face. He was drawing on his own childhood, remembering, evidently, how he played with dolls in the company of his cousin Sallie. And he was reconsidering his own dismissal of women as actors in their own right. You also have to ask, What impact did meeting Joan Crawford have on him? John Matthews suggests that writing for Crawford constituted a significant change in Faulkner's idea of what he could accomplish in Hollywood: "The simple presence of Ann may be read as the transformative force of the cinema itself in Faulkner's narrative. That is, Joan Crawford *is* the movie. I think Faulkner proved a quick study of the star-vehicle system; he must have understood that the female romantic lead exists to be desired as objects by the male audience, and to be identified with as desiring subject by female spectators."[46] "I think" and "must have" are too timidly academic. Hawks had already explained Crawford's importance in his man-to-man discussions with his screenwriter. Faulkner also came to terms with his insatiable need to idealize women as something *other* than men, as the sum of men's dreams of perfection, and his anger at or distrust of women who wanted to compete with men. He knew better, of course, than to devalue women because he knew Anita Loos, Dorothy Parker, and Lillian Hellman, and dated Leane Zugsmith.

But in his screenwriting Faulkner was now "forced to imagine a different space for women than he might be used to." That is putting it mildly. In Ann, we have "female desire" that is "sexually alluring, tragic and noble,"[47] not to mention independent—an unbeatable Hollywood combination and the counterpoise to Temple Drake. It is ironic that the advertising for the film touted that it was written "by the author of *Sanctuary*," since it portrays the very qualities absent from that novel—not only in the depiction of Ann but in the code of the gentleman that Gowan traduces and that Ronnie, Claude, and Bogard exemplify. In this context, their clipped dialogue is what results when Faulkner shears away Gowan's bogus chivalric rhetoric. The male triumvirate is centered on Ann—or, rather, Joan Crawford, the star, for whom Faulkner, albeit with the assistance of three screenwriters (Edith Fitzgerald, Dwight Taylor, and Ann Cunningham), serves as Hollywood host.

What is more, in Faulkner's treatment, Ann asserts her independence against male opposition, and Ronnie is unwilling to recognize Ann's power even as Claude capitulates: "Oh, she won't hurt anything. I suppose. Let her stay, so long as she doesn't muddy the water." Of course that is exactly what Ann is doing: disrupting the male preserve, dirtying up their romantic notions of themselves, as Caddy does. In this wonderfully unsentimental opening for a Hollywood film, Ronnie shoves Ann into the brook. He is as angry as Quentin Compson, who cannot abide even the possibility that his sister might get dirty. But unlike Quentin, Ronnie is not passive-aggressive. Claude, now determined to defend Ann's honor, "springs upon Ronnie. They fall to the ground, wrestling and pummeling one another." Then the soaking-wet Ann puts a stop to the fight by attacking Claude and saying, "You stop hurting Ronnie! You stop it, now!" The two boys ignore her and "soon the three of them are inextricable, rolling and surging, drawing nearer and nearer to the brook, until at last all three roll into the water and sit up." Claude is "whooping with laughter" while Ronnie remains unruffled, as ever in the guise of the leader. Whatever tensions trouble this threesome, they are a unit, almost military in their respect of rank, of Ronnie as the oldest. The fight breaks up when they hear the sound of an aeroplane: "As one they scramble out of the brook and rush out into an opening, looking up. The aeroplane passes overhead. It is a clumsy pusher, flying low. Yet to the children it is a thing of magic," as it was to the Falkner boys when they watched their first aeroplane and ran across fields to follow it. The aeroplane is also a foreshadowing of Bogard, an American aviator who will join but also disrupt this childhood reverie, who will bring the war home to Ann, who falls in love with him, although she has been promised to Claude, who later says during his wartime torpedo-boat horrors: "there's not any Eden anymore, and they wear khaki and not veils."[48]

"Turn About" returned to a favorite subject, the loss of innocence, but linked that loss powerfully to the war, creating a woman more engaged and forthright than Margaret Powers in *Soldiers' Pay*. Unlike Caddy, Ann does not have to run away. She is given the opportunity to challenge male privilege. If she acknowledges Ronnie as leader, as the one who sets the agenda, so to speak, she is unwavering in making him behave like a leader, not a bully. She makes him a better man without sacrificing her own sense of self-worth.

When the boys waver between a commitment to be aviators or sailors, Ann upbraids them: "You're scared, both of you." She is the one to say what the males dare not express.

Faulkner dilutes the power of this opening scene by lingering too long on the backstory of the children growing up in the years leading to war. The dramatic exposition, workable in a novel, simply takes too long to get to the war scenes and Bogard's entrance. When Faulkner turned in his screenplay to Hawks in late September 1932, both men knew it needed more work. Hawks tried to film the opening scene but found the children could not do the English accents, and perhaps he realized, as well, that as good as the opening scene was, it would make a much longer film than budgeted or that could be commercially exhibited to develop the psychological complexity Faulkner had introduced into an action-picture screenplay. The Bogard-Ann dynamic alone would make a good picture, and some of it did get into the released film, especially a somewhat muted version of Ann's initial hostility to Bogard, as a healthy American untouched by the war. Her independence and devotion to the British cause attracts the sensitive Bogard, who emerges as her worthy counterpart. When Ronnie, who encourages Bogard, takes him to Ann, Bogard frankly confesses, "I'm afraid." What is it about Ann? She can take the measure of a man, and that makes Bogard uneasy but also committed to serve, to fight, and to marry her. Bogard, the aviator, is also the hero who accompanies Ronnie and Claude on their dangerous torpedo run. In short, he is the complete hero.

Only in the pre-Code era could Faulkner have Ann actually go to bed with Claude before they are married. It is during a period when Ann has rejected Bogard because she remains loyal to Claude, and then believes a false report that Bogard had died in an air crash. Claude, too, may not survive the war, and believing there must be some kind of fulfillment of their childhood intimacy, she embraces him, saying: "But not love Claude! Not love!"[49] It is, paradoxically, her way of remaining true to Bogard. In a moment that is pure cinema, Ronnie arrives home, spots Claude's cap on the floor, and then, knocking and looking into Ann's room, he notices her "stockings and underthings, as though discarded hurriedly." He never says a word and never comments on his discovery, maintaining his discreet, understated style, realizing the depths of his sister's passions and her conflicts, which he has intensified by having introduced her to Bogard.

How to reunite Ann and Bogard after she discovers he has not died? Hawks, remembering the blind hero of *Soldiers' Pay*, suggested blinding Claude during an attack on the torpedo boat. Faulkner complied, and then had Claude and Ronnie launch a suicidal mission against a cruiser, even as

Bogard attempts the same attack from the air. The British team gets to the cruiser first and crashes into it, losing their lives before Bogard, in all likelihood, would have sacrificed his. The screenplay ends, predictably, with an Ann-Bogard marriage and in antiwar sentiment reminiscent of *A Fable,* with Bogard's bitter reaction against the leaders who have sent good men to perish: "If they had only all been there: generals, the admirals, the presidents, and the kings—theirs, ours, all of them!"

This promising screenplay reveals that Faulkner had begun to master cinematic form. Bruce Kawin points out the effective use of montage: "a series of glimpses of events, often augmented by superimposition, indicating the passage of time or the unfolding of a process. Faulkner's use of sound effects in these transitions is unconventional (most such sequences simply had music tracks) and quite beautiful."[50] He worked in the "sounds of warfare, letting them clarify the characters' thoughts."[51] For example, when Ann calls Bogard a coward before he has enlisted, they are near a window where the soldiers' tramping can be heard. Bogard listens as the tramping fades away in a scene that heightens the drama of two fraught lives against the mass movements of murderous war. It is impossible to say but also tempting to suppose that Faulkner's own distance from the actual fighting made such scenes especially poignant to him. He had been in Bogard's position but never had the opportunity to prove himself in combat.

The screenplay had plenty of faults, including some improbable scenes that Hawks cut, and dialogue so terse it seemed a mockery of British understatement. Hawks now needed Faulkner on-site to continue the revisions. In mid-October, Estelle reported to Hal Smith: "Billy has gone to California again—been away two weeks now, but says that he will be home by the 20th. I am sceptical! He swears he hates it—but his six weeks this summer lengthened into three months and only his father's death hastened his return." He could be as much a mystery to her as to others: "This time he motored out taking his mother and youngest brother to show them the world—or perhaps [to show] them the movies—who knows."[52] She was supposed to be one of the party but found herself pregnant and apparently did not want to risk her health. She helped Maud and Dean buy clothes for the trip, which, in the end, Maud does not seem to have enjoyed any more than her son said he did.[53]

Perhaps Faulkner wanted to bring his home with him, so speak, at a time when his recently deceased father left him suddenly on his own in a new way. However much father and son misunderstood one another, Faulkner's earlier letters home to his parents from Yale and Europe reflected his family fealty, the same fealty that motivates Ann's initial hostility to Bogard, who seems so American and foreign to her. She and Ronnie have lost both of their parents—the father to the war, their mother to her grief—making the brother-and-sister bond all the more precious but also fragile and too intense. The ebullient Claude seems a surrogate for Ronnie and a kind of antidote, but his obsessive drinking makes him effectively a dead man walking and ultimately unsatisfactory for Ann because he seems more like a brother than a lover whom a patient Ann has to nurse.

Hawks scrapped a good fourth of Faulkner's screenplay. Several sets of writers were put to work on jettisoning the backstory that provides the psychological underpinning of the characters, so that in the film as released their bond is simply a given. Only Gary Cooper remains to fulfill Faulkner's version of the sensitive American, a refutation of the pushy, cocky American stereotype. Bogard empathizes with the British and never imposes his temperament on his British associates. Cooper had a profound ability to play characters as observers with actions that arose out of careful contemplation that preceded passion.

The film was retitled *Today We Live* by November 28, and a full script, dated April 8, 1933, credits the story to Faulkner and the screenplay to Edith Fitzgerald and Dwight Taylor.[54] The final product, not as daring as Faulkner's screenplay, reflected Production Code pressures that resulted in censorship. Joseph Breen, enforcing the Code, advised that words like "hell," "damn," "God"—even "gad"—be eliminated from the script as well as two references to "Huns," since "it has become highly offensive with Germans," although Hawks managed to hold on to one "Hun." British censors later deleted derogatory references to British officers. Claude's drinking had to be minimized so as not to disgrace the uniform.[55] V. J. Hart wrote in a report on the film: "It is a revision of *Hell's Angels* [1930], much better done, with no vulgarity and with a tenseness of plot brought about by excellent dramatization without overdoing." The Howard Hughes film had two brothers, one a womanizer, and a duplicitous, evil woman, Jean Harlow. Under the heading "Code," Hart declared that the film "should not have any censor difficulties."[56] And that is the problem: revisions of the screenplay shaved off most of Ann's hard edges, and Crawford has to appear in an extravagant ensemble fit for a goddess whom Cooper has to appease. Franchot Tone and Robert Young as Ronnie and Claude appear as innocents never able to finish their sentences, or maintain their accents, even though they know one another so well and are so veddy British. The best that can be said is that their performances point to Faulkner's evocation of their claustrophobic upbringing that makes them unfit for a broader world, notwithstanding their bravery.

Near the end of October, Faulkner returned to Oxford, just as reviews of *Light in August* began to appear. Robert Sherwood, winner of a Pulitzer Prize for Drama three times and author of several screenplays, including *Abe Lincoln in Illinois* and *The Best Years of Our Lives,* left an indelible impression of Faulkner in Hollywood, in a letter to Kyle Crichton at Scribner's:

> Who do you think occupies the office next to mine and whose typewriter I can hear clicking at this moment? William Faulkner. He's a bewildering character all right. I expected him to be painfully diffident but such is not the case. I was talking to him about Arnold Bennett's early enthusiasm for Soldiers Pay and how the author of The Old Wives Tale had been the first vociferous shouter for Faulkner, and the latter said in the most calm matter of fact manner, "Bennett's about the only man I ever heard of who deliberately set out to be a second rate writer and succeeded." What a dismissal of the subject![57]

At home, Faulkner told his stepdaughter, Cho-Cho, now fourteen, a story of what it was like in Hollywood. At a Laurence Stallings party, Tallulah Bankhead arrived late with a male companion. She said, "Laurence, I'm late because this gentleman wanted to know if I was a true blonde and I had to show him." Then she pulled her skirt up to her waist. Stallings, wine glass in hand, put it up to his eye and said to her, "Say Ah, Tallulah."

Estelle walked out.[58]

15

The Black Shadow

Light in August, October 1932

> I had seen and known negroes since I could remember. I just looked
> at them as I did at rain, or furniture, or food or sleep. But after that I
> seemed to see them for the first time not as people, but as a thing, a
> shadow in which I lived, we lived, all white people, all other people.
>
> —Joanna Burden, *Light in August*

THE PAST AS PROLOGUE

More than ever, reviewers began by sizing up Faulkner's stature. "He has probably forgotten more about literary tricks than such writers as Ernest Hemingway or Sherwood Anderson will ever learn," James T. Farrell suggested in the
New York Sun (October 7), also praising the deft use of melodrama and the
"social implications of his tales." Farrell found fault, to be sure, with Faulkner's excessive use of metaphor and running words together, and the reviewer
could not resist holding back the tide: "Faulkner has been overpraised." The
Oxford Eagle (October 20) called *Light in August* Faulkner's greatest novel
and claimed that he had attained international fame.

Most reviewers found *Light in August* more accessible than earlier novels,
although they puzzled over its form and its "crisscrossed lives," as Fanny
Butcher put it in the *Chicago Tribune* (October 8). Some assumed, like Floyd
Van Vuren in the *Milwaukee Journal* (October 8), a linear progression that
"removed the taint of obscurity" that reflected "a sounder and a more mature"
writer. If he had not created "one perfect chrysoprase," he had come close,
announced Henry Canby in the *Saturday Review of Literature* (October 8).

While some fretted over the competing plots attached to certain characters—
Lena Grove, Joe Christmas, and Gail Hightower—Canby argued that the
novel "gathers up all plots, all characters, as it goes." Faulkner moved, as Lena
did, "with the grain of life." With no remit to write biography, reviewers nevertheless identified a new compassion and equilibrium. J. Donald Adams
in the *New York Times Book Review* (October 8) dared to go further: "Mr.
Faulkner's work has seemed to be that of a man who has, at some time, been
desperately hurt; a man whom life has at some point badly cheated. There are
indications in the book that he has regained his balance."

To Ted Robinson (*Cleveland Plain Dealer*, October 9), however, Faulkner
had allowed the "squeamish critics" of *Sanctuary* to "cramp his style," resulting in a conventional book not as psychologically significant or as innovative
as earlier novels. To be sure, *Light in August* had memorable characters and
was not "unworthy of Faulkner," but it did not have the pace and intensity
that Robinson had come to expect. George Marion O'Donnell (*Memphis
Commercial Appeal*, October 9) focused on the flashbacks, suggesting they
gave the narrative "a slight looseness that stands in the way of perfection," but
then seemed to contradict himself by saying the flashbacks did not "impair
the cumulative effect of the whole." In fact, no reviewer was prescient enough
to perceive the beginning of a new Faulkner who would reshape the past into
a new kind of history, although O'Donnell noticed the way Faulkner shifted
tenses from past to present, and from first to third person, amalgamating but
also going beyond the techniques of earlier novels.

Reviewers set precedents for novelists that great writers like Faulkner
ignore, and so a surprised O'Donnell noted that the "characters are more
human and less pathological than one expects Faulkner's characters to be."
For this reason, perhaps, O'Donnell concluded that *Light in August* "is more
mature, broader in outlook, nearer to the final, truthful revelation of human
potentialities for which the author is striving." A more condescending version
of this judgment, by Henry George Hoch in the *Detroit News* (October 16),
appeared in northern newspapers: "In his successive novels about the lowly,
ignorant and criminal peoples of the South, Faulkner gradually has risen
above utter horror and morbidity by bringing in more and more characters
who can command respect and affection."

Reviews in British newspapers showed the same mix of respect and repro-
bation. Richard Aldington in the *Evening Standard* (February 2, 1933): "The
narrative is constructed in chapters which all converge on the central figure
[Joe Christmas] like avenues on a round point." Compton Mackenzie (*Daily
Mail*, February 9) complained about "verbal indecency" in the coinage of
words like "adjacenting," and Helen Fletcher (*Time and Tide*, February 4)

about Faulkner's "fine disregard for tense," but Mercury Patten in the *New Statesman and Nation* (February 11) invoked Conrad and Crane (whose standing in England was very high) as a measure of the novel's achievement, even if Faulkner remained "reckless" with his rhetoric. Few critics on either side of the Atlantic seemed able to comprehend the unity of Faulkner's longest novel, even as they called it his most accessible work, which is to say the easiest to read. And no one realized it marked a departure from earlier work and a herald of the great novels to come.

The past in *Flags in the Dust/Sartoris* and *The Sound and the Fury* is a given. It may be remembered or characterized by different characters in different ways—by Miss Jenny, young Bayard, Mr. Compson, Quentin, and Jason, for example, but the past, as an object of fascination, a subject, does not truly enter Faulkner's fiction until the advent of Gail Hightower, who makes of the past a fetish that is erotic in its implications. The present, as it appears in the day-by-day journey of the Bundrens, is all-encompassing. So it becomes in the horrors of Temple Drake's encounters with Popeye, a rape that robs her of a standing built upon a past of class, status, and racial superiority. *Light in August* is the first novel to supercharge different ways of experiencing time, with Lena's journey and Joe Christmas's flight conveyed in the present tense, as time composed of one moment after another, as opposed to Hightower's ecstatic entrance into Jefferson as the embodiment of the past, of the thundering, galloping horses—the Civil War events—that echo forever in his mind as though they had created him, which, in a sense, they did, since they remain the locus of his identity. For Lena what matters is what is happening to her *now;* for Hightower, what matters is what has already happened and what he preserves in memory. Of course, that presentness of the past informs *Flags in the Dust/Sartoris,* but young Bayard's effort to live in the present and reject the past is bound to fail, and old Bayard renders himself moribund because all he can hold on to is his memory. Hightower is unequal to the determination that Lena Grove demonstrates in her pursuit of Lucas Burch, aka Joe Brown, who has impregnated and deserted her. Hightower can only advise Byron Bunch, who becomes Lena Grove's cavalier, to flee, an option that ought to appeal to Byron, who has spent a lifetime avoiding family commitments and other troubles. But Byron lives up to his namesake's reputation by repudiating the community's cant, championing a fallen woman, and deciding not to follow the outcast Hightower into exile. Hightower's own failed marriage, his wife's mental illness, and the community's rejection of him as their spiritual leader make him a reverend they cannot revere. This trauma drives Hightower even further into reveries of the past when his grandfather, like Colonel Sartoris and Colonel Falkner, displayed the savoir faire and Byronic insouciance to the pieties of the polity. That Byron should confide in Hightower is both an expression of their isolation from others but also Bunch's quest to force his friend to return to his role as moral exemplar.

Burch/Brown can change his name and identity in a way that is impossible for Joe Christmas, whose origins are occluded. Is he part black? The very idea destabilizes him. He cannot count on any sort of heritage. Without a past, he has no present. Ironically, Hightower's fixation on the past is such that he, too, cannot live in the present, although at key moments, he rouses himself: delivering a black child and, near the end of the novel, briefly harboring Joe Christmas, who has escaped custody and is pursued by the Percy Grimm–led lynching mob.

Race becomes a cynosure in *Light in August* that separates the novel from its predecessors. Although race is a ubiquitous feature of earlier fiction, it is not an ontological category. That Christmas might be part black unsettles him so much that he has to confess his suspected color to Bobbie, his first lover, to Joe Brown, and to his last lover, Joanna Burden. But race is a category that is itself unstable, as it is not in Faulkner's previous fiction. What constitutes Joe's blackness? Is it his parchment-colored skin? Hardly, since whites can be dark-complected. Is it his eyes or his hair, which he mentions to Bobbie, who associates his features not with black people but with foreigners? Faulkner was writing in the heyday of novels about black people passing as white, and his contribution to this genre is to create a character who regards the very idea of passing as problematic—not because he might be untrue to his own race but because he lives in a culture that demands that he identify as white or black, but not both. To be black, he understands, makes him an outcast. Yet the very notion of being black results in the same impasse: an inability to function entirely as white or black. Some reviewers did the novel an injustice by referring to Joe as a mulatto. The point is that he does not know if he is part black, and because he does not know, he cannot function as a whole man. That they missed the central dilemma of the novel is telling. They could not read race as a fundamental question of identity and therefore could not see that one's race endows one with a basic sense of self that characters like Lena or her suitor, Byron Bunch, take for granted. Never for a moment can Joe Christmas experience their kind of certitude. As a child he is singled out as "Negro" by the children who will not play with him; as an adult he has only that singularity on which to rely, so that he is permanently estranged from the rest of society and will not participate in its games.

The political thrust of *Light in August*—Faulkner's understanding of American fascism, an understanding that began in the mid-1920s during and after his trip to Europe—reaches its culmination at the end of the novel in the figure of Percy Grimm, a character who devolves from stories like "Mistral" and "Dry September." Certain details in Grimm's biography line up with Faulkner's: the regret over missing the action in World War I, performing poorly in school, a love of uniforms and parading around in them, and a father, the owner of a hardware store, who does not understand his son: "He [the father] thought that the boy was just lazy and in a fair way to become perfectly worthless, when in reality the boy was suffering the terrible tragedy of having been born not alone too late but not late enough to have escaped first hand knowledge of the lost time when he should have been a man instead of a child." The Civil War but also World War I thundered in Faulkner's imagination. But even worse for Grimm, as for Faulkner, the postwar "hysteria passed away and the ones who had been loudest in the hysteria and even the ones, the heroes who had suffered and served, beginning to look at one another a little askance, he had no one to tell it, to open his heart to." Grimm, like his creator, suffers from an acute awareness that the very cause he wants to serve has been deemed unworthy by those who served and whom he envies. Imagine, for example, what Faulkner felt listening in New York and Hollywood to Laurence Stallings, who lost a leg in wartime heroics and wrote the screenplay based on his hit play *What Price Glory?* that turned the war into farce as much as tragedy.

Light in August takes the measure of Faulkner as the man he did not become but understood very well. For Grimm, the military is a godsend:

> He could now see his life opening before him, uncomplex and inescapable as a barren corridor, completely freed now of ever again having to think or decide, the burden which he now assumed and carried as bright and weightless and martial as his insignatory brass: a sublime and implicit faith in physical courage and blind obedience, and a belief that the white race is superior to any and all other races and that the American is superior to all other white races and that the American uniform is superior to all men, and that all that would ever be required of him in payment for this belief, this privilege, would be his own life.

Grimm cannot leave behind the make-believe that once was so important to Faulkner: "he walked among the civilians with about him an air half belligerent and half the selfconscious pride of a boy." Ignoring the American Legion commander who says he does not need his help, ignoring the sheriff who says the same, Grimm clothes his vigilante mission in the uniforms of Legionnaires he manipulates into believing they have been called up to protect the community and defend its honor. "What does your legion stand for, if not for the protection of America and Americans?" Grimm asks. Faulkner understood that

Percy Grimm was a new, fascist phenomenon, although Faulkner never uses that term: "He was indefatigable, restrained yet forceful; there was something about him irresistible and prophetlike." Perhaps the "irresistible and prophet-like" Percy Grimm and the idea of an Aryan tormented by the suspicion he might have black blood is what appealed to the Nazis, who permitted the translation of *Light in August* while burning the books of Ernest Hemingway, Jack London, and Upton Sinclair.[1] Grimm was a blood-and-soil type that fascinated fascists, which would not have surprised Faulkner, who declared that figures like Percy Grimm were "everywhere, in all countries, in all people."[2] Just a few years earlier, in a William Fox film, Mussolini spoke in English to Americans, saluting them as the cutting edge of history.

The Germans were not alone in finding at least a latent fascist mentality in Faulkner, referred to as the "cult of cruelty," focused on horror, the grotesque, and the irrational, as several American critics put it. Black people and women, especially those who did not know their place, were the scapegoats of a southern traditionalist nostalgia for the pre-Reconstruction South. Critic Maxwell Geismar argued that Faulkner attacked women and black people the same way that fascists attacked Jews.[3] But Grimm is as much the antithesis of community sentiment as he is a harbinger of it, and he hardly emerges as a hero. He is a master manipulator, making the phlegmatic Legionnaires feel "sheepish . . . somehow they had fallen short of his own cold ardor." This is a man of action, not one who gives talks at the Rotary. Faulkner, a superb reader of political movements, catches exactly the way Grimm insinuates himself into a cynosure: "So quickly is man unwittingly and unpredictably moved that without knowing that they were thinking it, the town had suddenly accepted Grimm with respect and perhaps a little awe and a deal of actual faith and confidence, as though somehow his vision and patriotism and pride in the town, the occasion, had been quicker and truer than theirs." Faulkner, so susceptible to the sartorial, notes the way Grimm has tailored his reactionary force: "which was almost as palpable as the khaki would have been which Grimm wished them to wear, wished that they wore, as though each time they returned to the orderly room they dressed themselves anew in suave and austerely splendid scraps of his dream." And this is a boy's dream, a boy on a borrowed bicycle no less, who chases down Christmas and confronts him with "nothing vengeful about him either, no fury, no outrage. Christmas saw that, himself. Because for an instant they looked at one another almost face to face." Two displaced figures, for a fleeting moment, acknowledge their boyish consanguinity. Christmas is back in the schoolyard, his life coming to a close in another circle, the end of a deadly game that has a religious intensity. Grimm's "face had that serene, unearthly luminousness of angels in church windows." Like so many evil men,

Grimm believes God is on his side, and he gives every appearance of one who has been blessed in his mission. Three men, like disciples, follow Grimm's pursuit of Christmas, a fleeing deity, into Hightower's house: "their faces seemed to glare with bodiless suspension as though from haloes as they stooped and raised Hightower, his face bleeding, from the floor where Christmas, running up the hall, his raised and armed and manacled hands full of glare and glitter like lightning bolts, so that he resembled a vengeful and furious god pronouncing a doom, had struck him down."

How is it that Grimm and Christmas converge in the same imagery? For all their black and white differences, they have associated their masculinity with the power and the desire to dominate. They are both fascistic in rejecting weakness—for Christmas the subservience of women, white and black, whom he attacks, beginning with the black prostitute when he is a teenager, and also Bobbie, the white woman who, even after he beats her, tries to console him. To accept that consolation is to go soft, in Joe's mind. And for Grimm it is the same, although the target is the "Negro," upon which Grimm will prove himself to his father and community.[4]

Light in August creates different voices to array the diversity of temperaments in the polity that attempt to reckon with the ungovernable nature of Joe Christmas's life and death. These constituents of society cannot place Christmas, categorize him, any more than he can characterize himself—although Gavin Stevens, another late entrant in the novel, desperately tries to confine Christmas's story to the white blood–black blood color scheme, which is the only one he knows. Stevens is from an old Jefferson family, Harvard- and Heidelberg-schooled, and inevitably reminiscent of Phil Stone. He is steeped in the lore of the Civil War and his slave-owning land. He takes it upon himself, as Stone often did, to pontificate on racial psychology, here applied to Christmas:

> the black blood drove him first to the negro cabin. And then the white blood drove him out of there, as it was the black blood which snatched up the pistol and the white blood which would not let him fire it. And it was the white blood which sent him to the minister, which rising in him for the last and final time, sent him against all reason and all reality, into the embrace of a chimaera, a blind faith in something read in a printed Book. Then I believe that the white blood deserted him for the moment. Just a second, a flicker, allowing the black to rise in its final moment and make him turn upon that on which he had postulated his hope of salvation. It was the black blood which swept him by his own desire beyond the aid of any man, swept him up into that ecstasy out of a black jungle

where life has already ceased before the heart stops and death is desire and fulfillment. And then the black blood failed him again, as it must have in crises all his life. He did not kill the minister. He merely struck him with the pistol and ran on and crouched behind that table and defied the black blood for the last time, as he had been defying it for thirty years. He crouched behind that overturned table and let them shoot him to death, with that loaded and unfired pistol in his hand.

Informing this "educated" southerner's musings is a lifetime of framing the black American experience in phrases like "black jungle," in which it is presumed that white civilization saved black people from the savagery of Africa and gave them the Bible, "the printed book," as their spiritual guide and redemption. Ironically, it is Jefferson, as much as Christmas, that is associated with savagery. Grimm and his cohort invade the "stale and cloistral dimness" of Hightower's house, as though it were in fact a sanctuary they are defiling. And they pursue Christmas in the "savage summer sunlight which they had just left. It was upon them, of them: its shameless savageness." Faulkner's reading of texts like Frazer's *The Golden Bough* made him aware of the "savage roots of Christianity," its demand for a scapegoat and a redeemer. Grimm, leading his "sheepish" flock, is even called "a primitive priest of a blood cult." To acknowledge Christmas as simply a man, not a "nigger," would thwart the "yearning for a scapegoat, even, or perhaps especially—if it be our own son,"[5] or grandson, as is the case with Hines, who also murders Joe's father.

But Joe Christmas has been struggling with quite a different conflict that Stevens cannot begin to fathom. Race, religion, sexuality, and politics converge in the Joanna Burden–Joe Christmas affair. Joe has been on the run for fifteen years after assaulting the Calvinist McEachern, who has adopted him, and after Joe has been assaulted by the pimps who ridicule his devotion to Bobbie, the prostitute he wants to marry. Sex has been a need and a sickness and a punishment ever since, as an agitated young boy, he vomited from eating too much toothpaste when caught in the room where a couple is fornicating. Hectored by a fanatical janitor, Doc Hines (disclosed later as Joe's grandfather), and children who call him a nigger, Joe has spent his life alternating between white and black communities and expecting to be punished for it. Joanna Burden, the descendant of northern abolitionists, a middle-aged woman active in support of black colleges, allows Joe to take her to bed. Her tolerance troubles him, makes him feel he has been indulged like a slave and permitted to live in a "Negro" cabin, accepting her food and, in essence, her patronage. She does not see him as an individual but as "negro," the word she chants in their bed. She may be of abolitionist stock, but that does not mean that she, any more than her forebears, actually regards black people as equals. Like Joe's grandfather, Joanna's father has killed a Mexican who supposedly stole his horse.[6] Again and again, the very concept of individuality is destroyed in this closed society. In denying "basic human and civil rights to the black community, white society has denied its own members the right to act as individuals."[7]

When Joanna prays over Joe—adopting the patriarchal role he has spent his life rejecting—and then threatens him with a gun in a form of coercion that is also of a piece with his childhood, Joe's rage and self-loathing are projected onto her, and he strikes out with his razor, nearly decapitating her. This sudden violence originates from a man who has become the vector of racism, fundamentalism, and misogyny, driving him toward the novel's denouement, when Percy Grimm, frustrated over missing his heroic moment in World War I and desperately seeking some way to exert the authority of his race and community, captures and castrates Christmas, whose life, it seems, has been on the trajectory to tragedy as one of the damned his Calvinist elders have denounced. Joe's confusion and lashing out when he is cornered are reminiscent of Bigger Thomas in Richard Wright's *Native Son* (1940), a novel, written by a Mississippi native, that Faulkner admired.

But overlaying this intricate psychology is Calvinist theology, expressed in Faulkner's repeated references to "the Player," never identified as God but nevertheless as a figuration of predestination, with each character designed to enact an assigned role, just as Doc Hines declares in calls to lynch Christmas, calls that are the fated result of Hines's initial decision to place Christmas in the orphanage after his daughter gives birth to a child identified as Mexican, but whom Hines immediately deems black. So often in the novel, events are presented in flashbacks, as if to say the past is prologue and that to understand the present requires a recitation of history. It is as if Faulkner is saying this is a society, a world that thinks backward. Hightower is the epitome of this retrograde mentality, so it is no wonder that Joe, who cannot get beyond the curse of his childhood, finally seeks sanctuary with Hightower.

THE "GOOD NIGGER"

The Nelse Patton lynching is part of the background that informs *Light in August,* although Faulkner takes the typical lynching story and makes it not merely the shame of a community, of what it has done to a black man, but also the story of a complicity in evil that the victim himself cannot escape. No one can ever know what happened in that encounter between Patton and his victim, but there was some kind of intimacy—some claim made on the black man or the white woman, or both, that informed Faulkner's exploration of a character who is white and black by turns and turns on himself even as his community rejects and annihilates him. Jefferson cannot repudiate Joe Christmas without also repudiating itself. Joe, like Charles Bon in *Absalom, Absalom!*, is a passable white man who ultimately does not want to pass as one. His face is the parchment, the durable surface, on which his society writes his identity. But also like Bon, Christmas cannot content himself with the construct others impose on him. Is that what finally destroyed Nelse Patton? His sudden, overwhelming need to lash out at a community that thought it knew him as a "good nigger"? What did he say to the white woman he slashed? What did she say to him? Patton, a conduit, was carrying a message from her husband. Joanna Burden, the daughter of abolitionists who died while trying to secure voting and human rights for black people, tells an incredulous Joe Christmas that she wants him to be her messenger, to take on her responsibilities by acknowledging a "Negro" identity, schooling himself as a Negro lawyer, and helping the Negro community as one of their own. In effect, she is saying that this is his fate, to be defined by an identity he has been unable to accept for the thirty years of his existence. To Christmas, her high-handed program for his redemption is humiliating. Was Nelse Patton, in the final reckoning, unwilling to be defined as a white man's messenger boy? Did his razor slash reflect a sudden welling up of outrage over his fate? Patton's own story may have been much simpler than Christmas's, but the circumstances of such murders appeared like a black shadow in the novelist's imagination, a part of the truth his community tried to suppress.

When Joe Christmas is captured, after barbering and walking openly on a street in Mottstown, closing the circle of his life, returning to where he began, the populace is perplexed. "He dont look any more like a nigger than I do," says more than one person, and another calls him a "white nigger." Only when Joe does not strike back during an assault is he deemed appropriately black. In a scene reminiscent of the Nelse Patton lynching, the "sheriff made a speech, asking the folks to respect the law and [saying] that him and the Jefferson sheriff both promised that the nigger would get a quick and fair trial; and then somebody in the crowd says, 'Fair, hell. Did he give that white woman a fair trial?'" That Joe has returned home, to the very site of his racial branding, goes unrecognized, part of an unknown or unspoken history familiar to the Falkner family.

Even more than Nelse Patton, Joe Christmas has been implicated in the life of the white community, involved with a white woman who draws a gun on him before he murders her, a white woman who has said that both of them should die. She does not say why. But her despair seems to stem from the same isolation and thwarted love that has driven Joe Christmas nearly his entire life. She has been his lover but treated him as a "Negro," setting food out for him and providing a Negro cabin. He has become part of her property, part of her plans, and Joe revolts not merely against her but all the hegemonic forces that he can no longer evade. After running for days, no longer even wanting to eat, he presents himself as virtually an ascetic, beyond the cravings and sufferings of mortal flesh. But to the white community he is no longer himself but Negro—and worse, a product of miscegenation that had been undetectable.[8] For Christmas, the problem has been even more excruciating: How to live not beside the Negro but with what he dreads as the Negro within himself.

That is all Joe is to Percy Grimm, who castrates Christmas and proclaims, "Now you'll let white women alone, even in hell." The racist-theological axis of evil is complete. Grimm fulfills Hines's call for Christmas to be lynched as a way of saving the community. All along Grimm has seen himself as an instrument of justice, not as a man exercising free will. Joe himself has been schooled by McEachern to believe in a predestined life, and he seems to accept its culmination:

> For a long moment he looked up at them with peaceful and unfathomable and unbearable eyes. Then his face, body, all, seemed to collapse, to fall in upon itself, and from out the slashed garments about his hips and loins the pent black blood seemed to rush like a released breath. It seemed to rush out of his pale body like the rush of sparks from a rising rocket; upon that black blast the man seemed to rise soaring into their memories forever and ever. They are not to lose it, in whatever peaceful valleys, beside whatever placid and reassuring streams of old age, in the mirroring faces of whatever children they will contemplate old disasters and newer hopes. It will be there, musing, quiet, steadfast, not fading and not particularly threatful, but of itself alone serene, of itself alone triumphant. Again from the town, deadened a little by the walls, the scream of the siren mounted toward its unbelievable crescendo, passing out of the realm of hearing.

The black blood recalls Stevens's race-based theological psychology, enhanced by the biblical "slashed garments" and the "pale body" resurrected in death. Joe Christmas is finally released from all the pent-up years of a fraught, bifurcated life. Self and soul seem finally at one as Christmas passes from men into another realm beyond human anguish. How he dies, however, in that last phrase, "passing out of the realm of hearing," puts him beyond the pain of the society that has contrived his torment, not his salvation.

Christmas's epiphany is followed by Hightower's reckoning with his own failed life, his inability to live in the present, to minister to his wife, to make of Jefferson anything except a repository for his fantasies about the war, abetted by his faithful black servant, strongly reminiscent of Faulkner's Callie Barr. That Joe Christmas should end his life in Hightower's home, where his slaveholder grandfather and abolitionist father engendered his conflicted patrimony, links Hightower to Joe Christmas, Joanna Burden, and even Percy Grimm, who has seen himself as a Christian messenger. Hightower experiences a tremendous sense of release in the words that recall Christmas's passing: "Then it seems to him that some ultimate dammed flood within him breaks and rushes away. He seems to watch it, feeling himself losing contact with earth, lighter and lighter, emptying, floating. 'I am dying,' he thinks. 'I should pray. I should try to pray.' But he does not. He does not try. 'With all air, all heaven, filled with the lost and unheeded crying of all the living who ever lived, wailing still like lost children among the cold and terrible stars. . . . I wanted so little. I asked so little.'" Like Christmas, Hightower rejects prayer even as he welcomes his own oblivion, using Christmas's very words, "I wanted so little. I asked so little." But Hightower, dying or not, remains fixated on the past, as the last words of his reverie reveal: "it seems to him that he still hears them: the wild bugles and the clashing sabres and the dying thunder of hooves."

Neither Christmas's castration nor Hightower's elegiacal musings can serve as the novel's ending. Instead, we are on the road again with Lena and Byron Bunch, as rendered by a furniture repairer and dealer who tells his wife, in bed, about how he picked up the couple in his truck on the way to where they cannot say. Suddenly we see Byron and Lena and their story from the outside. Byron is the "kind of fellow you wouldn't see the first glance if he was alone by himself in the bottom of a empty concrete swimming pool." Did Faulkner see himself in Byron, the little man who takes on the burden of another man's woman? Is that why Byron has a poet's name? Faulkner seems to have been drawing on a memory of having been taunted in a Memphis brothel, when one of the customers asked the prostitutes if they have ever enjoyed "a good time with little Billy." Phil Stone witnessed the incident, and though Faulkner did not react to the provocation, Stone knew his friend resented remarks about his size.[9]

The furniture repairer wonders "how a young, strapping gal like her ever come to take up with" scrawny Byron. The couple travel from Jefferson, where, as the furniture repairer says, "they lynched that nigger." The point of the story is how Byron got up his nerve to bed Lena even as the husband is preparing to bed his wife, who is not as resistant as Lena but nevertheless is not prepared to let her husband have his way without considerable persuasion. Byron is the "little cuss," the underdog who has the furniture repairer rooting for him. Although Byron and Lena are ostensibly searching for Burch/Brown, who has run away from his family responsibilities, the furniture repairer surmises, "I dont think she had any idea of finding whoever it was she was following." She admonishes Byron for trying to sleep with her on the truckbed, but after going off in a funk he returns. The novel ends as her journey began, with Lena apostrophizing: "My, my. A body does get around. Here we aint been coming from Alabama but two months, and now it's already Tennessee."

And so she closes another circle, but one that leads her on and that promises if not exactly a happy ending, a new life and set of possibilities, and a world that does not seem quite so claustrophobic as the one that encompasses all that has gone before. The furniture repairer, like the subjects of his story, embarks on a new kind of history. The strapping Lena prevails, even though she is the member of the weaker sex in a fascist state, and so does Byron Bunch, that "little cuss," a surprising winner in a realm that regards him as a loser. If Lena has been fooled by the bigger and stronger and flashier Lucas Burch/Joe Brown, she is no fool. She is strong enough to pick up Byron and put him out of her bed but also smart enough to follow his lead. Faulkner emphasized other qualities not often mentioned in discussions of Lena Grove: her endurance and courage.[10] He might also have mentioned her droll humor. When Byron says, "I done come too far now . . . I be dog if I'm going to quit now," she answers, "'Aint nobody never said for you to quit." Lena may seem pathetic to others, or a fallen woman to still others, but she keeps her own counsel and never says more than is necessary to accomplish her purposes. She cannot be deflected or drawn into the furniture repairer's curiosity about the lynching. "She clammed up," he notes, assuming Byron told her not to talk about it. But it is just as likely that the careful Lena knows better than to say more. And this is not a new Lena. She has been this way all along, as economical with her biography as William Faulkner when asked a direct question: "How far you come from?" Henry Armstid asks her. She takes her time, suiting herself to the moment: "She expels her breath. It is not a sigh so much as a peaceful expiration, as though of peaceful astonishment. 'A right good piece, it seems now. I come from Alabama.'" The astonished Armstid cries out: "Alabama? In your shape? Where's your folks?" Lena, not willing to engage her interlocutor, "does not look at him" but simply announces, "I'm looking to meet him up this way." In one stroke she has established her mission even as she has refused to satisfy Armstid's curiosity or cater to his concern. While seeming to depend on the kindness of strangers, Lena remains in control. She never loses her composure. She is "obliged" to those who help her, and yet she never behaves like the weak women that Joe Christmas reviles and attacks.

Lena seems to have had her origins in the story of Dorothy Ware, a prostitute who had impressed Lee Brown, a Clarksdale gambler friend of Phil Stone's and Faulkner's. She had walked all the way from north Alabama to Memphis after her family had disowned her for consorting with a city man. Forever estranged from her kin, she made a life with Brown, who became her exclusive partner.[11] He was more like Lucas Burch/Joe Brown than Byron Bunch, but the very idea of a woman who could act so independently fascinated Faulkner. Dorothy Ware commanded a certain authority.

The novel begins and ends with Lena's story, in the present tense, as if it is still happening. She has come a "fur piece" in a body that gets around, establishing her as a kind of folk epic heroine, a fertility goddess, a part of the "natural strength of the earth,"[12] crossing the hot ground of a southern summer like those pastoral figures on Keats's urn. She is, as Faulkner said, "the captain of her soul."[13] She is eternal, unlike those fascist twins, Joe Christmas and Percy Grimm.[14] She never hardens or secludes herself, or shows the slightest self-pity. All plots become absorbed in hers: "We need only look at the whole structure to see that the book is not a tragedy with an inappropriate bit of farce tacked on at the end, but a comedy which contains a tragedy and assimilates it, as life assimilates disease and death."[15]

Toward a New Kind of History

Light in August represents a convergence and culmination of themes that had been building up the pressure of *Flags in the Dust/Sartoris, The Sound and the Fury,* the two versions of *Sanctuary,* and *As I Lay Dying.* None of these novels encompasses so many antinomies, the forces of past and present, white and black, good and evil, male and female, along so many different story fronts as the new novel did. Blackness hovers in *Sanctuary,* like the black razor-murderer in jail, like Popeye, whom Temple tries to dismiss as "a little black thing like a nigger boy," like the black people in the New Orleans sketches, a constituent of the scene and yet never fully exposed, like the old Colonel's black family, and like William Faulkner himself, the small, dark man of *Mosquitoes.* Race runs riot in "Dry September," and a razor-murderer haunts "That Evening Sun," but not until *Light in August* is Faulkner able, or perhaps willing, to interlock black and white lives, far more tightly than in *Flags in the Dust/Sartoris,* or even in *The Sound and the Fury.*

And yet why Faulkner should write *Light in August* after *Sanctuary* is no more apparent than why he wrote *As I Lay Dying* after *The Sound and the*

Fury. Intervening events seemed to have had an influence on his creative life: the Great Flood of 1927 covering so many lives, with its disproportionate impact on the poorest, has its outcome in the Bundren saga. *Sanctuary* has a European ending consonant with the burgeoning of fascism, first in the Italy Faulkner saw firsthand but also well under way in Germany, with corrupt corollaries at home. Faulkner's Nazi Percy Grimm must take a black life in order to feel in full possession of his own whiteness. The great fear of the other, embodied in the immigrant influx, in the very idea of foreignness that is so palpable in the responses to the little immigrant girl in *The Sound and the Fury,* becomes the crucible in which Joe Christmas is forged as a man who is an other to himself and a perplexity to his community. Does he rape Joanna Burden as a black man or as a white man? He thinks he might be black, and others say so, and thinking and saying make it so in the tautological universe of *Light in August.* Popeye is white, and yet Temple fantasizes him as black. Nelse Patton was a trusted black, so what was going on between him and that white woman? Something that did not make the papers but could be addressed in a novel. Joe cannot run away when, like Nelse Patton, he razors off a white woman's head. He runs in a circle toward his own fate as, in effect, Patton did as well. Patton carried a message to a white woman, and it was supposed he also wanted the woman who became the message. Did the woman lead him on—as is often alleged in rape cases? A white woman? It was, in Faulkner's day, an unbearable thought. But is it the thought, the question, that Faulkner considered when creating Joe's intercourse with Joanna Burden, the descendent of abolitionists, who themselves are murdered before they can consummate a more perfect union by securing the black right to vote?

And where in this turn of events did pregnant Lena Grove turn up? Why was she even needed in a story already as powerful, as grim as the burden that Joanna, Joe, and Gail Hightower, haunted by the Civil War, carry as the accretions of the past, of a slaveholding, war-ravaged South that drives their tortured trajectory in the present?

Something happened to Faulkner in Hollywood when Howard Hawks told him there had to be a woman in the story, and Joan Crawford told him that a woman would have to hold her own with men. She would not martyr herself to war in a series of reaction shots in a story about men any more than Lena plays the victim. There Lena is: stolid and persistent, trying to catch up with the wayward Lucas Burch aka Joe Brown while fending off the temperate, ironically named Byron Bunch, who is a Romantic once removed by virtue of his last name. Lena is serene, a calmative, the quiet melody of a society that may be riven by race but also rejuvenated by her journey, no matter how quixotic, and even pathetic. There is light in August, hope and harvest in the very heat of the season and its passions.

Until *Light in August,* the past functions in Faulkner's work as primarily a fixative, manipulated by memory but nevertheless remaining a kind of received lore and legend as stories to be repeated, elaborated, and exaggerated. But in *Light in August,* the very structure of the novel rewrites history, remaking it in many ways that lead to *Absalom, Absalom!,* the re-creation of war in the later Hollywood years, and in the reconception of the past in *Go Down, Moses, Requiem for a Nun, A Fable,* the Snopes trilogy, and *The Reivers.*

16

Hollywood at Home

October 1932–August 1933

HOLLYWOOD FIELD HAND

From the end of October 1932 to August 1933, William Faulkner moonlighted at home as a screenwriter, thanks to the good offices of Howard Hawks. To Hal Smith, Faulkner mentioned working on a movie script while he had been taking care of a sick Estelle and the children during the Christmas holidays. Then she had fallen down the stairs. No one, Faulkner admitted, would have been surprised if the accident had happened to him. Faulkner did not name Estelle's sickness, but by end of 1932, it was certain she had become pregnant, always a precarious condition for her.

Faulkner expected to get to work on a Snopes novel, a project he kept delaying, but his thoughts turned not to New York and literary matters but to Hollywood. He was a "mere four months' bride of the golden west" with the knowledge of "an amateur, no matter how eager and willing," he confided to Hubert Starr. That phantasmagorical hegira to Death Valley continued to bemuse Faulkner. It seemed like a "helioptical illusion," or some kind of allergic reaction—a "brick rash"? Where he might have been exposed to building construction dust, he did not say, but he obviously enjoyed his anthropological confusion: "What is the right term when making sign talk with the aborigines east of the SIERRA?" He liked to put on the persona of an aloof writer out of place in ersatz Hollywood, but his allusions to the contemporary scene, to a big-band leader, suggest he was much more engaged in his surroundings than he liked to let on to all but close confidants like Starr: "It was pretty bad, but from what I saw of Long Beach, I believe that some of the

381

buildings can be spared, and I dont think that all of the folks will be missed. Probably anyway when they reach the bottom of it, they will find it was only Melvin Holman falling down stairs with his trombones." Faulkner made lifelong friends in Hollywood, like the Elliotts, and indulged himself, at least in letter form, in a bit of swaggering worthy of Hemingway, telling Starr: "Give my best to Bill Elliott. I would have written him a Xmas card, but I knew he would be down at Deauville, in the ocean, and his hands would be too wet to read it. I will bring my fishing tackle when I come, and you can send word on up the mountain. Tell the trout that papa's coming home."[1]

On January 12, MGM's script department had in hand Faulkner's fully developed screenplay "War Birds," derived from the diary of a World War I aviator, John McGavock Grider, that had been rewritten after the pilot's death by Major Elliot White Springs and published in *Liberty* magazine in 1926. The diary had been a likely source for Faulkner's short story "Ad Astra," which featured the Sartoris twins. Grider, a southerner and the grandson of a Confederate army captain who later became a banker, had obvious appeal: "I hear that the Germans have the goods in airplanes and A.A. guns. I guess it's the North and South over again," the diarist notes.[2] He is eager for combat in France but is cautioned: "An English general made us a talk and said this war was no great adventure: you were either scared to death or bored to death all the time." While training in England, he indulges in wild drinking parties even as he realizes the precarious plight of men and their machines: "If you crash, the gas tank is right at your back like in a Camel and your legs are up under the motor. There's not much hope for the pilot." He watches even the best pilots—two or three a week—die in crashes without ever experiencing combat. Arnold Bennett makes an appearance, "getting some local colour for a book." Grider sees Chinese workers imported to dig trenches and wonders, "Why don't they go over and get two hundred and fifty thousand of our negroes?" The diary's casual racism is apparent in his comment on one of his white friends: "Cal is just like a nigger. He can wear anybody's clothes and does. He never worries about anything and hasn't a nerve in his body." Grider chafes at the delay, wishing to become "one of the elect," as he refers to the pilots in France. An increasingly bitter tone creeps into his entries: "It will never do to let the people at home find out the truth about this war. They've been fed on bunk until they'd never believe anything that didn't sound like a monk's story of the Crusades." The joy he took in shooting down Huns and executing brilliant aerial maneuvers gives way to nihilism: "The war won't prove anything." One dictator will be replaced with another, he declares. He considers his options: "I only hope I can stick it out and not turn yellow. I've heard of men landing in Germany when they didn't have to. They'd be better off dead because they've got to live with themselves the rest of their lives. I wouldn't mind being shot down; I've got no taste for glory and I'm no more good, but I've got to keep on until I can quit honourably. All I'm fighting for now is my own self-respect." Shortly thereafter an editor's note explains that Grider was shot down and respectfully buried by Germans.

What to do with this authentic-sounding, vivid, but also grim portrayal of the air war? MGM's reader recommended focusing on the thrilling air battles and the romantic, heroic quest of the aviators. Howard Hawks rejected a treatment with a silly love triangle that did not do much with the diary's depiction of war, and he turned to Faulkner, who, in effect, rewrote *Flags in the Dust,* with some elements of "Ad Astra" and "All the Dead Pilots," for the screen, with several remarkable changes. Bayard is the steady brother, a cool war ace, not the tormented suicidal figure of Faulkner's fiction. Bayard's twin, John, is the wayward one, recently married but still a philanderer, who dies in the air recklessly pursuing the enemy, feeling betrayed by his French mistress, Antoinette, whom he has discovered with another man. To complicate matters more, Bayard brings home Lothar, the German pilot who killed his brother, as well as Antoinette, both of whom Bayard befriends when, in their own way, they show a surprising fidelity to the memory of his dead brother. Antoinette, forced into becoming a kept woman, nevertheless remained devoted to John in ways that he would never know, becoming in effect his body servant as she launders his clothes. Lothar has also lost a brother in the war, and like his namesake in "Ad Astra," he understands the futility of war. Bayard stifles the impulse to shoot Lothar, thus ending the violent cycle of war, much as the Bayard in *The Unvanquished* renounces the right to retaliate against his father's murderer, thereby enacting his own Reconstruction. Faulkner could have been thinking of the South when he has Lothar tell Bayard, "Your brother is slain, but my country is slain; fallen from a greater height than any Camel has ever reached."[3]

Faulkner's willingness to reconstitute his characters and plots and settings rivals the Hollywood penchant for remakes. His script begins with John's son, Johnny, born before John could get home, realizing that his "uncle" Lothar is the German who shot down his father and that his "aunt" Antoinette was his father's mistress. John's mother, Caroline, has kept all knowledge of this family history from Johnny, but when her fourteen-year-old son guesses the truth, she shares with him John's diary, much of which is featured in the film in shots that show Caroline's hand turning diary pages in double-exposure dissolves that turn her hand into John's as he writes his diary. In effect, "War Birds" becomes the story of a writer, as Faulkner draws directly on Grider's work. "War Birds" is also about a writer/hero who becomes his family's integrating force, a role Faulkner claimed for himself.

In one of the first scenes, John writes in his diary that "Bayard's a better man than I am. . . . Funny we should be twins and still be so different." Funny, too, that the death of this man who cannot remain faithful to his wife, and who rejects his mistress when she has been unfaithful, inspires everyone connected to him to treat one another with such integrity and respect. John has always wanted to do the right thing, but he feels like a fraud. He has been too weak to follow Bayard's example, a brother who serves as John's conscience—really as an older brother, not a twin, much as William Faulkner behaved with Dean. Bayard is a genuine hero, if rather stiff and without John's winning personality. Perhaps in creating this version of Bayard, Faulkner had his own brother Jack in mind, who fought the battles that Billy could only invent for himself. John, for all his failings, believes in family fealty, as Faulkner did. John's diary becomes his testament to the value of love and loyalty, no matter how many times he has failed to fulfill his mission to be a good man. John is eloquent about his failings, confessing to Bayard: "I never was anything much but your shadow. So you can go back and be the man I never was and never will be. So they will say, well those Sartoris boys made one good man between them."

Faulkner's use of the term "double exposure dissolve" nine times throughout the script emphasizes a superimposition of images that reflect the simultaneity of events in the present and also between past and present. This cinema technique is the equivalent of italics in *The Sound and the Fury*. What happens now in the film also happened then, and what happens now dissolves into what happens next, as if any moment of time is a conduit of the past and future. This is the Bergsonian time that Faulkner said he believed in.

Exactly how Hawks might have shepherded this script through the censors is hard to imagine. Certainly John's line that "sooner or later I'll be in another jam, fumbling around under another skirt" would have been bowdlerized. But the story of John's redemption through the way others honor his life might, perhaps, have carried the day for the director, an expert in getting scripts approved that skirted propriety. As Caroline tells Antoinette, "Bayard says that in us he [John] is not dead, in the three of us and Johnny."

"War Birds" did not have a Hollywood plot, which is perhaps what sealed its doom. The story is couched in terms of John Sartoris's point of view, "his furious and unbelieving 'outrage' which eventually develops into a death wish syndrome." His despair is unrelieved by "Hollywood types: no good-bad girl, no red-blooded young men fighting for their country, no villain."[4] That Faulkner was willing to put his fiction at the service of his Hollywood job is significant, especially since he radically altered Bayard's nature. Early on, in other words, an inclination to redeem his characters, which became stronger as he matured as a writer, had its beginnings in Hollywood. The commercial demand for happy endings—in this case, the "ghost of John's ship" looks down at the reconstituted family, "his face bright, peaceful"—may be hokey, and yet it reflected a genuine side of Faulkner he had no fear of exploiting.

But Hawks did not find these southern characters congenial to his genius, and the no-flashbacks director did not have the patience or the interest to work on Faulkner's intricate screenplay. Hawks later said he got mad at Faulkner: "I got so sick and tired of the goddam inbred people he was writing about. I said, 'Why don't you write about some decent people for goodness' sake?' 'Like who?' I said, 'Well, you fly around, don't you know some pilots or something that you can write about?'"[5] Of course, that comment led to *Pylon*. But hadn't Hawks missed the point of "War Birds"? Wasn't Bayard's bringing home a French woman and a German, both sick of war, exactly the antidote to the inbred world the director deplored?

During the writing of "War Birds," Hollywood money had gone into another Rowan Oak bedroom and bath and paid for a paint job. Hollywood had become a Faulkner province, as he vouchsafed to Wasson: "You said something in Memphis about following through all my stories which you handle, into movies, etc. I would like you to do this, myself. But apparently I can do better for myself through Howard Hawks than agents can.... I would like to have you protect me from myself, but how to do it? I am under no written contract with anyone. This arrangement is like that of a field hand; either of us (me or M.G.M.) to call it off without notice, they pay me by the week and to pay a bonus on each original story."[6]

On March 18, 1933, Faulkner the field hand wrote to Will Bryant that although Hollywood money was fitful, he did not anticipate a "complete cessation of salary," and he still wanted to acquire four lots north of Rowan Oak for their agreed-upon price of $1,500. The property gave him a profound pleasure that he felt bound to share with Bryant: "Spring is here. From my window I can see three peach trees in bloom, and a struggling turkey gobbler and a hen with a brood of chickens, and across the pasture, a horse. There is no satisfaction like it anywhere under the sun, I believe." He even wanted to brag on himself a little: "Last year I had the best kitchen garden in town; this year I want to do even better." He would do Cash Bundren proud: "I have also framed the inside of the stable, and I am now hunting square hewn timbers to restore it." Hollywood might be calling, but Rowan Oak held him: "I intend to own as much of this property as I can get. I dont think that even a sheriff's paper could remove me now."[7] By April 11, banking on the $6,000 he had received from Paramount for the film adaptation of *Sanctuary*, Faulkner sent Bryant a check for $1,800 for more property, and with considerable pride, if also wariness, he declared: "My credit is good now, and I want to keep it so. Also, I want to use it, judiciously of course, as I believe a certain amount of debt is good for a young man. But I also know that credit, in the hands of one young in business as I am, can also be dynamite."[8]

Revamping Rowan Oak remained a costly enterprise and one that required some adjustments. After Faulkner installed a forced-air heating system, a strange odor pervaded the house. Mammy Callie, a heavy user of snuff, had been spitting in the open floor registers, a practice promptly halted.[9] John Phillips, a local black man who had done some carpentry at the home, saw Faulkner spreading gravel in the deeply rutted driveway and asked why Faulkner was doing the job himself. He had run out of money, he told Phillips, who in turn said he would do the work and Faulkner could pay him later. They agreed on a $1.50 per day plus dinner. Later, when Phillips was having an asthma attack, Faulkner drove him to the hospital and paid for his prescription at the Gathright-Reed Drugstore.[10]

"The Most Anticipated Motion Picture of the Current Season"

On April 12, *Today We Live* premiered in Oxford: "A short note to tell you that one of my pictured stories is to be shown here Wednesday and Thursday nights," Faulkner wrote to Will Bryant. Rowan Oak was in no shape for guests, but Faulkner wanted the Bryants to see the movie and offered to put them up in a hotel.[11] With or without the Bryants (they could have seen the film in nearby Water Valley on April 14), the film was shown at the Lyric Theater, owned by Bob Williams, the husband of Faulkner's cousin Sallie Murry. With family members present, and some of Faulkner's "hired help," Williams introduced Faulkner, who gave a short talk about the differences between screenplay and novel writing. He also joked that his family could see that he did work from time to time.[12] Actually, it was a sore point with a writer who hated interruptions when he was writing and looked like he was not doing much. Did he smile watching the Mickey Mouse cartoon and the newsreel that completed the evening's entertainment?

A laudatory review in the *Athens (OH) Sunday Messenger* (May 14) noted the story by "brilliant American writer William Faulkner" was the "most anticipated motion picture of the current season." Similar notices appeared across the country, including the *Laredo (TX) Times* (April 28), *Berkeley (CA) Daily Gazette* (May 13), *Salt Lake Tribune* (November 5), with the *Waterloo (IA) Daily Courier* mentioning Faulkner's "powerful story." Philip K. Scheuer sneered in the *Los Angeles Times* (June 2): "Britishers with Faulkner neuroses." Faulkner's name appeared frequently beside that of Hawks, already well established with *Scarface* (1932). The *San Antonio Express* (May 7) headlined "William Faulkner's 'Today We Live,'" even though he had been given story, not screenplay, credit.

A feature story in the *Greenwood (MS) Commonwealth* (April 22), "Hollywood Scared William Faulkner," quoted him as saying the "miles of stages and hundreds of thousands of dollars worth of equipment" had been "all too big for me." But a different angle on the war had given him courage to explore the role of women behind the lines, "risking their lives in a hail of shot and shell." The article portrayed him as writing "earthy" novels in longhand in an antebellum house with "sanitary conveniences . . . only in the backyard," oil lamps, and a recently installed telephone.

Critics consider *Today We Live* as second-rate—"intolerably heavy, noble, stout fellow style."[13] The two male leads, Franchot Tone and Robert Young, playing British sailors, sacrifice themselves in attacking a German ship so that the American flyer, Gary Cooper, does not have to die in the same operation. Instead he survives to marry Crawford, who no longer has to remain loyal to her lesser love, Young, who has been blinded in a previous mission. The impact on certain audiences and servicemen was palpable. A column, "Screen Life: Hollywood to Fairbanks," in the *Fairbanks (AK) Daily Miner* (December 6) quoted a general who had seen the picture:

> I do not know the Mr. Faulkner who wrote the story. I do not even know whether or not he was an ex-service man, but if he didn't get his information from actual experience, he must have received it from some one who was well informed. Time and time again we officers had to deal with matters that were not strictly official . . . matters that never went down on record . . . acting as father, brother, and even Father Confessor. . . . During the war we officers had the opportunity of seeing human nature in the RAW, and I must say that the humans involved in this production . . . are typical of the many which we met on and behind the lines. TODAY WE LIVE is a dignified picture, seldom theatrical.

However much Hollywood tampered with Faulkner's fiction and his script, dressing up Crawford in gowns by Adrian and setting her and Gary Cooper in awkward drawing room scenes, something had come through—enough, it seems, to have encouraged Faulkner to invite Will Bryant to see for himself. "The unexpected touches of this remarkable writer are prevalent throughout the picture," reported the *Jackson (MS) Clarion-Ledger* (May 16). The film opened to good attendance in New York and elsewhere, but box office receipts quickly dropped with mixed reviews.[14]

One feature of the Faulkner-Hawks collaboration has not received its due. Neither Tone nor Young can rival Cooper's physical stature and presence, and yet they are just as effective in war, not needing to exemplify the fascist idea of strength. Young, who seems silly and effete, proves just as capable as a gunner on one of Cooper's bombing runs as he is on the torpedo boat alongside Tone, his childhood companion. Later, Faulkner and Hawks would return to their antifascist attack by creating Eddie, the rummy in *To Have and Have Not,* who plays a pivotal role in saving hero Humphrey Bogart's life. Faulkner, for all his initial faltering in Hollywood, more than proved himself among the big shots.

An Amateur Who "Does Not Truly Know His Way About"

By April 20, after three months of instruction, and shortly after publishing his second poetry collection, *A Green Bough,* William Faulkner soloed. Pilot, homeowner, landowner, farmer, pater familias, screenwriter, novelist, and poet—all were in perpetual play. He was soaring and flush with movie money, even after his salary on his second MGM contract had been reduced by six hundred dollars to three hundred dollars a week. To celebrate, he purchased a Waco-210 monoplane.

Faulkner spent twenty hours learning to fly when about twelve was standard. He had the best instructor imaginable—Vernon Omlie, the "coolest flier" Navy Sowell, a mechanic and parachute jumper, had ever seen. The veteran pilot had a "weathered face, very kind." He was virile, fearless, but cautious. His wife, Phoebe, had a "scarred face like a map from the crashes and fires of those days."[15] She kept her hair cropped like a man's and provided Faulkner with a model for Laverne in *Pylon.*[16] Phoebe liked to watch Vernon and Bill kid one another. It was a sign of mutual respect, she thought, between men who realized they were important in their own professions.[17] The word for Faulkner's flying was "inconsistent." He would "fly extremely well one day and then the next day would flip rather badly." Navy thought Faulkner had his mind on other things and possibly had poor depth perception.[18]

Why Faulkner wanted a second and last collection of poetry published he did not say, except to remark to his publisher, "This is a fair sized book now, and the stuff does not seem so bad, on rereading," even if, he called it "2nd poetry."[19] He had been getting the book together over the past five years, although many of the poems were written much earlier. Perhaps Faulkner was using Smith's firm as a "last hurrah."[20] This handsome volume in green cloth, with its inlaid frontispiece, and two pictorial labels, may also have spoken to his earliest sense of bookmaking—in this case graced with Lynd Ward's woodcuts on the cover: a nude woman kneeling and bent forward with hair cascading to her knees and below her a nude male crouching with his head down and his hands uplifted, in scenes of enigmatic effulgence.

William Gorman's review in the *New York Sun* (April 21) quickly spotted influences: T. S. Eliot, Hart Crane, e. e. cummings, and A. E. Housman. This was accomplished if derivative work, not the "powerful 'original'" prose from Mississippi but a good antidote to that common notion of the author as a "slave to his corrosive vision of Southern Evil." D. J., the *Cincinnati Times-Star* reviewer (April 25), called Faulkner well-read but "callow," even if some lines approached the quality of Tennyson:

> She is a flower lightly cast
> Upon a river flowing, dimly going
> Between two silent shores where
> willows lean.

In the *Saturday Review of Literature* (April 29), William Rose Benét also found lines to admire but also much that was "merely empty rhetoric" in an amateur who "does not truly know his way about." Morris U. Shappes in *Poetry* (October) offered no higher verdict. Babette Deutsch in the October issue of *Virginia Quarterly Review* called *A Green Bough* full of "jangled but sometimes moving music." She quoted lines that she did not apply to Faulkner's prose but that emerge out of his obsession with a sense of the past as a faded martial glory that still provided solace and suffused the quietude, to use a favorite Faulkner word, of a historied sensibility:

> The sun sank down, and with him went
> A pageantry whose swords are sheathed
> At last, as warriors long ago
> Let fall their storied arms and breathed

> This air and found this peace as he
> Who across this sunset moves to rest,
> Finds but simple sense and sounds;
> And this is all, and this is best.

"Conventional Attributes and Uncontrollable Desires"

On May 22, a month after the publication of *A Green Bough*, *The Story of Temple Drake* received respectful attention in the *Jackson (MS) Clarion-Ledger,* which praised Miriam Hopkins for portraying with "perfect understanding the complexities of literature's most spirited character . . . a strange composite of good and evil forces, a curious mixture of conventional attributes and uncontrollable desires." This was surprising, since women's clubs had protested the making of the picture, and, as some film historians suggest, Hollywood thereafter subjected itself to self-imposed censorship by the Hays Office to police the treatment of sex and violence. George Raft, who had become a star in *Scarface* playing a gangster, turned down the high-profile role of Popeye, renamed Trigger, calling the role "career suicide." But handsome Jack La Rue, Raft's replacement, had a rewritten character with the sex appeal absent from Popeye. La Rue's Trigger still terrorizes Temple, and the film retains some of the novel's sinister atmosphere, as the *Greenwood (MS) Commonwealth* (June 8) noted. "You all know what this story is," announced the *Winona (MS) Times* on August 11, "so don't fail to see it." Popeye's impotence and the failure of Horace Benbow (renamed Stephen Benbow) to rectify the injustice to Lee Goodwin are erased in the film so that Stephen becomes a hero, urging Temple to confess to the truth and redeem herself at the end of Goodwin's trial.

Although Faulkner did no work for the film, he did meet with production assistant Jean Negulesco—later an important director. Negulesco, an art connoisseur and skillful draftsman, showed Faulkner black-and-white drawings of the rape scene. "Exactly what I had in mind," Faulkner said. Negulesco emphasized the play of shadow and light, and director Stephen Roberts used low-angle shots between Trigger's (Popeye's) legs as he moved toward Temple, menacing her. The film never loses focus on her even as it boldly portrays the rapist's point of view. Faulkner was impressed, calling the scene "brilliant." Later he asked Wasson to convey his thanks for making the story into a motion picture "I'm not ashamed of."[21]

Did *The Story of Temple Drake* have any impact on Faulkner?[22] The very idea would have been dismissed in an earlier age of Faulkner biography relying on his many contemptuous comments about Hollywood. And yet the ending of the film presages the sequel of Temple's moral rehabilitation in *Requiem for a Nun,* a novel Faulkner incepted before the end of 1933.[23] The filmmakers, at any rate, detected a humanity in Temple largely absent from *Sanctuary*'s ending, in which she appears in all her sullen imperviousness. That bleak denouement, it turned out, was not the end of the story, and Hollywood, not for the last time, would impinge on Faulkner's imagination.[24]

Faulkner left Oxford only once, it seems, in order to fulfill his Hollywood contract. In May, he spent a week in New Orleans working on a film eventually released as *Lazy River,* a story about a writer researching a story in the bayous. Tod Browning, famous for directing *Dracula* (1931), wired the studio: "BRILLIANT, CAPABLE MAN BUT HAD UNFORTUNATE START." The fiasco became one of Faulkner's parables about Hollywood. Even though on location, most of the time was taken up with long boat trips to a studio-built set. A frustrated Faulkner complained he got no cooperation from the other writers working on the movie. Then a telegram arrived: "FAULKNER IS FIRED, MGM STUDIO." Not to worry, Browning said, assuring the writer he would be rehired. Then a second telegram arrived: "BROWNING IS FIRED, MGM STUDIO." In truth, Faulkner could probably have stayed on the MGM payroll if he had been willing to return to Hollywood. He wrote Browning: "They want to can me, and I am ready to quit. Dont say anything more to the studio about keeping me on. Just let it go."[25] Faulkner's tall tale seems a perfect parable of his moonlighting, reflecting how quickly regimes in Hollywood could change.

POWER

Regime change, in fact, became the theme of his last work for MGM, "Mythical Latin-American Kingdom Story." Filed in the MGM script department on August 26, 1933, this ambitious original political scenario is like nothing he had written up to this point. It has been compared to Conrad's *Nostromo*,[26] a novel that creates a mythical Latin American country, Costaguana, dominated by foreign and material interests. Faulkner's script upends Conrad's patriarchal plot by centering on a revolt headed by a woman, Maria Rojas, a strident forerunner of Linda Snopes in *The Mansion*. Rojas aims to restore a deposed king by displacing the American agents who are exploiting the country's resources. Rojas explicitly rejects the role men have played in the country's politics: "Men, men, it is no wonder there is no stability in our country, since our mother land spawns only adolescents." When a girl laments, "Oh, if I were only a man just for a little while," Maria responds, "Will you be forever more a victim of man?" Why Rojas puts faith in the king is never explained, except that he is devoid of the male chauvinism and ineptitude that has dishonored the country: "It is chivalry, not love, for which we play this game," Maria declares. Rojas may seem a universe away from Caddy Compson, Addie Bundren, and Lena Grove, but she shares their self-sufficiency, and yet couples her independence with a quest for power.

The script is also an antiwar, antifascist indictment, beginning with a newsboy barking out headlines about American victories over Germany and confident proclamations of postwar prosperity and disarmament. The oppressed resort to their own thuggish tactics, however, suggesting Faulkner shared Conrad's skepticism about the merits of political liberation movements. Whatever crimes the occupiers have committed in exploiting the country's economy are matched by Rojas's brutal willingness to manipulate other women and men in her monomaniacal revolutionary program. Rojas preys on human vulnerabilities, making sure that the American pilot, Captain George Bowden, who brings in a gold shipment the revolutionaries will use in their cause, is discredited. She stages a scene in which his fiancé, Nancy, mistakenly supposes he has been bedding another woman, Marion, whom Rojas has tricked into meeting Bowden, who works for Nancy's mine-owner father. Rojas is so secretive it is not possible to fathom all of her maneuvers, but that is a consequence of her unwillingness to empathize with others, who simply become her tools. All that matters is that Nancy rejects Bowden and that the king, five years out of power, reasserts his sovereignty. While the king and his retinue follow Rojas's lead, they are aware that in the quest for power they may lose their humanity. Although much remains obscure and to be worked out in Faulkner's original draft, his Conradian dilemma is clear: remaining your own man apart from your employment and while engaging in politics is problematic.

Bowden, like the Americans in "Mistral," tries to avoid entanglements in the body politic, advising his mechanic, Otto Birdsong: "Dont tell anybody anything. Let them run their country like they want to. If they want to spend a holiday shooting each other, let them. And if anybody asks you what you think about it, say, no spika. Get that?" The very phrase "No spika" is the refrain of "Mistral," which Bowden repeats twice more in admonishing Birdsong, and which Birdsong desperately repeats as he is drawn into alcoholic conversations about what he is doing in the country. Otto foreshadows Eddie, the rummy, in Faulkner's other great antifascist screenplay for *To Have and Have Not*. Bowden has saved Birdsong's life in France during the war, but in this mythical political world neither man can save the other, and Birdsong can only drown his grief in drink, unable to articulate his agony, except to say "No spika." In short, "Mythical Latin-American Kingdom Story" has no redemptory ending, which is perhaps why it never made it to the screen.

That Bowden, a World War I ace, is reduced to carrying out the interests of a mine owner suggests how he has diminished himself. Faulkner's own plight as a hired hand, while it did not compromise his novels, nevertheless troubled him. He, too, worked for a pot of gold. Bowden, a man of few words, like Faulkner, keeps his own counsel and tries to wrest himself from Rojas's trap but in the end seems to realize he has become so implicated in the regime that he cannot exonerate himself. Even Nancy's father suggests as much, since he is willing to overlook Bowden's supposed infidelity to Nancy in order to maintain the business that controls the kingdom.

An MGM script reader dismissed "Mythical Latin-American Kingdom Story": "one or two characters that might have been very interesting if the author had taken the trouble to develop them." But Faulkner thought enough of this property to request Sam Marx's permission to use it as the basis of a novel. Faulkner did not follow up, but Marx, many years later, still thought the script filmmable.[27] In fact, he associated Faulkner's depiction of the king as a redeemer with a startling prefiguration of Castro at the beginning of his revolution when he seemed, said Marx, "an answer to everybody's prayer."[28] It should be taken seriously: "a complete screenplay," Bruce Kawin notes, "with no treatment or studio consultation whatever."[29]

17

Seeing It Both Ways

June 1933–December 1934

PAPPY WITHOUT A PENCIL

"Well, bud, we've got us a gal baby named Jill. Born Saturday [June 24] and both well," Faulkner wrote to Ben Wasson.[1] The anxious father had made sure Estelle had plenty of bed rest. The couple had wanted a boy, to be named Bill. When Estelle said she had disappointed him, he said, "No, there are too many Faulkner boys anyway."[2]

On the day of Jill's arrival, Faulkner dressed up in his RFC uniform, picked up his stepson Malcolm from school, and announced: "Mac, you are going with me to the hospital to see your little sister." The uniform, the announcement, typified Faulkner's sense of occasion. In Estelle's room, "Billy was standing there with a rare smile on his face and an aura of radiance about him," Malcolm remembered, watching his happy mama. They brought Jill home with a nurse, needed to spell Estelle during her recovery. Then another nurse, Narcissus McEwen, a "delightful, enormous, heavy set colored woman," became Jill's mammy for the next four years. As soon as Jill learned to talk, she called her father "Pappy," a name everyone then used for the head of the family.[3]

How much work Faulkner accomplished during this period is unclear. Malcolm said Pappy had no "set routine. . . . He never carried a notebook, or made any notes. He did not at any time carry a pencil or paper. He seemed to work largely from memory and observation." With Faulkner fully engaged in writing, the house remained "very quiet. No telephone, no radio and no door bell!" You could hear dogs barking, a rooster, a crow, a cow, and woodland sounds, but no traffic since the house was far enough away from the road. In the afternoon, he liked to take six-mile walks down Old Taylor Road toward Thacker Mountain and return home to his typewriter set up on a small table and commence composition.[4]

Faulkner's letters reveal that he did some work on a special, limited edition of *The Sound and the Fury,* to be produced in different-colored inks for the Benjy section, but the project proved too expensive to continue. "Working spasmodically at a novel," he told Ben Wasson.[5] Which one? He began on what would eventually become *Requiem for a Nun.* The Snopes saga always seemed to be on an intermittent boil. *Scribner's Magazine* saw Flem as a series character: "We want him triumphant to the point where everybody in America will hate him in unison. Then it will be time for his downfall." In short, the editor wanted a franchise, although he admitted that might involve turning Faulkner into a "Flem Snopes machine" that might hurt the writer "artistically."[6] Is this what Faulkner feared at a time when Hollywood was producing just this sort of serialization? Did the very clamor for more Snopes stories dissuade him?

Faulkner still had Hollywood in his system. Howard Hawks sent him an adaptation of "Honor," which Faulkner had looked over but did not "change . . . or do any work on."[7] But he wanted to know how Tod Browning was coming along with "Louisiana Lou" aka *Lazy River.* "I was getting pretty steamed up over it when I got the air. He's a fine fellow. Give him my best when you see him," Faulkner told Ben Wasson. That scripts and collaborative work did not engage him deeply proved not to be entirely true.

Dark Houses and Flying Visits

By the fall of 1933, he was broke again, worrying about taxes, his own and his mother's, and other obligations to Estelle's people, and what he could do for Dean. He worked on stories for the *Saturday Evening Post* and also projected a new collection of short fiction. In the midst of all this, he wrote to Hal Smith in early 1934 about yet another novel that began to erupt, set between 1860 and 1910, concerning the "violent breakup of a household or family." Initially titled "Dark House," it became the story of Thomas Sutpen, who "outraged the land, and the land then turned and destroyed the man's family." He would return to Quentin Compson, as narrator, who makes the story his own, projecting his suicidal feeling and bitterness over his sister onto the South, thus adding a dimension not to be found in conventional historical novels. Above all, Faulkner wanted to avoid the sentimentality and clichés, the "hoop skirts and plug hats."[8] This was not made-to-order work, or even in the nature of a sequel like *Requiem for a Nun,* or like the adventures of Flem Snopes, and it would take much time to layer the novel in terms of its time sequence and character development. The very originality of the work seemed to galvanize him. He was also beginning to "cook up"[9] the picaresque Civil War tales that he would later deepen and publish with a Reconstruction coda in *The Unvanquished.*

In November, accompanied by Dean and Vernon Omlie, Faulkner flew to New York to see Hal Smith, apparently to discuss plans for a Snopes novel, although it would take at least two years to complete, and in the meantime he was attempting to support himself with selling short stories. He also met with Bennett Cerf, still determined to get Faulkner on the Random House list, as were Harold and Alice Guinzburg and George Oppenheimer—all at Viking Press. Oppenheimer called Faulkner "one of the friendliest men I ever knew in my life, yet had an integrity of his own. He did want to give himself to too many. He came up from Oxford to renew himself, to go on binges and also to go on binges of cordiality. He had a quality of boyishness yet an enormous amount of Southern Chivalry. He played the country boy around the Algonquin."[10] Faulkner had turned down Bennett Cerf's offer to pay for an introduction to a limited edition of *The Sound and the Fury,* saying: "I would be proud to have you do THE SOUND AND THE FURY, and I hope that some day we can agree. But I dont need five hundred bad enough today to take that, when I believe that later we can both get more out of it."[11] On the November trip, he had evidently succumbed to another binge and wrote apologetically to Cerf: "I'm mighty sorry I made more or less of a fiasco of my part of the afternoon at your place. I was sick. It had started coming on soon after I got to New York, and I made the mistake of trying to carry on on liquor until I could get back home." The indulgent publisher replied: "Banish the thought that you made a fiasco of your part of the afternoon at my house. You gave a memorable performance and delivered several speeches that delighted your audience."[12]

Retrospectives and Prophecies

In the spring of 1934, on one of their frequent visits to the Peabody Hotel in Memphis, where they would dine with Aunt Bama, Estelle importuned her reluctant husband to arrange a visit to the brothel that had been featured in *Sanctuary.* She wanted to see one before she died. Aunt Bama had another engagement but took Estelle's side, and Faulkner agreed so long as Estelle did not make a fuss. Estelle remembered entering a "big, dull, empty parlour," to be received by a "big fat blowsy" madam of maybe forty-five or fifty. She began her day with beer and switched to gin at about four. She kept calling

Estelle "dearie." Like Miss Reba, she was enormous, with an elegant dress that covered her like a tent. But the visit had none of *Sanctuary*'s high drama. Faulkner seemed intent on confining his wife to the parlor. What went on elsewhere she did not see. After twenty minutes they left. Estelle doubted the woman knew that her establishment had figured in the novel, and Estelle supposed she would have been outraged at the use Faulkner had made of her and the business.[13]

The spring of 1934 also featured a Faulkner retrospective: two Phil Stone reminiscences in the April and June issues of *Oxford Magazine,* and the publication of a short-story collection, including some work dating back to the 1920s. Between 1933 and 1938 no recorded interviews with Faulkner or significant profiles appeared, making Stone's early notice a standout. He staked his claim, announcing that he knew more about Faulkner's literary history than anyone else alive—true, actually, to only about the late 1920s, when Faulkner shifted his attention to the East and West, attenuating their friendship. Stone wanted to portray the man who carried a handkerchief in his coat sleeve, the house painter, carpenter, and proficient amateur golfer who preferred the "company of simple unliterary people." The articles are a cloying and sententious performance—sort of like Gavin Stevens rambling on about Faulkner as a decent man but infuriating friend with a high talent but no genius. Stone devotes several pages to Faulkner as a descendent of frontier stock and to the changes in the economy as a consequence of the Civil War and Reconstruction. He retails the fraught legacy of old Colonel Falkner, with brief descriptions of latter-day Falkners. Of Faulkner's childhood, Stone permits himself only the testimony of a grandmother (father Murry's mother) that for "three weeks in the month he [Billy] was an angel and the fourth week he was a devil." Stone divulges the family's failed efforts to get Faulkner to be a banker or a success at any profession. In Stone's telling, Oxford becomes almost a character unto itself—like Faulkner—unconcerned with the world at large, content, and unimpressed with visitors. "Home means more in Oxford than it does in most places these days," Stone claims. Neighbors would just as soon entertain themselves on their verandas as attend the movies. Stone mentions a Faulkner letter from New York City, saying he felt sorry for all those millions who did not live in Oxford. Stone argues that Faulkner had the advantage of escaping the "dead hand of culture." He could grow up without models or precedents in the literary line—even in proximity to the university. Was Stone forgetting the old Colonel? Only Stone could serve as a mentor, one who, in his words, "stood [Faulkner] upon his feet to keep them on the ground." Beware of literary cliques and cultivate his own native soil, Stone admonished him, apparently reinforcing Faulkner's own desire to go it alone and not politick for recognition. Oxford used to tolerate Faulkner's ambitions with wry amusement, Stone notes, and now has some respect since Faulkner made money by writing. Stone ends his first installment with an ode to Oxford reminiscent of certain lines in *A Green Bough,* looking out at "rows on serried rows of far hills, blue and purple and lavender and lilac in the sun, hills upon which you can look day after day and year after year and never find light and shadow and color exactly the same."

Smith and Haas, a new partnership that brought in Robert Haas, who got on well with Faulkner, published another kind of retrospective, *Doctor Martino and Other Stories,* on April 16, 1934. Reviewers and later critics have deemed it an eclectic and uneven collection, with "Turnabout" as the outstanding story, according to Peter Monro Jack in the *New York Sun* (April 16). He quoted a passage that perfectly exemplified the inebriated nobility of Faulkner's characters and the toll taken on doing their duty: "The English boy made an effort then he pulled himself together, focusing his eyes. He swayed, throwing his arms about the policeman's neck, and with the other hand he saluted!" But no consensus emerged on which stories were best. Louis Kronenberger in the *New York Times Book Review* (April 22) even declared that this ephemeral magazine fiction would detract from Faulkner's reputation. In the *North American Review* (June) no more than the title of Faulkner's book was listed under the heading, "Others of Less Moment." Alvah Bessie in the *Brooklyn Daily Eagle* (May 6) did a body count: "Murder figures in six stories; death in ten," with three cases of comic relief.

"Dr. Martino," the title story, to most reviewers and subsequent critics seems minor Faulkner, especially compared to "Mountain Victory," "Elly," "Fox Hunt," and "Smoke," included in the same volume. "Dr. Martino" went through several revisions before he was pleased or at least content with the outcome.[14] It is assumed that "Dr. Martino" had some special significance for its author, but what is it? The story of an older man whose life is renewed or at least bolstered by a younger woman whose devotion to him defies her domineering mother and other conventionally minded characters would repeat itself in various versions of Faulkner's life, with Meta Carpenter, Joan Williams, and Jean Stein,[15] and in his work—the disturbing older man in "The College Widow," the obsessed barber in "Hair," and, much later, Gavin Stevens doting on Linda Snopes in *The Mansion.* So, too, Dr. Martino's exhortation to Louise King that she conquer her fears in order to feel fully alive finds its like in Faulkner's own persistent riding of horses into his sixties, admitting that he had to conquer his fears after he had fallen. But such persistence can also be seen as a self-destructive act. Like so much of Faulkner's life, his fiction is paradoxical.

Society aligns itself against the older man, no matter that Dr. Martino clearly means Louise no harm. He has no sexual interest in a woman described as "a little on the epicene," as Faulkner's ingénues tend to be in his drawings. But Dr. Martino's obsession with Louise is disturbing to others because she cannot seem to act without his approval, and because she seeks to prove herself by riding a dangerous horse, as she has already learned to swim, conquering her fear of drowning, and then testing herself once again by swimming in snake-infested waters. Louise appeals to Hubert Jarrod, a smug Yale student and oil-money heir, because she shakes up his complacency. In his "Yale nimbus . . . leading no classes and winning no football games" Hubert is attracted to the athletic, risk-taking Louise, a type of young woman that Hubert's psychology professor compares to "racing aviators . . . making a fast turn." She is situated, in other words, alongside the barnstorming women of Faulkner's stories and *Pylon*'s Laverne in his gallery of daring women. The professor suggests such women have a penchant for evil, like another fast woman, Temple Drake. But Louise is no belle, and unlike Temple, Louise is described as "beyond-looking" with a "tense expectation." Hubert realizes that she is "beyond him," but that is why he wants her. Unlike other women, she is in no hurry to give Hubert what he thinks is his due. "It seems I'm going to need psychology," he tells himself, realizing that he will have to follow Louise's lead to figure her out.

Complicating a response to the story are the actions of her manipulative mother, who tricks Hubert into believing Louise has renounced the ailing Dr. Martino, who takes nitroglycerin for his heart condition and seems to thrive on Louise's energy. Hubert thinks he can take control by visiting Dr. Martino and announcing his engagement to Louise, showing off her engagement ring. But Dr. Martino notes, "Your proof seems to be in the hands of the wrong party." Hubert also does not understand the warning that Mrs. King has deceived him: "'Young Mr. Jarrod, you have been conquered by a woman, as I have been. But with this difference: it will be a long time yet before you will realize that you have been slain.' And I said, 'If Louise is to do the slaying, I intend to die every day for the rest of my life or hers.' And he said, 'Ah; Louise. Were you speaking of Louise?'" Not Louise, but Mrs. King is the slayer. Doctor Martino dies as soon as Jarrod departs with her. Has Louise forsaken him for Jarrod—for comfort and security and conventionality—as Hubert hopes? Louise has also been duped by her mother, thinking that she has lost the inch-tall brass rabbit, the "shape of being afraid," that Dr. Martino has given to her as a prod to her courage and that Mrs. King has given to Hubert to return to Dr. Martino as a sign of Louise's capitulation to Hubert's proposal. But Louise, realizing she has been entrapped, still refuses Hubert's offer to return home before they are married. In fact, she urges Hubert to drive faster toward their new life together. Is she facing still another fear—marriage?—or has she run away from her own independence? How are we to interpret "her face . . . pale, white, her mouth open, shaped to an agony of despair and a surrender." Hubert thinks of the Martino imperative: "to be afraid, and yet to do. He said it himself: there's nothing in the world but being alive, knowing you are alive." Has Dr. Martino also become Hubert Jarrod's inspiration?

Is Hubert a knockoff of Hubert Starr, whom Faulkner first met at Yale but who had a University of Mississippi law degree and then also served as Faulkner's legal advisor and companion in Hollywood? Faulkner inscribed at least eight of his books to Starr, "my friend," including *Doctor Martino and Other Stories*.[16] The vulnerable writer in studioland counted on Starr, who had the Jarrod-like "rhinoceroslike sufficiency" of a Yale education, if not Jarrod's "oil-well veneer." Starr would yet prove to be a crucial advisor at a crisis point and would remain a friend forever. Faulkner's letters suggest he enjoyed their badinage, inscribing *Pylon,* "To Hubert Starr, / god damn him / Bill Faulkner."[17] Who knows? Turning Starr into the somewhat dense Hubert Jarrod might have amused both men.

Is there a kind of prophecy of the older man Faulkner would become, steering the lives of young women? He now had a daughter, and he would see to it that she would have her own horse, and she would become, in certain respects, as fearless as her Pappy. Faulkner found the plight of older and younger people poignant, saying that in middle age people were far less sympathetic. Critics claim "Dr. Martino" is an undeveloped and unresolved story. Do we side for or against Dr. Martino? Perhaps the very question reflects the divided sensibility of a man who saw it both ways. Louise herself remains elusive, and it is "possible she was so to the author, too."[18] That Faulkner identified with Louise seems likely, given critic Beatrice Lang's suggestion that in losing the metal rabbit, Louise is "torn away from the world of childhood and magic,"[19] which Faulkner prized in the stories he told children and in so much of his published fiction.

Breaking away from a mentor certainly informed Faulkner's experience. Beginning perhaps as early as his first prolonged stay in New Orleans, and certainly after his marriage to Estelle, Stone's influence over Faulkner eroded, and like Dr. Martino with his ailing heart incarcerated in a dark house, Stone, sunk in debt, was stuck in Oxford, gradually losing his own life force. His wife, Emily, would say she had married a burned-out man. Later a fire would damage the Stone house, effectively diminishing the evidence of Stone's efforts to elevate Bill Faulkner. Biographer Carvel Collins would poke among the ashes of this conflagration in a desperate effort to recover the papers that Stone alone had midwifed. Fragments of the fire were saved and preserved like sacred relics.

It is difficult to assess the true nature of Dr. Martino and his motivations,[20] and so it was with Phil Stone. Without question, he helped to create William Faulkner, the man and the writer, but Stone was also the possessive mother who did not want to let go and repeatedly reminded Faulkner's admirers that Stone had been there first, to author, indeed mother, the writer. The biographical undertow of the story may also reflect Faulkner's ambivalence about separating from Stone and cleaving to Estelle, rebelling against his very need for her that he had to work out in various affairs and stories. Like Louise, Faulkner had the "beyond-looking" intensity that set him apart. In those younger women whom Faulkner courted later on, he sought, perhaps, some replica of himself as a relief from the frustrations of home and family life. Louise complains that both her mother and Hubert let her down, and that is the way William Faulkner often felt. "He didn't get what he was entitled to in a wife, in a love affair, in critical recognition for a time, certainly in money," said David Hempstead, an assistant to screenwriter Nunnally Johnson, who worked on a project with Faulkner.[21] The letdown was palpable, and an air of grievance never left until, perhaps, his final days. Lang suggests Dr. Martino's unresolved air of mystery "sets the tone" for the stories of death and the occult to come[22]—and maybe for the life yet to unfold as well.

ON THE WAY TO SUTPEN'S HUNDRED

Fiction never paid enough to clear his debts, fund Faulkner's flying excursions, and to support a family that now included his own child and her nurse. Earning more money gave him more time to work on his ambitious novel. By July 1, 1934, he had returned to Hollywood for three weeks, making a thousand dollars per week, to work at Universal Studios with Howard Hawks on an adaptation of a Blaise Cendrars novel, *Sutter's Gold* (1926). The film began as a Sergei Eisenstein project at Paramount, which the studio rejected for two reasons: its projected $3 million cost and the subject matter, the 1849 California gold rush—dismissed as "history, past and dead now."[23] After the Russian director's departure, Hawks had commandeered the Eisenstein script and taken it to Universal for Faulkner to rewrite as a big-budget epic of the American West.[24]

A week later Faulkner reported from Hubert Starr's home that it was a "good place to hide out and work; he is alone now and I will have the house to myself all day long. I can put on bathing suit right in the house and walk

2 blocks to the beach." He liked the ale in a nearby German restaurant and watching the proprietor's daughter, "about 3 or 4, like a Dresden doll, with a toy violin helping them" to the accompaniment of "good German food and sentimental Bavarian music under a vine trellis."[25] Starr also took Faulkner to Ivan House, a restaurant run by a Starr client, Orsina, who had nowhere to wear her evening gowns except while presiding in her tea room providing minor entertainment. In her elaborate ensembles she served a "damn good meal for $1.00."[26] As always, Faulkner yearned for home, and though he never gave Estelle enough credit for holding everything together while he was away, he did manage to offer encouraging words: "I had both your letters at one time yesterday. They were the nicest ones I ever had from you because they sound happiest and like you had a good grip on yourself and are at peace. . . . I love you and miss you damn bad. God bless you and Cho and Mac and little baby Jill."[27]

By July 7, Faulkner had a synopsis to discuss with Howard Hawks, and five days later he had worked up a revision while reporting he might have another assignment, an adaptation of a play, *Mary of Scotland,* that did not materialize, and a script that has not survived for the actress Margaret Sullavan. Another week passed without much to report, except that Hawks had delivered some corrections for *Sutter's Gold.*[28] Faulkner's public statements provide no idea of the scope of his work for Hawks or how quickly he produced a 108-page ambitious screenplay treatment. If *Absalom, Absalom!* remained a priority, *Sutter's Gold* nevertheless deeply engaged the novelist's imagination, since it afforded the same kind of huge canvas and character that Faulkner now seemed to crave, beginning with projects like "Mythical Latin-American Kingdom Story."

How much *Sutter's Gold* meant to Faulkner is revealed in a long letter (September 4, 1934) to Will Bryant, who remained in Faulkner's confidence in ways not vouchsafed to others. If there is another letter evincing such enthusiasm for Hollywood work, I have yet to find it. Even the word Faulkner used for his stay in Hollywood, "expedition," is especially fitting in his pell-mell description of the picaresque Sutter:

> the Swiss immigrant who fled Europe in 1830 to escape debtor's prison, made an Odyssey across the American continent trying to reach California, reached Vancouver, could not get to California, went to Hawaii, got a Russian ship captain to take him back to Alaska, from there bought a small vessel and reached California at last, established a "New Helvetia" where people could find refuge from the oppression which drove him to desert his wife and children in Europe, became the richest man in the

world, when one day his carpenter found gold while building a flour mill. The Gold Rush of '49 overwhelmed him. He had title to all the land in the Sacramento basin, where the gold was found, yet he never got an ounce of it. His very land was taken away from him by claimstakers, so that when order was at last established, no government dared trying to dispossess the hordes of people, although Sutter's grant and title were admitted. He spent his fortune trying to get justice, was driven out of California by a mob, went to Washington and spent almost twenty years trying to get an audience with Congress and receive justice, became a pauper, was sitting on the Capitol steps one Sunday waiting for Congress to convene, when a newsboy, for a joke, told him that his claim had been allowed at last. He died of shock, and was buried by contribution by a small Moravian church congregation like our Southern negroes are buried sometimes.

It is a good story, I think, and I have just finished it (yesterday). I have worked at it pretty steadily. [29]

Sutter squatted in Faulkner's imagination, Sutter's New Helvetia a larger simulacrum of Sutpen's Hundred, the kingdom Sutpen had torn out of the earth he had purchased from the Chickasaw. Here, in Sutter, was a driven, displaced, and dispossessed man coming along, so to speak, at the very time that Faulkner worried about losing his own home and place in the world. To save himself, he had to do as Sutter had done, and set out on an expedition. What is more, Faulkner had to explain himself to his mortgagee, who had replaced, in important respects, the cranky Phil Stone, now scornful of Faulkner's pretensions and possessive about his role in fostering Faulkner's talent—not genius, Stone was quick to observe. Who else besides Will Bryant could have played such a supportive role? He could have foreclosed on Faulkner on several occasions but instead tolerated, even encouraged, Faulkner's plans. The fraught emotional weight that Faulkner carried when dealing with his financial and familial obligations could be eased in his letters and meetings with Bryant, which could include literary talk without embarrassment or excuse.

Faulkner followed closely Cendrars's portrayal of Sutter as a migrant, an obsessive, ruthlessly pursuing his design, notwithstanding family obligations or the ordinary ties that bind most men to their communities. In short, he is kin to the relentless Thomas Sutpen, who would dominate the storytelling in *Absalom, Absalom!* Sutter's story confirmed how important Faulkner's own novel was and how much it derived from history, even if Faulkner did not know that history before beginning *Absalom, Absalom!* Cendrars's Sutter, like Faulkner's Sutpen, refuses "to submit." Both ambitious men belong to "a hardy race of adventurers," as Cendrars puts it. Both men engage to work with others but ultimately go it alone. Sutter shows up in pre–gold rush California with an armed band of Kanakas (Hawaiian natives) forming a cordon around him like the passel of "wild niggers" who accompany Sutpen. Sutter even narrates his own downfall in clear, simple prose, without expatiation, much as Sutpen will do in chapter 7 (not yet written) in telling the events of his ruin.

But the Cendrars novel, via Eisenstein, became in Faulkner's adaptation a new original work that deserves comment beyond citing parallels between *Sutter's Gold* and *Absalom, Absalom!* In some ways, Eisenstein's version is closer to *Absalom, Absalom!* than Faulkner's own screen treatment. In Eisenstein, the "blackened face of Sutter," who "fights like a demon" and is a "dark figure," a "horseback emperor" with "hypnotising eyes," recalls Miss Rosa's portrayal of the charismatic, sulphur-reeking, "man-horse-demon." Sutter's destruction of the wilderness, accompanied by the "whistling of saws, and the falling of the trees,"[30] recalls passages in *Go Down, Moses* describing the shrinking big woods. Most astonishing is Eisenstein's scene with Sutter fighting with a black man, which does not appear in Faulkner's screen treatment, even though it is very like Sutpen's fights with his slaves.[31]

In his screenplay, Faulkner not only rewrote Cendrars; he also radically changed Eisenstein's cinematic conception of the story. Faulkner returned to his time in his grandfather's bank to focus on what it means to have a society based on money, and to his earliest understanding of movies that were *silent,* making the audience concentrate intensely on the pictorial even as they craved those title cards that not only dispensed vital information but became signposts, signifying where the film was headed and, in this instance, how Sutter sought his destiny. So many accounts of Faulkner's screenwriting emphasize that he wrote long speeches that did not suit the aesthetics of Hollywood film. To be sure, but not always.

The first three minutes of the film contain no dialogue and are about money changing hands:

Gold letters increase in size, filling the camera, FADE in behind letters: Four or five stacks of coins at close shot, filling camera. PAN slowly BACKWARD to: small scoops digging into coins, hands handling shovels, then arms. PAN back complete, reveals vault, clerks busily shoveling coins. TRUCK BACKWARD from vault through countingroom, clerks writing at high desks, one vacant desk in view but not emphasized yet. TRUCK on BACKWARD through lobby of bank, grilled windows, customers, etc. To: Street entrance of bank. Title letters decrease and DISSOLVE. RESOLVE SUPERPOSE: title:

(Town), Switzerland. January, 1830.

DISSOLVE title, PAN to: brass plate beside door:
German letters:

Rittsmueller Brothers

Civilization and the gold standard and the California gold rush—the sheer materiality of money dominates the film. But Sutter begins as a disciple of Rousseau, a believer in natural innocence and an opponent of a corrupt society. He does not pay his debts, and he does not take them seriously—a wonder in the world of William Faulkner when not a day seemed to pass when a debt was not due.

When we first see Sutter, we might as well be seeing a Swiss version of William Faulkner, except for the musical instrument: "He is young, with a clerklike, indoors, face, intelligent but impractical. He has a thin youthful moustache, carefully curled; there is something foppish about his appearance; he loves to wear his uniform; he is enjoying himself. *He is younger and more intelligent looking than the other members of the band.*" Faulkner understood that love of uniforms and of the sense of display that set him off from others. He presents Sutter the showman as his alter ego.

The first title card accomplishes what great silent films did so well, presenting not just exposition, or comment on action, or what characters say, but using language as emblematic of their natures:

He was born poor but he did not hate poverty; He earned his daily bread by handling other men's gold, but he did not covet it—

DOUBLE EXPOSURE of title to: title:

BECAUSE

DOUBLE EXPOSURE of title to: title:

To him gold was dross, and Liberty and Justice alone were gold.

The very words "Sutter's gold" take on a new meaning—his understanding of money—not what he possesses, at least not to begin with.

Sutter's first speech: "He speaks with impassioned eloquence and conviction, preaching Rousseau's philosophy of man's duty to his fellow man; of the honest rewards of honest toil and honest sweat, the Arcadian life of the soil. It is impassioned, sincere, and amateur." Such a man cannot provide for his family, and they are evicted, and Sutter is on the run. Nowhere do we see Eisenstein's dark figure, or any prefiguration of Thomas Sutpen. Sutter is fanatical but only in devotion to his natural-man ideology. Sutter is "calm, ecstatic, serene." But he is also haughty, vain, and more than a little preening—like young William Faulkner: "Unconsciously his other hand smoothes his uniform coat."

Sutter never lets go of the uniform—even after it is dirtied and bloodied and torn in beatings he suffers, Christ-like, in his devotion to Rousseau. He forsakes family and home and society, as summed up in the words of a title card that tells more than the character himself could say: "Speaking no language save his own, with neither purpose nor hope, fleeing not yet *to* anything or anyplace, choosing a ship bound for the new world not because he hoped yet to find less of injustice there than in the old." But in the new world he is "assaulted and robbed, his uniform's buttons and epaulettes jerked off." He perseveres, learns English, styles himself "Professor Sutter" and delivers lectures on "Liberty and Mankind." He opposes slavery, frees an octoroon, and after much trial and tribulation he leads a group of settlers west: "So he went beyond peace and found, not only life again, but purpose," as the title card says.

Sutter survives an Indian attack and gradually becomes the commander of a following that will fulfill his dream of a new state, New Helvetia. He has a new appearance and a new uniform: "now with beard and moustache, swaggering frontier style. He wears fringed hunter's shirt, with two pistols in belt, a new hat." In effect, he becomes a political force and eventually the embodiment of the state itself in a quasi-fascist manner—even selling the octoroon to further his empire, which encompasses, at least in his own mind, the whole of the Sacramento valley. He becomes an anti-Christ, crucifying three Indians, and he murders one of his friends and followers for reasons of state. He seems part Kurtz, part Stalin, pursuing an ideology that justifies mass murder as the only means of establishing a new world. This Rousseau gone awry is a refutation of Rousseau, of the idea that society corrupts natural innocence. The proud Sutter—too proud to honor his debts or to countenance society's other demands—has, in the end, re-created a society even worse than the one he escaped.

When gold is discovered on Sutter's land, he regards it as an "increase of his power." The gold rush, which he is vain enough to think he can control, is the corruption of his dream of justice and liberty. All ideals becomes subsumed in the materiality of digging for gold, which is like the scooping of coins at the beginning of film. Indeed, so many scenes in Faulkner's screen treatment are cyclical, returning again and again to Sutter's utter incomprehension of society and his role in it—a role Faulkner understood very well while working for Hollywood gold, after he, too, had spurned his grandfather's bank job. Sutter's world is one in which money changes hands, again and again, as opposed to man in a state of nature uncorrupted by society—a dream of Rousseau's destined to end in grief.

Sutter ends as a foolish figure, thinking he can get the president to honor his claim to all of the gold rush land. He arrives in Washington in uniform and delivers a "grandiose peroration. Everyone will have free land in California once his claim is settled. A large crowd gathers, laughing. When police stop him, he calls himself General Sutter." This self-bestowed honorific is reminiscent of Faulkner's own southern kin, maintaining their titles in memory of a lost cause. Lincoln is shown indulging Sutter's petition but also realizing he can hardly dislodge the squatters on Sutter's land. All Sutter receives is a pension and then the mockery of a newsboy who, as Faulkner told Will Bryant, dupes Sutter into believing that his claim had been allowed at last. Sutter dies of shock after the boy's announcement of fake news, but Faulkner does not include that last little bit in the letter to Will Bryant about Sutter's funeral, arranged "by contribution by a small Moravian church congregation like our Southern negroes are buried sometimes." The Sutter that Faulkner creates, at least in his letter to Bryant, rests beside the black people he once championed and then abandoned.

"Golden Land"

The intense job of work completed, Faulkner was "getting nervous and a little jumpy to get home, at the fingernail chewing stage. I wasted a whole week doing nothing at all; that's what frets me about this business." He consoled himself doing "a little on the novel [*Absalom, Absalom!*] from time to time." He also put a good deal of his anxiety and anger about remaining in Hollywood into a story, "Golden Land," which reveals that it was not just the work away from the novel, or even his time away from home, that troubled him but what Hollywood represented, which was, in effect, nothing. Ira Ewing, a hard-drinking real estate tycoon, makes money easily—too easily, his Nebraska mother tells him. He owns and sells land—properties—the way Hollywood moguls transacted business, with no inherent attachment to what they own, and none of the depth and desire that motivated Sutter. Like the Falkners, the Ewings are four generations removed from the frontier. They were sodbusters living in sod houses and log cabins who rooted themselves in Midwest soil. In California, there is nothing to hold on to, nothing that will last, not even the Ewing name, which his daughter has changed in a movie career move. As Faulkner wrote in the screenplay treatment he recapped for Will Bryant, you could come to California, like Sutter, and eventually amass property that extended from Sacramento to San Francisco and even have a deed to it, and yet others would squat on it and take it away from you, and not even the courts could make restitution. Screenplays were properties, like Ira Ewing's real estate, like the Eisenstein Sutter scenario that Faulkner worked over and that others, in turn, would rewrite, dispossessing Faulkner in a film eventually released in 1936 that did not credit him or Eisenstein.

It is also tempting to see other parallels between Ira Ewing and Faulkner himself. Both men are depressed alcoholics making their money a long way from home, estranged from their wives. Soon Faulkner would emulate Ewing with a mistress a decade younger than himself.[32] Ewing's impudent Filipino servant and Japanese gardener can be regarded as stand-ins for the recalcitrant black people Faulkner would sometimes complain about in his letters. Ewing's frequent visits to his dour mother seem a caricature of Faulkner's missions to Maud, who detested California on her one visit there. But the midwestern landscape Ewing's mother yearns for seems barren and cold. A return would be fatal, Ewing tells her, although at one point he seems to agree that he, too, would like to return. The family ought to be a bastion against a corrupt culture, but instead it reflects the same base behavior, with Ewing's promiscuous daughter and son who dresses in women's underclothing.[33] The children do not fulfill the father's expectations, although Ewing is willing to capitalize on his daughter's notoriety in ways unimaginable in Faulkner's own life. Ewing may express feelings that Faulkner sometimes held, but Ewing is more of a creature of this golden land than Faulkner ever was. That Faulkner drew on his own experience seems obvious, but to call the story a disguised autobiography seems to claim too much, while admitting the story "testifies to a deep anxiety about marriage, paternity, and family."[34]

Perhaps Faulkner rebuilt Rowan Oak partly to allay such anxieties. He made its former owners feel part of his enterprise, and they reciprocated his devotion by catering to his plans. This continuity did not obtain in Faulkner's California city, the parts of which seemed to be randomly put together— "scattered about the arid earth like so many gay scraps of paper blown without order." Hollywood was a disordered text, no matter how much it sparkled. Faulkner, like Ewing, breathed "its curious air of being rootless" and looked out on "houses bright beautiful and gay, without basements or foundations, lightly attached to a few inches of light penetrable earth, lighter even than dust and laid lightly in turn upon the profound and primeval lava, which one good hard rain would wash forever from the sight and memory of man as a firehose flushes down a gutter." This ephemeral existence so unnerves Ewing's mother, whom he has set up in a comfortable California home, that she wants to return to Nebraska's harsh, cold climate, just as Faulkner preferred the extreme weather of hot and humid Mississippi. The printed page

offered eternity, or some approximation of it, compared to combustible celluloid that had burned more than one studio down to the ground. The city in
"Golden Land" of "incalculable wealth . . . erected upon a few spools of a substance whose value is computed in billions" could be "completely destroyed
in that second's instant of a careless match between the moment of striking
and the moment when the striker might have sprung and stamped it out."
Working in Oxford on Hollywood scripts at least put some distance between
him and those fires. He could resume his visits every day to his mother, just as
Ira Ewing does in "Golden Land," as if to affix his identity, unmoored by his
occupation, to his origins.

Back home by the last week of July, he did more work on *Sutter's Gold*,
on short stories for the *Post* that would eventually be revised for *The Unvanquished*, but he had decided not to go back to *Absalom, Absalom!* pending
his need for cash.[35] In August, he confessed to Hal Smith, "I believe that the
book is not quite ripe." Instead, he might return to *Requiem for a Nun*. He
wanted his publisher close to hand: "How about coming Nov 20 and go on
to the deer hunt? I want you to come and stay a week this time. . . . I have not
had a drink since you left . . . and I want to show you the South: cotton and
niggers, etc., that I failed to show you before. We can spend three days in the
woods, and three more days looking at the Mississippi delta, where the cotton
grows; we can take the aero plane and go to New Orleans."[36]

By the fall, however, he had started on another novel, *Pylon*, based on a lost
short story, "This Kind of Courage," and he had completed it by the middle of
December. He had "worked forced draft," he told his agent, Morton Goldman,
who had taken over from Ben Wasson.[37] What did Faulkner mean, exactly, by
"worked forced draft"? That was the kind of language that might apply to one
of his screenplays, and it seems, in fact, that the Hollywood regimen had infil-
trated his Mississippi mind-set. To Goldman, he wrote again near the end of
the year: "I have sent in the novel manuscript to Smith. I think I will send a
copy of it to Howard Hawks, in California. I have not done it yet, though I am
writing him today. I will let you know what he says about it."[38]

Pylon, so it seems in retrospect, became a pivotal work in Faulkner's life
and career, marking a change in his outlook and prospects as he thought not
only about what he wanted to write but how it might serve a director as well.
In adapting to the taste and temper of another while remaining true to his
own interests and aesthetic, Faulkner fashioned a new sense of himself as a
writer—and, eventually, a public figure—that would dominate the second
half of his career.

Notes

Abbreviations

B	Malcolm Franklin, *Bitterweeds*
CCP	Carvel Collins Papers, Harry Ransom Humanities Research Center, University of Texas
CGBC	Louis Daniel Brodsky and Robert W. Hamblin, eds., *Faulkner: A Comprehensive Guide to the Brodsky Collection*
CWF	M. Thomas Inge, *Conversations with William Faulkner*
"DSF"	Dean Faulkner Wells, "Dean Swift Faulkner: A Biographical Study"
ESPL	William Faulkner, *Essays, Speeches, and Public Letters*
FB (1974)	Joseph Blotner, *Faulkner: A Biography* (1974)
FB (1984)	Joseph Blotner, *Faulkner: A Biography* (1984)
FC	Malcolm Cowley, *The Faulkner-Cowley File*
FL	Judith Sensibar, *Faulkner and Love*
FMGM	William Faulkner, *Faulkner's MGM Screenplays,* edited by Bruce Kawin
FWP	Floyd Watkins Papers, Emory University
JBP	Joseph Blotner Papers, Louis Daniel Brodsky Collection, Center for Faulkner Studies, Southeast Missouri State University
LDBP	Louis Daniel Brodsky Papers, Center for Faulkner Studies, Southeast Missouri State University
LG	Louis Daniel Brodsky, *William Faulkner, Life Glimpses*
LITG	James B. Meriwether and Michael Millgate, eds., *Lion in the Garden*
MBB	John Faulkner, *My Brother Bill*
MCR	Meta Carpenter recordings, UM
MFP	Malcolm Franklin Papers, Special Collections, Thomas Cooper Library University of South Carolina
NYPL	Berg Collection, New York Public Library
RHMP	Robert H. Moore Papers, University of North Carolina, Special Collections
SL	*Selected Letters of William Faulkner*
UM	Archives and Special Collections, University of Mississippi
UVA	William Faulkner Collection, Albert and Shirley Small Special Collections Library, University of Virginia
VJR	Recording of Louis Daniel Brodsky interview with Victoria Johnson, LDBP
WFCR	M. Thomas Inge, *William Faulkner: The Contemporary Reviews*
WFTF	William Faulkner, *William Faulkner at Twentieth Century-Fox: The Annotated Screenplays,* edited by Sarah Gleeson-White

Preface

1. Mike Granberry, "Bearing with Carvel Collins," *Los Angeles Times Magazine,* January 1987, 28.
2. Carvel Collins to Kana Parks Oberst, July 16, 1967, CCP.
3. Blotner to Goldman, March 12, 1967, JBP.
4. Blotner to Watkins, July 24, 1974, FWP.
5. Faulkner's own disparaging comments on his screen work have contributed to this lack of focus on film in previous Faulkner biographies. When Charles Nelson Jr., returning from service in World War II, met Faulkner on the street and told him he had just seen *To Have and Have Not,* Faulkner replied, "It's all right to see once, but not twice" (see Nelson and Goforth, 22). But in his *Paris Review* interview, he noted, "If I didn't take, or feel I was capable of taking, motion-picture work seriously, out of simple honesty to motion-pictures and myself too, I would not have tried." This is not the last word, to be sure, but for me the evidence is overwhelming that Faulkner did take the work seriously. For a superb overview of Faulkner and film scholarship, see the introduction to *WFTF.*
6. B. Robbins, "The Pragmatic Modernist," 241: "All artistic works are shaped by networks and conditions outside of themselves, despite their possible claims to autonomy."
7. B. Robbins, "The Pragmatic Modernist," 243.

1. Beginnings

1. Jack Elliott's research reveals that the family name occurred with and without the *u* at various points in its history. Faulkner's addition of a *u* to his name when he enlisted in the Royal Air Force in 1918 restored a spelling that had sometimes been used in earlier generations. See also https://hottytoddy.com/2014/07/28/the-real-story-behind-the-missing-u-in-faulkner/.
2. Minter, 4.
3. Duclos, xiv. Faulkner also did not seem interested in passing on the lore about his great-grandfather. "I know little on the Colonel as Pappy (William) has never told me & I probably spent more man hours with WF than anyone. I will help if I can for the Col. has always interested me," Malcolm Franklin, Faulkner's stepson, wrote to Duclos (February 2, 1957, Donald Philip Duclos Papers, William Patterson University).
4. Phil Stone to Donald Duclos, February 9, 1956, CCP; Hamblin, *Myself and the World,* 10.
5. Gray, 63.
6. See the Digital Yoknapatawpha link "Colonel Sartoris and Colonel Falkner?," http://faulkner.drupal.shanti.virginia.edu/node/8451?canvas#.
7. Robert Cantwell Papers, Special Collections and University Archives, University of Oregon Libraries.
8. Interview with Mrs. Thompson, March 15, 1965, JBP.
9. Interview with Aunt Bama, Mrs. Walter McLean, August 5 or 6, 1951, CCP.
10. Robert Cantwell Papers, University of Oregon Libraries, Special Collections and University Archives. I am quoting from Cantwell's handwritten notes, with

wording and some candid details that differ from the published version (see "The Faulkners: Recollections of a Gifted Family" in *CWF*, 30–41). Meriwether, "Early Notices of Faulkner by Phil Stone and Louis Cochran," 156.

11. Qtd. in Duclos, 95–96.

12. *CWF*, 65.

13. Williamson: "It would have been perfectly fitting for him to be genuinely surprised and unable to understand why Dick Thurmond had shot him, to respond as if he could not believe what had happened to him."

14. In *Simply Faulkner*, Weinstein asks if the murder was "also charged with racial and sexual tensions?"

15. My account of Colonel Falkner, his conflict with Richard Thurmond, and the likelihood that they had a falling out over a black woman who had been part of their households relies on an unpublished chapter of Joel Williamson's Faulkner biography (LDBP).

16. The plot of *The White Rose of Memphis:* Aboard a three-week cruise on a Mississippi riverboat headed to New Orleans, a masked ball becomes the occasion for a rodomontade of storytelling with figures dressed like the Queen of Sheba, Ivanhoe, the Duke of Wellington, Queen Mary, George III, and other royalty. But this make-believe is interrupted by Ingomar's picaresque tale. The central character is Edward Demar, orphaned at thirteen and accompanied by a foster brother and sister on a 221-mile walk to Memphis. Storms, rattlesnakes, and other perilous adventures beset the threesome, who are rescued by a kindly doctor and the benefactions of an heiress, Lottie, who, in turn, befriends Viola, courted by Harry, a promising lawyer, but their plans are wrecked when Viola is accused of poisoning her little brother in a scheme to inherit a family fortune. Edward, now a medical student, rushes from Philadelphia to Memphis. It is all a scramble with plots and counterplots, duels, brain fevers, and country jails, with Lottie reported dead, then alive, then half-dead, until all is explained in the exposure of the machinations of Ben Bowles, who began his nefarious career by attacking Lottie. Most interesting to readers of *Sanctuary* is Bowles's seduction of a thirteen-year-old he installs in a Memphis gambling hall. Coincidences and mistaken identities abound as staples of nineteenth-century melodrama. This curious blend of southern romanticism and corruption becomes, in a far more sophisticated form, the burden of William Faulkner's novels.

17. Hirsch.

18. McMillen, 23.

19. Personal correspondence with the author. Jimmy Falkner claimed the mulatto woman's visits resulted in a son named Dick Thurmond who twenty years later in 1910 was lynched after attempting to rape a daughter of Z. M. Stephens, a lawyer who had defended Thurmond in 1891. Jimmy, however, had clearly based his tale on an event that happened in Ripley not in 1910 but in 1898, in which year a black man named Dick Thurmond was lynched for the attempted rape of a daughter not of Stephens but of Lee Hines, part owner of the Ripley Railroad. If the black Dick Thurmond had been conceived during the nocturnal jail visits, he would have been only about eight years old when lynched.

20. Personal correspondence with the author.

21. Rhodes, 96.

22. "Simon's character?": http://faulkner.drupal.shanti.virginia.edu/node/8451?canvas#.

23. Young, *The Far Pavilion,* 53–54.

24. June 25, 1955, Donald Philip Duclos Papers, William Patterson University.

25. *FB* (1974), 36.

26. Duclos, 263.

27. Interview with Alabama McLean, August 6, 1951, CCP.

28. *SL,* 19–20.

29. Interviews with Maud Falkner and Mrs. Walter McLean (Aunt Bama) on April 13, 1950, and 1951 (no month or day specified), CCP.

30. Undated interview with Mac Reed, CCP.

31. *FB* (1974), 94. Faulkner kept the novel (see Blotner, *William Faulkner's Library: A Catalogue,* 27).

32. See Erin Blakesmore's fascinating "How the Confederacy Is Etched into American Roads," *Atlantic,* August 29, 2017, https://www.theatlantic.com/business/archive/2017/08/jefferson-davis-highways/538062/.

33. Robert Cantwell Papers, Special Collections and University Archives, University of Oregon Libraries.

34. *FB* (1974), 3, 31.

35. Letter from Kana Parks Oberst to Carvel Collins, qtd. in Carvel Collins's notes of October 11, 1966, and Carvel Collins to Kana Parks Oberst, August 3, 1970. The books by Mary L. Williamson, *The Life of Gen. Thos. J. Jackson "Stonewall." For the Young. In Easy Words. Illustrated* and *The Life of Gen. Robert E. Lee. For the Young. In Easy Words. Illustrated* (B. F. Johnson, 1899).

36. *CWF,* 39. This statement is not in Cantwell's handwritten notes.

37. "Mississippi," *ESPL.*

38. See *FL.*

39. Webb and Green, eds., 25.

40. Interview with Sallie Murry, August 19, 1964, JBP.

41. Young, *The Far Pavilion,* 61.

42. Blotner, *William Faulkner's Library: A Catalogue,* 58.

43. *FB* (1974), 78.

44. Interview with Robert Coughlan, December 30, 1964, JBP.

45. Interview with Jimmy Faulkner, November 14, 1966, JBP.

46. *LITG,* 16.

47. Interview with Murry (Jack) Falkner, December 2, 1964, JBP.

48. *FB* (1974), 106.

49. Interview with Ed Lowe, August, 1951, CCP.

50. Interview with Maud Falkner, April 13, 1950, CCP.

51. Blotner, "The Sources of Faulkner's Genius," in *Fifty Years of Yoknapatawpha,* ed. Fowler and Abadie, 252. Blotner mentions he was permitted to read through Murry's scrapbook, but he does not otherwise divulge his source.

52. Interview with Jimmy Faulkner, March 17, 1965, JBP. In an email to me, Jack Elliott has corrected Jimmy Falkner's account of this incident.

53. Jimmy Faulkner to Sallie Burns, n.d.; interview with Jimmy Faulkner, March 17, 1965, JBP.

54. Blotner to Noel Polk, November 7, 1979, listing Faulkner's statements that were not included in *Faulkner in the University,* JBP.

55. "DSF," 4.

56. See Bailey.

57. Interview with Dorothy Oldham, n.d., JBP.

58. Sallie Burns, Maud's niece, to Jimmy Faulkner, November 21, 1964, JBP. Sallie was not sure if it was a ride or a walk.

59. W. H. Hutchinson to Blotner, January 11, 1965, JBP.

60. *The Falkners of Mississippi,* 3–4. For more details about Oxford in the early 1900s, see Curnutt, chap. 1.

61. Robert Cantwell Papers, Special Collections and University Archives, University of Oregon Libraries.

62. The phrase is used in *Flags in the Dust* and in "My Grandmother Millard and the Battle of Harrykin Creek."

63. Williamson.

64. Interview with Mrs. Walter McLean, August 5 or 6, 1951, CCP.

65. Interview with Sallie Murry, August 19, 1964, JBP.

66. Interview with Sallie Murry, November 14, 1966, JBP.

67. So did his mother, who recalled that he had sold a number of subscriptions and won a uniform as a prize. As soon as it arrived he wanted a photograph taken, but his mother was not home and it was already evening and too dark to take one without a flash. He improvised some flashing powder from a number of shotgun shells. He instructed his brother John to light the powder with a match and click the shutter at the same time. The explosion singed off John's eyebrows but did no harm to Billy Falkner in his pristine regalia (interview with novelist Elizabeth Spencer, who roomed in Maud Falkner's house, n.d., CCP).

68. Fant and Ashley, 101.

69. W. Faulkner, *New Orleans Sketches,* ed. Carvel Collins.

70. Interview with Mrs. Robert X. Williams, November 26, 1963, CCP.

71. Estelle chose Joseph Blotner to write her husband's biography and told him this story. In his index she is identified as Mrs. William Faulkner.

72. See *FB* (1974), 85–86.

73. *FB* (1974), 110.

74. *FB* (1974), 109.

75. *FL.*

76. Williamson.

77. Interview with Sallie Murry, n.d., JBP.

78. Erikson.

79. Interview with Ed Lowe, August 1951, CCP.

80. Interview with Walter Johnson, August 1951, CCP.

81. Webb and Green, eds., 23.

82. Erikson.

83. *SL,* 111.

84. Interview with Ed Lowe, August 1951, CCP.

85. Webb and Green, eds., 169.

86. Karl, 28; see also Gray, 64; and Porter, *William Faulkner,* 12.

87. *FL.*

88. Cullen, 4.

89. Hubert Starr to Carvel Collins, May 14, 1965, CCP.

90. Interview with Sallie Burns, August 3, 1963, CCP.

91. Oates, 12–13.

92. Interview with Robert Farley, April 3, 1965, JBP.

93. Meriwether, ed., *A Faulkner Miscellany,* 145.

94. *MBB,* 70–71.

95. Interview with S. Bernard Wortis, August 17, 1965, JBP: "Dr. W felt that WF had not had enough love from his mother, but WF wouldn't talk about it. . . . He wanted so much to be loved."

96. Interview with Sallie Murry, November 14, 1966, JBP.

97. Karl, 31.

98. *FL.*

99. Porter, *William Faulkner,* 14.

100. Interview with Sallie Murry, n.d., JBP.

101. Interview with Jack Falkner, October 2, 1967, JBP.

102. This item appeared in the *Lafayette County Press,* September 9, 1908, and is quoted in Kinney, "Faulkner and Racism," 270.

103. Wolff and Watkins, *Talking about William Faulkner,* 53. Jimmy mentioned an autopsy that discovered a piece of metal in Mrs. McMillan's spine that matched a missing part of Patton's razor. No researcher has turned up a copy of the autopsy report, if there was one, and such a procedure would seem unusual in the Jim Crow South, when evidence seemed hardly to matter when it came to lynching a black man.

104. Interview with Mrs. James Kyle Hudson (former Katrina Carter of Oxford, a good friend of Estelle and William Faulkner and others of that generation), Memphis, n.d., CCP.

105. Hannon, "The Filming of *Intruder in the Dust,*" 75–76.

106. Most accounts relying on John Cullen's book, 89–98, repeat his remark that he was fourteen or fifteen. But his gravestone reads 1895, which would have made Cullen thirteen, a not insignificant point since Cullen quit school on his fourteenth birthday and did not see much of Faulkner for the next several years but was in a position in 1908 to share an account of his experience with his friend.

107. FWP. Cullen says two thousand, which seems unlikely.

108. McMillen, 248.

109. Qtd. in Doyle, 323. The most detailed accounts of the Nelse Patton lynching are in Blotner; Williamson; and Doyle. Their accounts, like mine, are drawn from contemporary newspaper articles, some of which are included in Cullen.

110. FWP.

111. FWP.

112. Wolff and Watkins, *Talking about William Faulkner,* 51. Jimmy Faulkner describes Patton as defending himself with a wooden stool.

113. FWP.

114. McMillen, 233.

115. Interview notes, August 5, 1963, CCP.

116. Wolff and Watkins, *Talking about William Faulkner,* 51–53.

117. Interview with Estelle Faulkner, February 13, 1965, JBP. "No one had liked the Cullen book," Joseph Blotner wrote to Harrison Smith on October 25, 1964, by

way of explaining why the Faulkner family had entrusted Blotner with writing the biography. But on October 23, 1961, Cullen wrote to Floyd Watkins: "I met William Falkner on the street some time ago. He stopped and shook hands with me in a very friendly manner. We had a few friendly words and he continued on up the street. I was talking with another friend at the time. So nothing can be made out of it, only that he has no resentment over our book. I am truly glad of that. I have had his number all the time. His reactions are just as I guessed. I am willing to bet he read our book but as I told you long ago he will never comment on it one way or the other." On March 27, 1969, Watkins wrote Richard Dee Utley: "Faulkner and Cullen, John tells me, met on the streets of Oxford some time after the book was published; they talked forty-five minutes or so and neither mentioned the book. Faulkner did not throw it in the trash, however, as he did much of his mail. The copy which Cullen sent to him is listed in his library as it is described in Blotner's book" (see FWP). See also SL, 434–35, where Faulkner calls the book part of the "scavenger school of writing [which] seems to have a following . . . and we hope he enjoys the profits." About Cullen, Faulkner said, "personally I like him."

118. Doyle, 323.
119. McMillen, 236.
120. See McMillen, xv, xix, 31.
121. See Kinney, "Unscrambling Surprises."
122. For a discussion of "dependency and disavowal," see Hannon, 92.
123. Hannon, 93.
124. Weinstein, *Becoming Faulkner*, 121.
125. Matthews, *William Faulkner: Seeing through the South*, 156.
126. See Peter Lurie's essay "Inside and Outside Southern Whiteness: Film Viewing, the Frame and the Racing of Space in Yoknapatawpha," 153–59.
127. Qtd. in Millgate, *Achievement*, 263.
128. See Towner and Carothers, 100.
129. Peters, 91.
130. A. G. Jones, "Faulkner and the Ideology of Penetration," 145.
131. A. G. Jones, "Faulkner and the Ideology of Penetration," 140.
132. Karl, 86.
133. Meriwether, ed., *A Faulkner Miscellany*, 146.

2. Apprenticeships

1. Interview with Kana Parks Oberst, October 11, 1966, CCP.
2. *MBB,* 73.
3. *CWF,* 131.
4. M. C. Falkner, *The Falkners of Mississippi,* 49–52. Folks, 173, connects Faulkner's characterization of himself in the essay "Mississippi" with Chaplin. Folks also cites many references to film and film characters and actors in Faulkner's first three novels.
5. *FB* (1974), 160.
6. Interview with Estelle Faulkner, September 9, 1965, JBP.

7. Phil Stone to Carvel Collins, April 11, 1950, CCP.

8. Interview with Dorothy Oldham, March 21, 1965, JBP.

9. Interview with Taylor H. McElroy, March 23, 1965, JBP.

10. Interview with Dr. Ralph Muckenfuss, April 9, 1967, JBP.

11. Interview with Sallie Murry, November 15, 1967. Taylor McElroy said Oldham "probably didn't know much law or how to try a case" (November 18, 1967, JBP).

12. Interview with Estelle Faulkner, December 9, 1964, JBP.

13. Interview with Sallie Murry, November 26, 1965, JBP.

14. Notes about an interview with Bill and Victoria Fielden, March 14, 1968, CCP, referring to a Mr. and Mrs. Ridden, who mentioned the Oldhams' hostility to Faulkner.

15. Interview with Sallie Murry, November 14, 1966, JBP. For a similar southern situation, sending the nubile daughter abroad to interrupt a romance with the local scapegrace, see Carl Rollyson, *Hollywood Enigma: Dana Andrews*.

16. October 8, 1943, LDBP.

17. Interviews with Victoria Fielden, October 27, 1964, and Estelle Faulkner, August 22, 1964, both in JBP.

18. Interview with Maud Falkner, n.d., CCP.

19. Stone to Judith S. Bond, February 18, 1955, LDBP.

20. Phil Stone to Robert Coughlan, April 15, 1954, LDBP.

21. The original text edited by Noel Polk (Random House, 1981), 59.

22. Qtd. in *FB* (1974), 164.

23. Gray, 78; *MBB*.

24. CC notes on interview with Phil and Emily Stone, June 25, 1948, CCP.

25. Snell, 7.

26. Interview with Dean Faulkner Wells, Fred Karl Papers, Special Collections, Thomas Cooper Library, University of South Carolina.

27. Blotner to Ashby Woodson, October 5, 1967, JBP.

28. McAlexander first pointed out the resemblance between Eugene Oliver and William Faulkner.

29. "College Student Suicide in the United States: Incidence Data and Prospects for Demonstrating the Efficacy of Preventative Programs," *Journal of American College Health* 37 (1988), http://www.tandfonline.com/doi/abs/10.1080/07448481 .1988.9939042.

30. Pilkington, *Stark Young*, 96.

31. Pilkington, *Stark Young*, 95–96.

32. Interview, August 24, 1966, CCP.

33. Interview with Robert Farley, March 1963, CCP.

34. Coughlan, 48.

35. One may dispute with Dr. Johnson, but I must say that several of my biographical subjects—notably Norman Mailer, Susan Sontag, Rebecca West, Amy Lowell, and Sylvia Plath—come close to justifying the Johnson dictum.

36. Ashby Woodson to Blotner, JBP.

37. Undated interview with Mac Reed, CCP.

38. Interview with Dorothy Commins, who said Faulkner talked to her about his boyhood, January 18, 1964, CCP.

39. The drawing is reproduced in *William Faulkner: Early Prose and Poetry*.

40. *MBB*, 103.
41. Ben Wasson interview notes, November 29, 1965, JBP
42. Phil Stone to Carvel Collins, July 17, 1948, CCP.
43. Interview with Dorothy Ware, January 26, 1963, CCP.
44. Qtd. in Gresset, *A Faulkner Chronology*, 11.
45. M. C. Falkner, *The Falkners of Mississippi*, 89.
46. Interview with Sallie Murry, November 14, 1966, JBP.
47. See Curnutt, chap. 2, for a different interpretation of Faulkner's dealings with Estelle's father. Some biographers suspect that Faulkner expected Major Oldham to reject the proposal of marriage and that Faulkner was relieved not to assume the responsibilities of married life.
48. Snell, 102.
49. Collins, "Biographical Sources of Faulkner's War Fiction," 112.
50. Compound and double compound steam engines had two and four cylinders that partly determined their power and efficiency. For my quotations from Faulkner's letters, see W. Faulkner, *Thinking of Home,* ed. Watson.
51. *MBB*, 29.
52. The mounting base for a steam engine.
53. *MBB*, 105–6.
54. Interview with Carl Cline, July 23, 1964, CCP.
55. Hubert Starr to Carvel Collins, February 16, 1966, CCP.
56. Hubert Starr to Carvel Collins, May 5, 1966, CCP.
57. Hubert Starr to Carvel Collins, March 5, 1968, CCP.
58. Margaret D. Rollins to Carvel Collins, July 9, 1963, CCP.
59. Hubert Starr to Carvel Collins, May 14, 1966, CCP.
60. Norah Smallwood, "An Impression of William Faulkner," *Listener,* August 2, 1962, 165–66.
61. Elmer O. Parker for Mabel E. Deutrich, Director, Old Military Records Division, General Services Administration, National Archives and Records Service, November 20, 1967, JBP.
62. *FB* (1974), 204.
63. See Watson, *William Faulkner: Self-Presentation and Performance.*
64. Leslie Scrivener, "U of T Back Campus Debate Invokes William Faulkner, Morley Callaghan," June 9, 2013, https://www.thestar.com/news/gta/2013/06/09/u_of_t_back_campus_debate_invokes_william_faulkner_morley_callaghan.html.
65. Ted Tebbetts to Carvel Collins, December 15, 1963, CCP.
66. Interviews with Reginald Rockwell and Ted Tebbetts, October 11 and 16, 1966, CCP.
67. Interview with Ben Wasson, March 13, 1950, CCP.
68. Faulkner's letter to Starr is postmarked January 2, 1919 (LDBP).
69. UVA.
70. Interview, n.d., CCP.
71. Hagood makes much of Faulkner's fascination with disability. It is difficult to ignore his remarkable range of impaired characters from Donald Mahon to Benjy to Linda Snopes.
72. *MBB*, 70.
73. *MBB*, 108–9.

74. M. C. Falkner, *The Falkners of Mississippi*, 90.
75. Wasson, 30. Lucy Somerville, part of Wasson's drama group, also remembered the widespread skepticism about Faulkner's war record (interview notes, January 7, 1965, CCP).
76. Stone to Glenn O. Carey, February 20 and April 5, 1950, LDBP.
77. Richardson, 42, 199.
78. Richardson, 59–60.
79. Richardson, 59–60.
80. Moser, 193.
81. *SL,* 4.
82. Karl, 124.
83. J. Watson Campbell to Franklin Moak, December 11, 1975, JBP.
84. "DSF," 40, 41. Dean interviewed her mother, Louise Meadows, in December 1974. Additional information from Dean's husband, Larry Wells.
85. *FB* (1974), 248; *FB* (1984); Parini, 48.
86. Wittenberg, *Faulkner: The Transfiguration of Biography,* 34; Minter, 35; Karl, 140; Williamson; Gray, 79.
87. Wasson, 30.
88. Interview with Gid Montjoy, November 23, 1962, CCP.
89. Jim Breyealle to Robert H. Moore, July 17, 1970, RHMP.
90. See Lowe's stimulating article "Fraternal Fury: Faulkner, World War I, and Myths of Masculinity," 70–101.
91. Sensibar, *The Origins of Faulkner's Art,* 38.
92. Hönnighausen, *William Faulkner: The Art of Stylization in His Early Graphic and Literary Work,* 18.
93. Hönnighausen, *William Faulkner: The Art of Stylization in His Early Graphic and Literary Work,* 32.
94. *Early Prose and Poetry.*
95. Richardson, 205.
96. Wasson, 18.
97. *FB* (1974), 253.
98. Interview with Ben Lumpkin, summer 1962, CCP.
99. Hönnighausen, *William Faulkner: The Art of Stylization in His Early Graphic and Literary Work,* 104.
100. *Early Prose and Poetry.*
101. *Early Prose and Poetry.*
102. https://archive.org/stream/olemiss24univ/olemiss24univ_djvu.txt.
103. See *FB* (1974), 264–75, for a detailed account of the Faulkner parodies and his response.
104. Snell, 118.
105. Snell, 120, quoting Phil Stone, "William Faulkner and His Neighbors," *Saturday Review,* September 19, 1942, 12.
106. Gray, 88.
107. Wasson, 41.
108. Interview with Ike Roberts, spring 1950, CCP.
109. Wasson, 47.
110. Robert Farley to Joseph Blotner, April 6, 1965, JBP.

111. Lind, "Faulkner's Uses of Poetic Drama," 68–69.

112. Williamson.

113. Snell, 55.

114. Shawhan and Swain, 13.

115. Shawhan and Swain, 2–19.

116. Notes from interview with Lucy Somerville, n.d., CCP.

117. *FL*.

118. These details about Lucy Somerville Howorth are drawn from Oral History Interview with Lucy Somerville Howorth, June 20, 22, and 23, 1975, Interview G-0028, Southern Oral History Program Collection (#4007), http://docsouth .unc.edu/sohp/G-0028/menu.html.

119. Shawhan and Swain, 30.

120. "The Faulkner I Knew," *Delta Review*, July–August 1965, 38–39, 73, UM.

121. The play was published for the first time in *Strand Magazine*, October–January, 2015, 4, 9, 10–12.

122. Lind, "Faulkner's Uses of Poetic Drama," 71.

123. Lind, "Faulkner's Uses of Poetic Drama," 73. I concentrate on the play's words. See Waid, 1–17, for an interpretation of the illustrations.

124. Wasson, 54.

125. Sensibar, *The Origins of Faulkner's Art*, 115.

126. Karl, 165.

127. Sensibar, *The Origins of Faulkner's Art*, xiiii. Her account of Pierrot in literature relies on Storey.

128. Sensibar, *The Origins of Faulkner's Art*, 12.

129. Preface to *The Marble Faun*, 7.

130. Faulkner to Braithwaite, February 25, 1927, Houghton Library, Harvard University.

131. See Karl, 168–74, for a detailed account of the poets who influenced *Vision in Spring*.

132. All quotations are from *Vision in Spring*, ed. Judith Sensibar.

133. Gray, 94. I concur with Gray's conclusion that Judith Sensibar inflates the importance of *Vision in Spring* as a significant step toward the major novels. It seems, instead, just one of several efforts of a floundering artist some years away from mastering his talent.

134. For Faulkner's letters to his mother during his New Haven and New York stays, see W. Faulkner, *Thinking of Home*, ed. Watson.

135. Young, *Stark Young: A Life in the Arts: Letters, 1900–1962*, ed. Pilkington, vol. 1, 164.

136. Anderson and Kelly, 40–42.

137. Anderson and Kelly, 41.

138. Margaret Silver, "A Visit with Miss Maud" [final draft], *McCall's*, May 1956, UM.

3. Postings

1. UM.

2. H. Edward Richard interview with Phil Stone, in Richardson, 34.

3. Phil Stone to Senator John Sharp Williams, May 1, 1922, UM. "It is true that his uncle, Judge John Falkner, of this place, is quite prominent in the faction opposed

to us in politics, but this young man takes no interest in politics whatever and never votes except when I go get him and make him vote the way I want him to. He is one of my dearest friends and, in fact, I persuaded Mr. Oldham and Mr. Daily to get him this appointment. . . . This young man is . . . I believe, a man of considerable talent who will develop into something worthwhile if he has the time and money to devote himself to his writing."

4. Interview with Ben Lumpkin, summer 1962, CCP.
5. Interview with Slim Billingsly, March 1963, CCP. Billingsly owned a barbershop in the building that housed the post office.
6. Richardson, 100, 112, points out wording that is reminiscent of *The Marble Faun* and other early poems.
7. Richardson, 101. Several critics have placed enormous importance on "The Hill" as a kind of key to the Yoknapatawpha fiction that would soon erupt in Faulkner's writing: Putzel, 65–70; Gresset, "Faulkner's 'The Hill,'"; Momberger, "A Reading of Faulkner's 'The Hill.'"
8. Brooks, *William Faulkner: Toward Yoknapatawpha,* 40.
9. Richardson, 212, quotes the Erikson passage.
10. Interview with Robert Coughlan, December 29, 1966, JBP.
11. Snell, 139, 141.
12. "The Faulkner I Knew," *Delta Review,* July–August 1965, 38–39, 73, UM.
13. Webb and Green, eds., 68–76.
14. RHMP, September 19, 1972.
15. Webb and Green, eds., 76.
16. I'm indebted to Barbara Barnett, Chevalier dans l'Ordre des Palmes Académiques, and Rosemary Clark for helping me to piece together the joke.
17. W. H. Hutchinson to Blotner, January 11 and November 17, 1965, JBP.
18. J. Allan Christian to Blotner, September 22, 1965, JBP.
19. *SL,* 6.
20. Wasson, 66.
21. Interview with Robert Farley, April 3, 1965, JBP.
22. *SL,* 7.
23. My account of this period during the publication of *The Marble Faun* draws on Snell, 151–58, and *FB* (1974), 362–66.
24. newspaperarchive.com.
25. See, for example, Snell, 154; and Oates, 36.
26. *LG,* 41.
27. Faulkner misspelled this word in a letter to Hal Smith.
28. Paul Rogers to Blotner, March 6, 1980, JBP.
29. Wasson, 66.
30. Interview with Emily Stone, November 30, 1965, JBP.
31. See Wasson, 60–71.

4. New Orleans

1. Dardis, *Firebrand,* 176–77.
2. Reed, 9.

3. Qtd. in Reed, 13.

4. Interview with Harold Dempsey, August 11, 1963, CCP.

5. La Farge, 125, 129.

6. For the whole song: http://www.horntip.com/html/songs_sorted_by_name /with_music/c/christopher_columbo/christopher_columbo.htm. T. S. Eliot was inspired to write his own pornographic poems that seem inspired by "Christopher Columbo": http://www.units.miamioh.edu/humanitiescenter/node/519.

7. See "Oliver La Farge: American Writer and Anthropologist," https://m.youtube .com/watch?v=RB_u9drQJfo.

8. *FB* (1984).

9. Eagle dance: http://encyclopedia2.thefreedictionary.com/Eagle+Dance.

10. Spratling's memoir of his friendship with Faulkner is included in the Kindle edition of *Sherwood Anderson and Other Famous Creoles*.

11. La Farge, 112.

12. Spratling, 30.

13. Luddington, 230. The biographer is quoting from Dos Passos's letters and diaries.

14. James K. Feibleman, qtd. in Holditch, 26.

15. Lillian Friend Marcus to Carvel Collins, November 1, 1951, CCP.

16. Karl, 194.

17. Anderson, *Sherwood Anderson's Memoirs,* 473. In *Sherwood Anderson and Other Famous Creoles*, Spratling drew a picture of himself and Faulkner, who sits in a chair beneath which can be seen three jugs of what is presumably corn liquor.

18. Interview, March 22, 1950, CCP.

19. Interview with Anita Loos, n.d., CCP.

20. July 27, 1925, CCP; ellipses are in the original.

21. Interview with Ben Wasson, n.d., CCP.

22. Reed, 109.

23. Kreiswirth, 4.

24. Snell, 151–52.

25. Notes on interview with Young, May 1950, CCP.

26. Qtd. in Carvel Collins's introduction to *New Orleans Sketches*.

27. Qtd. in Carvel Collins's introduction to *New Orleans Sketches*.

28. Qtd. in Carvel Collins's introduction to *New Orleans Sketches*.

29. Reed, 34.

30. Reed, 164–65

31. See Collins's informative introduction to *New Orleans Sketches*.

32. See the July 1921 cover shown in Reed, 41.

33. Interview with Emily Stone, January 27, 1963, CCP.

34. Snell, 172.

35. UM.

36. Still one of the best scholarly accounts of *The Marble Faun* and of Faulkner's other poetry is George Garrett, "An Examination of the Poetry of William Faulkner."

37. Qtd. in Reed, 33.

38. Qtd. in Reed, 33.

39. Brooks, *William Faulkner: Toward Yoknapatawpha,* 100, 106.

40. Reed, 61.

41. Owen Crump to Blotner, June 9, 1966, JBP.
42. Interview with Harold Dempsey, August 11, 1963, CCP.
43. Interview with John McClure, March 18, 1950, CCP.
44. Interview with Anderson, n.d., CCP.
45. Anderson, *Sherwood Anderson's Memoirs,* 462.
46. Anderson and Kelly, 100.
47. Interview with Harold Dempsey, August 11, 1963, CCP.
48. Reed, 18–19.
49. William H. Hoffman to Blotner, October 1, 1965, JBP.
50. Interview with Harold Dempsey, August 11, 1963, CCP.
51. Blotner (1984).
52. Interview with Feibleman, February 1, 1965, JBP.
53. Anderson and Kelly, 101.
54. Interview with Harold Dempsey, September 16, 1962, CCP.
55. Reed, 77.
56. Interview with Harold Dempsey, September 16, 1962, CCP.
57. See Holditch.
58. Reed, 75.
59. Interview with Caroline Durieux, March 26, 1963, CCP.
60. Notes on interview with Tichenor, CCP.
61. Interview with Ted. Liuzza, April 1963, CCP.
62. Reed, 14.
63. Qtd. in Reed, 15.
64. Interview with Margery Gumbel, March 22, 1968, CCP.
65. Interview with Margery Gumbel, April 5, 1963, CCP.
66. Two Jackson tales appear in W. Faulkner, *Uncollected Stories.*
67. Faulkner showed off his awareness of contemporary art in throwaway comments in "Mirrors of Chartres Street" (February 8, 1925), for example: "The moon had crawled up the sky like a fat spider and planes of light and shadow were despair for the Vorticist schools."
68. See Richardson, 130–33, for a discussion of how the imagery, themes, and techniques of Faulkner's poetry appear in his sketches.
69. Reed, 65.
70. Interview with Ted Liuzza, April 1963, CCP.
71. Skei, *William Faulkner: The Short Story Career,* 22, notes there is no typescript of the story but its setting and connection to other stories like "Don Giovani" and "Episode" is "sufficient evidence of a 1925 composition of them."
72. Carothers, "Faulkner's Short Story Writing and the Oldest Profession," 46.
73. Interview with Harold Dempsey, August 11, 1963, CCP.
74. *FB* (1984).
75. Interview with Harold Dempsey, August 11, 1963, CCP.
76. Ted Liuzza to Carvel Collins, May 22, 1967, CCP.
77. Reed, 227.
78. Reed, 199.
79. Reed, 169–70.
80. Reed, 9.

81. Reed, 214.
82. Interview with Ted Liuzza, April 1963, in Liuzza's New Orleans office, CCP. Liuzza worked on the *New Orleans Item* in the 1920s.
83. Interview with Joyce McClure, March 20, 1950, CCP.
84. Reed, 242–43.
85. Holditch.
86. Reed, 241.
87. Faulkner's introduction to the Modern Library edition of *Sanctuary* (1932), reprinted in the Library of America's *Novels 1930–1935*, 1029–30.
88. Anderson, *Sherwood Anderson: Selected Letters,* ed. Modlin, 69–70.
89. Interview with Mrs. Edward B. Martin, March 28, 1963, CCP.
90. *FB* (1984).
91. Moser, 198–99.
92. *FB* (1984).
93. Throughout I use the title the novel was given on first publication, even though Faulkner preferred *If I Forget Thee, Jerusalem,* first used in the Library of America edition of the novel.
94. Faulkner, *"Helen: A Courtship"* and *"Mississippi Poems"* 23.
95. Wittenberg, *Faulkner: The Transfiguration of Biography,* 51.
96. Snell, 161.
97. *FB* (1984).

5. Wanderjahr

1. Spratling, 30.
2. Bacigalupo.
3. All quotations from Faulkner's letters are from W. Faulkner, *Thinking of Home,* ed. Watson.
4. Interview with Else Jonsson, August 5, 1965, CCP.
5. Snell, 183, reports that Emily Stone saw a letter from T. S. Eliot, saying he had met Faulkner and "would pay more attention to him than he had before." This letter is supposed to have been destroyed in the 1942 fire in Stone's home.
6. *FB* (1974), 444.
7. Quotations are from the Cox edition; ellipses are in the original.
8. McHaney, "The Elmer Papers," 49, refers to Elmer's "aesthetic masturbation."
9. The ellipses are in the original.
10. Brooks, *William Faulkner: Toward Yoknapatawpha,* 117.
11. Skei, *William Faulkner: The Novelist as Short Story Writer,* 150.
12. Peek and Hamblin, eds., 225.
13. A. G. Jones, "Faulkner's War Stories and the Construction of Gender," 49.
14. Volpe, *A Reader's Guide to William Faulkner: The Short Stories.*
15. A. G. Jones, "Faulkner's War Stories and the Construction of Gender," 50.
16. *CGBC,* vol. 2, 5.
17. See *CGBC,* vol. 1, 42–43, for photographs of the poem's typescript.
18. Snell, 185–86.
19. *SL,* 27.

20. Richards, 23.
21. Simross.
22. Odiorne to Carvel Collins, March 15, 1963, CCP.
23. Unpublished Odiorne memoir, n.d., CCP.

6. Return

1. December 19, 1925, CCP.
2. Franklin Moak wrote out part of the minutes from the Rotary meeting for Carvel Collins on August 4, 1975, apparently in response to a conversation they had the day before.
3. This is my conjecture. See Paddock, "Trifles with a Tragic Profundity," 413, who notes that details in Faulkner's letter to his Aunt Bama in 1925 appear in the short story. However, he did not send out the story for publication until 1928.
4. Spratling, 33.
5. Volpe, *A Reader's Guide to William Faulkner: The Short Stories.*
6. Paddock, *Contrapuntal in Integration,* 57.
7. All quotations are from *Mayday,* introduction by Carvel Collins.
8. Typescript, NYPL.
9. Limon, 119.
10. Wittenberg, *Faulkner: The Transfiguration of Biography,* 44.
11. Kreiswirth, 63–64.
12. Brooks, *William Faulkner: Toward Yoknapatawpha,* 69–70.
13. Yonce, *William Faulkner: Annotations to the Novels: "Soldiers' Pay,"* 48.
14. Yonce, *William Faulkner: Annotations to the Novels: "Soldiers' Pay,"* 50.
15. "From Jazz Syncopation to Blues Elegy," 71.
16. Yonce, *Annotations to the Novels: "Soldiers' Pay,"* 161.
17. Yonce, *Annotations to the Novels: "Soldiers' Pay,"* 166.
18. Singal, 64.
19. Volpe, *A Reader's Guide to William Faulkner,* 52.
20. Snell, 187, 188.
21. *WFCR,* xi.
22. Bassett, ed., 3.
23. Cooperman, 160.
24. See Bledsoe.
25. Wasson, 72–73.
26. Mrs. McGehee to Robert H. Moore, April 15, 1970, RHMP.
27. Putzel, 27.
28. Interview with Harold Dempsey, August 11, 1963, CCP.
29. *The Letters of Sherwood Anderson,* 155.
30. Polk, "Faulkner: The Artist as Cuckold," 37. For other readings of the story, see Bradford, and Peterson, the only critic to suppose the story was written in 1926. Most date it from about 1931, when it was first sent out to magazines. Millgate, *Achievement,* 18–20, has a careful and shrewd interpretation of the Anderson-Faulkner relationship.
31. Hönnighausen, *Faulkner: Masks and Metaphors,* 90.

32. Irwin, "Not the Having but the Waiting," 154, 156.
33. Spratling, 29.
34. Anderson and Kelly, 102. Putzel, 77, mentions seeing a copy of the book bearing a "good-humored inscription" in Anderson's "own hand."
35. Qtd. in Snell, 188–89.
36. Interview with Mrs. Edward B. Martin, March 28, 1963, CCP.
37. All quotations are from *"Helen: A Courtship"* and *"Mississippi Poems."*
38. Interview with Mrs. Edward B. Martin, March 28, 1963, CCP.
39. Wasson, 79–81.
40. *FB* (1984). Karl, 268, referring to an undisclosed source, reports "Estelle became pregnant by a man not her husband." This claim, not followed up by any explanation of what happened to Estelle's pregnancy, is mystifying. Faulkner does not seem to have been the father, and I have seen no evidence that establishes whether or not he had sexual relations with Estelle before or during her marriage to Franklin.
41. *SL*, 35.
42. *FB* (1984).
43. *FL.*
44. *SL*, 35–36. Braithwaite was widely known for giving unknown poets an opportunity. Faulkner had counted three hundred new ones in Braithwaite's 1925 anthology, noting that so much writing was a "very healthy thing in America." Braithwaite assured Faulkner of his publisher's probity, but evidently Faulkner never did receive a check. Did Faulkner know that Braithwaite was an African American? It is impossible to say since so far as is known the two men never met, although Faulkner mentioned the possibility of coming to Boston.
45. *SL*, 34.
46. Minter, 65.
47. See Harrington for one of the most balanced accounts of the novel.
48. Spratling, 129; Anderson and Kelly, 117–21.
49. Interview with Marjorie Gumbel, n.d., CCP.
50. Brooks, *William Faulkner: Toward Yoknapatawpha*, 135.
51. Atkinson, 171.
52. Hönnighausen, *Faulkner: Masks and Metaphors*, 102.
53. See Kreiswirth, 82–87, for parallels between *Mosquitoes* and several Huxley novels.
54. Arnold, 84–85.
55. Freud is quoted in Arnold, 123.
56. For an analysis of the cuts, see Gwin, *"Mosquitoes'* Missing Bite: The Four Deletions." Feminist scholars have filled in the gaps left in the self-censored or simply obtuse earlier readings of the novel. See, for example, Michel, "Faulkner as Lesbian Author." In "Did Ernest like Gordon?" Gwin detects the oscillations between heterosexual and homosexual scenes, so that even Mr. Talliaferro, seemingly bent on pursuing women, is nevertheless attracted to Gordon, as Gwin notes, quoting suggestive sentences in which Ernest Talliaferro, a lingerie salesman, stands quite close to the sculptor, "examining with concern a faint even powdering of dust upon his neat small patent leather shoes." Later Mr. Talliaferro observes the

"rhythmic power" of Gordon's "back and arm," his "muscularity in an undershirt," compared to the observer's more feminine and symmetrical sleeve. Gordon even shoves his hard body against Mr. Talliaferro, not a very gentlemanly or, shall we say, Puritanical thing to do.

57. *SL,* 34.

7. Coming Home

1. *SL,* 37; Snell, 192.
2. Snell, 195.
3. All quotations are from *Father Abraham,* ed. Meriwether, 79–80.
4. Minter, 80.
5. March 22 [no year], JBP.
6. March 22 [no year], JBP.
7. Paul Rogers to Joseph Blotner, April 7, 1980, JBP.
8. Estelle's stories are in UVA.
9. My recapitulation of Estelle's life without Faulkner relies on and is a response to Judith Sensibar's perceptive account in *FL.*
10. Qtd. in *FL.*
11. *FL.*
12. Sensibar's interviews.
13. *SL,* 32.
14. Michel, 13.
15. Michel, 13.
16. Atkinson, 75.
17. Rado, 25.
18. Rado, 20.
19. *FL.*
20. Sensibar, "Writing for Faulkner," 362.
21. Sensibar, "Writing for Faulkner," 360.
22. Interview with Mrs. Weinmann, July 10, 1967, CCP.
23. Interview with Mrs. Weinmann, July 10, 1967, CCP.
24. Interview with "AP's daughter," JBP; *SL,* 42.
25. *SL,* 42.
26. Interview with Mrs. Weinmann, July 10, 1967, CCP.
27. Interview with Victoria Fielden, March 14, 1968, CCP.
28. Faulkner's letter: *CGBC,* vol. 2.
29. Ferguson, 27.
30. Interview with Sallie Murry, n.d., JBP.
31. Godwin, 129.
32. Ditsky, 63.
33. Snell, 264–65.
34. Ditsky, 63.
35. Brodsky, "A Textual History of William Faulkner's *The Wishing-Tree* and *The Wishing Tree,*" 341.
36. Wittenberg, 62.

37. Dean Faulkner Wells, "Faulkner Helped Young Brother Dean with Vocabulary Lesson," *Faulkner Newsletter & Yoknapatawpha Review* 2 (January–March 1982): 3, 73; interview with Ben Wasson, January 1975, CCP.

38. *FL.*

39. Snell, 200.

40. Dardis, *Firebrand,* 207.

41. *SL,* 37, 38.

42. *SL,* 38.

43. I quote from the Library of America text, which includes material that Faulkner added to *Sartoris* even as Ben Wasson was cutting about a fourth of *Flags in the Dust.*

44. Rhodes, 96, 98–99, 102.

45. McDaniel, 34–37.

46. Interview with Boyce Collins, November 27, 1965, JBP.

47. On Bayard as the name of the ideal knight in southern tradition, see McDaniel, 7.

48. Karl, 291.

49. Millgate, *Achievement,* 85.

50. Bailey, 72.

51. Karl, 297.

52. Bailey, 79.

53. Karl, 291.

54. Bailey, 75.

55. Peek and Hamblin, eds., 253–54.

56. Wittenberg, 68.

57. Interview with Victoria (Cho-Cho), October 17, 1964, JBP.

58. Thomas D. Clark to Robert H. Moore, September 19, 1972, RHMP.

59. Interview with Estelle Faulkner, November 27, 1964, JBP.

60. Wittenberg, 69.

61. Mrs. Edward Lee Whitten to Robert H. Moore, May 5, 1940, RHMP. She attended a Shakespeare class with John and later as a journalist interviewed him about his painting, after which they became friends.

62. Keiser, 62, 64.

63. *SL,* 39.

64. Several accounts refer to a story called "Twilight," but in fact all that is available looks like a beginning draft of *The Sound and the Fury.* See http://drc.usask.ca /projects/faulkner/main/related_texts/twilight.html.

65. See Towner and Carothers, 150–52, for a summary of the critical debate about the chronology of composition.

66. Momberger, "Faulkner's 'The Village' and 'That Evening Sun,'" 58.

67. John T. Matthews, in *Bloom's Major Short Story Writers,* ed. Bloom, 63. Originally published in Fowler and Abadie, eds., *Faulkner and the Craft of Fiction,* 78–79.

68. http://faulkner.drupal.shanti.virginia.edu/node/8455?canvas#.

69. Interview notes, August 5, 1963, CCP.

70. Volpe, *A Reader's Guide to William Faulkner: The Short Stories.*

71. M. C. Brown, 205.

72. Matthews, *William Faulkner: Seeing through the South,* 79–80.

73. December 21, 1927, addressed to "Sirs," in "Faulkner's Correspondence with the *Saturday Evening Post*," ed. Meriwether, 465.

74. Wasson, 86.

75. https://en.m.wikipedia.org/wiki/Sweet_Violets.

76. Wasson, 122–23; interview with Ben Wasson, n.d., CCP.

77. http://faulkner.drupal.shanti.virginia.edu/node/8504?canvas includes a lucid and succinct discussion of the novel's composition as well as listing the important studies of the manuscript, typescript, and publication history of *Flags in the Dust*.

78. Glick.

79. Alden Whitman, "Harrison Smith of the *Saturday Review* Is Dead," clipping file, CCP.

80. Interviews with Eric Devine, May 7, 1964, August 5, 1966, June 25, 1967, August 21, 1967, and Joel Sayre, March 26, 1968, CCP.

81. *SL*, 41

82. I found this reference to Smith (although he is not named) in a 1931 *New York World-Telegram* article, "William Faulkner, 'Literary Hope' from Mississippi Likens Himself in City to a 'Houn' Dawg under a Wagon,'" in a clipping file at UVA. In fact, Smith was not Faulkner's only friend. Eric Devine certainly qualifies as well.

83. Dardis, *The Thirsty Muse*, 52.

84. Confronted with a paucity of evidence, Dardis and Zugsmith's biographer (Ravitz, 10) retreat into supposing her zealous left-wing views put off a "politically indifferent" Faulkner. Possibly so, but Faulkner befriended radicals like Dashiell Hammett and Lillian Hellman and created a committed left-wing political activist, the impressive Linda Snopes, in *The Mansion*.

85. Interview with Devine, JBP.

86. Keiser, 49.

87. *FB* (1974), 562.

88. Keiser, 59.

89. *SL*, 43.

90. Dardis, "Harrison Smith," 166.

91. *SL*, 40.

92. Snell, 202–3.

8. Married

1. MCR.

2. UVA.

3. UVA.

4. VJR.

5. Two biographers, Joel Williamson and Jay Parini, mention a pregnancy and an abortion that William Faulkner helped procure for Estelle. Robert Hamblin has shown how weak the chain of evidence is for such a "fact" (see "Biographical Fact or Fiction? William Faulkner, Estelle Oldham Franklin, and Abortion").

6. *FL*.

7. Dardis, "Harrison Smith," 168.

8. Interview with Louise Bonino, who worked in Smith's firm, February 2, 1967, CCP.

9. Fred Karl Papers, Special Collections, Thomas Cooper Library, University of South Carolina.

10. Interview with Coughlan, December 30, 1964, JBP.

11. Interview with Estelle Faulkner, August 22, 1964, LDBP.

12. All quotations are from *B*.

13. Louise Hudson (Mrs. Almond Coleman), October 10, 1965, JBP.

14. November 15, 1967, JBP. See also interview with Dr. Ralph Muckenfuss, April 9, 1967, JBP.

15. Interview with Taylor H. McElroy, March 23, 1965, JBP.

16. The poem "To Lida" is handwritten on the stationery of Lemuel E. Oldham, Attorney at Law, Oxford, Mississippi. August 10, 1943, Fred Karl Papers, Special Collections, Thomas Cooper Library, University of South Carolina. Another copy of the poem is in LDBP.

17. Qtd. in Snell, 212.

18. Foreword to *B*.

19. *Faulkner Newsletter.*

20. Interview with Mrs. Leatherbury, September 1962, CCP.

21. Interview with Mrs. Leatherbury, September, 1962, CCP.

22. UVA.

23. Interview with Malcolm Franklin, September 26, 1966, CCP.

24. Interview with Mrs. Shepherd, March 30, 1963, CCP.

25. *SL,* 45.

26. *FL.*

27. There is a draft of the poem in pencil in Estelle's hand in LDBP.

28. VJR.

29. *FB* (1984).

30. Interview with Estelle Faulkner, February 23 [no year], JBP.

31. In the published novel, Temple wears "a spurious Chinese robe splotched with gold dragons and jade and scarlet flowers."

32. It is not clear why the women found the book shocking—that is, whether it was because of the comments about women or specifically the treatment of Temple's rape. Faulkner quoted Smith in the Modern Library edition of the novel and repeated Smith's remark at the University of Virginia: http://faulkner.drupal .shanti.virginia.edu/node/8456?canvas#.

33. Marshall Smith's interview in the *Bookman,* December 1931, reprinted in *LITG*, 13.

34. VJR, 135.

35. *FL.*

36. Snell, 213.

37. Noted in *FL*.

38. Other biographers present a bleaker picture (see Oates, 87–88; Karl, 380; and Weinstein, *Becoming Faulkner,* 17–20).

9. All in the Family

1. Wasson, 96–97.

2. Millgate, *Achievement,* 87–88.

3. Kreiswirth, 131. His chapter on the novel contains one of the best discussions of Faulkner's sources.
4. Polk, *Children of the Dark House.*
5. Kinney, *Critical Essays on William Faulkner: The Compson Family,* has a photo of the iron fence that has been associated with the Compson house.
6. Matthews, *William Faulkner: Seeing through the South.*
7. Bleikasten, *The Ink of Melancholy,* 94.
8. Wittenberg, 75.
9. Matthews, *William Faulkner: Seeing through the South.*
10. O. Vickery, 43.
11. Alexander, 184.
12. Williamson.
13. *FL.*
14. Matthews, *William Faulkner: Seeing through the South.*
15. See Wittenberg, 76. Minter, 94, is more circumspect.
16. Wittenberg, 80.
17. *FL.*
18. *FL.*
19. *FL.*
20. Dahl, 1027–28.
21. Dahl, 1026.
22. "DSF," 104.
23. Karl, 311.
24. Matthews, *William Faulkner: Seeing through the South.*

10. Desire and Death

1. Bleikasten, *The Ink of Melancholy.*
2. My account draws heavily on Luce, ed., *William Faulkner's "As I Lay Dying,"* xiii–xxiii, including her use of primary sources and interviews.
3. The urtext of *Sanctuary* announces that the Goodwin trial is in Yoknapatawpha County.
4. See Cullen, 84–86.
5. *LG,* 133, 135.
6. *LG,* 153.
7. Weinstein, *Becoming Faulkner.*
8. Bleikasten, *The Ink of Melancholy,* 89.
9. Wittenberg, 112.
10. See Luce, *William Faulkner: Annotations to the Novels: "As I Lay Dying,"* 1–4, for a discussion of the title.
11. Interview with Larry Wells.
12. http://faulkner.drupal.shanti.virginia.edu/node/8452?canvas#.
13. Gwynn and Blotner, eds., 115.
14. Scott, 78.
15. "Graphophone" was the trademark name for phonograph. The graphophone is mentioned three times in the novel. See Luce, *William Faulkner: Annotations*

to the Novels: "As I Lay Dying," for the appearance of the graphophone in other works that Faulkner may have read.

16. Scott, 86.
17. See the discussion of Faulkner's manuscript and typescript: http://faulkner .drupal.shanti.virginia.edu/node/8495?canvas.
18. Matthews, *William Faulkner: Seeing through the South,* 146.
19. Gray, 162.
20. Wittenberg, 108.
21. Qtd. in Oates, 89.
22. *SL,* 48.
23. Bassett, ed., 7.
24. *CWF,* 15, 16.
25. Bassett, ed., 59–60.
26. Bassett, ed., 62.

11. Old Days and New Ways

1. See the letters between Faulkner and the *Post,* October 4 and 9, in Meriwether, ed., "Faulkner's Correspondence with the *Saturday Evening Post,*" 468–69.
2. Gresset, *A Faulkner Chronology,* 29–30.
3. Meriwether, ed., "Faulkner's Correspondence with the *Saturday Evening Post,* 470.
4. *SL,* 46–47.
5. Towner and Carothers, 164. See also the entire issue of the *Faulkner Journal* 18 (Fall 2002–Spring 2003) devoted to the Indian stories.
6. http://faulkner.drupal.shanti.virginia.edu/node/8453?canvas#.
7. *SL,* 47.
8. Dabney, 109.
9. Parker, 84.
10. The following quotations are from Fletcher, 41, 42, 46, 51.
11. Fletcher, 51.
12. Thanks to my research associate Rosemary Clark, who discovered the girandoles: http://caseantiques.com/item/lot-174-cornelius-co-girandole-garniture-daniel -boone-indian-3-pcs/.
13. William Faulkner to William Bryant, March 22, 1930, in Trotter, 65.
14. A slave using the Spanish word is odd. Is it a word Issetibbeha picked up in New Orleans? Is calling the snake "grandfather" an allusion to the Eden in which humans met their mortality?
15. Dabney, 111.
16. Volpe, *A Reader's Guide to William Faulkner: The Short Stories.*
17. Dabney, 113.
18. Faulkner first considered another property, described on a lease contract drawn up by Phil Stone with Walter B. Mayfield "for house and land on Oxford and Toc-copola road, east of Oxford." Faulkner had the option to purchase (see Brodsky, *Selections from the William Faulkner Collection,* 57).
19. The spelling is often rendered as "Shegog," a spelling some members of the family used, but the deed of conveyance is made out to Robert B. Sheegog (see Trotter, 12).

20. Lawrence and Hise, 9, identify three other houses in Oxford that are "almost mirror images" of Rowan Oak.
21. Interview with Larry Wells.
22. Trotter, 9.
23. Trotter, 31.
24. Interview with Mr. and Mrs. William Fielden, March 14, 1968, CCP.
25. Trotter, 35.
26. Details are drawn from *B*, 21–26.
27. For the following account of the races in and near Bailey's Woods, I rely on Calvin Brown, "Faulkner's Manhunts," 389–91.
28. Fargnoli and Golay, 196.
29. Louis Cochran Papers, UM.
30. *LG*, 136–37.
31. Trotter, 75.
32. See Jackson, "Images of Collaboration," 33–34.
33. Interview with Ted Curtis, who saw firsthand bootlegging operations in New York City and Memphis, CCP. Carvel Collins tried to pin down real-life models for Ruby Lamar, one of whom had been Popeye's woman and later a devout Christian who moved to Florida and renounced her former life, which her husband, Collins realized, knew nothing about.
34. Matthews, *William Faulkner: Seeing through the South*, 44.
35. Polk, ed., *"Sanctuary": The Original Text*, 295. See Langford, 6–7, for a discussion of the flashbacks.
36. See Millgate, *Achievement*, 119–21.
37. Brooks, *William Faulkner: The Yoknapatawpha Country*, 136–37.
38. Gray, 167.
39. For details about Faulkner's sources for Popeye, see Rouselle, 4.
40. Interview with John Foley, July 10, 1953, CCP.
41. Weinstein, *Becoming Faulkner*, 15.
42. Gwynn and Blotner, eds., 21.
43. Chabrier, 34.
44. Rousselle, 44.
45. Alex Palmer, "The Segregated Railway Car Offers a Visceral Reminder of the Jim Crow Era," http://www.smithsonianmag.com/smithsonian-institution /segregated-railway-car-offers-visceral-reminder-jim-crow-era-180959383/. A Virginia law required that "there be no difference in the quality, conveniences, and accommodations in the cars": https://historyengine.richmond.edu/episodes /view/3273.
46. Kathleen Scheel advances the ingenious argument that the central event in *Sanctuary* is not Popeye's rape of Temple with a corn cob, but her rape at home, which is a repressed memory she alludes to in the traumatic scene at the old Frenchman place. Several problems arise in this analysis: Was Faulkner dealing at all with repressed memory? It had gained considerable currency when Scheel wrote her article but was also viewed with considerable skepticism, as she acknowledges. Scheel counts on the concept of repressed memory to elucidate Temple's "inexplicable behavior at the old Frenchman place." But it does not seem inexplicable to

me. She suffers a sort of psychic break, suddenly deprived of societal and familial support. Not a strong personality to begin with, Temple first puts herself under the protection of the inept Gowan Stevens and then entirely collapses when Popeye and the lawless world of the old Frenchman place bears down upon her. She cannot believe what is happening to her. Hence her plaintive cry that her father is a judge. He is a source of power that is no longer available to her, but it is her habit to identify with those who have power over her, and hence she substitutes Popeye's hegemony for her father's. Her status means nothing at the old Frenchman place, and that status is ironically restored at the end of the novel. Scheel is right that Temple can no longer trust her father to save her, but is it because, like Goodwin's father, Pap, who is blind but is there for the rape, Judge Temple refuses to acknowledge what is happening in front of him—that Temple is raped by her brothers? Isn't Temple's problem, instead, that she has allowed herself, like so many southern women, to be defined by male family members and authority figures? When Faulkner said he never read Freud, his denial was not so much a rejection of Freudianism or lack of interest but rather a distrust of consigning his work to becoming a gloss on Freudian theories.

47. Morell, 351.
48. Waggoner, 98.
49. "DSF," 119.
50. *MBB*, 128.
51. Trotter, 76.
52. *MBB*, 191.
53. Trotter, 76. Faulkner tended to think of the Chickasaws and Choctaws interchangeably.
54. Trotter, 36.

12. Sorrow and Scandal

1. JBP. *CGBC*, vol. 2, gives the date as January 19, but that is an error, as an examination of the original telegram shows.
2. Meriwether, ed., "Faulkner's Correspondence with the *Saturday Evening Post*," 474.
3. Karl, 432–33.
4. "Fetal Alcohol Syndrome: The Origins of a Moral Panic," *Alcohol and Alcoholism* 35 (May 2000): 276–82, https://academic.oup.com/alcalc/article/35/3/276/208920/FETAL-ALCOHOL-SYNDROME-THE-ORIGINS-OF-A-MORAL
5. Wasson, 108.
6. Blotner draws a parallel between the Faulkner marriage and "The Brooch." See also Karl, 424–25.
7. Robert Sherwood also had a whack at Bennett, remarking in *Scribner's Magazine* (April 1931) that Faulkner "writes rather like a fiend out of hell."
8. Polchin, 145.
9. Fargnoli, ed., 111.
10. Qtd. in *Brooklyn Eagle*, March 16, 1931.

11. For more on early notices of Faulkner's work, see Rollyson, "Faulkner's First Biographers."
12. Coughlan, 78.
13. "DSF," 120, 122.
14. *MBB,* 135.
15. Coughlan, 78.
16. Interview with Tom Kell, March 30, 1965, JBP.
17. *MBB,* 135.
18. Snell, 9.
19. Snell, 77.
20. Stone to Robert Daniel, April 6, 1942, CCP.
21. Snell, 127. Carvel Collins interviewed Dorothy Ware, who operated several houses of prostitution and saw a good deal of Faulkner in the company of Reno Devaux, another whorehouse proprietor. She could not remember Faulkner ever with "a girl."
22. Snell, 127.
23. *SL,* 43. Tanlac was a patent medicine cure-all (http://www.mydaytondailynews .com/lifestyles/gem-city-jewel-tanlac-dayton-patent-medicine/0Kvwfni CaHbULyM7agjIlL/), and Pinkham's Compound was for menstrual, meno-pausal, and other female problems (https://www.britannica.com/biography/Lydia -E-Pinkham).
24. Wolff and Watkins, *Talking about William Faulkner,* 86.
25. Snell, 109.
26. Snell, 149–50.
27. Reed's comments come from an undated interview, CCP.
28. *WFCR,* xiii.
29. Reed's comments come from an undated interview, CCP.
30. Trotter, 83.
31. Trotter, 84.
32. Trotter, 85.
33. *CGBC,* vol. 2, 11–12.
34. Snell, 221–22.
35. *SL,* 48.
36. *FB* (1984).
37. *SL,* 51.

13. Fame

1. *SL,* 34.
2. Faulkner's remark is mentioned by Anthony Buttita in *Contempo,* February 1, 1932, 3.
3. Millgate, *Achievement,* 261–62.
4. See Paddock, *Contrapuntal in Integration,* 9–69, for an extensive discussion of the book's structure.
5. See Maya Jasanoff's *The Dawn Patrol: Joseph Conrad in a Global World.* She does not mention Faulkner, but the precedent Conrad sets for Faulkner's fiction is palpable.

6. Paddock, *Contrapuntal in Integration,* 25–26.
7. *SL,* 51.
8. *SL,* 52.
9. *LG,* 139.
10. UVA. Only part of the letter is reprinted in *SL.*
11. *SL,* 52.
12. Anderson, *Sherwood Anderson: Selected Letters,* ed. Modlin, 42–43.
13. Minter, 133.
14. *SL,* 56.
15. *LITG,* 17–18.
16. Karl, 456.
17. Williamson has one of the best accounts of the Charlottesville conference.
18. *LITG,* 18.
19. *SL,* 75.
20. *LITG,* 18.
21. Bennett Cerf Papers, Butler Library, Rare Books and Manuscripts, Columbia University.
22. Interview with Anthony Buttita, December 27, 1966, CCP.
23. I found these items in two databases: newspapers.com and newspaperarchive.com.
24. http://www.hansenwheel.com/custom-showcase/custom-vehicle-showcase/spring-wagon-democrat-wagon.
25. *CWF,* 15.
26. *SL,* 52–53.
27. Trotter, 90.
28. The interview is reprinted in *LITG,* 19–22.
29. *LITG,* ix.
30. See, for example, "5 Things Virginia Schools Taught about Slavery and the Civil War during the Confederate Monuments Boom," https://pilotonline.com/news/local/education/public-schools/things-virginia-schools-taught-about-slavery-and-the-civil-war/article_3b6f9dbd-fdfd-5265-9585-01f965b1cfee.html.
31. *SL,* 53.
32. *SL,* 53.
33. Wasson, 112–13.
34. Notes from interview with Hellman, January 29, 1952, CCP.
35. Klopfer's oral history, Butler Library, Columbia University.
36. Interview with Hellman, January 17, 1965, JBP.
37. Interview with Lillian Hellman, n.d., CCP.
38. Interview with Ben Wasson, March 28, 1965, JBP.
39. Interview with Eric Devine, August 31, 1967, CCP.
40. For more on Woollcott and Faulkner, see Ryan, "Fabbulous Monsters."
41. http://www.millionairesunit.org/index.php?option=com_content&task=view&id=26&Itemid=36.
42. Interviews with Lovett and Wasson, March 28 and August 26, 1965, JBP; Wasson, 125. Ramsey, "'Turnabout' Is Fair(y) Play," 67, accuses Blotner of "whitewashing" Faulkner, of removing anything that might question Faulkner's gender identity. But it is clear from Blotner's notes that Wasson said he did not stay the night. Why

Wasson changed his story, nearly two decades after Blotner interviewed him, I do not know. Was Wasson doing whitewashing that he later decided to remove?

43. Nauman.
44. Ramsey, "'Turnabout' Is Fair(y) Play," 72–73.
45. JBP, interview with Mrs. Sewell Haggard April 23, 1965.
46. Interview with Mrs. Rudolph Weinmann, July 10, 1967, CCP.
47. Smith's interview with Estelle Faulkner is in *LITG*, 25–27.
48. Wasson, 126.
49. F. P. Adams, 1036.
50. Interview with Estelle Faulkner, February 19, 1965, JBP. Blotner's notes record two reactions from Estelle, saying that at first she thought her husband was amused, then that he was annoyed. Blotner chose the second option in *FB* (1974) and omitted the account from *FB* (1984).
51. Wasson, 107.
52. Bezzerides, 68.
53. Volpe, *A Reader's Guide to William Faulkner: The Short Stories.*
54. Wasson to Cerf, December 8, 1931, JBP.
55. Interview with Estelle Faulkner, May 29, 1967, JBP.

14. Home and Hollywood

1. *SL*, 54.
2. Interview with Morton Goldman, August 2, 1967, CCP. Goldman called the treatment "Night Birds," but a treatment Faulkner did for MGM is titled "Night Bird" (see *FMGM*).
3. UVA.
4. Rotary club minutes transcribed on August 4, 1975, for Carvel Collins by Frank Moak, Division of Student Personnel, University of Mississippi.
5. Smith's interview in included in *LITG*, 28–32.
6. *SL*, 56, 60.
7. Interview with V. P. Ferguson, June 29, 1965, CCP: "V. P. says that Faulkner owned and liked Lynd Ward's 'novel' which was all done in wood cuts and called something like *Mad Man's Drum*. Faulkner with pleasure told V. P. that the same man had done another book of the sort [perhaps *Gods' Man*]."
8. Ward, "On *Gods' Man*," in Spiegelman, 786.
9. Cohen, 191.
10. Spiegelman, xii.
11. W. Faulkner, *Thinking of Home,* ed. Watson, 196.
12. Interview with Hubert Starr, January 11, 1968, CCP.
13. "Stallings says that Faulkner did have extremely and effectively penetrating eyes. When I told him what E. O. Champion had said about Faulkner's 'reading you' Mr. Stallings said that certainly was true" (n.d., notes, CCP).
14. Interview with Mrs. Ralph Elliott, January 30, 1968, CCP.
15. Throughout my discussion of Faulkner's first four treatments I rely heavily on *FMGM*.
16. *FMGM*, 55.

17. *FMGM*, 57.
18. *FMGM*, 59.
19. *SL*, 64.
20. Interview with Laurence Stallings, January 11, 1968, CCP.
21. *FMGM*, 76.
22. Interview with Budd Schulberg, November 17, 1950, CCP.
23. *FMGM*, 77.
24. *FMGM*, 81.
25. Both Blotner and Collins conducted interviews that corroborated Fuchs.
26. Karl, 405.
27. This undated letter written on a Thursday from Hollywood with the penciled dates May 25 and June 1 is in CCP.
28. Hubert Starr to Carvel Collins, May 22, 1966, CCP.
29. Interview with Sam Marx, January 11, 1968, CCP.
30. Interview with Bob Buckner, June 8, 1966, JBP.
31. Interview with Frank Gruber, June 12, 1965, JBP.
32. Volpe, *A Reader's Guide to William Faulkner: The Short Stories.*
33. McCarthy, 178.
34. For slightly different versions of the Hawks-Thalberg exchange, see Kawin, *Faulkner and Film,* 76; and McCarthy, 178.
35. McCarthy, 177.
36. McBride, *Focus on Howard Hawks,* 57.
37. Interview with Frank Gruber, June 12, 1965, JBP.
38. Kawin, *Faulkner and Film,* 77.
39. Spoto, 104.
40. Interview with Sallie Murray, October 17, 1967, CCP.
41. Interview with Dorothy Oldham, January 17, 1967, CCP.
42. Interviews with Sallie Murry, March 19, 1965; October 17, 1967, CCP.
43. *SL*, 65.
44. *SL*, 66.
45. *FMGM*, 129.
46. Matthews, "Faulkner and the Culture Industry," 66.
47. Ramsey, "Stars, Fashion, and Authorship in *Today We Live,*" 100.
48. *FMGM*, 194. In his notes, 116, Kawin identifies a pusher as "an airplane driven by a propeller mounted on the rear end of the engine or propeller shaft, behind the plane's main supporting surfaces."
49. *FMGM*, 190.
50. *FMGM*, 117.
51. *FMGM*, 120.
52. A copy of the letter, in CCP, seems to have been written about October 17.
53. Interview with Howard Hawks, June 3, 1965, JBP.
54. Turner/MGM script file, Academy of Motion Picture Arts and Sciences.
55. Academy of Motion Picture Arts and Sciences production files: James Wingate to Irving Thalberg, December 2, 1932; April 11, 1933; Wingate to Mr. E. J. Mannix at MGM, May 19, 1933; Geoffrey Shurlock MGM memo, May 19 and July 6, 1933, reporting British censors' requests.

56. April 12, 1933, Academy of Motion Picture Arts and Sciences.
57. Andrew Turnbull quotes from the Sherwood letter in a letter to Carvel Collins, February 5, 1965.
58. Interview with Cho-Cho (Victoria), January 17, 1965, CCP.

15. The Black Shadow

1. Spoth, 241.
2. *FC*, 32.
3. Brinkmeyer, 177–79.
4. Fowler, "Joe Christmas and 'Womanshenegro,'" 148.
5. Hlavsa, 127–39; Vickery and Vickery, 35.
6. See Lind, "The Calvinistic Burden," 90, for the parallels between Joe and Joanna. Their names suggest they are twins.
7. Pruitt.
8. Bleikasten, *William Faulkner*, 190.
9. Snell, 128.
10. http://faulkner.drupal.shanti.virginia.edu/node/8457?canvas#.
11. Snell, 127.
12. *CWF*, 75.
13. *LITG*, 253.
14. See Atkinson, 152–54, for more about Grimm as a fascist character, although Atkinson does not seem to see Christmas's behavior in the same light.
15. R. Adams, 203.

16. Hollywood at Home

1. Postmarked March 20, 1933, NYPL.
2. All quotations from "War Birds" are from the Kindle edition.
3. All quotations from the screenplay are from *FMGM*.
4. Sidney, 265.
5. Qtd. in McCarthy, 186.
6. *SL*, 70–71.
7. Trotter, 95.
8. Trotter, 99.
9. Interview with Louise Meadow, July 8, 1975, CCP.
10. Interview with John Phillips, July 8, 1976, CCP.
11. Trotter, 98.
12. *FB* (1984).
13. McBride, ed., *Focus on Howard Hawks*, 84.
14. McCarthy, 185.
15. Interview with Louise Meadow, n.d., CCP.
16. Interview with Louise Meadow, November 17, 1965, JBP.
17. Interview with Phoebe Omlie, November 24, 1963, CCP.
18. Interview with Navy Sowell, July 12, 1967, CCP. Faulkner's pilot's log at UVA records fewer than eight hours before he soloed on April 20, but perhaps this is an

incomplete record. Murry Spain also spoke of Faulkner's poor depth perception that sometimes resulted in his trying to land too soon (interview with Murry Spain, early June, 1960, CCP).

19. *SL,* 54; Faulkner to Smith, n.d., CCP.
20. Karl, 72.
21. Interview with Ben Wasson, JBP; Capula, 17.
22. Faulkner liked Florence Eldridge's performance as Ruby, but what he thought of the film is not clear (interview with Ben Wasson, August 1, 1963, CCP).
23. Phillips, 73; *SL,* 75.
24. See Barker, 71, who also argues that *The Story of Temple Drake* had an impact on Faulkner's writing of *Requiem for a Nun.*
25. *FMGM,* xxvi.
26. *FMGM,* 431.
27. *FMGM,* xxxvii.
28. Interview with Sam Marx, January 11, 1968, CCP.
29. *FMGM,* xvii.

17. Seeing It Both Ways

1. *SL,* 71.
2. Interview with Estelle Faulkner, April 27, 1965, JBP.
3. *B,* 45–47.
4. *B,* 33–34.
5. *SL,* 71.
6. Qtd. in Solomon, 42, who suggests Faulkner's reuse of characters was akin to the Hollywood star system, employing the same recognizable personality in picture after picture. See also K. S. Crichton to Faulkner, August 20, 1931: "Well, we finally got our Flem Snopes but, damn it. It is the last (underlined) Flem Snopes and we don't feel like killing the grand character off that quickly. You are really missing a great chance to carry on the character until the point where he gets his come-uppance. What we are very anxious for is a few more Snopes stories in which he is triumphant, bringing out all the meanness and caginess in his make-up. If you print this story now it will mean that others of the type I am referring to won't be possible." Carvel Collins appends a note: "suggests possibility that this story is Centaur in Brass and that Flem died in this version."
7. *SL,* 73. In the Howard Hawks Papers at Brigham Young University, there is a continuity script with Faulkner's name on it, "with dialogue by Harry Benn and Jules Furthman," dated March 30, 1933, although Kawin's examination of the script affirms Faulkner's letter.
8. *SL,* 79.
9. *SL,* 80.
10. Interview with George Oppenheimer, April 16, 65, JBP.
11. *SL,* 69.
12. Faulkner's undated letter to Cerf and his December 12, 1933, reply: UVA.
13. Interview with Estelle Faulkner, March 2, 1965, JBP.
14. Skei, *William Faulkner: The Short Story Career,* 69–70.

15. Karl, 435–36, is the only biographer to discuss autobiographical elements in "Dr. Martino." He sees the shades of Phil Stone and the Oldhams in the story as well.
16. See *CGBC,* vol. 1, 46, 51, 54, 57, 63, 67, 80, 93, 97. These are the extant copies; others may not have survived.
17. *CGBC,* vol. 1, 97.
18. Skei, *William Faulkner: The Novelist as Short Story Writer,* 125. For a comprehensive survey of the critical reaction to "Dr. Martino," see Diane Brown Jones, 411–22.
19. Lang, 24.
20. Lang, 23.
21. Interview with David Hempstead, n.d., CCP.
22. Lang, 30. She has made the strongest case for the unity of *Doctor Martino and Other Stories.*
23. Montagu, 109, 110.
24. See Gleeson-White, "William Faulkner, Screenwriter," 435, for parallels between the Eisenstein and Faulkner screenplays.
25. *SL,* 81.
26. Interview with Hubert Starr, February 16, 1966, CCP.
27. July 12, 1934, UVA. Blotner omitted virtually all signs of affection for Estelle in *Selected Letters,* ostensibly because he wanted to focus on Faulkner as writer. The unfortunate result, however, is that she is diminished as his wife and as a person in her own right while making Faulkner appear to be absorbed only in his own activities.
28. *SL,* 82.
29. Trotter, 102.
30. The screenplay is included in Montagu, 150–206.
31. For more on Eisenstein's influence on Faulkner, see Gleeson-White, "Auditory Exposures." Did Faulkner draw on these Eisenstein details for his novel even as he omitted them from his screenplay?
32. Here Faulkner seems prophetic, since he wrote the story before meeting Meta Carpenter.
33. See Ramsey for a check on the tendency to read Ewing as Faulkner's stand-in.
34. Grimwood, 279.
35. *SL,* 83.
36. The undated letter seems to have been written in August 1934, UVA.
37. *SL,* 85–86.
38. *SL,* 86.

Bibliography

Abdur-Rahman, Aliyyah I. "What Moves at the Margin: William Faulkner and Race." In *The New Cambridge Companion to William Faulkner,* edited by John T. Matthews. Cambridge University Press, 2015. Kindle.

Adams, Franklin Pierce. *The Diary of Our Own Samuel Pepys.* Vol. 2. Simon and Schuster, 1935.

Adams, Richard. "Myth and Motion." In *"Light in August" and the Critical Spectrum,* edited by John B. Vickery and Olga W. Vickery. Wadsworth, 1971.

Agee, James. *Film Writing and Selected Journalism.* Library of America, 1996.

Aldridge, John. *The Devil in the Fire: Retrospective Essays on American Literature and Culture, 1951–1971.* Harper and Row, 1972.

Alexander, Marshall. "Faulkner's Metaphysics of Absence." In *Faulkner and Religion,* edited by Doreen Fowler and Ann J. Abadie. University Press of Mississippi, 1991.

Anderson, Elizabeth, and Gerald R. Kelly. *Miss Elizabeth: A Memoir.* Little, Brown, 1969.

Anderson, Sherwood. *Sherwood Anderson: Selected Letters.* Edited by Charles E. Modlin. University of Tennessee Press, 1984.

———. *Sherwood Anderson's Memoirs: A Critical Edition.* Edited by Ray Lewis White. University of North Carolina Press, 1969.

Arnheim, Rudolf. *Film as Art.* University of California Press, 2006.

Arnold, Edwin T. *Annotations to "Mosquitoes."* Garland, 1989.

Atkinson, Ted. *Faulkner and the Great Depression: Aesthetics, Ideology, and Cultural Politics.* University of Georgia Press, 2006.

Bacigalupo, Massimo. "New Information on William Faulkner's First Trip to Italy." *Journal of Modern Literature* 24 (Winter 2000–2001): 321–25.

Bailey, Kevin. "*Flags in the Dust* and the Material Culture of Class." In *Faulkner and Material Culture,* edited by Joseph R. Urgo and Ann J. Abadie. University Press of Mississippi, 2004.

Barker, Deborah. "Demystifying the Modern Mammy in *Requiem for a Nun.*" In *Faulkner and Film,* edited by Peter Lurie and Ann J. Abadie. University Press of Mississippi, 2014.

Bassett, John, ed. *William Faulkner: The Critical Heritage.* Routledge and Kegan Paul, 1975.

Beck, Warren. *Man in Motion: Faulkner's Trilogy.* University of Wisconsin Press, 1961.

Bezzerides, A. I. *William Faulkner: A Life on Paper.* University Press of Mississippi, 1980.

Black, Victorian Fielden. "Faulkner and Women." In *The South and Faulkner's Yoknapatawpha,* edited by Evans Harrington and Ann J. Abadie. University Press of Mississippi, 1977.

Bledsoe, Erik. "Margaret Mitchell's Review of *Soldiers' Pay*." *Mississippi Quarterly* 49.3 (Summer 1996): 591–93.

Bleikasten, André. *The Ink of Melancholy: Faulkner's Novels from "The Sound and the Fury" to "Light in August."* Indiana University Press, 2016. Nook.

———. *Most Splendid Failure: Faulkner's "The Sound and the Fury."* Indiana University Press, 1976.

———. *William Faulkner: A Life through the Novels.* Indiana University Press, 2017.

Bloom, Harold, ed. *Bloom's Major Short Story Writers: William Faulkner.* Chelsea House, 1999.

Blotner, Joseph. *Faulkner: A Biography.* Random House, 1974.

———. *Faulkner: A Biography.* University Press of Mississippi, 2005. Kindle.

———. *William Faulkner's Library: A Catalogue.* University Press of Virginia, 1964.

Bradford, Melvin J. "An Aesthetic Parable: Faulkner's 'Artist at Home.'" *Georgia Review* 27 (Summer 1973): 175–81.

Brinkmeyer, Robert H., Jr. *The Fourth Ghost: White Southern Writers and European Fascism (1930–1950).* Louisiana State University Press, 2009.

Brister, J. G. "*Absalom, Absalom!* and the Semiotic Other." *Faulkner Journal* (Fall 2006/Spring 2007): 39–55.

Broach, Vance. *Grande Dame: A Tribute to Bama Falkner McLean.* Privately printed, n.d.

Brodsky, Louis Daniel. "A Textual History of William Faulkner's *The Wishing-Tree* and *The Wishing Tree.*" *Studies in Bibliography* 38 (1985): 330–74.

———. *William Faulkner, Life Glimpses.* University of Texas Press, 1990.

Brodsky, Louis Daniel, and Robert W. Hamblin, eds. *Faulkner: A Comprehensive Guide to the Brodsky Collection.* Vol. 1: *The Bibliography.* University Press of Mississippi, 1982.

———, eds. *Faulkner: A Comprehensive Guide to the Brodsky Collection.* Vol. 2: *The Letters.* University Press of Mississippi, 1984.

———, eds. *Faulkner: A Comprehensive Guide to the Brodsky Collection.* Vol. 3: *The De Gaulle Story.* University Press of Mississippi, 1984.

———. *Faulkner: A Comprehensive Guide to the Brodsky Collection.* Vol. 4: *Battle Cry.* University Press of Mississippi, 1985.

———, eds. *Faulkner: A Comprehensive Guide to the Brodsky Collection.* Vol. 5: *Manuscripts and Documents.* University Press of Mississippi, 1988.

———, eds. *Selections from the William Faulkner Collection of Louis Daniel Brodsky.* University Press of Mississippi, 1979.

Broncano, Manuel. "Reading Faulkner in Spain, Reading Spain in Faulkner." In *Global Faulkner,* edited by Annette Trefzer and Ann J. Abadie. University Press of Mississippi, 2009.

Brooks, Cleanth. *William Faulkner: The Yoknapatawpha Country.* Yale University Press, 1966.

———. *William Faulkner: Toward Yoknapatawpha and Beyond.* Yale University Press, 1978.

Broughton, Panthea Reid. "An Interview with Meta Carpenter Wilde." *Southern Review* 18.4 (October 1976): 776–801.

Brown, Calvin S. "Faulkner's Manhunts." *Georgia Review* 20.4 (Winter 1966): 388–95.

Brown, May Cameron. "Voice in 'That Evening Sun': A Study of Quentin Compson." In *Critical Essays on William Faulkner: The Compson Family,* edited by Arthur F. Kinney. G. K. Hall, 1982.

Campbell, William K. "A Consideration of the Contrasting Opinions of William Faulkner's Attitude toward the Negro." Master's thesis, State University of Iowa, June 1951. UVA.

Capula, Michelangelo. *Jean Negulesco: His Life and Films.* McFarland, 2017.

Carothers, James B. "Faulkner's Short Story Writing and the Oldest Profession." In *Faulkner and the Short Story,* edited by Evans Harrington and Ann J. Abadie. University Press of Mississippi, 1992.

———. "The Road to *The Reivers.*" In *A Cosmos of My Own: Faulkner and Yoknapatawpha 1980,* edited by Doreen Fowler and Ann J. Abadie. University Press of Mississippi, 1981.

———. *William Faulkner's Short Stories.* UMI Research Press, 1985.

Carter, William C., ed. *Conversations with Shelby Foote.* University Press of Mississippi, 1989.

Chabrier, Gwendolyn. *Faulkner's Families: A Southern Saga.* Gordian, 1993.

Cohen, Martin. "The Novel in Woodcuts: A Handbook." *Journal of Modern Literature* 6.2 (1977): 171–95.

Coleman, Rosemary. "Family Ties: Generating Narratives in *Absalom, Absalom!*" *Mississippi Quarterly* 41.3 (Summer 1998): 421–31.

Collins, Carvel. "Biographical Sources of Faulkner's War Fiction." In *Faulkner and the Short Story,* edited by Evans Harrington and Ann J. Abadie. University Press of Mississippi, 1992.

Commins, Dorothy. *What Is an Editor? Saxe Commins at Work.* University of Chicago Press, 1978.

Cooperman, Stanley. *World War I and the American Novel.* Johns Hopkins University Press, 1967.

Coughlan, Robert. *The Private World of William Faulkner.* Harper and Brothers, 1954.

Cowley, Malcolm. *The Faulkner-Cowley File: Letters and Memories, 1944–1962.* Viking, 1966.

Cullen, John B. *Old Times in the Faulkner Country.* University of North Carolina Press, 1961.

Curnutt, Kirk. *William Faulkner.* Reaktion, 2018. Kindle.

Dabney, Lewis M. *The Indians of Yoknapatawpha: A Study in Literature and History.* Louisiana State University Press, 1974.

Dahl, James. "A Faulkner Reminiscence: Conversations with Mrs. Maud Falkner." *Journal of Modern Literature* 3 (April 1974): 1026–30.

Dardis, Tom. *Firebrand: The Life of Horace Liveright.* Random House, 1995.

———. "Harrison Smith: The Man Who Took a Chance on *The Sound and the Fury.*" In *Faulkner and Popular Culture,* edited by Doreen Fowler and Ann J. Abadie. University Press of Mississippi, 1990.

———. *Some Time in the Sun: The Hollywood Years of F. Scott Fitzgerald, William Faulkner, Nathanael West, Aldous Huxley, and James Agee.* Limelight Editions, 2004. Kindle.

———. *The Thirsty Muse: Alcohol and the American Writer.* Ticknor and Fields, 1989.

Davis, Ronald L. *Zachary Scott: Hollywood's Sophisticated Cad.* University Press of Mississippi, 2006.

Davis, Thadious M. *Faulkner's Negro: Art and the Southern Context.* Louisiana State University Press, 1983.

———. "From Jazz Syncopation to Blues Elegy: Faulkner's Development of Black Characterization." In *Faulkner and Race,* edited by Doreen Fowler and Ann J. Abadie. University Press of Mississippi, 1988.

Degenfelder, E. Pauline. "The Film Adaptation of Faulkner's *Intruder in the Dust.*" *Literature/Film Quarterly* 1 (Spring 1973): 138–49.

Delson, Susan. *Dudley Murphy: Hollywood Wild Card.* University of Minnesota Press, 2006.

Dickerson, Mary Jane. "'The Magician's Wand': Faulkner's *Compson Appendix.*" *Mississippi Quarterly* 28 (1975): 317–37.

Ditsky, John. "William Faulkner's *The Wishing Tree.*" *Lion and the Unicorn* 2.1 (1978): 56–64.

Doyle, Don H. *Faulkner's County: The Historical Roots of Yoknapatawpha.* University of North Carolina Press, 2001.

Duclos, Donald Philip. *Son of Sorrow: The Life Works and Influence of Colonel William C. Falkner, 1825–1889.* International Scholars Publications, 1999.

Eagles, Charles W. *The Price of Defiance: James Meredith and the Integration of Ole Miss.* University of North Carolina Press, 2014.

Earle, David M. "Faulkner and the Paperback Trade." In *William Faulkner in Context,* edited by John T. Matthews. Cambridge University Press, 2015.

Elliott, Jack. "Looking for Callie Barr." *Mississippi Quarterly* 65.3 (Summer 2012): 423–35.

Erikson, Erik. *Childhood and Society.* Norton, 2013. Kindle.

Fadiman, Regina K. *Faulkner's "Intruder in the Dust": Novel into Film.* University of Tennessee Press, 1978.

Falkner, Murry C. *The Falkners of Mississippi: A Reminiscence.* Louisiana State University Press, 1968.

Fant, Joseph L., and Robert Ashley. *Faulkner at West Point.* University Press of Mississippi, 2002.

Farber, Manny. *Farber on Film: The Complete Film Writings of Manny Farber.* Edited by Robert Polito. Library of America, 2009.

Fargnoli, A. Nicholas, ed. *William Faulkner: A Literary Companion.* Pegasus, 2008.

Fargnoli, A. Nicholas, and Michael Golay. *William Faulkner A to Z.* Checkmark, 2002.

Faulkner, John. *My Brother Bill.* University of South Carolina Press, 2010.

Faulkner, William. *The Collected Stories of William Faulkner.* Random House, 1950. Kindle.

———. *"Country Lawyer" and Other Stories for the Screen.* Edited by Louis Daniel Brodsky and Robert W. Hamblin. University Press of Mississippi, 1987.

———. *Early Prose and Poetry.* Random House, 1963. Kindle.

———. *Elmer.* Edited by Dianne L. Cox. Seajay, 1983.

———. *Essays, Speeches, and Public Letters.* Random House, 2011. Kindle.

———. *Father Abraham.* Edited by James B. Meriwether. Random House, 1983.

———. *Faulkner's MGM Screenplays.* Edited by Bruce Kawin. University of Tennessee Press, 1982.

———. "Helen: A Courtship" and "Mississippi Poems." Introductory essays by Carvel Collins and Joseph Blotner. Tulane University and Yoknapatawpha Press, 1981.

———. The Marionettes. Edited by Noel Polk. University Press of Virginia, 1977.

———. Mayday. Introduction by Carvel Collins. University of Notre Dame Press, 1976.

———. New Orleans Sketches. Edited by Carvel Collins. University Press of Mississippi, 2002. Kindle.

———. Thinking of Home: William Faulkner's Letters to His Mother and Father, 1918–1925. Edited by James G. Watson. Norton, 1992.

———. The Uncollected Stories of William Faulkner. Edited by Joseph Blotner. Vintage, 2011. Kindle.

———. Vision in Spring. Edited by Judith Sensibar. University of Texas Press, 1984.

———. William Faulkner at Twentieth Century-Fox: The Annotated Screenplays. Edited by Sarah Gleeson-White. Oxford University Press, 2017.

Ferguson, James. Faulkner's Short Fiction. University of Tennessee Press, 1991.

Fletcher, Matthew L. M. "Red Leaves and the Dirty Ground: The Cannibalism of Law and Economics." American Indian Law Review 33 (2008–9): 33–52.

Folks, Jeffrey J. "William Faulkner and the Silent Film. In The South and Film, edited by Warren French. University Press of Mississippi, 1981.

Ford, Corey. The Time of Laughter. Little, Brown, 1967.

Fowler, Doreen. Faulkner: The Return of the Repressed. University Press of Virginia, 1997.

———. "Joe Christmas and 'Womanshenegro.'" In Faulkner and Women, edited by Fowler and Ann J. Abadie. University Press of Mississippi, 1986.

Fowler, Doreen, and Ann J. Abadie, eds. Fifty Years of Yoknapatawpha. University Press of Mississippi, 1980.

Franklin, Malcolm. Bitterweeds: Life with William Faulkner at Rowan Oak. Society for the Study of Traditional Culture, 1977.

Fulton, Keith Louise. "Linda Snopes Kohl: Faulkner's Radical Woman." Modern Fiction Studies 34 (1988): 425–36.

Garrett, George. Afterword to The Road to Glory, by Joel Sayre and William Faulkner. Southern Illinois University Press, 1981.

———. "An Examination of the Poetry of William Faulkner." In William Faulkner: Four Decades of Criticism. Michigan State University Press, 1973.

Gleeson-White, Sarah. "Auditory Exposures: Faulkner, Eisenstein, and Film Sound." PMLA 128.1 (2013): 187–200.

———. "William Faulkner, Screenwriter: 'Sutter's Gold' and 'Drums along the Mohawk.'" Mississippi Quarterly 62.3–4 (Summer 2009): 427–42.

Glick, Evelyn Harper. The Making of William Faulkner's Books, 1929–1937: An Interview with Evelyn Harper Glick. Southern Studies Program, University of South Carolina, 1979.

Godden, Richard. "Absalom, Absalom! and Faulkner's Erroneous Dating of the Haitian Revolution." Mississippi Quarterly 47.3 (Summer 1994): 489–95.

———. "Absalom, Absalom! and Rosa Coldfield: Or, What Is in the Dark House?" Faulkner Journal 8.2 (Spring 1993): 31–66.

Godwin, Hannah. "'Who Are You?': Modernism, Childhood, and Historical Consciousness in Faulkner's The Wishing Tree." In Faulkner and History, edited by Jay Watson and James G. Thomas Jr. University Press of Mississippi, 2017.

Gray, Richard. *The Life of William Faulkner: A Critical Biography.* Blackwell, 1994.

Grider, John MacGavock. *War Birds: Diary of an Unknown Aviator.* Texas A&M Press, 2000. Kindle.

Gresset, Michel. *Fascination: Faulkner's Fiction, 1919–1936.* Duke University Press, 1989.

———. *A Faulkner Chronology.* University Press of Mississippi, 1985.

———. "Faulkner's 'The Hill.'" *Southern Literary Journal* (Spring 1974): 3–18.

———. "A Public Man's Private Voice." In *Faulkner: After the Nobel Prize,* edited by Gresset and Kenzaburo Ohashi. Yamaguchi, 1987.

———. "Weekend, Lost and Revisited." *Mississippi Quarterly* 31 (1968): 173–78.

Grimwood, Michael. "Faulkner's 'Golden Land' as Autobiography." *Studies in Short Fiction* 23.3 (Summer 1986): 275–80.

Guetti, James. "*Absalom, Absalom!:* The Extended Simile." In *William Faulkner's "Absalom, Absalom!": A Critical Casebook,* edited by Elisabeth Muhlenfeld. Garland, 1984.

Guttman, Sondra. "Who's Afraid of the Corncob Man: Masculinity, Race, and Labor in the Preface to *Sanctuary.*" *Faulkner Journal* 15.1/2 (Fall 1999/Spring 2000): 15–34.

Gwin, Minrose C. *The Feminine and Faulkner: Reading (Beyond) Sexual Difference.* University of Tennessee Press, 1990.

———. "*Mosquitoes'* Missing Bite: The Four Deletions." *Faulkner Journal* 9 (Fall 1993/Spring 1994): 31–41.

———. "Racial Wounding and the Aesthetics of the Middle Voice." *Faulkner Journal* 20.1–2 (Fall 2004): 21–35.

Gwynn, Frederick L., and Joseph Blotner, eds. *Faulkner in the University: Class Conferences at the University of Virginia, 1957–1958.* University Press of Virginia, 1959.

Hagood, Taylor. *Faulkner, Writer of Disability.* Louisiana State University Press, 2014.

Hall, Donald. *A Carnival of Losses: Notes Nearing Ninety.* Houghton Mifflin Harcourt, 2018. Kindle.

Hamblin, Robert W. "Biographical Fact or Fiction? William Faulkner, Estelle Oldham Franklin, and Abortion." *Mississippi Quarterly* 60.3 (Summer 1997): 579–87.

———. "Faulkner and Hollywood: A Call for Reassessment." In *Faulkner and Film,* edited by Peter Lurie and Ann J. Abadie. University Press of Mississippi, 2014.

———. "Lucas Beauchamp, Ned Barnett, and William Faulkner's 1940 Will." *Studies in Bibliography* 32 (1979): 281–83.

———. *Myself and the World: A Biography of William Faulkner.* University Press of Mississippi, 2016.

Hamilton, Ian. *Writers in Hollywood: 1915–1951.* Harper and Row, 1990.

Handley, George B. *Postslavery Literature in the Americas: Family Portraits in Black and White.* University Press of Virginia, 2000.

Hannon, Charles. "The Filming of *Intruder in the Dust.*" In *Essays on William Faulkner's "Intruder in the Dust": A Gathering of Evidence,* edited by Michel Gresset and Patrick Samway. St. Joseph's University Press, 2004.

Harrington, Gary. *Faulkner's Fables of Creativity: The Non-Yoknapatawpha Novels.* University of Georgia Press, 1990.

Hemingway, Ernest. *Ernest Hemingway: Selected Letters 1917–1961.* Edited by Carlos Baker. Scribner's, 1981.

Hickman, Lisa C. *William Faulkner and Joan Williams: The Romance of Two Writers.* McFarland, 2006.

Hillier, Jim, and Peter Wollen, eds. *Howard Hawks: American Artist.* British Film Institute, 1996.

Hirsch, Arthur. "Ghosts of the South." *Baltimore Sun,* September 21, 1997.

Hlavsa, Virginia H. "Crucifixion in *Light in August.*" In *Faulkner and Religion,* edited by Doreen Fowler and Ann J. Abadie. University Press of Mississippi, 1991.

Holditch, W. Kenneth. "William Faulkner and Other Famous Creoles." In *Faulkner and His Contemporaries,* edited by Joseph R. Urgo and Ann J. Abadie. University Press of Mississippi, 2010.

Hönnighausen, Lothar. *Faulkner: Masks and Metaphors.* University Press of Mississippi, 1997.

———. *William Faulkner: The Art of Stylization in His Early Graphic and Literary Work.* Cambridge University Press, 1987.

Inge, M. Thomas, ed. *Conversations with William Faulkner.* University Press of Mississippi, 1999.

———. *The Dixie Limited: Writers on William Faulkner and His Influence.* University Press of Mississippi, 2016.

———. *William Faulkner.* Overlook, 2006.

———, ed. *William Faulkner: The Contemporary Reviews.* Cambridge: Cambridge University Press, 1995.

———. "William Faulkner, James Avati, and the Art of the Paperback Novel." *Illustration* 56 (2017): 46–58.

Irwin, John T. *Doubling and Incest/Repetition and Revenge: A Speculative Reading of Faulkner.* Expanded ed. Johns Hopkins University Press, 1996.

———. "Not the Having but the Waiting: Faulkner's Lost Loves." In *Faulkner at 100: Retrospect and Prospect,* edited by Donald M. Kartiganer and Ann J. Abadie. University Press of Mississippi, 2000.

Izard, Barbara, and Clara Hieronymus. *"Requiem for a Nun": On Stage and Off.* Aurora, 1970.

Jackson, Robert. "'If It Still Is France, It Will Endure': Faulknerian Projections from Hollywood to Stockholm." For the "Faulkner and World Cinema" program arranged by the William Faulkner Society, Modern Language Association of America Convention, December 28, 2007. http://faulknersociety.com/mla07jackson.doc.

———. "Images of Collaboration: William Faulkner's Motion Pictures Communities." In *Faulkner and Film,* edited by Peter Lurie and Ann J. Abadie. University Press of Mississippi, 2014.

Jenkins, Lee. *Faulkner and Black-White Relations: A Psychoanalytic Approach.* Columbia University Press, 1981.

Johnson, Glen M. "*Big Woods:* Faulkner's Elegy for Wilderness." *Southern Humanities Review* 14 (1980): 249–58.

Jones, Anne Goodwyn. "Faulkner and the Ideology of Penetration." In *Faulkner and Ideology,* edited by Donald M. Kartiganer and Ann J. Abadie. University Press of Mississippi, 1995.

———. "Faulkner's War Stories and the Construction of Gender." In *Faulkner and Psychology,* edited by Donald M. Kartiganer and Ann J. Abadie. University Press of Mississippi, 1994.

———. "'The Kotex Age': Women, Popular Culture, and *The Wild Palms.*" In *Faulkner and Popular Culture,* edited by Doreen Fowler and Ann J. Abadie. University Press of Mississippi, 1990.

Jones, Diane Brown. *A Reader's Guide to the Short Stories of William Faulkner.* G. K. Hall, 1994.

Jones, Dorothy B. "Novel into Film." *Quarterly of Film, Television, and Radio* 8.1 (Autumn 1953): 51–70.

Jones, Lennis Miears. "Racial Relations in the Fiction of William Faulkner: A Study of Meaning." Master's thesis, University of Iowa, August 1957. UVA.

Kang, Hee. "A New Configuration of Faulkner's Feminine." *Faulkner Journal* 8 (1992): 21–41.

Karem, Jeff. "Fear of a Black Atlantic? African Passages in *Absalom, Absalom!* and *The Last Slaver.*" In *Global Faulkner,* edited by Annette Trefzer and Ann J. Abadie. University Press of Mississippi, 2009.

Karl, Frederick. *William Faulkner, American Writer: A Biography.* Ballantine, 1990.

Kartiganer, Donald M. "The Role of Myth in *Absalom, Absalom!*" In *Faulkner and His Critics,* edited by John N. Duvall. Johns Hopkins University Press, 2010.

Kaufman, Linda. "A Lover's Discourse in *Absalom, Absalom!*" In *Faulkner and His Critics,* edited by John N. Duvall. Johns Hopkins University Press, 2010.

Kawin, Bruce. *Faulkner and Film.* Ungar, 1977.

———, ed. *To Have and Have Not.* University of Wisconsin Press, 1980.

Keiser, Merle Wallace. "*Flags in the Dust* and *Sartoris.*" In *Fifty Years of Yoknapatawpha,* edited by Doreen Fowler and Ann J. Abadie. University Press of Mississippi, 1980.

Kinney, Arthur F., ed. *Critical Essays on William Faulkner: The Compson Family.* G. K. Hall, 1982.

———. "Faulkner and Racism." *Connotations* 3.3 (1993/94).

———. "Faulkner's Narrative Poetics and *Collected Stories.*" *Faulkner Studies* 1 (1980): 58–79.

———. "Unscrambling Surprises." *Connotations* 15.1–3 (2005/2006): 17–29.

Knox, Robert Hilton. "William Faulkner's *Absalom, Absalom!*" Ph.D. diss., Harvard University, April 1959.

Kodat, Catherine Gunther. "Writing *A Fable* for America." In *Faulkner in America,* edited by Joseph E. Urgo and Ann J. Abadie. University Press of Mississippi, 2001.

Kreiswirth, Martin. *William Faulkner: The Making of a Novelist.* University of Georgia Press, 1983.

Ladd, Barbara. *Nationalism and the Color Line in George W. Cable, Mark Twain, and William Faulkner.* Louisiana State University Press, 1996.

La Farge, Oliver. *Raw Material.* Houghton, Mifflin, 1945.

Lang, Beatrice. "'Dr. Martino': The Conflict of Life and Death." *Delta* 3 (1976): 23–32.

Langford, Gerald. *Faulkner's Revision of "Sanctuary": A Collation of the Unrevised Galleys and the Published Book.* University of Texas Press, 1972.

Latham, Sean. "Jim Bond's America: Denaturalizing the Logic of Slavery in *Absalom, Absalom!*" *Mississippi Quarterly* 51.3 (Summer 1998): 453–63.

LaValley, Albert J., ed. *Mildred Pierce.* University of Wisconsin Press, 1980.

Lawrence, John, and Dan Hise. *Faulkner's Rowan Oak.* University Press of Mississippi, 1993.

Limon, John. *Writing after War: American War Fiction from Realism to Postmodernism.* Oxford University Press, 1994.

Lind, Ilse Dusoir. "The Calvinistic Burden." In *"Light in August" and the Critical Spectrum,* edited by John B. Vickery and Olga Vickery. Wadsworth, 1971.

———. "Faulkner's Uses of Poetic Drama." In *Faulkner, Modernism, and Film,* edited by Evans Harrington and Ann J. Abadie. University Press of Mississippi, 1978.

Lowe, John. "Fraternal Fury: Faulkner, World War I, and Myths of Masculinity." In *Faulkner and War,* edited by Noel Polk and Ann J. Abadie. University Press of Mississippi, 2004.

Luce, Diane Cox. *William Faulkner: Annotations to the Novels: "As I Lay Dying."* Garland, 1990.

———, ed. *William Faulkner's "As I Lay Dying": A Critical Casebook.* Garland, 1985.

Luddington, Townsend. *John Dos Passos: A Twentieth-Century Odyssey.* Dutton, 1980.

Lurie, Peter. "Inside and outside Southern Whiteness: Film Viewing, the Frame and the Racing of Space in Yoknapatawpha." In *Faulkner and Whiteness,* edited by Jay Watson, 153–59. University Press of Mississippi, 2011.

———. *Vision's Immanence: Faulkner, Film, and the Popular Imagination.* Johns Hopkins University Press, 2004.

Matthews, John T. "Faulkner and the Culture Industry." In *The Cambridge Companion to William Faulkner,* edited by Philip Weinstein, 51–74. Cambridge University Press, 1995.

———. "Faulkner's Narrative Frames." In *Faulkner and the Craft of Fiction,* edited by Doreen Fowler and Ann J. Abadie. University Press of Mississippi, 1989.

———. "Many Mansions: Faulkner's Cold War Conflicts. In *Global Faulkner,* edited by Annette Trefzer and Ann J. Abadie. University Press of Mississippi, 2009.

———, ed. *The New Cambridge Companion to William Faulkner.* Cambridge University Press, 2015.

———. *William Faulkner: Seeing through the South.* Wiley-Blackwell, 2012. Kindle.

McAlexander, Hubert, Jr. "William Faulkner—The Young Poet in Stark Young's *The Torches Flare.*" *American Literature* 43 (January 1972): 647–49.

McBride, Joseph, ed. *Focus on Howard Hawks.* Prentice Hall, 1972.

———. *Hawks on Hawks.* University of California Press, 1982.

McCarthy, Todd. *Howard Hawks: The Grey Fox of Hollywood.* Grove, 1997.

McClelland, Doug. *Forties Film Talk: Oral Histories of Hollywood with 120 Lobby Posters.* McFarland, 1992.

McDaniel, Linda Elkins. *Annotations to William Faulkner's "Flags in the Dust."* Garland, 1991.

McHaney, Thomas L. "The Elmer Papers." In *A Faulkner Miscellany,* edited by James B. Meriwether. University Press of Mississippi, 1974.

———. *William Faulkner's "The Wild Palms": A Study.* University Press of Mississippi, 1975.

McMillen, Neil R. *Dark Journey: Black Mississippians in the Age of Jim Crow.* University of Illinois Press, 1989.

Meade, Marion. *Dorothy Parker: What Fresh Hell Is This?* Villard, 1988.

Meriwether, James B. "Early Notices of Faulkner by Phil Stone and Louis Cochran." *Mississippi Quarterly* 17 (Summer 1964): 136–48.

———, ed. *A Faulkner Miscellany*. University Press of Mississippi, 1974.

———, ed. "Faulkner's Correspondence with *Scribner's Magazine*." *Proof* 3: 256–60.

———, ed. "Faulkner's Correspondence with the *Saturday Evening Post*. *Mississippi Quarterly* 30 (Summer 1977): 464–66.

———. *The Literary Career of William Faulkner*. University of North Carolina Press, 1971.

Meriwether, James B., and Michael Millgate, eds. *Lion in the Garden: Interviews with William Faulkner*. Random House, 1968.

Michel, Fran. "Faulkner as Lesbian Author." *Faulkner Journal* 4.1 & 2 (Fall 1988/Spring 1989): 5–18.

Millgate, Michael. *The Achievement of William Faulkner*. University of Georgia Press, 1989.

Minter, David. *William Faulkner: His Life and Work*. Johns Hopkins University Press, 1980.

Momberger, Philip. "Faulkner's 'The Village' and 'That Evening Sun': The Tale in Context." In *Bloom's Major Short Story Writers: William Faulkner,* edited by Harold Bloom. Chelsea House, 1999.

———. "A Reading of Faulkner's 'The Hill.'" *Southern Literary Journal* (Spring 1977): 16–29.

Monaghan, David M. "Faulkner's Relationship to Gavin Stevens in *Intruder in the Dust*." *Dalhousie Review* 52 (1972): 449–57.

Montagu, Ivor. *With Eisenstein in Hollywood*. International, 1969.

Moore, Michelle. "Vampires, Detectives, and Hawks: A History and Analysis of William Faulkner's Unpublished Screenplay *Dreadful Hollow*." *Literature/Film Quarterly* 45.3 (July 2017). http://www.salisbury.edu/lfq/_issues/45_3/vampires_detectives_and_hawks.html.

Morell, Giliane. "The Last Scene of *Sanctuary*." *Mississippi Quarterly* 25.3 (Summer 1972): 351–55.

Morland, Agnes Louise. "The Negro in the Fiction of William Faulkner." Master's thesis, University of Washington, 1953. UVA.

Moser, Thomas C. "Faulkner's Muse: Speculations on the Genesis of *The Sound and the Fury*." In *Critical Reconstructions: The Relationship of Fiction and Life,* edited by Robert M. Polhemus and Roger B. Henkel. Stanford University Press, 1994.

Mullener, Elizabeth. "Joan Williams and William Faulkner: A Romance Remembered." *New Orleans Times-Picayune,* September 19, 1982, 8–18.

Murphet, Julian. *Faulkner's Media Romance*. Oxford University Press, 2017.

Nauman, Hilda. "How Faulkner Went His Way and I Went Mine." *Esquire,* December 1967.

Nelson, Charles, and David Goforth. *Our Neighbor, William Faulkner*. Adams, 1977.

Nuechterlein, Donald E. *A Cold War Odyssey*. University Press of Kentucky, 1997.

Oates, Stephen B. *William Faulkner: The Man and the Artist: A Biography*. Harper, 1987.

Owada, Eiko. *Faulkner, Haiti, and Questions of Imperialism*. Sairyusha, 2002.

Paddock, Lisa. *Contrapuntal in Integration: A Study of Three Faulkner Short Story Volumes*. International Scholars, 2000.

———. "'Trifles with a Tragic Profundity': The Importance of 'Mistral.'" *Mississippi Quarterly* (Summer 1979): 413–22.

Parini, Jay. *One Matchless Time: A Life of William Faulkner.* HarperCollins, 2009. Kindle.

Parker, Robert Dale. "Red Slippers and Cottonmouth Moccasins: White Anxieties in Faulkner's Indian Stories." *Faulkner Journal* 18 (Fall 2002/Spring 2003): 81–100.

Peek, Charles A., and Robert W. Hamblin, eds. *A Companion to Faulkner Studies.* Greenwood, 2004.

Peters, Erskine. *William Faulkner: The Yoknapatawpha World and Black Being.* Norwood, 1983.

Peterson, Richard F. "An Early Judgement of Anderson and Joyce in Faulkner's 'Artist at Home.'" *Kyushu American Literature* 18 (1977): 19–23.

Phillips, Gene D. *Fiction, Film, and Faulkner: The Art of Adaptation.* University of Tennessee Press, 1988.

Pilkington, John. *Stark Young.* Twayne, 1985.

Polchin, James. "Selling a Novel: Faulkner's *Sanctuary* as a Psychosexual Text." In *Faulkner and Gender,* edited by Donald M. Kartiganer and Ann J. Abadie. University Press of Mississippi, 1996.

Polk, Noel, ed. *"Absalom, Absalom!": Typesetting Copy and Miscellaneous Material.* William Faulkner Manuscripts 13. Garland, 1987.

———. *Children of the Dark House.* University Press of Mississippi, 1998. Kindle.

———. "Faulkner: The Artist as Cuckold." In *Faulkner and Gender,* edited by Donald M. Kartiganer and Ann J. Abadie. University Press of Mississippi, 1996. Reprinted in *Children of the Dark House,* by Polk.

———. *Faulkner's "Requiem for a Nun": A Critical Study.* Indiana University Press, 1981.

———, ed. *"Requiem for a Nun": Preliminary Holograph and Typescript Materials.* William Faulkner Manuscripts 19. Garland, 1987.

———, ed. *William Faulkner: "Sanctuary": The Original Text.* Random House, 1981.

Polk, Noel, and Neil R. McMillen. "Faulkner on Lynching." *Faulkner Journal* 8 (1992): 3–14.

Porter, Carolyn. *Seeing & Being: The Plight of the Participant Observer in Emerson, James, Adams, and Faulkner.* Wesleyan University Press, 1981.

———. *William Faulkner.* Oxford University Press, 2007.

Pruitt, Claude. *The Well-Wrought Urn: Faulkner and Jefferson on the Practice of Freedom.* CreateSpace Direct, 2015. Kindle.

Putzel, Max. *Genius of Place: William Faulkner's Triumphant Beginnings.* Louisiana State University Press, 1985.

Rado, Lisa. "A Perversion That Builds Chartres and Invents Lear Is a Pretty Good Thing: *Mosquitoes* and Faulkner's Androgynous Imagination." *Faulkner Journal* 9.1 (Fall 1993): 13–30.

Ragan, David Paul. "'Belonging to the Business of Mankind': The Achievement of Faulkner's *Big Woods.*" *Mississippi Quarterly* 36 (Summer 1983): 301–17.

Ramsey, Matthew. "'All That Glitters': Reappraising 'Golden Land.'" *Faulkner Journal* 21.1/2 (Fall 2005/Spring 2006): 51–68.

———. "Stars, Fashion, and Authorship in *Today We Live.*" In *Faulkner and Material Culture,* edited by Joseph R. Urgo and Ann J. Abadie. University Press of Mississippi, 2007.

———. "'Turnabout' Is Fair(y) Play: Faulkner's Queer War Story." *Faulkner Journal* 15.1 (Fall 1999/Spring 2000): 61–81.

Ravitz, Abe C. *Leane Zugsmith: Thunder on the Left*. International, 1992.

Reed, John Shelton. *Dixie Bohemia: A French Quarter Circle in the 1920s*. Louisiana State University Press, 2012.

Rhodes, Pamela E. "Who Killed Simon Strother and Why? Race and Counterplot in *Flags in the Dust*." In *Faulkner and Race*, edited by Doreen Fowler and Ann J. Abadie. University Press of Mississippi, 2007.

Richards, Gary. "Male Homosexuality and Faulkner's Early Prose. In *Faulkner's Sexualities*, edited by Annette Trefzer and Ann J. Abadie. University Press of Mississippi, 2010.

Richardson, H. Edward. *William Faulkner: The Journey to Self-Discovery*. University of Missouri Press, 1969.

Robbins, Ben. "The Pragmatic Modernist: William Faulkner's Craft and Hollywood's Networks of Production." *Journal of Screenwriting* 5.2 (2014): 239–57.

———. "William Faulkner's *Requiem for a Nun* and Hollywood Cold War Melodrama." *Genre* 50.3 (2017): 343–70.

Robbins, Deborah. "The Desperate Eloquence of *Absalom, Absalom!*" *Mississippi Quarterly* 34.3 (Summer 1981): 315–25.

Roberts, Diane. "Eula, Linda, and the Death of Nature." In *Faulkner and the Natural World*, edited by Donald M. Kartiganer and Ann J. Abadie. University Press of Mississippi, 1999.

Rollyson, Carl. "Faulkner's First Biographers: Early Notices." In *Faulkner and Print Culture*, edited by Jay Watson, Jaime Harper, and James G. Thomas Jr. University Press of Mississippi, 2017.

———. "Faulkner's Shadow: Hollywood, Hemingway, and *Pylon*." In *Faulkner and Hemingway*, edited by Christopher Rieger and Andrew B. Leiter. Southeast Missouri State University Press, 2018.

———. *Lillian Hellman: Her Legend and Her Legacy*. St. Martin's, 1988.

———. *A Real American Character: The Life of Walter Brennan*. University Press of Mississippi, 2015.

———. *Rebecca West: A Modern Sibyl*. iUniverse, 2009.

———. *Uses of the Past in the Novels of William Faulkner*. Open Road, 2016.

Rose, Julie. "Faulkner's Horror and the American Gothic Cultural Imagination (1930–1945)." Ph.D. diss., New York University, 1999.

Rouselle, Melinda McLeod. *William Faulkner: Annotations to the Novels: "Sanctuary."* Garland, 1989.

Ryan, Tim. "Fabbulous Monsters: Faulkner, Alexander Woollcott, and American Literary Culture." In *Faulkner and Print Culture*, edited by Jay Watson, Jaime Harker, and James G. Thomas Jr. University Press of Mississippi, 2017.

Sanderson, Jane. "A Kind of Greatness." *Delta Review* 1 (July/August 1965): 15, 17.

Saunders, Rebecca. "Faulkner's *Absalom, Absalom!* and the New South." In *Faulkner and His Critics*, edited by John N. Duvall. Johns Hopkins University Press, 2010.

Schoenberg, Estella. *Old Tales and Talking: Quentin Compson in William Faulkner's "Absalom, Absalom!" and Related Works*. University Press of Mississippi, 1977.

Scott, Susan. "*As I Lay Dying* and the Modern Aesthetics of Ecological Crisis." In *The New Cambridge Companion to William Faulkner*, edited by John T. Matthews. Cambridge University Press, 2015.

Sensibar, Judith. *Faulkner and Love: The Women Who Shaped His Art, A Biography.* Yale University Press, 2009. Kindle.

————. *The Origins of Faulkner's Art.* University of Texas Press, 1984.

————. "Writing for Faulkner, Writing for Herself: Estelle Oldham's Postcolonial Fiction." *Prospects* 22 (October 1997): 357–78.

Shawhan, Dorothy S., and Martha H. Swain. *Lucy Somerville Howorth: New Deal Lawyer, Politician, and Feminist from the South.* Louisiana State University Press, 2006.

Sidney, George. "Faulkner in Hollywood: A Study of His Career as a Scenarist." Ph.D. diss., University of New Mexico, 1959.

Silver, James. *Running Scared: Silver in Mississippi.* University Press of Mississippi, 1984.

Simross, Lynn. "Memories of a Bohemian in Paris, 1924." *Los Angeles Times*, April 14, 1977.

Singal, Daniel J. *William Faulkner: The Making of a Modernist.* University of North Carolina Press, 1997.

Skei, Hans. *William Faulkner: The Novelist as Short Story Writer.* Universitetsforlaget, 1985.

————. *William Faulkner: The Short Story Career.* Universitetsforlaget, 1981.

Snead, James A. "The 'Joint' of Racism: Withholding the Black in *Absalom, Absalom!*" In *William Faulkner's "Absalom, Absalom!,"* edited by Harold Bloom. Chelsea House, 1987.

Snell, Susan. *Phil Stone of Oxford: A Vicarious Life.* University of Georgia Press, 1991.

Solomon, Stefan. *William Faulkner in Hollywood: Screenwriting for the Studios.* University of Georgia Press, 2017.

Spiegelman, Art, ed. *Lyn Ward: "Gods' Man," "Madman's Drum," "Wild Pilgrimage."* Library of America, 2010.

Spoth, Daniel. "Totalitarian Faulkner: The Nazi Interpretation of *Light in August* and *Absalom, Absalom!*" *English Literary History* 78 (Spring 2011): 239–78.

Spoto, Donald. *Possessed: The Life of Joan Crawford.* HarperCollins, 2010. Kindle.

Spratling, William. *File on Spratling: An Autobiography.* Little, Brown, 1967.

Starr, Kenneth. *Material Dreams: Southern California through the 1920s.* Oxford University Press, 1990.

Stecopoulos, Harilaos. *Reconstructing the World: Southern Fictions and U.S. Imperialisms, 1898–1976.* Cornell University Press, 2008.

Stein, Jean. *West of Eden: An American Place.* Jonathan Cape, 2016.

Stempel, Tom. *Screenwriter: The Life and Times of Nunnally Johnson.* A. S. Barnes, 1980.

Storey, Robert. *Pierrots on the Stage of Desire: Nineteenth-Century French Literary Artists and the Comic Pantomime.* Princeton University Press, 1985.

Sundquist, Eric. *Faulkner: The House Divided.* Johns Hopkins University Press, 1983.

Taylor, Herman E. *William Faulkner's Oxford: Recollections and Reflections.* Rutledge Hill, 1990.

Taylor, Walter. "Faulkner's *Reivers:* How to Change the Joke without Slipping the Yoke." In *Faulkner and Race,* edited by Doreen Fowler and Ann J. Abadie. University Press of Mississippi, 1986.

Torchiana, Donald T. "Faulkner's *Pylon* and the Structure of Modernity." In *Faulkner and His Critics,* edited by John N. Duvall. Johns Hopkins University Press, 2010.

Towner, Theresa M. *Faulkner on the Color Line: The Later Novels.* University Press of Mississippi, 2000.

Towner, Theresa M., and James B. Carothers. *Reading Faulkner: Collected Stories.* University Press of Mississippi, 2006.

Trotter, Sally Stone. *Rowan Oak: A History of the William Faulkner Home.* Nautilus, 2017.

Urgo, Joseph R. "*Absalom, Absalom!:* The Movie." *American Literature* 62.1 (1990): 56–73.

Urgo, Joseph R., and Ann J. Abadie, eds. *Faulkner and Material Culture.* University Press of Mississippi, 2007.

Urgo, Joseph R., and Noel Polk, eds. *Reading Faulkner: "Absalom, Absalom!"* University Press of Mississippi, 2010.

Vickery, John B., and Olga W. Vickery, eds. *"Light in August" and the Critical Spectrum.* Wadsworth, 1971.

Vickery, Olga. *The Novels of William Faulkner: A Critical Interpretation.* Louisiana State University Press, 1964.

Volpe, Edmond L. *A Reader's Guide to William Faulkner.* Octagon, 1964.

———. *A Reader's Guide to William Faulkner: The Short Stories.* Syracuse University Press, 2004. Kindle.

Waggoner, Hyatt H. *William Faulkner: From Jefferson to the World.* University of Kentucky Press, 1959.

Waid, Candace. *The Signifying Eye: Seeing Faulkner's Art.* University of Georgia Press, 2013.

Wald, Jerry. "Faulkner and Hollywood." *Films in Review* (March 1959): 129–33.

Walton, Anthony. *Mississippi: An American Journey.* Knopf, 1996.

Warner, Jack L. *My First Hundred Years in Hollywood.* Random House, 1965.

Wasson, Ben. *Count No 'Count: Flashbacks to Faulkner.* University Press of Mississippi, 1983.

Watson, James G. "'If Was Existed': Faulkner's Prophets and the Patterns of History." In *Faulkner and His Critics,* edited by John N. Duvall. Johns Hopkins University Press, 2010.

———. *The Snopes Dilemma: Faulkner's Trilogy.* University of Miami Press, 1968.

———. *William Faulkner: Letters & Fictions.* University of Texas Press, 1987.

———. *William Faulkner: Self-Presentation and Performance.* University of Texas Press, 2000. Kindle.

Watson, Jay. *Forensic Fictions: The Lawyer Figure in Faulkner.* University of Georgia Press, 1993.

Webb, James, and A. Wigfall Green, eds. *William Faulkner of Oxford.* Louisiana State University Press, 1965.

Weinstein, Philip. *Becoming Faulkner.* Oxford University Press, 2009. Kindle.

———. "Marginalia: Faulkner's Black Lives." In *Faulkner and Race,* edited by Doreen Fowler and Ann J. Abadie. University Press of Mississippi, 1987. Kindle.

———. *Simply Faulkner.* Simply Charly, 2016. Kindle.

Welling, Bart H. "Faulkner's Library Revisited." *Mississippi Quarterly* 52 (1999): 365–420.

Wells, Dean Faulkner. "Dean Swift Faulkner: A Biographical Study." Master's thesis, University of Mississippi, 1975.

———. *Every Day by the Sun: A Memoir of the Faulkners of Mississippi.* Crown, 2010. Kindle.

———. "Faulkner Helped Young Brother Dean with Vocabulary Lesson." *Faulkner Newsletter & Yoknapatawpha Review* 2 (January–March 1982).

Wilde, Meta Carpenter. "An Unpublished Chapter from A Loving Gentleman." Mississippi Quarterly 30 (1977): 449–60.

Wilde, Meta Carpenter, and Orin Borsten. "A Loving Gentleman." Typescript. Berg Collection, New York Public Library.

———. *A Loving Gentleman: The Love Story of William Faulkner and Meta Carpenter.* Simon and Schuster, 1976.

———. "An Unpublished Chapter from *A Loving Gentleman.*" *Mississippi Quarterly* 30 (1977): 449–60.

Williamson, Joel. *William Faulkner and Southern History.* Oxford University Press, 1993. Kindle.

Wittenberg, Judith. *Faulkner: The Transfiguration of Biography.* University of Nebraska Press, 1979.

———. "*The Reivers:* A Conservative Fable?" In *Faulkner: After the Nobel Prize,* edited by Michel Gresset and Kenzaburo Ohashi. Yamaguchi, 1987.

Wolff, Sally. *Ledgers of History: William Faulkner, an Almost Forgotten Friendship, and an Antebellum Plantation Diary.* Louisiana State University Press, 2010.

Wolff, Sally, and Floyd Watkins. *Talking about William Faulkner: Interviews with Jimmy Faulkner and Others.* Louisiana State University Press, 1996.

Wood, Robin. *Howard Hawks.* Doubleday, 1968.

Yonce, Margaret. "'Shot down Last Spring': The Wounded Aviators of Faulkner's Wasteland." In *Critical Essays on William Faulkner: The Sartoris Family,* edited by Arthur F. Kinney. G. K. Hall, 1985.

———. *William Faulkner: Annotations to the Novels: "Soldiers' Pay."* Garland, 1990.

Yoshida, Michiko. "Faulkner's Comedy of Motion: *The Reivers.*" In *Faulkner: After the Nobel Prize,* edited by Michel Gresset and Kenzaburo Ohashi. Yamaguchi, 1987.

Young, Stark. *The Far Pavilion: Of People and Times Remembered, Of Stories and Places.*

———. *Heaven Trees.* Scribner's, 1926.

———. *So Red the Rose.* J. S. Sanders, 1993. Kindle.

———. *Stark Young: A Life in the Arts: Letters, 1900–1962.* 2 vols. Edited by John Pilkington. Louisiana State University Press, 1975.

———. *The Torches Flare.* Scribner's, 1928.

Zender, Karl. "Two Unpublished Letters from William Faulkner to Helen Baird." *American Literature* 63.3 (September 1991): 535–38.

Illustration Credits

Index

Clytemnestra, 277

Cochran, Louis, 65, 297

Coffeeville, Mississippi, 295, 296, 297

Coindreau, Maurice, 314, 333, 343

Colbert, Claudette, 357

Collier's, 201

Collins, Carvel, x, xiii, 7, 12, 55, 59, 92,
110, 118–19, 122, 123, 124, 126, 127, 142,
204, 225, 342, 400, 434n33, 436n21,
439n25, 441n6

Collins, Wilkie, "The Woman in White,"
142

Commins, Dorothy, 418n38

Compson, Quentin (*The Sound and
the Fury; Absalom, Absalom!*), 13, 35,
43, 44, 50, 52, 67, 77, 81, 88, 89, 102,
104, 124, 142, 143, 145, 146, 211–15,
235, 236–38, 239, 240, 241, 242–51,
252, 253, 254, 255, 256, 257, 258, 259,
260, 261, 262, 263, 264, 265, 266, 267,
268 70, 271, 272–73, 285, 317, 328, 353,
360, 367, 395

Compson family (*The Sound and the
Fury*): Benjamin (Benjy), 8, 13, 53, 91,
120, 211, 231, 235, 236, 237, 238–42, 243,
244, 246, 248, 249, 250, 253, 256, 257,
258, 259, 260–61, 264–65, 271, 330,
395, 419n71; Caddy, 13, 19, 44, 98, 199,
211, 214–15, 235–36, 237, 239, 240–42,
243, 244, 245–51, 252–54, 256, 258,
260–61, 262, 264–65, 266, 267, 269,
272, 275–76, 353, 359, 360, 391; father,
44, 146, 151, 214, 235, 242–43, 248,
251, 256, 257, 367; Jason, 13, 21, 211,
214–15, 235–36, 237, 239–41, 242, 243,
244–45, 246, 247, 250, 251–55, 256,
257, 258–59, 260–61, 262–65, 268, 269,
270, 272, 273, 276, 279, 285, 306, 343,
367; mother, 98, 240, 244, 246, 248,
249, 251, 253, 256, 257, 258, 260, 262,
263; Quentin (Caddy's daughter), 251,
254, 255, 258, 262–63, 273, 276. *See also*
Compson, Quentin

Columbia University, 70

Confederate army, 1, 11, 205

Confederate flag, 15, 210

Confederate monuments, 160

Confederate soldiers, 9, 12, 69, 111, 244,
294, 315, 382

Confederate States of America, 153

Conrad, Joseph, v, 17, 22, 73, 137, 265, 301,
315, 328, 334, 367, 391, 392, 436n5

Contempo, 332, 344

Cooper, Gary, 18, 356, 357, 363, 387, 388

Cooper, Monte, 106, 112–13

Coughlan, Robert, 46, 226, 229

"Count No 'Count," 68, 248

Cowley, Malcolm, v, 24, 261, 287

Crane, Hart, 111, 389

Crane, Stephen, 114, 327, 367

Crawford, Joan, 356, 357, 358, 359–60,
363, 379, 387

Crichton, Kyle, 364, 441n6

Crump, Owen, 219, 339

Cullen, Hal, 28

Cullen, Jenks, 28, 29

Cullen, John, 25, 27–29, 34, 274,
416nn106–7, 416n109, 416n117

Cullen clan, 207

Culley, John, 311

Culloden, 9, 262

Cunningham, Ann, 360

Damuddy. *See* Butler, Lelia

Daniel, B. O., 46

Daniel, Robert, 318

D'Anunzio, Gabriele, 45

Dardis, Tom, 222, 430n84

Dashiell, Alfred, 189, 342

Davidson, Donald, 159, 180, 221

Davis, Jefferson, 9

Dawn Patrol, The (film) 355

Death Valley, 348–49, 381

Degas, Edgar, 130

Dempsey, Harold, 101, 122–23

Detective Story, 218

Devine, Eric (Jim), 217, 218–19, 337,
430n82

Dial, 87

Dickens, Charles, 23, 77, 137, 173, 253, 331

Dietrich, Marlene, 356, 357

Disney, Walt, 348

lynching, 26–34, 110, 144, 195, 261, 314, 333–34, 368, 373–74, 375, 376, 377, 413n19, 416n103, 416n109
Lyric Theater, 346, 386

Madora, Willie, 8
Majorca, Spain, 167
Manet, Édouard, 130
Man Who Came to Dinner, The (Kaufman and Hart), 316
Marble Faun, The, 35, 41, 59–60, 75–77, 94, 95, 96, 97, 111; reviews of, 111–14, 134, 138, 171, 322–23, 422n6, 423n36
Marcus, Lillian Friend, 104, 117
Marion, Virginia, 329
Marionettes (theater group), 69, 73
Marlow (in *Chance*), 301
Marlowe, Christopher, 137
Marx, Sam, 342, 347, 348, 349, 350, 355, 358, 393
Mary Baldwin College, 38, 39
Mary of Scotland (play), 402
Matthews, John T., 215, 239, 271, 284, 300, 359
Mayer, Alice, 160
Mayfair, 137
McBride, Joseph, 356
McClure, John, 101, 102, 105, 111–12, 116, 161, 180
McClure, Joyce, 105, 124
McEwen, Narcissus, 394
McLean, Alabama (Bama), 3, 7, 8, 19, 70, 127, 131, 135, 183, 196–97, 203, 208, 217, 218, 220, 311, 396
McMillan, Mattie, 26–30, 416n103
Melville, Herman, 325
Memphis, 5, 40, 48, 49, 51, 58, 61, 72, 89, 94, 96, 113, 196, 226, 275, 299, 302, 305, 306, 310, 311, 323, 333, 354, 376, 378, 385, 396, 413n16, 434n3
Mencken, H. L., 111, 138, 334, 341
MGM (Metro-Goldwyn-Mayer), 342, 345, 346, 348, 355–56, 358, 382, 383, 388, 391, 393, 438n2
Mickey Mouse, 348, 358, 386
Milan cathedral, 130

Millay, Edna St. Vincent, *Aria Da Capo,* 87
Millgate, Michael, xii, 327, 328, 426n30
Milton, John, 135, 262
Min and Bill (film), 353
Mississippian, 63, 65, 66, 67, 68, 70, 82, 87, 98, 111
Modern Library, 299, 302, 314, 331, 345, 431n32
Modern Times (film), 348
Monjoy, Marc, 194
Monroe, Harriet, 40
Montjoy, Gid, 62
Morris, Mary, 317
Morris, William, 63, 64
Moser, Thomas, 59–60
Mosquitoes, 100, 101, 104, 115, 119, 125, 126, 127, 130, 132, 166, 167, 169, 171–80, 187, 188, 189, 190, 201, 207, 223, 273, 330, 336, 378, 427n53, 427n56; reviews of, 180–81
Moulin Rouge, 132
Mussolini, Benito, 129, 144, 145, 174, 370

Negulesco, Jean, 390
Nesbit, Evelyn, 142, 143
New Albany, Mississippi, 18
New Haven, Connecticut, 49, 50, 51, 54
New Orleans, 51, 89, 95, 99–127, 131, 132, 133, 161, 164–65, 167, 172–73, 178, 187, 188, 194, 202, 212, 219, 231, 268, 288, 292, 302, 330, 336, 378, 390, 400, 409, 413n16, 433n14
New York City, 43, 44, 50, 53, 58, 70, 71, 80, 81, 82–84, 95, 109, 110, 112, 114, 118, 125, 139, 140–41, 162, 187, 216, 218–20, 299, 306, 321, 324, 329, 331, 332–42, 369, 381, 387, 396, 397
Niles, Henry C. (judge), 22, 267, 303
Nolia, 21–22, 267
North, 4, 6, 9, 71, 121, 306, 332, 382
northern abolitionists, 372
northerners, 9, 106, 107, 108, 270, 290
northern newspapers, 366
Notre Dame, 130